'Hoodbhoy's richly textured inquiry into Pakistan's evolution from early days onward brings out reality, myth, hope. With penetrating insight and scrupulous care he explores and dismantles multiple poisonous fallacies. But this is no Jeremiad. The cures, he shows, exist as do hopes for a much brighter future.'

Noam Chomsky, *Professor of Linguistics (Emeritus), Massachusetts Institute of Technology (USA)*

'A hard-hitting and truth-seeking analysis of how Pakistan came to be what it is today with the conclusion, first, that the very idea of Pakistan must be rethought, and second, suggestions as to how this might be done.'

Francis Robinson, *Professor of the History of South Asia, University of London (UK)*

'The effort which has gone into writing this book can only be called monumental. It is highly recommended to all who are interested in truthful history and is especially recommended to those who disagree with the author – if only to promote rational, intellectual debate on the subject of Pakistan's origins and identity.'

Tariq Rahman, *Linguist, Humboldt Laureate, Distinguished National Professor of Social Sciences, HEC (Pakistan)*

'In a bold sweep, Pervez Hoodbhoy seeks to analyze Pakistan's nationhood, its origins, its present, and its future, as also figures critical to the country's formation. The result is a clinical and candid book, yet one that is also constructive and very readable.'

Rajmohan Gandhi, *Author, Biographer, Peace Activist, IIT Gandhinagar (India)*

'The book unabashedly lays bare facts of history that in the past were only just whispered. A brave exposé and, equally, a desire for a different Pakistan that few dare talk about.'

Ayesha Siddiqa, *Author of* Military Inc.: Inside Pakistan's Military Economy

'As a scientist, Hoodbhoy weighs evidence as he fearlessly digs into explaining and resolving crucial issues that present-day Pakistanis face. His scholarship is meticulous and wide-ranging, laying a foundation for an extraordinarily insightful exploration of Pakistan's history and its social, cultural, and political dynamics extending into the present day. Withal, he reaches out to the reader with straightforward and clear questions, inviting informed revision of the conventional understanding of Pakistan.'

Philip K. Oldenburg, *Research Scholar, South Asia Institute, Columbia University (USA)*

'Agree with it or not, Pervez Hoodbhoy's book demands to be read. It provides the most thorough reversal of existing narratives about Pakistan's origins. A bracing and counter-intuitive interpretation of nationalist history.'

Faisal Devji, *Professor of Indian History, University of Oxford (UK)*

PAKISTAN

This book is an accessible, comprehensive, and nuanced history of Pakistan. It reflects upon the state and society in Pakistan and shows they have been shaped by historical forces and personae. Hoodbhoy expertly maps the journey of the region from many millennia ago to the circumstances and impulses that gave birth to the very first state in history founded upon religious identity. He documents colonial rule, the trauma of Partition, the nation's wars with India, the formation of Bangladesh, and the emergence of Baloch nationalism. The book also examines longstanding complex themes and issues – such as religious fundamentalism, identity formation, democracy, and military rule – as well as their impact on the future of the state of Pakistan.

Drawing on a range of sources and written by one of the foremost intellectuals of the region, this book will be indispensable for scholars, researchers, and students of history, politics, and South Asian studies. It will be of great interest to the general reader interested in understanding Pakistan.

Pervez Hoodbhoy taught physics at Quaid-e-Azam University in Islamabad (1973–2021) as well as other Pakistani universities (Lahore University of Management Sciences and Forman Christian College) for nearly five decades. He was visiting professor at the Massachusetts Institute of Technology (MIT), Carnegie Mellon University, and the University of Maryland, and a post-doctoral research fellow at the University of Washington.

PAKISTAN

Origins, Identity and Future

Pervez Hoodbhoy

LONDON AND NEW YORK

Designed cover image: Felice Beato

First published 2023
by Routledge
4 Park Square, Milton Park, Abingdon, Oxon OX14 4RN

and by Routledge
605 Third Avenue, New York, NY 10158

Routledge is an imprint of the Taylor & Francis Group, an informa business

© 2023 Pervez Hoodbhoy

The right of Pervez Hoodbhoy to be identified as author of this
work has been asserted in accordance with sections 77 and 78 of the
Copyright, Designs and Patents Act 1988.

All rights reserved. No part of this book may be reprinted or reproduced
or utilised in any form or by any electronic, mechanical, or other
means, now known or hereafter invented, including photocopying and
recording, or in any information storage or retrieval system, without
permission in writing from the publishers.

Trademark notice: Product or corporate names may be trademarks
or registered trademarks, and are used only for identification and
explanation without intent to infringe.

British Library Cataloguing-in-Publication Data
A catalogue record for this book is available from the British Library

Library of Congress Cataloging-in-Publication Data
Names: Hoodbhoy, Pervez, author.
Title: Pakistan : origins, identity and future / Pervez Hoodbhoy.
Description: Abingdon, Oxon ; New York, NY : Routledge, 2023. |
Includes bibliographical references and index. |
Identifiers: LCCN 2022049221 (print) | LCCN 2022049222 (ebook) |
ISBN 9781032270234 (hardback) | ISBN 9781032458953 (paperback) |
ISBN 9781003379140 (ebook)
Subjects: LCSH: Pakistan--History. | Nationalism--Pakistan--History.
| National characteristics, Pakistani.
Classification: LCC DS382 .H66 2023 (print) | LCC DS382 (ebook) |
DDC 954.91--dc23/eng/20221017
LC record available at https://lccn.loc.gov/2022049221
LC ebook record available at https://lccn.loc.gov/2022049222

ISBN: 978-1-032-27023-4 (hbk)
ISBN: 978-1-032-45895-3 (pbk)
ISBN: 978-1-003-37914-0 (ebk)

DOI: 10.4324/9781003379140

Typeset in Bembo
by Deanta Global Publishing Services, Chennai, India

CONTENTS

Foreword		*ix*
Preface		*xiii*
Acknowledgments		*xxi*
Introduction		1

PART ONE
Long Before the Two-Nation Idea   **19**

One	Identity Formation in Ancient India	21
Two	The British Reinvent India	43

PART TWO
A Closer Look at Pakistan's Three Founder-Heroes   **75**

Three	Founder I: The Lonely Modernizer	77
Four	Founder II: Poet–Preacher–Politician	102
Five	Founder III: Liberal, Secular, Visionary?	139
Six	Jinnah Trounces His Muslim Opponents	171

viii Contents

PART THREE
Postnatal Blues

197

| Seven | Stubborn Angularities I: East Pakistan | 199 |
| Eight | Stubborn Angularities II: Balochistan | 219 |

PART FOUR
Five Big Questions

237

Nine	Was Partition Worth the Price?	239
Ten	What Is the Ideology of Pakistan – and Does It Matter?	260
Eleven	Why Couldn't Pakistan Become an Islamic State?	276
Twelve	Why Is Pakistan a Praetorian State?	311
Thirteen	Identity: I'm Pakistani, but What Am I?	346

PART FIVE
Looking Ahead

379

Fourteen	Three Physical Perils up Ahead	381
Fifteen	The Paths Travelled Post-1971	394
Sixteen	Replacing the Two Nation Theory	420

| *Index* | 441 |

FOREWORD

Christophe Jaffrelot

Pervez Hoodbhoy's book does not belong to any established genre: it is not a standard history of Pakistan but deals extensively with the making and trajectory of Pakistan from the 19th century onwards. While focusing on certain episodes, it is not intended as a linear account. Nor is it just an essay: its arguments are copiously supported by empirical evidence. There is more than one thesis in these hundreds of pages which explore the Pakistani story by using just a few well-chosen entry points. This makes it an original chrono-thematic volume whose outstanding quality lies in the author's capacity to call a spade a spade. Hoodbhoy excels in deconstruction of the official narrative whose sincerity is nourished by his personal memory on more than one occasion. Indeed, he peppers his very erudite manuscript with personal anecdotes that are all very revealing – after all, he is almost a midnight child whose life is nearly as long as Pakistan's existence.

On the origins of Pakistan, he exposes the state's history textbooks by showing that in fact Hindus and Muslims did not form two nations in India until political and religious leaders encouraged ordinary people to think in this way. It was not for defending Islam that *some* Muslims rallied around Jinnah for creating a separate country: it was for promoting their interests. These people formed elite groups (often descending from the Moghul aristocracy) which felt threatened by the rise of the Hindus (be they better educated or more entrepreneurial), especially in the provinces of the Raj where Muslims were in a minority. But these elites used Islam to mobilize the masses in the name of the Pakistan movement. Using the work of several historians, Hoodbhoy demonstrates that they could only succeed because of the support they received from *pirs* and other religious figures who, therefore, expected some payback from the Muslim League after 1947; some of the attendant debates in the Constituent Assembly of Pakistan about the role of Islam in the new state are very well analyzed by Hoodbhoy.

x Foreword

While Hoodbhoy organizes his narrative around personalities, including Syed Ahmed Khan, Iqbal, Jinnah, Maududi, Azad and Khan Abdul Ghaffar Khan, his analysis of the making of Pakistan from the late-19th century till 1947 elucidates the social rationale of a process that had very little to do with religion. This power-oriented dynamic remained the order of the day until the Muhajirs, who had detached the territory they needed to have a state to rule, were in turn dislodged by the Punjabis. Indeed, identities and interests of ethno-linguistic groups turned out to be very resilient and sometimes even prevailed over Islam – as evident from the strength of Pashtun and Baloch nationalisms as well as the sentiments which gave birth to Bangladesh. This ethnic factor lost some of its political influence under Zulfikar Ali Bhutto. Indeed, in the early 1970s his Pakistan People Party (PPP) made inroads into Punjab in spite of its Sindhi roots, a clear indication that something like a national political arena was taking shape (I'll return to this issue below). Imran Khan's Pakistan Tehreek-e-Insaf (PTI) has shown a similar capacity to go beyond ethno-regional perimeters to acquire a national aura. But in his case, as Hoodbhoy convincingly argues, that was because of the army's support.

The role of the army in the Pakistani story is described in this book in a clinical manner. Hoodbhoy is at his best when he demonstrates that since the 1950s, even if civilians sometimes governed the country, the military have ruled it constantly – for many reasons, as he shows, including that of American support. While external actors are not systematically factored in, the role of the U.S. is described here in a very eloquent manner.

If Hoodbhoy is not defending any thesis, one question crosses the book: what is Pakistan, how can one make sense of its identity, of its reality, and of its future? This inquiry naturally emerges from the country's genesis because the concept of Pakistani nation lacked substance. It was an ideological state created by elite groups in quest of a territory – and finally captured by men in uniform. But this inquiry also results from the rather uncertain profile of a country that is neither a democracy nor a dictatorship and neither secular nor theocratic.

Certainly, Pakistan looks like an anomaly to many observers, but its trajectory is not so atypical: like many other countries, Pakistan tries to emulate the model of an ethnic nation-state, and such a project is particularly painful and difficult given the diversity of the Pakistani society in terms of religions, languages, and cultures. Pakistan embarked on this inevitably violent journey before India, but this is the route those who rule in New Delhi are now following. Hoodbhoy's book, here, is fascinating as it shows how Hindu nationalists are converging with the makers of Pakistan by emulating some recipes of ethno-religious nationalism. Even the vocabulary is the same: for both sides, Hinduism and Islam are more than religions, they are "ways of life", and can therefore endow citizens with a complete identity – which means that they have to reduce "angularities", the word Jinnah used in 1947 and that M.S. Golwalkar used too in the 1960s to describe the work of the RSS, his organization.[1] Provincial identities were the angularities Jinnah was obsessed with – and that Pakistan is still fighting because centralization and concentration of power in the hands of Punjabis, and more precisely of Punjabi officers, instead of defusing tensions have exacerbated centrifugal forces and, therefore, "angularities".

As early as 1947, Jinnah wanted every Pakistani to speak Urdu and forget Bengali, Sindhi, Pashto, etc. Apart from that, as Hoodbhoy points out, he was so enamored with the unitary pattern of nation-building that he recommended to the Muslims who had stayed behind in India to learn Hindi. Maududi went one step further: not only the inhabitants of Pakistan and India had to embrace two different, specific national cultures which were to emerge from the old Hindustani mix, but they had to accept the dominant social order too. In 1954, summoned before the Justice Munir Commission because of his role in the anti-Ahmadi agitation, he argued – as Hoodbhoy demonstrates – that while the Muslims should follow the rules of an Islamic state in Pakistan, it would be normal for the "Muslims of India [to be] treated in that form of Government as *shudras* and *malishes* and [that] Manu's laws are applied to them, depriving them of all share in the Government and the rights of a citizen".

Not to "be reduced to the status of Shudras" and to become "slaves of Hindus" was precisely one of the main reasons why Jinnah wanted to create a separate Pakistan – as Hoodbhoy shows. But once he got it, he would not care for the Muslims who had remained in India except the Kashmiris, of course. Why? Simply because of the logic of ethnic states which implies that only the dominant community enjoys citizenship rights.

Hoodbhoy concludes that such a nation-state is bound to be badly affected by all kinds of tensions – like Israel, another "ideological state" to which Pakistan is often compared. But like Israel, Pakistan may persist in its present form not only because of the strength of the establishment and majority community, but also because of the constant disinformation to which society is exposed. When people believe, for instance, that India started the 1965 war (a personal anecdote that Hoodbhoy recalls), they can more easily be maintained in a state of fear. And the fear of a big neighbor is one of the best glues for keeping together a divided nation-state.

In one of the last chapters of the book, Hoodbhoy asks: "I'm a Pakistani, but what am I?" and the short answer, seventy-five years after Partition, can still be: "I'm someone who fears India". However, this negative definition needs to be qualified because national integration has also made progress thanks to the promotion of Urdu, because of the making of a national education system, because of the presence of Pakistan in all kinds of international fora (including the world cup of cricket), and last but not least because of the making of a national, political arena in which power-hungry competitors fight for resources. Till they are hopeful to get a fraction of the pie, they will not try to secede – and will help those who rule to repress the secessionists. After all, this is one of the reasons why most Sindhis have given up on the idea of forming a separate nation-state since Zulfikar Ali Bhutto's first election.

Pakistan will probably survive nolens volens and so Hoodbhoy's last chapter is worth reading for one to know how a better Pakistan – and a more viable

xii Foreword

one – could be built. The author pleads for the end of legalized discrimination, a redistribution of wealth, more federalism, gender equality, a more independent education system, a questioning of the country's obsession with Kashmir, and a purely civilian regime. It may sound utopian, but Pakistan itself seemed to be a utopia when the idea emerged in the 1930s.

Christophe Jaffrelot

Professor of Indian Politics and Sociology
King's College London, Research Director at CERI-SciencesPo/CNRS
and President of the French Political Science Association

Note

1 Golwalkar considered that the RSS "gives the individual the necessary incentive to rub away his angularities, to behave in a spirit of oneness with the rest of his brethren in society and fall in line with the organized and disciplined way of life by adjusting himself to the varied outlooks of other minds" (Cited in C. Jaffrelot, *The Hindu Nationalist Movement and Indian Politics*, London, Hurst (1996), p. 60).

PREFACE

> There has existed throughout history an ironic relationship between the past and future. Those who glorify the past and seek to recreate it almost invariably fail while those who view it comprehensively and critically are able to draw on the past in meaningful and lasting ways. People who have confidence in their future approach the past with seriousness and critical reverence. They study it, try to comprehend the values, aesthetics, and style which invested an earlier civilization its greatness or caused it to decline. They preserve its remains, and enshrine relevant, enriching images and events of the past in their memories both collectively and individually.
>
> — *Eqbal Ahmad in* Between Past and Future[1]

In writing this book I started out thinking I should record my half-century-long experiences as a teacher and professor in Pakistan, a nuclear physicist opposed to nuclear weapons, a science popularizer in a science-unfriendly country, a rationalist who disputes hearsay and seeks evidence, and a worker for peace between Pakistan and India. But by the time I was done — and this was well after the Taliban took over Afghanistan — the book before me was absolutely not that. Rather than tell stories about myself, to reflect upon state and society in Pakistan and to see how they have been shaped by historical forces and personae was so much more important.

Looking back into history through the dispassionate lens of rationalism can help us understand why the Pakistani state instinctively fears cultural and religious diversity, is palpably averse to establishing a people's democracy, has failed to create meritocratic institutions, and continues to support and perpetuate a feudal order rather than seek its eradication. While one hopes for better in the decades ahead, I want to understand and explain why Pakistan has been unable

xiv Preface

to create a viable education system, achieve progress in science, establish trust in government, and earn respect for lawful authority.

Even more tragically and dangerously, there remains a bitter residue of pain and resentment from Partition that separates the peoples of Pakistan and India. This toxic residue is being passed down through generations, a combustible material well suited for those eager to reignite inherited grievances. In both countries, reliance upon religion for nation-building is bringing up contradictions in new and unexpected forms. In Pakistan, religious groups actively cultivated by the state launch the fury of their faith from time to time against non-Muslims. Whether in the form of Deobandi militancy (as up to a decade ago) or in the present form of blasphemy-obsessed Barelvi fanatics, these powerful armed groups have boomeranged on the Pakistani establishment which refuses to learn from the past and continues to nurture them as political tools.

For these reasons, this book eventually turned out to be analytical and academic, not a personal account. However, where it can add value here or there, I do slip in an occasional recollection or observation. The book's journey starts from many millennia ago but then centers quickly on the circumstances and impulses that gave birth to the very first state in history founded upon religious identity. Thereafter, it moves on to the present epoch and considers its myriad puzzlements. It ends with brief prognostications on the perils ahead and how to navigate past them.

A book like this one should rightfully have been written by a full-blooded historian of South Asia. Only one requirement would be strictly non-negotiable – that of being scrupulously honest and sticking to facts as best as we know them. Unfortunately, this is a near-impossible condition to expect from all but a few academics in the history departments of Pakistan's universities. Our professors have mostly stayed clear of genuine fact-finding, choosing instead to serve the needs of power. Referring to the obsequious behavior of some of his contemporaries and colleagues, the late K.K. Aziz – author of *The Murder of History* – once sardonically remarked that like governments, a people get the historians they deserve. Of course, there are brilliant exceptions to an overall mediocre lot that fill our universities but, well, exceptions are always exceptions. The good ones confine themselves to what is academically respectable – a narrow, detailed examination of some person, issue, or period of history. They refuse to assign causes or, if they do, surround their arguments with so much fluff that the reader is exhausted by the time they arrive at conclusions. Many so-called historians are silent spectators and publish nothing of consequence. Still, they are not as bad as the ones who are greedy for paychecks and complicit in supporting false narratives.

Understanding the present in light of the past is best done by those best equipped academically by training for this task and who also have easy access to large libraries across the world. These have shelves with everything you might want to know including excruciatingly careful descriptions of historical events, personae, and phenomena covering almost every aspect of South Asian history.

Preface **xv**

I have much admiration for the true professionals who base their work upon perspicacious primary research. Still, there seems to be little by way of a grand synthesis in the existing literature. Most importantly, it seems that no one has really tried to understand just why the theory of two distinct nations emerged. What caused people who lived together as reasonably peaceful neighbors for centuries to violently hate each other so suddenly? The enormous spread of information needs distillation into a coherent narrative – one that is both broad and deep enough for understanding our present.

In doing justice to a book that ranges so widely, the ideal author should be an expert of South Asian history. However, that alone would be insufficient. She or he should also be a political scientist, sociologist, ethnographer, economist, and someone well-rounded in world affairs and history. Maybe someone someday will do a much better job, but I simply could not wait for the right expert to come along. And so, knowing well that I was biting off more than I could chew, I took the plunge anyway. The truth needs to be told, and told well.

Wait a minute! Truth is one thing – and absolutely crucial – but what shall guide us when there are competing and mutually incompatible versions of history? Who are we to believe? While researching archives and writing, I was ever conscious that each of us is shaped by the place we fell to Earth. This explains the repetitive patterns of human behavior and, equally, the slowness and incredible stupidity humans demonstrate when it comes to evaluating collective social behavior. Prejudice warps not just history but also what we see around us at this very moment. This makes it so difficult to evaluate the actions of one's own nation or tribe. Say what you will about Da'esh, Taliban, Boko Haram, and their ilk. They are victims of sheer ignorance, more to be pitied than condemned. But take white Americans: even after the storming of the Capitol in Washington – with every detail recorded on video – large parts of Middle America continue to believe the Illuminati, Birthers, QAnon, and others that the takeover was the work of communist provocateurs. And, amazingly, the most scientifically advanced nation in the world has a population that largely refuses to believe climate science…and then there are "the anti-vaxxers". At times, one despairs whether humans have enough time left to adapt to this planet.

It's far worse when it comes to historical accounts where there are only papers and books but no pictures or videos. I have piles of books on my desk that describe the pre-Partition period. The same events are described so very differently by those with different persuasions. To give just one example: a series of Communal Award Round Table Conferences were held between 1930 and 1932 in London. One historian writes that they plainly exposed Congress's obduracy and Muslim flexibility. Another refers to the same records but sees in them nothing but Muslim obduracy and Congress's magnanimity. Each rightly points to hard-liners on the other side while conveniently forgetting the zealots from his own side These are different but informed perspectives on the same historical events. To make one's case, each must be understood and responded to.

xvi Preface

History, Voltaire is said to have famously remarked, is the lie commonly agreed upon. Or, to put it differently, majoritarian consensus determines how we look at the past. But like most nice-sounding aphorisms, this one too needs to be taken with more than just a pinch of salt because such dire pessimism precludes the possibility of knowing anything at all about the past, or for that matter, anything about anything. Damn! Then we must all give up. But this is clearly false. We certainly know a lot about a lot of things, even if imperfectly in places.

We don't even know why we know what we know. In fact one of philosophy's most profound questions was posed by Bertrand Russell. I was stunned after reading it at age sixteen and then barely able to comprehend it: How comes it that human beings, whose contacts with the world are brief and personal and limited, are nevertheless able to know as much as they do know? And, yes, let's not be overly modest – we humans know a lot.

Clearly, if the world external to an individual wasn't objectively describable at some level, then we would end up knowing nothing. We wouldn't be able to even agree upon what is a chair, tree, or dog. So is a reasonably fair, objective, and scientific assessment of human affairs possible? This book optimistically accepts this as an ab initio premise. We can know history even if some lies are bigger than others, and some truths are clearer than others. In this book I have attempted to identify the bigger and the clearer truths as well as some outright falsehoods and, hopefully, have added in a pinch of clarity.

I have asked myself whether the world really needs yet another book about Pakistan and can stomach yet another attempt to understand the tortuous history of India's partition. No matter which way I looked at it, the answer came out to be: yes. For one, those times are so imbedded into our consciousness that even in daily discourse in newspapers and television there is frequent reference to them. And, for another, I believe that the present brings out certain features which, although they had always existed, had nevertheless not been examined for those particularities which have become so enormously relevant today. Like in a fractal structure, one finds repetition of a basic pattern over and over again. My contention is that Pakistan's failure to develop universities and institutions of learning can only be understood after a critical examination of what happened as the Mughal Empire fell apart, the differential development of Muslims and Hindus under the impact of British colonialism, and the division of the subcontinent. Further, that division happened because once-powerful Muslims lagged Hindus in competing for jobs which demanded modern education.

I now have to tell you what really drove me to write this book. It's because I am angry and I have been angry for decades. And yet, I promise, I know my first duty as a scientist is to be objective and not let feelings interfere when it comes to facts.

I am first-generation Pakistani, born in Karachi three years after Pakistan. Perhaps even more enthusiastically than most boys my age, I too greedily absorbed nationalism and militarism. I was a hugely thrilled eight-year-old when General Ayub Khan seized power after a military coup in 1958. Soldiers had set up camp in our neighborhood's park near Soldier Bazar; I crawled under the barbed wire so that I could see them up close. It was a high point for me when one friendly soldier allowed me to touch his Bren gun.

Then, at age twelve, I had a terrible fall while playing cricket. On the way to the hospital, bleeding profusely with four front teeth knocked in, my elder brother Samir whispered in my ear that General Eisenhower had just promised to provide Pakistan with 12 B-57 Canberra bombers. I loved aircraft madly, bombers almost as much as fighters. My pain disappeared, at least for a while.

The martial law regime and the tall, handsome President Ayub Khan – who by now had promoted himself to Field Marshal – seemed to eight-year-old me as the best thing that could happen to Pakistan. From a special supplement of *Jang* newspaper, I carefully snipped out Ayub's picture poster, together with eight smaller ones of his other generals, to decorate my room. Then on 6 September 1965 our English teacher at Karachi Grammar School, Mrs. Raheela Masood, announced in class that India had invaded Pakistan and that the president had declared war because of India's "unprovoked aggression". Pakistan would now give India a "befitting response" – a term typically used by army people even today. I burst into whoops of joy; Mrs. Masood had a hard time shutting me up. I am particularly appalled that I shouted, "the only good Hindu is a dead Hindu". That's because I loved reading about Wyatt Earp, Roy Rogers, and the cries, "the only good Injun is a dead Injun".

Actually there was no way I could have hated Hindus. My father, a Sindhi Muslim, had only Hindu buddies in his school days. They had to flee to India after Partition and, although I could never meet any of them, we nevertheless reverentially addressed them as uncles. My delight at the declaration of war came instead from the delicious anticipation of the battles now to be fought with fighter aircraft, tanks, and warships. Best of all, we'd now get to see more deeds of valor and more heroes of war like Major Tufail Muhammed, my number-one hero. For years I had collected accounts of his epic last stand after scouring various newspapers and magazines. Machine-gun bullets had ripped through his stomach while his company was fighting off Indian intruders from across the border into East Pakistan. But the valiant Major Tufail kept throwing grenades and finally killed an enemy commander by pounding him with his helmet.

The declaration of war seemed too good to be true. Pumping the pedals furiously, I bicycled the distance from Soldier Bazar to the far off air force recruiting center on Ingle Road in record time. Disappointed at being told I was too young to enlist in the Pakistan Air Force, I rushed to Napier Barracks on the other side of Karachi only to have a friendly major chuckle as he refused my proffered services to the army. We don't take boys with spectacles, he said. And so my neighborhood's civil defense team was the highest to which I could rise. Hearing ack-ack guns firing at Indian bombers over Karachi was as close as I ever got to seeing action. As darkness fell and the city was blacked out, our family would gather around a radio to hear Alam Lohar on Radio Pakistan singing the Punjabi ditty *jang khaid na'ee hundi zananiyan dee* (war is not a game to be played

xviii Preface

by the effeminate). It said one brave Muslim soldier was worth five cowardly Hindus; soon Delhi's Red Fort would be ours. Fifty years ago I "knew" Pakistan had not only thwarted an unprovoked Indian attack upon our territory but that we had won – and won handsomely. Dammit: how could it not be true?

As Winston Churchill famously said, *a lie can travel half way around the world while the truth is putting on its shoes.* States can easily peddle lies, small and big, as and when needed. This particular one was a whopper. If I hadn't been such a blockhead at age fifteen, I'd have known the truth sooner. Things just didn't add up: if we were on the point of winning, why wrap up the war so suddenly and have disappointed people take to the streets? Pakistan had won the air war (we actually did), so why did we capture less territory than India?

The biggest shocker was finding out that India hadn't started the war, Pakistan had! Code-named Operation Gibraltar, President Field Marshal Ayub Khan had embraced the suggestion of his foreign minister, Zulfikar Ali Bhutto, to liberate Kashmir. And so infiltrators were prepared for sending across the border into Occupied Kashmir. Eighteen years later, the same General Muhammad Musa whose portrait once decorated my room together with others, and who oversaw Gibraltar as Chief of Army Staff wrote in his autobiography that their job was to sabotage military targets, disrupt communications, etc. As a long-term measure, arms would be distributed to the people of Occupied Kashmir and a guerrilla movement started as a prelude to a full-scale uprising in the valley. Operation Gibraltar was to be followed by Operation Grand Slam with regular troops, tanks, and fighter-bomber support from the Pakistan Air Force. But the civilians of Indian-administered Kashmir were not only unprepared for mass rebellion, they actually suffered at the hands of the intruders. Soon the commandoes were isolated; some were captured, others fled. A month later, India attacked across the international border.

Fast forward forty years during which people change and change…so did I. In 2004 while making a video documentary on Kashmir that sought an objective appraisal of the conflict, I interviewed Pakistan's much decorated national hero, Air Marshal Asghar Khan (1921–2018), on camera in his Islamabad residence. He was perfectly forthright about how the 1965 war began:

> We started the damn thing (war) by moving into Indian occupied Kashmir. I was the commander of the air force only six weeks before that but I had no idea they were doing this. And when I saw in the (news)papers that our tanks were moving into Indian occupied Kashmir, I saw Ayub Khan on the third of September, three days before the Indians attacked and I said to him, I think you've decided to go to war. He said, no not at all – who told you that? I said nobody told me but reading the newspapers you've sent the army into occupied Kashmir and therefore India is bound to react. They will react in the Punjab. He said no, no, this will not happen. We've been assured by the foreign office this is not likely to happen. It will be localized conflict. And of course, three days later Indian forces moved into

Pakistan…we didn't win the war nor did the Indians. The air force did very well indeed. In the first four days we had knocked the Indian air force out. They were not able to fly over Pakistan.

External pressure forced the war to a halt. With 3000–4000 dead on each side, the war caused approximately equal damage on both sides. Nevertheless, both countries claimed victory, pointing to their gains while ignoring their losses. Every year on 6 September Pakistan celebrates. At this century's beginning, these celebrations had been fairly modest. But with a rejuvenated army running Pakistan, they have become gala festivals with a national holiday, gun salutes, airpower displays, and prayer ceremonies. Each year there is a rededication to the idea of eternal war with India. On the Indian side, in the years before the rise of militant Hindutva, the date had been largely forgotten. But now India too insists on celebrating victory. It is strange that one war should have two victors. Surely, militarism everywhere finds easy converts – especially if you can catch them young.

Decades later, I can coolly reflect upon my earlier enthusiasm for blood and sacrifice. As a warrior child, I had within me what a lot of young people everywhere have within them. It's just that I was a tad ahead of many. War, aggression, and territoriality are primordial instincts that all primates – particularly libidinous males – have inherited from our early ape ancestors. Equipped by nature with a limbic system, a primitive part of our brains operates below the horizon of consciousness. Survival needs had made it necessary for humans to be programmed to feel fear and rage, making it easy to kill when emotions are suitably aroused. National states have learned to capitalize on this urge and seek to inspire their young men into joining their army. As a boy, I had been no different. It was only through reading voraciously – and facility with English – that I gradually came to a different understanding of the world.

Do young people in Pakistan today see the 1965 war just as I saw it fifty years ago? Sadly, the answer is, yes. I know this because from time to time I am invited to speak to students at various Pakistani universities and colleges – at least in places where I am not yet banned from campuses. At a lecture in the main auditorium of the elite Ghulam Ishaq Khan Institute of Engineering Sciences and Technology in 2017, I asked the audience how many there believe that India had started the 1965 war. Most hands went up. Then I asked: how many of you have heard of Operation Gibraltar? From the podium I saw faces blank out. Some students turned to their smart phones, presumably to google whether this was some kind of spoof question or whether some such thing had actually existed. From that audience of approximately 300, eleven hands went up. Repeating the same question in 2018 elsewhere, I found that at Quaid-e-Azam University only one student from the 180 present was aware of Operation Gibraltar (and he thought that it had been a fine idea, improperly implemented). At Government College-University (Lahore), only 3 out of 200 students from social science departments had heard of it.

xx Preface

As a kid I had been lied to. But surely I was not the only one taken for a ride. Large numbers embrace a worldview based upon belief in some unblemished, mythical past. Of course, Pakistan and India are not unique – look at how successfully Vladimir Putin has roused his people to a war of aggression against Ukraine. Even more than in earlier decades, today's social environment is characterized by primal yearnings for moral renewal, new glory, and vengeance. College-degree holders are generally no less invested in such myths than those considered uneducated. This is unsurprising because a tradition of open debate and discussion is yet to be established in our institutions of learning. In every authoritarian society, free speech and critical thought is unwelcome, and Pakistan's shaky democracy has failed to protect these fundamental rights. The critical need for alternative discourses – such as in this book – cannot be overstated.

The task of truth telling needs many knowledgeable people to tell their tales because each of us can know only a small piece of some larger story. So much is unknown and might never be known because many of those who actually knew left this world without telling their stories. Most Pakistanis still don't know why and how East Pakistan separated; what happened in the Ojhri Camp tragedy when an ammunition dump hidden inside Rawalpindi city blew up in 1988 (it killed three times more people than the 2020 port explosion in Beirut); what thinking lay behind Pakistan's Kargil invasion of 1999 and what was expected to follow; who organized and oversaw the 2008 Mumbai massacre; why Osama bin Laden was found in Abbottabad in 2011; why Sindhis and the Baloch are upset with the Centre; who abducted the thousands still missing in Balochistan and Waziristan; and how Pakistan's deep state operates through militant religious forces. Now that the Taliban are Pakistan's neighbors and Pakistan is seeing a revival of religious terrorism, it is hugely important to understand how that came to be.

Self-delusion is bad for individuals because it beclouds their judgment. It's much worse for a country. All countries of the world exaggerate their successes and understate their failures; they delude themselves to differing degrees. They all need a truth serum, but Pakistan does so more than most.

Learning has been slow for all humankind, and still slower for some than others. But at least we are not flotsam and jetsam in some metaphorical stream of history. As agents of change, we are endowed with reason and silently guided by some deeply hidden species survival mechanism. The more we ponder upon our origins and wonder how we got to where we happen to be, the better.

Note

1 E. Ahmad, *Between Past and Future: Selected Essays on South Asia*, Pakistan, Oxford University Press (2004).

ACKNOWLEDGMENTS

I am awed, surprised, and grateful that some of the finest and most respected scholars and professional historians of South Asia, most of whom I have never met in person or had prior correspondence with, readily agreed to my request to read this book's manuscript as it slowly took shape. I name them alphabetically by first name: Ali Usman Qasmi, Ayesha Siddiqa, David Gilmartin, Faisal Devji, Francis Robinson, Noam Chomsky, Philip K. Oldenburg, Rajmohan Gandhi, Romila Thapar, and Tariq Rahman. Each was pressed for time in teaching and research and could easily have ignored a request from someone so distant from their respective areas of professional expertise. It is my good fortune that they did not. By subjecting this book to their rigorous scrutiny, I was able to avoid mistakes and factual errors that could have been embarrassing. Still more importantly, their deep knowledge helped me investigate directions that I had been hitherto unaware of. However, the views expressed in this book are mine only, not theirs.

I acknowledge Shaheryar Azhar for his unstinting enthusiasm for the book project. He carefully read the manuscript, detailed its shortcomings, pointed to places where my arguments needed to be strengthened, added his sharp political insights, advised me on the reorganization of some sections and – meriting a separate acknowledgment – also contributed a Zen poem (see Chapter Thirteen)!

I am grateful to Sadia Manzoor for her love but, almost as much, for her occasional scathing and insightful comments that helped me moderate the book's tone in places where it had been unnecessarily abrasive. Nayyar Afaq, with his extensive knowledge of literature and poetry, helped me locate and type certain Urdu poems, while Hajra Ahmad and Abdul Hameed Nayyar read and commented on some chapters. The Balochistan chapter benefited from comments by Kaiser Bengali and Amir Rana. Zia Mian's withering critiques of the book's very earliest drafts eventually led to structural changes in the book's

xxii Acknowledgments

layout. His invitations to visit Princeton University at the Program on Science and Global Security gave me valuable access to the university's library resources. Bilal Zahoor carefully read the manuscript and suggested improvements and additions. I appreciate his efforts to nudge me leftwards, even if I could not always comply. Hareem Fatima not only indexed the book but also pointed out repetitions (now removed) and asked sharp questions. Ranjit Powar helped locate various sources and suggested a cover design for the forthcoming local edition.

INTRODUCTION

Nations can lie, exaggerate, invent false narratives, or create myths. Of all these, myths are the most complicated, an entirely different kind of beast. They are often neither wholly true nor wholly false. Instead, they are hardy creatures because they often contain a kernel of truth thereby making them persistent, stubborn, and memorable. Academic jargon speaks of a variety of myths: imagined realities, imagined communities, social constructs, or deep fiction. And yet – just think about it – myth-making and religion is the hallmark of intelligence. Chimpanzees, our nearest living relatives, have no religion and are unable to invent myths or spread fictions. This is also why they are unable to cooperate in the large numbers that mark human society. Yuval Noah Harari points to our imaginative fecundity as the reason why humans are able to communicate on such a large scale. The talent for developing myths is what he calls the cognitive revolution, the point at which "history achieved independence from biology".

Pakistan, more than any other country on earth, looks for a myth to justify its existence. It is certainly not the rebirth of some former Muslim nation. In fact the name "Pakistan" was invented in 1933 at the University of Cambridge by a young student, Chaudhry Rehmat Ali. It was a flight of imagination because there never had been any kind of Muslim state in India. So, while the Mughals had ruled India for centuries, the population had been dominantly Hindu. Although Muslims were spread everywhere across India's vastness in those times, in no sense did they form a nation. Yet the myth of the Two Nation Theory (TNT) emerged towards the tail end of the British Raj and had both Muslim and Hindu versions. The Muslim version came with a sense of entitlement, persuading Muslims into implicitly believing that since they had ruled India for

DOI: 10.4324/9781003379140-1

2 Introduction

centuries they were not just different from those they had ruled over but could rightfully rule forever. On the other hand, the Hindu version told Hindus that they belonged to an ancient, much superior, civilization now on the verge of freeing itself of the shackles of Muslim and Christian invaders. With enormous explosive power, these myths fueled political movements that ultimately led to new political boundaries and a reconfiguration of the Indian Subcontinent.

Myths of a nation's origin

Any kind of myth can be incredibly powerful if and when it grips the popular imagination. A young man I once met in distant Hunza, when told about his tribal ancestors from many thousand years ago, spoke of how he felt the knowledge "course through him, make fire in his veins, and illuminate his heart". Those stories gave to him his personal identity. On the other hand, collective identity is generated by myths of a nation's origin. To define that body of people, there is invented a heroic past, great men, and glory. For any newly established state, it becomes important to create the illusion of its origin as just one single people – a nation. Thus every nation-state has a unique genealogy around which it builds a mythology. This romantic notion helps shape that nation's self-image and sense of direction.

Sometimes, national myths can be as totally innocuous as the cartoonized Hägar the Horrible. But, unless you're Scandinavian, who cares if this now popular character actually existed? On the other hand, some myths can be terribly dangerous because certain facts can be excised from them and false memories deliberately inserted. They then become enormously powerful tools with which political movements construct, strengthen, and perpetuate fictitious narratives. Once a myth catches on fully, one must bid goodbye to reason, commonsense, and compassion. "Land without a people for people without a land" is a stunningly clear example. Popularized by the early 20th-century Zionist movement, it was used methodically to take over an already settled land. A people historically settled there for centuries were ultimately thrown out and today count among the world's most tragically dispossessed refugees.

Myths underlie the struggles of Uyghurs in China, Chechens in Russia, Armenian separatists of Nagorno-Karabakh, and Kurds spread over Iraq, Iran, and Turkey. These insecure minorities are demanding breakup of their common ancestral lands, believing that coexistence with the dominating and domineering majority will suffocate them. All make claim to a separate homeland on the basis of a shared culture and language (but not religion). Closer to home, Baloch nationalists see themselves struggling against Pakistan much as the Kashmiris are out fighting India. Each nation – whether or not it succeeds in carving out geographical space for itself – creates its own set of myths and is saturated in myth. This creates a cushion from reality and gives strength to struggle.

The myth of Mother India prevails across BJP-led India today. It is based on the fiction which assumes that from time immemorial there had existed a pure indigenous Aryan culture – a mother culture if you will – which predated all invaders including, of course, Muslims. The golden age of Chandragupta is so imagined as to put all other civilizations to shame. The claimed achievements of ancient India boggle the mind: Hindu civilization is supposed to have performed incredible feats which modern civilization is now only barely able to duplicate. An ethnically pure Sanskrit-speaking ancient India supposedly flew airplanes before the Wright brothers, initiated the practice of plastic surgery, learned how to cure cancer, and invented both calculus and the law of gravity long before Newton. The five vital forces or 'panchapraanas' known to ancient sages are claimed to encompass all known forces of Nature and go even beyond present scientific knowledge, whereas from the Bhagavatapurana we learn that the wise ancients knew of Einstein's relativistic time dilation well before Einstein and used it for traveling between planets. The Muslim invader allegedly destroyed it all – and Hindu temples in particular – and so Hindu India must now assert its historical right to avenge its humiliation. Underlying Hindu nationalism, this version of two nations is now state ideology in India. In its extreme version, it demands the destruction of symbols of Muslim rule – such as the Babri Mosque – and imposition of a Hindu order upon all who live on Indian soil.

We shall see in this book how and why the myth of the Two Nation Theory emerged. As articulated by Pakistan's founders, this asserts that Muslims have constituted a separate nation ever since Arab Muslims set foot on the Indian Subcontinent some 1300 years ago. Even if they lived side-by-side with Hindus since that time, Hindu–Muslim antipathy was claimed to be deep and unalterable. Wouldn't Hindus seek to avenge the thousand years of domination by Muslim invaders? This fear increased – some would say it was relentlessly exploited – as British imperial rule lost its grip. Thus the next logical step was to seek separate abodes. Pakistan would be the final outcome of a Muslim struggle against Hindu domination and a victory over conspiracies hatched by British rulers.

Invention of the Muslim TNT and the Hindu TNT was for diametrically opposite reasons: one was to split India and the other to enforce Hindu hegemony on a united India. The Indian National Congress, though Hindu-dominated and with more than just a few hardliners in its ranks, was steered by the eclectic Nehru into rejecting both forms of the TNT before and after Partition. The task of popularizing the respective versions of TNT fell upon the Muslim League and the Hindu Mahasabha. The consequences were stupendous. The ensuing bloodbath remains etched into the minds of even those who never saw it happen. Films like *Garam Hawa* and novels like *Udas Naslain* drive home the poignancy and tragedy of creating new borders and splitting asunder a land that was once home to all.

No intelligent and reasonably informed person today can defend either version of the TNT on the basis of reason and evidence. It was perhaps a pardonable mistake when communal temperatures had reached the skies as in the first half of the 20th century. But can it be pardoned now? Can anyone really believe that Mother India is the fount of all civilization and Muslims were the only invaders? The older generation of Indians had largely rejected that view but I'll let the citizens of Narendra Modi's India sort that one out. The focus of this book is Pakistan, and the intended audience is that of Pakistanis (although I admit that only a few will read a counternarrative such as this one). For us Pakistanis there

4 Introduction

is a question that is still more important and puzzling: did the subcontinent's Muslims ever constitute a single indivisible unit in the sense described to them in Jinnah's epic speech of 1940 in Lahore? This gives birth to other questions: Are Pakistani Muslims still one nation? More interesting: if not a nation today, can they ever become one?

From a rational viewpoint, the subcontinent's Muslims were one nation only if someone is willing to engage in self-deception or chooses to be duped. Any objective historical assessment will reveal that the Muslims of the Indian Subcontinent have never been together as a single nation. Nor are they one nation today. After 1971 the Bengali Muslim has shown emphatically by word and deed that he will have no truck with the Punjabi Muslim. The Punjabi Muslim and the north Indian Muslim – both as they stood then and as they stand today – considered the Bengali Muslim to be derived from inferior stock. What of Hazaras, Makranis, Kafiristanis, and the diverse peoples of the Northern Areas? Perhaps the Bengali Muslim issue has become moot after 1971 and the total severance of contact with what was once East Pakistan. But mainstream Pakistanis are also unwilling to admit all co-religionists into their own fold.

To see this, simply ask a participant at any one of many mammoth rallies that happen every year after the month of Muharram. These draw tens of thousands where the crowd roars *Shia-kafir, Shia-kafir*! Randomly choose some member of the crowd – likely a Sunni Muslim belonging to the *Tehreek-e-Labbaik Pakistan* – and ask whether he considers Shias, Ismailis, Zikris, or Ahmadis as a member of his own nation. His answer is likely to be unequivocal, spontaneous, and likely to be accompanied by a strong expletive. As for the Hazara people, no public outcry has ever followed whenever religious fanatics butcher them, or when their houses, shops, and meeting places in Quetta are destroyed.

Nevertheless, few Pakistanis – particularly those from Punjab – are willing or brave enough to challenge a manifest untruth. The Two Nation Theory is mandatory for teaching in school and the Civil Service curriculum for Pakistan Studies centers upon it. To challenge the TNT is treasonable under the law and doing so in public can invite not just the wrath of the state but can make an individual feel very unsafe. As a result of teaching distorted history in schools, countless inconvenient truths have been wiped clean. For example no Pakistani student today knows that the most popular leader in their history – second only to Jinnah – was Sheikh Mujib-ur-Rehman.

Ah! But can one Pakistan become a nation in the future? That's a different question altogether to which we shall revert in later chapters.

The danger of any open-minded investigation, as in this book, is that multiple myths such as that of two nations will crumble in the light of properly investigated facts. Myth busting is anathema wherever it is perceived as challenging a country's fundamentals because interpreting the past has enormous consequences. Pakistan is not unique in this regard. The powerful propaganda machinery of nation-states and their frequent reliance upon exclusivism encourages their populations to take caricatures of history as serious fact without subjecting them to historical or logical scrutiny. This helps states to consolidate their political, social, and cultural power.

Exclusivism as philosophy

Every exclusivist philosophy is predicated on the assumption that humankind is divided into diverse, fundamentally incompatible groupings each character-ized by ethnicity, history, language, culture, tradition, and – most importantly – religion. It assumes that these cannot mutually coexist peacefully. Beliefs that conflict holds sway over cooperation are as old as human history. By its very nature, exclusivism is a pessimistic view of the world in which universal human values cannot exist, democracy and participation are not always to be cherished, and accident of birth is more important than any other determinant. In pre-Enlightenment Europe, countless mutually hostile groupings fought each other for centuries. Some countries have moved towards inclusivism, only to take half a step back. Brexit stands before us.

The Two Nation Theory is all about exclusivism. A clear articulation of this genre of beliefs came from Samuel Huntington, a much sought-after professor at Harvard back in the days of the Vietnam War. He proposed that one naturally allies with one's "own kind", and so cultural and religious identities would be the primary source of conflict between peoples once the communist ideology had fallen. Henceforth, he said, all future conflicts would be civilizational and largely religious. This would be so because the world was rapidly shrinking, and so there would be more interaction among people who share your "real" identity and origins. Local identities would therefore be diluted and replaced by something bigger. That bigger thing would "come from the guts". It would be primordial – civilization and culture. For Huntington, the survival of the West depends on Americans, "reaffirming their Western identity and Westerners accepting their civilization as unique not universal, and uniting to renew and preserve it against challenges from non-western societies".

One can keep adding to Huntington's list and end up with a world full of conflicts between groups of every variety. I will not debate Huntington here, although I must confess to being present among the dozens of students in the early 1970s who semipeacefully protested in Harvard Yard his role in adding to the carnage of the Vietnam War. Huntington's civilizational thesis has been demol-ished over and over again. The critiques are powerful and persuasive: Edward Said emphasizes that it is far simpler to opt for bellicosity than to patiently sort out the complexity of reality. Mobilizing collective passions – as Huntington does – is easy through "othering". Much more difficult is to reflect upon and examine a conflict at its roots. This requires somehow becoming mature enough to step outside of ourselves and view things from a perspective other than simply us-versus-them. To phrase a conflict in terms of labels and cultural generaliza-tions can become the source of the problem itself. Equally, reducing multiple identities to a single one is deeply dangerous.

6 Introduction

This is exactly how things started going wrong on the subcontinent. Multiple conflicts were phrased in essentialist terms: it was all to be understood as Hindu versus Muslim. Only the differences and conflicts between Hindus and Muslims were spotlighted, while similarities and syncretic assimilations were downplayed. Feudalism, exploitation of peasantry and labor, ethnic differences, and political rivalries were shoved into the background although they were rampant throughout India. And so, around the beginning of the 20th century, most political debate and discussion in north India took place between emerging Hindu triumphalism and the retreating Muslim elite – the remnants of those who had once been victorious rulers. This helped consolidate the myth that Hindus and Muslims have been nations at daggers drawn from time immemorial. Purged from memory were the long periods of peaceful coexistence.

The effort it took to widen the Hindu–Muslim divide should not be underestimated. At the corners of history's grand triangular clash stood British imperialism, Indian nationalists, and Muslim separatists. All undertook clever political engineering. Who would win or lose and in what measure was uncertain until almost the end. The mathematical theory of games says outcomes cannot be stably predicted in any situation where complex conflicts are artificially reduced to a two-player game. We know this also from experience with war gaming – a part of training in every military war college. Communal cheerleaders and those who sought the division of India banked on particular strategies. Looking back, one can charitably assume that they did not anticipate the bloodbaths that ultimately followed and may have desisted had they known. But antagonisms, when fed into febrile minds, have a tendency to generate their own dynamic. Misperceptions become inevitable when you guess at your opponent's next move; subjective assessments can become just as important as material reality, and threat perceptions can be freely manipulated upwards or downwards. As happens in football matches, excess of testosterone puts physical violence just around the corner after which the myth gets closer to reality and becomes self-fulfilling. As grounds for conflict become more fertile, a calculus of gains and losses takes shape with the zero-sum game emerging almost inevitably.

A striking example of zero-sum gaming is that of pre-Partition hostage bargaining – one that Jinnah endorsed – where the deal was that if you kill so many Muslims on the Indian side (where they were in the minority), we will allow so many Hindus and Sikhs to be killed on the Pakistani side. The claim was that an eye for an eye and a tooth for a tooth would ensure the security of minorities in both countries. Morally, this is indefensible and amounts to collective punishment. If Shia assassins kill a Sunni leader, can Sunnis rightfully extract revenge upon all Shias (and vice versa)? If a Palestinian kills an Israeli soldier or settler, is it okay for Israel to take out a whole Gaza neighborhood? In any case, this perverse logic of mass retribution did not work, and the subcontinent was left awash in blood. An atrocity committed by Hindus inspired a second atrocity committed by Muslims and the cycle kept repeating itself. Once two large groups of people

Introduction **7**

were up in arms, the theory of two nations became self-fulfilling, at least for those times and for some decades thereafter.

Hostility towards other groups and their othering was a survival necessity that derives from our caveman past. But we miss the point by looking at conflict only because it is cooperation, not conflict, that lies at the core of human civilization and progress. How did we miss this obvious fact? Why do old beliefs persist in the face of flatly contradictory evidence? This is a deep puzzle for evolutionary biologists to answer, not for us. Albeit it does suggest that Darwinian evolution has installed certain flawed substructures in our brains.

Was Partition accidental?

There was nothing inevitable about Partition. Post facto it might so appear, but imagine two small shapeless puffs of smoke. Over time they accreted material from the surroundings and grew bigger but were still largely formless. Had a gust of wind come along they might have dispersed, broken into smaller puffs, or merged into one. Who knows? As it turned out, the wind turned the puffs into two ghosts who, just as after Macbeth murdered Banquo, wandered around the house whispering to all: sleep no more, the enemy is nigh! And so eventually a large number of people were convinced into believing that India was inhabited by two mutually hostile nations that could never live together. From there the emergence of two nation-states with defined boundaries was just a step away.

Happenstance could still have prevented Pakistan from being made. Imagine that Jinnah had died of tuberculosis two years earlier, or that Nehru and Patel had been wiser and accepted the power-sharing formula of the Cabinet Mission, or that a more thoughtful last viceroy had been appointed instead of the vain glory-seeking Mountbatten, or a thousand other such "ifs". But such speculations are just a waste of time because they teach us nothing.

While the notion of two nations was initially a false, manufactured one, with the passage of time it went on to acquire some elements of reality. Who made this happen, just how it happened, and what led up to it is extremely instructive. In fact, much of this book seeks to understand and explain precisely this. This is not some arcane issue that can be dumped as belonging to history alone; we stand to imperil our understanding of the present if we do not explain why this idea gained currency. As we shall see, although the idea of Hindus and Muslims being essentially separate categories had already started to grow in the decades after 1857, there were real material causes that led religious identities to solidify. It was at a second stage that they were leveraged for attaining definite political ends. Jinnah, Gandhi, Nehru, and Patel were doubtless important actors, but Hindu–Muslim differences were not invented by these individuals. Nor were they solely the result of machinations by a receding colonial power. They eventually assumed elements of reality.

What caused the solidification of religious identities? As everywhere, economics has much to do with it. How wealth is created and distributed largely

8 Introduction

determine how societies behave as a whole. Traditional Marxists claim that "the material world determines our ideas, rather than our ideas determining the material world". Of course, this cannot be fully true and today only the most doctrinaire among Marxists will insist on rigorous historical determinism. But sophisticated historians like E.P. Thompson have adapted and modified previous rigid beliefs in Marxism and look towards material forces for interpretation and understanding. This is perfectly fair because it leaves enough room for happenstance – that over which no one has control.

Informed by such debates, progressive historians of India have also looked for material causes. They stress that a meaningful history of India cannot be simply a sequence of chronologically ordered episodes involving kings, dynasties, and their challengers. In understanding social and political change, we can thus understand why historians held in high esteem, such as Irfan Habib, Romila Thapar, Mushir-ul-Hasan, Hamza Alavi, D.D. Kosambi, Ram Sharan Sharma, and others, have used an entirely different paradigm that requires studying local geography, land ownership, and caste relations. Economic history – the changing means of production – provides a much sounder understanding of social dynamics than just religion or politics alone. And yet all elements can become important in certain circumstances – it would certainly be erroneous to exclude religion because socialization into a group gives it a powerful hold over people's minds.

The book's expeditionary map

With a view to keeping the chronological order of events intact, and with linked ideas placed as close as possible to each other, this book is divided into five parts. The first four seek to understand the present by looking at the past. The fifth and final part looks at future challenges. It asks what must be done if Pakistan is to ever emerge as a viable and prosperous country.

Part One: *Long Before the Two-Nation Idea*. This part begins with a broad sweep of history over the last millennium that covers the formation of political communities in theoretical, anthropological terms. Historians of ancient India give us hard evidence that religious identities had once been ill-formed and amorphous. Even in the centuries that followed the first Muslim invasion in AD 712, a man would be known by where he lived and his occupation rather than his religion. Romila Thapar, distinguished historian of ancient India, points out that up until the 13th century local sources did not use the undifferentiated term Muslim for foreigners. Instead, references to foreigners were in political rather than religious terms. For example, Turks were Turushkas and Arabs were Yavanas; that they were both Muslims was secondary.

From the time of the first Muslim invasion of India to the arrival of the British is roughly a thousand years. This period saw periods of religious violence between the invaders and local peoples, but also periods of cooperation and the spread of multiple cultures that syncretized local Hindu and Muslim customs. Divisions were blurred with Hindus managing many key functions of the

Mughal state. Cross marriages were common. Adoption of Hindu ways eventually drew the ire of such Muslim purifiers of the faith such as Shaikh Ahmad Sirhindi (1564–1624) during the time of Emperor Akbar (1542–1605). When Emperor Aurangzeb (1658–1707) seized the Mughal throne, the purifiers – Shah Waliullah and later his son Abdul Aziz – got a huge boost. These conservative clerics railed against the accretion of Hindu beliefs into Islam and called for treating Hindus as a conquered people who must pay the *jizya* tax. Centuries later they are held up as models of Islamic scholarship and behavior.

But try as they did, the impact of faith purifiers was limited because the needs of governance trumped those of faith. Aurangzeb, too, had to employ Hindu generals and high functionaries, just as the Mughal rulers before him. Until mid-Mughal times and even until much later, religious identities had been amorphous and their boundaries ill-defined. Many Muslims and Hindus had more in common with each other than with their co-religionists. Hindu and Muslim landlords and government servants had a common mentality because their political connections were based on pursuing identical interests. In fact because of syncretic practices, in some cases it was not even clear how to define Muslim or Hindu. So how, when, and why did hugely different varieties of people who had lived together – sometimes comfortably and sometimes not – start to think that they belonged to only one of two camps?

Awareness of religious identities was sharpened by European colonizers of the 18th century. In fact they were far more effective in creating divisions than the faith purifiers. Of course, making deliberate distinctions between peoples worked naturally to their advantage because it helped to divide and rule. But to entirely attribute growing Hindu–Muslim differences upon them would be incorrect because there was another reason as well. It is one that is rarely emphasized these days, but the rapidly turning wheels of progress had brought to India new issues and contradictions. Old professions had become redundant, and new professions were demanding new skills. These changes brought into question the relative speeds of adaptation by Hindus and Muslims to new ways, knowledge, and an alien language. These sharpened religious differences which were quickly highlighted by a recent addition: fast communications allowed 19th century faith preachers to travel by rail as well as send out literature by post. We shall dwell on this point later.

Therefore, as our next step, in seeing how Hindus and Muslims diverged, we must investigate their different responses to the challenges of modernity. The upshot: with the systematization introduced by the British, religious boundaries became sharper and sharper in a land where they had been fuzzy and ill-defined just two centuries ago. In particular, the gathering of census data categorized by religion by civil service functionaries turned out to be astonishingly important.

Chapter Three takes the year 1857 as the anchor point for such an investigation. This is when centuries of Mughal rule over India had ground to an end. Pakistan was born just ninety years later. This year is so important that historians are wont to divide British rule in India into two parts – that before and after it. Tens

10 Introduction

of thousands of Muslim and Hindu peasants armed with primitive swords and spears had buried their differences in the War of Independence – also known as the Great Mutiny – to battle the cavalry, infantry and artillery regiments of the British East India Company. The failed uprising was crushed with extreme brutality. Never in a thousand years had India's Muslims felt so demoralized and lost.

The Scottish historian William Hunter (1840–1900) noted in 1876, "A hundred and seventy years ago it was almost impossible for a well-born Mussulman in Bengal to become poor; at present it is almost impossible for him to continue rich". Muslims, even more than Hindus, became targets of British revenge. From mighty conquerors they had been whittled down to mere subjects. Even after the uprising was defeated, those Muslims who were no longer a threat and, instead, humbly supplicated the Raj's benevolence were distraught at finding their appeals spurned. Getting any kind of job was enormously difficult. To cap it all, even a military career was now no longer an employment option. With Muslim history being steeped in military prowess and generations having spent their lives in service of some ruler or the other, there could not have been a bigger blow. Getting a commission in the British Army was next to impossible (although much was made of a certain Captain Hidayat Ali who was brought forward on the recommendation of Colonel Rattray for staunch defense of the British during the Great Mutiny).

Imperialism had come not to spread enlightenment in India. Rather, it sought to plunder India's wealth and seek new markets for European capitalism. Nevertheless, it willy-nilly also brought in tow new rules for the new age. Ruling the empire meant that the British needed natives who knew English sufficiently well and could be taught the right skills. Your race and religion did matter, but job competence was crucial. Without education and skills, you could not land one. Apart from the English language, also needed was a certain amount of flexibility in social matters. The Muslim nobility – the *ashrafiyya* – could not fit in well into the new scheme of things. It had little to offer to the Company. Their cultured manners with frills and flourishes befitted an aristocracy, but their refined Urdu and Persian had little functional value. The Company's profit-seeking goals were better served by having more suitable employees as part of its administrative apparatus.

That apparatus was being built upon quantitative reasoning. In the present age of supercomputers, we know the huge latency carried by Big Data. This, of course, was not known when the first ever census was carried out in India in 1872. It then fulfilled a British administrative need. Until that point, how many local inhabitants were Muslim and how many Hindu was a matter of guesswork, but careful bookkeeping became possible after the census. Henceforth, vague qualitative ideas would give way to numbers gathered by surveys carried throughout the length and breadth of India. Although the initial goal may have been to govern efficiently, once colonial authorities used this data for administrative purposes – jobs, services, and seats for public offices – communal cartography subsequently became firmly embedded into the scheme of things.

The system of separate electorates caused the Hindu–Muslim difference to grow from a crack to a chasm. The web of jobs and religious affiliation got linked together. Whether this was formally so or informally, religious affiliation now began to matter.

Perhaps unwittingly, modernizing movements such as Brahmo Samaj amplified differences. These helped Hindus adopt European values and managed to ameliorate the appalling inequities of the caste system. While Hindu traditionalists resisted the suggested reforms, their resistance was relatively weak because modern education was seen as the way to get employment in government and hence attractive. By 1831 there was more demand for English education than the Committee of Public Instruction was able to meet.

With Muslims it was different. Over the millennia, there have been countless wars and defeats and after every war defiance and hurt are natural responses to defeat. Although once-powerful conquerors find it difficult to accept that the times had changed, it generally happens that after a period of hesitation and resistance the defeated adapt to the ways of the victors. On the other hand, there are others who persist in refusing because they are convinced of their intrinsic superiority – the ones chosen by God to rule others.

That latter conviction was strong with *ashrafiyya*. The glory days of Mughal India were long gone, but they still hankered for those times. Memories of greatness went back to the earlier Muslim conquests of India and even to the glories of the Arab Golden Age. An overwhelming majority was psychologically unwilling to accept that things had changed forever and they had been overpowered. Convinced that Islam was the only true religion, and superior to every other, they saw the present state of Muslims simply as a temporary setback. There was no introspection. By the end of the 19th century, a sense of orphanhood – the mentalité of having lost protective parents – fueled the search for a new identity and, ultimately, Pakistan. The faith in a messiah who would unite all Muslims into victory remained undiminished. It is a hope that the passage of centuries has left intact for some even today.

As the Muslim predicament sharpened, they blamed this upon British prejudice who sought to assuage them by giving jobs. In turn, Hindus would protest that the jobs given to Muslims were undeserved and amounted to appeasement; some unfounded stories were created that Muslims were actually agents of the British who secretly served their every need. On the other hand, many Muslims feared – as large numbers do to this day – that western education would take their children away from Islam. Western ways being considered obnoxious, few families were willing to send their children to secular schools. The Hindu–Muslim economic disparity that derived from a difference in education levels ultimately snowballed. Some cultural boundaries got redrawn, while existing ones became sharper.

With education and skills becoming increasingly more lopsided on the religious balance, I argue in this chapter that the Two Nation Theory was by now well on its way. Two antagonists emerged eventually by the end of the 19th century; the puffs

12 Introduction

of smoke were becoming like Hamlet's ghosts that wandered around the encampment suggesting that each necessarily belongs to one camp or the other. Still, matters were far from simple. There was little enthusiasm for the notion of Pakistan in the first thirty years of the 20th century. Understanding the emergence of the Two Nation Theory in cultural terms – as has been done in this book – is such a hot potato that most Pakistani historians do not touch it. Instead of focusing on what prevented Muslims from being competitive, their emphasis is on emphasizing grievances, discrimination, and Hindu domination as primary causes.

By the time 1947 came along, the Two Nation Theory had acquired a life of its own. The myth was now the mainstream, accepted by most Muslims and also by many Hindus. In fact, your life could depend on whether you were Hindu or Muslim. How exactly this emerged is extremely important to understand in detail and worth spending many pages on. I have dwelt upon this in such detail not for arcane historical reasons but because the very processes by which religious divisions are enhanced – such as those between Pakistani Muslims – remain operative today as well and need to be understood.

Part Two: *A Closer Look at Pakistan's Three Founder-Heroes*. This part is about the trinity of Pakistan's founding figures. I have devoted a chapter each to three towering individuals – Syed Ahmad Khan, Muhammad Iqbal, and Muhammad Ali Jinnah. All are celebrated in Pakistan as heroic figures for having advocated a separate national Muslim identity. Countless hagiographies have wrapped multiple myths around them, hiding the complexities of these three iconic figures. I will not give detailed biographies because some excellent scholarly and reliably researched works exist on each. They will, of course, be referenced in due course. Instead, my purpose here will be to use as far as possible the original writings and speeches of these men for charting their intellectual evolution amid the peculiar circumstances of their times. In particular, for each individual the following key questions will be investigated:

1. What he perceived as primarily responsible for the plight of India's Muslims.
2. His attitude towards modernity, science, and European civilization.
3. How and why he ultimately transitioned from universalism to communalism.
4. How he saw Islam relating to the needs of the time.
5. His politics with respect to the Muslim masses, Hindus, and the British.
6. How he visualized the future of the subcontinent's Muslims.

Lifting the curtain brings out unfamiliar truths. Sir Syed was by far the most progressive Muslim of his time. As a proselytizer for modernity and science, he ran into bitter opposition from orthodox Muslims. And yet he sided fully with the orthodox in opposing the education of women or even poor Muslim men. Even though he eventually saw Muslims and Hindus to be different, he often found more commonality with the rich Hindu than with any Bengali Muslim. This complex personality was a product of his time. He deserves a nuanced understanding.

So does Iqbal who is often hugely misunderstood – often deliberately – by his awestruck admirers. So great are his contradictions that one is tempted to say there were actually two Iqbals, one liberal and the other reactionary. One does not see them talking to each other. He is so important and relevant a figure to contemporary Pakistan that the longest chapter of this book is on him.

As for Jinnah, he too was Janus-like. His utterances are freely used by cherry-pickers to justify whatever point of view they want. Although by no means an orthodox Muslim, his iconic status among Pakistani liberals of being liberal and secular fails to survive rigorous scrutiny. There exist at least two dozen books on Jinnah, including scholarly tomes. Popular hagiographies as well as the rants against him are legion. So what possible goal can be served by yet another account? In defense, I offer two reasons. First, any attempt to understand Pakistan would be incomplete without a reasonably thorough account of Jinnah's role. Second, instead of the mythical Jinnah, we need to know the real Jinnah who lies scattered across different books.

The subsequent chapter looks at those Muslims who opposed Jinnah's plan for creating a new state for Muslims. I have chosen to concentrate on just three of his key opponents here: Abul A'la Maududi because he saw Islam as universal and argued that an Islamic state with defined borders was improper; Abul Kalam Azad because he surmised that the Muslims of India would be collectively weakened by the separation; and Khan Abdul Ghaffar Khan because he was against the very idea of communal politics. Even if Jinnah triumphed over these men, much can be learned from their critiques and experiences. I wish other important figures such as Maulana Husain Ahmad Madani, Maulana Syed Muhammad Sajjad Bihari, and many others could have been included, but the three chosen opponents tell us much about the mood of those times.

Part Three: *Postnatal Blues*. The aftermath of creating ab initio the modern world's first religious state left the subcontinent awash in blood. By the time India had been divided, nearly a million corpses lay strewn on each side. Accurate numbers will never be known, but in the greatest mass migration in centuries, an estimated 14–15 million people crossed the new border. By comparison, even the 21st century's Syrian or Rohingya refugee crises were small ones. Communal frenzy took over the minds of men; neighbor turned on neighbor and childhood friends became enemies. Trains carrying refugees between the two new nations arrived with compartments stuffed with only the dead; all aboard had been waylaid and slaughtered by mobs chanting religious slogans. They confirm what Blaise Pascal, the 17th century philosopher and mathematician, had concluded: men never do evil so completely and cheerfully as when they do it for religious conviction.

Nevertheless, in spite of such bloody beginnings, Pakistan's future could have been bright. Let's recall that the white man had slaughtered millions of America's native inhabitants and the Jew had chased away the Palestinian Arab. Still, both the United States and Israel eventually became powerful nation-states. Similarly, in spite of the carnage of 1947, one could still have hoped that the birth pangs of

14 Introduction

a new nation would eventually subside and another Shining City on the Hill – as the Puritan John Winthrop dreamed while on board the *Arbella* – would emerge from the darkness. Those who dreamed of Pakistan hoped for no less. They thought that centuries of Muslim decline would be reversed once the waves of incoming refugees were accommodated somewhere or the other. Here would be a model state where all Muslims would thrive. Jinnah went even further with his famous post-Partition words, "Hindus would cease to be Hindus and Muslims would cease to be Muslims, not in the religious sense, because that is the personal faith of each individual, but in the political sense as citizens of the State." This exceptional country was to be, literally, Land of the Pure. All differences would be subsumed into one supra-identity. Pakistan's official motto became – and remains – Faith, Unity, Discipline.

Once the euphoria subsided, bitter realities set in. Chapters Seven and Eight in Part Three center upon "angularities". This word features prominently in Jinnah's famed address of 11 August 1947 wherein he dismissed cultural, linguistic, and ethnic differences as mere warts and lumps – minor irritants that would fade rapidly in the new dispensation built on Muslim unity and the Two Nation Theory. But, contrary to hopes, this did not happen.

Chapter Seven details developments in East Pakistan where it turned out that Islam was not strong enough to glue two disparate peoples together. Trouble began to grow within the first few months even while Jinnah was alive. Had he died much later, or had another statesman miraculously emerged from within the Muslim League, a natural union would still have been difficult if not impossible. In any case, upon Jinnah's death, the Muslim League degenerated into a free-for-all, and successive governments were unstable and corrupt. As the only stable, modern institution, the military became steadily more dominant. Insulated from the people, it pursued its own institutional interests and agenda. Under President General Ayub Khan, and then President General Yahya Khan, East Pakistan became convinced it had been colonized by West Pakistan. In 1971 it sought separation, and, after the military action, it demanded and got a total divorce.

Chapter Eight tackles Balochistan – Pakistan's perennial problem from day one. This also turned out to be an angularity with a vengeance. Nomadic and tribal for many millennia, Balochistan had a Muslim majority that was ruled from far away Delhi which had once been the seat of the Mughal Empire and, later, of the Raj. Given the imminent British departure, it was not an attractive possibility for the Baloch to be under Punjabi or Muhajir domination. Nevertheless, upon Jinnah's written assurance that the state of Kalat would be acknowledged as sovereign and independent, the Khan of Kalat opted for Pakistan. After Jinnah went back on his guarantee of an independent Kalat state, the military was called in for the first time and all of Balochistan was forcibly made to accede to Pakistan. Balochistan was wedded at gunpoint and that's how it remains today. This messy situation was like with other princely states. But had things not been so thoroughly mishandled, they would have been as bad as they later turned out to be. This chapter asks what went wrong and what might be needed to set things right.

Of course, East Pakistan and Balochistan were not the only troublesome angularities. Other problems also emerged with time – Sindhi nationalism earlier, and now also in the areas of Pakistan at the periphery of Punjabi power. Tribal Waziristan, where the Pakistani deep state had helped the Taliban to establish their base after 911, stands largely alienated. The northern areas of Pakistan have a myriad different cultures and languages. The fifth province of Gilgit–Baltistan is in the making.

Part Four: *Five Big Questions*. Addressed in this part are five vexatious questions that appear and reappear in different guises and shapes at different times. Where possible I give a definitive answer, and where it is not possible my goal will be to explore possibilities as broadly as I can. For some questions, we cannot ever know the true answers but can still hold opinions that are reasoned. Those opinions will become still more reasonable and refined as we probe the past more critically. To do so is extremely important because such speculations influence our attitudes to much of what matters today: militarism, democracy, human rights, education, and science. Indeed, to understand these from the roots upward is the purpose of this book.

First: Was Partition worth the price in Muslim blood? Far from becoming the homeland of all the subcontinent's Muslims, Pakistan now hosts less than one-third. Some gained, including those who had been the most privileged among Muslims. The ones who probably lost the most were the Muslims who stayed behind in India. But there were others too, and we must do a full tally of plusses and minuses. Since the future can only be speculated upon, one cannot be categorical. Perhaps dividing India saved it from a fate still more terrible. Who knows? I will leave the reader to judge after putting possibilities on the table.

Nearly twenty years after Partition, the incomparable left-wing poet, Faiz Ahmad Faiz, composed his famous Urdu melancholia *yeh daag daag ujala* of a faded, darkened dawn and of promises betrayed. It so captured the mood of the people that many committed it to memory. But, in retrospect, the Pakistan depicted in Faiz's sorrowful soliloquy of some fifty years ago appears idyllic and peaceful. Back in the 1960s, the fanatical suicide bomber of the 21st century was unimaginable, the abbreviation IDP (Internally Displaced Person) was unknown, university students lynching a fellow student accused of disrespecting Islam would have been unthinkable, and none could have conceived of mobs chasing terrified Ahmadis and Christians and burning them alive. Who could have anticipated that Shias – of whom Jinnah, the founder, was one – would also become marginalized and be considered non-Muslims by roughly half of today's Pakistanis?

Second: What is the ideology of Pakistan and why does it matter? To contest this quantity today is legally a crime and few dare. But there is – at least as yet – no legal definition of what it is. Equally, none may dispute the Two Nation Theory which, figuratively speaking, is the placenta of Pakistan's birth – without it there would have been no Pakistan. For humans, this organ becomes redundant once a child is born and is thrown away. But does a country need to retain the relic of

16 Introduction

its birth eight decades later? The TNT became not only redundant but was also exposed as factually false after 1971. So why does the state insist on retaining it? These questions have relevance because all school textbooks are officially required to devote large sections towards teaching the TNT. This naturally invites the question of whether Pakistan needs an ideology in some shape or form and, correspondingly, what might happen if it chooses to dispense with having any.

Third: Why couldn't Pakistan become an Islamic state? There certainly has been no lack of trying. Jinnah may or may not have wanted one, but General Zia-ul-Haq's *Nizam-e-Mustafa* and Imran Khan's *Riyazat-e-Medina* were most certainly aimed at turning Pakistan into an Islamic state. These have remained unfulfilled yearnings and, as I shall argue, are certain to remain unfulfillable for multiple reasons. For one, the past offers no relevant blueprint. The Qur'an is silent on statehood. Further, there's no indication of what the Prophet of Islam may have wanted after his death. And yet, this has not stopped Islamists from yearning for an Islamic state because they want Islam to be everywhere and not just in the mosque or at home. I speculate on what might result if they happen to get their wish someday.

Fourth: Why is Pakistan a praetorian state? The military in Pakistan sees itself as a permanent part of the ruling establishment and is quite upfront about it. Of course, many emerging countries have also suffered periods of military dictatorship – Indonesia and Argentina are examples – but there was enough learning, and military rule did not recur. Pakistan appears to be different. As things stand, the ruling establishment sees no way to preserve itself except through a large military. Because the question of Kashmir has no foreseeable resolution, the Army has resolved to keep the country in a state of mind just short of war; this issue gives sanction to the military's dominance over every other institution. Civilian leadership is not allowed to challenge this basic, written-in-stone rule. Where and when needed, fanatical religious groups – Deobandi earlier and Barelvi later – are to be cultivated and used as per the need of the moment. But when they get out of hand, they must be confronted and crushed.

Fifth: Just what are Pakistanis and how do they self-identify? Is Pakistan the land and people inside a certain geographical boundary or, instead, is it a nation? If not, is it moving towards becoming one? The beginnings were not auspicious: the Two Nation Theory demanded elimination of all that people had inherited from the past with only their religious identity retained. In reality this has proved to be impossible. A nation implies a cultural or social community whose members share an identity, mental makeup, sense of history, or perhaps a common ancestry, parentage, or descent. This is why Pakistanis are confused about whether they should identify with the invaders of the last millennium or, instead, consider themselves linked to the source of their genetic pool, South Asia. How should Pakistanis think of themselves? I shall give my personal opinion after thoroughly discussing various past and ongoing searches for identity.

Part Five: *Looking Ahead*. This is the shortest section of this book – and for good reason: the future is far harder to predict than the past! In all likelihood, the next few years will be no different from those that preceded them. Absent some catastrophic event, normalcy will prevail. Notwithstanding the breakup of the alliance between Imran Khan and the military, a civil–military hybrid political system will muddle along, dependency on foreign powers will be no less than in previous decades, gated communities will keep the poor away from the rich, public facilities will shrink, and quality education will become still rarer. Of course, everything could be totally different from this, but in the short run this appears most plausible.

But what after that? A somewhat longer time scale – perhaps a decade or more – shows that even this level of normality will be faced by serious challenges. Chapter Fourteen identifies three outstanding physical perils. The first is climate change, the effects of which we are just beginning to see. The second is explosive population growth, a fact that all in every successive government have done their best to ignore. But this elephant in the room is growing by the day, squeezing everyone into narrow, cramped, and ever dirtier quarters. Still, the next generation of Pakistanis will live life as they do now assuming, of course, deliberate or accidental nuclear war can be avoided.

What if one wishes to break with a system that, at best, can provide only more of what presently exists? But before discussing this speculative question it is important to briefly step back and examine past experiments which followed the catastrophic events leading to December 1971 and the end of a united Pakistan. At that point Pakistan had to somehow reinvent itself. The fall of Dacca was not just a military defeat; it also led to ideological collapse and an existential dilemma. The notion of two nations had become irrelevant because Hindus of Muslim majority provinces had mostly fled to India and had been reduced to an insignificant minority. So what could be sufficient reason for a religiously homogeneous but culturally heterogeneous Pakistan to continue existing as a unit? The Baloch, Sindhis, and even the privileged Muhajirs were chafing at Punjabi domination. The road ahead was murky.

Chapter Fifteen discusses four distinct experiments to repurpose Pakistan. Bhutto called for vengeance against India, Zia-ul-Haq for full-blown Islamization, Musharraf for enlightened moderation, and Imran Khan was for a hybrid civil–military government that would somehow turn Pakistan into a replica of the Medina state. Every experiment relied on the military for protecting the state from its own people. None has worked because the starting assumptions have been wrong.

Chapter Sixteen – the very last chapter – is a manifesto for change. As a *gedanken* experiment, imagine being given a magic wand. How to fix Pakistan? It's almost a no-brainer: make peace with Pakistan's neighbors; let civilians, not soldiers, rule the country; decentralize massively but intelligently; choose trade over aid; redirect education towards skill enhancement and enlightenment; stop official efforts at political or religious indoctrination; give women a voice; allow labor and students a role in the democratic process; eliminate large land holdings through appropriate legislation; collect land and property taxes based upon

18 Introduction

current market value; speed up the courts and make them transparent; and make meritocratic appointments in government.

If the future is not to be an even worse continuation of the present, then the very idea of Pakistan must be rethought. To be what it was in 1947 is simply impossible. Learning anew means that much will have to be first unlearned and abandoned. To imagine a progressive and happy Pakistan is possible – else why bother with reading this book? But the steps to be taken are not what have been taken so far. Hopefully the outline here will have some value, at least to those who believe in a better future. As for implementation, it is for political movements to own and work towards this or some similar vision.

Whether this book has succeeded is for the reader to decide. Rather than a linear map, it must be read as a series of thought-circled pieces that return in their own ways to a single thread: how we got here with an occasional pointer towards exit locations.

PART ONE

Long Before the Two-Nation Idea

One

IDENTITY FORMATION IN ANCIENT INDIA

We started human life as hunter-gatherers, where contact with others, kin and non-kin, was the center of human life, social and moral. Begin by holding hands and talking, face to face, recalling our shared evolutionary history, and the importance of human nature.

> — Marc Hauser, evolutionary biologist,
> Harvard University[1]

To talk of an India with two nations was once an absurdity because there was not even a single one. In fact there were exactly zero nations. So where did the Two Nation Theory (TNT) spring from? Searching for answers to this fundamental question can help us understand why India was ultimately partitioned into three modern nation-states on the basis of this theory. In searching for the roots of separation, the present chapter begins from ancient India, follows up with the Muslim invasions, and ends just before the British took over. On this journey we shall encounter a concatenation of myths. Today's Hindu nationalists want us to believe that India was a primordial Sanskrit-speaking civilization with Sanskrit, its holy language, being of indigenous origin. They would also have us think that Muslims did nothing save loot, smash temples, and humiliate Mother India. On the other side of the divide is the myth of the noble Muslim who came across the seas to end caste discrimination, save desperate women from being exploited, and spread the light of Islam. Young Pakistanis are told that the heroic young Arab general Muhammad bin Qasim laid the foundation for Pakistan. Although deeply antagonistic to each other, two nation theorists on both sides of the Hindu–Muslim divide are united in their insistence that their respective nations are real entities grounded in historical fact. But the claims of both protagonists are false. Anthropology tells us the concept of nation is purely

DOI: 10.4324/9781003379140-3

22 Identity Formation in Ancient India

an imagined one. Far from having roots in reality that stretch back into eternity, the idea of nations is an invented one.

As we embark upon the quest for Pakistan's origins, there is a real danger of losing one's way in a jumble of facts. Imagine being inside a forest where all you can see are the branches and leaves. To go in circles is easy, and to think that there is little beyond was how forest dwellers thought about their habitat. So instead of barging straightaway into the minutiae of history, we shall step back to look at the grander picture: anthropogenesis and the manner in which human society on planet Earth arrived at the idea of nation. Perched on a hill above the seashore makes it far easier to understand that the earth is round, not flat.

In today's highly polarized debates over culture and civilizational heritage, a sizeable number of Hindus and Muslims of the subcontinent are like flat-earthers. They would like to believe that their origins stretch deep back into the impenetrable mists of time. Hindu nationalists in today's India promote the notion that Hindus are a primordial people, i.e., people of the soil who came from nowhere else. This 20th century development is one that historians and anthropologists tell us is absurd. Pre-modern Indians were far too fragmented to associate themselves with a readily identifiable Hindu identity. In fact religious and cultural boundaries on the Indian subcontinent had once been exceedingly fuzzy and ill-defined, different in different places, and shifting over time even in one particular area.

Equally, there had been no sense of Muslim-ness and, as we shall see time and time again in this book, this too had to be steadily cultivated. Periods of violence and confrontation between invaders and locals, as well as times of intimate and peaceful coexistence – both are abundantly found over the last 1300 years. Most Muslim rulers did not impose harsh sanctions, demand conversion by the sword, or commit genocide. But, as in traditional empires, each incident of rebellion was met by war, and opposition could not be brooked.

The herd instinct

Everything – including the Two Nation Theory – starts from our desire to live in groups. As we learn in *Social Psychology 101*, group identity is what the Homo sapien instinctively hankers for. Some 40,000–50,000 years ago our hunter-gatherer ancestors lived in tribes towards which they felt strong emotions of loyalty.[2] Viewed as evolutionary strategy, it made sense. Individual survival is increased by passionate attachment to one's own group, self-sacrifice for the sake of the group, and willingness both to die and to kill while defending your group from its enemies. Richard Dawkins makes the case that even altruism ulti-mately comes from group survival, transmitted – somewhat paradoxically – via our selfish genes.[3] Even if there was some inner sense of right or wrong among individuals, it had to be suppressed. Instead, there had to be a sustained belief that in case of a conflict one's own group is always in the right. Within their own group, individuals are generally kind to their own children and sometimes

Identity Formation in Ancient India **23**

willing to sacrifice their own lives for the sake of others within the group – an extreme example of altruism. But competing groups can exhibit terrible aggression against each other. Such intergroup conflicts are the most severe where boundaries between groups are sharpest, particularly where marriage or mating is forbidden across the boundaries.

This particular view of social evolution and population dynamics was first introduced into the study of population genetics between 1918 and 1932 by R.A. Fisher, J.B.S. Haldane, and Sewall Wright. In so doing, these researchers accomplished a formal mathematical synthesis of Darwin's natural-selection mechanism with the principles of Mendelian inheritance.[4] Earlier on, these involved tedious calculations, but modern computers make it almost trivial to implement such rule-based models for population growth and gene-transmission. The results can be compared against animal populations, and they seem to bear up.

For human populations no such models are available. The problem is that evolution has been hugely speeded up for humans because they are naturally endowed with the language faculty which permits cultures to evolve. Avery stresses that cultural evolution (as opposed to genetic evolution) is a new form of evolution. Information is passed between generations not in the form of a genetic code (i.e., DNA sequences) but in the form of linguistic symbols such as speech, writing, printing, and finally electronic signals.[5] The evolutionary success of humans is largely a success of cultural evolution.

The enormous "software" advances made by humans notwithstanding, you and I carry a huge amount of chemical baggage from the past. Loyalties to narrow interests are etched into our genes and hence the instinctive recourse to an "us" (or the in-group) and a "them" (or the out-group). Social scientists have studied the mental processes involved. These take place in a particular order: categorization, social identification, and social comparison.[6] Strong group identification remains intact even when survival is not what is at stake. On your side, there can be your football or cricket team, criminal gang, corporate entity, racial group, religion, or nation. Each group can be made to feel that it is intrinsically superior to the other, or vulnerable and helpless before the machinations of the other. The instinct to belong had once served us well; earlier in the evolutionary game, it advantaged *Homo sapiens* to cooperate against external foes and thus to survive in hostile environments. But in the age of nuclear nationalism and a warming earth, the evolutionary advantage of identifying with a particular group has become less clear.

India without nations

To venture into the history of ancient India is like walking into a minefield. The experts are divided and mercilessly attack each other. That's because for long centuries India was known to the outside world only through stray references in classical Greek and Roman literature. The historian D.N. Jha reminds us that Indology – the systematic study of Sanskrit-based Indian cultures – began

24 Identity Formation in Ancient India

only in the 18th century and was initiated by officers of the British East India Company.[7] Nevertheless, there are certain broad features that most historians do agree upon and which can be a reasonable basis for discussing here.

India was once a petri dish teeming with an uncounted number of communities of people who, within each community, could identify with each other and know the difference between "us" and "them". As yet there was no sense of having some overarching religious identity. Gilmartin and Lawrence note the changing meaning of the term Hindu as often denoting a non-religious category of people:

> Arabic and Persian use of the term *Hindu* had a range of meanings that changed over time, sometimes denoting an ethnic or geographic referent without religious content. By the same token, Indic texts referring to the invaders from the northwest used a variety of terms in different contexts, including *yavanas, mlecchas, farangis, musalmans,* and *Turks.* Such terms sometimes carried a strong negative connotation, but they rarely denoted a distinct religious community conceived in opposition to Hindus.[8]

Romila Thapar, historian of ancient India and the author of a dozen influential books, concurs with the above while observing that the notion of a uniform, religious community readily identifiable as "Hindu" was a rather late introduction:

> The first occurrence of the term Hindu is as a geographical nomenclature and this has its own significance…. It refers to the inhabitants of the Indian land across the Sindhu or Indus river. Al-Hind was therefore a geographical identity and the Hindus were all the people who lived on this land. Hindu thus essentially came to mean "the other" in the eyes the new arrivals. It was only gradually and over time that it was used not only for those who were inhabitants of India but also for those who professed a religion other than Islam or Christianity.[9]

Had you asked an ordinary villager in India from ancient times if he was Hindu, would he have even understood your question? Most likely the response would have been a blank stare. People identified themselves by where they lived, occupation, caste, ethnicity, language, and other markers. As Thapar emphasizes, the word Hindu is not to be found in any holy text; its roots derive from proximity to a river – the Indus. Pre-modern and pre-capitalist societies had pastoralists, peasants, and townsmen. Religion was far from what it is understood to be today. A bewildering mosaic of deities, beliefs, sects, and ideas defied any notion of commonality:

> Even when such religious sects attempted to constitute a larger community, the limitations of location, caste and language, acted as a deterrent to a single, homogeneous Hindu community. In the continuing processes of

Identity Formation in Ancient India   **25**

either appropriation or rejection of belief and practice, the kaleidoscopic change in the constitution of religious sects was one which precluded the emergence of a uniform, monolithic religion.[10]

Ancient era Indians were too fragmented to associate themselves with an identity that was readily identifiable as Hindu. But let us also observe how al-Biruni (973–1052) describes the people he encountered. His memoirs are readily available on the internet and make for fascinating reading.[11] They are significant because they record the very first interaction between a Muslim scholar and the locals of India. His aim was to understand how Hindus regarded the natural world and to make it possible for Muslims "to converse with the Hindus, and to discuss with them questions of religion, science, or literature, on the very basis of their own civilization".[12] For thirteen years he traveled in northern India, observing, questioning, and studying. His observations carry great credence since he was an amazingly astute and perspicacious observer who learned Sanskrit, a difficult language for an Arabic speaker.

Note al-Biruni's era: this was a full two centuries *after* the first Muslim invasion of AD 712. By now there was also a sizeable community of Arabs in India on the west coast, many of them settled from pre-Islamic times. By the 9th century, these had developed into various sects of mixed religions such as Bohras, Khojas, Mapillas, etc. But because their customs seemed so strange to him, al-Biruni lumps these Muslims with the rest by calling them Hindu! After all, they too belonged to al-Hind. For him the *real* Muslims were Arabs, Turks, and Persians – local Muslims were just too different to be properly called Muslim. This gnawing feeling of inferiority bedevils a good fraction of Muslims on the subcontinent even today, a topic that we shall revisit in some detail in Chapter Thirteen.

How al-Biruni came to India is not without irony: he had accompanied Sultan Mahmud of Ghazni (967–1030) for his plunder of the Somnath Temple which, together with other temples, offered rich pickings. However, al-Biruni grabbed his sultan's offer so that he could learn from India about its culture, religion, philosophy, science, and mathematics. More to the point: in describing the majority of India's inhabitants, al-Biruni uses religious terms:

Secondly, they totally differ from us in religion, as we believe in nothing in which they believe, and *vice versa*. On the whole, there is very little disputing about theological topics among themselves; at the utmost, they fight with words, but they will never stake their soul or body or their property on religious controversy. On the contrary, all their fanaticism is directed against those who do not belong to them – against all foreigners. They call them *mleccha. i.e.* impure, and forbid having any connection with them, be it by intermarriage or any other kind of relationship, or by sitting, eating, and drinking with them, because thereby, they think, they would be polluted.[13]

26 Identity Formation in Ancient India

This is a significant observation for two reasons. First, as Thapar puts it, this indicates that some religious doctrines that came to define Hinduism did not invariably conform to the same pattern of belief as the others. Nor were doctrines sufficiently well-defined at all times so as to provide the basis for a single, monolithic, uniform body. Many aspects of Hindu belief and worship were articulated in the form of sects with minor or major differences. The entire belief system did not go back to the identical set of events or a single historical founder or a canon that every sect acknowledged, as is true for Abrahamic religions.

Second, Hinduism was too amorphous by itself to have generated a description of who was a believer versus who was not. Thus the Sanskrit word *mlechha* (in Urdu it has morphed into *maleech* and means impure) was used for all peoples who were unfamiliar with Aryan culture, including those tribes living in parts of northern and central India that spoke a non-Aryan language. These were the earliest *mlecchas*. Later used to describe Muslim invaders, *mleccha* had more of a cultural connotation than a religious one. More refined, separate religious identifications emerged only after the establishment of Turkish political power in India.

Hinduism's polytheistic nature meant that even the gods were not fixed. Accordingly, new rituals and gods would pop up even as old ones died. No blood was shed by Hindus in doctrinal religious wars against each other (compare this against monotheistic beliefs). There was only a vague concept of a central overarching divinity under which there was a multiplicity of hierarchies. Idols of different statures abounded. Patronage of local rulers determined the status of a particular group of believers. With no historical founder or a single sacred text, it was caste that mattered more than anything else. In Vedic orthodoxy the Brahman stood at the apex, with all others required to pay due deference. In lieu of a strict ideology, there were religious customs such as daily rituals, festivals, and pilgrimages that must be strictly adhered to.

The amorphous nature of belief and the absence of a central core remained until much later. So, for example, the 8th-century Bhakti (devotion) movement was a theistic devotional trend that emerged somewhere in South India and developed around different gods and goddesses. Thapar notes that the conflation of Bhakti-ism with Hinduism, as touted by India's present rulers, is actually a doubtful one. There was never a shared creed, catechism, theology, or ecclesiastical organization:

> The consciousness of a similarity in ritual and belief in different geographical regions was not always evident. Thus bhakti cults were confined to particular regions and were frequently unaware of their precursors or contemporaries elsewhere. Recourse to historicity of founder and practice was confined within the sect and was not required of a conglomeration of sects which later came to be called Hinduism. This is in part reflected in

the use of the term *sampradaya* for a sect where the emphasis is on transmission of traditional belief and usage through a line of teachers.[14]

Bhaktis evoked shared religiosity, direct emotional and intellection of the divine, and the pursuit of spiritual ideas without the overhead of institutional superstructures. One notes that Guru Nanak, the first Sikh Guru and the founder of Sikhism, was a Bhakti saint. Modern-day Hindutvas claim of some unified Hindu nation that existed prior to the Muslim invasion surely hangs by the thinnest of threads. Mythology, not verifiable fact, lies at its core.

The Sanskrit controversy

Hindu nationalists claim that Aryans were indigenous to India and hence that Hinduism has timeless origins with Vedic Aryans inhabiting India since ancient times. The Vedic Foundation website states:

> The history of *Bharatvarsh* (which is now called India) is the description of the timeless glory of the Divine dignitaries who not only Graced the soils of India with their presence and Divine intelligence, but they also showed and revealed the true path of peace, happiness and the Divine enlightenment for the souls of the world that still is the guideline for the true lovers of God who desire to taste the sweetness of His Divine love in an intimate style.[15]

Advocates of indigenous Aryanism claim that the notion of Aryan invasions was manufactured by Europeans to serve their imperial conquests because, quite obviously, it leads to the notion of an India that had been invaded by outsider from the very beginning. In imperialist historiography a white race is depicted as subduing the local darker-colored population. While politically expedient for Hindu nationalists, the Indigenous Aryan theory appears to have no support in mainstream scholarship. For a careful description of various positions based upon available evidence, I refer the reader to Edwin Bryant's, *The Quest for the Origins of Vedic Culture – The Indo-Aryan Migration Debate*.[16]

Indigenous Aryanism and the 20th-century Hindutva movement claim that Sanskrit is a homegrown language that actually developed within the Indian Sanskrit-based civilization and spread out westward only later. Why is this Out-of-India theory so dear to revivalists? Thapar says that's because, "if the Hindus are to have primacy as citizens in a Hindu Rashtra (kingdom), their foundational religion cannot be an imported one".[17] The theory of the indigenous origin of the Aryans is unacceptable to most scholars but is at the core of Hindutva ideology for obvious reasons. It bases itself on the argument that Hindus are all of Aryan descent and have to belong to the subcontinent. Also, that the Vedic religion – which is foundational to Hinduism – has to be indigenous.

28 Identity Formation in Ancient India

So was there an Aryan migration into India that brought Sanskrit along with it? Or did Sanskrit radiate outward from India? The second is a conviction that goes under the name Out-of-India. It seemed to have little basis, but new evidence demolishes it entirely. Solid genetic data tells us that about 4000 years ago the Aryans who came from the north were actually Sanskrit speakers, bringing with them to India the holy language of the Vedas. This research is based upon data on Y chromosomes (or chromosomes that are transmitted through the male parental line, from father to son). In a peer-reviewed journal, 16 scientists led by Prof. Martin P. Richards of the University of Huddersfield, U.K., concluded:

> Genetic influx from Central Asia in the Bronze Age was strongly male-driven, consistent with the patriarchal, patrilocal and patrilineal social structure attributed to the inferred pastoralist early Indo-European society. This was part of a much wider process of Indo-European expansion, with an ultimate source in the Pontic-Caspian region, which carried closely related Y-chromosome lineages... across a vast swathe of Eurasia between 5,000 and 3,500 years ago.[18]

The abstract of a 2019 paper with 117 authors published in *Science*, a publication of the American Association for the Advancement of Science, is consistent with this conclusion and reads as follows:

> The primary ancestral population of modern South Asians is a mixture of people related to early Holocene populations of Iran and South Asia that we detect in outlier individuals from two sites in cultural contact with the Indus Valley Civilization (IVC), making it plausible that it was characteristic of the IVC. After the IVC's decline, this population mixed with northwestern groups with Steppe ancestry to form the "Ancestral North Indians" (ANI) and also mixed with southeastern groups to form the "Ancestral South Indians" (ASI), whose direct descendants today live in tribal groups in southern India. Mixtures of these two post-IVC groups—the ANI and ASI—drive the main gradient of genetic variation in South Asia today.[19]

A team led by Richards concludes that the prevalence of the R1a haplogroup[20] in India was "very powerful evidence for a substantial Bronze Age migration from central Asia that most likely brought Indo-European speakers to India".[21] Most modern South Asians are therefore some mix of Ancestral North Indian and Ancestral South Indian with the former being Steppe pastoralists who had migrated from grasslands in Eastern Europe corresponding to modern-day Ukraine, Russia, and Kazakhstan.

A very readable recent semitechnical account[22] of today's South Asian population genetics explains that once the Steppe people entered India, they mixed

Identity Formation in Ancient India **29**

with the Indus Valley people to create what is now called the Ancestral North Indian grouping. However, a significant portion of the people of the Indus Valley Civilization was pushed south when the Steppe people entered. They then mixed with the Ancient Ancestral South Indians to form a group known as the Ancestral South Indian population after which a "great churning" occurred and Indians interbred freely for the next 2000 years. Eventually the caste system put an end to this, and Indian society started calcifying into groups that did not marry across caste lines.

The conclusions of population geneticists specializing on South Asia rest on their own substantive research as well as a vast trove of new data and findings that have become available in recent years through the work of other genetic scientists around the world. In a nutshell: yes, there had most probably been an Aryan migration which brought into India a people and a language that was not indigenous. One can expect more precise genetic data in the future and a still firmer conclusion.

This scientific research is telling us something very definite: Mother India was not a virgin. In fact the factual evidence for an immaculate conception is about as strong as that of Mary having conceived Jesus without a father. There was no indigenous Indian primordial nation which had existed on Indian soil since the beginning of time. Indigenous Aryanism – or the so-called Out-of-India proposition – is a myth unsupported by mainstream scholarship and scientific evidence. But where evidence doesn't matter, anything can be believed no matter how far-fetched.

That Sanskrit, the liturgical language of Hinduism, was spoken in Syria before it came to India should rightly pull the rug out from under Hindutva advocates, at least those who claim to believe in reason.[23] Syria provides written evidence of the presence of speakers of Aryan in the 14th century BC. That evidence comes from a treaty between two contending forces, both equipped with horses and both speaking Aryan. The writing refers to some of the deities that are also referred to in Vedic sources and the language resembles Indo-Aryan. However, this is insufficient evidence on which to build a definitive theory of invasion. The chronology remains uncertain. It is likely that the Syrian evidence is earlier than the Indian if we argue that the *Rigveda* – the earliest source for the presence of Aryan speakers in India – was composed in the latter part of the second millennium BC. But some would prefer an earlier date. The chronological uncertainty makes it difficult to be categorical about which form of Aryan was earlier – the Syrian or the Indian.[24] While science will ultimately provide definitive answers, it is most likely that Aryan-speaking people migrated slowly from the north probably speaking a form of Indo-European from which Indo-Aryan/ Vedic Sanskrit evolved.

The bottom line: everyone has come from somewhere else. Therefore, a multicultural narrative makes much more sense than one that insists on racial purity. One simply must understand India as a rich tapestry born of migrations, invasions, and conversions.

30 Identity Formation in Ancient India

Muslim invasions

Invasions are a staple of history to which religion sometimes provides cover. Thus, for example, in the Hebrew Bible the Canaanites are the bad guys and so, as we learn from the Book of Joshua, Joshua's Israelites invade Canaan. God tells Joshua that the Israelites will possess the whole land between Lebanon and the Euphrates (Joshua 1:1–9) and personally promises Joshua help in expelling the Canaanites, Hittites, Hivites, Perizzites, Girgashites, Amorites, and Jebusites beyond the Jordan River (3:7–11). God remains faithful to His word to help Joshua on the battlefield. To let Joshua do his job well, He orders the sun and moon to stop moving which, of course, they promptly do. Thereafter, Joshua proceeds to slaughter the bad tribes.[25]

To moralize about historical events and judge them in the light of modern values leads one to a dead end. It is pointless to praise, condemn, or bear grudges for the wars waged by Alexander the Great, invasion of Britain by the Vikings, Peloponnesian War, invasion of Korea by Japan, the conquest of Scotland by the English, and a thousand other bloody episodes of history that shaped the world into what it is today. Instead, if it becomes necessary to look at any one particular region or episode, facts must be placed foremost and looked at dispassionately.

Our concern here is with Arab invasions of the Indian subcontinent. These were preceded by Arab traders well before the advent of Islam. These Arabs had come to India and settled all along the western coast. They were peaceful traders. In fact there had been a long history of trade between the west coast of India and the coast of Southern Arabia and the Red Sea – what is sometimes referred to as the Indo-Roman trade. Some Arabs were employed by the administration of the Rashtrakutas, a royal dynasty ruling large parts of the Indian subcontinent between the 6th and 10th centuries.[26] There was no history of temple raiding.

With the coming of Islam, things were to change. The entire Arabian Peninsula was conquered by Muslims, who were led into battle by Prophet Muhammad between AD 622 and AD 632. Upon his death in AD 632 at age 61, the leadership role was transferred to the Rashidun (righteous) caliphs who from AD 632 to AD 661 further extended Islam's eastern borders to Persia and Afghanistan. Thereafter, it did not take long for Arab Muslims to arrive at India's doorstep. First they came as traders and emissaries, and only later as invaders looking for wealth. Idol destruction – a religious requirement – was thrown in as a bonus. On the other hand, Turks and Afghans came to northern India primarily as invaders, not traders.

That India was filled with temples and idols provided holy justification for conquest because *shirk* (polytheism) is a cardinal sin in Islam, while *but-shikinee* (idol-breaking) is a virtuous act.[27] Iconoclasm, of course, is not unique to Islam. The story of the golden statue of a calf is shared between Judaism, Christianity, and Islam. It is, therefore, perfectly likely that early Muslim invasions of India were propelled by missionary zeal just as much as by the normal urge for conquest, plunder, and expansion of trade.

Identity Formation in Ancient India   **31**

Does that mean Hindu kings did not plunder the riches of other Hindu kings or destroy their temples? In his essay, "Indian Art Objects as Loot", Richard H. Davis, professor of Religion and Asian Studies at Bard College, points out kings in medieval India proudly and repeatedly proclaimed their expropriation of objects from other kings.[28] The *dharmashastra* of Manu – which long preceded Islam – specifies a code of conduct that, in the event of war, allows "Chariots, horses, parasols, money, grain, cattle, women, all kinds of goods, and base metals all belong to the one who wins (*jayati*) them" [Ibid. 7.96].

Why would a Hindu ruler destroy or appropriate a temple? We need to recall that ancient kings often associated their own legitimacy with their royal temple – typically one that housed an image of a ruling dynasty's state-deity, or *rashtra-devata* (usually Vishnu or Shiva). Destroying, looting, or redefining that temple was therefore a political act. A book by Richard Eaton, professor of Indian history at the University of Arizona, *Temple Desecration and Muslim States in Medieval India*, points out that temples that were not so identified, or temples formerly so identified but abandoned by their royal patrons and thereby rendered politically irrelevant, were normally left unharmed.[29] So, for example, the famous temples at Khajuraho south of the Middle Gangetic Plain were abandoned by their Candella royal patrons well before Turkish armies reached the area in the early 13th century.

Focused solely on Muslim invasions, while ignoring local fragmentation and internecine conflict, Hindu nationalists would obviously rather see history through a simple us-versus-them perspective rather than bother about tricky historical details. Had there existed a consciousness of being Hindu, surely there would have been attempts to jointly repel the Muslim invaders. Raja Dahir would have been joined by other Hindu rulers to fight bin Qasim, but there were none. Fragmented opposition was all that there was.

A high-pitched propagandistic tract – "Heroic Hindu Resistance to Muslim Invaders (636 to 1206 AD)" by Sita Ram Goel – typifies Hindutva views of foreign invasions. Goel purports to tell the story of "the greatest civilization which the world has known, and later of Hindu heroism which fought and ultimately frustrated all foreign invaders".[30] These invaders included Aryans, Iranians, Greeks, Parthians, Scythians, Kushans, Turks, Persians, Portuguese, Dutch, French, and British. Goel's pamphlet-sized book, available on the internet, was written around the time when the 400-year-old Babri Mosque in Ayodhya had been torn apart brick-by-brick by religiously charged Hindu mobs. He focuses on Muslims for razing Hindu temples, breaking Hindu idols, and amassing plunder as per divine order of their god.

There cannot be any dispute that such narratives have a kernel of truth. Yet one must heed the caution expressed by genuine historians of ancient India before accepting them at face value. "Claims of many thousands of such instances of temple destruction are outlandish, irresponsible and without foundation," according to Eaton. The Mughals are thought to have torn down only about two dozen temples.[31] He underscores the fact that much of the evidence cited

32 Identity Formation in Ancient India

by Hindu nationalists is found in Persian materials translated and published during the rise of British hegemony in India. Especially influential has been the eight-volume *The History of India, As Told by Its Own Historians,* first published in 1849. Edited by Sir Henry M. Elliot and completed by John Dowson, this was a particularly self-serving account of history because Elliot was keen to compare and contrast what he understood as the mildness, equity, justice, and efficiency of British rule against the cruelty and absolute despotism of Muslim rulers who had preceded the British. He wrote in the book's original preface,

> The common people must have been plunged into the lowest depths of wretchedness and despondency. The few glimpses we have, even among the short extracts in this single volume, of Hindus slain for disputing with Muhammadans, of general prohibitions against processions, worship, and ablutions, and of other intolerant measures, of idols mutilated, of temples razed, of forcible conversions and marriages, of proscriptions and confiscations, of murders and massacres, and of the sensuality and drunkenness of the tyrants who enjoined them, show us that this picture is not overcharged.[32]

Propagandists like Goel allege irrefutable evidence of a persistent pattern of villainy and fanaticism on the part of the medieval Indo-Muslim conquerors and rulers. One must take a measured position here. While conversion at the point of the sword certainly did happen, it cannot tell the full story. Sufis gained popularity through much of northern India, offering a way out of the caste system. Gradually, the invaders settled into the new land, living mostly among their own kind initially. But over time exclusivity was lost. They did not plan on returning to where they had come from.

I repeat: one does not need to dispute temple destruction by Muslims – that obviously did happen. But, as Eaton's research has uncovered, there are also sometimes serious misinterpretations of such "evidence" that can only be rectified by careful primary research, such as in the case of the alleged destruction of a Hindu temple by one Abdullah Shah Changal during the reign of Raja Bhoja, a king who had ruled over the region from 1010 to 1053. This is a particularly relevant piece of research because it turns out that one of Goel's chapters is titled, "From the Horse's Mouth", wherein he refers to Changal as a temple destroyer. But, upon careful examination of the inscription in Persian on Changal's tomb, it turns out that the "evidence" quoted by Goel – who does not read Persian – was quite off the mark. The inscription is, in fact, a narration and celebration of Changal as a Sufi saint.[33] How embarrassing !

MS Jayaprakash, professor of history at Kollam, has an interesting take on the systematic destruction of Buddhism by Hindus in earlier centuries: "Hundreds of Buddhist statues, stupas and viharas have been destroyed in India between 830 and 966 AD in the name of Hindu revivalism.... Spiritual leaders like Sankaracharya and many Hindu kings and rulers took pride in demolishing Buddhist images aiming at the total eradication of Buddhist culture".[34]

Identity Formation in Ancient India **33**

Today's Hindu and Muslim nationalists, though deeply antagonistic toward each other, are nevertheless united in their insistence that their nations had existed eons ago. What they both miss, however, is that the notion of nation was born just yesterday. The historian William R. Polk reminds us just how slow the process of self-identification has been for Muslims:

> Had you asked a Nineteenth Century Egyptian what was his "nation", he would have given you the name of his village. The Bedouin would not even have understood the question. In Persian, Turkish and Berber as in other African and Asian languages, no word fit the new need. The word that the Arabs first pressed into this service was *watan*, but *watan*, like the French word *pays*, meant village. It took not only a linguistic but also a mental leap to change village to nation. Farsi (Persian) and Turkish use a word for nation that is derived from the medieval practice of assigning minority peoples of a common faith, often called a "confession", a separate status. In Farsi, it is *mellat* and in Turkish it is *millet*. Both are derived from the Arabic word *millah* which in classical Arabic meant rite or [non-Muslim] religion. The majority community members referred to themselves not as a Millah but as Muslims.[35]

On the Indian subcontinent, the absence of a coherent Muslim identity has been commented upon by many historians. Francis Robinson, distinguished professor of South Asian History at the University of London, says that even as recently as the 18th century, Muslim group identity was unpronounced:

> Amongst Muslims who were descended from, or who liked to claim that they were descended from, those who had migrated to India to seek service at its many Muslim courts – Turks, Persians, Arabs, Afghans – their Muslim identity was not a matter of overriding concern. At the courts of the Mughals they divided not into Hindu and Muslim factions but into Turkish and Persian ones. They shared their Persian high culture with Hindus, including their poetry which rejected Indian life and landscape as fit subjects for poetic response and found its imaginative horizons in Iran and Central Asia.[36]

Nevertheless, much of modern historiography continues to be essentialist, further entrenching differences as natural and as normative. But what does Muslim rule in Sind have in common with that of the Delhi Sultanate or the later Moghuls? Persianized Turkic invaders tended to look down upon Indian Muslims. Considered as locals of little merit, they did not receive top military ranks or high political appointments. Bengalis were rock bottom on the list, but Muslims of Punjab and Sind were also considered inferior. Rajputs, on the other hand, were well thought of because they were good fighters. Having been the local royalty and aristocracy of medieval times, they had high status in the local

34 Identity Formation in Ancient India

society of northern India. Thus high ranks in government went to those from high-ranking Rajput families or to those Muslims of good lineage.

It is particularly noteworthy how Islam came to Bengal. As argued by Eaton, Muslim expansion during Mughal times was principally driven by the need for workers to clear and domesticate the lands in the east, where the rainfall was plentiful. And so,

> Mughal representatives (*nawāb* s) and their land-owning dependents sent in local adventurers to plow and reclaim the land, and to settle and populate it. Such people were typically Muslim holy men (local judges, *pīr* s [popular mystics], and *shaikh* s [teachers]), who taught Islam by example and whose memories were hallowed by those with whom they worked. Such a historical perspective discounts four outmoded conceptions about Bengal and Islam: we now know that the Mughal period was not one of decline, Islam is not monolithic, Muslims are not primarily urban, and the emergence of a noticeable community of Muslims does not necessitate as a precondition a political regime encouraging conversion.[37]

For the most part, those who had converted to Islam from local beliefs became members of local Sufi cults. However, their claimed connection with Arabia was tenuous:

> Despite their hagiographers' efforts to portray them as directly connected to Arabia, none of the major historical Sufi saints, known as 'Shaykhs', ever made the Hajj to Mecca and Medina. Their land was India and, as their disciples maintained their *dargahs* there, they made India sacred for Muslims. From these mystical centres that disciples visited *en masse*, the Shaykh exerted a 'spiritual jurisdiction over a specific territory' or *wilayat* and extended his protection over entire cities—like Delhi in the case of the Chishtiyyas. The power attributed to the Sufi saints over their *wilayat* was bound to attract the pan-Islamic connections attention of local Muslim rulers who quickly cultivated a specific relationship with the Shaykhs.[38]

Attracted by the egalitarian and participatory nature of Sufi thought, and relieved at having to shed the burden of caste, their Islam was a curious admixture of local traditions from centuries past and the newly imbibed Muslim theology. Robinson notes:

> Amongst Muslims who were descended from converts to Islam, that is the vast majority of Muslims who expressed themselves through the regional cultures and languages of India – Bengali, Tamil, Malayalam, Gujarati, Sindhi, Punjabi and so on – the distinctions of language, metaphor and behaviour between Muslims and the wider society in which they moved have seemed so slight to some that they have referred to an Islamic

syncretistic tradition in Bengal or one Indian religion expressed through different religious idioms in the Tamil country of the south.[39]

Robinson's observations receive support if one looks at Indonesia where it expressed itself through the idioms of Hinduism, Buddhism, and animism. Unlike in South Asia, Islam did not come to Southeast Asia with sword in hand. Instead, it traveled with spices and silk. There is no evidence of any kind of major Muslim conquest. Instead of iconoclasm, there was an adaptation of Islamic teachings to the local culture. Pakistani Muslims are generally shocked to see Hindu god-like figures at Muslim festivals in Indonesia but, "Puppet shows are a big part of Indonesian culture. So what the Muslim scholars did was they changed the characters of Ramayana to Muslim figures — showing the companions of the Prophet and so on. That was a very effective way for people to convert to Islam".[40]

That there were predatory invasions by foreigners is a fact of history. But how foreign the foreigners were is another question whose answer cannot be readily provided. Says Thapar:

> North-western India was constantly in contact with Afghanistan and the Oxus plain. The Kushans with their base in Bactria – the Oxus plain – came as far as the middle Ganges plain. There were continuing trade contacts with the horse trade and the silk trade. These large scale comings and goings never stopped. Kashmir employed Turkish mercenaries in its army and Mahmud had contingents of Hindu soldiers under their Hindu general. Buddhism was the prevalent religion in Central Asia until the early centuries of the second millennium when Islam arrived on the scene. The Buddhist contacts were very close on both sides of the frontier regions. The return invitation to the Sufis was equally successful and close.[41]

Differing from region to region, syncretic here and relatively pure there, this is what the Indian landscape looked like in earlier centuries. It was as far as could possibly be from a neat division of two peoples, each a nation, inhabiting the same geographical region.

The bottom line: a mature attitude towards ancient foreign invasions would be to simply accept them clinically as facts of history. They should be investigated and absorbed without either glorification or condemnation. Doing otherwise is pointless. No one living today can be held responsible for the actions, good or bad, of their ancestors. Moreover, the ravages of time have forever destroyed most evidence, leaving us with only a few pieces of a complex jigsaw puzzle.

Mughal era purifiers of Islam

Around AD 700, when the first Muslims came to India with sword in hand, their goal had been no different from that of other conquerors in history. As contended

36 Identity Formation in Ancient India

earlier, Islamic religious zeal helped to justify plunder, but they actually came for land and treasure. All who stood in the way, whether Hindu or Muslim, had to be overcome. So, for example, when the first Mughal emperor Zahiruddin Babur (1483–1530) arrived as conqueror his rival was Ibrahim Lodhi, a local Muslim ruler whom he defeated at the First Battle of Panipat (1526). Although Babur was an alien from Central Asia, successive Mughals steadily became more "Hindustani". Over time, they created for the very first time a consolidated political entity in India, one of the most prosperous countries in the world. Robert Orme (Clive's companion and imperial historian) wrote in the 1760s that European traders came to India for wealth, and mariners for jobs, because of "the magnificence of the richest empire of the globe".[42]

Muslim conquerors used violence for establishing their hegemony over an alien land. To create acceptance of their rule, conquered peoples were indeed forcibly converted to Islam. But after a stable empire had been created in north India by the Mughals the proselytizing zeal dampened and Hindus remained a large majority. The late Mushirul Hasan noted that medieval sultans may have wanted to erect a uniform religio-cultural system and impose religious authority from 'great' or 'middle' traditions, but long distances and syncretic beliefs and practices inhibited them from doing so. The Faraizis in Bengal, the *mujahidins* in the northwest, and other itinerant preachers sporadically imposed their will in certain areas, but their impact was transient as well.[43]

The institutions of governance created by some conquerors were essentially secular. Under Mughal rule, they gave India its most magnificent architecture and works of art. New forms of music, poetry, painting, lawmaking, food, and dress habits came from a cross breeding of cultures. Although first-generation Mughals were invaders from Uzbekistan, subsequent emperors were born in India. In Mughal courts, numerous Hindus held positions as chief counsellors, governors, rulers of their states (in accordance with treaties with the Muslim rulers), and sharing of customs and traditions. For the first time, most of India was unified by Mughal rule, the role of religion was relatively reduced, and multiple identities began to emerge.

During the reigns of Akbar and Shahjehan, Hindu–Muslim intermarriages became fairly common. For example, Jodha Bai's marriage to Akbar eased Akbar's relations with the Rajputs, particularly because Jodha Bai remained Hindu. Through such marriages, Hindu culture diffused into the Red Fort (now a major tourist attraction in Delhi). Cross marriages to Rajput and Persian princesses led to mixed blood: Emperor Akbar (1542–1605), a Sunni Hanafi, was one-half Persian (his mother was of Persian origin), Jahangir was one-half Rajput and one-quarter Persian, and Shah Jahan was three-quarters Rajput.[44] Hindus would participate alongside Muslims in *Muharram* processions, *Eid* festivities, and they would worship at some of the same shrines.

Over time, the conqueror-invaders absorbed local traditions. As they Indianized, their understanding and practice of Islam changed as well. The accretion into Islam of various Hindu beliefs and traditions reached the apogee of syncretism during Akbar's reign. A ruler from his teens onward, he brought two-thirds of the Indian subcontinent into an empire which included Afghanistan, Kashmir, and all of present-day Pakistan and India (with the South excluded). Faced with governing a vastly diverse empire, he dispensed with *jizya* (tax for non-Muslims) imposed by his predecessors, and he proclaimed *sulh-i-kul* (universal peace) as imperial administrative policy. Philosophically inclined in spite of little early education, he invented the so-called *din-e-ilahi*, a cocktail of various religions. Akbar met Portuguese Jesuit priests and sent an ambassador to Goa asking them to send two missionaries to his court so that he could understand Christian doctrines better.

This deviation from scriptural Islam did not go unnoticed. The backlash came from the orthodox Sunni *ulema*, chief among whom was Shaikh Ahmad Sirhindi (1564–1624). Sirhindi is revered by the Sunni orthodoxy as the first purifier of Islam to have outright challenged an emperor. He complained bitterly that, under Akbar, the pillars of Islam were being demolished:

> Cow-slaughter is impeded, although it is one of the chief rites of Islam in India. Mosques and shrines are being demolished. The temples of the infidels and their customs are being venerated. In short, erasing the rites and precepts of Islam, the customs of the infidels and their vain faiths are being circulated in order to annihilate Islam.[45]

Believing that God had made him the *mujaddid alf-i-thani* (renewer of the second millennium of Islam), Sirhindi welcomed Akbar's death from dysentery and wrote to some nobles of his son and successor, Emperor Jehangir (1569–1627), demanding that Akbar's secular policies be reversed.[46] But Jehangir, although he had sought to seize power from his father, was deep in alcohol and opium and not attracted to orthodox Islam. Both Akbar and Jehangir had allowed individuals to freely choose their own faith – Muslim, Hindu, Sikh, or any other.[47] Although this liberal policy was discontinued by Shahjehan, Jehangir's successor, the aura of a just ruler – the *adl-e-jehangiri* – was associated with Jehangir.

It was Aurangzeb (1658–1707), the sixth Moghul emperor, who largely abandoned the earlier policy of pluralism of his predecessors and sought to purge Islam of impurities acquired from Hinduism and other local influences. *Jizya* tax on Hindus was reimposed and some temples were destroyed as per policy, thus creating a deep religious divide that was to grow. But having to govern such a large empire forced a measure of pragmatism upon him. As a concession to power politics, he employed significantly more Hindus in his imperial bureaucracy than his predecessors had. High-caste Hindus joined his administration, and among his wives was a Rajput princess of Kashmir. Remarkably, after Akbar no Mughal emperor was born of a Muslim mother. Yet his zealotry alienated his non-Muslim subjects, fueling rebellions and causing central authority to melt down. Mughal decline had begun, never to reverse itself. The delicate cultural mosaic put into place by Akbar was disintegrating.

38 Identity Formation in Ancient India

Among history's "what if" questions is one that is particularly interesting: how would events have unfolded if Aurangzeb's brother, Dara Shukoh (1615–1659), a philosophically inclined prince, had succeeded in becoming emperor instead? Dara was favored over Aurangzeb as a successor by his father and his older sister, Princess Jahanara Begum. Like his great-grandfather Akbar, his approach to religion was adaptive, eclectic, pluralistic, and inclusive. For him, the mullah epitomized all that had gone wrong with Islam:

بهشت آں جا که ملائی نباشد

جہاں خالی شود از شورِ ملا

در آں شہرے کہ ملا خانہ دارد

زملا شور و غوغائی نباشد

زفتوئ باش پروائ ی نباشد

در آنجا ہچ دانائی نباشد

Paradise is where no Mullah abides	No stormy loud confusions there
Absent will be his pointless shouts	None there will heed his Fatwas
In the city where a Mullah resides	Missing are all men of wisdom

Dara Shukoh's tome *Sirr-e-Akbar* (The Greatest Secret) contends that to understand the hidden (*batini*) meaning of the Qur'an, one also needs to study the Upanishads which Dara, with the help of Pandits, translated from Sanskrit to Persian. Aurangzeb, who was his ideological opposite and more savvy politically, won the bitter two-year-long war of succession. Aurangzeb disposed of all his three brothers in the race for the throne, but Dara's popularity with masses did not allow for a public stoning to death. Instead, by one account:

> One of the murderers having secured Sipah Shikoh, the rest fell upon Dara, threw him down, and while three of the assassins held him, Nazir decapitated his wretched victim. The head was instantly carried to Aureng-Zebe, who commanded that it should be placed in a dish, and that water should be brought. The blood was then washed from the face, and when it could no longer be doubted that it was indeed the head of Dara, he shed tears, and said, 'Ai Bad-bakht ["Bed-bakt"]! Ah wretched one! Let this shocking sight no more offend my eyes, but take away the head, and let it be buried in Humayun's tomb'.[48]

Born in Aurangzeb's time was the most prominent purifier of Islam of the Mughal era, Shah Waliullah (1703–1762). His impact can be felt even upon contemporary religio-political movements like *Jamiat Ulema-e-Hind* or *Jamaat-e-Islami* and, earlier, the jihadist movement of Syed Ahmad Barelvi. A product of the *Madrassa-e-Rahimiyya*, Waliullah rejected the philosophy of rationalism (*ma'aqulat*) in favor of tradition (*manqulat*) and blamed the loss of Muslim power upon an excessive absorption of Greek philosophy by the ulema. The modern-day Taliban are Waliullah's ideological descendants and scions, while Hussain Ahmad Madani, Abul A'la Maududi, and Syed Qutb are his intellectual heirs. Waliullah despised local traditions and Hindus, famously declaring,

"We [Hindustanis] are an Arab people whose fathers have fallen in exile in the country of Hindustan, and Arabic genealogy and the Arabic language are our pride".[49]

Waliullah reasoned that wealth had become concentrated in the hands of Hindus because of the excessive leniency of rulers like Akbar. By this time, corroded by conspicuous consumption coupled with the rise of Maratha power, the Mughal Empire was nosing downward and in terminal decline. As a last ditch effort, Waliullah called on the Afghan ruler Ahmad Shah Abdali (d. 1772), also known as Ahmad Shah Durrani, to invade India and subdue the Marathas in the south:

> We beseech you (Abdali/Durrani) in the name of the Prophet to fight a jihad against the infidels of this region. This would entitle you to great rewards before God the Most High and your name would be included in the list of those who fought jihad for His sake. As far as worldly gains are concerned, incalculable booty would fall into the hands of the Islamic ghazis and the Muslims would be liberated from their bonds. The invasion of Nadir Shah who destroyed the Muslims left the Marathas and Jats secure and prosperous. This resulted in the infidels regaining their strength and in the reduction of the Muslim leaders of Delhi to mere puppets.[50]

Having invaded India several times earlier, Abdali happily obliged and returned to India from Afghanistan. With the help of local Muslim allies, he defeated the Marathas at the Third Battle of Panipat (1761). But this was no religious war, as the Muslims of north India discovered at their cost. Shias were slaughtered by the invading Sunni Afghans, and the spoils of war extracted from all – Muslim, Hindu, or Sikh – who lived along the path of the invaders as they returned home victorious.

The push by Shah Waliullah, his son Shah Abdul Aziz, and many others for an idealized, pristine Islam free from Hindu accretions came at a time when Muslims were seeking to understand why and how their absolute power was being lost. Waliullah could claim that ills and weaknesses came from insufficient observance of the true faith and spurious accretions from Sufism. That authority was weakened by wars of succession to the Mughal throne. Aurangzeb's authority was being challenged through uprisings by Rajputs, Marathas, Bundelas, Jats, and Sikhs.

Even if Hindus and Muslims were two broad categories towards the end of the Mughal Empire, boundaries had been greatly blurred because of pluralism and cultural assimilation. This assimilation – wherein the "pure" became mixed with the "impure" – caused great anguish to the orthodox. It led Sayyid Ahmad Dehlawi (1846–1918) to complain bitterly,

> All the customs of Muslim women, and because of them the customs of Muslim men, are almost all of Hindu origin. Some of the customs have

40 Identity Formation in Ancient India

been adopted without any change; for some, though original names have been retained, their styles have been changed. In some cases change is only in name; some have been integrated even in religious matters with only a slight change in the nomenclature.[51]

While Islam's purifiers caused quite a stir among the learned ones of the time, they were not game-changers because of the sheer diversity of local beliefs. Mughal central authority, which on the whole worked toward plurality, had been weakened. And yet this was far from sufficient to reverse centuries of assimilation.

Conclusion

Imagine for a moment trying to make a geographical, cultural, or political map of India from about AD 700 to around AD 1700, i.e., from around when the first Muslims came, to when European colonialism began to assert itself.[52] Landscape pictures taken from an orbiting satellite would have been identical to those of a thousand years before. Even the largest city then would have been barely the size of a medium-sized town today. Rivers ran their full courses, there were no dams, and jungles were intact. Political boundaries were fluid, changing, or disappearing after every century or two. Northern India in AD 700 had a smattering of small kingdoms like Takkas, Gujars, Kanaujiyas, and Maghadis, while towards the south were Chalukyas, Gangas, Pallavas, and Pandyas. One thousand years later, about two-thirds was under Mughal rule, with Marathas still holding their own in the south.

But did these political boundaries really matter beyond the names of the ruler and ruled? There was a strong continuity – the present looked like the past with only some modifications. There was a structural symmetry between you and your enemy. All cultures were pastoral, agrarian, and medieval. Winners and losers manufactured and used the same weapons, traded in comparable goods, and professions were similar. They were tillers of the soil, metal workers, artisans, priests, and soldiers. All were subject to the vagaries of nature in the same way. When rivers changed their course, some towns and settlements died while new ones came up.

Arguably the more important history of those times was not political, but economic – how changes came about in the means of production, and response to ecological and natural changes. D.D. Kosambi pithily remarks that, in writing history, "it is more important to know whether a given people had the plough or not than to know the name of their king".[53] History thus-defined becomes a sequence of successive changes in the means and relations of production, and culture must then be a description of the entire set of ways of a people of which religion is only a part. In seeking to explain the formation of military alliances, wars, and other significant events, a non-communal view of history has greater explanatory power. Those in power would look to see how their hard material interests would be served rather than secondary factors like kinship, caste, and religion.

But maps that had once stayed unchanged for centuries were to change very fast, very soon. The India of a thousand nations was soon to lose some of its diversity in just a couple of centuries. Fueled by the Industrial Revolution and a capitalist spirit, European maritime imperialism had set sail for destinations across the globe in search of raw materials and markets. It was about to remake the world. Whether by deliberate design or otherwise, there would come to exist new antagonistic social formations that would go on to divide India forever.

Notes

1 https://fs.blog/massively-distilled-wisdom/
2 J.S. Avery, *The Origin of Cooperation*, 12 July, 2012, Countercurrents.org and references therein.
3 R. Dawkins, *The Selfish Gene*, 30th anniversary edition, New York, Oxford University Press (2006).
4 R.A. Skipper, Revisiting the Fisher-Wright Controversy. *Transactions of the American Philosophical Society*, New Series, 99, no. 1 (2009): 299–322.
5 Avery, op. cit.
6 H.Tajfel, J.C. Turner, W.G. Austin, and S. Worchel, An Integrative Theory of Intergroup Conflict. *Organizational Identity: A Reader* (1979), pp. 56–65. See also, S.A. McLeod, *Social Identity Theory*, 24 October 2019, Simply Psychology, https://www.simplypsychology.org/social-identity-theory.html
7 D.N. Jha, *Ancient India in Historical Outline*, revised and enlarged edition, Delhi, Manohar Books (2009).
8 D. Gilmartin and B.B. Lawrence (eds.) *Beyond Turk and Hindu – Rethinking Religious Identities in Islamicate South Asia*, Florida, University Press of Florida (2000), p. 5.
9 R. Thapar, Imagined Religious Communities? Ancient History and the Modern Search for a Hindu Identity. *Modern Asian Studies*, 23, no. 2 (1989): 222. See also, Romila Thapar, *Communalism and the Writing of Indian History*, Delhi, Peoples Publishing House (1969).
10 R. Thapar, Imagined Religious Communities, op cit, 215.
11 *Alberuni's India*, English edition by Dr. Edward C. Sachau, London, Kegan Paul, Trench, Trübner & Co. (1910). Electronic reproduction. Vol. 1. New York, Columbia University Libraries (2006).
12 *Alberuni's India*, op. cit.
13 Ibid.
14 Thapar, op. cit.
15 http://www.thevedicfoundation.org/bhartiya_history/index.html
16 E. Bryant, *The Quest for the Origins of Vedic Culture – The Indo-Aryan Migration Debate*, Oxford University Press (2001).
17 R. Jain and T. Lasseter, Special Report: By Rewriting History, Hindu Nationalists Aim to Assert Their Dominance over India, Reuters article, 6 March 2018.
18 A Genetic Chronology for the Indian Subcontinent Points to Heavily Sex-biased Dispersals, *BMC Evolutionary Biology*, March 23, 2017.
19 V.M. Narasimhan et al., The Formation of Human Populations in South and Central Asia, *Science*, 365, no. 6457 (6 September 2019): p. eaat7487, DOI: 10.1126/science.aat7487.
20 A haplogroup is a group of genes originating from a common ancestor.
21 Richard et al quoted in https://www.thehindu.com/sci-tech/science/how-genetics-is-settling-the-aryan-migration-debate/article19090301.ece For a very readable analysis of their technical paper, see R. Venkataramakrishnan, Aryan Migration: Everything You Need to Know about the New Study on Indian genetics, 13 August 2018.
22 S. Daniyal, *Two New Genetic Studies Upheld Indo-Aryan Migration. So Why Did Indian Media Report the Opposite?*, Scroll.in, 15 September 2019.

23 S. Daniyal, *Fact Check: India Wasn't the First Place Sanskrit Was Recorded – It Was Syria*, 30 June 2015. https://scroll.in/article/737715/fact-check-india-wasnt-the-first-place-sanskrit-was-recorded-it-was-syria

24 Romila Thapar in private communication to this author.

25 If you are a fundamentalist Jew or Christian and watch the evangelical TV star Jimmy Swaggart – as I sometimes do – you will learn about this "fact" and more.

26 Romila Thapar in private communication to this author.

27 K. Armstrong, *Islam – A Short History*, Random House (2002).

28 R.H. Davis, Indian Art Objects as Loot, *The Journal of Asian Studies*, 52, no. 1 (1993): 22–48. doi:10.2307/2059143.

29 R.M. Eaton, *Temple Desecration and Muslim States in Medieval India*, Delhi, Oxford University Press India, Hope Publications (2004), p. 32.

30 S.R. Goel, *Heroic Hindu Resistance to Muslim Invaders (636 AD to 1206 AD)*, Delhi, Voice of India (1994).

31 Thousands of mosques targeted as Hindu nationalists try to rewrite India's history, The Guardian, 30 October, 2022.

32 H.M. Elliot, quoted in Eaton, op. cit., pp. 11–12.

33 Eaton, op. cit., pp. 13–14.

34 M.C. Menon, quoted in Hinduism and Talibanism.

35 W.R. Polk Muslim Memories of West's Imperialism, 4 September 2015, *The Politics of Ghar Wapsi, Manjari Katju, Economic and Political Weekly.*

36 F. Robinson, The British Empire and Muslim Identity in South Asia, *Transactions of the Royal Historical Society*, 8 (1998): 271–289.

37 https://www.encyclopedia.com/environment/encyclopedias-almanacs-transcripts-and-maps/bengali-religions

38 C. Jaffrelot (ed.) *Pan-Islamic Connections – Transnational Networks between South Asia and the Gulf*, Oxford University Press (2017), pp. 3–4.

39 Robinson, op. cit.

40 S. Hasan, How Islam Came to Dominate Indonesia, TRT World, 25 August 2020.

41 Romila Thapar in private communication to this author.

42 R. Orme, *A History of the Military Transactions of the British Nation in Indostan, From the Year MDCCXLV; to Which Is Prefixed a Dissertation on the Establishments Made by Mahomedan Conquerors in Indostan*. Vol 2, London, John Nourse (1778); reprinted in New Delhi by Today's and Tomorrow's Printers and Publishers, n.d., p. 7.

43 M. Hasan, *Legacy of a Divided Nation India's Muslims since Independence*, Westview Press (1997), p. 30.

44 D. Collier, *The Great Mughals and Their Mughals*, Hay House (2016), p. 15.

45 *Hazrat Mujaddid and His Critics,* a translation from the Urdu *hazrat Mujaddid aur unkay naqedeen,* published by Progressive Books, Lahore (1982). https://www.irfi.org/articles/articles_901_950/emperor_mogul_akbar_and_shai.htm

46 S.A.A. Rizvi, *Shah Wali-Allah and His Times – A Study of Eighteenth Century Islam, Politics, and Society in India*, Australia, Ma'rifat Publishing House (1980), pp. 62–63.

47 A. Eraly, *The Mughal World – Life in India's Last Golden Age*, Penguin Books (2007), p. xiv.

48 F. Bernier, *Travels in the Mogul Empire, AD 1656–1668*, translated by Archibald Constable on the basis of Irving Brock's version, ed. by Vincent A. Smith. Delhi, Low Price Publications (1994) [1934].

49 Cited in A. Schimmel, *Islam in the Indian Subcontinent*, Leiden (1980), p. 121.

50 Rizvi, op. cit., p. 305.

51 S.A. Dehlawi, *Rasum-e Dehli*, Delhi, Mukhzan Press (1905), pp. 37–41.

52 Amateur historian Thomas Lessman has created a series of maps of India from AD 1 till the rule of the Delhi Sultanate, https://scroll.in/article/722369/the-changing-map-of-india-from-1-ad-to-the-20th-century

53 D.D. Kosambi, *The Culture and Civilisation of Ancient India in Historical Outline*, Vikas Books (1964). This is an encyclopedic account of ancient Indian cultural history.

Two
THE BRITISH REINVENT INDIA

Take up the White Man's burden,
Send forth the best ye breed,
Go bind your sons to exile,
to serve your captives' need;

Take up the White Man's burden,
The savage wars of peace,
Fill full the mouth of Famine
And bid the sickness cease;
And when your goal is nearest
The end for others sought,
Watch sloth and heathen Folly
Bring all your hopes to nought.

Rudyard Kipling, The Times (London), 4 February 1899

Colonialism came to India to plunder its wealth and to seek new markets for European capitalism, but it also brought along multiple ambiguities and contradictions. A handful of Englishmen needed large numbers of Indians to govern a vast subcontinent. This called for creating an efficient administrative apparatus that strictly followed meritocratic principles. As per the dictum of evolutionary theory, how well a group – Hindu or Muslim – could adapt to the new dispensation determined its chances for prosperity and success. This chapter makes the case that Indian Muslims, encumbered by historical baggage and attitudes that they were reluctant to shed, lost the race for jobs in the colonial administration and failed to modernize fast enough. . With the decline of Mughal power, a world where identities and cultures had once been fluid began to solidify. I examine how

DOI: 10.4324/9781003379140-4

44 The British Reinvent India

there was a parting of ways not just between Muslims and Hindus, but also between Muslims themselves. Some took up arms against the British invaders, while a few went on a different track to seek modernization in the hope of getting jobs and lands. No one at the time could have guessed that a supreme paradox would eventually shape up: as it turned out, it was not Islamic conservatives but Islamic modernists who would succeed in creating the first Muslim state in history.

For Kipling, the novelist and apologist-in-chief of the English ruling class, imperialism was a moral duty and a Christian jihad aimed at liberating the world from medieval heathen thought. Through education, immigration, transportation, irrigation, and administration, the mother country would transform the colony into a civilized nation. Napoleon also claimed Egypt in the name of "freedom and equality"; for the French it was their *mission civilisatrice* (civilizing mission) that gave moral sanction for capturing the lands of those who they said were inhabited by backward peoples in Algeria, West Africa, and Indo-China.

And yet Kipling's ennobling "The White Man's Burden" made the 1800s a terribly dismal time for Indians. After visiting India in 1930, Will Durant, the American historian and philosopher, wrote that he had come across the greatest crime ever in history and was astonished "any government could allow its subjects to sink to such misery". Under British rule there were famines by neglect as well as famines by design: Bengal, Madras, Chalisa, Agra, Orissa, Bihar, and Bombay saw suffering beyond description. Durant wrote:

> I have seen a great people starving to death before my eyes, and I am convinced that this exhaustion and starvation are due not, as their beneficiaries claim, to overpopulation and superstition, but to the most sordid and criminal exploitation of one nation by another in all recorded history. I propose to show that England has year after year been bleeding India to the point of death, and that self-government of India by Hindus could not, within any reasonable probability, have worse results than the present form of alien domination.[1]

More recently Shashi Tharoor, Indian writer and politician, has written and spoken extensively on how the British saw India as a cash cow.[2] They exacted payments from Indians far beyond what they could afford, resorted to robbery and murder, and were unashamed of their cupidity and corruption. On his first return to England, Robert Clive – who started out as a small-time British East India Company employee but rose to become a founder of the British Empire in India – took home £234,000 from his Indian exploits (£23 million in today's money, making him one of the richest men in Europe). This systematic expropriation of wealth led to a once-rich India vulnerable to famine, poverty, and suffering. Clive's companion and imperial historian, Robert Orme, wrote in the 1760s that European traders came to India for wealth, and mariners for jobs, because of "the

The British Reinvent India **45**

magnificence of the richest empire of the globe."[3] Britain gorged itself with the treasures it had discovered, making the natives pay for their expropriation. By the 19th century every British soldier posted to India had to be paid, equipped, fed, and eventually pensioned by the Government of India, not by Britain.

It was not just India that had come under the heel of colonialism. Three Muslim empires fell in quick succession almost simultaneously and, by the middle of the 18th century, the so-called Gunpowder Empires – Ottoman, Safavid, and Mughal – had collapsed. (The historian Marshall Hodgson had invented this term because the rise of these empires to power depended critically upon the use of cannons and small arms.) In the early modern period, these empires had been the strongest and most stable economies. They boasted cities such as Lahore and Delhi which were wealthier, larger, and more organized than Paris or London at the time. Mughal collapse was partly because of internal revolts; the wealth in the cities and the magnificent architecture of tombs and gardens came from exploiting the peasantry who fought against the central authorities through powerful dissident local landlords. As the center ceased to hold, birds of prey from Europe – Portuguese, Dutch, French, and English – descended to feed upon the dying empire. To paraphrase Yeats:[4]

Turning and turning in the widening gyre
The falcon cannot hear the falconer;
Things fall apart; the centre cannot hold;
Mere anarchy is loosed upon the world,
The blood-dimmed tide is loosed, and everywhere
The ceremony of innocence is drowned;
The best lack all conviction, while the worst
Are full of passionate intensity.

Starvation and defeat faced once-mighty conquerors. With just a few thousand troops, Europeans could be victorious against entire native populations. Better weaponry and advanced technology was part of the reason but, even more, Europeans came armed with a system of organized thought based upon a rational approach to life, a modern system of justice, and a new set of social relations. Modern means of communication – telegraph, railways, press, and post – ultimately made it possible for a mere island in the North Sea to run an empire over which the sun never set.

Colonialism did not just substitute one set of rulers for another, it went on to change the very way in which people think of themselves. In a recent work provocatively titled, *The Loss of Hindustan – The Invention of India*, professor Manan Asif of Columbia University argues that the British actively worked against the idea of a shared political ancestry of those who they now governed.[5] For the imperial purpose to be seen as a force for the general good, obfuscated versions of history had to be developed. These compartmentalized the works of native historians who were selectively read and excerpted. What emerged was a subcontinent that prior to the Muslim invasions had "timeless, history-less Hindus",

46 The British Reinvent India

a land of primitive people without agency. Eventually, the idea of Hindustan went missing, to be taken up with a faith-differentiated version of history. We shall return to this again later in this chapter.

Colonialism quietly sneaks in

The English did not rudely barge into India. They politely knocked at the door and then gained a foothold through obsequious prostrations before local rulers and kings. Later they duly supplicated and flattered the emperors in Delhi who at the time controlled most of India. But, after establishing a corporate entity, they also sought to displace Maratha power in the south and Sikhs in the Punjab. Initially called the Honorable East India Company, this joint-stock company was out for profits not political power. M. Monier-Williams (1819–1899) wrote that until the 1680s:

> The position of the English in India was that of a company of commercial speculation, who had invested a large amount of hard cash in their speculation and wanted a good dividend. Money was their motive, money was their guiding principle, money was their end, intrigue and negotiation, their modus operandi.[6]

Later the Honorable East India Company's name was changed to the British East India Company or, more simply, the "Company". The appellation "Honorable" was eventually dropped. This was indeed appropriate: the Company violated with impunity the solemn pledges it had made to Muslim rulers. The immediate goal of the Europeans was to obtain trade concessions and permission for building trading settlements along the coast. Since the smaller Indian rulers and rajas had to rule their territories through local appointees who often shortchanged them, the Europeans began to act as tax collectors for the rulers. In this process they acquired land and property. Mughal rulers paid no attention to sea power and willingly elected the Company to protect them from the Dutch, Portuguese, and French. India was won province-by-province. By the time the locals understood that the British were actually aiming to take over India rather than to simply trade, it had become too late.

Remarkably, the Company fought only two major battles – that at Plassey (1757) and Buxar (1764) – to establish its complete victory over India's powerful Muslim emperors and kings. The sizes of the forces involved on the Mughal and British sides were in the few thousands only, far fewer than the subcontinent's major wars. The subsequent dethroning of Siraj-ud-Daulah and installation of the puppet Mir Jafar by Robert Clive is known to every Pakistani schoolchild; the word traitor and Mir Jafar are interchangeable. The only credible resistance the British met was in the south of India at the hands of Hyder Ali (1720–1782) and his eldest son Tipu Sultan (1750–1799). For the Company's militias, it would have been very hard to take on any large, well-organized army. Therefore, the Company's cunning

The British Reinvent India **47**

servants opted for a strategy that would steadily whittle down Muslim power by encouraging local political rivals and governors to eliminate one another. Separate treaties were signed with rajas and maharajas on the one hand, and with nawabs and nizams on the other. These worked well. In 1833 the Company removed the name of Mughal Emperor Shah Alam II from its rupee coin, and in 1835 it issued the first one that bore the head of the British sovereign. Formally, India still belonged to the Mughals but the pretense kept getting thinner.

Like the giant multinationals that rule the world today, the Company thought far ahead of its times. It strategized that treating natives on the basis of their religion would sharpen cleavages. In 1776 Nathaniel Brassey Halhed, a British grammarian working for the Company translated the authoritative law book *Manu Smriti* into English titled, "A Code of Gentoo Laws or Ordinations of the Pundits". Pandits were associated with British judges to administer Hindu civil law and maulvis to administer that of Muslims. Thapar observes that separate laws inevitably led to the sharpening of identities:

> The East India Company's interest in locating and codifying Hindu law gave a legal form to what was essentially social observance and customary law. The concept of law required that it be defined as a cohesive ideological code. The Manu Dharmasastra, for example, which was basically part of Brahmanical *smrti* was taken as the laws of the Hindus and presumed to apply universally. In the process of upward social mobility during the late eighteenth and early nineteenth centuries, traders and artisanal groups emerged as patrons of temple building activities and the trend to conform to the brahmanical model was reinforced by this comprehension of Hinduism.[7]

Colonialism was accompanied by proselytizers and so a Christian undertone could be found even in the translation of texts from Sanskrit into English, where religious concepts were frequently articulated in a new way. These stayed; the process of selecting excerpts from holy texts can have its own very definite political purpose. Psychological warfare had been invented.

With every passing year, a company designed for commerce was becoming more deeply involved in the business of administering a country. The Indian Civil Service (ICS) was created for ruling over the vastness of a subcontinent with a minimum number of Britishers. This required creating a competent, scientifically minded bureaucracy that over time became known as India's steel frame. Earlier on, the Company – and later the British government – had recruited ICS officers by patronage with preference given to those of high birth. However, the British public had begun to protest the hold of the English aristocracy and insisted on a more equitable system. Therefore in 1806, the Company set up its own college at Haileybury, England, with magnificent buildings, huge lawns, and teachers drawing salaries comparable to those at Oxford and Cambridge. The curriculum, though wide, was functionally directed: political economy, history, mathematics, natural philosophy, classics, law, humanities, and philology.

48 The British Reinvent India

Languages included Arabic, Persian, Urdu, Bengali, Sanskrit, Telugu, etc. This broad education helped create modern methods of governance and devise new solutions to new problems. Competitive examinations identified the more capable ones. After the Company's dissolution in 1858, King's College London was tasked with organizing competitive exams into the ICS.

The aspiring young British rulers of India had to be given a sense of its history, but that history had not yet been written into textbooks. The ten volumes of *History of British India* by James Mill (1773–1836) must be counted as the most influential of books in this regard. Mill set the stage for interpreting India's past to the would-be servants of the Company.[8] He claimed a clear temporal divide between the indigenous Hindu-India and the Muslim-invaded India. Mill split Indian history into three parts: Hindu, Muslim, and British. As such he was the first writer ever to use this classification. It seemed reasonable and so it stuck. He claimed – without ever having been to India – that in India there were three different and distinct worlds situated far apart. Those educated at Haileybury imbibed this division of history quite naturally as though this was how India had actually been. But the impact went much further. Even if analytic and descriptive categories invented were mere conveniences, these half-truths and stereotypes became encoded into official tracts.

Mill expressed some regret at never having set foot in India at any time in his life but argued that "A duly qualified man can obtain more knowledge of India in one year in his closet in England than he could obtain during the course of the longest life, by the use of his eyes and ears in India."[9] Nevertheless, he took upon himself the task of writing the tome. Today's professional historians consider Mill's work poorly researched and unsatisfactory. It has been described as "a classic of colonial self-congratulation which contains a complete denunciation and rejection of Indian culture and civilization and which both exhorts and extolls the civilizing mission of the British in the subcontinent"[10]. Nevertheless, Mill was attractive for many because he allowed everything to be neatly pigeonholed. For other Europeans – German, French, and Dutch – comprehending the ethnography and history of the new colonies was also important. This made Mill the most influential among the historians of India – or Hindustan, as it was generally referred to in those times.

Nevertheless, colonial administrators, soldiers, and casual visitors found the facts on the ground to be much more complicated than had been portrayed in Mill's books. The late Mushirul Hasan, historian and former vice-chancellor of Jamia Millia Islamia in Delhi, notes the enormous variety of local, heterodox traditions that had evolved over time.[11] Divisions were blurry between Hindu and Muslim. Although they tried hard to create an Islamic monoculture, revivalist zealots had failed to prevent a hugely diverse ecosystem from coming into existence.

> Charles Alfred Elliot reported from Unnao, close to Lucknow in UP, that there was a strong tendency among Muslims to assimilate in all externals with their Hindu neighbours. He found them wearing dhotis and using Ram

Ram as the mode of salutation. Fuller, likewise, wrote on Hindu influences among Muslims: in purely agricultural districts, he commented, the people not 'only understood each other's systems, but the systems seemed to overlap'. Hindus and Muslims cheerfully attended each other's festivals and sang each other's songs. Lytton, Bengal's governor in the 1920's, commented on the rank and file of the communities in the province getting on well with each other in all daily business of life. O.M. Martin, having served in Bengal from 1915 to 1926, emphatically stated that Hindu-Muslim mutual dependence and friendship were an old and cherished tradition.[12]

An extensive account of the writing of Indian history in British times and the misconceptions it spawned is given by Columbia University professor, Manan Asif.[13] He traces developments from the early 17th century onward, beginning with a Persian text *Tarikh-e-Firishta* (history according to Firishta) by Muhammad Qasim Firishta, a court functionary of the Deccan ruler Adil Shah II in the early years of the 17th century. This was picked up by a certain Lt. Col. Alexander Dow (1735–1779) who understood the text wrongly. Dow thought it was sanctioned and authenticated by the Mughal rulers of north India. Hindus, as he saw it, had mythology as contained in the Mahabharata but no authentic history. Therefore, to Firishta's account Dow added on a "Dissertation Concerning the Religion and Philosophy of the Brahmin", before presenting it as a complete history of Hindustan to King George III. This simplified "History of Hindostan" was an immediate sensation in Europe and was rendered into French and German in 1769. Other "soldier scribes" followed Dow, and Mill too was deeply influenced by Dow. These writings helped establish the paradigm of a 5000-year-old history and a Hindu Golden Age. Asif notes that it was because of colonial era historians that the dual configuration of Ashoka as representative of the Golden Age, and of Mahmud Ghazni as heralding India's Dark Ages has come to be widely accepted in India today.

It was in British interest to establish that Muslim conquerors and rulers had displayed a persistent pattern of villainy and fanaticism in desecrating and demolishing Hindu temples.[14] It was particularly convenient to adopt this point of view when describing those Indian rulers who fought against the British, as was the case of Tipu Sultan (1751–1799), also known as Tiger of Mysore. Based in South India, he was a pioneer of rocket artillery and a brilliant tactician but was nevertheless defeated and killed on the battlefield by the British as he defended his capital, Seringapatam, in 1799. In British historiography, he comes across as a cruel and relentless enemy as well as an intolerant bigot and furious fanatic.

A very different picture emerges when the nuances of that period of history is properly investigated. Kate Brittlebank, in her book, *Tipu Sultan's Search for Legitimacy: Islam and Kingship in a Hindu Domain*, sets out in detail how Tipu had appropriated both Muslim and Hindu practices into his rule.[15] While he was ruthless in persecuting his political opponents, he made regular endowments to Hindu temples and made appointments of Hindus to key posts. Brittlebank

50 The British Reinvent India

argues that in Mysore prior to 1860 there was perhaps no identifiable religious identity – Muslim, Sikh, or Hindu – and Tipu's attitudes reflected that. On the basis of Tipu's patronage of certain temples, she concludes that their "size and style gives the lie to the notion that Hindus, solely because they were Hindus, suffered discrimination or persecution at his hands".[16]

The British had their reasons to denigrate Muslim rule in India and Hindu right-wingers have their own. Writing on the pernicious influence that such biased understandings of medieval Indian history have had on subsequent generations, the eminent historian Mohammad Habib once remarked: "The peaceful Indian Mussalman, descended beyond doubt from Hindu ancestors, was dressed up in the garb of a foreign barbarian, as a breaker of temples, and an eater of beef, and declared to be a military colonist in the land where he had lived for about thirty or forty centuries. The result of it is seen in the communalistic atmosphere of India today".[17]

The Great Mutiny – a watershed

Historians are wont to divide British rule in India into two parts – that before and after the bloody year of 1857. Tens of thousands of peasants armed with primitive swords and spears had risen up in the War of Independence – also known as the Great Mutiny – and battled with the cavalry, infantry, and artillery regiments of the East India Company. The East India Company's Bengal Army was at the forefront of the 1857 Sepoy Mutiny with over 150,000 sepoys taking up arms against their masters. They were following other mutinous sepoys – Indian soldiers recruited into the Company's army – who had been pushed beyond bearable limits of mistreatment and discrimination. From Meerut to Delhi to Calcutta and spreading southwards, large numbers stood up in a final act of defiance against the Company's imperial might.

The uprising, spontaneous and disorganized, failed after almost one year of battle. Muslims, even more than Hindus, became targets of British revenge. Rebels had targeted white men indiscriminately but also their women and children. The British response was disproportionate. Vengeful soldiers looted architectural treasures, carrying whatever they could with them. Delhi resounded to gunpowder blasts as the victors blew up palaces, houses, and mosques. Corpses, mostly Muslim but also Hindu, lay in heaps on the streets, some trampled under carriages. The poet Ghalib chronicled those times graphically:

> Here it seems as if the whole city is being demolished…. Some of the biggest and most famous bazaars – the *Khas Bazaar*, the *Urdu Bazaar* and the *Khanum ka Bazaar*, each of which was practically as a small town, have all gone without a trace. You cannot even tell where they were. Householders and shopkeepers cannot point out to you where their houses and shops used to stand…. Food is dear, and death is cheap, and grain sells so dear that you would think each grain was a fruit.
>
> – *Letters of Mirza Ghalib, Delhi (1857)*

The British Reinvent India   51

Summoned from his house to appear before a certain Colonel Brown, Ghalib was one of those inhabitants lucky enough to be spared. Later, he wrote:

بس کہ فعال ما یرید ہے آج   ہر سلح شور انگلتاں کا

گھر سے بازار میں نکلتے ہوئے   زہرہ ہوتا ہے آب نساں کا

چوک جس کو کہیں وہ مقتل ہے   گھر نمونہ بنا ہے زنداں کا

شہر دلی کا ذرہ ذرۂ خاک   تشنۂ خوں ہے ہر مسلماں کا

Now every English soldier that bears arms
Is sovereign and free to work his will
Men dare not venture out into the street
And terror chills their heart within them still
Their homes enclose them as in prison walls
And in the Chowk the victors hang and kill
The city is athirst for Muslim blood
And every grain of dust must drink its fill[18]

In a display of unity that shocked the British, Muslims and Hindus stood together to fight the British. Dead Hindus had beef stuffed into their mouths, but Muslims were treated yet harsher since they were seen as wanting to get rid of the British and bring back Mughal rule. Ghalib relates that Hindus were allowed to return to Delhi as early as January 1858, but it took another year before any Muslims were permitted, and even then their numbers were no more than one thousand. As the thick, dark stench of death lay heavy in the air, Britain debated whether the city should be obliterated. The public in England was favorably inclined towards Lord Palmerston's suggestion that "every civil building connected with the Mohammedan tradition should be leveled to the ground without regard to antiquarian veneration or artistic predilections".[19] So was the viceroy, Lord Canning. Cannons were ordered to take up positions, but the orders were never given.

The causes of the Mutiny were several: heavy taxation of land, confiscation of jagirs, and low pay for the sepoys on the Company's payroll. But perhaps just as much, or perhaps more, was the widespread feeling that the British were overbearing and arrogant, disrespectful of local traditions and religion. Muslim fears of being proselytized into Christianity flared up in 1855, when a letter by a certain Reverend E. Edmond (of whom not much else seems to be known) was circulated publicly from Calcutta. A copy of that letter had been sent to all the principal officials of government. Edmond called for massive conversions to the faith,

All Hindustan was now under one rule, that the telegraph had so connected all parts of the country that they were as one, that the railroad had brought them so near that all towns were as one, the time had clearly come when there should be but one faith; it was right therefore, that we should all become Christians.[20]

52 The British Reinvent India

The rumor spread that this circular was written by order of the government. The conversions were to begin with government servants and then spread to the mass of the people. Thereafter, the ground began to shake under the feet of many Muslims. Edmond's circular is counted among the reasons for the 1857 uprising. It certainly did not help that soldiers were required to bite open a paper cartridge designed for their Lee Enfield rifles that was covered with a grease variously claimed to contain pork or beef fat. But historian Irfan Habib says the reasons go far beyond the putative composition of the cartridges.[21] The bulk of those who rose up came from the highest taxed part of the country. The peasantry as well as the "village zamindars", he says, had been made subject to an ever rising burden of tax under the *Mahalwari* system established in 1822. In *Mahalwari* areas, not only were the settlements made for twenty years only, but the revenue-rate could be changed at any time. There was also collective responsibility for payment: even if a peasant or landholder paid his tax but his neighbor did not, then his own land could also be forfeited to the government.

The unity showed by Muslim and Hindu troops during the Great Mutiny had the British greatly worried. The Governor of Bombay, Lord Elphinstone, wrote in 1859 that henceforth "our only safe military policy in India" would be through separating companies. "*Divide et impera* was the old Roman motto, and it should be ours".[22] Brigadier John Coke, experienced from fighting in Frontier, had an identical opinion:

> By mixing the castes in one corps they become amalgamated, and make common cause, which they never do if kept in separate corps. Hindoos and Musselmans are natural enemies, the same with Sikhs; yet the result of mixing them in one corps has been to make them all join against the Government, and not only the soldiers but through them the Hindoo and Musselman zame-endars [landowners] were incited to make common cause, which they would never have done had the races been kept in distinct corps. Our endeavor should be to uphold in full force (the fortunate for us) the separation which exists between the different religions and races, not to endeavor to amalgam-ate them. *Divide et impera* should be the principle of the Indian government.[23]

This pointed to an obvious policy: use the enormous diversity of peoples and creeds in India to prevent another 1857 from ever happening. But did the British need to use this in full seriousness? Or could other differences also be leveraged to prevent unity?

Demoralized Muslim *ashrafiyya*

> A hundred and seventy years ago it was almost impossible for a well-born Musalman in Bengal to become poor; at present it is almost impossible for him to continue rich.
>
> — *W.W. Hunter (1876)*[24]

Well before 1857 Muslim authority had diminished sharply even in Delhi, once the seat of Mughal power. The last noteworthy Mughal was Emperor Shah Alam II who died in 1806. Under the terms of agreement with the British, Emperor Bahadur Shah Zafar could still maintain a level of pomp-and-show and ride his elephants through the city to attend lavish weddings. But, in fact, his power did not extend beyond the walls of the Red Fort. Reduced to an Indian pope ruling inside his own Vatican City, Zafar kept busy managing his considerable harem, dealing with Delhi's court intrigues, organizing poetry and music sessions, and meeting with visitors – all under the watchful eye of the British Resident, Sir William Metcalfe. In his poignant account, *The Last Mughal*, William Dalrymple's pen magically brings to life the dying days of a once mighty empire that had ruled much of India. Under the shadow of Zafar's palace there lay a sea of misery:

> Besides the senior princes, there were over two thousand poor princes and princesses – grandchildren and great-grandchildren and great-great-grandchildren of previous monarchs – most of whom lived a life of poverty in their own walled quarter of the Palace, to the south-west of the area occupied by Zafar and his immediate family. This was the darker side of the life of the Red Fort, and its greatest embarrassment; for this reason many of the *salatin* (palace-born princes and princesses) were never allowed out of the gates of the Fort, least of all on so ostentatious an occasion as the very public festivities in Daryaganj.[25]

Zafar turned out to be the last Mughal. Banished to Rangoon, his poems of suffering and anguish stand ready on the lips of aficionados of Urdu poetry:

Hear not this tale of woe from some raconteur	یہ قصہ وہ نہیں تم جس کو قصہ خواں سے سنو
Hear my tragedy from me and me alone	مرے فسانۂ غم کو مری زباں سے سنو

Even before 1857, the British had viewed Muslims with suspicion. The Mutiny was seen as an attempt to reestablish Muslim supremacy, and so the punishment meted out to Muslims was even harsher than to Hindus. There is hard evidence of a special British dislike of Muslims in apportioning of privileges in times after 1857. Chughtai notes that in Punjab, river waters were allocated preferentially to Sikhs and Hindus.[26] In Sind, a preponderantly Muslim province, there was not a single Muslim among the subordinate judges. In the Northern Division, there were 1930 Muslims serving in the police department, of which only 57 belonged to the salary group of 30 rupees and upwards. (However, as we shall see shortly, the situation in the United Provinces was quite different.)

Sir Alfred Lyall (1835–1911), a literary historian and poet who joined the British Civil Service a year before the Mutiny, wrote that post-1857:

The English turned fiercely on the Mahomedans as upon their real enemies and most dangerous rivals; so that the failure of the revolt was much
more disastrous to them than to the Hindus. The Mahomedans lost almost
all their remaining prestige of traditionary superiority over Hindus they
forfeited for the time the confidence of their foreign rulers; and it is from
this period that must be dated the loss of their numerical majority in the
higher subordinate ranks of the civil and military services.[27]

A petition presented by the local Muslims to the Divisional Commissioner of
Orissa for government jobs reveals their plight:

The Orissa Muhammadans have been levelled down and down, with no
hope of rising again. Born of noble percentage, poor by profession, and
destitute of patrons, we find ourselves in the position of a fish out of water.
The penniless and parsimonious condition which we are reduced to, con-
sequent on the failure of our former Government service, has thrown us
into such an everlasting despondency, that we speak from the very core
of our hearts, that we would travel into the remotest corners of the earth,
ascend the snowy peaks of the Himalaya, wander the forlorn regions of
Siberia, could we be convinced that by so travelling we would be blessed
with a Government appointment of ten shillings a week.[28]

Perhaps the most well-documented account of the plight of Indian Muslims
comes from a civil service officer from Scotland who was assigned to distant
Bengal in 1877. There he wrote a book that has informed the subcontinent's
historians for generations. Sir William Wilson Hunter's originally titled it, *The
Indian Musalmans: Are They Bound in Conscience to Rebel Against the Queen?* He then
retitled it more simply as, *Our Indian Musalmans.* This newer edition describes
the Muslim plight thus: "A hundred and seventy years ago it was almost impossible for a well-born Musalman in Bengal to become poor; at present it is almost
impossible for him to continue rich".[29] The situation closer to a once-wealthy
city was scarcely much better:

At Murshidabad a Muhammadan Court still plays its farce of mimic state,
and in every District the descendant of some line of princes sullenly and
proudly eats his heart out among roofless palaces and weed-choked tanks.
Of such families I have personally known several. Their ruined mansions
swarm with grown-up sons and daughters, with grandchildren and nephews and nieces, and not one of the hungry crowd has a chance of doing
anything for himself in life.[30]

Hunter was not sympathetic to those he wrote about, remarking at one point that
Muslims are a "persistently belligerent class", which successive British governments have rightly declared to be a source of permanent danger to the Indian

The British Reinvent India   **55**

Empire. But somewhat grudgingly he admits Muslims are "a race ruined under British rule".[31] Under the Raj, he says, Hindus had slowly but surely gained the upper hand,

> A hundred years ago, the Musulmans monopolized all the important offices of State. The Hindus accepted with thanks such crumbs as their former conquerors dropped from their table, and the English were represented by a few factors and clerks... the proportion of the race which a century ago had the monopoly of Government, has now fallen to less than one-twenty-third of the whole administrative body... and, in fact, there is now scarcely a Government office in Calcutta in which a Muhammadan can hope for any post above the rank of porter, messenger, filler of inkpots, and mender of pens.[32]

Earlier, the source of income for Muslims derived from their being tax collectors, police officers, and running the courts of law which they, by virtue of command over Persian, monopolized. But most of all there was the Army, where the officers did not fight wars but who "enrolled their peasantry into troops, and drew pay from the State for them as soldiers". But with the establishment in 1793 of a new land tenure system and a new means for the collection of revenue, these sources of revenue disappeared. Hunter reflects upon their situation:

> If ever a people stood in need of a career, it is the Musalman aristocracy of Lower Bengal. Their old sources of wealth have run dry. They can no longer sack the stronghold of a neighbouring Hindu nobleman; send out a score of troopers to pillage the peasantry; levy tolls upon travelling merchants; purchase exemption through a friend at Court from their land-tax; raise a revenue by local ceases on marriages, births, harvest-homes, and every other incident of rural life; collect the excise on their own behoof, with further gratifications for winking at the sale of forbidden liquors during the sacred month of Ramazan.[33]

Hunter has been criticized for being excessively partial towards Muslims and as a progenitor of the British scheme to divide and rule. However, his data on Muslim employment in Bengal is consistent with that in other parts of India.[34] The large and growing Hindu–Muslim imbalance in the army and civil service was to become the cause *célèbre* uniting Muslim groups. Seeking to increase their share of jobs, such pressure groups were successful at times, but lobbying could benefit only certain individuals or small groups without changing the lot of the majority.

As Muslim complaints of being discriminated against became louder, the British conceded some appointments to them. These were at the relatively high level of Deputy Magistrate, Deputy Collector, and *Munsif* (judge). This had high visibility, but entrance at the lower levels was meritocratic and determined by impartially administered examinations. There, Muslims lost out badly. Hunter writes,

56 The British Reinvent India

> It is, however, in the less conspicuous Departments, in which the distribution of patronage is less keenly watched by the political parties in Bengal, that we may read the fate of the Musulmans. In 1869 these Departments were filled thus: In the three grades of Assistant Government Engineers there were fourteen Hindus and not one Musulman; among the apprentices there were four Hindus and two Englishmen, and not one Musulman. Among the sub-Engineers and Supervisors of the Public Works Department there were twenty-four Hindus to one Musulman; among the Overseers, two Musulmans to sixty-three Hindus. In the offices of Account there were fifty names of Hindus, and not one Musalman; and in the Upper Subordinate Department there were twenty-two Hindus, and again not one Musalman.[35]

To summarize, in 1871 gazetted officers in Bengal were mostly Europeans followed by Hindus with Muslims a distant third. Although Bengal as a whole had at the time roughly comparable numbers of Hindus and Muslims, a statistical analysis of the Judicial, Magisterial, and Collectoral appointments in the Bengal Presidency (today's Bengal, Assam, Bihar, Meghalaya, Orissa, Tripura) showed that, out of 485 natives of India holding these appointments, only 19 were Muslims.

The situation of Muslims in other parts of India was not very different from that in Bengal (I shall come to the Uttar Pradesh (UP) later as a special case). Chughtai[36] points out that about a year after the publication of Hunter's book, a certain Lord Hobart wrote his minutes on the situation of Muslims in the Presidency of Madras. Muslims in Madras, said Hobart, had almost disappeared from the public service in the Presidency, and in education they were far behind the Hindu community. Hobart's view was that this would create disharmony among Muslims and would lead to their feelings of being deliberately disadvantaged by the British. This would be detrimental to British interests and so should be avoided. In a letter to the Secretary of State for India, Hobart wrote:

> I found that the Muhammadans were... in a position of decided inferiority to the rest of their fellow subjects, in regard (1) to education, (2) to the employment in the public service; and my object was to rectify this inequality. In writings, in speeches and by every other means in my power, I have since endeavoured further to impress upon them that the purpose was not to prefer them but only place on equality with others, and that they need expect neither privilege nor favour: and I believe that I have completely succeeded. I can hardly conceive a greater error on the part of a Government than to show partiality to any class of the community: and I trust that after this explanation, you will acquit me of a course of conduct which would have proved me quite unworthy of the position which I hold.[37]

Note the defensive tone of Hobart's letter. By now, Hindu interest groups had become more assertive and powerful. Hobart was accused by these groups of being pro-Muslim and had to defend himself after having appointed a Muslim as Police Magistrate in Madras (a committee found this man was actually a capable candidate).

The British Reinvent India   **57**

Being scientifically minded administrators, to rule more effectively the British wanted clarity in a land of strange customs and beliefs. How many were the inhabitants of India and in what categories? To this end, a major step was taken in the first British census of 1872. Prior to this, demographics depended entirely on guesswork and conjecture. Technically, the census was a huge undertaking given the basic nature of 19th-century communication technology, and its successful completion was an administrative triumph. One result was a categorization along religious lines. Now there could be separate job quotas for Hindus and Muslims. While the initial intent of the census may not have been to consciously accentuate differences between peoples but, as we know today, quantification of characteristics can have huge consequences. This fact was just being discovered in the 19th century when colonial authorities used it for administrative ends. The numbers below indicate the huge lopsidedness in Bengal that existed between Hindus and Muslims in 1871. Only a tiny fraction of Muslims had any decent jobs.

Distribution of State Patronage in Bengal, April 1871

	Europeans	Hindus	Muslims	Total
Covenanted Civil Service (appointed by the crown in England)	260	0	0	260
Judicial officers in the Non-regulated Districts[1]	47	0	0	47
Extra Assistant Commissioners...	26	7	0	33
Deputy-Magistrates and Deputy-Collectors...,	53	113	30	196
Income-Tax Assessors	11	43	6	60
Registration Department	33	25	2	60
Judges of Small Cause Court & Subordinate Judges	14	25	8	47
Munsifs	1	178	37	216
Police Department, Gazetted Officers of all Grades	106	3	0	109
Public Works Department, Engineering Establishment,	154	19	0	173
Public Works Department, Subordinate Establishment,	72	125	4	201
Public Works Department, Account Establishment				
Medical Department, Officers attached to Medical Colleges, Jails, Charitable Dispensaries,	22	54	0	76
Sanitation and Vaccination	89	65	4	158
Establishments, and Medical Officers in charge of Districts, etc.				
Department of Public Instruction	38	14	1	53
Other Departments, such as Customs, Marine, Survey, Opium[2], etc.	412	10	0	422
Total	1338	681	92	2111

Source: W.W. Hunter.

[1] This and the following grades receive their appointments from the Local Government.

[2] But exclusive of the Ecclesiastical Establishment. Some of the Opium Officers are not gazetted.

58 The British Reinvent India

Exception: the United Provinces

That the British preferred Hindus over Muslims is undoubtedly correct. The British had snatched away an empire from Muslims, not Hindus. However, the extent of prejudice can be debated interminably. Favoring Hindus had to be kept within bounds because the British were anxious to not inspire open revolt; they were canny enough to know that a large organized ethnic and religious group could not be ignored or visibly discriminated against without endangering the entire colonial apparatus. Only a few thousand Englishmen in the Royal Army and Government were available for governing India's several hundred million people. Thus, the art of government necessitated carefully balancing the demands of various colonized peoples and playing one group off against the other.

The situation of Muslims in the United Provinces (Uttar Pradesh today) reflected the above described priorities and made it different from the rest of India. Jaffrelot has estimated the *ashrafiyya* in this province numbered around 2.5 million, a rather small circle but one with outsized impact.[38] UP was special in many ways. It is here where some of the most divisive politics of the 19th century was played out: the agitation for banning cow slaughter, the Hindi–Urdu controversy, the emergence of Nadwatul Ulama in Lucknow, etc. Deoband, Firangi Mahal, and the Aligarh Movement all belong to UP. This is also the land of Aryavarta, the claimed birthplace of Ram and Krishna, and home to several holy places. Proximity to Delhi – the heart of political power – gave Muslims leverage, enabling them to extract privileges that were not possible for those far away. Because of Sir Syed Ahmad Khan (to be covered in Chapter Three), UP Muslims became the most advanced of all of India's Muslims. That these Muslims were somehow less privileged (as in the rest of India) is strongly dismissed by historian Paul Brass who maintains that:

> There was unevenness of development between the two communities – but it was the Muslims who were the more advanced community and the Hindus the less advanced. Muslims in the UP in the nineteenth century constituted a cultural and administrative urban elite whose language dominated in the courts and primary schools of the province. The rates of change among Muslims in several respects, including urbanisation, literacy and government employment, continued to keep ahead of rates of change among Hindus till 1931. The Muslims of the UP took the leading role in Muslim separatism because they were a privileged minority and their leaders were determined to maintain their privileges.[39]

Brass also dismisses Hunter's depiction of Muslims as having shunned Western education – and so having been eliminated from government jobs – at least so far as the UP is concerned. On the contrary, he says UP Muslims were more advanced than Hindus and formed the dominant administrative and cultural elite. He claims that the faulty arguments made by Hunter became imbedded in the minds of Muslims, and so they began to feel persecuted. Brass's paper

The British Reinvent India **59**

shows that, in terms of relative population sizes, in the UP, Muslims and Hindus had roughly comparable percentages employed in Trade (bank managers, money lenders, etc.), Public Force (army, police, etc.), and Professions and Liberal Arts (lawyers, medical practitioners, teachers, letters and the arts, etc.). The reader is referred to Brass's paper for details.[40] Even more significantly, Brass shows statistics that UP Muslims had higher literacy rates than Hindus. As one indicator, there were about 20 million illiterate Hindus versus 3 million illiterate Muslims.

Tariq Rahman, Pakistani linguist and historian, agrees with Brass that the Muslims of UP were not a suppressed community: "However, their own perception of their condition was different. They had been the privileged elite and nostalgia rather than realism dominated their worldview. They were convinced that their religion, culture, language, literature, etc. were intrinsically superior to those of other Indians".[41] Indeed, the *ashrafiyya* maintained its position of privilege until the elimination of landed estates. Language played a key part: in 1839 English had replaced Persianized Urdu as the court language. However, as Rahman notes, in the UP, the British attitude on this matter was more flexible. This undoubtedly helped maintain a lead of Muslims over Hindus in several areas. But do the relative employment and education statistics tell the true state of development of the two communities? Or was it political exigencies that compelled the British to favor Muslims in the UP?

In my opinion, Brass's analysis of Muslim education superiority crucially misses out on something fundamentally important. He looks at numbers but does not go into the content of education and what at the time was considered worthy of being taught. While Muslim and Hindu literacy figures in the UP were comparable, there was relatively little attention paid by Muslims to modern knowledge and the English language was frowned upon by the religious orthodoxy. Brass does not sufficiently take into account attitudes towards learning that led to widening differences. We see this in the fact that even in the heartland of Urdu, the difficult job of translating legal and technical texts from English into Urdu was done by individuals who were mostly Hindu.

As an example, consider the case of the Thomason College of Civil Engineering at Roorki in UP (now known as IIT, Roorki). Established in 1847, it was India's first college dedicated exclusively to engineering. In view of the linguistic background of the students and perhaps the state of development of local languages, the British college administration decided that Urdu – the language associated with Muslims – should be the language of instruction. Until 1870 when the decision was made to convert to English, Urdu remained the College's mainstay. This, being the first major effort to engage with the language of the Industrial Revolution, was significant. To enable the use of Urdu, at the College's inception, a translation program had been launched. Although records have been imperfectly preserved, a recent investigation by Nizami located 34 technical books, 33 of which were translated by Hindus with just one slim volume of 42 pages being associated with a Muslim translator.[42] Teachers and professors were almost exclusively British or Hindu; Muslims were nearly absent from the

60 The British Reinvent India

faculty in spite of being allegedly better educated. But why were Muslims by and large at a disadvantage not just in engineering but all professions associated with the modern age?

The Muslim predicament

One must not think that Muslim resistance in India to modernity was simply because they were the injured ones and so avoided adopting the ways of their conquerors. From Mughal days there had been little appetite among India's Muslims for philosophy, science, and reason. In fact let's go back still further: ever since the 13th century, Islam's mainstream had rejected its earlier acceptance of Hellenistic thought. That incursion into tribal Islam had made Muslim lands scintillate with achievements in astronomy, mathematics, physics, and medicine. Starting from the mid-9th century, for another 400 years Muslims were at the forefront of rational knowledge. But the rise of an anti-rationalist religious orthodoxy – often associated with Imam Al-Ghazali (1058–1111) – had led to a closing of the Muslim mind and ended the Islamic Golden Era.[43] As science and secular learning receded, scholarship was increasingly confined to religious matters. Thus, when Islam was exported to India, it came sans its former intellectual vitality.

The Mughals showed no interest in learning from a Europe that, at the time, was undergoing a revolution of discovery and invention.[44] In 1615 the British ambassador to India, Sir Thomas Roe, brought telescopes and reading spectacles to Emperor Jehangir's court as a gift. He was delighted to see how far and clearly he could now see. It soon became a prestige item. Many of the nobility became interested in buying them but none asked what made them work or sought to duplicate them. The strategic importance of the telescope was also lost upon the Mughals. Institutionalized curiosity was absent. The printing press did not stir excitement. Mughal culture had beautiful gardens, dancing girls and boys, poetry and colorful clothing, but not much scholarship. So while Mughals made beautiful mosques and tombs, they created no universities. Art, particularly under Jehangir, featured exotic birds and animals, but there was no attempt to systematically document, categorize, and study their habits and breeding patterns. A great empire that lasted over three centuries had produced no new knowledge or shown any scientific inclination. Lack of curiosity led to lack of interest in seafaring, and so there was no Mughal navy. Instead, European navies were put under contract to defend the empire from other Europeans. This would prove to be a fatal weakness.

Complacency may be a big reason. For centuries the Muslim *ashrafiyya* had relied critically on managing the *jagir* system (a system yet to be abolished in today's Pakistan). Probably devised by the Rajputs in the 13th century, rules for *jagirdari* were revised 300 years later by Akbar. Basically a small territory, the *jagir* would be allotted by the ruler to an army chieftain in recognition of his military service. Agricultural surplus was extracted from peasants, and the income distributed among the dominating classes. The *jagirdar* would pay a tithe which went into the royal treasury, and from which Mughal emperors maintained their courts and retainers Thus the wealth and income of the Muslim elite derived from patronage, not from mastery of particular skills. But they were now in for a rude shock.

The encounter with modern imperialism armed with the products of scientific thinking left India's Muslims distraught and disoriented. Once patronage disappeared, ruin followed. They who believed themselves to be under God's exclusive protection and the most superior of all men wondered what had gone wrong. Had God abandoned them? That the Qur'an is the most superior and complete book of knowledge was central to their belief. They knew they were the chosen ones but to their deep chagrin they found themselves utterly unprepared for what had come from across the seas. The grandest periods of Islamic history had nothing that matched the firepower, technology, depth of organization, or the sheer size of the imperial apparatus. After the Mutiny, there were no jobs to be had for them but, worse, it was still harder to deal with the new ideas and social institutions introduced by Western conquest. For all this, many still cherished the fond hope that once the *firangis* were driven away, Muslim political authority would be restored to its pristine glory. A conquering race would somehow win again.

But the times had changed and there was no going back. In Europe steel from the Bessemer process, hydraulic press, macadamized roads, printing press, and the telegraph had revolutionized life. The steamship carried these into India and soon the industrialization of India was on the horizon. The days of the bullock cart and elephant were numbered. Elaborate railway networks were being constructed with bridges over wide rivers, and tunnels made through forbiddingly high mountains.

Traditional *madrassa* education left Muslims ill-equipped for the modern age. The dull rote memorization of past centuries was no longer useful. Teaching about the greatness of kings and emperors was replaced by ideas of the parliamentary and legal system. The child in a modern school would learn trigonometry and logarithms, the properties of solids and gases, and of experiments that showed these obeyed certain laws. The change of curriculum was not easy to digest. The *zamindar* and *jagirdar* could see little reason or use for it even when his boys were sent to school and, as happened occasionally, to Oxford and Cambridge where very few opted for the sciences or other forms of hard learning. Most learned the airs and graces that would assure their social position back home.

The language policy enforced by the British in Bengal was no less than an earthquake. It caused the Muslim upper- and middle classes there to disappear. With English as the official language instead of Persian, those with a traditional education had been driven out with one stroke of the pen. Hindus, who had taken to English with less resistance, gained relative to Muslims. Muslim access to jobs plummeted. The statistics tell a shocking story:

62 The British Reinvent India

Until 1839 Muslim lawyers (pleaders) were almost as numerous as the Hindus and English put together, the proportion being 6 of the former to 7 of both of the latter. But, since 1851, the scene started to change. Different fitness tests were introduced; of 240 pleaders of the Calcutta High Court admitted from 1851 to 1869, 239 were Hindus and only one was Muslim. Among the attorneys, proctors, and solicitors of the High Court in 1869, there were 27 Hindus and not one Muslim; among the barristers-at-law were three Hindus and not one Muslim. Again, in 1868, the statistics regarding the medical profession indicated: (a) among the graduates of medicine in the Calcutta University there were 4 doctors, 3 Hindu, one English, and no Muslim; (b) among 11 bachelors of medicine, 10 were Hindus and one English; (c) the 104 licentiates of medicine consisted of 5 English, 98 Hindus, and 1 Muslim.[45]

While race and religion certainly played a role with the British in selecting candidates, they came second. Employees, whether Hindu or Muslim, were expected to take orders and demonstrate some modest amount of initiative as well. British rulers chose those best-suited for the job. Those without education, skill, and professional competence would find employment difficult to get and to maintain. Facility with the English language was crucial, and this turned out to be an employment bottleneck.

Modernity impacts Muslims

Resistance to learning and speaking the English language was widespread among the Muslim *ashrafiyya*. Some of the more conservative ones suggested rinsing one's mouth (*kuli*) thrice and saying *naoozobillah* after speaking English to purify oneself. To an extent more flexible Muslims broke through this barrier but relatively few Muslims developed reasonable facility in the language. Knowledge of English had already become important by the beginning of the 19th century. Although as yet it had not quite become the sine qua non for a job with the Company, the writing was on the wall.

I have already alluded above to the catastrophic effects upon Muslim employment once the Persian language lost its earlier status as the language of the courts. Thereafter, enrollment of Muslim students in schools dropped because there was a view that education should be essentially religious and taught through the medium of Persian. Resistance to English was therefore natural. The report of the Indian Education Commission of 1882 painted a grim picture:

> ...[In 1835], after the introduction of English into the course of studies, the Council of Education had to confess that "the endeavour to impart a high order of English education" to the Muhammadan community had completely failed. Forty years later again, the condition of the Muhammadan population of India "as regards education had of late been frequently pressed upon the attention of the Government of India. The Muhammadans

The British Reinvent India **63**

were not even competing on equal terms with the Hindus for employment under Government, nor had the endeavour to impart to them a high order of education been attended by any adequate success... A considerable proportion of Muhammadans were learning English [by 1882]... But the high English education was not cultivated, in any appreciable degree, more extensively than it had been in 1832.[46]

Rahman maintains that no fatwa barred the Muslims of united India to study the English language but, given the vastness of India and multiple sources of authority, this is not a verifiable statement. On the other hand, there was clearly great suspicion.[47] Thus, for example, Rashid Ahmad Gangohi gave a ruling that it was lawful to learn English but only if there was no danger to religion.[48] The fact that such a fatwa had to be issued shows that the matter occupied the minds of people at the time. In fact, as Pakistan swings to the right, that suspicion has begun to grow again and English as a means of communication is narrowly restricted to the upper classes.

Why exactly did Muslims object to sending their children to government schools and colleges? And how can they be persuaded to take advantage of facilities offered by the government? To explore this further in December 1870, an essay competition was organized on this topic by the Committee for the Better Diffusion and Advancement of Learning among Muhammadans of India.[49] Thirty-two essays were received. The reasons given were: (1) the want of religious education, (2) disbelief in religion, especially Islam, (3) corruption of morals and absence of traditional politeness and courtesy among modern students, (4) depressed economic status of Muslims. Some essayists deplored the teaching of English which consumed many years without producing any mastery of the language. Both the essayists and their assessors noted, "that in the works of canon law, *ulum aqlia* (rational sciences) as well as *ilm-ul-kalam* (scholastic theology) have been declared unlawful".[50]

Shutting out modern education was seen by the majority of the Muslim elite as protection of their religion and culture. A protest petition signed by 8312 Muslims, including the *ulema* and leading gentlemen of Calcutta was submitted to the authorities.[51] They argued therein for support of *madrassas* and *maktabs* but that was rejected. Muslim participation in education began to decline yet further. In West Bengal there were roughly three Hindus to every one Muslim, but the participation ratios were highly skewed. In 1893 out of 44 Deputy Inspectors of Schools in Bengal Presidency only 2 were Muslims, out of 181 Sub-Inspectors only 9 were Muslims, and out of 279 teachers in government high schools only 11 were Muslims.[52] Differences in Hindu–Muslim educational achievement increased over time at every level – school, college, and university. This was to profoundly affect the future of both communities, widening distances between them, and ultimately becoming an important cause for the partition of India.

At the school level, there were far fewer Muslim students enrolled as compared to Hindus. In Bengal the number of students enrolled in government colleges and schools in 1841 was 751 Muslims against 3188 Hindus.

64 The British Reinvent India

In 1856 this nosedived to 731 Muslims against 6448 Hindus.[53] For higher education, the statistics are eye-opening: the University of Calcutta was the first secular western-style university in India and set standards as far away as Punjab. Only a few Muslims applied or qualified for admission, the requirements being rigorous by the standards of the time. Although the populations were commensurate in size, just two Muslims passed the first B.A. examination held in 1858.[54] The first Muslim graduate passed his B.A. in 1861 with the next one graduating in 1865. Out of a total of 250 graduates by 1870, only 12 were Muslim. The university calendar up to 1868 shows only one Muslim had passed the Bachelor of Law examination.[55] The table below compares educational attainment data for Hindus and Muslims across India, 1850–1878. The difference is staggering, greater than even the employment statistics encountered above.

Education Level	Total Graduates	Muslim Graduates
Doctor in Law	6	0
Honours in Law	4	0
Bachelor in Law	705	6
Licentiate in Law	235	5
Bachelor in Civil Engineering	36	0
Licentiate in Engineering	51	0
Master of Arts	326	5
Bachelor of Arts	1343	30
Doctor in Medicine	4	0
Honours in Medicine	2	0
Bachelor in Medicine	58	1
Licentiate in Medicine and Surgery	385	8
Total	**3155**	**55**

Comparison of Education Levels of Hindus with Muslims (1850–1878) from Data Submitted to Government of India in 1878.[56]

Such statistics are seen to repeat over and over in different parts of India. The decline of Muslim schools in areas with large Muslim populations had a direct effect on education at higher levels – and ultimately jobs – as well.[57] The Calcutta University examination of 1871 shows how bleak things had become:

Name of Examination	Hindus Successful	Hindus Unsuccessful	Muslims Successful	Muslims Unsuccessful
Entrance Exam	504	859	27	44
First-Year Arts	166	268	1	18
Bachelor of Arts	56	95	0	2

Source: National Archives of India, Government of Bengal, Home Department, Education of Bengal for 1876–1877, January 1878, Proceedings No. 45–48, quoted in Paul.[58]

Had Muslims responded differently to the demands of modern civilization, the subcontinent's history would have been very different. But, even after past glories had faded away, a false sense of entitlement stood in way of Muslim progress. The Muslim *ashrafiyya*, though in dire straits, refused to surrender their notions of absolute superiority over non-Muslims. Were we not born to rule, they asked, and will we not rule again? Has not the Qur'an declared Islam as the last and final religion, and that the ultimate victory shall be that of Islam? Decades later, Allama Iqbal – as we shall see in Chapter Four – was to give powerful poetic voice to these aspirations.

The upshot of these attitudes was, for the most part, a rejection of the education which the British wanted for India. There was deep discomfort at moving Muslim children away from *maktabs* and *madrassas* towards secular ones. Assimilation into the modern world through school and college education was for lesser peoples, fit only for those who had been ruled over but not for those who had gloriously ruled India for centuries. Akbar Allahabadi (1846–1921), known for his wittily scathing poems, captures the mood of his times by staging a fictional encounter between the epic lover *Majnun* and the mother of his beloved, *Laila*.

کہ بیٹا تو اگر کر لے بی اے پاس   کہا مجنوں سے یہ لیلٰی کی ماں نے

بلا دقت میں بن جاؤں تری ساس   تو فوراً بیاہ دوں لیلٰی کو تجھ سے

کجا عاشق، کجا کالج کا بکواس   کہا مجنوں نے یہ اچھی سنائی

کجا ٹھونسی ہوئی چیزوں کا احساس   کجا یہ فطرتِ جوشِ طبیعت

ہرن پہ لادی جاتی ہے کہیں گھاس   بڑی بی آپ کو کیا ہو گیا ہے

مجھے سمجھا ہے کوئی ہرچرن داس   یہ اچھی قدردانی آپ نے کی

Said Laila's mother to Majnun	Son, were you to pass your BA exam
Happily would I wed to you my Laila	And become your ever dear mother-in-law
Said Majnun, no ma'am I'm surprised	I'm an amorous one no college nonsense for me
Here I am naturally eager and willing	But certainly unwilling to carry a useless burden
What's the matter with you, old lady?	Would you make a gazelle carry grass?
Is that how much you value me?	Am I just some damn Harcharan Das?

Majnun is indignant that he must become college educated to be considered worthy of his beloved. Only Hindus – typified by the Hindu name *Harcharan Das* – go to college, not Muslims! Locked into visions of past grandeur and vainglorious pride, the *ashrafiyya* lacked the skills – or even willingness – to acquire those skills critically needed for the new age. Having the outlook of a *zamindar* rendered one unfit for the professions. Not going to college meant that very few Muslims could compete in civil service or university entrance exams. Within the administrative apparatus and professions, opportunities for Muslims kept shriveling.

Modernity posed countless other challenges too: could one use electric lights in a mosque? Wear shirts and pants? Use a knife, fork, and spoon? Eat while sitting at a table with a Christian? Deposit money in a bank, take a loan, or use a

66 The British Reinvent India

money order? Use a urinal when the express instruction from the *Hadith* is to crouch down? The relevance of some questions remains even in the 21st century. While there is no longer a taboo against English, the unpopularity of urinals is noticeable in present-day bus and airport terminals.

Perhaps the greatest challenge of modernity was the role of Muslim women in society. In her PhD dissertation, Karin Deutsch examines politics, law, and identity of women in 19th-century India.[59] In the upper classes, *purdah* was practiced by both Hindu and Muslim women albeit with different kinds of restrictions. Although the *burqa* was a marker for Muslims only, it is unclear which form of *purdah* – Hindu or Muslim – was more restrictive. Arguably the social and legal position of women in Islam was better than in traditional Hinduism, at least such as had existed for a millennium. In fact this was held up to underscore both the difference and the superiority of Muslims vis-à-vis Hindus. Deutsch remarks that,

> Hindu social reformers, eager to find causes for the present 'degraded' position of Hindu women as opposed to their notionally pure and exalted status in ancient India, fixed upon purdah as a scapegoat: it had been brought to India by Muslim invaders and its adoption by the Hindu community had marked the decline in women's position. By designating purdah as a Muslim practice, Hindus were able to distance themselves from it and thus support its abolition with greater ease, as it was not considered to be a part of 'traditional' Indian culture. This discourse was adopted by some British writers as well who took up the theme that purdah was a Muslim institution.[60]

The relative success of Hindu reformers in dispensing with *purdah* for Hindu women allowed for rapid distancing of Hindu women from other traditions as well. On the other hand, the Muslim *ashrafiyya*, particularly in the UP, were much more conservative. The seclusion of women was seen as the ideal behavior for Muslim women and a marker of Muslim identity. Muslim women could not be permitted the freedoms of western women or even that of modernized Hindu women; their place was at home as wives and mothers. When the government recommended education for girls, the overall Muslim response was hugely negative. Educating girls was seen as a travesty of modesty. The veil and polygamy were seen as parts of culture that must be defended against cultural incursion.[61]

Modernity impacts Hindus

By 1765, the East India Company was ruling Bengal and repatriating large profits to the home country. But what was being done to educate the natives? Though pressured by some enlightened members of the public and Christian missionaries, the Company's directors refused to take responsibility, stating that it should be left to private initiatives. Nevertheless, some half-way steps were taken with

The British Reinvent India **67**

the establishment of Calcutta Madrasa in 1781 and Sanskrit College in 1791 at Benares. These were limited to oriental learning.

As with Muslims, at the time there was no significant demand for western style education. Adapting to colonial rule and modern ideas did not come easily to most Hindus. We have already noted above that traditional Hinduism's treatment of women reflected patriarchal values no less than among Muslims. Caste distinctions were rigid, and discrimination was written into the law: in any dispute, a Brahmana was to be tested by a balance, a Kshatriya by fire, a Vaishya by water, and a Shudra by poison.[62] Legally, Shudras could appear as witnesses only for members of their own caste. Pre-puberty marriages were common as was widow-burning (*sati*). Women were no more than chattels. British conservatives, such as Bishop Samuel Wilberforce, were full of contempt for all Indians, Hindus, and Muslims: "Our Christian religion", he told the members of Parliament, "is sublime, pure and beneficent. The Indian religions system is mean, licentious and cruel. It is one grand abomination!".

While Hindu traditionalists opposed western education and modern ideas, adaptation came easier to Hindus than to Muslims because they possessed some critical skills. Under Mughal rule Hindus had maintained footholds in the empire's administrative and commercial life to a greater extent than Muslims. It is they who kept the accounts of Muslim kings and emperors for which simple mathematics was a crucial tool. Because of the Islamic prohibition against usury, Hindus found themselves an important vocation – money-lending. In this sense, they were in a similar position to the Jews of Europe. Success in this profession required a set of skills very different from farming and the traditional trades. Some, surely, were social: cultivating connections, winning over trust. But it also required cognitive skills – a fluency in mathematics and some dexterity with numbers. Traditional Hindu merchant classes were skilled in trade and commerce, did almost all of the money-lending and banking, and were bookkeepers and agents. They took a portion of the collected revenue before passing on the proceeds to their superior Muslim officers. This was a relatively unimportant function earlier on, but it became hugely important once the British dismissed the Muslim link between the actual collector and the government. The Cornwallis-Shore reforms, as they came to be known, effectively diverted wealth from Muslim to Hindu hands enabling Hindus to become landowners.[63]

Adaptation to the new dispensation was helped along by reformist social and religious Hindu movements such as Brahmo Samaj (which literally means the society of the worshippers of One True God). Raja Ram Mohan Roy (1772–1883), Raja Radhakanta Deb (1784–1867), and Debendranath Tagore (1817–1905) are among those who sought British help to educate their communities. Roy, Brahmo's founder, was a strong individual remembered for campaigning against *sati*, dowry, and child marriage and for being a powerful advocate of English education and thought.[64] A Bengali Brahman who rebelled against his priestly clan and widely prevalent superstitions, he had studied Persian and Arabic in a *madrassa* but was also intricately familiar with Sanskrit, Hindi, and

68 The British Reinvent India

his mother tongue, Bengali. Remarkably, among other books he wrote a tract, *Tuhfat-ul-Muwahhidin* (A Gift to Monotheists), in Persian with an introduction in Arabic. It was part of his effort to show the oneness of all religions.

At least part of Roy's insistence on reform had a pragmatic origin: "The present system of Hindoos is not well calculated to promote their political interests.... It is necessary that some change should take place in their religion, at least for the sake of their political advantage and social comfort".[65] This line of thinking resonated well with the Hindu community leaders, and so in rapid succession Roy was able to secure help in setting up various schools and colleges: Hindu College (1817), Anglo-Hindu School (1826), Vedanta College (1826), and Scottish Church College (1830).

Reform movements were critical in creating modernized and articulate Hindu middle classes that went on to virtually monopolize government jobs and modern professions. Hindus turned to modern ideas faster than Muslims because a relatively greater fraction was able to see tangible benefits in terms of personal advancement and access to jobs and professions. There was also less of a psychological barrier for them in political terms. For most Hindus, the advent of British rule involved merely changing one master for another; both were conquerors. Thus they could adapt faster than Muslims to the new dispensation and be of greater help to the British rulers.

Evidence for this attitude is abundant. For example in 1827 – a full thirty years before the Great Mutiny – Hindu princes, chieftains, and gentlemen belonging to the western part of India subscribed 215,000 rupees for "founding one or more Professorship for teaching the languages, literature, sciences and moral philosophy of Europe".[66] There is no record of prominent Muslims having made similar grants. As Hunter observed in 1871, "our system of public instruction, which has awakened Hindus from the sleep of centuries, and quickened their inert masses with some of the noble impulses of a nation, is opposed to the traditions, unsuited to the requirements, and hateful to the religion of Mussalmans".[67]

Ways begin to part

I have chosen 1857 as a convenient breakpoint in Indian history but, of course, there cannot be an exact time. Major changes had been set in motion a decade or two earlier as well as later. One change – dealt with in detail in the preceding sections – had been a massive widening of the Hindu–Muslim split and a parting of their ways. But within Muslims, ways had also parted with the emergence of two sharply different tendencies. While the *ashrafiyya* beseeched the British for jobs and lands, a militant religious-based movement was out fighting the colonizers but, at other times, also Hindus and Sikhs. These were the Wahhabis who fought for the faith and had adherents in the seminary in Deoband as well.

In the climate of growing Muslim conservatism and defeatism, the doctrine of Wahhabism had received a very warm welcome in India upon its arrival from across the seas. Wahhabi opposition to British rule had already started to worry colonialists

The British Reinvent India **69**

because it offered the most serious and well-planned challenge to British supremacy in India around 1830–1870.[68] Named after an 18th- century preacher, Muhammad ibn Abdul Wahhab (1703–1792), Wahhabism – also known as Salafism – calls for interpreting the Qur'an in literal terms and expunging widespread Sunni practices such as visiting tombs or venerating holy men or idols (*shirk*). Among Wahhabism's key concepts was *bid'ah* (Arabic) or *bid'at* (Urdu); i.e., in religious matters, novelty or invention is forbidden. It announced itself an implacable opponent of modernity. Its declared enemies were Shias as well as the Sufis who had accreted local traditions over the one thousand years of Muslim rule in India and were considered tainted by Hindu influence. In the Indian context, Wahhabism was directed as much against the British as against Sikhs, Hindus, and "corrupted Muslims".

The man credited with importing Wahhabism into India is Syed Ahmad of Rae Barelvi (1786–1831), who returned from pilgrimage in Mecca in 1824 to begin a holy war against the Sikhs aimed at restoring the Punjab to Muslim rule.[69] However, this may be somewhat of a mischaracterization because he had already accepted the basic tenets of Wahhabism long before sailing to Arabia. Syed Ahmad was a student of the *Madrassa-i-Ramiyya* religious seminary in Delhi and a star pupil of its leader, Shah Abdul Aziz (who we have already encountered in the previous chapter). Aziz was more militant than his father, Shah Waliullah, declaring India to be *Dar-ul-Harb* (land of unbelief) that would have to be converted into *Dar-ul-Islam* (land of Islam). In *Risalah Jihaddiyah* (treatise on war), he exhorts Muslims to jihad:

> Jihad is mandatory for you, O! Muslims,
> Prepare at once for it if you have faith, O! Muslims.
> The warrior whose feet became dusty on the battlefield's sod,
> Escaped from hell, and became free from hell's fire.
> The warrior who fought briefly for Allah's truth,
> Won the adorned sepulchre of the Paradise.[70]

Syed Ahmad Barelvi became the undisputed Wahhabi leader. Bitterly anti-Shia, he repeatedly destroyed their *taziyyas* and other mourning symbols. Although based in the tribal North Western Frontier Province (today Pakistan's Khyber Pakhtunkhwa province), Barelvi's outreach extended as far as Hyderabad, Madras, Bengal, Uttar Pradesh, and Bombay. Jihad was declared against the Sikh kingdom of Ranjit Singh in Punjab. Barelvi captured Peshawar in 1830 but then lost it to the Sikhs in the following year. He was killed in battle a year later and is buried in Balakot. His mausoleum is visited by Pakistani tourists today. According to Olivier Roy, Barelvi was "the first person to realize the necessity of a movement which was at the same time religious, military, and political".[71] In essence the Wahhabi movement was a movement of Muslims by Muslims and for Muslims. Though also directed against the British, the movement's principal enemy was the Sikhs. Under its influence, Barelvi had created a sharia state in areas that are now parts of Khyber Pakhtunkhwa and Afghanistan.

70 The British Reinvent India

Despair can make one clutch at straws. Religious orthodoxy was an attractive alternative because it offered a cut-and-dried explanation for why Muslims had lost out – they had disobeyed Allah by having deviated from the righteous path of the Qur'an and Sunnah. Ancient glories, it proclaimed, could be revived only by returning to the unblemished past and following the Prophet of Islam. In Bengal, the Faraizi Movement led by Haji Shariatullah (1781–1840) preached against polytheism and against *bid'at*.[72] No longer must one succumb to pleasures of the flesh. Horse and sword alone could resurrect past glories. This message has never really gone away: some Pakistani school textbooks in the 1950s and 1960s regretted that Muslims had forgotten the art of warfare:

O' Muslim come forth to the battlefield	اے مسلماں! تجھے میدان میں آنا ہو گا
Unleash once again the power of your sword	پھر تجھے جوہر شمشیر دکھانا ہو گا

Easier communication – a by-product of modernity – was a game changer no less than the census alluded to earlier. Old inhibitions against the printing press had come down, and so making religious pamphlets or books became easy. They could be sent by postal service to different parts of India. Religious leaders could take the train going from town to town and spread their particular message. Princeton history professor Qasim Zaman notes that,

> Between 1861 and 1946–47, railway tracks had grown from 1,587 to 40,524 route miles; already by 1902, India was "the world's fourth largest railway system measured by route length." The number of passengers traveling by trains had grown from 19,283,000 in 1871 to 1,189,428,000 in 1946–47... Two examples are instructive here. Jama'at Ali Shah (ca. 1841–1951), a Sufi master belonging to the Naqshbandi order, had taken to traveling by rail from his base in the Punjab for months on end to visit groups of disciples all across the Indian subcontinent... the Deobandi Sufi and scholar Ashraf Ali Thanawi (1863–1943) spent much of the first four decades of the twentieth century at his Sufi lodge in Thana Bhawan, a small town not far from Deoband, and it was there that throngs of visitors came to him, thanks again to the small railway station that connected his lodge to the rest of the subcontinent.[73]

Since the Wahhabis were the inveterate enemies of colonialism, one might be tempted to believe that British were against all conservative Muslims. This is not true and they too had their "good Taliban" and "bad Taliban". Muslim conservatism was encouraged by at least some top British administrators. As a matter of policy, the distribution of canal colony land grants in Punjab did not extend to religious leaders and *pirs*. In fact the colonial administrator H. J. Maynard is said to have objected to the Pir of Makhad (Attock District) being included among the "landed gentry", whom the British considered among their closest allies. But

The British Reinvent India **71**

the Lieutenant-Governor, Sir Michael O'Dwyer, answered that whether they were truly "landed gentry" or not, the influence of such religious heads could not be ignored.[74] The Pir of Makhad, he pointed out, was "regarded with veneration by many of the leading Frontier and western Punjab chiefs," and such influence had to be taken into account. *Sajjada nashins,* whose hereditary religious influence might be put to useful political purposes, were therefore given grants as well. O'Dwyer, lest it be forgotten, had approved the massacre at Jallianwala Bagh in 1919 and was assassinated by Udham Singh in London twenty-one years later.

Ironically those Indian Muslims who were the most conservative and fought hardest against the British for the glory of Islam got nowhere. Instead, it was the modernist Muslims of India – the ones who chose English education and modernity – who actually succeeded in carving out Pakistan. Our next goal post is therefore to study key Muslim movers and shakers of the 19th and 20th centuries: Sir Syed, Iqbal, and Jinnah.

Notes

1 W. Durant, *The Case for India*, New York, Simon & Schuster (1930), pp. 1–2.
2 S. Tharoor, *An Era of Darkness – the British Empire in India*, Rupa Publications (2016).
3 R. Orme, *A History of the Military Transactions of the British Nation in Indostan, from the year MDCCXLV; to Which Is Prefixed a Dissertation on the Establishments Made by Mahomedan Conquerors in Indostan*. Vol. 2. London, John Nourse (1778); reprinted in New Delhi by Today's and Tomorrow's Printers and Publishers, n.d., p. 7.
4 *The Collected Poems of W. B. Yeats* (Wordsworth Poetry Library).
5 M.A. Asif, *The Loss of Hindustan – The Invention of India*, Harvard University Press (2020).
6 M. Monier-Williams, *Modern India and the Indians*, London (1879), pp. 268–269.
7 R. Thapar, Imagined Religious Communities? Ancient History and the Modern Search for a Hindu Identity, *Modern Asian Studies* 23, no. 2 (1989): 218.
8 John Mill, *The History of British India* (5th ed.), 10 vols., edited by H. H. Wilson. London, James Madden (1858), OCLC 893322163.
9 John Marriott, *The Other Empire: Metropolis, India and Progress in the Colonial Imagination*, Manchester University Press (2003), p. 133.
10 Wikipedia, the free encyclopedia.
11 M. Hasan, *Islam in the Subcontinent*, Manohar Books (2002), pp. 38–41.
12 Ibid, pp. 41–42.
13 Asif, op. cit.
14 R.M. Eaton, *Temple Desecration and Muslim States in Medieval India*, Oxford University Press India (2004), Dehli, Hope Publications, p. 12.
15 K. Brittlebank, *Tipu Sultan's Search for Legitimacy – Islam and Kingship in a Hindu Domain*, Oxford University Press (1997).
16 Ibid, pp. 152–153.
17 K.A. Nizami (ed) *Politics and Society during the Early Medieval Period: Collected Works of Professor Mohammad Habib*, New Delhi, People's Publishing House (1974), p. 1:12.
18 All translations from Urdu are the author's own.
19 E. Stokes, *The Peasant Armed: The Indian Revolt of 1857*, ed. C.A. Bayly, Oxford (1986), p. 92.
20 Sir Sayyid Ahmad Khan, *The Causes for the Indian Revolt* (1858).

72 The British Reinvent India

21 I. Habib, *Commemorating 1857: The Role of the Bengal Army in the First War of Independence*, Outlook, 24 May 2017.
22 N. Stewart, Divide and Rule: British Policy in Indian History, *Science & Society*, 15, no. 1 (1951): 54.
23 Ibid, p. 55.
24 W.W. Hunter, *The Indian Musalmans*, London, Trubner and Company (1876), p. 94.
25 W. Dalrymple, *The Last Mughal – The Fall of a Dynasty, 1857*, Bloomsbury Publishing (2006), p. 87.
26 Munir-ud-din Chughtai, Post-1857 Economic and Administrative Policies of the British in India and the Muslims, *Pakistan Economic and Social Review*, 12, no. 3 (Autumn 1974): 243–254.
27 Sir A.C. Lyall, *Asiatic Studies: Religious and Social*, second edition, London, John Murray (1884), pp. 239–249.
28 Ibid.
29 Hunter, op. cit., p. 94.
30 Ibid, p. 150.
31 Ibid, Hunter in his dedication.
32 Ibid, p. 170.
33 Ibid, p. 94.
34 For a discussion of Hunter per se, see: Hunter's "The Indian Musalmans": A Re-Examination of Its Background by Mohammed Mohar Ali, *The Journal of the Royal Asiatic Society of Great Britain and Ireland*, no. 1 (1980): 30–51.
35 Hunter, op. cit., p. 168.
36 Munir-ud-din Chughtai, op. cit.
37 Salisbury Papers (i.e., The Papers of the Third Marquis of Salisbury, Secretary of State for India, February 1874 to April 1878, deposited in the Library of Christ Church, Oxford), Hobart to Salisbury, 12 January, 1875.
38 C. Jaffrelot, *The Pakistan Paradox – Instability and Resilience*, Oxford University Press (USA), Translated by Cynthia Schoch (2015), p. 23.
39 P.R. Brass, Muslim Separatism in United Provinces: Social Context and Political Strategy before Partition, *Economic and Political Weekly*, 5, no. 3/5 (1970): p. 167.
40 Ibid.
41 T. Rahman, *Language and Politics in Pakistan*, Oxford University Press (1997), p. 68.
42 S. Nizami in *The Particle*, SBASSE, Issue No. 15, July–September 2020.
43 P. Hoodbhoy, *Islam and Science – Religious Orthodoxy and the Battle for Rationality*, London, Zed Books (1991).
44 T.E. Huff, *Intellectual Curiosity and the Scientific Revolution – A Global Perspective*, Cambridge University Press (2011).
45 Hunter, op. cit., pp. 169–180.
46 S. Nurullah and J.P. Naik, *A History of Education in India*, Bombay, Macmillan and Company, Ltd. (1951), p. 139, quoted in Education, the Muslim Elite, and the Creation of Pakistan by Alan Peshkin, *Comparative Education Review*, 6, no. 2 (1962): pp. 152–159. https://www.jstor.org/stable/1186691
47 No Fatwa on English during Sir Syed's time, *The Express Tribune*, 14 October 2017.
48 Hasan, op. cit., p. 104.
49 H. Malik, *Sir Sayyid Ahmad Khan and Muslim modernization in India and Pakistan*, Columbia University Press (1980), p. 126.
50 Ibid, p. 133.
51 S. Murtaza Ali, Quoted as Report of Madrassah Education Committee, 1941, p. 149 in Muslim Education in Bengal 1837–1937, *Islamic Studies*, 10, no. 3 (September 1971): pp. 181–199. Published by: Islamic Research Institute, International Islamic University, Islamabad.
52 Ibid.
53 Ibid.
54 Ibid.

The British Reinvent India **73**

55 Ibid.
56 T. Hasan, *The Aligarh Movement and the Making of the Muslim Mind*, Rupa Publications India Pvt. Ltd. (2006), p. xxvi
57 N. Paul, *Muslim Education and Communal Conflict in Colonial Bengal: British Policies and Muslim Responses from 1854 to 1947*, doctoral thesis, West Virginia University (2016).
58 Ibid.
59 K.A. Deutsch, *Muslim Women In Colonial North India Circa 1920–1947: Politics, Law And Community Identity*, doctoral thesis, University of Cambridge (July 1998).
60 Ibid, p. 40.
61 See, for example, the outrage expressed by Sir Syed on such cultural matters and particularly on educating girls in: *Writings and Speeches of Sir Syed Ahmad Khan-7*, compiled and edited by Shan Mohammad, foreword by Rai Gopal, Bombay, Nachiketa Publications Limited (1972), p. 24.
62 D.N. Jha, *Ancient India in Historical Outline*, revised and enlarged edition, Dehli, Manohar Books (2009).
63 *The Cambridge History of the British Empire*, Vol. IV British India 1497–1858, edited by H.H. Dodwell, Cambridge University Press (1929), p. 451.
64 *The Life and Letters of Raja Rammohun Roy*, compiled and edited by Sophia Dobson Collet, second edition edited by Hem Chandra Sarkar, Calcutta (1914), p. 160.
65 Brahmo Samaj, Arya Samaj, and the Church-Sect Typology, Gauri Shankar Bhatt, *Review of Religious Research*, 10, no. 1 (Autumn 1968): 24. https://www.jstor.org/stable/3510669
66 Parulekar, quoted in T. Rahman, *Language and Politics in Pakistan*, Karachi, Oxford University Press (1996), p. 31.
67 Hunter, op. cit., p. 106.
68 Wahhabis in Delhi in *Ledlie's Miscellany* by J. Parks Ledlie, Delhi (1852).
69 C. Allen, The Hidden Roots of Wahhabism in British India, *World Policy Journal*, 22, no. 2 (Summer 2005): 87–93.
70 Quoted in H. Malik, *Sir Sayyid Ahmad Khan and Muslim Modernization in India and Pakistan*, Columbia University Press (1980), p. 46.
71 O. Roy, *Islam and Resistance in Afghanistan*, Cambridge University Press (1985), p. 56.
72 Banglapedia – National Encyclopedia of Bangladesh. http://en.banglapedia.org/index.php?title=Shariatullah,Haji
73 M.Q. Zaman, *Islam in Pakistan: A History*, Princeton University Press (2018), p. 21.
74 D. Gilmartin, Religious Leadership and the Pakistan Movement in the Punjab, *Modern Asian Studies*, 13, no.3 (1979): 495. http://www.jstor.org/stable/312311

PART TWO

A Closer Look at Pakistan's Three Founder-Heroes

Three

FOUNDER I: THE LONELY MODERNIZER

Unique among Pakistan's founders is Sir Syed Ahmad Khan. Once a deeply orthodox Wahhabi-inspired Muslim, he traveled to the other end of Islam's intellectual universe to become its leading modernist. As such he was the only prominent Muslim of the subcontinent to have figured out why the magnificent ship of Mughal times had foundered. Muslim backwardness came not from British or Hindu conspiracies, he said, but from Muslim reluctance to accept evidence-based ways of thinking, modern science, and their obstinate attachment to tradition. His exegetic work, *Tafsir-ul-Quran*, radically reinterpreted Muslim theology in the light of modern European science. But did he distort Islam while doing so? And just how influential were his reinterpretations? On the political and social front, much controversy surrounds him: for one, progressives generally dismiss him as a colonial flunky. How true is the accusation? Was he the true voice of all Muslims of his time or just that of the rapidly decaying north Indian Muslim elite? Was he for Hindu–Muslim amity or a communalist? Although he was once a hero, why has he fallen from favor in the eyes of those who run Pakistan today? This chapter unwraps the mythology around the first significant Muslim leader who proposed that Hindus and Muslims form separate nations and locates him appropriately within the context of his times.

Mughal rule was over but its music and poetry lived on. Delhi's cold wintry nights would see the city's Muslim literati gather at *mushairas*, comfortably ensconced in the *baithaks* of crumbling *havelis* savoring the last remnants of a splendid past grandeur. Servants kept alive glowing *angeethees*, periodically removing ashes and silently adding on fresh coals. From time to time rapt listeners would burst out in appreciative refrain. The poetics themes were fairly well defined: unrequited love, forbidden pleasures of wine, the meaning of life, *qasidas* (odes to heroes and ancestors), and *marsiyas* (elegies to the Karbala tragedy). As incomes shrank further and jobs became fewer, the times grew grimmer and so

DOI: 10.4324/9781003379140-6

78 Founder I: The Lonely Modernizer

did the poetry. A poem of Altaf Hussain Hali, *madd-o-jazr-e-Islam* (the rise and fall of Islam), was a surefire tear-jerker that would leave audiences weeping in distress:

Not privy to the secrets of government are we	نہ اہل حکومت کے ہمراز ہیں ہم
Not welcome to the corridors of power are we	نہ درباریوں میں سرافراز ہیں ہم
Not known for great feats of learning are we	نہ علموں میں شایان اعزاز ہیں ہم
Not distinguished for skills or industry are we	نہ صنعت میں، حرفت میں، ممتاز ہیں ہم
Not well placed for employment are we	نہ رکھتے ہیں کچھ منزلت نوکری میں
Not welcome in business and trade are we	نہ حصہ ہمارا ہے سودا گری میں
In sorrowful decline and ruination are we	تنزل نے کی ہے بری گت ہماری
Known far and wide for our perdition are we	بہت دور پہنچی ہے نکبت ہماری
Honor is lost, lost to the world are we	گئی گذری دنیا سے عزت ہماری
Doomed never to rise again are we	نہیں کچھ ابھرنے کی صورت ہماری
We live but having just one single hope	پڑے ہیں اک امید کے ہم سہارے
That up above the clouds is heaven	توقع پہ جنت کے جیتے ہیں سارے

Syed Ahmad Khan (1817–1898) belonged to this traumatized and despondent world of Muslims, one filled with sighs, sobs, and lamentations of decay and decline. Although Pakistan was born a half-century after his death, he set into motion a sense of Muslim nationalism that seemingly offered a way out to India's Muslims. For this, alongside Iqbal and Jinnah, he was once placed in the holy trinity of Pakistan's founders. His friend and acolyte, Maulana Altaf Hussain Hali, paid eloquent tribute: "The world has seen how one man has aroused a whole land, one man saved a caravan from destruction, and small boats sinking ships to the shore... Hidden among the gravel there are pearls to be found; and mingled in the sand are particles of gold".[1] Indeed, Sir Syed's picture is still to be seen in Pakistan Independence Day newspaper supplements.

With time, however, Sir Syed has been silently demoted. As Pakistan becomes more Punjabi-run and *muhajir* influence fades, Sir Syed gets less attention. When his services towards the creation of Pakistan are extolled, they lie strictly in a single dimension – that of being the originator of the Two Nation Theory and the architect of Muslim separatism. Schoolbooks list his other accomplishment as empowerment of Muslims through education, advocacy of Urdu over Hindi, founding of Aligarh Muslim University, and support for various Muslim causes. To be fair, he is not entirely uncelebrated today in Pakistan. His earlier days of popularity have resulted in a small university bearing his name, a housing colony, at least two major roads, and a railway express train. However, unlike with Jinnah or Iqbal, one does not see an airport, large hospital, major highway, or artery named after Sir Syed. Newspaper columnists generally fail to notice his birth and death anniversaries.

Why and what happened? This chapter is about a man whose life and times need demythologizing. In doing so, we shall gain much insight into the world of

Founder I: The Lonely Modernizer **79**

north Indian Muslims of the 19th century – the ones who imagined Pakistan and carried it through to fruition. The idea of belonging to some place other than their native soil was then a new one. It arose well over a century after British imperial power had arrived willy-nilly from across the oceans. Communal and political disputes that had earlier been seen in caste, class, and regional terms became increasingly couched in religious terms. A Hindu–Muslim communal divide emerged as each party sought the best deal from the English. Eventually, the days of peaceful coexistence would end, and important Hindu and Muslim leaders would proclaim for the very first time that India was inhabited by two nations.

Henceforth in this chapter, Syed Ahmad Khan shall be referred to simply as Sir Syed. This implies neither respect nor disrespect. I do so because all literature in Urdu – even that which judges him harshly – identifies him as such and so I will use it here as well. As for the spelling: this is how he chose to write his name. In the Mutiny Papers there is a letter of Sir Syed to Sir John Kaye signed in this way.

At one level, Sir Syed was the boldest and most vigorous advocate of science, education, and philosophy from among all Muslim reformers of the 19th century, whether in India or in Egypt or Turkey. His influence was strongest in north India. In Bengal, Muslims had been similarly encouraged towards modernization by Nawab Abdul Latif (1828–1893) and by Syed Ameer Ali (1849–1928). But probably because of their greater distance from Delhi and from having come a little later, their influence on the national life of Indian Muslims was nowhere near that of Sir Syed. Among Muslims of the time, the mood was either one of resignation and defeat or of revival through a return to old ways. There seemed no way for them to escape from a vicious downward spiral. Sir Syed's importance comes from being the very first to insist that Muslims had no alternative but to engage with the modern world and meet the challenges of western science and philosophy. To wallow in self-pity and hark back at past Islamic glories is pointless, he said. No other Muslim reformer has ever been so loud, unequivocal, and clear.

Sir Syed – who opposed education of Muslims in *madrassas* – can be compared with Raja Ram Mohan Roy (1772–1833) who preceded him by about half a century. This polyglot radical Hindu reformist and proponent of modern education held that a return to traditional ways of life was unsuited and so had opposed the setting up of Sanskrit College in 1823. Instead, as founder of the Brahmo Samaj movement, Roy fought for reform and modernization of Hindu thought and targeted practices such as *sati*, polygamy, child marriage, and the caste system. Perhaps the biggest difference between the two men is that Roy was resisted much less fiercely by Hindus than Sir Syed was by Muslims. Indeed, one finds reformers other than Roy among Hindus but, apart from Sir Syed, there is no other prominent name among Muslims.

Starting out as a traditional and deeply conservative Muslim, Sir Syed's natural perceptiveness forced him to explore ideological alternatives. His was a long journey beginning from arch-conservativism that went through multiple twists and turns, but which ended with him advocating a radical reinterpretation of

80 Founder I: The Lonely Modernizer

Muslim theology and a new direction for Muslim politics. Readers are referred to my Urdu essay for more details.[2] While there were other contemporary Muslim modernists – Muhammad Abduh (1845–1905) and Rashid Rida (1865–1935) in Egypt and Ziya Gökalp (1876–1924) in Turkey – Sir Syed's reinterpretation of Islamic theology in the light of scientific modernity and prescriptions for Muslim progress came earlier than theirs. His prescriptions were also bolder and sometimes to the point of being extreme. In particular, while seeking to reconcile Islam with science, he pushed the boundaries of Islamic theology to a level well beyond what his contemporaries in the Muslim world had contemplated or would agree with. Then, as now, orthodox Muslims despised him as a hell-bound heretic. Yet he stoutly maintained that his explorations were well within the limits set by Islam.

Both in his times as well as today, Sir Syed evokes a plethora of different feelings. Socialists and liberals abhor him as a class enemy representing interests of the decadent Mughal *ashrafiyya* (upper classes, also called *shur'fa*). Feminists see him as typifying patriarchy because, in his opinion, female education was unnecessary and dangerous. But the strongest attacks on him came from Muslim nationalists of the time. Among them was Jamaluddin Afghani, a secular Muslim and tireless anti-imperialist. Afghani, who was sent to India by Turkey's Sultan Hamid II to drum up enthusiasm for pan-Islamism, was a colorful and somewhat mysterious character frequently traveling around in the Middle East and India. Afghani disparagingly referred to Sir Syed as a *nechari* (one who believed that physical law rather than God ran the world) and accused him of being a groveling apologist for the Raj.

Early years

My goal in this subsection is not to give yet another account of some great man's life or to extol some individual's virtues or lack thereof. Of much greater import is to see how Muslim attitudes were conditioned by the political and economic environment of the post-Mughal era and, most importantly, to examine the similarities and differences with those attitudes today. In looking at the life of an individual who helped set the direction of things, there is much to be learned about how and why Pakistan came to be what it is today.

All biographical information in this subsection (except when indicated) is selected from selections taken from *Hayat-e-Javed*, his authorized biography penned by his friend, Maulana Altaf Hussain Hali.[3] There are an uncounted number of commentaries and books on Sir Syed, including many hostile ones. The reader may enjoy a largely sympathetic account by Rajmohan Gandhi.[4] The books by Christian Troll and Hafeez Malik (see references) are well researched, authoritative accounts.

Syed Ahmad Khan was born in a deeply religious family of Delhi's Muslim *ashrafiyya* towards the tail end of the Mughal dynasty. His father, Mir Muttaqi, was a functionary in the court of Akbar II and had taken *bayat* (oath of allegiance)

Founder I: The Lonely Modernizer **81**

to the saint Hazrat Shah Ghulam Ali. Muttaqi was essentially disconnected with domestic matters and a dropout from the royal court (but with assured income) who spent much of his time at the shrine. His deeply religious wife, also the saint's follower, took responsibility for the boy's education. Immediately after the *bismillah* ceremony – a rite for boys that normally happens around five years of age among Sunni Muslims – she arranged for a *moulvi* who taught him the Qur'an. Home-tutored in Urdu, Persian, and Arabic, he had no access to the modern subjects that a few Muslims had begun to receive in Delhi's Christian missionary schools. To keep his Urdu pronunciation pure and proper, he was kept away from street boys who spoke all kinds of dialects.

Then came puberty and the hormones started kicking in. For this youthful young man, Delhi wasn't all that dull. In the evenings, the young scions of a degenerated Mughal court bureaucracy would gather where beautiful girls sang and danced, swinging to and fro with the music. The wine flowed freely until midnight after which it was time for greater intimacy. Hali, his acolyte, tries hard to sweep these dark aspects under the carpet but does not deny what was known. Lest the young man become a compulsive pleasure seeker, his worried family married him off at the tender age of nineteen but his trips to forbidden parts of the city continued nevertheless. As Sir Syed later conceded, "I still did not escape [this debauchery] and slept so deeply that even the angels could not awake me".[5] Hali notes that Sir Syed's first victory was to cleanse his own self. The death of his father was a big jolt. A remorseful Sir Syed returned to moral purity and close attention to prayer and rituals.

With ever-declining income from properties, it was now imperative for this 22-year-old to find a calling in life. The imperial court, which his ancestors had served, still existed but only in name. So, although his Imperial Highness Akbar II, Emperor of India, lived in royal splendor and continued to bestow impressive titles and royal honors, the family income was limited to the meager stipend allotted by the East India Company. Worse, there were terrible rumors that the Emperor himself was deep in debt, and that the usurious money lenders of Delhi were clamoring to get their money back from him.

For the young Syed to follow family tradition and become a royal flunky would have been stupid. Working for the Company wasn't supposed to be politically correct, but the smarter ones among the Muslim nobility well knew where their future lay. Starting out from the low rank of a lawyer's apprentice, Sir Syed's diligence rapidly moved him up the ladder. He was appointed by the Company to the administrative post of *sadr-e-amin* in Fatehpur Sikri near Delhi. It was a leisurely job that gave prestige, power, and a handsome amount of money. By all measures, the young man had climbed up the ladder.

Sir Syed was to become a strong advocate of learning the English language. At the beginning of his career, he knew that to get a Company job you had to know English – which this young man did not know. All his formal training was only in Islamic languages, which may be why he never learned English well enough. Although his able mind was quick in picking up the language's essentials, his

82 Founder I: The Lonely Modernizer

writings are exclusively in Urdu with some Persian phrases thrown in. One hint of difficulty with English comes from the toast that was dedicated to him by Lord Lytton at the launch of MAO College in 1877. Syed Mahmud, his Cambridge-educated son, responded to the toast and explained that his father was not comfortable speaking in English.

It's okay to eat mangoes

With plenty of time on his hands while at Fatehpur Sikri, Sir Syed could indulge in what had become his favorite pastime – reading Islamic religious tracts. A precocious devourer of religious literature of every sect, he re-read those books to which he had paid inadequate attention during his early education. The local *ulema* were more than happy to engage with a young man in authority, and they steadily deepened his knowledge of prophetic traditions as well as the four schools of Islamic law. With his able pen, he now started to address religious questions using the classical style of argumentation, gradually creating an attentive band of followers who plied him with questions.

An early issue was to prove that Earth is stationary and does not move around the sun. This doctrine was taught in the *madrassas* of the time, was advocated by learned Qur'anic scholars, and has never totally gone away[6]. Religious scholars appearing on Pakistani television channels continue to insist on its truth and quote supporting Qur'anic verses. But modern science, which had led many Muslims of the day worried, says the opposite. What is the truth? In a booklet *Qaul-e-Mateen dar Abtal-e-Harkat-e-Zameen* (Firm Refutation of the Motion of the Earth, 1848), Sir Syed demolishes Copernican astronomy using a quaint mixture of Greek syllogistic logic and Qur'anic verses. He argues: if I throw something exactly straight upwards, how is it possible that it does not return exactly to the original point? Thus motion of the earth is impossible. By such "thought experiments", he proved to his satisfaction and those around him that Earth was just as still and unmoving as the Qur'an said it was. It took over a decade before Sir Syed ruefully admitted he had written his essay while under the influence of Wahhabism and that it deserves to be thrown away.

With his fascination for religious disputations and literature, Sir Syed had come to admire the Wahhabi brand of Islam. This had already made its debut into India some decades earlier. Much of Wahhabism is concerned with determining precisely what is allowed or forbidden. In particular, *bid'ah* (innovation) is a cardinal sin – you may not perform any action that the Prophet himself had not. Many questions arise from this. For example, is it permissible for a Muslim to eat mangoes? This became a test case.[7]

The question grew out of discussions at a religious forum held in the house of Maulana Sadruddin Azurda in Delhi.[8] Since mangoes do not grow in desert climes, clearly the Holy Prophet could not have eaten them. Hence, one wondered if eating this fruit would constitute *bid'ah*. Sir Syed ponders on this question in a 30-page tract, replete with references to the Qur'an, Hadith, and earlier scholars. His considered opinion is that it is probably not sinful to eat mangoes. However, a Muslim who resists this temptation will be amply rewarded by having his feet kissed by angels on the Day of Judgement. The reward, of course, is limited to those who have desisted from eating mangoes purely for religious reasons and not because they don't like the taste or for medical reasons.

Sir Syed was not only a religious conservative, but also a conservationist of culture and cultural artifacts. He therefore could not fully buy into Wahhabi teachings that insist on spurning holy relics and even destroying them. His task: how to preserve Muslim culture and safeguard a grand inheritance? How were the last remnants of grand Mughal architecture, the elaborate court language and customs, well-developed mannerisms, painting of miniatures, and music of the famous Tan Sen to be preserved? The classic tract *Ain-e-Akbari*, a comprehensive record of the times of Akbar the Great that included a description of extant laws and practices, had turned nearly incomprehensible because it contained an archaic mixture of Persian, Arabic, Turkish, Urdu, Hindi, and Sanskrit languages.

Sir Syed had intuitively grasped that Akbar's period was the grand one, not that of arch-conservative Aurangzeb. This was a telling sign of his disposition even at this early stage of his career. Rewriting this book into Urdu after much toil and effort, Sir Syed regarded it as his crowning scholarly achievement. The proud author promptly sent off the manuscript to Delhi's unparalleled master of Urdu verse, Mirza Asadullah Ghalib, asking him to write a *taqriz* for the book. The *taqriz* is a short customary praise of a book written in the then-fashionable flowery and convoluted form of Urdu. He expected Ghalib – whom he informally would address as *chacha* (uncle) – to comply.

To Sir Syed's great shock, he received – for publication – a stinging riposte written as verses in Persian telling him not to waste his time on praising and preserving that which had become effete and degenerate. The modern age offered far better. Forget Akbar and Abul Fazl, said Ghalib, and look at the *sahibs* of England. See how logically they make their rules and laws and, more importantly, see how they are conquering nature:

صاحبان انگلستان را نگر شیوہ و انداز ایناں را نگر

زیں ہنرمنداں ہنر بیشی گرفت سعی بر پیشینیاں پیشی گرفت

گہ دخاں کشتی بہ جیوں می برد گہ دخاں گردوں بہ ہاموں می برد

از دخاں زورق بہ رفتار آمدہ باد و موج، ایں ہر دو بیکار آمدہ

نغمہ ہا بے زخمہ از ساز آورند حرف چوں طائر بہ پرواز آورند

ایں نمی بینی کہ ایں دانا گروہ در دو دم آرند حرف از صد کروہ

رو بہ لندن کاندراں رخشندہ باغ شہر روشن گشتہ در شب بے چراغ

مردہ پرور دن مبارک کار نیست خود بگوکاں نیز جز گفتار نیست

Go look at the sahibs of England
Go learn from them their skills and ways

84 Founder I: The Lonely Modernizer

> From their hands have wonders and wonders
> Go try and see if you can excel them
>
> What a spell they can cast upon water
> That mere smoke propels a boat on water
>
> How speedily that smoke can make the boat go
> Helpless before it are the wind and waves
>
> They touch not a string but music begins to play
> And words begin to fly like the birds
>
> Have you not seen how these clever people
> Get news from afar in a couple of breaths
>
> Go to London and see the brightly lit gardens
> The city shines bright in the night without candles.
>
> Worshipping the dead shall get us nowhere
> Ask yourself what good will come of that

Mortified, Sir Syed did not include Ghalib's *taqriz* in *Ain-e-Akbari*. But, by the time the book had been published, his disagreement with Ghalib had disappeared. Years later, to assuage the great master who might have been offended by the *taqriz's* non-inclusion, Sir Syed invited Ghalib to his home while he was passing through Muradabad where Sir Syed was the local administrator. The poet turned up promptly on time, but to Sir Syed's embarrassment, he came with a bottle of wine in hand which he promptly placed upon the mantle for all to see! It was an in-your-face statement of Ghalib's rejection of cultural norms. For all that, no longer would Sir Syed ever refer again to *Ain-e-Akbari*. He was fast becoming a different man.

Metamorphosis to modernity

Syed Ahmad Khan, a deeply conservative Muslim religious scholar, eventually turned into the Muslim world's foremost proponent of modernity and science. How did this astonishing transition happen?

The voluminous *Hayat-e-Javed* – Sir Syed's officially sanctioned biography – does not indicate any particular transformative moment. Rather, it seems to be the result of interacting with modern ideas, spread out over many years. Asked by Reverend J.J. Moore to translate a textbook on mechanics from Persian into Urdu, Sir Syed readily assented and then went on to translate others as well. His frequent visits to Agra from Moradabad and Fatehpur Sikri, and his interactions with Englishmen, must have played at least an equal role. In the process he

Founder I: The Lonely Modernizer **85**

started to understand basic principles of science, filling the gaps of his childhood education. And yet, in spite of being the foremost proponent of science among Muslims, Sir Syed's knowledge of science, in particular of Darwin's theory published in 1859, was rather rudimentary.[9] Nevertheless, he was quick to grasp that this put the concept of Adam and Eve as well as the Great Flood – alluded to both in the Bible and Qur'an – as being in contradiction with science and hence to be interpreted allegorically.[10] The Aligarh Scientific Society translated works of science but could not add to the corpus of knowledge itself. As it turned out in later years, Aligarh Muslim University was undistinguished in science, both teaching as well as research.

Ambitious and quick of mind, Sir Syed was just past his youth when he started suspecting that the Muslims of India had false explanations for the end of Islam's golden age. The common ones running through Delhi's literary gatherings were that religious rituals had been insufficiently observed or Muslims had succumbed to pleasures of the flesh, while others held that invaders – in particular the sacking of Baghdad in 1258 by the Mongols – had dealt the death blow. At some point Sir Syed must have stopped buying into this.

In a radically different analysis, Sir Syed argued in his famous *Tahzeeb-ul-Akhlaq* essays that desperate new remedies were needed if Indians were ever to become anything more than "stable boys, cooks, servants, hewers of wood, and drawers of water".[11] Muslim misfortune, concluded Sir Syed, owes to a basic misunderstanding of the Islamic faith, rejection of *ma'aqulat* (reason), and blind acceptance of *manqulat* (tradition). This had atrophied thought through the rejection of fresh ways of thinking. Without forcing a deep attitudinal change towards religion, nothing would work in these modern times. By now he had reluctantly come over to Ghalib's position. The way forward lay in learning the English language, practicing the scientific method, accepting that physical phenomena are explainable by science only, and rejecting superstition. Unless Muslims could learn to relearn their religion in the light of modern science, they would remain stuck forever.

It was a difficult challenge. The period after Akbar the Great's reign had been one of unbroken anti-science and anti-rationalist conservatism. Some 200 years before Sir Syed, Sheikh Ahmed Sirhindi and other influential religious figures who followed Imam Al-Ghazali had issued *fatwas* against mathematics and the secular sciences and demanded that the education of Muslims be limited to religious books. But the books that Sir Syed had read, re-read, and was deeply influenced by now appeared to him empty and barren. This turned him into an ideologue for modernity who wanted to make Islam compatible with post-Renaissance Western humanistic and scientific rationalism. He set about seeking a new *ilm-ul-kalam* that would allow Muslims to leapfrog dead centuries and to somehow extract the "*thet* (pure) Islam" from fossilized dogma. In *Tahzib-ul-Akhlaq*, he writes:

> Yes, if the Mussulman be a true warrior and thinks his religion correct, then let him come fearlessly to the battleground and do unto Western

86 Founder I: The Lonely Modernizer

> knowledge and modern research what his forefathers did to Greek philosophy. Only then shall our religious books be of any real use. Mere parroting and praising ourselves will not do (*apnay moon mian mithoo kahney say koee fayda nahin*).... The blind prejudice of Muslims is preventing them from emulating [Western] education, sciences, and technology; Muslim society erroneously admires the blindness of those who are stubborn and haughty and consider all nations except their own inferior.[12]

To balance modern science against Qur'anic theology was a task that few could have taken on. Every Muslim must necessarily believe that the Qur'an is the literal word of God and therefore infallible. Sir Syed, while agreeing with this, nevertheless appealed to Islam's forgotten *Mua'tizila* tradition of rational inquiry as in the works of Ibn-e-Rushd (Averroes) who had famously disagreed with the arch-conservative Imam Ghazali on the role of agency and reason in human affairs. When Islam is suitably reinterpreted, said Sir Syed, it becomes a religion that is completely consistent with nature (*tabiya*). There simply could not be any contradiction between the Word of God (Qur'an) and the Work of God (Nature).

And yet a literal reading of the Qur'an leads to sharp contradictions with science. Modern science totally rejects the notion of seven heavens, man coming from a clot of blood, all living beings existing in pairs, shooting stars as projectiles to drive away the devil, and mountains as pegs created to keep the earth from shaking. To resolve these, Sir Syed argued, one must perform a deep study of the Quran's etymology while keeping in mind the context within which the verses were revealed. By this prescription, the rigorous exegete must learn the meaning of every word in the Qur'an as had been understood at the time of revelation, and only then fit together modern science with Islam. So, in other words, make whatever interpretation you want but force it to fit science. This meant that *taqleed* (imitation) must therefore be abandoned in favor of *ijtihad* (intellectual effort/adaptation). Various creatures mentioned in the Qur'an such as *jinns*, *hoors*, and *yajooj-majooj* (Gog and Magog) are to be understood as symbolic only, he claimed.

But what if, at the end, the Qur'an and science cannot be reconciled together and we are left with a flat contradiction? Dealing with miracles was a particularly big problem because modern science rejects that very notion; accepting their existence would amount to giving up on search for natural laws and a universe that follows principles and patterns. On the other hand, it is a cornerstone of faith that Muslims are required to accept as factual. Here, Sir Syed took a firm stand: apart from the Qur'an being a miracle, no other miracles really happened. Instead, they must be understood as purely allegorical and symbolic. In arriving at this view, Sir Syed was essentially borrowing from the Enlightenment tradition in repeating the theistic argument that the laws of physics were actually promises made by God to man – and God always kept his promises. By this logic, miracles couldn't really have happened since this would make God less than perfect. It is therefore impossible that God should make the laws of physics and then capriciously violate his own laws.

The conclusions derived from such reasoning were mind-blowing for those with a traditional religious upbringing. Sir Syed was claiming that the *mair'aj* (Prophet Muhammad's ascension to heaven on the back of a steed, *buraq*) was just a beautiful dream; that the Great Flood of Noah as related in the Qur'an has no supporting geological evidence and so must be understood allegorically; and that the story of Adam and Eve as well as the various miracles of Jesus were also symbolic. God had used such allusions in His holy books knowing the simple people of ancient times would otherwise fail to understand His word.

Sir Syed's other conclusions were no less radical and provocative: that every religion needs to be judged for its truthfulness on the touchstone of reason and evidence; that it is permissible for Muslims to eat at the same table and use the same utensils as Christians; that a deep study of the Bible would inevitably prove that Christianity is Unitarian and not Trinitarian; that Islam actually forbids polygamy and amputation of limbs; and that slavery has no place in Islam. Such interpretations earned him the hostility of the *ulema*, and the keeper of the Holy Kaaba declared him *wajib-ul-qatl* (deserver of death). It is said that there were 5,555 calls for his execution. But this precise number appears purely polemical.

A deep pragmatist, Sir Syed knew his thoughts were far too bold for his times, and so he recommended[13] that some of his own writings should be kept away from the students of Mohammadan Anglo-Oriental (MAO) College, an institution which he founded in 1875 and which provided the nucleus of the Pakistan Movement in the 1940s. In this way he was able to achieve a compromise with the Deobandi *ulema*, or at least some of them. Deoband was primarily a center occupied by matters of religious purity, with its curriculum of studies being that of *Dars-i-Nizami*. It was anti-British, associating itself with the views and aspirations of Jamaluddin Afghani and his pan-Islamic movement.

Even after he expressed willingness to compromise, many religious leaders thought Sir Syed had gone much too far. Conscious of their hostility, he offered to have no role in matters of religious instruction in MAO College and invited leading clerics to prepare the syllabus. But even this extreme measure worked only partially. Maulana Qasim Nanautvi and Maulana Yaqoob of Deoband shot down his proposal saying they could not associate with an institution which would have Shia students on the campus.

The anger that Sir Syed inspires among the orthodox even today can be judged from books that are published from time to time. A 2013 publication from Lahore, *Sir Syed Ahmad Khan ka asli roop* (The real face of Sir Syed Ahmed Khan) contains attacks from well-known *moulvis* spanning the range from Barelvi, Deobandi, Salafi, and Wahhabi. Starting from relatively minor accusations such as *kabootar baazi* (keeping pigeons) and frequenting *mujras* (dance performances), the book moves on to allege major ones: refusing to accept the existence of Gabriel the Angel, making fun of the pleasures of heaven, denying the existences of *jinns* and the devil, refuting the need for jihad, not acknowledging miracles of the Holy Prophet and other messengers of God, denying the

88 Founder I: The Lonely Modernizer

miraculous nature of the Black Stone of the Kaaba, and claiming that Muslims are permitted to eat non–halal food.[14]

Siding with the British

That Sir Syed bent over backward to exonerate the British from their every unjust and cruel action cannot be doubted. This was a choice made out of pragmatism. He, like almost all Indians, could not foresee that British rulers would be forced out of India just ninety years later; at the time the imperial colossus appeared as permanent as time itself. Self-rule was utterly undesirable. "To form a parliament from the natives of India is of course out of the question", he wrote, "It is not only impossible, but useless".[15] Be loyal to the state, he lectured to Muslims, for the state is your protector and benefactor. Flatly going against the fiery Abdul Aziz (Shah Waliullah's son, encountered in the previous chapter) and others who had declared jihad against the British, he argued that the religion of India's rulers does not matter since they are just to their subjects. The Indian National Congress's demand for self-rule was seditious, he said. Sir Syed's loyalty to the Crown was amply rewarded with power and positions, culminating with his knighthood in 1888.

Still, one must not rush to judgment. Historical personae must be evaluated by the standards of their time, not those of the present. Back in the 1800s, the invincible British behemoth towered so high that none could then reasonably believe that India would ever be free. It was a thought beyond imagination – you may as well wail in anger or shake your fist impotently at the sky. Among prominent Indians who thought this way was the young Mohandas Gandhi who believed that India's emancipation could only come from staying within the Empire, and who in 1899 called for defending the British Empire during the Boer War. Things changed only after the First World War and then even more after Britain was mortally wounded forty years later by Hitler. Ram Mohan Roy and the early Congress leaders also sang praises of the Raj, praying only that England may gradually change the character of her rule in India.

Syed Ahmad Khan, then a Company employee, did not support the 1857 uprising against the British. His open endorsement of British rule, and his insistence on loyalty to the colonizers, drew criticism from his supporters. Still, he hoped that weaning Muslims away from a position of opposition to one of acceptance would change the government's attitude away from its policy of suppression towards one of benevolent paternalism. He was thus able to draw upon his increased personal influence upon the British to win concessions. This included the saving of many Muslim lives, including those of his relatives in Delhi. Months after the uprising, the British had retaken Delhi and were wreaking vengeance.

We learn from Hali that about two years before the uprising Sir Syed had been transferred from Delhi to Bijnor as *sadr amin* (local chief administrator). Bijnor was a large district of about 1800 square miles with a population of 500,000

Founder I: The Lonely Modernizer **89**

Hindus and 240,000 Muslims. As soon as the news of the rebellion reached Bijnor, he went to the house where twenty whites, including women and children, were hiding in fear of the rebel onslaught. To emphasize that his stand was unambiguous, he patrolled the street outside the house with gun in hand. A large man with a slight stoop, he was immediately identifiable.

A year later, Sir Syed was to publish an apologia for Muslim behavior in 1857. The English version is the "Loyal Mohamedans of India", followed by a differently titled tract in Urdu, *Asbab-e-Baghawat-e-Hind* (Causes of the Indian Mutiny). Therein he attempted to explain away the rebellion as the act of a few who had stupidly acted against the larger interests of India's Muslims. The uprising was not, he said, a reflection of common Muslim sentiment against the British but that of subversives who had exploited the religious sensibilities of ignorant soldiers and convinced them into disobedience,

> The turmoil of violence which happened was only a punishment for the ungratefulness of the Hindustanis... you people were not acquainted with the injustice and oppression that used to take place in the days of past (Muslim) rulers. If you had been acquainted with the injustice and excesses of those past days, you would have appreciated the value of English rule and given thanks to God. But you were never grateful to God, and remained always discontented. God has punished you Hindustanis for this ungratefulness, and allowed you to experience again a sample of the Government of former times, after he suspended English rule for a short time.[16]

The English were a superior civilization beyond challenge, said Sir Syed. This view was multiply reinforced upon his visit to England in 1869 where he was invited to dine with lords and dukes, visited museums and engineering works, walked on the decks of warships which he described "as one mile long", and saw ordinary people, too – but that was from a distance. Although he never ventured into the dingy, rat-infested parts of cities like Staffordshire or Liverpool where the working class toiled in horrific conditions, English civilizational superiority was clear as day to him,

> Without flattering the English I can truly say that the natives of India, right and low, merchants and petty shopkeepers, educated and illiterate, when contrasted with the English in education, manners, and uprightness, are as like them as a dirty animal is to an able and handsome man.[17]

For Sir Syed, self-rule was highly undesirable because Indians were unready for that. The British, he reasoned, alone could preserve law and order. Their departure would empower local leaders who would descend into communal conflict. There would be chaos and mayhem. So the only solution was for Indians to remain British subjects. Self-rule was undesirable:

I do not wish to enter into the question as to how the ignorant and uneducated natives of Hindustan could be allowed a share in the deliberations of the Legislative Council or as to how they should be selected to form an assembly like the English Parliament. These are knotty points. All I wish to prove here is that such a step is not only advisable but absolutely necessary, and that the disturbances were due to the neglect of such a measure.[18]

Natives could appeal for fair treatment but should not participate in political decision-making or interfere in the executive decisions of the government:

It is our earnest desire that the English Rule in India should last not only for a long, long time but that it should be everlasting and eternal. This desire of ours is not for the sake of the English nation itself, but for the sake of our own country; it is not for the sake of flattering the English people but it is for the prosperity and welfare of our own country.[19]

The Englishman had to be followed in every possible way – including his attire – but with one crucial difference. Islam, not Christianity, must be followed. During his visit, the idea of a new college grew in him. It had to be British in style and manner, modeled on the lines of Oxford and Cambridge. The curriculum would be western, English would be the medium of instruction, and the college principal would be English, as would be most members of the staff. However, in this residential college, prayers five times a day would be made compulsory. It was to be a unique synthesis of east and west:

I may appear to be dreaming and talking like *Shaikh Chilli* [a legendary boaster], but we aim to turn this Mohammedan Anglo Oriental College into a University similar to that of Oxford or Cambridge. Like the churches of Oxford and Cambridge, there will be mosques attached to each College... It will be mandatory on boys in residence to join the congregational prayers (namaz) at all the five times. Students of other religions will be exempted from this religious observance. Muslim students will have a uniform consisting of a black alpaca, half-sleeved *chugha* and a red Fez cap... It will be strictly enforced that Shia and Sunni boys shall not discuss their religious differences in the College or in the boarding house. At present it is like a day dream. I pray to God that this dream may come true.[20]

At a time when India's Muslims were rallying towards defending the caliphate based out of Turkey, Sir Syed was speaking out strongly against it. This made him suspect in the eyes of pan-Islamists who subscribed to an Islam without borders. Even close friends broke away from him. The reasons he gave for his opposition were several. For one, the notion of caliphate requires that all those united in faith to have one ruler. But Sir Syed had already pledged allegiance to the

British. Moreover, he had long been convinced of the incompatibility between traditional Muslim thought and modernity. The caliphate would simply prolong the misery of Muslims. Perhaps just as importantly he did not subscribe to the caliphate's goal of producing a global community of Muslims. If he could not feel kinship with the Bengali Muslim, how could he and a Muslim from some distant alien culture feel that they were the same people?

An unabashed elitist

Sir Syed was successful in his endeavors both because the British wanted to weaken the emerging Hindu bourgeoisie of Bombay and Calcutta who stood as a more important challenge to the Raj than Muslims and, equally, because he received the support of his class – the Muslim *ashrafiyya*. He was overtly for his own kind.

The *ashrafiyya* were the heirs of the long decadent Mughal nobility comprising men of high rank (*mansabdars*), the descendants of judges (*qazis*), jurists (*muftis*), scholars, and poets. It would be tragic, he said, "if these noble families disappeared from India and the nouveau riche replaced them. India would eventually suffer and be deprived of enduring prestige".[21] Sir Syed's prescription was that the native elite, both Muslim and Hindu, needed greater appreciation from the government and allowed to participate in local affairs. Hence Indians ought to be admitted into the Viceroy's Legislative Council, albeit under the watchful eyes of the British.

For Sir Syed, class and rank were just as important, if not more, as Muslim identity. A committee that he headed concluded that in deciding the relative levels of education between Muslims and Hindus one should not include the lowly tribes of India including "the Bhangis, Chamars, Bheels, Phansias, Kanjars, and Babarias [who were] beyond the pale of civilization".[22] With this simple trick of counting, he concluded that Muslims were no less educated than Hindus. Sir Syed's opinion of Bengalis, whether Muslim or Hindu, was one that would be deemed racist by today's standards:

> Every people, not just Muslims, but all this country's Hindus, honored kings and brave Rajputs who worship the swords of their fathers, will they tolerate the command of the Bengali who falls from his chair upon seeing a table knife? Not a piece of this country will remain where faces other than Bengali ones will be seen at the table of command and justice. We say we are happy that only our Bengali brother should progress, but the question is, what will happen to the state of the country's administration? In your opinion, can the Rajput or fiery Pathan, who do not fear the noose, the police, or the army, live peacefully under the Bengali?[23]

There was a very different perception of Sir Syed among those who saw inequities of power and wealth in India as more dangerous than the communal split. Dhulipala[24] gives an interesting account of some idealistic young Muslims who had gone to British universities and, while studying there, had turned into staunch anti-colonialist socialists and communists. For such leftists, the Muslim community's biggest misfortune was its betrayal at the hands of putative modernizers like Sir Syed who actually thwarted political modernization by insisting that British imperialism was a welcome bulwark against Hindu majoritarian domination. Instead of fighting against imperialism, Muslims were instructed to rally around the *zamindars* and the *ashrafiyya* class.

Indeed, Sir Syed not only spoke for the *ashrafiyya*, he also spoke to them. To meetings in Lucknow or Delhi, the riff-raff was not invited. It is instructive to note the composition of one of his meetings. Those attending included,

> The taluqdars of Oudh, members of the Government services, the Army, the professions of Law, the Press and the Priesthood; Syeds, Shaikhs, Moghals, and Pathans belonging to some of the noblest families in India; and representatives of every school, from orthodox Sunni and Shiah Maulavis to the young men trained in Indian colleges or in England.[25]

Sir Syed's MAO College – which underwent a name change in 1920 and became Aligarh Muslim University (AMU) – had class built into its very structure: in AMU's early days, there were two different messes. One mess was for "commoners" and the other for sons of the *shur'fa* (*ashrafiyya*).[26] This practice carried over into the decades ahead – even in 1947 character certificates issued to school students would have to specify that the holder of the certificate belonged to a "*sharif khandaan*", i.e., a good, well-to-do family.

The non-communal Sir Syed

Sir Syed started his political journey as a non-communal Muslim.[27] Here the word "communal" requires clarification in the Indian context. Communalism is a state of the mind wherein an individual identifies – whether largely or exclusively – on the basis of his religion while subordinating all other attributes such as personality, class, language, color, profession, caste, etc. In other words, the pure Indian communalist cares for a single data point – whether you are Muslim or Hindu. Nothing else matters. Of course, in reality multiple identities compete against one another.

Communalism is associated directly with the Arabic word *qaum*, which flows freely in Sir Syed's speeches and writings. In normal usage it means a *nation* – but that of Muslims only. In his earlier phase, Sir Syed perhaps meant that sense of Indian nationhood which could transcend the subcontinent's diverse languages, cultures, sects, and perhaps religions as well. When challenged before mixed audiences of both Muslims and Hindus, he made explicit its meaning,[28]

> By the word *qaum*, I mean both Hindus and Muslims. That is the way in which I define the word nation (*qaum*). In my opinion, it matters not

whatever be their religious beliefs, because we cannot see anything of it; but what we see is that all of us, either Hindus or Muslims, live on one soil, are governed by one and the same ruler, have the same sources of our benefits, and equally share the hardships of a famine. These are the various reasons why I designate both the nationalities by the term "Hindu" – that is, the nation (*qaum*) which lives in India.[29]

In another exhortation he says,

O, Hindus and Muslims! Do you live in any country other than India? Don't you get cremated on or buried under the same soil? If you do, then remember Hindu and Muslim are merely religious terms. The Hindus, the Muslims and even the Christians constitute one nation by virtue of living in the same country.[30]

Speaking at Patna on 27 January 1883, Sir Syed declared:

Now both of us live on the air of India, drink the holy waters of the Ganga and Jumna. We both feed upon the products of the Indian soil. We are together in life and death; living in India both of us have changed our blood, the colour of bodies has become the same, our features have become similar; the Musalmans have adopted numerous Hindu customs; the Hindus have accepted many Muslim traits of conduct; we became so fused that we developed the new language of Urdu, which was neither our language nor that of the Hindus. Therefore, if we except that part of our lives which belongs to God, then undoubtedly, in consideration of the fact that we both belong to the same country, we are a nation, and the progress and welfare of the country, and of both of us, depend on our unity, mutual sympathy, and love, while our mutual disagreement, obstinacy and opposition and ill-feeling are sure to destroy us.[31]

Addressing the Hindus of the Punjab, he complained that they did not regard him as one of them: "you have used the term Hindu for yourselves. This is not correct. For, in my opinion, the word Hindu does not denote a particular religion, but, on the contrary, everyone who lives in India has the right to call himself a Hindu. I am, therefore, sorry that although I live in India, you do not consider me a Hindu".[32] Should one be shocked? As pointed out in Chapter One, eight centuries earlier the Arab traveler Al-Biruni understood "Hindu" in strictly geographical terms rather than in terms of religion. In 2018, the RSS chief Mohan Bhagwat reportedly quoted from Sir Syed's speech at an Arya Samaj function: "I am very upset that you did not consider me one of your own. Am I not a son of Mother India? Nothing has changed except our ways of worship".[33]

Perhaps Sir Syed's best-known saying on Hindu–Muslim unity is when he compares India to "A beautiful bride blessed by two attractive eyes, the Hindus

94 Founder I: The Lonely Modernizer

and the Muslims. If they maintain enmity or hypocritical (*nifaq*) relations with each other, [the bride] will look one-eyed. So! Inhabitants of India, do as you will".[34]

In present times, because of attacks on Indian Muslims by BJP officials and the Hindu right wing, it has become politically necessary to stress Sir Syed's non-communal side and to refer to numerous attacks on him by the Muslim clerics both within and outside India such as, for example, the Imam of Mecca's bitter criticism for having established MAO college (later Aligarh Muslim University). There is no shortage of examples. Altaf Hussain Hali quotes a fatwa given by the *ulema* of Saudi Arabia who declared that it was every Muslim's duty to give no assistance to the College and to destroy it if it is ever established. In 2017 the vice-chancellor of NALSAR University of Law, Hyderabad, noted the irony after the University Grants Commission proposed removing "Muslim" from AMU's name. In defense of Sir Syed, he wrote:

> The Scientific Society which was founded by Sir Syed in 1863 was really national in its complexion and character. Apart from the British Members, it had 82 Hindu and 107 Muslim members. Even the Managing Committee of MAO College which comprised 22 members had six Hindu members on it. The first second master of the school was Sri Baijnath who was no. 2 in the administrative hierarchy. The famous mathematician J.C. Chakravarty joined as professor in 1888 and subsequently was elevated to the coveted post of registrar. The first graduate of the university was Ishwari Prasad; the first MA was similarly one Amba Prasad. Legendary cricketer Lala Amarnath too studied there.[35]

Nonetheless, the lessons of the 1857 uprising had not slipped Sir Syed's attention. The British had lost control between May and September of that year, anarchy had descended, and primal instincts burst forth. In Bijnor he saw from up close that Hindus and Muslims clustered into separate groups, unable to make common cause against British rulers and instead took advantage of the situation to settle scores against the other. Maintaining his position as an important leader of India's Muslims required he change his attitude in important ways.

Sir Syed communalizes

With time, and with British support, Sir Syed had become the most important Muslim leader in India. His position on Hindu–Muslim issues had been accommodative and inclusive until the 1880s.[36] But thereafter one sees that his efforts turned towards benefitting the Muslim *ashrafiyya*. On Hindu–Muslim issues his position steadily became insular, turning eventually into "us versus them", an assertion of primordial identities. Here is why:

First: The Indian National Congress, with mostly Hindu members, had emerged in 1885 in response to dissatisfaction with British colonial governance practices.

Its demands for reforms were scarcely radical, but any change towards self-rule was disliked by the British. With the 1857 uprising having put Muslims under suspicion, and his rise as a Muslim leader resting upon British support, Sir Syed did not want Muslims to be associated in any way with any organization that would be seen as anti-colonial. Indeed it cannot be doubted that among the Congress were some leaders who welcomed British rule because it destroyed Muslim supremacy. They wanted the last vestiges of Muslim political authority to be wiped out, after which Hindus would rule over all of India. Sir Syed therefore considered self-rule for India as highly undesirable both because Indians were incapable of governing themselves, and because Muslims would thereafter become a minority. Understandably, this logic did not endear him to anti-colonialists.

In 1888 a disappointed 23-year-old passionate supporter of the Congress wrote a series of four open letters to Sir Syed. Declaring himself an admirer of Sir Syed's past efforts, and signing himself as "The Son of an Old Follower of Yours", Lala Lajpat Rai reminded him of his earlier stance:

> Thirty years ago, you advocated the institution of a Parliament, and yet you chide us saying that we want an Indian Parliament, notwithstanding that we protest that for the present, and for a long time to come, we do not claim any such thing? Mark the difference. India is no longer what it was thirty years ago. In the course of this period it has made a marked advance towards a higher civilization. The natives of India are no longer, with very few exceptions, ignorant or uneducated. The rays of education are penetrating and shedding their wholesome light inside most Indian homes; hundreds of thousands of Indians are as well educated as any average English gentleman, and we see scores of our countrymen every year crossing the "black waters" to witness with their own eyes the proceedings of the great British Parliament, and personally familiarize themselves with the political institutions of the English nation.[37]

As Wilfred Cantwell Smith points out, Sir Syed was by now an old man, fixed in his ways and outclassed by progressive Hindus who were calling for political and social change even more effectively than he had done earlier for Muslims. Smith explains why he refused to join the Congress and why his reactions became increasingly more harsh and bitter:

> Now for the first time Sir Sayyid found his position of total and joyous acceptance of the British challenged not only by those behind him, the reactionaries who could not share in or could not appreciate his progress, but also by those who had outstripped him, progressives like himself, but who had even more initiative and more progress than had he.[38]

Rajmohan Gandhi shares Cantwell Smith's position but disputes that Sir Syed had turned communalist or that his aloofness from Congress was linked to its alleged Hindu character: "There is no reference in Sayyid Ahmed's numerous criticisms of Congress to its supposed Hindu-ness. He was against Congress because he did not want to disturb the Raj-*qaum* equilibrium for which he had carefully and successfully labored".[39] Gandhi is carefully considerate of Sir Syed's position:

> Not synonymous with Hindus but largely representing them, Congress was, we saw, ungenerous in that crucial year, 1937. Blindness lay behind its failure to give Muslims a visible share in its ministries. It did not realize that Congress rule could be taken as Hindu rule by the bulk of the "qaum". This blindness was not new. We saw in Sayyid Ahmad's story that as far back as the 1880's most Hindus associated with the founding of Congress were unaware of Muslim fears of one-man-one-vote.[40]

Well, true enough, but Sir Syed's opposition was crucial in turning a majority of Muslims away from joining the Congress. No longer did he emphasize Hindu–Muslim unity. Fear of one-man-one-vote led Sir Syed to create the Muslim *qaum*. Separatism initiated a process that culminated in the Two Nation Theory (*do qaumi nazariyya*), making him Pakistan's godfather.

Second: Sir Syed was keenly aware that the demands of meritocracy favored the Hindus because they were better educated. Thus the Congress's demand for competitive examinations into the bureaucracy would place Muslims at a disadvantage. Instead, he argued, British administrators should make appointments taking into account the pedigree of applicants. Aristocratic backgrounds should be preferred; this was the principle agreed to during Mughal times and that's how he believed it should stay. Educated Bengali Hindus, who outperformed others, should be excluded and left to their own devices because they were pusillanimous, incapable of leading properly. Instead well-born north Indians from both religious communities should handle administrative affairs.

Third: Hindu revivalism was becoming ever more on display in the 1880s with new temples, street processions, gaushalas (cow protection centers), and schools. Socio-religious movements like the Arya Samaj were promoting a more aggressive Hinduism. A ban on the killing of cows would threaten a large section of the Muslim population engaged in meat production. However, as a measure to avoid losing Hindu support for his educational efforts, Sir Syed banned cow-slaughter within the premises of the MAO College which he founded at Aligarh in 1875.

Fourth: The question of whether vernacular education should be in Urdu or Hindi became a major friction point between Muslims and Hindus. It was perceived that in the well-being of their language lay the future of a community. Sir Syed was outraged that Hindu members of his Scientific Society had suggested that the Society's journal be published in the Devanagari (Hindi) script rather than the Urdu–Persian script. He was particularly upset with Raja Jaikishan Das who was now in charge of the Scientific Society and, with the rise of the

Hindi–Urdu controversy, wanted the Society's journal to be in Hindi rather than Urdu. He wrote:

> This proposal would destroy cooperation between Hindus and Muslims. Muslims would never accept Hindi and if Hindus persist in demanding the adoption of Hindi in preference to Urdu it would result in the total separation of the Muslims from Hindus.[41]

Whereas both languages are similarly structured and understandable in most part to speakers of the other, Urdu (in Persian script) was strongly associated with Muslims and Hindi (in Devanagari script) with Hindus. Sir Syed, whose primary language was Urdu, insisted upon Urdu being the glue that would hold the *qaum* together. Fifty years later, Pakistan would have to pay a heavy price in Bengal, where Urdu was imposed upon Bengalis. Then, as now, language could unite but also divide.

This chapter has provided background for the evolution of thoughts that led up to the Two Nation Theory. Until 1857 there had been no identification of the subcontinent's Muslims with a Muslim nation. However, the stage was ready for one to emerge. A simmering subterranean animosity was brewing, fueled by a Hindu–Muslim differential in access to jobs and lands. With the passage of some more decades, tensions rose dangerously high in the 1920s. The Khilafat and Non-Cooperation Movements (1919–1922) enabled Hindu–Muslim fraternization, but it was strictly temporary. From 1923 to 1926 there were as many as 72 communal riots against 16 in the course of twenty years from 1900.[42]

Sir Syed's mixed legacy

> One of the author's earliest memories is of the arrival in our ancestral village in northern India of three young men carrying the Muslim League flag – the Islamic crescent and star on a deep green background. The three were students from Aligarh University. They planted the flag in the village square and a crowd of little boys gathered around them…. Within an hour our quiet village had been turned into a "Pakistan Village"…. Every piece of green material our mother could find was made into Muslim League flags…. A few months later they [parents] all walked in their bare feet and some carried their aged and sick parents on the backs to the polling booth four miles away to vote for Muslim League and Pakistan. This was repeated all over India. Seldom in history have so few inspired so many with so little effort.
>
> *Kalim Siddiqui,* Conflict, Crisis & War in Pakistan[43]

A hub of the movement for Pakistan was Aligarh Muslim University (AMU), Sir Syed's creation. Clearly he had succeeded brilliantly in identity politics, and his lasting legacy was to articulate a sense of Indian Muslimness – soft communalism

98 Founder I: The Lonely Modernizer

if you will – that established a set of visible markers distinguishing interests of the Muslim elite from those of Hindus. The All-India Muslim League (AIML), founded nearly a decade after Sir Syed's death, was the vehicle which would channel Muslim resentment. AMU would headquarter AIML. Indeed, the university was a petri dish for a teeming Muslim nationalism. Its professors, teachers, and students went in large numbers to the Punjab to campaign for AIML and Pakistan. In 1941 a heavily garlanded Mohammad Ali Jinnah spoke at AMU and described it as "an arsenal for Pakistan". Others have complimented AMU for producing the *mujahideen-e-Pakistan*. In 1945 a young university lecturer, Manzar Alam, enthusiastically proclaimed, "Aligarh being the arsenal of Muslim India, must also supply the ammunition in the battle for the freedom of the Great Muslim Nation".[44]

After 1947 the story becomes sadder.[45] Aligarh's Muslim nationalists became strangers in their own land taunted by the Hindu majority: why don't you also go away? Yet, notwithstanding the large-scale exodus of the faculty and alumni to Pakistan, the university continued to nurture Muslim ethnicity in north Indian states, Uttar Pradesh and Bihar in particular. Though the catchment area for attracting students shrank, AMU insisted upon flaunting its Muslim character. Although conceived as a vehicle for modernizing the Muslim mind, it increasingly veered towards becoming a Muslim ghetto. Inbreeding, illiberalism, and Islamic revivalism are threatening to remove it from the mainstream of Indian and international academia. The path of secular knowledge and universal truths has steadily narrowed.

Over a full century of existence, AMU has produced little new thought or deep scholarship in either the humanities or sciences. Allowing large number of *madrassa* students into AMU has impacted the atmosphere. Ariful Islam, a retired professor of statistics from AMU, noted that: "I too am for reforms in madrassa education. But instead of modernizing the madrassas, they are turning a modern institution like AMU into a madrassa".[46] Revived Muslim politics has provoked a Hindu reaction. AMU is currently in the crosshairs of right-wing BJP activists. In May 2018 they demanded that Jinnah's portrait be removed from the student union hall at AMU where it had been hanging for decades. Dozens of students who resisted were injured; the portrait was temporarily removed. An aggressive and militant Hindu right-wing perceives every assertion of Muslimness with jaundiced eyes and sees in AMU an outpost of Pakistan.

While Sir Syed did communalize in the last part of his life, through MAO College – and thus Aligarh Muslim University – he succeeded in creating an educated Muslim middle class. Indeed, Sir Syed's educational efforts were directed primarily towards Muslims, but Hindus featured prominently in them as well. In 1859, he founded the *Moradabad Panchayat Madrasa* where the medium of instruction was Persian. The first batch of this school included 72 Hindus and 103 Muslims. The idea of students doing politics was anathema for him. His opposition to Congress should not be conflated with a desire to separate Hindus from Muslims. For one, he had never wanted – or perhaps never even have imagined – that the Raj would end one day, and India's natives could be left without

British protection. While his primary loyalty lay with upper-class Muslims, at no point in his life was he a hard anti-Hindu communalist – one who sees a mongoose–snake relationship between communities or as a zero-sum game where only one or the other could survive.

Sir Syed would likely not have sought or approved of physically separating the two communities through a violent partition. But, as is sometimes the case, ideas take on a life of their own. Decades later, these led to the notion of two mutually incompatible nations perpetually in a state of strife. In today's Pakistan questioning its correctness is tantamount to heresy. Mutual incompatibility of Hindus and Muslims fills schoolbooks and is taught in all military colleges. One runs the risk of being labeled a traitor and anti-Pakistan for not subscribing to it.

The complexities and nuances that led to Sir Syed's actions and positions are absent from every Pakistani history book. However, these do need to be inserted there both for historical accuracy as well as for a proper understanding of the mood of those times. In this chapter, I have tried to fill in what has gone missing there. One should really begin from Sir Syed's early days when, as a conservative young man with Mughal parentage, he was thoroughly imbued with religious teachings. As a passionate Wahhabi and literalist, he had argued that Earth was stationary and rejected every form of modern ways and behavior. It is therefore truly remarkable that from there onwards he journeyed towards becoming the foremost – and most radical – of all subcontinental leaders and argued for the need to reinterpret Islamic theology in the light of science and modern knowledge. But Sir Syed's legacy as a rationalist is barely remembered today. It faded during his lifetime because, to sustain his college, he had to stay within the traditional Muslim milieu. Thus he had to essentially give up on his attempt to refine and modernize Islam. His spectacular failure is evident from the fact that today it would be dangerous to publicly discuss Sir Syed's ideas of interpreting miracles or that the Qur'an must be consulted for spiritual matters only, rather than for those concerning law, politics, and science.

As I turn the pages of *Tahzib-ul-Akhlaq*, the magazine that Sir Syed created for propagating his ideas in the 19th century, I shake my head in disbelief. Such boldness would be unthinkable in our times. Would Pakistan's godfather have survived the bullet or the suicide bomber? Perhaps the only religious scholar of the 21st century who even remotely resembles Sir Syed and has a substantial following is Javed Ahmad Ghamidi, a disciple of the nearly forgotten Ghulam Ahmad Pervez. Faced with attempts on his life while in Pakistan, Ghamidi has lived abroad in exile for well over a decade.

Notes

1 *Musaddas-e-Hali*, pp. 83–85, quoted in Mushirul Hasan, *Islam in the Subcontinent – Muslims in a Plural Society*, Manohar Books (2002), p. 18.
2 P. Hoodbhoy, *Sir Syed Ahmad Khan – Qadamat Say Jadeedeat Tak ka Safr*. http://eacpe.org/sir-syed-ahmed-khan-from-archconservative-to-radical-reformer/
3 A.H. Hali, *Hayat-e-Javed* (1901).

4 R. Gandhi, *Eight Lives: A Study of the Hindu-Muslim Encounter*, SUNY Press (1968).
5 Ibid.
6 See, for example, https://raza-e-khushtar.org/articles/concerning-the-creation/the-earth-is-stationary/
7 Sir Syed in *Tasanif-i-Ahmadi*, Vol. 1, part 1 (1870), p. 135.
8 C.W. Troll, *Sayyid Ahmed Khan – A Reinterpretation of Muslim Theology* (1978), p. 41.
9 M. Riexinger, Responses of South Asian Muslims to the Theory of Evolution, *Die Welt Des Islams*, New Series, 49, no. 2 (2009): 212–247. Accessed May 2, 2021. http://www.jstor.org/stable/27798302.
10 *Adna halat se a'la halat par insan ki taraqqi*, Syed Ahmad Khan in *Maqalat-e-Sir Syed*, Vol. IV.
11 Syed Ahmad Khan, *Tahzib-e-Akhlaq*, quoted in Sibt-e-Hasan, *Naveed-e-Fikr*, Karachi, Danial Publications (1983), p107.
12 Ibid, p. 109.
13 Sheikh Muhammad Ikram, *Modern Muslim India and the Birth of Pakistan*, Lahore, Institute of Islamic Culture, p. 54.
14 *Sir Syed Ahmad Khan ka asli roop*, Moulana Mufti Muhammad Rashid Qadri Rizvi, Maktaba Noor-e-Baseerat, Lahore (2013).
15 H. Malik, *Sir Sayyid Ahmad Khan and Muslim Modernization in India and Pakistan*, Columbia University Press (1980), p. 119.
16 *Tarikh-e-Sarkashi-e-Zilla Bijnor* (History of the Bijnor Rebellion), Syed Ahmad Khan, translated by Hafeez Malik and Morris Dembo.
17 A. Read and D. Fisher, *The Proudest Day – India's Long Road to Independence*, W.W. Norton (1978), p. 76.
18 S. Hay, *Sources of Indian Tradition: Modern India and Pakistan – Modern India and Pakistan*, Columbia University Press (1988), p. 164.
19 *Writings and Speeches of Sir Syed Ahmad Khan-7*, compiled and edited by Shan Mohammad, foreword by Rai Gopal, Bombay, Nachiketa Publications Limited (1972), p. 178.
20 Aligarh Institute Gazette, 5 April 1911.
21 H. Malik, Sir Sayyid Ahmad Khan's Contribution to the Development of Muslim Nationalism in India, *Modern Asian Studies*, 4, no. 2 (March 1970): 129–147.
22 Ibid, p. 127.
23 Syed Ahmad Khan, Taqrir bajawab address-e anjuman-e Islamiyya Rae Bareilly, *Khutbat-e Sir Sayyid*, vol. 1: 365–369.
24 V. Dhulipala, *Creating a New Medina – State Power, Islam, and the Quest for Pakistan in Late Colonial North India*, Cambridge University Press (2015), pp. 52–58.
25 W.C. Smith, *Modern Islam in India – A Social Analysis*, Lahore, Minerva Books (1943), p. 22.
26 T. Hasan, *The Aligarh Movement and the Making of the Muslim Mind*, Rupa Publications India Pvt. Ltd. (2006), p. 126.
27 Malik, op. cit.
28 Sharif-ul-Mujahid, Sir Syed Ahmad Khan And Muslim Nationalism, *India Islamic Studies*, 38, no. 1 (Spring 1999): 87–101. Published by: Islamic Research Institute, International Islamic University, Islamabad.
29 Sayyid Iqbal Ali, *Sayyid Ahmad Khan Ka Safar-e-Punjab*, Aligarh (n.d.), p. 140, 167.
30 Ibid, p. 161.
31 *Majmua Lectures-e-Sir Syed* (Urdu), Munshi Sirajuddin edition, Balaji Press (1892), pp. 117–121.
32 Ibid.
33 How Sir Syed Ahmed Khan helped bring in Indian renaissance, *The Times of India*, 13 October 2018.
34 S.A. Khan, *Madressa al-Ulum Key Zarurat*, Taqriri Maqalat, p. 120.
35 https://indianexpress.com/article/opinion/columns/misreading-sir-syed-ahmad-khan-aligarh-muslim-university-4893795/

36 Malik, op. cit.
37 Lala Lajpat Rai, Letter 1: Open Letters to Sir Syed Ahmed Khan (1888) by Lala Lajpat Rai, http://www.columbia.edu/itc/mealac/pritchett/00islamlinks/txt_lajpat-rai_1888/letter01.html
38 Smith, op. cit., p. 16.
39 Gandhi, op. cit.
40 R. Gandhi, *Understanding the Muslim Mind*, Dehli, Penguin Books (1987), p. 311.
41 Syed Ahmad Khan to Mahdi Ali Khan Muhsin al-Mulk, 29 April 1870, in Maktubat-e-Sir-Syed, ed. Shaikh Muhammad Isma'il Panipati, Lahore, Majlis Taraqqi-e-Adab (1959), p. 103.
42 V. Datta, Iqbal, Jinnah and India's Partition: An Intimate Relationship, *Economic and Political Weekly*, 37, no. 50 (2002): 5035.
43 K. Siddiqui, *Conflict, Crisis & War in Pakistan*, quoted in M. Hasan, *Islam in the Subcontinent*, Manohar Books (2002), p. 253.
44 Dawn, 18 October 1945.
45 A. Maheshwari, *Aligarh Muslim University: Institution of Learning or Identity (Centenary Year) 1920–2020*, to be published.
46 M. Wajihuddin, *Aligarh Muslim University: The Making of the Modern Indian Muslim*, quoted in Scroll.in, 10 December 2021.

Four

FOUNDER II: POET–PREACHER–POLITICIAN

> I cannot become an object of worship – so deeply is ingrained in me the instinct of a worshipper. But if the innermost thoughts of my soul are ever revealed to the public, if what lies concealed in my heart is ever expressed, then I am sure the world will worship me someday after my death. They will forget my sins and give me the tribute of a tear.
>
> – Muhammad Iqbal, Letter to Atiya Faizee,
> 7 July 1909[1]

Allama Iqbal, Pakistan's revered national icon, was a poet par excellence and the most celebrated Muslim thinker of the 20th century. His disciples, enthralled by the beauty of his Urdu and Persian verse, have wrapped him in multiple layers of hagiographic fiction. Therefore, given his continuing presence as an inspirational figure, it becomes important to disaggregate, demystify, and separate fact from fabrication. In this chapter I maintain that while his works of poetry and occasional prose are soul-stirring, to look therein for a consistent political narrative or a vision for Muslims is hopeless. Among many misconceptions about Iqbal is that he was a philosopher. While he had a doctoral degree in philosophy and was doubtless an original thinker, he was not a philosopher in the sense of modern academia nor wanted to be regarded as one. Here a calmer, more measured assessment is undertaken on multiple other matters as well: how and why he journeyed from being an Indian nationalist towards soft communitarianism and towards eventually becoming an Islamic supremacist; his critique of reason and peremptory dismissal of Golden Age Muslim rationalist thinkers; his aversion to science and reason as manifested in his various commentaries on 20th-century science; his prescription for a Muslim revival through valorization of jihad and the sword; his rejection of secularism; and his vision of India as a theodemocracy – or perhaps multiple theodemocracies.

DOI: 10.4324/9781003379140-7

Muhammad Iqbal (1877–1938), reverentially known as Allama Iqbal, knew he was destined to become an icon of worship. In his 1909 letter (quoted on the preceding page) to lady-friend Atiya Faizee, he predicted that all else – foibles and inconsistencies included – would eventually be washed away. He was spot on. But what may have surprised (and doubtless pleased him) is the size and fervor of his following.

Today, upon entering any government office in Pakistan, you will notice three adorned portraits. That of the current president of Pakistan is framed lightly because it will get tossed out the very day he leaves office. The other two are the permanent furniture: Muhammad Ali Jinnah, who founded Pakistan, and Muhammad Iqbal, now on par with Jinnah. Across Pakistan, Iqbal looms large. A man pictured deep in thought, head resting to one side on a closed fist fills school textbooks, military recruiting centers, and colleges and universities. Literary societies, housing blocks, roads, hospitals, Lahore's airport, and countless schools all bear his name. Iqbal is everywhere. Though quintessentially Punjabi, he is Pakistan personified.

Variously called the Prophet of Muslim Renaissance, *sha'ir-e-Mashriq* (Poet of the East), *mufakkir-e-Pakistan* (Savant of Pakistan), and *hakeem-ul-Ummat* (Sage of the Ummah) Iqbal is officially designated as Pakistan's national poet (although the Iqbal Academy's website peevishly claims he was just as much a philosopher as poet). Some universities have departments of *Iqbaliat* offering PhD and other degree programs. His birthday, like that of Jinnah, is a national holiday. Iqbal's status in Pakistan rose hugely during the 1980s – a period of rapid Islamization under General Zia-ul-Haq. Earlier, he had been portrayed as one of the ideological forces behind Pakistan. But later, as per the state's changed needs, he was elevated to the position of its co-founder. Jinnah, who had once been seated alone upon that throne, must perforce share the glory with Iqbal on days of national celebration. Some laudatory speeches on the 74th anniversary of Pakistan placed him a notch above Jinnah.

Many hundreds of local authors have described Iqbal in hagiographic terms: great poet, great philosopher, great thinker, great Muslim, great visionary…a breathless list of "greats". On the other side only a sprinkling of authors in Urdu – Sibte Hasan, Mubarak Ali, and Ali Abbas Jalalpuri – have dared to examine him in the light of facts. A recent book by Mahboob Tabish that seeks to look systematically at common misperceptions surrounding Iqbal is also a rare exception.[2]

Iqbal's genius lay in his exquisite poetic compositions. He said what people in his community wanted to hear and so can be cherry-picked for any given purpose or even for the very opposite one. Which one of his putative visions or expressions is authentic one does not know. Cult followers worship their leader and so it is with Iqbal. Many appear perfectly comfortable in letting go of accepted rules of logic and good judgment, gladly ignoring his contradictions and zigzags. Instead, these are hailed as a sign of deep wisdom. Certainly, perfect consistency cannot be expected of any human, and contradictions, if mild, are not always bad. They may well be tolerable and even welcome as mid-course corrections.

104 Founder II: Poet–Preacher–Politician

In fact any person would be rightly considered excessively rigid were he or she to rigidly adhere to a point of view and choose to remain uninformed or unaffected by circumstance. But working around a formidable mountain of metaphysical confusion is sometimes very hard.

There is a resolution to these inconsistencies provided one accepts that what we need to deal with is two Iqbals. Iqbal-A is the relatively unknown but high-minded Iqbal, which he was before leaving in 1905 to study in the West. Iqbal-B is the man who returned transformed and eventually commanded a mass following. But because his followers insist upon merging the two into one single individual, they fall into a pit of self-deception while imagining they have developed a new, profound, and some "multidimensional" insight into the man they worship.

That Iqbal was a man of genius is beyond doubt. His Urdu and Persian diction, richness of imagery, and strong sense of purpose have immortalized him. But esthetics aside, hard questions must be asked about his intellectual contributions: What did he add to philosophy? Was he equipped to comment on matters that relate to the intersection of science and philosophy? In matters of society and politics, one would like many answers from him. Would Iqbal have been for – or perhaps against the Taliban – and if so, why? Could one have expected him to support or oppose Pakistan's blasphemy laws? Would he have justified or condemned the persecution of Ahmadis and other religious minorities? Are the calls for fulfilling Iqbal's dreams actually what Pakistan needs today? And what might be the consequences if some of his more radical ideas were taken seriously and become reality?

For this iconic figure standing at the apex of Pakistani nationalism, the paucity of calm, measured assessments calls for deconstructing decades-old beliefs. To know the true Iqbal – as opposed to the Iqbal of popular mythology – is therefore the task of this chapter.

Everyone loves Iqbal

People across the board find this man of genius useful. Mullahs and mullah-bashers, communalists and universalists, nationalists and anti-nationalists, secularists, democrats and fascists – all can find in his poetry that which best suits them. Pakistanis will often clinch an argument by quoting one of Iqbal's verses. The intoxicating poetic beauty is such that many assume some profound truth to be hidden beneath the imagery, music, and rhythm. Politicians, generals, scholars, and teachers while seeking to inspire audiences quote his angst-laden verses. His ideas and sayings are also used as sanctification of ideas, to silence critics and legitimize indefensible policies.

Cricketer–politician Imran Khan, who became prime minister in 2018, declared Allama Iqbal his mentor and said that "Naya Pakistan" shall be "Iqbal's Pakistan". Others speak of fulfilling "Iqbal's dream", although what any person dreams – unless subsequently written down – can only be guessed at by others.

Founder II: Poet–Preacher–Politician **105**

Militant Islamists also count among Iqbal's admirers today. Khadim Hussain Rizvi, the recently deceased fiery, foul-mouthed, and wheelchair-bound cleric who founded the extremist *Tehreek Labbaik Pakistan* had appropriated Iqbal as perhaps no one else has in recent history.[3] As he led charged anti-blasphemy and anti-minority mobs across the country, Rizvi honed the use of Iqbal's selected verses into a fine art. With barely hidden support provided by the Pakistan Army, he shut down Islamabad in 2017 and eventually helped cause the Nawaz Sharif government to fall.

Elsewhere too, Iqbal inspires – and sets on fire – a large section of Muslims who see the world a stage where civilizations clash. His brilliant verses in *shikwa* dwell upon past Muslim pride, calling for a return to the Faith as the way towards the future. The hypermasculine *mard-e-momin* is an idealized Muslim male; a remodeled superman along Nietzschean lines who craves martyrdom in service of the faith. Alone capable of rescuing Muslims from internal decay and predatory colonialism, Iqbal likens his superman to a *shaheen* (falcon) aloof from all worldly desire. The *shaheen* seeks its abode on mountain rocks, refuses to make a nest, and returns to fight again and again (*jhapatna, palatna, palat kar jhapatna*). Likewise, with sword in hand and the Qur'an on his lips, the Musulman must seek to conquer the world once again for Islam.

In the shadow of the sword have we been weaned	تیغوں کے سائے میں ہم، پل کر جواں ہوئے ہیں
Our proud symbol is the crescent's dagger	خنجبرِ ہلال کا ہے، قومی نشاں ہمارا

Iqbal's epic poem *Tariq Ki Dua* is about the early Muslim conqueror Tariq bin Ziyad (670–720) who landed hugely outnumbered on the coast of Andalusia but ordered his boats burned and fought to ultimate victory. Again and again Iqbal passionately addresses his Urdu audience for a Muslim land without borders. He is far more circumspect in his English writings where he comes across as sober and thoughtful. Therein he disparages the notion of a caliphate and supports Ataturk's decision to disband this centuries old institution. This dualism runs through his works; even as he praised Ataturk's *ijtihad*, he dwells on the idea of divine retribution. His poems arouse Muslim supremacy, calling upon ascetic warriors to lead the world:

Martyrdom is all that the true believer seeks	شہادت ہے مطلوب و مقصودِ مومن
Not for him is the booty of war or other splendors	نہ مالِ غنیمت، نہ کشور کشائی

In imploring Allah, Iqbal asks that He not forget the services rendered unto Him by his followers:

Who was it that smashed the idols of worship?	توڑے مخلوق خداوندوں کے پیکر کس نے
Whose sword was it that defeated the unbeliever?	کاٹ کر رکھ دیے کفار کے لشکر کس نے

106 Founder II: Poet–Preacher–Politician

Such nostalgic appeals to lost glory go down well with right-wing political leaders in Pakistan, as well as various Islamic militant groups such as the Pakistani Taliban whose pamphlets sometimes use his verses. Pakistan Army recruiting centers are inscribed with Iqbal's poetry and the *shaheen* emblem. Although the Army and Islamic militants go to war against the other from time to time, for both sides he is the warrior–poet par excellence. Arguably, no other poet has so directly impacted the world of Muslim politics. In 1986 Iran's supreme revolutionary leader Ayatollah Khamenei declared that Iran was "exactly following the path that was shown to us by Iqbal".[4]

Germany remembers Iqbal too. He had stayed in Heidelberg for six months to learn German for his PhD thesis. In deference to this important person, a prominent street sign there bears the name Iqbal-Ufer with an explanation beneath: Dr. Mohammad Iqbal (1877–1938), Pakistanischer Dichter und Nationalphilosoph. However, the impact of Herr Professor Dr. Iqbal on German academia in Heidelberg or Munich appears limited; a Google search does not reveal anything much. According to Duriya Hashmi, "Students in Heidelberg University have keine ahnung (no idea) about Pakistan's national philosopher-poet".[5]

Biographical sketch

Muhammad Iqbal of Sialkot was born in 1877 to parents who were uneducated but deeply religious. The family was Kashmiri Brahmin in origin, having converted to Islam some generations earlier. His father, a tailor, sent the four-year-old off to learn the Qur'an at a nearby mosque, then to the Scotch Mission College where he learned the Arabic language. After matriculation, and subsequently receiving his Intermediate Diploma, he enrolled at age nineteen in Government College Lahore where he obtained a Bachelor of Arts degree in philosophy and then a Master of Arts degree in 1899. Because of his outstanding academic record he was soon selected as junior professor of philosophy, again at the same college. Here he was guided by Thomas Arnold (later knighted), a British orientalist and historian of Islamic art, who was a longtime friend of Sir Syed Ahmad Khan. [6]

The youthful Iqbal had already begun attracting attention on the Lahore literary scene around 1903–1904 with his powerful poetry. As Wilfred Cantwell Smith notes, the themes were fairly conventional: verses on nature and unrequited love, a long ode to the recently departed Queen Victoria called *khuda ka saya*, in praise of the glorious land of Hindustan, and poems strongly expressive of Hindu–Muslim solidarity. He also wrote Islamic poems and was a regular visitor to the *Anjuman-e-Himayat-e-Islam*. But even in his appearances there, he pleaded against communalism and for coexistence between Hindus and Muslims.

Arnold was quick to recognize Iqbal's exceptional talents and advised him to apply for his studies at Cambridge University. In 1905 Iqbal departed for England, obtaining a Bachelor of Arts degree from Cambridge in 1906. He then submitted his dissertation, entitled *The Development of Metaphysics in Persia*,

Founder II: Poet–Preacher–Politician **107**

to Munich University in 1907 which was then published as a book in 1908 by Luzac & Company (London). Professor Hommel, one of Iqbal's thesis supervisors wrote, "So far as I am aware, it is the first attempt that has been made to trace the continuous development of ancient Iranian speculation as they have survived in Muhammadan Philosophy."[7] It was judged to be a good PhD thesis but not a path-breaker. Sir Thomas Arnold, Iqbal's teacher in Lahore and London, had put in a good word for Iqbal. The work was treated as a "dissertation in oriental philology and not philosophy because the committee was not satisfied with its quality in the latter area".[8] Iqbal never followed up on it thereafter and was not keen about having it translated into Urdu (although it did get translated later).

The Iqbal who had set out to Europe and the Iqbal who returned were two very different persons.

As with other visitors and students from India, Iqbal was initially awestruck by the enormous vitality of the West, the relentless search for new knowledge, the freedom to speak and act as one wants, and the willingness of people to change what they did not like. In contrast, he saw India as static, its people passive and fatalistic, quite unable to take charge of their own destiny. But as the months passed, he became increasingly uncomfortable. It became evident that in spite of being better read and superior in intelligence than most people around him, he as an Indian and a colonial subject was not going to be accepted as an equal to white Europeans. This discrimination made him increasingly more resentful.

Iqbal relates one example: shortly after beginning studies at Cambridge University, he chanced upon a fundraiser addressed by a Christian missionary who painted the bleakest possible picture of an India consumed by ignorance and poverty.[9] Incensed, Iqbal rose and sought permission to speak and for the next twenty-five minutes he passionately described pre-colonial India as prosperous and cultured, rich in tradition and knowledge; a land now reduced to servitude and destitution by its colonial masters. Iqbal's command of English was replete with idioms and his inventory of facts expansive. The meeting burst out in applause and Iqbal found himself surrounded by awestruck newfound admirers. The missionary went back empty-handed.

Even as he enjoyed the splendour of Cambridge and London, Iqbal's shame and anger at his being a colonial subject continued to grow. Thirty years earlier, Sir Syed had been uncritically appreciative of these very places but for Iqbal the dark side of the West began to grow ever darker. He disliked the frenetic pace of life, finding it dehumanizing and stressful, and leaving little time for thought and reflection. But more importantly, prior to the First World War, the clouds could be seen gathering on the horizon. Capitalistic competition and jingoistic nationalism had begun pitting one European country against the other. In just another few years, Germany would see the rise of Hitler's Third Reich.

It is tempting to compare Iqbal with Syed Qutb (1906–1966), the Egyptian Islamic theorist who left an enduring legacy in the Islamic world. For Qutb, as with Iqbal, living in the West turned out to be transformational. Qutb spent two years (1948–1950) on a scholarship in the United States to study its educational

108 Founder II: Poet–Preacher–Politician

system. He also came back convinced that the dazzling lights of the materialist West had blinded people everywhere to what was sacred and true. The real apex of human civilization, said Qutb, was that created by Prophet Muhammad and thereafter spread by the Four Righteous Caliphs. Through jihad, Muslim lands must be cleansed of infidels and their ideology. Modernity was not progress, for it enslaved man and left him numb to "faith in religion, faith in art and faith in spiritual values altogether." Qutb died by hanging after being found guilty of plotting to assassinate President Gamal Abdel Nasser. His books and writings, published in Saudi Arabia, inspired millions including Ayman al-Zawahiri and Osama bin Laden.

Iqbal had greater intellectual depth than Qutb and recognized that the West had huge achievements in every field – scientific, philosophical, and cultural. This compelled all, including Indians, to admire them. But as his own world appeared inferior and British rule hung heavy over India, his poetry took an increasingly more strident anti-West tone. Like Qutb, Iqbal had eventually concluded that European civilization needed to be rejected in its totality, both culturally and philosophically. It was naught but the glitter of fake jewels, a phony construction built upon shifting sands. Truth, he said, could only be found in faith:

Dazzling is glitter of today's civilization	نظر کو خیرہ کرتی ہے چمک ــ تہذیب حاضر کی
'Tis but a mosaic of cleverly crafted fake jewels	یہ صنّاعی مگر جھوٹے نگوں کی ریزہ کاری ہے
In enslavement useless is sword and strategy	غلامی میں نہ کام آتی ہیں شمشیریں، نہ تدبیریں
Faith alone can cut the chains	جو ہو ذوقِ یقیں پیدا تو کٹ جاتی ہیں زنجیریں

Iqbal set up his law practice after returning to Lahore in 1908. But by now his heart had turned towards using his poetry in the service of Islam and the Muslims of India. These Muslims had to be whipped into action and recover their lost heritage through reviving the concepts of *ijtihad* (reinterpreting Islamic doctrines according to current needs) and *ijma'* (consensus of the community). Altered by his European experience, he declared that secular democracy was anathema to Islam, and Muslims must live in a state guided by the Islamic principles. He attempts to elaborate upon these principles in his English writings but not in Urdu prose.

This changed stance also created a sharp break with his poetry of the years prior to becoming a powerful political figure. Earlier he had tuned his verses alternately towards praising monarchy, fascism, socialism, and communism. This immature phase ended with his decrying these systems as materialist and soulless. Nevertheless, long after he stopped writing such erratic and contradictory paeans, his inspirational poetry continued to mesmerize leftists, Ahmadis, and women. The complicated relationship they have with him will be evident below and in other chapters of this book.

The flirtation of communists and socialists with Iqbal is a particularly interesting one. Progressives would often claim him to be one of their own. Faiz

Ahmad Faiz, Pakistan's left wing poet of the revolution, saw in Iqbal an ally for building a theistic case against capitalism. Like other leftists, he took seriously the odes to communism written in Iqbal's earlier days. Several have titles that speak for themselves: *Karl Marx Ki Awaz* (Voice of Karl Marx), *Bolshevik Roos* (Bolshevik Russia), *Lenin Khuda Ke Huzoor Mein* (When Lenin Was Summoned By God), and *Sarmaya-o-Mehnat* (Capital and Labor) is a noninclusive list. Iqbal also wrote a powerful poem urging peasants to revolt against their landlords and burn down their fields. This was written well before he joined with big landlords of the Punjab Muslim League and was elected president of the All India Muslim League. An Indian communist, Shamsuddin Hasan, commenting in the Zamindar of 23 June 1923 on the arrest of his communist co-workers wrote:

> If supporting Bolshevik thought is a crime our country's greatest poet, Sir Muhammad Iqbal cannot escape legal action...even a person of average intelligence will soon see by a careful study of Sir Muhammad Iqbal's Khizr-i-Rah (The Journey's Guide) and Payam-i-Mashriq (The Message of the East), that Allamah Iqbal is not only a communist but communism's high priest.[10]

Iqbal, who had by now been knighted by the Crown, panicked and immediately rushed to deny any communist affiliation. The very next day, the Zamindar published the following response from Iqbal:

> I am a Muslim and believe, on the basis of logical reasoning, that the Holy Qur'an has offered the best cure for the economic maladies of human societies...Russian Bolshevism is a strong reaction against the selfish and short-sighted capitalism of Europe. But in fact the European capitalism and the Russian Bolshevism are two extremes. The happy middle path is what the Holy Qur'an has shown to us and to which I have alluded above. The equitable Shariah aims at protecting one class from the economic domination of the other, and in my belief, the path chosen by the Holy Prophet (P.B.U.H.) is the one best suited for this purpose.[11]

The brief progressive phase of Iqbal's life ended as he became more religiously conservative and increasingly eager to deny his earlier advocacy of socialism and communism. Henceforth he would often conflate them with atheism. In a letter to Jinnah, he warned against Congress's growing influence among Muslims and their willingness to support what he described as the "atheistic socialism" championed by Nehru.[12] A lifelong member of the All India Muslim League, which had by now become highly influential with the north Indian elite, he was elected from his Lahore constituency to the Punjab Legislative Assembly. Soon thereafter he wrote to Jinnah recommending that one of Punjab's largest landlords, the Nawab of Mamdot, be invited to join the Punjab Muslim League. Some leftist

110 Founder II: Poet–Preacher–Politician

progressives nevertheless continued to adore Iqbal, a testimony to the bewitching power of his verse.

Interestingly, those who eventually received the roughest treatment from Iqbal's pen also continue to inspire themselves and others with his verses. Stockholm syndrome? Ahmadis, by far Pakistan's most persecuted religious minority, still quote the prose and poetry from Iqbal's early days. They proudly note that Iqbal's father and elder brother had taken the Ahmadiyya *bay'at* (pledge). Also, as we shall see in a later section, Iqbal was an unapologetic patriarch. Nevertheless women also memorize his verses in awestruck admiration. They either do not know, or perhaps prefer not to know, how differently he related to western women as compared to eastern women, including his own wives and daughter. More will be said on this point later.

Philosopher or just philosophical?

Iqbal was an extraordinarily thoughtful and gifted individual. But although he is celebrated as the "Philosopher of the East", he was not a philosopher in the sense that the world of academic philosophy can accept. The Indian subcontinent knows of other distinguished thinkers such as Rabindranath Tagore, who won the Nobel Prize in literature and has a Wikipedia description as "poet, writer, playwright, composer, philosopher, social reformer and painter". Similarly, Swami Vivekananda, who conjoined western esoteric traditions with selected parts of Hinduism, is also called a philosopher by his devotees. But, in the sense to be explained below, it would be improper and inaccurate to say that Iqbal, Tagore, or Vivekananda were philosophers.

Colloquially, "philosophy" can be just about anything involving thought. The fact that I have a philosophy does not qualify me to being a philosopher. On the other hand, academic philosophy has a well-defined meaning in academia. Its characteristic is exercise of rigour together with arguments drawn from earlier works in the subject. To get an academic position in a university's philosophy department, one needs solid evidence of work done in some field of philosophy with detailed arguments supported by references and footnotes. But Iqbal's only work that could qualify in this regard was his doctoral thesis on metaphysics in Persia. This too was a historical survey rather than an original exposition of a philosophical viewpoint. Iqbal did not publish any book or monograph on philosophy, or a paper in any professional philosophy journal.

Far more importantly – and this is a point missed by all who adamantly insist upon calling Iqbal a philosopher – is that he was not interested or willing to transgress the limits set by faith. To be thus limited runs contrary to the very nature of philosophy. By definition, philosophy is the unfettered questioning of the nature of knowledge, reality, and existence in which all presuppositions are reduced to the barest minimum. Even philosophers who are considered to have a religious bent – Immanuel Kant and Søren Kierkegaard being examples of believing Christians – have approached epistemological questions with open,

Founder II: Poet–Preacher–Politician **111**

skeptical minds. A philosopher may, of course, eventually arrive at a definitive conclusion at the end of all argumentation that may affirm or deny the truth of his particular faith. But Iqbal shied away from questioning the religion of his birth, choosing to look only at affirmations and confirmations of what he believed to be true. At no point in his life did he challenge the basic precepts of his particular faith, inquire into conditions necessary for validating true knowledge from false knowledge, or engage in the kind of careful, critical discourse expected of a professional philosopher. And, as will be discussed in detail later in this chapter, while Iqbal wrote very evocative and suggestive poetry, he was not sufficiently knowledgeable in matters of science to make any meaningful contribution on matters related to the nature of space, time, energy, and the universe's origins. Indeed, after his doctorate, Iqbal's interest in philosophy waned drastically.

Upon his return to Lahore, Iqbal increasingly saw himself as a Muslim public intellectual rather than an academic philosopher. In fact he turned down the lectureship in philosophy offered to him by Government College, Lahore. Preaching and politics through the medium of poetry is what occupied him for the rest of his life. In his letter of 8 December 1919 addressed to his sister, Kareem-bi, he made clear his preference:

> As I look back over my life, I so regret at having wasted my time studying European philosophy. God has given me an exceptional mind (*quwa'ey dimaghi*). Had I studied *deeni uloom* (Islamic theology) instead of philosophy I would have been able to serve the Holy Prophet (PBUH). It pains me even more when I recall that our father actually wanted me to study theology... So even if I done some service it is not enough. I really should have dedicated my entire life to the Holy Prophet (PBUH).[13]

In the same letter, Iqbal puts down his belief that Allah alone can save ignorant Muslims: "It is my faith that Allah will infuse a new spirit among those who have kept his word alive. They will never be disappointed. The best sword we Muslims have is prayer and so we must pray constantly and send blessing to the Holy Prophet (PBUH)".[14]

Iqbal selects languages selectively

Iqbal was equally expressive in Urdu, Persian, and English – apart from being a native speaker of Punjabi. Yet he chose English only when wishing to convey a serious, well-thought-out message instead of an emotional, polemical one. This is exemplified by *The Reconstruction of Religious Thought in Islam*.[15] Briefly, this is a set of six chapters, later extended by an additional one, which appeared in 1934. In these lectures, undertaken at the request of the Madras Muslim Association and delivered at Madras, Hyderabad, and Aligarh, he creates a new 20th-century vision for Muslims. It is his only book wherein he deals with matters of Islamic

112 Founder II: Poet–Preacher–Politician

teachings, science, politics, law, and society. The lectures are in English, and, significantly, Iqbal did not repeat the contents elsewhere in Urdu or Persian. Parts of these lectures will be discussed later in this chapter.

Why English, a language not understood by most of Iqbal's constituency? There could be three reasons. First, the choice of English bestowed erudition and gravitas upon Iqbal, elevating him above other orthodox Muslims who were also bitterly critical of science and reason but who could express themselves only in Urdu and Persian with a dash of Arabic thrown in. Being limited to these languages meant that other critics had no real access to European ideas, and hence their criticism was that of the uninformed. Second, Iqbal feared that some thoughts he had expressed in *Reconstruction* or elsewhere could potentially stir controversy if they were expressed in Urdu. He could clearly have translated these effortlessly given his extraordinary gift for languages but chose not to do so. Third, he continued to seek admiration from the West and so wrote in English prose because prose in any language is far more suitable than poetry for conveying exact ideas. This led to his Janus-like existence where one face faced the past and fired up the masses, while the other face looked to the future and appeared eminently reasonable and balanced to the Western world.

Given this dualism, I think the reader of Urdu and the reader of English get very different pictures of Iqbal's personality. The Islamic narcissism filling his Urdu verses goes subterranean, and the dagger and sword return to their sheaths when he writes in English. In response to an Englishman's criticism of the glorification of blood and gore in his *shikwa*, Iqbal responded tangentially:

> I am afraid the old European idea of a blood-thirsty Islam is still lingering in the mind of Mr. Dickinson. All men and not Muslims alone are meant for the Kingdom of God on earth, provided they say good-bye to their idols of race and nationality, and treat one another as personalities... Leagues, Mandates, treaties and Imperialism, however, draped in democracy, can never bring salvation to mankind.... That Muslims have fought and conquered like other peoples, and that some of their leaders screened their personal ambitions behind the veil of religion, I do not deny, but I am absolutely sure that territorial conquest was no part of the original programme of Islam. As a matter of fact, I consider it a great loss that the progress of Islam as a conquering faith stultified the growth of those germs of an economic and democratic organization of society which I find scattered up and down the pages of the Quran and the tradition of the Prophet.... The object of my Persian poem is not to make a case for Islam; my aim is simply to discover a universal social reconstruction.[16]

The above reply – perfectly reasonable and well argued – could be accepted at face value. But it scarcely seems to be written by the same author whose verses inspired strong militant dreams among the bulk of his followers. We have encountered some such couplets earlier and will encounter some more below.

In the remainder of this chapter, I shall draw upon some of Iqbal's best-known Urdu poems (again with my own, inadequate translation). His Urdu poetry continues to have far greater impact than his Persian poetry because Persian is barely understood in today's Pakistan. Moreover, Iqbal's classical Persian is formal and quite different from the lived version in Iran.

Iqbal on faith versus reason

> I have… found it necessary to deny knowledge, in order to make room for faith.
>
> *Immanuel Kant, in preface to* Critique of Pure Reason *(1787)*

In the first chapter of *Reconstruction*, Iqbal attacks the foundations of modern science, dismissing science as "mere" pragmatism and says that religion is "far more anxious to reach the real than science". The methodology of free inquiry is fundamentally flawed, he says, because it could end up with one denying the existence of God:

> The spirit of philosophy is one of free inquiry. It suspects all authority. Its function is to trace the uncritical assumptions of human thought to their hiding places, and in this pursuit it may finally end in denial or a frank admission of the incapacity of pure reason to reach the Ultimate Reality.[17]

Iqbal trenchantly warns against thought that strays outside religious confines,

Imperiled stands the nation that allows doubt	اس قوم میں ہے شوخیِ اندیشہ خطرناک
Where thought is freed from all rules	جس قوم کے افراد ہوں ہر بند سے آزاد
Though God's reason has lit up the world	گو فکرِ خداداد سے روشن ہے زمانہ
Freedom of thought is the Devil's invention	آزادیِ افکار ہے ابلیس کی ایجاد

Iqbal is unsympathetic to the *Mu'tazila* (Muslim rationalists) and, in places, is frankly critical of them. These rationalists had imported Hellenic science and learning into Islamic civilization beginning in the 9th century and extending well into the 13th century. Through translation of works in Greek, and through inviting scholars of all faiths to understand and improve upon them, *Mu'tazila* caliphs such as Haroon-ul-Rashid, Al-Mamun, and Abd-al-Rahman II had ushered in the Islamic Golden Age of scientific and intellectual achievements. Without Islamic rationalism, Islam would have been remembered for its sword but not the pen[18]. Although Iqbal appreciates and understands this, he thinks the cost of rationality was far too great:

> Greek philosophy has been a great cultural force in the history of Islam. Yet a careful study of the Qur'an and the various schools of scholastic theology that arose under the inspiration of Greek thought disclose the remarkable

114 Founder II: Poet–Preacher–Politician

fact that while Greek philosophy very much broadened the outlook of Muslim thinkers, it, on the whole, obscured their vision of the Qur'an.[19]

Iqbal criticizes two iconic rationalist figures of the 10th century, Avicenna (Ibn Sina) and Al-Farabi, known as pioneers of medicine and mathematics. In *Tulu'-e-Islam* (Rise of Islam) he pours scorn upon them for failing to understand how it was the faith of Islam that had made Muslims great:

Through the dead East ran this life-blood of faith	عـــروقِ مردۂ مشرق میں خونِ زندگی دوڑا
But Avicenna and Farabi couldn't fathom this secret	سمجھ سکتے نہیں اس راز کو سینا و فارابی

On the other hand, Iqbal has high praise for the anti-rationalist Asharites and Imam Ghazali, who denied causation and stressed on man's inability to understand the physical universe. Averroes (Ibn-e-Rushd), whose work served as an inspiration for the European Enlightenment, also comes into his crosshairs. Averroes, says Iqbal, "unwittingly helped the growth of that enervating philosophy of life which obscures man's vision of himself, his God, and his world".[20] Iqbal rejects the scientific method saying the essence of knowledge is lost if one insists upon rigorous objectivity and repeatability of experiences. To accept the normal level of human experience as fact and reject mystical and emotional experiences is wrong in his opinion.

To demonstrate the superiority of Islam over these human constructs, Iqbal creates an imagined dialog between Faith and Reason, one that weighs in heavily on the side of Faith[21]:

Reason said to me Faith is but absurdity	علم نے مجھ سے کہا عشق ہے دیوانہ پن
Faith said to me Reason is but conjecture	عشق نے مجھ سے کہا علم ہے تخمین و ظن
Lost are you in conjecture! Be not lost in books	بندۂ تخمین و ظن! کرمِ کتابی نہ بن
Faith reveals Truth; Reason hides Truth	عشق سراپا حضور، علم سراپا حجاب
Faith's power explains the miraculous universe	عشق کی گرمی سے ہے معرکۂ کائنات
Reason explains detail; Faith explains the whole	علم مقامِ صفات، عشق تماشائے ذات
Faith yields tranquility; Faith explains life and death	عشق سکون و ثبات، عشق حیات و ممات
Reason raises only questions; Faith explains it all	علم ہے پیدا سوال، عشق ہے پنہاں جواب

True knowledge, says Iqbal, is that which only the heart can divine and must therefore not be subjected to the same criteria:

> The "heart" is a kind of inner intuition or insight which, in the beautiful words of Rumi, feeds on the rays of the sun and brings us into contact with aspects of Reality other than those open to sense-perception... The revealed and mystic literature of mankind bears ample testimony to the fact that religious experience has been too enduring and dominant in the history of mankind to be rejected as mere illusion.[22]

Let us now reflect further upon *ishq* – which I translated loosely above as "faith". This gets broadened in other parts of Iqbal's poetry to cover an entire spectrum of concepts ranging from those grounded in theism to those which are non-theistic and nonreligious such as Marxism. If one tries to peer through the veil of deliberately constructed ambiguity – that which every major poet has in his toolbox – *ishq*/faith can be disaggregated into at least four identifiable components: the affective (providing existential confidence in life and purpose), the cognitive (special nontransferable knowledge derived from individual experience), the entitling (a gift from above to chosen recipients only), and the practical (the necessity of having an organizing principle for popular movements). Iqbal flits from one to the other effortlessly; this is one of the secrets for his success as a poet. So far as the last mentioned is concerned, one cannot dispute that exercise of reason alone did not move millions in history to sacrifice their lives and wealth for causes they believed to be right. It goes without saying that no logical process of thought led people to follow Gandhi, Golwalkar, Bacha Khan, Jinnah, Nehru, etc. In that sense, yes, one needs more than a direct application of reason to change the world. Emotion releases immense forces within individuals. But as an assertion that "I know it's right because I feel it from inside me that it's right" can bring disaster in countless situations.

The insufficiency of reason occupies Iqbal and he dwells at length and in different places on this topic. Faith on the other hand, he says, is not similarly limited and so can leap across the boundaries set by reason and logic. Hence it is intrinsically far more powerful and allows humans to enter into realms otherwise not accessible. Personal revelation alone brings forth the fire of living conviction. Reason is also dangerous, according to Iqbal. Even if it brings science and material well-being, it also brings the doubt which corrodes the foundations of faith. Hence Iqbal insists that reason must be subordinated to faith.

There is nothing even slightly original in this argument. In fact this is a thoroughly commonplace objection raised by theists of every variety. For centuries, biblical and ecclesiastical tracts have sought to convince believers that it is futile to look for reason in what is divinely ordained. It is God and God alone who knows why the world is what it is. One is also told that reason cannot ever tell you why a compassionate God has filled the world with terrible suffering. Nor can reason explain to the physically or mentally malformed why God made them so, and why they must endure a life of torture without having had even a chance to sin. Although such issues properly belong to the realm of philosophy, Iqbal does not touch them. Instead, he substitutes the beauty of metaphors where serious argument is called for.

But wait! Faith cannot work at the level of epistemological inquiry because individual subjectivity then becomes the touchstone of determining right from wrong, true from false. Other than your intuition, what markers can tell you if you are being rightly guided and are on the right track? Do all believers in some faith believe in the same thing, come to the same conclusion, or agree on what their inner feelings have convinced them of? The answer, of course, is negative.

116 Founder II: Poet–Preacher–Politician

In fact although people keep trying, there is usually no way to mediate a religious dispute. This is why different sects exist within a religion, with each sect believing it alone has the monopoly of truth. As a concrete example, try convincing a Sunni to abandon his faith and convert into the Shia faith or vice versa. This is mission impossible in almost all cases. Each feels and knows from "within himself" what the real truth is. Their heart is speaking!

Philosophers generally attempt to grapple with difficult questions – what happens when two different, deeply held intuitions collide? Although Iqbal systematically downgrades empirical evidence, he makes no attempt to acknowledge that this basic dilemma exists, much less propose a solution. Faith derives from the particular environment and personal experiences of an individual. This raises a fundamental difficulty: if the belief system I acquired at my birth is different from the belief system given to you at your birth, how is one to judge which one is correct? While Iqbal is convinced of having found the correct faith (or that the right faith found him), he does not provide us even a hint of what others should do. Sure, listen to the heart. But what if my heart is a jumbled mess and everybody started following their own jumbled messes?

A case in point is the search for the right god. In old times, tribal peoples would simply switch over into worshipping the winner's gods after losing a war. This made sense – one god was more powerful than another and so had to be the right one. The genealogy in *Zindah Rood* says Iqbal's great-grandparents had been polytheistic Kashmiri Pandits before they converted to monotheistic Islam which was then on the ascendancy. Then somewhere along the chain of descent, the Ahmadiyya faith also came into the family. In his book on the Ahmadiyya movement, Spencer Lavan writes that, "Muhammad Iqbal's father, Shaykh Nur Muhammad (d-1929), formerly from Sialkot, entered the *bay'at* of Ghulam Ahmad in 1891. In their youth, Muhammad Iqbal and his brother Ata Muhammad considered themselves members of the Ahmadiyya community and spoke of their faith in Ahmad as *masih maw'ud*".[23] However, Iqbal's own relationship with Ahmadiyyat evolved over time. It appears plausible that Iqbal, whose native Sialkot hosted a larger Ahmadiyya milieu, had indeed flirted with Ahmadiyya ideology even if briefly only. The daily *Nawa-i Waqt* – a right-wing Urdu newspaper from Lahore that frequently carries quotes from Iqbal on its editorial pages – wrote on 15 November 1953 that, "in 1897, Sir Muhammad Iqbal took the (Ahmadiyya) pledge". Ahmadis claim that he had earlier on written several articles proclaiming Ghulam Ahmad "as the greatest religious thinker among modern Indian Muslims" and, even more significantly, that he made a *bayat* with Ahmad in 1897.[24] Because there do not seem to be any surviving writings carrying Iqbal's name wherein he praises Ahmadiyyat, this claim should be taken with a grain of salt. Ahmadis claim that these writings were destroyed in a massive witch hunt.

After his return from the West, Iqbal reassessed his earlier position and strongly denounced the Ahmadiyya faith as heretical, seeing it as even more dangerous than Bahai'ism because of the closeness of its beliefs and practices to mainstream Islam. He called upon the British to declare it as a separate faith.

Founder II: Poet–Preacher–Politician **117**

His fervent opposition to this faith is well known. In 1934, he wrote "Qadianis and Orthodox Muslims" in which he argued that Ahmadis ought to declare themselves a separate community from Indian Muslims.[25] One year later, Nehru responded to Iqbal through a series of pieces in the *Modern Review of Calcutta*, calling into question Iqbal's presuppositions about religion. Iqbal followed up with "Islam and Ahmadism" in 1935, a still more trenchant attack.

Whatever the truth about Iqbal's earlier religious leaning, for the sake of argument, suppose that Iqbal's great-grandfathers had not converted to Islam from Brahmanical Hinduism. Would he have then engaged in writing his brilliant poems in worship of Lord Shiva or Kheer Bhawani? What if he had followed his brother and father into Ahmadism? Iqbal does acknowledge that most people simply carry the faith of their parents but does not tell us why he was able to follow the correct faith. So, if faith can be arbitrarily selected without guidance from reason, how can one possibly know which is the right way for one to go?

While Iqbal gives reason a low status, the chances of agreement between people are slim unless they agree to its use. This is why scientists hail from every part of the world, are of different races, colors, and ethnic origins, and yet can easily work together. Using reason and empirical inquiry, we are no longer at the mercy of some holy text or inspired individuals and so everyone can agree on whether or not the Earth is flat or the sun circles the Earth. Reason is the mother of mathematics, and without mathematics there could not be science. Take away science and there would be no Industrial Revolution, no machines, no factories, no life-saving medicines, and no cars or computers. Science is enormously successful simply because it doesn't care about your likes and dislikes, fears or hopes, and beliefs or convictions. In describing how nature works, we assume that there are laws in place that care nothing about our existence and so nature does what it does whether we like it or not. Science has no room for holy men or personal revelations because these are neither repeatable nor verifiable.

This is the very opposite for other worldly affairs. Here the consequences of dogma can be deeply pernicious and dangerous. Carried away by the power of faith, men are known to commit the most terrible of atrocities. The Bible speaks of the Israelites killing every man, woman, child (and beast) in Jericho at the command of their god Yahweh and performing other gruesome deeds in the confident belief that they were privileged by being His Chosen People (*Deuteronomy 6:21*). And in Syria and Iraq, the grisly deeds of the Islamic State owe to Salafists who have sworn to protect the purity of the Qur'an. One wonders, what would Iqbal have to say about them? Now that Afghanistan is under rule of the Taliban, would Iqbal have had second thoughts? Have the members of Da'esh and Boko Haram not listened to their hearts? To quote Steven Weinberg, Nobel Prize winning physicist, "With or without religion, good people can behave well and bad people can do evil; but for good people to do evil – that takes religion."

Or to take another example: if revelation is indeed the giver of truth, should we also accept that God told President G.W. Bush to invade Iraq? Of course he

118 Founder II: Poet–Preacher–Politician

could be lying but how can we be sure? Iqbal errs fundamentally in placing the heart at the center – even if the heart is understood as being symbolic of something else. It is well known today that different physical states of the brain – and emotions in particular – can be induced through the environment or consuming various substances and it is experimentally verified that these result in different moods. Neuroscience is making ever more precise the nature of emotions, to the point that specific areas can be watched in 3-D for electrical activity.

Once objectivity is lost, all that remains is feeling and intuition. Science becomes impossible, but Iqbal is unconcerned. He is not interested in seeking to make Islam consistent with science and knowledge – his goal is to Islamicize these, a theme that remains popular today. Of course, one might argue that a world without science would be a better world – there would be no nuclear weapons or threat of catastrophic climate change – but you cannot dispute that modern civilization would be impossible without reason and science. Bertrand Russell put it eloquently:

> If Homer and Aeschylus had not existed, if Dante and Shakespeare had not written a line, if Bach and Beethoven had been silent, the daily life of most people in the present day would have been much what it is. But if Pythagoras and Galileo and James Watt had not existed, the daily life not only of Western Europeans and Americans but of Russian and Chinese peasants would be profoundly different from what it is. And these profound changes are still only beginning.[26]

Humanity is undoubtedly still searching for answers to fundamental questions, and philosophers do not pretend to know the absolute truth. The challenges of modernity are enormous. Russell notes that "scientific technique advances like an army of tanks that have lost their drivers, blindly, ruthlessly, without goal or purpose. This is largely because the men who are concerned with human values and with making life worthy to be lived are still in imagination in the old pre-industrial world".[27] Unless guided by compassion, reason alone cannot answer every question. While faith may give answers to all questions, we cannot know whether these are the right ones. Humanism, while it relies upon the power of reason and science, well knows that scientific discoveries must be supplemented with ethical and moral values that allow us to live with these advances.

Iqbal's physics/math criticisms

> The great achievements of Muslim scholars in mathematics, sociology, medicine and physics are still locked up in different libraries of the world. It is urgent to bring these to light…ideas that western scholars found new and novel had actually been discovered by Arab scholars centuries ago. *Einstein's theory of relativity was new for Europe but Islamic scholars had already discovered its basic premises hundreds of years earlier*[emphasis added].

Founder II: Poet–Preacher–Politician **119**

To understand Bergson's philosophy of differentiation you need to read Ibn-e-Khaldun first.[28]

— Muhammad Iqbal: presidential address, Hailey Hall,
Punjab University, 15 April 1933

A genius when it comes to expressing feelings and beliefs, Iqbal is at his very weakest when he attempts to comment on matters of physics and mathematics. Just as a house physician or veterinarian is unprepared for performing cardiac or neurosurgery, so also was Iqbal when he challenged the mightiest of science's giants of his times. Perhaps if he had studied these subjects at the college level – which he did not – he might not have attempted his sweeping critiques, some of which are detailed below in this section. Noted scholars of Iqbal educated in the liberal arts have nevertheless sought to outdo each other with their panegyrics and, like ordinary readers, have been awed by his references to the great scientific minds of his times. Thus they have looked no further and have wrongly assumed that Iqbal had somehow mastered the concept of infinity as used in the mathematical sense, as well as understood the nature of space–time in Einstein's theory of special and general relativity. These are unfounded assumptions. In this section, using direct quotes from Iqbal, I will show that he was appallingly uninformed of math and physics fundamentals and thus unequipped to make the remarks that he did make.

Before coming to Iqbal's specific statements, it is important to know that while blithe references to infinity are common, in fact there are an infinite number of types of infinities (defined by what is called their cardinalities). This was established by George Cantor (1845–1918) and then carried further by mathematical giants such as Kurt Gödel (1906–1978). The concepts are so difficult to master that students take years to reach the level where the subtleties can be understood. Physics has a similar story. Relativity grew naturally from developments in the theory of electricity and magnetism, codified into what are now known as Maxwell's equations. These equations are barely three hundred years old. As for Einstein's General Theory of Relativity: this presupposes knowledge of tensor calculus in curved spaces, a still later 19th-century creation of the mathematical genius, Bernhard Riemann. To comment on the nature of space–time without the arduous effort needed to learn these difficult subjects is not meaningful.

Iqbal's claim during his lecture at Punjab University (quoted at the beginning of this section) that Einstein's Relativity Theory was known to ancient Islamic scholars is patently absurd. By asserting cultural and religious pride in this manner, Iqbal opened the doors to multiple spurious claims. Today it is far from unusual to hear that the Big Bang theory is contained in the Qur'an, or that space travel and quantum mechanics were long anticipated in the holy book. One is also sometimes told that calculus is actually an Arab invention, as is the idea that humans can fly. Freed from fact, and driven only by the heart, wishful thinking soars into the skies. These claims are no less ridiculous than those of Hindu fundamentalists who say that Vedic period civilization possessed cars, had means

120 Founder II: Poet–Preacher–Politician

of interplanetary travel, and invented plastic surgery as well as the internet. By letting cultural and religious pride overwhelm him, Iqbal unwittingly set the stage for many such later claims.

In *Reconstruction*, Iqbal attempts to marshal his arguments on the inadequacy of science by quoting an impressive range of western mathematicians, philosophers, and scientists. A few of those he casually names include Einstein, Russell, Kant, Whitehead, Cantor, Berkeley, Descartes, Bergson, Haldane, Driesch, Ouspensky, Hocking, and William James. But he did not have the necessary grounding to absorb their technical and scientific arguments, and he shows little understanding of their actual work. In parts of *Reconstruction*, he largely confines himself to quoting what one scientist said about another hoping that they are in contradiction with each other. But then it steadily gets worse: Zeno's Paradox, Cantor sets, and General Relativity all get thrown into a meat grinder – what emerges on the other side is a mass of confusion.

Let me now come to some specific claims made by Iqbal which are either factually false or empty of content.

> Thus physics, finding it necessary to criticize its own foundations, has eventually found reason to break its own idol, and the empirical attitude which appeared to necessitate scientific materialism has finally ended in a revolt against matter…the concept of matter has received the greatest blow from the hand of Einstein.[29]

This is wrong! The concept of matter did not receive a blow from Einstein. In the Special Theory of Relativity (1905), he merely refined its meaning and showed that matter and energy are convertible into each other (that's what led to the bomb and, equally, a variety of modern medical diagnostics such as PET scans now commonly available in hospitals). Then, in the General Theory of Relativity (1916), Einstein showed that matter is a source of the curvature of the space–time in which we live. This was both a clarification of what matter can do and an advance on Newtonian gravity. General Relativity is a highly mathematical subject and something that no person untutored in non-Euclidean geometry can really understand (although popular accounts do exist today for the layman). It is senseless to speak about a "revolt against matter" as Iqbal alleges.

Even if one agrees to forgive this as a solitary mistake, more worrying is that Iqbal seems unaware of the Baconian scientific method and how science is eternally evolving – a fact which is the source of its strength, not weakness. Science *always* seeks deeper foundations by relentlessly testing its assumptions and subjecting them to severe critique. In fact, science recognizes ideas and individuals for their importance; they are not religious idols to be worshipped and preserved. Iconic figures and theories are replaced from time to time in the natural course of things. Far from scientists being frustrated when science had to "break its own idols", the world of science saw it as a matter of

Founder II: Poet–Preacher–Politician **121**

great pride and achievement when Newtonian mechanics was proved inadequate using the very tools that were invented by Newton and his successors. Although the older mechanics was supplemented by Einsteinian mechanics, this was improved upon but did not negate the older theory in its domain of applicability.

In his Second Lecture in *Reconstruction*, Iqbal's lack of formal training in physics and mathematics is evident when he brings up Zeno's Paradox and then attempts to relate it to the nature of space–time:

> The criticism of the foundations of the mathematical sciences has fully disclosed that the hypothesis of a pure materiality, an enduring stuff situated in an absolute space, is unworkable. Is space an independent void in which things are situated and which would remain intact if all things were withdrawn? The ancient Greek philosopher Zeno approached the problem of space through the question of movement in space.[30]

In the above-quoted paragraph three different, unconnected issues are wrongly conflated with each other, giving the impression of profundity. In fact these are three stand-alone unconnected sentences dealing with very different things. Let's look at them one by one.

The first sentence: "The criticism of the foundations of the mathematical sciences has fully disclosed that the hypothesis of a pure materiality, an enduring stuff situated in an absolute space, is unworkable". Iqbal's reference here to pure materiality is a reference to something called the ether hypothesis. This was a substance that was assumed to be weightless and transparent filling all space, hypothesized to make possible the transmission of light. This hypothesis was disproved by experiment (the Michelson–Morley experiment in 1887), not by mathematical science as Iqbal seems to think. In fact, mathematics would have no problem with the existence of ether or, equally, of its nonexistence.

The second sentence: "Is space an independent void in which things are situated and which would remain intact if all things were withdrawn?". If Iqbal had actually understood the principles of General Relativity, he would never have asked this question. General Relativity says most emphatically that space does not remain intact by the introduction of matter. Exactly how much it changes is measured by the extent of modification or curvature of space, and this amount is exactly determined by Einstein's equations.

The third sentence: "The ancient Greek philosopher Zeno approached the problem of space through the question of movement in space". One is puzzled by what this sentence has to do with the preceding two quoted sentences or with earlier parts of the chapter. Zeno's paradox (actually there are several paradoxes named after Zeno, and more have been invented in recent times) has to do with the nature of mathematical infinity, continuity, and the theory of numbers. It was a theoretical question posed within what mathematicians call a space with fixed metric – i.e., a rigid or Euclidean space–time.

To see the irrelevance of the quoted paragraph, imagine for yourself that someone randomly sprayed red, blue, and green paint on a canvas. Even by the relaxed standards of abstract art, does that make a painting? The three sentences I have dwelt upon above have no connection at all with each other. Yet Iqbal's awestruck admirers have not probed his writings on science and philosophy for meaningful content; they simply gasp in amazement at the "deep" questions he raises.

As two final examples from *Reconstruction*: "The mathematical conception of continuity as infinite series applies not to movement regarded as an act, but rather to the picture of movement as viewed from the outside".[31] Any undergraduate student who has taken a course in mathematical topology would know that this is a meaningless comment. Movement in time is irrelevant in matters of continuity, and infinite series have absolutely nothing to do with the continuity of functions. Similarly anyone familiar with relativity theory will immediately fault Iqbal's statement, "Substance for modern Relativity-Physics is not a persistent thing with variable states, but a system of interrelated events".[32] But an event is mathematically a point in space–time and exists independent of substance. An undergraduate physics student learns that at the very beginning of a course on Relativity.

In his attempt to philosophize and appear knowledgeable, Iqbal went out of his depth. No philosophical journal of repute would have considered such observations worthy of its pages. They would have been rejected even in a student term paper. Unsurprisingly, Iqbal never published professionally as a philosopher.

Iqbal's "higher" communalism

> Communalism *in its higher aspect* (emphasis added), then, is indispensable to the formation of a harmonious whole in a country like India. The units of Indian society are not territorial as in European countries. India is a continent of human groups belonging to different races, speaking different languages, and professing different religions... The principle of European democracy cannot be applied to India without recognising the fact of communal groups. The Muslim demand for the creation of a Muslim India within India is, therefore, perfectly justified.
>
> *– Dr. Muhammad Iqbal, presidential address at the 25th annual session of the All-India Muslim League, on the afternoon of Monday, 29 December 1930, at Allahabad, British India*

Communalism, as is generally understood, is a negation of universalism. What then are we to make of Iqbal speaking of a "higher aspect" of communalism? Iqbal is perfectly correct in stating that India is fragmented, far from homogeneous. Indeed, there were and still are countless differences between the many different peoples of India of every kind – religious, linguistic, caste, and color. They cannot be wished away. This very question had also vexed Rabindranath

Founder II: Poet–Preacher–Politician **123**

Tagore[33]. He was conscious that the extended human family would live in an overall public space, but there was also the need for special types of individual and group space. Tagore wrote,

> There is a private corner for me in my house with a little table, which has its special fittings of pen and inkstand and paper, and here I can do my writing and other work. There is no reason to run down, or run away from this corner of mine, because in it I cannot invite and provide for all my friends and guests. It may be that this corner is too narrow or too close, or too untidy, so that my doctor may object, my friends remonstrate, my enemies sneer… My point is that if all the rooms in my house be likewise solely for my own special convenience, if there be no reception room for my friends or accommodation for my guests, then indeed I may be blamed. Then with bowed head I must confess that in my house no great meeting of friends can ever take place.[34]

In acknowledging the need for separate communities to inhabit separate spaces, Tagore was a communalist – albeit of a higher kind. He is arguing for a private space, yet insisting that the public space – where all communities may live – must also exist. So how should we think of Iqbal? Was he a communalist – also perhaps of an enlightened kind?

The early Iqbal is still remembered in India for singing praises to the beauty of a land that knew no division between its peoples. He was truly a universalist in that phase:

Proud indeed of Ram is Hindustan	ہے رام کے وجود پہ ہندوستاں کو ناز
Men of wisdom know Him as head of Hind	اہل نظر سمجھتے ہیں اس کو امام ہند

His best known poem is *tarana-e-Hindi* (anthem of Hindustan), written for children in the *ghazal* style of Urdu poetry and published in the weekly journal *Ittehad* on 16 August 1904. Iqbal recited it in the following year at Government College Lahore. Thereafter, it became enormously popular and was sung as an anthem of opposition to the Raj. But even more, it was a passionate call for people to reject their division by religion.

Better than the entire world is our Hindustan	سارے جہاں سے اچھا، ہندوستاں ہمارا
We are its nightingales, and it's our garden abode	ہم بلبلیں ہیں اس کی، یہ گلستاں ہمارا
O' flowing waters of the Ganges recall you that day	اے آبِ رودِ گنگا! وہ دن ہے یاد تجھ کو؟
When our caravan first disembarked by your side?	اترا ترے کنارے، جب کارواں ہمارا
To divide ourselves is not religion's teaching	مذہب نہیں سکھاتا، آپس میں بیر رکھنا
We are of Hind, our homeland is Hindustan	ہندی ہیں ہم، وطن ہے ہندوستاں ہمارا

In this poem everyone was accommodated, and both individuals and groups could come together in ever-widening circles of inclusion and integration. Although

124 Founder II: Poet–Preacher–Politician

growing Hindutva sentiment may not allow this for long, the celebration of diversity in *tarana-e-Hindi* is still popular in India and taught in schools. But upon returning to India in 1908 – and certainly by 1910 – Iqbal had become a man possessed with very different sentiments. To negate *tarana-e-Hindi* he wrote *tarana-e-milli* (anthem of the community). He made it a point to use the same stanza and meter. Its content could not have been more angry, militant, and rejectionist:

China and Arabia are ours; Hindustan is ours	چین و عرب ہمارا، ہندوستاں ہمارا
Muslims are we; the world is ours	مسلم ہیں ہم، وطن ہے سارا جہاں ہمارا
In the shadow of the sword have we grown	تیغوں کے سائے میں ہم، پل کر جواں ہوئے ہیں
The scimitar of the crescent stands as our emblem	خنجر ہلال کا ہے ، قومی نشاں ہمارا
The valleys of the West reverberated with the *azan*	مغرب کی وادیوں میں، گونجی اذاں ہماری
None could stem our onward flow	تھمتا نہ تھا کسی سے، سیلِ رواں ہمارا

Iqbal's biographer, his son Javaid Iqbal, says his father could not stand the sight of blood and would not watch cows or goats being sacrificed. But now Iqbal's poetry steadily dwelt upon the greatness of Islam and conquests through blood, gore, scimitar, sword, and dagger. He seeks metaphors in Qur'anic verses that call the true believer to war. This martial poetry, accompanied by martial music, or perhaps sung by accomplished singers like Nur Jehan, was on the lips of Pakistanis (like myself!) during the 1965 war with India.

O' warriors, fighters for the Faith	یہ غازی، یہ تیرے پر اسرار بندے
They to who You have granted Belief	جنہیں تو نے بخشا ہے ذوقِ خدائی
Who cleave through land and river	دو نیم ان کی ٹھوکر سے صحرا و دریا
Whose terror turns mountains into dust	سمٹ کر پہاڑ ان کی ہیبت سے رائی
The true believer longs for martyrdom	شہادت ہے مطلوب و مقصودِ مومن
He desires neither booty nor luxury	نہ مالِ غنیمت، نہ کشور کشائی

One of Iqbal's outstanding poems is *shikwa* (complaint), written a year after his return from Europe. As in Samuel Huntington's famous clash of civilizations thesis, Iqbal puts it all in stark us-versus-them terms. He extols the role of early Islam where, with sword and dagger in hand, Muslims conquered the globe in Allah's name and brought truth to the world. Why has an Omnipotent and Omniscient Allah become indifferent to the suffering and defeat of his worshippers, allowing them to be trampled under the feet of unbelievers? Iqbal reminds God of the sacrifices rendered:

Our *azan* reverberated in the cathedrals of Europe	دیں اذانیں کبھی یورپ کے کلیسائوں میں
And over the burning sands of Africa's deserts	کبھی افریقہ کے تپتے ہوئے صحرائوں میں
We cared not for earthly pomp and show	شان آنکھوں میں نہ جچتی تھی جہاں داروں کی
Instead we prayed in the shadow of our swords	کلمہ پڑھتے تھے ہم چھاؤں میں تلواروں کی

Founder II: Poet–Preacher–Politician **125**

For all the fiery Islamism here, the orthodoxy was not amused about Iqbal complaining to God about God not having redeemed his promises. This is not what the faithful are permitted to do. Taken aback by their displeasure, Iqbal crafted *jawab-e-shikwa* (reply to the complaint). God's answer came back loud and clear – you have been insufficiently good enough Muslims so seize now upon the Faith and all shall be well. This mollified the clergy sufficiently, and so the dual-set of poems is now a venerated part of Urdu literature.

Let me return to the question posed earlier: was Iqbal a communalist and, if so, was he one of a "higher order"? Did he want the rebirth of both communities, Muslim and Hindu, or was he committed only to Muslims? Asked whether his prescription for seeking answers in faith was universal for all times and all peoples or limited to Muslims only, Iqbal responded:

> My real purpose is to look for a better social order and to present a universally acceptable ideal (of life and action) before the world, but it is impossible for me, in this effort to outlive this ideal, to ignore the social system and values of Islam whose most important objective is to demolish all the artificial and pernicious distinctions of caste, creed, color and economic status.... when I realized that the conception of nationalism based on the differences of race and country was beginning to overshadow the world and that the Muslims also were in danger of giving up the universality of their ideal in favor of a narrow patriotism and false nationalism, I felt it my duty as a Muslim and a well-wisher of humanity to recall them back to their true role in the drama of human evolution. No doubt, I am intensely devoted to Islam but I have selected the Islamic community as my starting point not because of any national or religious prejudice but because it is the most practicable line of approach.[35]

Iqbal assured Hindus that creating separate Muslim states would allow Hindus and Muslims to prosper separately, and Muslim states would not impose religious rule (i.e., the sharia) upon Hindus. It is unclear how that could be possible because Iqbal abhorred the secular state, which was the very reason he opposed reform in Hinduism as well as those Hindu reformers who sought to secularize Hinduism by liberating it from orthodox practices.[36] He even called for the British to protect traditional Hinduism: "I very much appreciate the orthodox Hindus' demands for protection against religious reformers in the new constitution. Indeed this demand ought to have been first made by the Muslims".[37]

In the last phase of his life, Iqbal took on a completely Muslim identity and sought to distance himself from every symbol of a non-Muslim culture and civilization. His son recalls that Iqbal would lose his temper if he (Javaid) did not wear the traditional *achkan* and *shalwar*.[38] Pants were not allowed. He was allowed to watch only two movies, both historical ones. Daughter Munira, then 10–11 years old, was told to stop parting her hair and braiding it. When she asked why, he simply replied – because Jews do that.[39]

Iqbal's earlier enthusiasm for Hindu–Muslim unity dissipated as he got deeper into politics. Initially he advocated two separate electorates but then increasingly

126 Founder II: Poet–Preacher–Politician

saw them as two nations that must no longer live together. At political rallies he would stress in fiery speeches that Hindus and Muslims were different to the core and began to use the word "mullah" to denigrate Muslim scholars like Maulana Abul Kalam Azad and Maulana Hussain Ahmed Madani because of their belief that Muslims did not need a separate territory to practice Islam:

Just because he is allowed to pray in Hindustan ملا کو جو ہے ہند میں سجدے کی اجازت

The foolish mullah thinks that Islam has been liberated ناداں یہ سمجھتا ہے کہ اسلام ہے آزاد

Over the years, Iqbal became a powerful orator who addressed crowds at Bhatti Gate in Lahore, the popular venue for public demonstrations. In 1930 he was elected president of the Muslim League. Iqbal is often said to be the first Muslim leader to have made a demand for Pakistan. However, this is factually false since many lesser-known persons – Chaudhry Rehmat Ali in particular – had from time to time made the demand for a separate Muslim state.

Iqbal on women

Almost all great scientists and philosophers, poets and writers, have had complex, personal lives. Iqbal was no exception. With one true love, three wives, and married four times (twice to the same woman) he was not a happy man for much of his life. Many have written on his personal life.[40] To pursue this further here would be inappropriate since my intent is to discuss his messages to society. But an important question demands an answer: why did Iqbal, a man of exceptional intelligence and exposure to liberal philosophy, have such an exceedingly low opinion of the female sex? Of his contempt there can be little doubt:

Not veil or education whether new or old can suffice نے پردہ ، نے تعلیم ، نئی ہو کہ پرانی

Man alone can guard woman's femininity: نسوانیتِ زن کا نگہباں ہے فقط مرد

A nation oblivious to this living truth جس قوم نے اس زندہ حقیقت کو نہ پایا

Is doomed to see its sun grow pale اس قوم کا خورشید بہت جلد ہوا زرد

Iqbal conceived of man taking charge of his own destiny and struggle for an ever better life by obtaining still higher levels of consciousness. In developing this noble concept of *khudi* (ego, self-worth), the ideal Muslim would be so firm of purpose and determination that even God would have to acknowledge the strength of his inner will. The *khuda mard* (or a Muslim Übermensch) would defeat men of all other faiths and create an Islamic utopia. But, alas, woman was to have no part in Iqbal's reconstructed universe. Wilfred Cantwell Smith remarks,[41]

> Even at his most poetic, his most progressive, his most inclusively uto-pian, he never wished that the new values should apply to more than half the human race. He never understood, and he constantly fought against, those who deem that women too might share in the brave new world. He imagined European women heartless, hating maternity, love, and life; he

wanted women 'pure' and in subjection. For women he wanted no activism, no freedom, no vice-regency of God...she should remain a means to an end. Iqbal kept his own wives in purdah and untiringly he preached to the world his conception of the ideal woman:

In his collection of Persian poems, *ramuz-e-beykhudi*, Iqbal identifies Fatimah, the Holy Prophet's daughter, as the ultimate to which any woman can aspire:

The chaste Fatimah is the harvest of the field of submission	مــزرع تسلیم را حاصل بتول
The chaste Fatimah is a perfect model for mothers.	مادراں را اسوہٴ کامـل بتول
She who might command the spirits of heaven and hell	نوری وہم آتشی فرمانبرـش
Merged her own will in the will of her husband.	گم رضایش دررضاۓ شوہرـش
Her upbringing was in courtesy and forbearance;	آں ادب پروردہ صبر ورضا
And, murmuring the Qur'an, she ground corn.	آسیاگردان و لب فتـرآں سرا

Malala Yusafzai is surely not one who Iqbal would be enamored by; he was deeply uncomfortable with Indian Muslim girls seeking an education in English schools and, heaven forbid, learning English!

Girls are learning English these days	لڑکیاں پڑھ رہی ہیں انگریزی
Driven by the fashion to become modern	ڈھونڈلی قوم نے فلاح کی راہ
So afflicted by westernism are they	روشِں معنربی ہے مدِ نظر
Eastern tradition appears to them as a sin	وضع مشرق کو جانتے ہیں گناہ
How will this drama play out?	یہ ڈراما دکھاۓ گا کیا سین؟
Just wait until they lift the veil/curtain	پردہ اٹھنے کی منتظـر ہے نگاہ

Was Iqbal's opinion about women so low because his wives were intellectually far inferior to him? Though he married Karim Bibi at the age of eighteen and fathered two children, Iqbal had strictly a formal and traditional relationship with her and his subsequent two wives. One feels that Javaid Iqbal, his son, had to steer a difficult course in writing his father's biography, *Zindah Rood*. On the one hand, he must be reverential of a father who stands tall in recent history and therefore spends several pages indignantly repudiating allegations that Iqbal had curried favor with the British, was a wine drinker, and refutes allegations that he had murdered a prostitute. On the other hand, he does not suppress recollections of his troubled childhood and his mother's unhappiness. Surely, in discussing something as delicate as his father's relationship with other women, he has chosen to be extremely circumspect, perhaps defensive.

Nevertheless, Javaid Iqbal still writes enough for the reader to know that when in Europe, Iqbal was perceived as a witty, charming young man whom women were much attracted towards. Waitresses in pubs and teahouses would greet him in familiar terms. Equally, he sought their company. Much in demand at social events

128 Founder II: Poet–Preacher–Politician

because of his sharp witticisms, he would be surrounded by beautiful white English women who would engage him on matters of philosophy and poetry. Upon going to Germany, it took almost no time for him to make other women friends. At one of many picnics in the countryside, Iqbal joyfully recalls long walks with his friends to where "we held hands, walked in two's and three's, and reached Heidelberg happy and exhausted".[42] In India's conservative society, holding hands publicly with any woman would be unthinkable. Remarkably, even as he was entering into the anti-West phase of his life, Iqbal wistfully recalls those Heidelberg days as his happiest.

No woman attracted Iqbal more than Atiya Faizee. A Gujarati-speaking Sulaimani Bohra from the Tyabjee-Faizee family, she was born in Constantinople where her father served as chamberlain at court. Educated in London, she was the first woman from South Asia to have attended the University of Cambridge. A modern western woman of high culture, she was attractive and unveiled and had just graduated from a teachers' training college. Atiya and Iqbal met often in Cambridge, taking long walks together. It was a meeting of minds, but not just that. Her letters – many of which she destroyed because they may have conveyed excessive intimacy – suggest that their relationship had grown well beyond the intellectual. Soon after leaving England, Iqbal invited her to visit Heidelberg. Atiya promptly accepted.

Iqbal separated from Sardar Begum, Javaid Iqbal's mother, soon after his return to Lahore. Perhaps it had become impossible to be with her after he had encountered women who were educated, intelligent, and free. Although he could not bear to have her around the house, he agreed to keep supporting her financially. Desperately unhappy, he kept up his correspondence with Atiya for many years. But he never proposed to her. Javaid Iqbal offers the following explanation:

> Iqbal may have wanted her [Atiya] to become his life partner but he felt his household had too crude a lifestyle for her to fit in. Then, he was not in good financial shape and there were uncertainties. He was also now getting deeply involved with his worldly (*duniya-darana*) work. Add to all this the fact that although he respected Atiya's high education and intellectual capability, a woman of this kind would be prone to think that freedom (*azadi*) was her right. But freedom was something that Iqbal could not countenance in his world. So this love affair was ultimately unsuccessful. [43]

Wilfred Cantwell Smith was incorrect in asserting that Iqbal "imagined European women heartless, hating maternity, love, and life". He clearly did not think of Atiya Faizee in this way, or of Emma Wegenast, his German philosophy teacher with whom Iqbal had also developed a close friendship. That he considered Indian Muslim women as worthy of becoming good mothers and no more is because he could not conceive of them as equals; to believe so would overturn all that he had worked for.

Until the very end, Iqbal remained committed to upholding the values of a patriarchal society of ancient Arabia. He more than suspected that Atiya wanted

Founder II: Poet–Preacher–Politician **129**

to marry him, but he did not want to risk disapproval from his community. Since he had become a man of destiny whose contribution to India's Muslims would remain inscribed in the annals of history, why risk that just for a marriage? This may be why in his letter addressed to "My Dear Miss Atiya!" he wrote, "I am sure the world will worship me someday after my death. They will forget my sins and give me the tribute of a tear".[44] Whether Miss Atiya chose to forgive we cannot know.

Iqbal on theocracy

On 29 December 1930, Iqbal gave his presidential address in English before the Muslim League's 25th annual session. It was the first articulation by the Muslim League for a separate national state:

> Personally…I would like to see the Punjab, North-West Frontier Province, Sind and Baluchistan amalgamated into a single State. Self-government within the British Empire, or without the British Empire, the formation of a consolidated North-West Indian Muslim State appears to me to be the final destiny of the Muslims, at least of North-West India.

Whereas Bengal may have crossed his mind, he believed it was at too great a cultural distance. Like Sir Syed, he did not consider Bengalis a valorous race. The virile and martial races of what later became West Pakistan were more likely to produce his *mard-e-momin* and the *shaheen*.

One must not think that Iqbal's demand for a separate state with defined boundaries necessarily arose out of some religious requirement. On the contrary, as discussed earlier in this book, religious scholars have strongly disagreed on whether Islam mandates any specific kind of state for Muslims. The Qur'an, by omitting any mention of state, leaves the door open for all kinds of social and political formations. Just a few years earlier, Iqbal had inveighed against the concept of nationalism which, he said, was detrimental to the concept of the *ummah* – a universal brotherhood of Muslims that knew or recognized no geographical boundaries.

Of the new gods the biggest is Nation	ان تازہ خداؤں میں سب سے بڑا اس کا وطن ہے
Its cloak is naught but Religion's death shroud	جو پیرہن اس کا ہے، وہ مذہب کا کفن ہے

All this changed when Iqbal recognized the enthusiasm of Indian Muslim nationalism. He now sought a new state for Muslims that would separate them from Hindus. But what kind of state would it be? As we shall see in Chapter Eleven, Islam does not provide a unique answer to this. Would it be democratic, run by the will of its people? We are left guessing because Iqbal gives no clear answer. One might have expected that the word "democracy" would occur repeatedly in Iqbal's major work in political philosophy, *The Reconstruction of Religious Thought in Islam*.

130 Founder II: Poet–Preacher–Politician

However, searching the text reveals that it occurs only once in a phrase where he states, "spiritual democracy, which is the ultimate aim of Islam." What does it mean? Could it mean conversion to a state of mind where all become identical? To derive any kind of operational meaning from this phrase appears difficult.

In his Urdu poetry, Iqbal is far clearer – he pours contempt upon a system where all citizens are equal in political terms. It amounts to, he says, accepting the tyranny of the masses.

Democracy is a certain way of governing wherein جمہوریت اک طرزِ حکومت ہے کہ جس میں

Men are merely counted, not weighed بندوں کو گنا کرتے ہیں تولا نہیں کرتے

With democracy thus disparaged, one is left with the question: is Iqbal suggesting that monarchy or dictatorship is to be preferred? We do not hear a clear answer in his Urdu poetry. This very fact has hugely reduced his political relevance – people everywhere today, including Pakistan, want representative political rule. While they pay lip service to arcane issues of Islamic ethics and the ideal Medina state, what they actually want is a system of governance and a means of choosing leaders. Iqbal does not have a plausible scheme to offer.

In poem after poem, Iqbal flays western democracy for having separated religion from politics:

For me this politics is atheistic مری نگاہ میں ہے یہ سیاستِ لادیں

The devil's mistress, greedy and without conscience کنیزِ اہرمن و دوں نہاد و مردہ ضمیر

The "false democracies" in the West that prize economic opportunities over morality are merely farcical, he says, and can offer no hope. He denounces nationalism as idolatry and blames democracy for having created imperialism. Elsewhere he equates secular democracy with barbarism because it separates faith and politics:

Be it monarchy or the circus of democracy حبلال پادشاہی ہو کہ جمہوری تماشا ہو

Politics separated from faith is *changezi* جدا ہو دیں سیاست سے تو رہ جاتی ہے چنگیزی

The word *changezi* features often in Iqbal's Urdu poetry, especially with reference to European nationalism and imperialism. Derived from Changez Khan (Genghis Khan), it signifies ruthless expansionism, bloody tyranny, and ambition.

Wasn't Iqbal aware of counterexamples within Europe, with Iceland being one example? As the world's oldest parliamentary democracy, it has Lutheranism nominally as its state religion but has a firmly secular democratic constitution. Anyone is eligible to vote or can stand for parliament. Iceland is only one of many countries. Today, secular democracies across the world – Sweden, Norway, Denmark, Italy, Germany, Britain, and France, to name some – are peaceful countries towards which Muslim refugees flee and, in doing so, often risk their lives. How could one possibly confuse secularism with *changezi*? Iqbal reiterates his point of view repeatedly, most notably in his famous 1930 Allahabad address:

Is religion a private affair? Would you like to see Islam, as a moral and political ideal, meeting the same fate in the world of Islam as Christianity has already met in Europe? Is it possible to retain Islam as an ethical ideal and to reject it as a polity in favour of national politics in which religious attitude is not permitted to play any part?[45]

In *Reconstruction*, Iqbal advocates that Muslims create modern national states built around the following three principles: (1) No separation would be permitted between the spiritual and temporal, (2) All laws would have to be consistent with Qur'an, and (3) New legislation that is appropriate for the modern era would be prepared through applying the principle of *ijtihad* wherein consistency with Islamic precepts would be the guide.

Iqbal was a reformer – the state he envisioned would be run by a grand *ijtihad* council that would deliberate on new legislation for civil and criminal matters. A parliament, which would include non-Muslim members, would be elected by ordinary men (Iqbal could find no way around that, but he does not mention votes by women). Modernization of Islam would follow – polygamy and slavery would be forbidden by the state and a new set of Islamic rules would be defined. These were modest changes but had the result of drawing the orthodoxy's ire. This is almost certainly the reason why Iqbal chose to express these thoughts in English, a language that most mullahs could not read.

In creating the concept of a shared community, how does one deal with vast differences between the rich and the weak, the powerful and the weak? Iqbal's answer was: to belong to the *ummah* is more important than seeking to address these differences. And so Mahmood (the king, Mahmood Ghaznavi) and his faithful slave (Ayyaz) by standing in the same prayer line, become equals before God:

Standing side by side were Mahmood and Ayyaz	ایک ہی صف میں کھڑے ہو گئے محمود وایاز
None was small and none was great	نہ کوئی بندہ رہا اور نہ کوئی بندہ نواز
Weak and strong, servant and patron	بندہ و صاحب و محتاج و غنی ایک ہوئے
Before Thee they bowed and became one	تیری سرکار میں پہنچے تو سبھی ایک ہوئے

Where would non-Muslims fit into this picture? Iqbal is silent on that. And how did he plan to deal with the centuries-old Shia–Sunni problem? For one who had seen pluralism at work and been its beneficiary, did he not know how important it was to have a framework in which diverse peoples could live together as equals in peace?

Since Iqbal's utopia involves an elected parliament, it might be better termed as a *theodemocracy* instead of a theocracy. Theodemocracy is an idea put forward by Joseph Smith (1805–1844) for his planned Mormon paradise. In Smith's system, God was to be the ultimate power and would give law to the people who would then exercise it on the principles underlying a liberal democracy. Sovereignty would reside jointly with the people and with God. For the most part, it would be men who would rule it through a Supreme Council, debating issues until consensus is reached. The limits to what the Supreme Council is allowed to do

132 Founder II: Poet–Preacher–Politician

would be set by the Supreme Ruler (Smith). This is close to what Iqbal demands in *Reconstruction*. When Ayatollah Khamenei said Iran was "exactly following the path that was shown to us by Iqbal", he was unaware of Smith!

In calling for a theodemocracy – or perhaps even multiple theodemocracies – Iqbal simply states his ideological position but does not argue why that is correct or how this could lead to a more moral, peaceful, and successful society. He dares not attempt to grapple with historical or practical realities such as existed in his time. Let us see what his ideas might mean in the context of today's world.

1. Iqbal critiques western secularist democracy as soulless. One must ask: would countries in Europe be better off if they brought Christianity back into their national political systems? Presumably Germany should become a Lutheran-Protestant-Catholic-Calvinist state, France should revert to Catholicism, Britain should formally declare itself run by Anglican-Catholic law, etc. But Europe, which was ravaged by a series of religious wars that included the Hundred Years War and the Thirty Years War, has no appetite for interstate conflict based on religion. It has even less patience for intrastate religious conflict. Except for lingering Catholic–Protestant feuding in Northern Ireland, Europe has dispensed with this scourge and would gain little by inserting religion back into politics.

2. European countries – more so today than in Iqbal's times – have large Muslim populations and are magnets for peoples everywhere, particularly from Muslim countries. While a level of discrimination exists after terrorist attacks by extreme Islamic groups, by law, Muslims enjoy the same rights, protections, and privileges as others. These can exist only in a secular state where the religious affiliation of a citizen is irrelevant. If today's Europe comprised Christian states where Christianity is fully practiced, peoples of other faiths living there would have long turned into second-class citizens – as indeed non-Muslims are in Pakistan.

3. In recommending theocracy as the preferred state of government, was Iqbal not aware of the bitter Sunni–Shia division that would be exacerbated if one party saw itself as being treated unequally, or if that party was made to live under some brand of theocracy that is not its own? The Shias reject the notion of caliphate. In fact they bitterly resent the first three caliphs who followed Prophet Muhammad. Today, as religion plays a larger role than five to six decades ago, the *ummah* finds that it is at war with itself. What other way is there to describe the brutal bloodletting by Muslims of Muslims in Syria, Iraq, Libya, Yemen, Afghanistan, Turkey, and, of course, Pakistan. While this is not all Shia–Sunni conflict, there is certainly plenty of that.

Iqbal on blasphemy

There is scarcely an issue in contemporary Pakistan more sensitive than that of blasphemy and the blasphemy law that awards death – and less – to those

Founder II: Poet–Preacher–Politician **133**

convicted. Scores of convicted blasphemers are presently awaiting their turn on death row. This number is small compared to the hundreds accused of blasphemy who have been killed while in jail or by lynch mobs. Certainly, no case has had greater visibility than that of Punjab governor Salman Taseer, assassinated in 2011 by his security guard Malik Mumtaz Qadri. Five years later, Qadri was hanged. He now enjoys the status of martyr with a shrine having been constructed in Islamabad, visited by tens of thousands every year. The movement around Qadri is today known as the TLP, Tehreek Labbaik Pakistan. Its central demand is that the Prophet's honor be protected and capital punishment inflicted upon blasphemers. According to votes cast in the 2018 national elections, TLP was listed sixth in terms of the number of votes won.[46] In October 2021, TLP succeeded in closing down Lahore.[47]

Qadri's case is often compared to that of Ilm Din, a 19-year-old illiterate son of a carpenter in Lahore. In 1929 Ilm Din stabbed and killed the Hindu publisher of the provocatively titled book *Rangeela Rasool* (The Colourful Prophet) which was disrespectful of Prophet Muhammad and had inflamed communal sentiment. After a trial, Ilm Din was found guilty of murder and executed by the British. In Pakistan he is venerated by a mausoleum over his grave in Lahore. In the KPK province, he is eulogized in school textbooks and multiple myths are wrapped around him. One book published in 2016 says Ilm Din's body remained fresh for fifteen days after the execution.

In 1929 the Ilm Din affair had aroused communalist passions, and Iqbal was then at the center of Muslim politics. He therefore became deeply involved in the public protests to have the offending author and publisher punished. To get a sense of events and moods of the time, I have translated relevant sections of Javaid Iqbal's biography of his father:

> In his book Rangeela Rasool, a certain Hindu of Lahore by the name of Rajpal had insulted the Holy Prophet and his trial lasted about two to two-and-a-half years. But in June 1927 Lahore High Court justice Dilip Singh ruled in favor of Rajpal. This upset Muslims greatly. The Muslim notables of Lahore, which included Iqbal, met with the governor to demand that a law be passed banning any book that could hurt religious sentiments. Instead, the government, fearing communal violence, imposed Section 144. But the Khilafat Committee decided to disobey. To ponder upon the implications of this decision, on 8 July 1927 the notables of Lahore held a meeting at Mohammedan Hall that was presided over by Sir Abdul Qadir. At this meeting Iqbal strongly criticized the book, saying that he did not even want to utter the despicable word Rajpal. But he also said that, given the sensitivity of the moment, civil disobedience would not be appropriate. Then, speaking at another rally on 10 July 1927 at the Shahi Masjid he declared,
>
> "For a Muslim there cannot be anything more hurtful than Rajpal's book. I do not want to take this abominable man's name who has hit the most sensitive part of a Muslim's heart".

134 Founder II: Poet–Preacher–Politician

Together with this, Iqbal again pleaded that at this stage civil disobedience would be unwise. To prevent blasphemy against prophets, or leaders
of the faith, he said he had moved a resolution in the Punjab Council.
Then, two years later, a young man from Lahore, Ilm Din, murdered
Rajpal. Upon hearing the news, Iqbal spontaneously said in Punjabi:
اسی گلاں کردے رے تے ترکھاناں دا منڈا بازی لے گیا "We did nothing but talk. This young
son of a carpenter scooped us."

Ilm Din was arrested, tried in court, and sentenced to death. Upon his
execution, Muslims were very upset. The government feared disturbances
and so refused to hand over his body. Iqbal, together with other Muslim
notables, met with the governor and assured him that peace would be
maintained. The governor agreed. The crowd of 100,000 at the burial of
Ilm Din Shaheed dispersed peacefully after funeral prayers.

Iqbal was undoubtedly jubilant after the murder of Rajpal. It is therefore natural
to speculate how he would have reacted to the assassination of Governor Taseer.
Columnists in Urdu newspapers discussing the issue have claimed that Iqbal, had
he been alive, would have praised Qadri no less than Ilm Din. But this could
well be an unwarranted extrapolation. Taseer had not denigrated any religion
or religious figure and had merely sought a way to modify and prevent misuse
of the existing law. On the other hand, Rajpal's book came at a time of high
Hindu–Muslim tensions, and it raised these still more by deliberately seeking to
insult the Holy Prophet. It was therefore a mischievous act, and so it is hard to
draw a direct parallel between the cases of Qadri and Ilm Din. The only certain
thing one can say is that Iqbal had publicly approved the extra-judicial killing of
someone seen as a blasphemer by the Muslims of that time.

Iqbal and Sir Syed compared

Spaced roughly half a century apart, neither lived long enough to see the birth
of the new Muslim state, but both are venerated in today's school textbooks as
the spiritual founders of Pakistan. Iqbal shares many commonalities with Sir
Syed – the subject of the previous chapter. Both Iqbal and Sir Syed advocated
purdah for Muslim women, and both were scornful of the mullah and *pir*. They
saw the custodianship of Islam as properly belonging to creative individuals like
themselves, who could help interpret Islam for a new age. They would have
also agreed upon rule by privileged elites: as Iqbal famously said, democracy is
a system where people are counted but not weighed. Both had strongly traditional religious backgrounds, both represented the class interests of the Muslim
bourgeoisie. Both eagerly accepted knighthood for their services to the British
Empire although Sir Syed had seen the genocidal fury of the British in 1857, and
Iqbal's award came four years after Jallianwala Bagh's massacre in 1919. That
Tipu Sultan, Subhas Chandra Bose, Bhagat Singh, or Hasrat Mohani could have
been similarly rewarded by the British is inconceivable. While Sir Syed never

Founder II: Poet–Preacher–Politician **135**

criticized imperial rule, Iqbal occasionally did so but only in Urdu and somewhat tangentially. He was careful to keep his anti-imperialism within bounds, pragmatic and unwilling to take personal risks especially when it came to challenging the British on matters that they considered important at a given moment. Tahir Kamran notes that in the effort to keep Iqbal "clean", the Pakistani state is careful not to let anti-colonial resistance come into public view.[48] He notes that in a newspaper article Iqbal had argued that, "An ideal for the Muslims is not the building of an empire but the spreading of their *deen* (faith) and the British government does exactly that".[49]

This softness on the British has also been noted by Baloch[50], who observes that Iqbal refused to lend his support at critical moments to the Khilafat Movement in spite of his enthusiastic pan-Islamism[51]. Muslims, who looked up to Iqbal for guidance, were disappointed. But, saddled with family responsibilities, Iqbal was not inclined to take up cudgels with the British. That he was knighted by King George V in 1922 for services rendered to the British Empire disappointed his acolytes – more so because it came after the massacre at Jallianwala Bagh by British soldiers in 1919 (Tagore had refused knighthood for this reason). But they denied that he had lobbied for the award and claimed it simply came out of the blue to recognize his achievements as a poet. Iqbal remained silent on Palestine although this was intensely debated at the time and Gandhi had come out strongly against the creation of Israel.[52] Asked why he chose not to speak against the British, Iqbal lightly dismissed his role saying he was only a *guftar ka ghazi* (a soldier who fights only with words).[53] Earlier in this chapter, certain similarities between Syed Qutb and Iqbal had been noted. But, although both reacted against the West, Qutb took his convictions to the hangman's noose.

The differences between Iqbal and Sir Syed are just as striking as the similarities. If Sir Syed's journey can be characterized as away from ultra-conservatism towards progressivism, Iqbal's went exactly the other way. Sir Syed envisioned that the rebirth of Muslim greatness in India would come only from learning European science and the English language, returning to the rationalism of the *Mu'tazila*, reviving the spirit of critical inquiry, and, most importantly, reinterpreting Muslim theology in the light of newly discovered scientific facts. His analysis led him to dedicate half his life towards promoting modern education and science among Indian Muslims of his times, albeit in a manner consistent with Muslim traditions.

Iqbal, on the other hand, does not exhort Muslims to educate themselves or engage with the world of science. In fact, he breathes contempt against westernization. In seeking to prove that western science is an inferior form of knowledge, his attitude towards science and modern learning is condescending at best and quite often oppositional. Ignoring the fundamental contributions made by other civilizations – Babylonian, Egyptian, Chinese, and Hindu – he wrongly claims that modern science is a mere continuation of Arab science. What *khudi* (ego) really means – and its relevance if any to the present – should be left to his clan of

136 Founder II: Poet–Preacher–Politician

admirers to explain. Mirza Mahmood Sarhadi (1913–1968), a poet who did not belong to Iqbal's fan club, was openly sarcastic:

We obeyed what the great Iqbal had said	ہم نے اقبال کا کہا مانا
And kept ourselves poor and starving	اور فاقوں کے ہاتھوں مرتے رہے
Those who swallowed their pride kept thriving	جھکنے والوں نے رفعتیں پائیں
On empty stomachs we kept our *khudi* high	ہم خودی کو بلند کرتے رہے

In the battle for Pakistan's soul, Sir Syed's rational approach was eclipsed by the Allama's call to the faith. In his final phases, Iqbal became an unabashed Muslim supremacist who believed in the superiority of Islam over all other religions. This aspect of Iqbal remains concealed in his English writings but is starkly evident in his Urdu poetry and public speeches. He was influenced by the sharp Hindu–Muslim polarization of his times but also contributed to it in the latter parts of his life. Taking literally his exclusionary world view – wherein *dar-ul-Islam* stands in sharp distinction to *dar-ul-harb* – makes impossible the coexistence of Muslims with non-Muslims. The world rightly fears Jewish, Hindu, and Christian supremacists. All cultural narcissists, and all who possess political power and who believe in the intrinsic superiority of their respective faiths, cannot be trusted to be fair to others. There is no reason to think that Muslim supremacists are different.

To conclude: Iqbal's poetry stirs our souls, makes us search within ourselves, and encourages us to confidently rise and meet the challenges of the world. Abandon the mentality of slaves and be your own selves, he says. This carries such universalism that people who think in diametrically opposite ways can feel equally inspired. The earlier part of his life was free of the bitterness and craving for past greatness that was to come later. His negative experiences in Europe somehow outweighed the positive, and so he left us without the tools to lift ourselves and achieve an impartial and factual understanding of the world. Sadly, his misunderstanding of science and passionate denigration of reason leave us defenseless in a world where the way forward is through reason and science guided by compassion and positive human values. Iqbal's loathing of the West blinds him to the reasons why a century later Muslims seek to migrate to countries where freedom of lifestyle and freedom of thought are valued and protected. By opting for communalism over universalism, railing against education for females, praising the killing of blasphemers, and demanding that politics be conjoined with religion, he takes us a step backward from the general trend of humanity. A man of his genius could have shown the way forward. Instead, Iqbal left a confused, uncertain legacy and no clear path for Pakistan.

Notes

1 Muhammad Iqbal, Letter to Atiya Faizee dated 7 July 1909, p. 51, Victory Printing Press, Jyoti Studios Compound, Bombay, 7 February 1947.
2 M. Tabish, *Iqbal – khush gumanian, ghalut fehmian*, Lahore, Fiction House (2019).

Founder II: Poet–Preacher–Politician **137**

3 Iqbal Poetry By Allama Khadim Hussain Rizvi "Pakturk", https://www.youtube .com/watch?v=WSR6TveGWZM

4 Speech delivered by President Sayyid Ali Khamenei at the opening session of the First International Conference on Iqbal, Tehran, 10–12 March 1986, on the occasion of the 108th birth anniversary of the Poet of the Subcontinent. Translation from Persian by Mahliqa Qara'i.

5 D. Hashmi, *Footprints: Finding Iqbal in Germany*, Dawn, 9 November 2015.

6 In the same speech referred to earlier, Ayatollah Khamenei also remarks that Sir Syed had "never done anything positive for Islam and Indian Muslims".

7 Iqbal's Doctoral Thesis, by M. Siddiq Shibli, http://www.allamaiqbal.com/publications/journals/review/apr89/3.htm

8 S. Khalid, *Iqbal: "The Metaphysics" and "The Reconstruction"– Part I*, The News, 9 November 2019.

9 Allama Iqbal ki khidmat main chand lamhay by Dr Ashiq Husain Batalvi in Asaar-e-Iqbal, ed. Ghulam Dastgir Nazir, pp. 39–41, n.d.

10 Sarguzash-i-Iqbal, published in Iqbal and Communism by Waheed Ishrat, http://www.allamaiqbal.com/publications/journals/review/oct91/6.htm

11 Muhammad Iqbal, Letter in Zamindar, Lahore, 24 June 1923. http://www.allamaiqbal.com/publications/journals/review/oct91/6.htm

12 Iqbal Letter to Jinnah of 28 May 1937 in G. Allana, *Pakistan Movement Historical Documents*, Karachi, Department of International Relations, University of Karachi (n.d. [1969]), p. 130.

13 Zindah Rood, *Dr. Javed Iqbal*, Lahore, Sang-e-Meel Publishers (2014), p. 323.

14 Ibid.

15 M. Iqbal, *The Reconstruction of Religious Thought in Islam*, London, Oxford University Press (1934).

16 S.H. Razzaqi, *Discourses of Iqbal*, Lahore, Iqbal Academy (1979), pp. 204–205.

17 Iqbal, Reconstruction, op. cit., p. 1.

18 P. Hoodbhoy, *Islam and Science – Religious Orthodoxy and the Battle for Rationality*, London, Zed Books (1990).

19 Iqbal, Reconstruction, op. cit., p.4.

20 Ibid, p. 4.

21 I have translated *ishq* here to mean *faith* rather than *love* because this is what Iqbal seems to suggest, i.e., love of the Creator and his Prophet. Similarly Iqbal appears to use *ilm* in the sense of *reason* rather than *knowledge*. However, Iqbal's verses have been translated by many, and the reader may instead prefer to choose from among them.

22 Iqbal, Reconstruction, op. cit., p.15.

23 S. Lavan, quoted in *The Ahmadiyah Movement – A History And Perspective*, Dehli, Manohar Book Service (1974), p. 172.

24 Ibid.

25 T. Purohit, Muhammad Iqbal on Muslim Orthodoxy and Transgression: A Response to Nehru, *ReOrient*, 1, no. 1 (2015): 78–92. Accessed May 2, 2021. doi:10.13169/reorient.1.1.0078.

26 B. Russell, Repr. *Fact and Fiction – The Reasoning of Europeans a Talk on the B.B.C. Overseas Service* (1957).

27 Ibid.

28 Rood op. cit., p. 568.

29 Iqbal, Reconstruction, op. cit., p.32.

30 Ibid, p. 33.

31 Ibid, p. 34.

32 Ibid, p. 36.

33 K.M. O'Connell, *Utsav-Celebration: Tagore's Approach to Cultivating the Human Spirit and the Study of Religion*, ISSN 1563-8685 at Parabaas.com.

34 Ibid, quoted in O'Connell, The Centre of Indian Culture in *Towards Universal Man*, New York, Asia Publishing House (1961), pp. 228–229.

138 Founder II: Poet–Preacher–Politician

35 M. Younus, Muhammad Iqbal, quoted in *The Rise of the Crescent: The Sacred Clash*, BookSurge (2006), p. 133.

36 The context here is very specific: Iqbal is suggesting that the British ban the Ahmadiyya faith, which he has come to disagree with by now.

37 Wilfred Cantwell Smith, *Modern Islam in India – A Social Analysis*, Lahore, Minerva Books (1943), p. 160 attributes this to Iqbal quoted in Jawaharlal Nehru, *Orthodox of All Religions, Unite!* In Iqbal's *Islam and Ahmadism*, this point of view is not denied.

38 Rood, op. cit., p. 675.

39 Ibid.

40 R. Zakaria, *Iqbal's Love, Iqbal's Life*, Dawn, 23 November 2013. K. Sohail, *Allama Iqbal – Ek Mehbooba, Teen Beewiyan, Chaar Shadiyan*, published in HumSub (2017, Urdu), translated by Ale Natiq. *Letters and Diary of Atiya Faizi*. Translation by Ziauddin Ahmad Burni, Karachi, Iqbal Academy (1969). Abdul Majeed Salik, *Zikr-e-Iqbal*, Delhi, Chaman Book Depot. *R. Aftab Iqbal and His Elder Son, Aftab Iqbal*, Karachi, Ferozsons (1999).

41 Smith, op. cit., p. 165.

42 Rood, op. cit., p. 148.

43 Ibid, p. 217.

44 Iqbal, Letter to Atiya Faizee, op. cit.

45 Sir Muhammad Iqbal's Presidential Address to the 25th Session of the All-India Muslim League Allahabad, 29 December 1930, Iqbal Academy (Lahore), 1977 [1944], 2nd ed., revised and enlarged.

46 Election Commission of Pakistan, https://www.ecp.gov.pk/frmVotebank.aspx

47 *TLP Protest, Long March: Lahore, Islamabad, Pindi Partially Sealed*, The News, 23 October 2021.

48 Kamran, Tahir, Problematising Iqbal as a State Ideologue, in *Revisioning Iqbal as a Poet and Muslim Political Thinker*, edited by Gita Dharampal-Frick, Ali Usman Qasmi, and Katia Rostetter, Germany, Draupadi Verlag (2010).

49 Ibid.

50 Paisa Akhbar, 24 June 1911.

51 I. Baloch, Caliphate and Iqbal in *Revisioning Iqbal as a Poet and Muslim Political Thinker* (op. cit.).

52 M.K. Gandhi, *Jews & Middle-East*, November 1938.

53 Baloch, op. cit., p. 152.

Five

FOUNDER III: LIBERAL, SECULAR, VISIONARY?

I want the Muslims of the Frontier to understand that they are Muslims first and Pathans afterwards and that the province will meet a disastrous fate if it does not join the Pakistan Constituent Assembly.

– Mohammed Ali Jinnah, 29 June 1947[1]

You may belong to any religion or caste or creed – that has nothing to do with the business of the State.

– Mohammed Ali Jinnah, 11 August 1947[2]

Jinnah remains at the center of a tug-of-war between Pakistan's liberals and Islamists. Each claims him as their own. The country's embattled religious minorities desperately appeal to his seminal speech of 11 August 1947 which stressed citizenship over religious faith in public matters. And yet the reality is more complex. We shall see in this chapter that Jinnah did not always allow his inner liberalism to interfere with his political goal of creating Pakistan by partitioning India. Many questions about what he "really wanted" have only ambiguous answers. Still, we must ask what plans he had proposed – apart from escaping the tyranny of majoritarian Hindu rule – for saving the Muslims of India. Did he have somewhere a blueprint for constructing a new state ab initio? Having chosen to fuse religion with politics in a landmark shift that dates to 1937, could one reasonably expect that the new state would be able to separate constitutional and administrative matters from matters of belief? Do away with the Sunni–Shia conflict or at least send it into dormancy? Perhaps the most puzzling fact is that sometimes Jinnah called for an Islamic state and sometimes a Muslim state, but he always insisted that he would not tolerate a theocracy. Seventy-five years into Pakistan, these mutually incompatible demands continue to puzzle but remain important and relevant.

DOI: 10.4324/9781003379140-8

140 Founder III: Liberal, Secular, Visionary?

Without Mohammad Ali Jinnah there might never have been a Pakistan. He is the heroic *Quaid-e-Azam* (the Great Leader) for all who sought to carve out a Muslim majority state. For opponents, he is the villain who vivisectioned Mother India. With boundless energy and steely will, Jinnah was a grandmaster on the political chessboard of British India. Without ever going to jail – as did all major political leaders of those times – he succeeded in wrenching Pakistan from the hands of the Indian National Congress and the retreating British, famously remarking that it was he alone, with the help of his secretary and typewriter, who won Pakistan for the Muslims of India.[3]

While man-worship may be too strong a term, there is no doubt of the approbation Jinnah receives in the country he founded. Anwar Syed has collected some of the qualities attributed to him from papers presented in December 1976 at Islamabad, the grand centenary celebration of Jinnah's birth:

> handsome, elegant, eloquent, successful, wealthy, shrewd, prudent, frugal; hard-working and persevering; tough, grave, disciplined, orderly; competent organizer, skillful negotiator, able tactician, master of detail; unafraid, proud, assertive, willful; unselfish, honest, incorruptible; rational, logical, modernist, constitutionalist; tolerant of honest criticism, democratic, covenant-keeper; dedicated to his people's welfare; servant of Islam.[4]

In her much acclaimed book, *The Sole Spokesman*, history professor Ayesha Jalal writes that Jinnah saw himself the sole spokesman of Indian Muslims everywhere, not just those in the northwest and the northeast where they were in a majority, but also for the geographically dispersed Muslim minorities in the rest of India.[5] Indeed, within the subcontinent's tiny educated Indian Muslim elite there was none who could so dexterously navigate the treacherous minefields of Indian politics or had the power of his legalistic logic, forceful expression in English, personal incorruptibility, determination, and propensity to pursue single-mindedly a set of self-set goals. These qualities equipped him for taking on the political heavyweights on the other side: Nehru and Gandhi as well as the British viceroys Linlithgow, Wavell, and Mountbatten. There was no question that his Congress opponents intensely despised him. In his diary on 28 December 1943, Nehru wrote: "Instinctively I think *it is better to have Pakistan* almost anything if only to keep Jinnah far away and not allow his muddled and arrogant head from interfering continually in India's progress".[6] The Congress insisted on immediate transfer of power, ridiculed the cry for Pakistan and expected that it would sort out the communal question after the British exit. Gandhi, in a moment of frustration, is said to have called Jinnah an evil genius.

After 1947, Jinnah governed Pakistan directly through the well-oiled administrative machinery inherited from British India, its much vaunted "steel frame". After appointing himself governor-general, he controlled the executive, cabinet, and assembly and personally chaired cabinet meetings. Even military

Founder III: Liberal, Secular, Visionary? **141**

dictators have not enjoyed such plenitude of power. What he said was more than just the law – it was what had to be. In spite of his failing health, he traveled and made his presence known wherever he felt it was essential. In 1957 the political scientist Keith Callard wrote, "By his own order he could amend the existing constitution and promulgate laws that would be beyond the effective power of any court".[7] When some disaffected members of the Constituent Assembly complained about being bypassed on some matters of great importance, Prime Minister Liaquat Ali Khan told the assembly: "under the present constitution, the man who has been vested with all powers is the Governor-General. He can do whatever he likes".[8]

Jinnah could perhaps be called the Ben-Gurion of Pakistan. But how closely do the two resemble each other? Pakistan and Israel are the only two states in the world created ab initio from religious identity, a fact made possible because of the collapse of imperial order. The comparison is therefore significant. Like Israel, Pakistan was ungrounded in any historic connection between land and people; both were concrete manifestations of an abstract idea of nationhood – the belief of some preexisting primordial political community which now needs a nation-state. Both claim to have been ordered into existence by God. In *Muslim Zion*, a provocatively titled book by Faisal Devji, the author underscores their essential similarity: both countries emerged from situations in which minority populations, dispersed across vast geographical areas, sought to escape majorities whose persecution they rightly or wrongly feared.[9]

But there the similarity stops: David Ben-Gurion, Israel's founder and first prime minister, was a socialist, and Israel was once the beacon of a modern socialist Jewish state whose paradigmatic building block was the kibbutz, a utopian commune that fused egalitarianism, agriculture, and aggressive Zionism. Now that Israel has swerved to the far right and abandoned its earlier dreams of utopian socialism, Ben-Gurion's vision for Israel – like Nehru's for a socialist India – may well be dead or have entered deep hibernation. Still, in all fairness, it must be said that Ben-Gurion's views were clear and unequivocal. For many decades they guided Israel through the General Federation of Labor (known as the Histadrut) into becoming a socialist and democratic state – albeit democratic for Jews only and not for Arabs. Ben-Gurion's clarity of vision helped Israel defeat the Arabs militarily and, being well-read and well-rounded with an understanding of what drives the modern world, he helped Israel become a leader in the world of science by drawing upon a long tradition of Jewish intellectual achievements.

Jinnah was also clear-sighted and his personal liberalism led many to assume that the new country would reflect his social preferences and political beliefs. But the state he created remains mired in confusion. To explain this fact, for seventy-five years Pakistanis have lamented that if only Jinnah had lived longer, he would have set Pakistan on its path towards a glorious destiny. The disappointed ones insist that it was bad people and bad luck that must be blamed. They call for a return to the vision of the *Quaid* (Leader). Browsing a long litany of exhortations and lamentations in various newspapers, one sees: "How Pakistan Betrayed its Founder", "Betrayal led to our Quaid's Death", "A Vision Unfulfilled", "Quaid's Betrayed Legacy", "How Pakistan Betrayed its Founding Father's Legacy", "11th August – Jinnah's Promise Betrayed", "Quaid – We're So Sorry", etc. Betrayal and disappointment runs through such ruminations. We must therefore examine if such feelings are indeed warranted and what Jinnah envisioned for Pakistan.

Did Jinnah Have a Plan?

In contrast to Ben-Gurion or Jawaharlal Nehru, we can only guess how Pakistan's founder envisaged his country-to-be. Or, if one uses the jargon of marketing or business school graduates, we cannot know for sure what his "business plan" was. This is because Jinnah wrote no books or substantive missives and instead communicated through his speeches that focused on issues of the moment. Even in these he did not address critical matters of organization and policy: Would land reform be pursued and should/could the *jagirdari* system be dispensed with? Was the new country to be a federation or confederation, and what would be the degree of central control? How, in a world increasingly defined by science and technology, and with Muslims being hugely educationally backward, could the country be brought up to speed? What resources were crucially needed for survival, and how to get them?

Still more significantly, the role of religion in Pakistan was left unspecified and ambiguous. Some find in Jinnah's speeches a liberal and secular voice, others an articulation of Islamic values. Jinnah was largely indifferent at a personal level to religious belief. If Ben-Gurion can be described as an incidental Jew, Jinnah was an incidental Muslim. But there is a crucial difference: Ben-Gurion made no appeal to the theology of Judaism in his bid to create Israel. On the other hand, Jinnah was flexible and allowed the force of circumstance to guide his position. Ayesha Jalal concedes that "Jinnah's appeal to religion was always ambiguous... evidence suggests that his use of the communal factor was a political tactic, not an ideological commitment".[10] This may well be true, but for the Pakistan movement this turned out to be defining.

While the notion of a Muslim nation on Indian soil was the work of Sir Syed and Iqbal, it is Jinnah who articulated it in the clearest and most explicit terms. In a letter to Gandhi he wrote:

> We maintain and hold that Muslims and Hindus are two major nations by any definition or test of a nation. We are a nation of a hundred million, and what is more, we are a nation with our own distinctive culture and civilization, language and literature, art and architecture, names and nomenclature, sense of value and proportion, legal laws and moral codes, customs and calendar, history and traditions, aptitudes and ambitions – in short we have our own distinctive outlook on life and of life. By all cannons of international law we are a nation.[11]

Founder III: Liberal, Secular, Visionary? **143**

These words and thoughts would come back to haunt the subcontinent. Without insisting that Hindu and Muslim are fundamentally different and incapable of living together in peace, Jinnah simply could not have succeeded in making Pakistan. But once uttered, the words of a revered leader are taken seriously by his followers. They cannot simply be tossed away at will at some later time when political circumstances have changed.

Indeed, Jinnah's above-quoted insistence on separate identities – which posits things in black and white – stands in stark contrast with his famous 11 August 1947 speech, delivered just three days before independence at the first meeting of the Pakistan Constituent Assembly, the members of which had been elected almost a year earlier. This speech was exemplary, noted far and wide, with its most quoted line being, "You may belong to any religion or caste or creed – that has nothing to do with the business of the State". It was strong and unequivocal, visible as a landmark because it clearly stated that the yet to be formed Pakistan would have an inclusive and impartial government, equal treatment for people of different religions, and rule of law would prevail equally for all who lived within its borders. This was a covenant to build a new nation, create a consensus governing all citizens, and a decisive move away from the bitter divisiveness of the preceding decade. In the speech, Jinnah did not mention his Two Nation Theory or about rescuing Islam from some imminent danger. Instead, he momentarily had returned to his quintessentially liberal, relaxed, and inclusive stance of the 1920s.

Hindus, Sikhs, Christians, and Parsis in Pakistan were understandably thrilled at the speech, but Muslim League (ML) activists were left scratching their heads. This unusual speech was such a stark deviation from Jinnah's earlier pronouncements about the incompatibility of Muslims and Hindus that many stalwarts wondered why the fight for Pakistan had been fought. Some scrambled to invent reasons, arguing that Islam does not discriminate between religions and that it does not call for imposing the sharia. In the decades that followed, certain well-known historians[12] excised it altogether from the pages of their books and collections of the *Quaid-e-Azam*'s speeches. Whether it was because of secret orders of high-ups or the spontaneous surreptitious acts of right-wingers, the speech disappeared from public view and has been restored relatively recently in school textbooks. Curiously, the original audio recording of the speech is missing from Radio Pakistan's archives. Although these archives contain an otherwise full record of Jinnah's utterances, this particular one could not be located even after Radio Pakistan's director-general in 2008 ordered a full search. Thereafter, he requested his Indian counterpart to search Indian archives, but this too proved unsuccessful.[13] Only the written record survives.

A chapter in a recent book on Jinnah by Ishtiaq Ahmed, a Pakistani historian based at Stockholm University, combs through the 11 August speech in detail while, at the same time, setting the context in which it was delivered.[14] Ahmed offers three possible explanations for why this speech differs so dramatically from Jinnah's prior speeches. First, that Jinnah was fearful that a massive deluge of

144 Founder III: Liberal, Secular, Visionary?

Muslim refugees fleeing the Indian side would swamp the nascent administration's capacity. Therefore, by way of this speech, he sought to assure the Indian side that Pakistan's minorities were not about to be forced out. Second, that his message was aimed towards an apprehensive foreign audience with the intent of reassuring them that Pakistan was not going to become some fearsome theocracy run by archaic laws. Jinnah well knew that, to even survive, Pakistan needed much help from the United States and Britain. Not only were some foreigners physically present when he delivered his speech before the Constituent Assembly, it was also broadcast overseas by radio. Third – and here Ahmed speculates – Shankar Roy, a Congress leader, had implored Jinnah to become a leader of all Pakistanis and not just Muslims. This, says Ahmed, may have touched Jinnah's ego and guided his choice of words.

The reasons behind Jinnah's famed speech can only be guessed. But it seems to me that reading too much into it would not be correct. Jinnah never repeated the contents with anything resembling the same force at any other time. Eloquence takes one only so far. A one-off speech cannot establish a principle that would force the divisive religious genie back in the bottle. But more importantly, words spoken without a supportive document cannot substitute for a carefully crafted draft constitution, the details of which could have been debated and approved by the Pakistan Constituent Assembly. Jinnah, who thought along precise juridical lines, could easily have created such a document for Pakistan. Instead, after Partition he chose to plunge into day-to-day administrative matters. Left hanging was Jinnah's business plan for the new state – now well into its first few months.

If he was too busy now, what about having planned the path for Pakistan prior to Partition? In the decade that preceded the creation of Pakistan, Jinnah had not only been quiet on this matter, but he also insisted that others should refrain from debating the nature of the state-to-be. Speaking at Aligarh Muslim University, he expressly forbade such discussions between his followers. Acquiring territory was all that should be presently talked about:

> We are told by one party or another that we must have a democratic or socialistic or a "nationalistic" form of government in Pakistan. These questions are raised to hoodwink you. At present you should just stand by Pakistan. It means first of all you have to take possession of a territory. Pakistan cannot exist in the air. When you have once taken possession of your homelands the question will then arise as to what form of government you are going to establish. Therefore, do not allow your mind to be diverted by these extraneous ideas. Let us concentrate all our attention on the question of taking possession of our homelands.[15]

In unambiguous terms, Jinnah put down his philosophy: make the country first, deal with problems later! In 1945, when Maulana Hussain Ahmad Madani wanted to know the Muslim League's plan for the future state and of the fate of Muslims to be left behind in India, Jinnah responded similarly:

Founder III: Liberal, Secular, Visionary? **145**

We shall have time to quarrel ourselves and we shall have time when these differences will have to be settled, when wrongs and injuries will have to be remedied. We shall have time for domestic programs and policies, but first get the government. This is a nation without any territory or any government.[16]

Jaffrelot points to how differently G.M. Syed, president of the Sindhi chapter of the AIML, envisioned the state to be.[17] Like all Sindhi nationalists, he was well versed in the poetry of Shah Abdul Latif Bhitai but also admired Sind's other historical heroes including the last Hindu king, Raja Dahir (661–712). Even as he supported the 1940 Lahore resolution, he took to heart its message that the entities comprising the new state would be "autonomous and sovereign". But this was not to be so in Jinnah's Pakistan, a fact that led to G.M. Syed becoming an icon of Sindhi nationalism and being put behind bars for close to twenty-eight years.

But choosing not to look ahead and focusing on the immediate meant that one becomes the proverbial ostrich which buries its head in the sand rather than face danger. Adding to the lack of planning and vision was that following the division of India, Pakistan won a meager poor 17.5% of the existing financial reserves, although it had 23% of the undivided land mass. Administratively, mass confusion was to follow in the years ahead. A glimpse of the political culture of the times after Partition can be had from Anwar Syed's article titled, "Factional Conflict in the Punjab Muslim League, 1947–1955", where the author examines the rivalry between the Muslim League feudal stalwarts Mian Mumtaz Mohammed Khan Daultana and Nawab Iftikhar Hussain Khan of Mamdot and later with Malik Firoz Khan Noon.[18]

At the time of the conflict Jinnah was sick but tried hard to patch things up between Daultana and Mamdot.[19] He failed, and their mutual enmity increased yet further. Unable to handle the situation he left it up to Sir Francis Mudie, the first Governor of Sind in the newly formed Pakistan, to impose a solution. But soon after Jinnah's death, the Governor was pushed out by Liaquat Ali Khan, and chaos continued. Liaquat, a Muhajir, had a significant Urdu-speaking Muhajir constituency but entirely lacked a Punjabi one. He found himself in a partisan war with Mamdot, a wealthy landlord who had extensive properties in East Punjab. This happened soon after he decided to align with Daultana, Mamdot's archrival in an effort to increase his base. Equally bitter turf battles broke out in Sind and NWFP. On 16 October 1951, Liaquat Ali Khan was assassinated in Rawalpindi. Ayub Khan wryly notes in his autobiography that the remaining cabinet ministers did not seem particularly upset at this. A game of musical chairs led to there being six prime ministers between 17 October 1951 and 7 October 1958. This means on average each prime minister spent less than thirteen months in office.

Khalid bin Sayeed, whose volumes are entitled, *Pakistan – the Formative Years*, are considered authoritative works in the field and presently used in hotly

146 Founder III: Liberal, Secular, Visionary?

contested CSS examinations, traces Pakistan's failure to Jinnah's early days as governor general and his deliberate use of the vice-regal system inherited from the Raj. But what mattered still more was the absence of an overall plan. Sayeed quotes extensively from letters obtained from Governor Mudie's collection. Mudie is crystal clear in assigning blame to various individuals as they battle each other and Pakistan drops into chaos. Sayeed's final reflections: the breakdown after Partition happened because there was no coherent political framework other than unifying Muslims in the face of a Hindu majority:

> This indicates that certain cleavages existed in the horizontal coalition of regional and economic interests that Jinnah had hastily put together. There was neither fundamental agreement among the landlords of the same Province nor did there exist any clear understanding based on a political programme between the rural and the urban interests of a Province. When the refugees poured into Pakistan they brought with them another source of future conflict between themselves and the local landlords. *All this meant that Islam was enough to unify the Muslims against the Hindus, but as a mere symbol it could not act as a cementing force among conflicting interests after the establishment of Pakistan.* [emphasis added] The Muslim League had also been unable to achieve much vertical integration in its organization. The social structure in the villages and the districts was semi-feudal or traditional, and virtually under the control of the Deputy Commissioner and the landlords. Muslim League party workers, most of whom were from urban areas, did succeed in arousing the political consciousness and support of the rural people, but they had not been able to build a viable political organization or change the power structure in the countryside. They needed an economic and social programme designed to mobilize both the support of the landowners and the peasants. The Muslim League had neither a programme nor an adequate mechanism within its organization to resolve or adjust the conflict of interests and views that existed between different social and economic classes.[20]

Jinnah had kept his deck of cards close to his chest in the earlier years. E.J. Benthall, president of the Bengal Chamber of Commerce, felt that any hint at what the future Pakistan might be would embroil him in matters of detail. In March 1940, after an hourlong conversation during which Jinnah adamantly refused to commit himself to any kind of constitutional framework for Pakistan, Benthall wrote: "his main interest was to keep Congress out while he builds up power and influence".[21]

There is no lack of people who still speak and write wistfully about Jinnah's vision for Pakistan and how it has been lost. There may well be a parallel universe where he articulated that vision but, so far as I can see, it is not the one we happen to live in. Former Senator Javed Jabbar, an ideologue of the Two Nation Theory, emphatically disagrees. The interested reader is referred to a ten-part series by Anjum Altaf on Jabbar's disagreements with me.[22]

Founder III: Liberal, Secular, Visionary? **147**

Anticipating Dependence

How would the new state of Pakistan find resources to sustain itself? This question was posed to Jinnah in September 1947 by Margaret Bourke-White, who was a correspondent and photographer for *Life* magazine during the Second World War years. Bourke-White had gone to Pakistan where she met Jinnah. She wrote about this meeting in her book, published in 1949. Reproduced below is an excerpt:

> Pakistan was one month old. Karachi was its mushrooming capital. On the sandy fringes of the city an enormous tent colony had grown up to house the influx of minor government officials. There was only one major government official, Mahomed Ali Jinnah, and there was no need for Jinnah to take to a tent. The huge marble and sandstone Government House, vacated by British officialdom, was waiting. The Quaid-i-Azam moved in, with his sister, Fatima, as hostess. Mr. Jinnah had put on what his critics called his "triple crown": he had made himself Governor-General; he was retaining the presidency of the Muslim League — now Pakistan's only political party; and he was president of the country's lawmaking body, the Constituent Assembly.
>
> What plans did he have for the industrial development of the country? Did he hope to enlist technical or financial assistance from America?
>
> "America needs Pakistan more than Pakistan needs America", was Jinnah's reply. "Pakistan is the pivot of the world, as we are placed" — he revolved his long forefinger in bony circles — "the frontier on which the future position of the world revolves." He leaned toward me, dropping his voice to a confidential note. "Russia", confided Mr. Jinnah, "is not so very far away".
>
> This had a familiar ring. In Jinnah's mind this brave new nation had no other claim on American friendship than this — that across a wild tumble of roadless mountain ranges lay the land of the Bolsheviks. I wondered whether the Quaid-i-Azam considered his new state only as an armored buffer between opposing major powers. He was stressing America's military interest in other parts of the world. "America is now awakened", he said with a satisfied smile. Since the United States was now bolstering up Greece and Turkey, she should be much more interested in pouring money and arms into Pakistan. "If Russia walks in here", he concluded, "the whole world is menaced".[23]

The above account has been reproduced at length above because this fascinating episode does not seem to be generally well known. Pakistan's position on the map would be a major source of income — Jinnah's prescience proved to be extraordinarily accurate. During the Cold War, America's need for forward bases gave to Pakistan economic and military assistance that otherwise would have been impossible.

148 Founder III: Liberal, Secular, Visionary?

Jinnah was again proved spectacularly correct when in December 1979 – a full thirty-two years later from the date of the above-quoted interview – the Soviet Union invaded Afghanistan in what turned out to be the largest, longest, and costliest military operation in Soviet history. The United States, in support of the Afghan resistance, waged an exceedingly elaborate, expensive, and ultimately successful covert war. For Pakistan this brought a windfall. Thereafter, for many decades it was able to trade its strategic position for American weapons and money. Today, although the geopolitical circumstances are entirely different from those of the Cold War, Pakistan's particular geographical location has brought to it the China–Pakistan Economic Corridor (CPEC).

Collecting rent based on a country's geographical location comes at a cost – dependency and the deference to the needs of the patron. The highest bidder for our strategic location will then control what it does. So while Jinnah was astute enough to see that Pakistan's position on the map was a money-spinner, this is by no means a proper, viable strategy for national development. Why did Jinnah not ever come up with a plan even after being in politics for so many decades? Or put together a task force to plan ahead once Partition had become likely? This elicits many explanations. A common one is that around that time he was sick with tuberculosis with sharply depleted energies. True enough, but no one can expect to live forever.

The absence of a clear vision meant that Pakistan would continue to wallow in confusion, unable to fix its national priorities and goals. Even within his own Muslim League, party members who would earlier not dare to speak up fearlessly challenged him now. Riven by internal conflicts, the Muslim League slowly disintegrated. By 1953 it had shattered and disappeared from view.

In seeking to explain the Muslim League's speedy demise, people choose their favorite villains. Frequently named are Liaquat Ali Khan, Mumtaz Daultana, Nawab Mamdot, M.A. Khuhro, Chaudhry Khaliquzzaman, Qayyum Khan, Ghulam Mohammed, Mohammed Munir, Iskander Mirza, as well as others who came later. In the decades to come, Pakistan would be run by those with personal and regional agendas – or by the military. There were to be no land reforms, no effective education system, and no stable democratic government. Not so far, that is.

Is this merely a value judgment? No, this is how things happen to be – unalterable historical fact. Jinnah had many other virtues, but he did not have a blueprint charting out the future of Pakistan. As a tactician he was brilliant. But he was not a strategist and so the plaintive calls for implementing his vision are futile. It is to the future and not towards the past that Pakistan must look.

Did Jinnah Not Want Pakistan?

> Pakistan is not only a practical goal but the only goal if you want to save Islam from complete annihilation in this country.
>
> – *Mohammed Ali Jinnah speech, 10 March 1941*[24]

Founder III: Liberal, Secular, Visionary? **149**

Jinnah did not have a strategic plan – a business model – for Pakistan. Could that be because he had not actually expected to win Pakistan? This might seem to be the case since he chose to accept the power-sharing Cabinet Mission Plan of March 1946. This plan, however, was shot down by the Hindu-dominated and hubris-filled Congress which had initially agreed to a version of it. In the next chapter we shall see how Abul Kalam Azad, who stayed with the Congress through thick and thin, rued the mistakes of the leadership particularly that of his friend Jawaharlal Nehru. Congress leaders feared that the Muslim League would make governance impossibly difficult. There is no way of knowing whether these fears were justified. Jinnah seized upon the Congress's move, making Pakistan certain.

It has been suggested that Jinnah merely sought protection for Muslims and did not want the partitioning of India. This possibility – which amounts to a truly extraordinary claim – has been championed most prominently by Ayesha Jalal. She argues that there were two steps in Jinnah's strategy to secure Muslim advantage in undivided India:

> The first was the consolidation of Muslim majority areas behind the All-India Muslim League and then to use undivided Punjab and Bengal as a weight to negotiate an arrangement for all the Muslims at an all-India level. But the Congress had Punjab and Bengal partitioned [to frustrate the first element of his strategy]. *Jinnah did not want Partition, in case people have forgotten that.* Similarly, when the United Bengal plan was floated, Jinnah said it was better that Bengal remained united. He said what was Bengal without Calcutta? It was like asking a man to live without his heart. So we ended up with a mutilated Pakistan that Jinnah had rejected out of hand.[25] [italics added]

Did not want Partition? As the astronomer Carl Sagan once said, extraordinary claims demand extraordinary evidence. Here there is both a lack of evidence and a preponderance of counterevidence. One notes that for a full five years between 1942 and 1947 Jinnah had spared no opportunity to make the case for a physical division of India, rejecting the possibility of a power-sharing agreement between the Congress and Muslim League. Going through a collection of Jinnah's speeches in this period, one sees several in which Jinnah is unequivocal in his stand. For example, on Pakistan Day, 23 March 1945, he was perfectly explicit: "In Pakistan lies our deliverance and honour…We shall never accept any constitution on the basis of a united India".[26]

Rejecting the claim that Jinnah had Partition thrust upon him, historian Ishtiaq Ahmad says that Jinnah should be credited with what he is normally credited for, and that a position such as Jalal's serves merely to exonerate the British of a disaster of epic proportions:

> For too long confusion has been generated by products of the colonial school of history centred in Cambridge and Oxford where a novel idea was

150 Founder III: Liberal, Secular, Visionary?

pedaled – that Jinnah did not want partition; it was the Congress leaders who did. It found supporters in India as well, notably among right-wing individuals wanting to make India a Hindu Rashtra (Hindu State) which is "secular" the same way as Jinnah's Pakistan was Islamic and secular. Jinnah and his relentless demand for partition leading to partition was thus blamed ingeniously by those who opposed it and languished in jails for years against it: the leaders of the Congress Party. What the colonial school of history and its products have also successfully prevented thus far is to identify the British as the villains. Without them deciding in favour of partition and implementing it in a great hurry there would be no Pakistan and no partition and most certainly not the bloodshed and forced migration it caused.[27]

But there is a flip side to this debate: if Jinnah was indeed expecting the creation of Pakistan, why did he continue to buy property and shares in India? This continued almost to the very end. For example, the compilation of Jinnah Papers contains the following letter from Jinnah for the purchase of shares in Indian National Airways. I think the date on the letter (8 June 1947) is very significant:

Re. the purchase of Air India or better 'Indian National Airways' shares:
8 June 1947
M.A. Jinnah to Messrs Goval Brothers,
Dear Sirs,
With reference to your notice of call dated 5th May, towards the first call of Rs. 1,800 for 1200 Shares Ordinary, I am sending you herewith a cheque for Rs. 1,800 ... I am also enclosing the notice form entire as desired by you. Please acknowledge receipt and oblige. M.A. Jinnah
Note: Goval Brothers are the Managing Agents of Indian National Airways ltd., Scindia House, New Delhi. The reference in the Jinnah Papers is F.910/324.[28]

The above-referenced volume of Jinnah Papers has a number of other references to the purchase of shares in March in both Bombay and Calcutta. Jinnah also refers to his property in Kashmir and was interested in the purchase of two houseboats. These purchases are certainly puzzling and go in favor of Jalal's thesis that Jinnah had not really envisaged a physical partition with hard borders. It could well be that Jinnah thought that India–Pakistan relations would be so amicable that easy travel would be possible across borders, or that monies and properties could be traded and sold without difficulty. Clearly one does not know the answer. But there can be no doubt that Jinnah was not worried about the safety of his investments, whether or not Pakistan became reality.

On balance it appears to me that if Jinnah could comment on this historical debate, he would support Ahmad's position rather than Jalal's. Scrolling through Jinnah's voluminous speeches, one can find unequivocal statements such as that

Founder III: Liberal, Secular, Visionary? **151**

of 10 March 1941 where Jinnah had put things in the starkest possible terms: "Pakistan is not only a practical goal but the only goal if you want to save Islam from complete annihilation in this country".[29] He explicitly refuted the notion that the demand for Pakistan was tactical. Could these have been just tactics? Possible but unlikely.

That Pakistan was a British creation appears a simplistic claim that has great appeal for Indian nationalists as well as Hindutva. From the British perspective, there were both pros and cons to having Pakistan. On the pro side, it would be certainly simpler to exert residual influence from afar if there was to be one country rather than two. On the other hand, it is true that they had never found a need to imprison Jinnah or ML leaders. Some in the British establishment, who wished to avoid a too hasty departure, had indeed found in Jinnah a willing ally against the Congress and its insistence that the British must leave without delay. Others were looking towards Britain's role in a post-war world. Churchill was consumed by the gnawing fear that India under the socialist Nehru would ally with the Soviet Union upon attaining freedom or remain neutral. He was, in fact, proved correct. The partitioning of India with a strongly pro-West and anti-communist Pakistan eventually worked out in the British interest. However, these were peripheral concerns. More than anything else, it was the ground reality – a reality that was created by relentless exploitation of communal feelings – that made Pakistan inevitable. After Direct Action Day on 16 August 1946, a united India had become impossible.

Jinnah – the Man

> Quaid-i-Azam was brave and honest. He was leader of Pakistan Movement. He was not afraid of enemies of Islam like Hindus or English people. Quaid-i-Azam said Pakistan is to be Islamic state because we are all Muslims. Quaid-i-Azam is great man and made many sacrifices to give us beloved country.
>
> – *Class 6 Social Studies (English, inside cover), Sind Government Textbook Board (2008)*

Mohammed Ali Jinnah's massive marble mausoleum, one of Karachi's few tourist attractions, is a scant fifteen-minute walk from our family home. When he died in 1948, hundreds of thousands lined the streets to pay tribute. I was born two years later, but remember being told as a boy that Jinnah would sometimes visit my businessman uncle, Suleman Hoodbhoy, at our common family home at 303, Ashoka Street, Garden East. The house is among the few in the neighborhood that in 2023 is still standing (the street sign disappeared 30–40 years ago). I can visualize Jinnah entering the gates and then walking up the steps! Uncle Suleman spent a considerable amount of his time in Africa proselytizing for the Ismaili *jamaat*.

Jinnah was a Khoja Isna-Ashari Shia Muslim, not a Khoja Ismaili Shia Muslim – this difference might seem arcane, but politically it made a big difference

152 Founder III: Liberal, Secular, Visionary?

because every Khoja Ismaili must accept the Ismaili Hazir Imam (imam of the present) as his spiritual leader and mentor. At the time, the Ismaili Hazir Imam was Sultan Mohammed Shah, one of the founders of the Muslim League. For a political leader to rub shoulders with his spiritual leader of his own sect could have been problematic, but this was not the case here: Jinnah dealt with Sultan Mohammed Shah as a non-Ismaili and hence as a non-follower who could be on equal terms. Nevertheless, it was maliciously whispered that some of Jinnah's relatives were Ismailis. One must not give such rumors credence. Ismaili Shias and Isna-Ashari Shias have always been at loggerheads, but the astute Jinnah still liked to keep his finger on the pulse everywhere.

Jinnah's political career prior to Partition spanned four decades and went through two distinct phases: before 1937 he was a liberal, critical of bringing religion into politics. In fact he began his political career as an exponent of Hindu–Muslim unity and as the leader of the liberal left wing of the Indian National Congress. His efforts culminated in the Lucknow Pact of 1916 between the Congress and the Muslim League that helped bridge Hindu–Muslim differences. Khalid bin Sayeed, one of his more respected biographers, argues that in the period of 1929–1935 Congress's intransigence was a major factor that changed him from an "idealist" into a "realist" who saw no future for Muslims – and his own political career – in a united India.[30] Bin Sayeed's evidence is persuasive: Congress had broken from reality and lost sensitivity to Muslim fears of being overrun by the Muslim majority, convinced that the future of India lay with it alone and that Hindu–Muslim communal problems were peripheral to the main goal of forcing the British out of India. This initiated Jinnah's next phase (1937–1947) in which he insisted on a separate Muslim political identity.

Prior to this new phase Jinnah had spurned religious distinctions and prohibitions: as the most Westernized political leader in Indian Muslim history, Jinnah was culturally and socially far more at ease with the high society of cosmopolitan Bombay and metropolitan London than with those people whom he led and represented. In the early 1930s Jinnah lived in a large house in Hampstead, London, and had an English chauffeur who drove his Bentley, together with an English staff to serve him.[31] With Victorian manners, this impeccably dressed secular and anglicized man had a connoisseur's appreciation of fine foods and wines. His culinary choices – which included ham and pork – outraged the strict Muslim. His speeches to the Muslim League and before large gatherings were delivered in the King's English with faultless pronunciation and emphasis. Unable to read any Islamic language – Arabic, Persian, or Urdu – he was incapable of having a reasonable conversation in any of these or even some local Indian language. His sister Shirin Bai could barely communicate with him because "Mr. Jinnah was not conversant in Gujarati or Urdu, she was not fluent in English".[32] Culturally, Jinnah was more British than Indian. Those of strong religious faith despised him.

Decades later, this personal profile deeply embarrassed General Zia-ul-Haq's spinmasters on Pakistan Television. They were tasked with forcing the long dead Jinnah into Islamic garb and stripping him of all liberal qualities. But like much

Founder III: Liberal, Secular, Visionary? **153**

else they took this into their stride and so in the 1980s Pakistanis were treated to a steady stream of profound pieties emanating from a stern, sherwani-clad man (he rarely wore them and must have complained when he finally had to wear "native costume"). The newly resurrected Islamic Jinnah was never shown in one of his elegant suits from Savile Row; reference to his marriage to a Parsi woman and Parsi daughter was also redacted.

Jinnah's cultural distance from the ordinary man, together with little apparent knowledge or insistence of specific Islamic doctrines, paradoxically turned out to be hugely advantageous in political terms. In the public eye, he was identified as a Muslim, but not with any particular region or any set of customs or a particular Islamic sect. People could see, as the saying goes, that he had no dog in the fight. One must remember that this was at a time when Muslim parties in different parts of India were riven by bitter rivalries within parties and between them, with some making alliances with Hindus while others announced their implacable opposition. Thus he enjoyed the trust of more Indian Muslims than any other leader. Allama Iqbal saw this and extended his support and confidence to Jinnah.[33] As *angraiz bara sahab* by lifestyle, Jinnah did need authentication from true Muslim representatives. He duly received a stamp of approval from Iqbal, who had captured the imagination of the masses with his passionate calls for an Islamic revival and was widely respected.

How did Jinnah, who in his student days hoped to be a professional actor in Shakespearean plays, end up leading a movement based on religious identity? How might he have justified it to himself and sold the idea to others? One can only speculate. Perhaps he hoped that: (a) People in his Muslim League would not notice his liberal lifestyle too much, (b) the contribution he was making to the welfare of Muslims – by helping level the playing field with Hindus – would dominate everything else, or (c) a liberal, secular Pakistan would one day follow once the messy business of Partition was over with and the whipped up religious fervor could be finally dispensed with.

Compromise, they say, is the art and essence of politics. Arguably most great men of history have had to make compromises. Thomas Jefferson, one of America's greatest, is celebrated for his fight against human trafficking and the institution of slavery but actually owned over 600 slaves of which he freed just seven. Similarly Martin Luther fought against the extreme corruption and cruelty of the Roman popes but opposed giving basic rights to peasants and was also a fierce antisemite.

Jinnah's flexibility was evident to all who chose to see. Even as he fought for a Muslim/Islamic state, he fought against the Indian National Congress's attempt to prohibit alcohol sales in Bombay Presidency.[34] Danish Khan points out that the Muslim League wanted to be seen visibly protecting pro-business interests, particularly those of the Parsi community who were heavily invested into alcohol production and distribution. In this way, the ML was able to garner support from Gujarati-speaking trading communities of Khojas, Bohras, and Memons. This also struck a chord with the landlords and urban elites across India.

154 Founder III: Liberal, Secular, Visionary?

Once things got going, even more flexibility became necessary when presenting himself at public meetings. To show that he was of Muslim soil became all important:

> In April 1943 the League session took place in Delhi, where an atmosphere reminiscent of lost splendour was the perfect scenario for this theatrical performance. Attended by over a lakh of persons it took place in a *pandal*, where pictures of Jinnah dominated the scenery. A map of Pakistan was placed at the head of the dais. The Karachi session, in the following December, displayed even more grandeur. Jinnah, wearing a traditional Muslim dress, was taken in a long procession, preceded by camels and horses ridden by hajis in Arab costumes.[35]

Did Jinnah Want Secularism?

Jinnah's definitive chronicler was the late Dr. Zawar Hussain Zaidi, head of the Quaid-e-Azam Academy and the editor-in-chief of the massive Quaid-e-Azam Papers Project. A devotee of Jinnah, he once told his wife that he eats with Jinnah, speaks with Jinnah, sits with Jinnah, and sleeps with Jinnah. It could scarcely be otherwise – classifying and compiling all of Jinnah's pronouncements during 1934–1948, and most of his letters and speeches during the pre-1934 period, was his life's work. He was so thorough that even Jinnah's weekly shopping lists in London – two bottles of wine and slices of ham – did not escape his scrutiny. He hoped to publish 30 volumes out of the 140,000 documents he had access to.[36] Far more than Stanley Wolpert or Herbert Bolitho – westerners who guessed at Jinnah from afar – he knew what Jinnah was all about and still loved him.

In the early 1990s, I spent several pleasant evenings in Islamabad with Dr. Zaidi, a thoroughly decent man whom I met through my mentor and friend Eqbal Ahmad. Eqbal had been Dr. Zaidi's student sometime in 1955–1956 and was duly deferential to his teacher. At one point I entered a conversation between them and asked Dr. Zaidi if he knew of any instance where Jinnah had pleaded for a secular state. His answer was firm and unequivocal: he had not detected the word "secular" (in the sense of signifying an ideology) in any of Jinnah's papers or utterances. Nevertheless, he confidently assured me that the *Quaid-e-Azam* had a secular Pakistan in mind. I wondered how and would have liked a little proof. Why had Jinnah not opened up the Muslim League to non-Muslims? But in our culture we must defer to seniors; this conversation could not be pursued further.

There is no known instance of Jinnah having criticized Hinduism. Of course he did attack Hindus bitterly for not accepting his demands and for not recognizing him as the sole spokesman – or perhaps the sole legal counsel – of Muslims. But this does not make him either pro- or anti-secularism, it merely shows that his actions had nothing to do with the particularities of a system of

Founder III: Liberal, Secular, Visionary? **155**

religious beliefs. Indeed from his speeches and writings it is unclear how much knowledge – or even interest – he had of Hinduism or, for that matter, Islam as well. Jinnah read multiple newspapers assiduously every morning, but one wonders whether he had time to read books because he rarely quotes from them.

Two of Jinnah's speeches – suppressed from public view during Zia's times – do however suggest a secular outlook. They belong to the arsenal of every liberal Pakistani who seeks to defend inclusivism. His presidential address of 11 August 1947 to the Constituent Assembly has already been discussed earlier in this chapter and is quoted more than any other speech:

> You are free; you are free to go to your temples, you are free to go to your mosques or to any other place of worship in this State of Pakistan. You may belong to any religion or caste or creed – that has nothing to do with the business of the State.... You will find that in course of time Hindus would cease to be Hindus and Muslims would cease to be Muslims, not in the religious sense, because that is the personal faith of each individual, but in the political sense as citizens of the State.

Earlier, in an interview with Doon Campbell, Reuter's correspondent in New Delhi in 1946, Jinnah made clear that, unlike Iqbal, it was Western-style democracy that he wanted for Pakistan: "The new state would be a modern democratic state with *sovereignty resting in the people* [my emphasis added here] and the members of the new nation having equal rights of citizenship regardless of their religion, caste or creed".[37] There was no talk of a *Majlis-e-Shura* or any such thing.

Note the highly significant phrase "sovereignty resting in the people" and contrast it with "sovereignty rests with Allah", the latter being frequently associated with the requirement for an Islamic state. Logically, therefore, Jinnah is rejecting the basis for a theocratic state. This is stated even more explicitly in his 1946 speech before the Muslim League convention in Delhi: "What are we fighting for? What are we aiming at? It is not theocracy, nor a theocratic state".[38] The historian K.K. Aziz has remarked that "on the record of their writings and speeches, Jinnah comes out to be far more liberal and secular than Gandhi".[39] After Partition, in a broadcast talk addressed to the people of the United States in February 1948, Jinnah retains and amplifies upon his position:

> Pakistan is not going to be a theocratic state to be ruled by priests with a divine mission. We have many non-Muslims-Hindus, Christians and Parsis – but they are all Pakistanis. They will enjoy the same rights and privileges as any other citizens and will play their rightful part in the affairs of Pakistan.

Jinnah did indeed reject theocracy; on this he was firm and never equivocated. Theocracy, says the dictionary, is a government "by ordained priests, who wield

156 Founder III: Liberal, Secular, Visionary?

authority as being specially appointed by those who claim to derive their rights from their sacerdotal position". Jinnah most certainly did not want the clergy running a country of which he would be head. This is understandable. But a common fallacy is to believe that a rejection of theocracy is an automatic endorsement of secularism. In fact there is no binary here.

Let's step back for a bit and reflect. Secularism is just as much about the nature of law as it is about the state treating citizens of different faiths equally. As a philosophy, secularism is fundamentally a post-Enlightenment belief that laws governing human activities and decisions should be based upon the concept of reasonableness, not a divine text. Secular laws are devised by humans according to their perception of society's needs. Because needs change according to times and circumstances, the laws in a secular society must necessarily change from time to time rather than being immutable.

One hears that Jinnah privately pledged (to an American diplomat) that Pakistan would be a "secular state" and used these words without qualification or equivocation. There is no way to either affirm or deny this. But in public gatherings he never mentioned secularism. Then, as now, secularism was a politically offensive word that was conflated with atheism by its opponents. Therefore, as a good tactician, Jinnah evaded questions on the matter. The following extracts from his 17 July 1947 press conference suggest extreme caution:

Question: "Will Pakistan be a secular or theocratic state?"

Mr. M.A. Jinnah: "You are asking me a question that is absurd. I do not know what a theocratic state means".

When another journalist suggested that the questioner meant a state run by 'maulanas', Jinnah retorted, "What about [a] Government run by Pundits in Hindustan?"

Question: A correspondent suggested that a theocratic state meant a state where only people of a particular religion, for example, Muslims, could be full citizens and non-Muslims would not be full citizens.

To this he replied,

Mr. M.A. Jinnah: Then it seems to me that what I have already said is like throwing water on a duck's back (laughter). When you talk of democracy, I am afraid you have not studied Islam. We learned democracy thirteen centuries ago.[40]

To conclude: Jinnah was a political leader first and liberal second. Once Pakistan was achieved, there was no further need or time for stirring the communal pot and so he stopped referring to the Two Nation Theory. He may well have wanted a secular Pakistan all along, but he was not prepared to pay the political cost he would have incurred. To be stamped a secularist in pre-Partition times would have been political suicide because he would have then been in competition with the secular Indian National Congress under the leadership of its highly effective leader, Jawaharlal Nehru. Consequently, Jinnah would have lost his leadership of the Pakistan Movement leaving Indian Muslims leaderless and directionless.

Founder III: Liberal, Secular, Visionary? **157**

Hence, ambiguity was the preferred option. But at the same time, Jinnah drew the line on theocracy and mullah rule. In fact, some of his fiercest opponents were certain mullahs and *pirs*.

Jinnah Fuses Politics with Religion

> Never before in South Asian history did so few divide so many, needlessly.
> — *Mushirul Hasan (1949–2018)*

Bringing religion into Indian politics generally pays quick dividends; the crowds soon come out roaring. This is true now in both India and Pakistan but was still truer a century ago when education levels were still lower. Mohandas Gandhi proved this when he sided with Muslims in the Khilafat Movement (1919–1924), an agitation by Indian Muslims to pressure the British government into preserving the Ottoman Sultan as Caliph of Islam. Seeking this as an opportunity to end British rule over India, Gandhi had asked the Congress and Hindus in 1920–1921 to generally support India's Muslims in their unhappiness over European/Christian control of Islam's holy places (Mecca, Madina, Najaf, Karbala). As he saw it, such an opportunity for a united Hindu–Muslim effort only comes "once in a hundred years". We need recall that all Indians – Hindu, Sikh, and Muslim – were appalled by the Jallianwala Bagh massacre in Amritsar in April 1919. Muslims were then agitated by the Khilafat issue as well. Although Gandhi has been accused of bringing religion into politics – and factually this is the case – he did so because it was a rare political opportunity to weaken British hold over India through his Non-Cooperation Movement.

The Khilafat issue being generally construed as a religious cause, there was plenty of religious symbolism in the speeches and declarations of leaders. Jinnah was uninterested in befriending Muslim leaders whom he saw as radical, anticipating correctly that a deeply divisive view of the world would emerge once the Khilafat Movement ran its course. He did not object to the use of religious symbols per se. When the terms of discourse did eventually shift that way, Jinnah used religious symbolism freely. As India approached independence, leaders with an overtly sectarian outlook such as Sardar Vallabhbhai Patel and Rajendra Prasad gained commanding positions in the Congress.

The idea of tying political demands with religion had initially repelled Jinnah. This had inspired a remark from Gopal Krishna Gokhale that Jinnah "has true stuff in him and that freedom from all sectarian prejudice which will make him the best ambassador of Hindu–Muslim Unity".[41] Earlier Jinnah, a member of both the League and Congress, had made known his opposition to a separate electorate system for Hindus and Muslims. This system was the brainchild of the Aga Khan and his colleague, Nawab Mohsin-ul-Mulk, who were then in command of the Muslim League. But Jinnah soon came around to their point of view. As the principal architect of the Lucknow Pact in December 1916, he dropped his earlier opposition and endorsed separate votes for Hindus and Muslims.

158 Founder III: Liberal, Secular, Visionary?

Under Gandhi's influence, the Congress had decided it would call for an end to British rule through *satyagraha*, a form of nonviolent resistance through civil disobedience. In 1920 Jinnah resigned from the Congress. One can speculate on what may have been the real reason: his feeling that departure of the British would put Muslims at a disadvantage relative to Hindus, his personal dislike for Gandhi, a genuine fear that violence would result, or that this was an opportunity to score points with the British.

The early 1930s saw a resurgence in Indian Muslim nationalism. In 1933 Choudhry Rehmat Ali had by then proposed the idea of Pakistan. But the League was in terrible shape and was routed in the 1937 elections where it could win only 109 seats out of the 492 reserved for Muslims. The performance in Punjab was even more disastrous where it garnered only two out of seven seats. Jinnah, as the League's president therefore chose a new stratagem – that of demanding exclusive Muslim rights. Still, even if he had crossed over to the other side of the bridge, mobilizing Muslims even on communal grounds was not simple. A sense of national identity was missing and had to be created ab initio. Faisal Devji notes that there was an essential contradiction in Jinnah's insistence on Muslims constituting a nation and their inability to behave as one: "Thus in the same breath that he proclaimed India's Muslims to be a nation after 1937, Jinnah could also bemoan their lack of such an identity and counsel them to achieve it by copying the Hindus, who he thought had achieved the kind of political integrity to qualify as one".[42] Indeed, one hears Jinnah complaining about the lack of communal spirit within Muslims:

> Today you find – apart from the fact whether the Congress's claims are right or wrong – today you find that the Hindus have to a very large degree acquired that essential quality – moral, cultural and political consciousness, and it has become the national consciousness of the Hindus. This is the force behind them. That is the force I want the Muslims to acquire. When you have acquired that, believe me, I have no doubt in my mind, you will realise what you want. The counting of heads may be a very good thing, but it is not the final arbiter of the destiny of nations. You have yet to develop a national self and national individuality.[43]

The Muslim League had been nearly kicked out of politics after its rout in the 1937 elections. Muslims in provinces where they were in the majority had little use for a party and its leader from another part of India. But this election actually turned out to be a turning point, not the League's demise. Chastened by defeat, it started using a frankly communal message and so learned how to draw together most Muslims, both rich and poor. Henceforth, the League would assert that all Muslims of India were one nation united not just by one religion but also one language (Urdu), one culture, and one destiny. The message was that if you want to vote for Islam, then you must vote for the League!

Founder III: Liberal, Secular, Visionary? **159**

Earlier apologia for using religion in politics disappeared – Jinnah had converted from secular to religious politics after the election debacle. Henceforth, politics would all be about creating a siege mentality. In his January 1938 address to Gaya Muslim League Conference, Jinnah began laying out his new strategy:

> When we say "This flag is the flag of Islam" they think we are introducing religion into politics – a fact of which we are proud. Islam gives us a complete code. It is not only religion but it contains laws, philosophy and politics. In fact, it contains everything that matters to a man from morning to night. When we talk of Islam we take it as an all embracing word. We do not mean any ill. The foundation of our Islamic code is that we stand for liberty, equality and fraternity.[44]

As the next step up the communal ladder, Jinnah set about systematically increasing his political capital among Muslims by explicating and amplifying upon his Two Nation Theory, the clearest articulation of which emerged during his landmark presidential address before the Lahore Session of Muslim League in March 1940:

> The Hindus and Muslims belong to two different religious philosophies, social customs, and literature. They neither intermarry nor interdine together, and indeed they belong to two different civilisations which are based mainly on conflicting ideas and conceptions. Their aspects on life, and of life, are different. It is quite clear that Hindus and Mussalmans derive their inspiration from different sources of history. They have different epics, their heroes are different, and different episodes. Very often the hero of one is a foe of the other, and likewise their victories and defeats overlap.[45]

Jinnah's letter to Gandhi of 17 September 1944 reiterated his Two Nation stance:

> Mussalmans (Muslims) came to India as conquerors, traders, and preachers and brought with them their own culture and civilization. They reformed and remolded the sub-continent of India. Today, the hundred million Mussalmans in (British) India represent the largest compact body of the Muslim population in any single part of the world. We are civilization, language, and literature, art and architecture, names and nomenclature, value and proportion, legal laws and moral code, customs and calendar, history and traditions, aptitude and ambitions, in short, we have our distinctive outlook of life and on life. By all canons of international law, we are a nation.[46]

In his Eid message of September 1945, Jinnah endorsed the "complete code of life" view of Islam:

> Everyone, except those who are ignorant, knows that the Quran is the general code of the Muslims. A religious, social, civil, commercial, military,

160 Founder III: Liberal, Secular, Visionary?

judicial, criminal, penal code, it regulates everything from the ceremonies of religion to those of daily life; from the salvation of the soul to the health of the body; from the rights of all to those of each individual; from morality to crime, from punishment here to that in the life to come, and our Prophet has enjoined on us that every Musalman should possess a copy of the Quran and be his own priest. Therefore Islam is not merely confined to the spiritual tenets and doctrines or rituals and ceremonies. It is a complete code regulating the whole Muslim society, every department of life, collective[ly] and individually.[47]

Addressing the Pathans, he said:

Do you want Pakistan or not? (shouts of Allah-o-Akbar.) Well, if you want Pakistan, vote for the League candidates. If we fail to realize our duty today you will be reduced to the status of Sudras (low castes) and Islam will be vanquished from India. I shall never allow Muslims to be slaves of Hindus (cries of Allah-o-Akbar).[48]

The cry "Islam is in danger" became a popular one at Muslim League rallies, whipping crowds into fury. After the 1937 election debacle, this slogan was used again and again, particularly in the Muslim-majority provinces where the League as yet had little support. The fortnightly confidential report of 22 February 1946 sent to Viceroy Wavell by the Punjab Governor Sir Bertrand Glancy says that in public meetings and mass contact campaigns, the Muslim League openly employed Islamic sentiments, slogans, and heroic themes to rouse the masses:

The ML (Muslim League) orators are becoming increasingly fanatical in their speeches. Maulvis (clerics) and Pirs (spiritual masters) and students travel all round the Province and preach that those who fail to vote for the League candidates will cease to be Muslims; their marriages will no longer be valid and they will be entirely excommunicated... It is not easy to foresee what the results of the elections will be. But there seems little doubt the Muslim League, thanks to the ruthless methods by which they have pursued their campaign of "Islam in danger" will considerably increase the number of their seats.[49]

Playing the communal card completely changed the League's fortunes. In the 1937 elections only 4.6% of India's Muslims voted for the League, winning only 3 out of 33 seats reserved for Muslims in Sind, 2 out of 84 seats in Punjab, 39 out of 117 seats in Bengal, and none in NWFP. Just ten years before it actually happened, the Muslims of India had decisively rejected the notion of partitioning India. But with the vigorous use of Islam-in-danger and Muslim-in-danger line, the League's ranks swelled and Jinnah became the supreme leader. With evident satisfaction, in 1945 he declared:

Founder III: Liberal, Secular, Visionary? **161**

The Frontier Pathan is now wide awake. He is out of the Congress snare now. But you must work and work hard and make the Muslim League still stronger. By doing so, you will contribute substantially not only to the honour of the crores of Muslims, but to the crystallisation of a free Muslim state of Pakistan where Muslims will be able to offer the ideology of Islamic rule.[50]

In 1946, the League polled a whopping 75% of the Muslim vote – a far cry from the mere 4.6% just nine years earlier. Addressing Pathans of the NWFP in June 1947, Jinnah bluntly asked Muslims to think along communal lines.

I want the Muslims of the Frontier to understand that they are Muslims first and Pathans afterwards and that the province will meet a disastrous fate if it does not join the Pakistan Constituent Assembly.[51]

Professor Sharif-al-Mujahid, honorary director of the Freedom Movement Archives at Karachi University and author of an award winning book on Jinnah identifies occasions when, as head of the state he had just founded, Jinnah spoke in the same vein.[52] He talked of securing "liberty, fraternity and equality as enjoined upon us by Islam" (25 August 1947); of "Islamic democracy, Islamic social justice and the equality of manhood" (21 February 1948); of raising Pakistan on "sure foundations of social justice and Islamic socialism which emphasized equality and brotherhood of man" (26 March 1948); of laying "the foundations of our democracy on the basis of true Islamic ideals and principles" (14 August 1948); and "the onward march of renaissance of Islamic culture and ideals" (18 August 1947). He called upon the mammoth Lahore audience to build up "Pakistan as a bulwark of Islam", to "live up to your traditions and add to it another chapter of glory", adding, "If we take our inspiration and guidance from the Holy Quran, the final victory, I once again say, will be ours" (30 October 1947).

Addressing specific institutions of the new state, Jinnah exhorted the armed forces to uphold "the high traditions of Islam and our National Banner" (8 November 1947); and commended the State Bank research organization to evolve "banking practices compatible with Islamic ideals of social and economic life" and to "work our destiny in our own way and present to the world an economic system based on true Islamic concept of equality of manhood and social justice" (1 July 1948). I have taken all the above quotes from al-Mujahid.[53]

With pirs, *sajjada nashins*, and *makhdooms*, Jinnah had to go the extra mile for their support. For details I refer the interested reader to Ishtiaq Ahmed's recent book.[54] He quotes sources that the Pir of Manki Sharif founded an organization of his own, the *Anjuman-us-Asfia*, which promised to support the Muslim League on condition that sharia be enforced in Pakistan. To this Jinnah agreed. As a result, the Pir Amn-ul-Hasanat of Manki Sharif declared jihad to achieve Pakistan and ordered the members of his organization to support the League in the 1946 elections. Jinnah, without specifying what might be construed as

162 Founder III: Liberal, Secular, Visionary?

"contrary to Islamic ideals and principles" but without committing himself to sharia law assures the Pir that the constitution will be according to Islam:

> I am greatly thankful to you for the powerful support which you have been pleased to give to the All India Muslim League...as regards your preliminary question of Pakistan being established is settled, it will not be the Muslim League that will frame the constitution of Pakistan but inhabitants of Pakistan in which 75% will be the Musalmans and, therefore, you will understand that it will be a Muslim government and it will be for the people of Pakistan to frame the constitution under which the Pakistan government will come into being and function. Therefore, there need be no apprehension that the Constitution Making Body, which will be composed of overwhelming majority of Muslims, can be ever establish any constitution for Pakistan other than one based on Islamic ideals, nor can the government of Pakistan when comes into being act contrary to Islamic ideals and principles.[55]

Post-Partition and with Pakistan achieved, the Muslim League still did not see it fit to open its membership to Hindus and Christians. It was then – and remained – a party of exclusion. The only non-Muslim member was a Dalit and follower of Dr. Ambedkar, Jogendra Nath Mandal. As such he was one of the 96 founding fathers of Pakistan, but in 1950 he submitted his resignation to prime minister Liaquat Ali Khan as a protest against the treatment of Dalits and Hindus in Pakistan. To evade arrest, he fled to India and died there in 1968.

Jinnah and the Islamic state

The mother of all questions was still hanging by the time Jinnah died: what was Pakistan to be? Did his Muslim League want to create a Muslim majority state where individuals, whether Muslim or otherwise, would be free to live their lives as in other countries? Or instead to create a state governed by 7th-century sharia law? If so, what exactly would such a state look like in the 20th century where science and technology had created an unrecognizably different world? Could secular principles apply in the functioning of whatever state he was proposing, or would they run afoul of certain religious principles and precedents? We now turn to these questions because they were important not just at the time of General Zia-ul-Haq, but also because Imran Khan continues to promise Pakistanis an Islamic state in the form of *Riyasat-e-Madina*. When Khan finally exits the political scene others will likely have to promise some such thing. It is difficult to conceive of a future leader staying clear of religious sloganeering.

From the early days of the Pakistan Movement, Jinnah's calculated ambiguity on the Islamic state had led to differences between him and the more religious young Muslim Leaguers, who had responded wholeheartedly to the League's call for Pakistan. There was, in fact, a long difference of opinion between Jinnah and

Founder III: Liberal, Secular, Visionary? **163**

the Raja of Mahmudabad, also a Shia and major source of financial support to the League, who happened to be the youngest member of the League's working committee. The Raja writes in his memoirs:

> I was one of the founder members of the Islamic *Jamaat*. We advocated that Pakistan should be an Islamic state. I must confess that I was very enthusiastic about it and in my speeches I constantly propagated my ideas. My advocacy of an Islamic state brought me into conflict with Jinnah. He thoroughly disapproved of my ideas and dissuaded me from expressing them publicly from the League platform lest the people might be led to believe that Jinnah shared my view and that he was asking me to convey such ideas to the public. As I was convinced that I was right and did not want to compromise Jinnah's position, I decided to cut myself away and for nearly two years kept my distance from him, apart from seeing him during working committee meetings and other formal occasions. It was not easy to take this decision as my associations with Jinnah had been very close in the past. Now that I look back I realize how wrong I had been.[56]

In the above we hear the Raja saying he wanted an Islamic state in Pakistan. Jinnah, however, refused. Pakistanis of the post-Zia generation who were brought up to believe that Pakistan was indeed conceived as a sharia state might be surprised at this. It is therefore of some importance to figure out just what Jinnah may have meant, or at the very least, to give context to his various utterances regarding the Islamic state.

No reference that Jinnah made to the Islamic state suggests any indication of familiarity with the literature on this subject. None contain specific references to the *hadith*, or even to the works of classical scholars such as Ibn-Khaldun, Al-Mawardi, and Al-Tabari who wrote on government and state from an Islamic perspective. Instead, there are vague generalities only when he alludes to any religious matter. Without relating any of the standard anecdotes generally used for demonstrating Islamic principles of fair play and justice, he uses a typical populist and rhetorical style. For example, to the Sibi Darbar in 1948, Jinnah said:

> Let us lay the foundations of our democracy on the basis of truly Islamic ideas and principles. Our Almighty has taught is that our decisions in the affairs of the state shall be guided by discussion and consultations.[57]

Jinnah used the terms "Muslim state", "Islamic state", and simply "state" rather loosely and interchangeably. Even if they mean very different things, all three are sometimes used in the same speech. But there is a strong correlation between his choice of words and the audience before him. For instance, in a press statement on 31 July 1947 addressed to the Tribal Areas, Jinnah said:

164 Founder III: Liberal, Secular, Visionary?

> The Government of Pakistan has no desire whatsoever to interfere in any way with the traditional independence of the Tribal Areas. On the contrary, we feel *as a Muslim State* [emphasis added], we can always rely on [the] active support and sympathy of the tribes.[58]

But, concluding his statement, Jinnah chose to use the term "Islamic state" instead:

> In the end, I would appeal to all the different elements in the Frontier Province and in the Tribal Areas to forget past disputes and differences and join hands with the Government of Pakistan in setting up a truly democratic *Islamic State*.[59]

He used similar terminology – referring to Pakistan as a "Muslim State" – in a statement of assurance to the people of Balochistan.[60] But, in another press statement (which was not addressed to any specific audience) about the question of minorities in Pakistan, which appeared two days before the one quoted above, Jinnah urged people to "make the building of Pakistan, as one of the greatest States in the world, successful".[61] In a broadcast address to the people of the United States in February 1948 (ironically, in the same speech where Jinnah came out forcefully against theocracy), and later to students at King Edwards Medical College, Jinnah described Pakistan as "the premier Islamic State".[62]

In brief: all along the movement to achieve Pakistan, Jinnah consciously sought ambiguity on the nature of the state he was fighting for. It was one thing on one day, and another on another day. It is impossible to know what he really meant. He appears not to have studied relevant texts nor ever defined the meaning of Islamic state. Of course, to be unclear was also a political necessity: insisting upon any one particular model in a clear and definite way would alienate one or the other of his supporting groups. This he simply could not afford. One the one hand, he had vehemently disagreed with Raja Mahmudabad who had passionately argued for an Islamic state. On the other hand, his statement of a Pakistan wherein sovereignty would rest in the people (democracy, wherein laws are man-made) was flatly contradicted by his calls for an Islamic state wherein, by definition, sovereignty lies with Allah (i.e., laws have been already given in the Holy Book). Equally, his warning: "I want the Muslims of the Frontier to understand that they are Muslims first and Pathans afterwards" conflicts with his famous utterance just one year later that "You may belong to any religion or caste or creed – that has nothing to do with the business of the State". Political compromises are made for the moment, but the confusions they generate remain forever.

Jinnah's Shia Problem

Jinnah parried questions on matters of his personal belief, whether he was Shia or Sunni. "Was the Holy Prophet Shia or Sunni?", he would ask rhetorically. This

Founder III: Liberal, Secular, Visionary? **165**

prompted accusations that he was practicing *taqiyya*, a Shia device permitted for purposes of self-preservation where one might publically deny being Shia. On the rare occasions where he was seen praying in public, it was with his hands folded as per the Sunni tradition, and not with his hands down as the Shia way demands. Nevertheless, upon his death his sister, Fatima Jinnah, claimed inheritance according to Shia law.[63] All this had to be done very delicately, and Jinnah's funeral prayers were performed privately with a Shia prayer leader, but the state funeral was led by a Sunni Deobandi *alim*, Shabbir Ahmed Usmani, a fact that Shias find distasteful even today. A conservative anti-Shia Deobandi scholar, Usmani had campaigned hard to wrench Muslim support away from Congress in NWFP and Punjab. After Jinnah's death, Usmani spearheaded the Objectives Resolution in 1949, a first step towards creating a state based on religion.

For Jinnah, a culturally Western man with no religious training, the theological Sunni–Shia dispute was quaintly antediluvian. But in the 1940s he was faced by extreme Shia nervousness about a future Sunni Islamic state that may target Shias along with Hindus and Sikhs. In earlier times – 1908, 1930, and 1935 – there had been major Shia–Sunni riots in Lucknow. Ultimately both *tabarra* (considered provocative by Sunnis) and *madhe-sahaba* (considered provocative by Shias) were banned by the British. If Pakistan was created, could Shias be going from the frying pan into the fire? Sections of the Shia *ulema* had already denounced the Muslim League as a Sunni organization. For this reason, Jinnah's friend, the Raja of Mahmudabad, had become less and less enthusiastic about creating Pakistan as an Islamic state. In fact, at the very end he opted to stay on in India after Partition.

In his recent book Simon Fuchs studies in detail the pre-Partition predicament of Shiism and contends that most scholars of the period have not fully understood how serious and widespread Shia worries were.[64] They had, in fact, demanded that for official purposes the British categorize Sunni and Shia as belonging to two separate religions, but this request had been rejected. Two months after the Lahore Resolution of 1940 in which Jinnah made the demand for Pakistan, the All-India Shia Conference had speaker after speaker denouncing the idea of Pakistan.[55] In October 1945, a Shia activist wrote:

> I am a Shia first and a Muslim afterwards. I do not believe in any abstract conception of Islam. We are either Sunnis or Shias...I emphatically say that we [Shias] represent true Islam and if we are doomed Islam is doomed. Now let me say that the religious, economic, political and social rights of the Shias have never been so much endangered in the country as they are now – not at the hands of the Hindus or the Congress but at the hands of your Muslim League and your Quaid-i-Azam, Mr Jinnah.[66]

Restrictions placed upon *azadari* and *tazia* processions in Punjab and Bihar were blamed on Muslim League members in high official positions. Jinnah was asked by Shia leaders for guarantees that they would be protected from

166 Founder III: Liberal, Secular, Visionary?

Hanafi interpretations of the *fiqh*. He refused, giving vague assurances of fair play and justice for all, including Shias. Thereafter the All-India Shia Political Conference's mouthpiece *Sarfaraz* published an editorial questioning the need for Pakistan:

> If our life will be limited to protest and sacrifice [*ihtijaj aur qurbani*], what sort of need do we have for Pakistan? A united Hindustan is way better for us, because the Hindus do not mind if we proclaim that Ali was the immediate successor of the Prophet [*khilafa bi-la-fasl*] or engage in mourning rites.[67]

In spite of such reservations, and the AISPC ultimately supporting the Congress, the mood of the times was such that enthusiasm for Pakistan captured the Shia majority. Dhulipala notes that in 1945,

> A new feature of Moharram *alams* and *tazias* that year was the prominence of the Pakistan map in front of every group of processions and the mounting of ML flags on elephants. The usual Moharram slogan of *Ya Ali* was replaced by the ML war cry *"le ke rahenge Pakistan"*.[68]

When a bandwagon starts rolling, those who do not get on board become mere bystanders. The question of whether Shias are Muslims — or whether Ahmadis are Muslims — became irrelevant once they became convinced that following the British departure Hindus would crush all Muslims, both Sunni and Shia. Shia leaders assured their followers that in the new country of Islam, the relationship between Sunni and Shia would change for the better. With such fears allayed, the success of the Pakistan Movement drew closer.

A Master Tactician Not Strategist

Six years before Partition, on 19 January 1940, Jinnah had written of two nations "who both must share the governance of their common motherland".[69] Now let us imagine a formula for shared governance within a confederation or, alternatively, that Jinnah's insistence on a large Pakistan had been accepted thereby averting a "moth-eaten Pakistan" and preventing the mostly non-Muslim districts in Bengal and Punjab from being partitioned away. Would either have worked and lifted the Muslims of India out of their malaise?

My personal opinion is that this could not have sufficed. Missing entirely from the Pakistan Movement was the realization that prosperity for countries in the modern world comes from modern education and a change of attitude that welcomes rational, scientific thinking. There was no introspection into why Muslim rule had been wiped out by the British. There was no attempt to build institutions such as they brought with them — institutions built upon modern ways of thinking that would be much larger and outlast their founders. Unlike Sir Syed, Jinnah had been so preoccupied with daily matters of politics that he

Founder III: Liberal, Secular, Visionary? **167**

never made a forceful pitch for Muslims to understand what attitudes had disadvantaged them relative to Hindus.

Even in a politically reconfigured India, it is hard to see how the Hindu–Muslim difference would have decreased without stressing modernization of the Muslim mind and Muslim practices. In contrast to Jinnah, beginning with land reform Nehru took every opportunity to stress what a modern country required of its citizens. Today his stamp upon Indian science can be seen across the length and breadth of India in the form of dozens of scientific institutes and universities that owe their existence to him. India is probably the world's only country whose constitution explicitly declares commitment to the "scientific temper" – a quintessential Nehruvian notion formulated during his years in prison.

Jinnah was a modern man who well understood the power of modern institutions and the system of thought that gave rise to them. But politics came first. So, for example, while inaugurating the State Bank of Pakistan in Karachi on 1 July 1948, he felt constrained to make vague allusions to an Islamic economic system instead of emphasizing the need for a modern banking system:

> The adoption of Western economic theory and practice will not help us in achieving our goal of creating a happy and contended people. We must work our destiny in our own way and present to the world an economic system based on true Islamic concept of equality of manhood and social justice. We will thereby be fulfilling our mission as Muslims and giving to humanity the message of peace which alone can save it and secure the welfare, happiness and prosperity of mankind.[70]

But wait! An intelligent man like Jinnah surely knew that there is no such thing as "Western economic theory". Both in theory and practice, the varieties of capitalism, socialism, and communism are as different as can be and simply cannot be lumped together. Nordic countries have systems unrecognizably different from those of the United States. What then is the "Western economic system"? As for an Islamic economic system in modern times, no one has yet figured out what that might be. Is the oil economy of Saudi Arabia run by westerners to be taken as Islamic? Do Iran, Turkey, Morocco, Egypt, Malaysia, or Indonesia have economies that can be called Islamic? Or, for that matter, Pakistan? More to the point: landlordism and serfdom manifestly prevent millions of Pakistanis from "creating a happy contented people", and yet in 1989 the Shariat Appellate Bench of the Supreme Court declared agrarian reform as un-Islamic.[71]

Jinnah was a pragmatic political leader and a brilliant tactician. But he was not a visionary or deep thinker. His interest in Islamic history was perfunctory. Rarely did he make any connection with historical events or draw upon either the individuals or glories of the Islamic Golden Age or, closer to home, those of the Mughal Empire and its achievements in centralized administration, art, and architecture. Instead he looked at the case of Muslims in India just as a first-rate lawyer would in trying to secure the best possible deal for his clients. As a politician, he was like

168 Founder III: Liberal, Secular, Visionary?

a juggler throwing up many balls simultaneously, concentrating upon those still up there and ignoring the ones he had dropped. To save Muslims from the tyranny of the Hindu majority's domination was Jinnah's one and only clear purpose. As for what the new country would be, he simply assumed – wrongly as it turned out – that time would sort things out. He was also wrong in assuming that somehow Sunni–Shia and India–Pakistan differences would be ironed out in due course.

But it is unfair to demand that Jinnah alone should provide the idea and vision of Pakistan and to be its sole champion of modernity. Surely this monumental task cannot be one man's work alone. After four decades of political struggle, a cadre of able deputies should have been ready by 1947. That was theoretically possible but difficult. The Muslim political class in India was small and Sir Syed's efforts had not led to any prominent modernist reformers. Nevertheless, had Jinnah emphasized modernism as a desirable goal in earlier stages, it may have drawn more modern men like Mian Iftikharuddin around him. Once Pakistan had been achieved, it was far too late for him to set direction even if he now had something definite in mind. His role was basically over.

Arrayed before Jinnah were a host of dedicated opponents – all Sunni Muslims – who thought differently. They opposed creating a separate country for Muslims and had to be defeated. Although Jinnah ultimately trumped them, their opposition was for varied reasons and each deserves separate, careful consideration. We turn to them next.

Notes

1 M.A. Jinnah, Illustrated Weekly of India, 29 June 1947 (Late News Supplement), p. 1.
2 M.A. Jinnah, speech of 11 August 1947, Government of Pakistan official website, http://www.pakistan.gov.pk/Quaid/quotes_page2.html.
3 C.H. Philips and M.D. Wainwright (eds.), *Partition of India – Policies and Perspectives 1937–1947*, Cambridge, Mass., MIT Press (1970), p. 32.
4 A.H. Syed, *The Discourse and Politics of Zulfikar Ali Bhutto*, London, Macmillan Press (1992), p. 5.
5 A. Jalal, *The Sole Spokesman: Jinnah, the Muslim League, and the Demand for Pakistan*, Cambridge University Press (1994), p. xv.
6 *Selected Works of Jawaharlal Nehru*; First Series: Vol. 13, p. 324.
7 K. Callard, *Pakistan – A Political Study*, The Macmillan Company (1957), p. 20.
8 R. Khan, *The Role of Military – Bureaucratic Oligarchy*, www.roedad.com.
9 F. Devji, *Muslim Zion – Pakistan as a Political Idea*, Harvard University Press (2013), p. 4.
10 Jalal, op. cit., p. 5.
11 A. Beg, *The Quiet Revolution: A Factual Story of Political Betrayal in Pakistan*, Karachi, Pakistan Patriotic Publications (1959), p. 34.
12 Ahmed (see Jinnah, p496) has noted that this speech is missing from a book collection of Jinnah's speeches 1947–1948 authored by Pakistani historian M. Rafique Afzal in 1966. Significantly, this was well before General Zia-ul-Haq who is accused of hiding the speech from public view.
13 India says it does not have Jinnah's 1947 speech, published 8 June 2012, https://www.bbc.com/news/world-asia-india-18363958
14 I. Ahmed, *Jinnah: His Successes, Failures and Role in History*, Penguin Viking (2020), pp. 483–504.

Founder III: Liberal, Secular, Visionary? **169**

15 Speech at a meeting of the Aligarh Muslim University Union, Aligarh, 9 March 1944.
16 M. Shafique, *Islamic Concept of Modern State*, Gujarat, The Centre for Islamic Research (1987), p. 34.
17 C. Jaffrelot, *The Pakistan Paradox – Instability and Resilience*, Oxford University Press (USA), Translated by Cynthia Schoch (2015), p. 86.
18 A.H. Syed, Factional Conflict in the Punjab Muslim League, 1947–1955, *Polity*, 22, no. 1 (1989): 49–73. Accessed October 11, 2020. doi:10.2307/3234846.
19 I. Talbot, *Pakistan – A Modern History*, *Hurst and Company*, London (1998), pp. 125–147.
20 K. bin Sayeed, *Pakistan—The Formative Phase*, eighth edition, Karachi, Oxford University Press (2000), p. 298.
21 E.J. Benthall papers, File Nos. 12&19, CSAS, Cambridge, quoted in M. Hasan, *Islam in the Subcontinent*, Manohar Books (2002), p. 211.
22 A. Altaf, *Javed Jabbar vs. Pervez Hoodbhoy: Round by Round*, May 20, 2020, https://eacpe.org/javed-jabbar-vs-pervez-hoodbhoy-round-by-round/
23 M. Bourke-White, *Halfway to Freedom: A Report on the New India*, New York, Simon & Schuster (1949), pp. 91–92.
24 *Some Recent Speeches and Writings of Mr. Jinnah*, Edited by Jamil-ud-Din Ahmad and published by Sh. Muhammad Ashraf, Lahore, 1942. A selection of speeches, writings and statements of Jinnah from 1935 to 1942, p. 230.
25 *Jinnah Did Not Want Partition: Ayesha Jalal*, interviewed by Ali Usman Qasmi, Herald, 13 April 2017.
26 *M.A. Jinnah*, reported in Dawn, 23 March 1945.
27 I. Ahmed, *Muslims against the Muslim League: Critiques of the Idea of Pakistan*, Daily Times 11 November 2017.
28 Z.H. Zaidi, *Jinnah Papers: Pakistan in the Making 3 June–30 June 1947*, First Series, Vol. II, Islamabad, National Archives of Pakistan (1994), p. 115.
29 *Some Recent Speeches and Writings of Mr. Jinnah*, op. cit..
30 K. bin Sayeed, Personality of Jinnah and his Political Strategy, in Philips and Wainwright, *Partition of India*, op. cit., pp. 276–293.
31 A.S. Ahmed, *Jinnah, Pakistan and Islamic Identity – The Search for Saladin*, Routledge.
32 *Shirin Jinnah Remembers Her Brother – the Quaid-i-Azam*, Dawn, 25 December 1976.
33 C.M. Naim, *Iqbal, Jinnah, and Pakistan: The Vision and the Reality*, http://www.columbia.edu/itc/mealac/pritchett/00litlinks/naim/ambiguities/13iqbaljinnah.html#n12
34 D. Khan, *The Politics of Business: The Congress Ministry and the Muslim League in Bombay, 1937–39, Bombay Before Mumbai*, Hurst Publishers, (2019), p. 285.
35 S. Casci, Muslim Self-determination: Jinnah-Congress Confrontation, 1943–44, *Politice*, 63, no. 1(184) (1998): p. 70. http://www.jstor.org/stable/43101775
36 Eighteen volumes have so been published, each is around 1200 pages.
37 M. Munir, *From Jinnah to Zia*, Lahore, Vanguard Books Ltd. (1980), p. 29.
38 J. Ahmed, *Recent Writings and Speeches*, p. 248.
39 K. K. Aziz, The Making of Pakistan, Islamabad: National Book Foundation, 1976.
40 Jinnah: Speeches and Statements 1947 – 1948; Oxford University Press Karachi; pp. 13 and 15. Jinnah Papers, ed. Zawar Zaidi, Vol. III, doc# VIII.2 (in Appendix VIII), p.1005.
41 S. Wolpert, Jinnah of Pakistan, Stanley Wolpert, Oxford University Press (2005), ppg 34–35.
42 F. Devji, Muslim Zion - Pakistan as a Political Idea, Harvard University Press, p106, (2013).
43 J. Ahmad, *Some Recent Speeches and Writings of Mr Jinnah*, p. 59, https://archive.org/details/SomeRecentSpeechesAndWritingsOfMr.Jinnah-JamiluddinAhmad/page/n25/mode/2up
44 *We Are a Nation: Excerpts from the Speeches and Statements of Quaid-i-Azam Mohammad Ali Jinnah (1937–1947)*, Mirza, Sarfaraz Hussain (ed.), Lahore, Nazaria-i-Pakistan Trust (2010), pp. 2–3.

45 Quaid-i-Azam Mohammad Ali Jinnah at Lahore Session of Muslim League, March, 1940, Islamabad: Directorate of Films and Publishing, Ministry of Information and Broadcasting, Government of Pakistan, Islamabad (1983), pp. 5–23.

46 R.J. Booney, Jinnah to Gandhi, 17 September 1944 in *Three giants of South Asia: Gandhi, Ambedkar, and Jinnah on Self-Determination* (2004), p. 193.

47 J. Ahmed, Speeches and Statements of Mr. Jinnah, Lahore: M. Ashraf, 1968, pp. 208–209.

48 J. Ahmad, Speeches and Writings of Mr. Jinnah – Vol. 2, Lahore: M. Ashraf, 1960, p. 243.

49 L. Carter, Punjab Politics, 1 January 1944–3 March 1947: Last Years of the Ministries, Governors' Fortnightly Reports and Other Key Documents, New Delhi, Manohar, p. 171.

50 Reported in The Eastern Times, Lahore, 27 November 1945. See Yusufi, Khurshid Ahmad Khan (ed.), *Quaid-i-Azam, Muhammad Ali Jinnah: Some Rare Speeches and Statements 1944-1947*, Lahore, Research Society of Pakistan, University of the Punjab (1988), pp. 98–99.

51 Cited in Illustrated Weekly of India, 29 June 1947 (Late News Supplement), p. 1.

52 S. al Mujahid, *Jinnah's Vision of Pakistan*, available at http://www.progress.org.pk/jinnahs-vision-of-pakistan-by-sharif-al-mujahid/

53 Ibid.

54 I. Ahmed, *Jinnah: His Successes, Failures and Role in History*, Penguin Viking (2020).

55 Letter to Pir Amn-ul-Hasanat of Manki Sharif, 18 November 1945. Quoted in: Khan, Israj and Begum, Toheeda, Quaid-e-Azam Muhammad Ali Jinnah and Pir Amin-ul-Hasanat of Manki Sharif, *Abasyn Journal of Social Sciences*, 4, no. 2, p. 402.

56 Raja of Mahmudabad, Some Memories, in his Political Strategy, in Philips and Wainwright, *Partition of India*, op. cit., pp. 388–389.

57 S.M. Burke and S. Qureshi, *Quaid-i-Azam Mohammad Ali Jinnah His personality and His Politics*, Karachi, Oxford University Press (1967), p. 369.

58 Jinnah Papers, op. cit. doc# VIII.4, p. 524.

59 Ibid.

60 Ibid. This statement appeared in The Pakistan Times on 13 August 1947, reproduced in the Jinnah Papers, doc# VIII.8, p. 527.

61 Ibid. This statement appeared in The Pakistan Times on 29 July 1947, reproduced in the Jinnah Papers, doc# VIII.2, p. 522.

62 http://www.pakistan.gov.pk/Quaid/speech25.htm

63 Devji, op. cit., pp. 215–220 details how Jinnah and his sister tackled the question of their Shia identity.

64 S.W. Fuchs, *In a Pure Muslim Land – Shi'ism between Pakistan and the Middle East*, The University of North Carolina Press (2019).

65 *Kalb-i'Abbās, Rū'idād-iijlās-i-sīyum-i-All India Shī'ah Conference*, quoted in Ibid, p. 17.

66 Ibid, p. 45.

67 Ibid, p. 43.

68 V. Dhulipala, *Creating a New Medina - State Power, Islam, and the Quest for Pakistan in Late Colonial North India*, Cambridge University Press (2015), p. 445.

69 M.A. Jinnah, article in *Time and Tide* (London), 19 January 1940.

70 M.A. Jinnah, speech on the occasion of the inauguration of the State Bank of Pakistan at Karachi, 1 July 1948.

71 S. Aziz, *A Leaf From History: Shariat Court Strikes Down Land Reforms as 'un-Islamic'*, 13 November 2016.

Six

JINNAH TROUNCES HIS MUSLIM OPPONENTS

> I must confess that the very term Pakistan goes against my grain. It suggests that some portions of the world are pure while others are impure. Such a division of territories into pure and impure is un-Islamic and is more in keeping with orthodox Brahmanism which divides men and countries into holy and unholy – a division which is a repudiation of the very spirit of Islam.
>
> – Abul Kalam Azad[1]

How terribly confusing: most of the traditional Muslim *ulema* in India supported the Indian National Congress, while most modernized Muslims opted for Pakistan through the All-India Muslim League (AIML). Jinnah, the liberal, got his Pakistan in spite of his Muslim opponents. Those who opposed him had reasons that varied: some thought Jinnah's lifestyle was insufficiently Muslim for him to argue for a Muslim state. Others disagreed with AIML's mission on the grounds of Islamic ideology while yet others feared AIML as an organization that would sow Hindu–Muslim discord. With the British rulers about to leave after ruling for nearly two centuries, India's Muslims feverishly grappled with the problem of identity, religious diversity, and personal politics. While that story is important academically for understanding the lead-up to Partition, my principal concern in this chapter will be to look at the legacies some of Jinnah's strongest opponents left behind. These remain visible and important even today. Here we shall be concerned with three individuals who became the most prominent: Abul Ala Maududi because, apart from despising Jinnah for his anglicized ways, he saw Islam as universal and argued that an Islamic state with defined borders was improper; Abul Kalam Azad because he surmised that the Muslims of India would be collectively weakened if they were to be physically distanced; and

DOI: 10.4324/9781003379140-9

Khan Abdul Ghaffar Khan because of his commitment to peace and opposition to communal politics.

As he expertly navigated the dark web of Indian politics, a personally secular but politically communalist Jinnah encountered a variety of hostile Muslim reactions to the making of a separate Muslim state. Of all who opposed Jinnah, three individuals stand out: Syed Abul Ala Maududi, Abul Kalam Azad, and Khan Abdul Ghaffar Khan. But these persons must be chosen from a long list that would include Malik Khizar Hayat Tiwana (premier of Punjab and leader of Unionist Party), Khan Abdul Qayyum Khan (later first chief minister of NWFP), Allah Baksh Soomro (chief minister of Sind), Maulana Attaullah Shah Bukhari, Nawabzada Nasrullah Khan, Maulana Hussain Ahmed Madani, Obaidullah Sindhi, and scores of others. Some opposed Pakistan because they shunned all politics and dedicated themselves solely to religious pursuits. Others were religious and emphatically rejected Jinnah, the man. Then there were Muslim organizations and political parties that believed in a united India. A partial list would include All-India Azad Conference, All-India Jamhur Muslim League, All-India Shia Political Conference, All-India Momin Conference, All-India Muslim Majlis, Jamiat Ahl-e-Hadith, Khudai Khidmatgars (NWFP), and Unionist Party of Punjab.

In this chapter I have chosen to concentrate on only Maududi, Azad, and Ghaffar Khan. This is both because they are sufficiently different from each other and they represent sufficiently important oppositional strands from those times. Still more importantly their legacies are clearly visible today across the subcontinent and their words ring loudly and clearly. An honest appraisal of oppositional leaders is largely missing from the literature, but an excellent recent book, *Muslims against the Muslim League – Critiques of the Idea of Pakistan*[2] gives a broader spectrum and more detailed analysis than is possible here.

At one level, it is quite astonishing that believing Muslims should have opposed the creation of a Muslim state that would privilege their own kind. It is all the more remarkable because present day *ulema* in Pakistan are loudly insistent that Islam and Pakistan be conjoined at every point. One might be tempted to dismiss Muslim opponents of a Muslim state as being Muslim in name only. However, it is hard to dismiss their Islamic credentials because among them were distinguished authors of Islamic religious texts who were fluent in Urdu, Persian, and Arabic. They could quote from Islamic history and traditions and freely recite verse and chapter from the Qur'an and Hadith.

Many of Jinnah's Muslim opponents had large followings. Barely a month after he demanded Pakistan in his March 1940 Lahore speech, the Azad Muslim Conference was held in April 1940. It was a formidable array of Muslim organizations opposed to the Muslim League's demand for the division of India along Hindu–Muslim lines. It was attended by delegates from Jamiat Ulama-i-Hind, Majlis-i-Ahrar, the All-India Momin Conference, the All-India Shia Political Conference, Khudai Khidmatgars, the Bengal Krishak Praja Party, Anjuman-i-Watan Baluchistan, the All-India Muslim Majlis, and Jamiat Ahl-e-Hadis.[3]

Jinnah Trounces His Muslim Opponents **173**

After Partition, those opposing groups that remained in India could claim having spoken up for Indian nationalism and so managed to escape the worst. On the other hand, those who sought to reestablish themselves in Pakistan had to eat their words, deny them, appeal to "context", or simply go out of existence.

Maududi Was Jinnah's Nemesis

> Islamic civilization did not aim at producing Tansen, Behzad and Charlie Chaplin but Abu Bakar, Omar, Hussain, Abu Dharr Ghaffari and Rabia Basri.
>
> *— Abul Ala Maududi*[4]

Syed Abul Ala Maududi (1903–1979), founder of the Jamaat-e-Islami, loathed the anglicized Jinnah as well as the entire leadership of the All India Muslim League. He spent much of his time during the years 1941–1943 excoriating them for what he considered impious behavior, westernized ways and un-Islamic personal lifestyles. Like many other clerics of his time, he strongly felt that any movement in India in the name of Muslims should have real Muslims in the driving seat, not those whom he considered to be Muslim only in name.[5]

> The westernized Indian Muslims cannot understand divine truths. Even if they chatter about an Islamic state their slavish mentality and western education does not allow them to think beyond a nation state.[6]

In January 1947 Maududi referred to the "Pakistan of the Muslim League" as *faqistan* (the land of the famished) and *langra* Pakistan (crippled Pakistan).[7] At a time when the AIML was gathering speed, this led to his political marginalization.

Maududi observed Jinnah and the Muslim League leadership only from afar and seems never to have met any in person (although assertions to the contrary started emerging much later). But his opposition to the partitioning of India went still deeper. The Islamic faith, he said, does not recognize nationalism. This being a European construct, the call for a separate state for Muslims is spurious since the entire world belongs to Muslims anyway. Logically speaking, said Maududi, "Muslim nationalism is as contradictory a term as 'chaste prostitute'".[8] This was consistent with rightist literature of pre-Partition times which would sometimes use derogatory words such as *napakistan* or *paleedistan* for the proposed state.[9] At Jinnah's funeral, apart from Jamaat-e-Islami, the foremost religious right-wing political parties – Jamiat Ulama-i-Hind, Majlis-i-Ahrar, and Khaksar – were conspicuously absent.

In 1937 Maududi had migrated from Hyderabad Deccan to Pathankot and then two years later to Lahore, where he established the Jamaat-e-Islami (or the Jamaat) in the locality of Ichra. Founded in 1941 as an alternative to the Muslim League, the Jamaat was too small to play any significant role in the movement for or against Pakistan. After partition, members were expressly forbidden to pledge

174 Jinnah Trounces His Muslim Opponents

loyalty to the new state until such time as it became properly Islamic. Their animus to the League and to Jinnah in particular continued to grow. Though sympathetic to the idea of liberating Kashmir from India, the Jamaat refused to join in or support Pakistan's first Kashmir war in 1947. Only an Islamic government, said Maududi, can call for jihad – and Jinnah's government was manifestly not. The government, in turn, accused the Jamaat of treason and incarcerated several leaders including Maududi.

But things brightened up in a matter of years. Maududi became important in helping the country move away from its confused but relatively secular beginnings. His axe first fell upon the Ahmadis, who Jinnah had considered indistinguishable from Muslims and who had supported the Pakistan Movement without reservation.[10] In 1953 Ahmadis were targeted in a popular agitation led by Maududi and other clerics. They demanded removal of Zafarullah Khan (appointed by Jinnah as foreign minister) as well as all other Ahmadis from top government positions. Most importantly, the clerics insisted that Ahmadis be declared non-Muslim. Thousands of houses were set on fire and, depending on whom you believe, between 200–2000 Ahmadis were killed. Martial law was declared in Lahore for seventy days; this marked the military's first foray into the civilian domain. Maududi's initial death sentence was soon commuted to life imprisonment. A full pardon followed: a year later he walked out of prison, a free man.

The Jamaat had successfully brought to national politics the demand that Islam must play the dominant role in matters of the state. The constitution of 1956 reflected the demands of the Jamaat and its allies, in which they insisted on a complete Islamization of all state institutions. This constitution, however, was set aside by the 1958 coup led by General Ayub Khan. Maududi's real chance did not come until the 1977 coup that brought General Zia-ul-Haq to power. Whatever earlier reservations Maududi had on Pakistan thereafter disappeared. He supported Zia's decision to hang Bhutto and Islamicize Pakistan, his party becoming one of Zia's principal instruments of social control. In recognition, Maududi was accorded the dignity of a senior statesman, albeit an ailing one now. He breathed his last in April 1979 while seeking medical treatment in the United States. Paradoxically, that was the very country which he had spent much of his life excoriating as godless.

Let's take a closer look at this man.

Born in India's southern state of Hyderabad, Maududi's stock goes back to the Chishtia line of saints. As in a traditional Muslim environment, he was home-schooled in religious matters and developed excellent skills in Urdu but was unexposed to secular subjects like science and English. All around him Muslims were gripped by acute despair. Their ancient glories had long dissipated with just their traces now visible. Although the rulers of the Hindu-majority state of Hyderabad were Muslims and could still provide some modicum of protection, they had been reduced to cyphers by the British. That the Hindus of British India had done relatively much better was still more galling. They were manifestly

Jinnah Trounces His Muslim Opponents   **175**

wealthier, more prosperous, and educated. At one point Maududi sorrowfully remarked that when Hyderabad was ruled by Nizam Usman Ali Pasha, all the commerce was handled by Hindus. Among Muslims there was no clear sense of direction. With the departure of the British now on the horizon, what would happen to Muslims now shorn of their protection?

Vali Nasr, Maududi's patient and perceptive biographer, notes that around the time of the Khilafat Movement Maududi had flirted with Indian nationalism and was attracted by the pan-Islamism of Maulana Azad and his struggle against the British.[11] It was, of course, the British who had brought down Muslim power on the subcontinent, and it was scarcely unusual for the colonized to despise their colonizers. But Maududi's dislike of the Hindu was deeper and more visceral. He had no direct contact with the British, but Hindus were all around him. They would remain and form a majority once the British left, and so democracy was pointless. Secularism was out of the question because Islam was superior to Hinduism; it was unacceptable that both should be treated at par by a religiously neutral state – assuming that one could be made. Maududi watched with alarm Gandhi's growing political influence not just among Hindus but also sections of the Muslim intelligentsia. The last straw proved to be the emergence of the revivalist *Shuddhi* and *Sangathan* Movements seeking to reconvert Muslims into becoming Hindus again. Eventually Maududi built a communalist wall excluding any possibility of dialogue or coexistence between communities.

Meanwhile, Maududi's able pen, first as a journalist and then as an ideologue, was bringing repute to this young man. At age twenty-three he started writing *Al Jihad Fil Islam*, completed in three years, and then followed it up with *Islam ka Qanun-i-Jang* (Islamic Laws of War). These were a clarification of the rules, and equally a strident call to war, that received acclaim from Allama Iqbal as well as the Indian *ulema*.[12] His lack of formal *madrassa* training led the traditional clergy to haughtily dismiss the honorific *maulana* that would be eventually attached to his name. Nevertheless, his grasp of Islamic texts and literature was wider than that of most. In the early 1930s his writings also caught the attention of Nawab Salar Jung (1889–1949) then prime minister for the 7th Nizam-ul-Mulk of Hyderabad. The enormously wealthy Jang – his personally owned Salar Jung Museum stands today in grand memorial to him – took it upon himself to request that Maududi prepare a grand plan for propagating Islam in Hyderabad. Roy Jackson, one of Maududi's biographers, writes, "Such a request seems reminiscent of Dion's request for Plato to go to Syracuse and create a Platonic state".[13]

Maududi excoriates nationalism (*wataniyyat*) as a western concept. Muslims, he says, are one people by virtue of faith, and this transcends all other differences between them such as race, color, language, or economic status. He is unequivocal that a state with borders violates Islamic teachings. In *Tarjuman-ul-Qur'an* he writes:

> No river, mountain, ocean, language, race, color, and no power on earth has the right to draw a line of distinction in the circle of Islam and separate

176 Jinnah Trounces His Muslim Opponents

one Muslim from another. Every Muslim, whether a resident of China or Morocco, black or white, speaks Hindi or Arabic, Semite or Aryan, subject of one government or the other, is part of the Muslim *qaum*, member of the Islamic society, citizen of the Islamic state, soldier of the Islamic army and protected under the Islamic law.[14]

A secular state would be the antithesis of what Islam commands and, given that the British were about to leave, the thing to be feared most. There is no need, he said, to celebrate past Islamic achievements because they are irrelevant. Islam enjoins its followers to be faithful only to Islam, not to culture or nation defined in any sense except Islam. Therefore, an Indian Muslim could be as faithful a citizen of Egypt, and an Afghan could be as valiant in his fight for Syria as he was for Afghanistan.[15]

As it turned out, Jung's efforts were overambitious and generated little enthusiasm among people. Jang himself showed little interest in jihad, and a disillusioned Maududi concluded that he was wasting his time with rich rulers. Saving decrepit Muslim monarchies was not the way to go. Still, he was disinclined to support the demand for a separate Muslim state because Islam does not recognize physical borders and boundaries. Muslims could, he believed, eventually convert all of India to Islam. Simply finding a separate corner for Muslims would take away from this challenge and constitute a disservice. This, together with his dislike for the Muslim League leadership, is why he had initially opposed the demand for Pakistan.

From Nasr's careful biographical work, we learn that the deleterious economic impact of colonialism was not what mattered most to Maududi. Lack of jobs for Muslims in the colonial economy concerned him but did not enrage. Colonialism was evil because it propagated the twin menace of secularism and nationalism, both of which he saw as contrary to Islamic teachings. But, more than anything else, it was in the realm of culture that western ideas and practices – as well as Hindu accretions into Muslim culture – had to be fought most fiercely.

Although Jinnah had grandly insisted that Muslims and Hindus belonged to separate nations with separate cultures, he was vague about just how the two cultures were different. Nor did Jinnah's personal lifestyle set a convincing example of Islamic culture, especially after his marriage to the beautiful Bombay socialite, Rattanbai Petit. The daughter of a wealthy Parsi industrialist, Sir Dinshaw Petit, the vivacious young woman's dress, diet, language, and mannerisms were anathema to a conservative Muslim. The cultural space that Jinnah left empty, Maududi filled by specifying exactly what constituted proper Islamic behavior:

> The real place of women is the house and she has been exempted from outdoor duties…She has however been allowed to go out of the house to fulfil her genuine needs, but whilst going out she must observe complete modesty. Neither should she wear glamorous clothes and attract attention,

Jinnah Trounces His Muslim Opponents **177**

nor should she cherish the desire to display the charms of the face and the hand, nor should she walk in a manner which may attract attention of others. Moreover she should not speak to them without necessity, and if she has to speak she should not speak in a sweet and soft voice.[16]

The way forward became clear. What was needed, Maududi reasoned, was a new view of Islam. Exemplars from Islamic history — except for when the first four pious caliphs held sway — were useless at best and harmful at worst. Apart from these first twenty-nine glorious years of Islamic history, the rest amounted to *jahilyah*; Maududi therefore strongly recommended against the teaching of Islamic history for any other periods.[17] Indeed, Islamic history is not taught at the school level in Pakistan, probably due to the Jamaat's influence in the educational system. Remarkably, although Pakistan's National Curriculum of 2023 is steeped in religious matters — to the point that even science subjects have religious content[18] — there is no attempt to teach Islamic history.

Reckoning that only 1% of all Muslims really knew what Islam is, it became incumbent upon Maududi to show others the light. Once they got to know the true Islam, Muslims would become a uniform monolith and they would end forever the internal divisions which had left them weak and emaciated. Maududi gradually donned the mantle of *mujaddid* — one who would revive and revise Islamic theology as per the needs of the times. Did he see himself as Shaikh Ahmad Sirhindi who was in opposition to the times? Before him was the monumental task of figuring out what Islam was actually about and, most importantly, figuring out who could justly be called Muslim and who could not.

Maududi, like Golwalkar who preceded him, was fascinated by Hitler's success and saw himself as the philosopher behind the transformation to come: "German Nazism could not have succeeded in establishing itself except as a result of the theoretical contributions of Fichte, Goethe and Nietzsche, coupled with the ingenious and mighty leadership of Hitler and his comrades".[19] The result of Maududi's intellectual labors is a clear definition of Muslim, one which few other Muslim thinkers have dared to provide. Islam, he said, is a complete code of life and the cure of all ills, both personal and societal. Therefore, a Muslim is one who obeys unquestioningly the totality of divine law as revealed in the Qur'an. It is insufficient, he stresses again and again, to simply state your belief in the oneness of God and acceptance of Mohammad as his prophet (*shahada*). That does not make you a Muslim.

Denial of choice is essential for one to become Muslim, says Maududi. Once a man accepts the *shuhada*, he accepts becoming a slave of God. His logic continues: just as no slave may leave his master, no Muslim may leave the faith. Therefore, the penalty for apostasy can only be death: "In our domain we neither allow any Muslim to change his religion nor allow any other religion to propagate its faith".[20] Similarly, Maududi argued, since Allah has so ordained, women cannot choose to be unveiled — the only remaining issue to be debated is "whether the hands and the face (of women) were to be covered or left uncovered".[21] The

178 Jinnah Trounces His Muslim Opponents

Muslim woman, having accepted *shuhada*, may not leave the house unless absolutely necessary. Her primary duty is to bear children and bring "the greatest possible comfort and contentment to her husband".[22]

It is important to see how Maududi's *tajdeed* (revival) of Islam was different from those of the other *ulema* of his time. Instead of focusing on prayer and individual salvation – which he saw as narcissistic – Maududi wanted action: the Jamaat, he said, "is not a missionary organization or a body of preachers or evangelists, but an organisation of God's Troopers".[23] The function of ideology would be to generate collective social action and his Jamaat-e-Islami would be the Bolsheviks of the coming revolution, blazing the trail to utopia – the Islamic state – where man becomes God's slave:

> It must now be obvious that the objective of the Islamic jihad is to eliminate the rule of an un-Islamic system, and establish in its place an Islamic system of state rule. Islam does not intend to confine its rule to a single state or a hand full of countries. The aim of Islam is to bring about a universal revolution. Although in the initial stages, it is incumbent upon members of the party of Islam to carry out a revolution in the state system of the countries to which they belong; their ultimate objective is none other than world revolution.[24]

We now turn to an interesting debate in the 1980s on the Maududi–Iqbal relationship. This was particularly important at the time when history books were being revised and rewritten to suit the new post-coup political dispensation.[25] The effort started in earnest in 1981, when General Zia-ul-Haq declared compulsory the teaching of Pakistan studies to all degree students, including those at engineering and medical colleges.[26] On the one hand, there was a concerted effort made to repaint Jinnah and Iqbal as ultraconservatives. On the other, at a smaller scale, Maududi's followers – who now occupied the highest posts in the education sector – sought to establish that their party's founder had been a close confidante of Iqbal. Clearly any association with such an iconic symbol – whose fame as sage and philosopher had spread across India – would enhance the fortunes of an ascendant political party now aligned with the Zia regime. How true was the second claim?

To cut a long story short,[27] there certainly was a connection between Iqbal and Maududi, but it was nowhere as close or deep as claimed by the latter's followers. Iqbal had met Maududi once in 1929 in Hyderabad where Iqbal was lecturing. He was later to know of Maududi through his *Al-Jihad fi'l-Islam* and through his monthly journal *Tarjuman*, but there is no evidence that Iqbal was particularly in the thrall of Maududi's revivalist agenda. Still he did agree to appoint Maududi as head of an institution, Dar-ul-Islam, that Iqbal envisioned as the center for training a new generation of capable Muslim students where the curriculum would include modern subjects. Nasr remarks that Iqbal saw Maududi as a minor figure only:[28]

Even after the two met again in 1937, Iqbal's opinion of Mawdudi was guarded. Mian Muhammad Shafi', Iqbal's secretary, recollected that he referred to Mawdudi as "just a mullah [low-ranking cleric]", someone more suited to lead the prayers at the Badshahi mosque than to oversee a pioneering educational project. When *Daru'l-Islam* began, it had a staff of some twelve people, not the educated leaders that Iqbal had intended (besides Mawdudi only four other educated men were involved), but mainly people from nearby towns and villages. No person of consequence joined. When on April 21, 1938, Iqbal died, Mawdudi was greatly dismayed, but at least Iqbal's death freed him from the restrictions to which he had acceded in Lahore.[29]

Iqbal, discussed in detail earlier, was a clear cut above the home-grown, home-schooled Maududi. Sophisticated, well-read, and well-traveled, his intellectual universe ranged from classical texts in Persian and Arabic to Spengler, Spencer, and Nietzsche. It would be natural that he would not agree with Maududi on many specifics or think highly of his ideas on the nature of the Islamic state and the role of sharia. But there are deep similarities as well:

They can both be described to a certain extent as Islamists, purists, believers, or devout. They both see Islam as a comprehensive way of life governing the spiritual and the temporal through a system of belief and law. To some extent they both blame the failure of the Muslim society on its departure from "the straight path", and both fear the demons of secularization and Westernization. They believe that the renewal of Muslim society and the salvation of humankind (Asia) are dependent on Islamic religiopolitical and social reformation drawing its inspiration from the Quran. In seeking to restore God's rule, Western inspired civil codes must be replaced by Islamic law which is the only acceptable blueprint for Muslim society. Yet while Westernization is rejected, modernization is accepted when subordinated to Islamic belief. They both call on dedicated and trained individuals to set an example by joining the struggle against corruption and social injustice. Finally both agree that religion is integral to state and society.[30]

Some people believe that Maududi ultimately failed, or that he is just a minor figure. Indeed even seventy years later, his Jamaat fared quite poorly as a political force and has never won more than a handful of seats in any national or provincial election. Even after passions had risen sky high after the 2002 invasion of Afghanistan by the United States, the total votes cast to all religious parties, including the Jamaat, went from a meagre 2% to an all-time high of a mere 11%. Although it has been a part of coalition governments in the provinces, this has only been as a junior partner. In the 2018 elections, the Jamaat's needle barely moved.

180 Jinnah Trounces His Muslim Opponents

But electoral victory is only one criterion. It is an inadequate and misleading metric in judging the influence that Pakistan's religious parties have had on state and society. Take, for one, the Ahmadi issue. Having raised the temperature sufficiently high, the Jamaat eventually succeeded in their street agitations and forced Bhutto to declare the Ahmadis as non-Muslim in 1974. In later years, even though Maududi had passed away, the Jamaat successfully pushed through the shariat and blasphemy bills into legislation. This was a big victory. Of still greater significance is the deep penetration of the Jamaat into Pakistan's education system and the creation of a national consensus on the importance of religion in matters of the state.

Azad the Prescient Cleric

The erudite Abul Kalam Muhiyuddin Ahmed Azad (1888–1958) travelled a long personal journey that took him from being an orthodox Muslim scholar to becoming the most powerful Muslim voice for a secular Indian polity. Jinnah considered Azad a turncoat Muslim who had ganged up with Hindus and would disparagingly refer to him as Congress's showboy. On other occasions, Jinnah called him Lord Haw Haw – a derogatory term used for William Joyce, an Englishman who turned into a propagandist and broadcaster for Nazi propaganda during the Second World War. Azad earned these epithets for having fought Jinnah ferociously. As head of the Indian National Congress, he opposed Jinnah's communalism and his call to partition India. In 1923, Azad was thirty-five years old when he was elected president of the Indian National Congress. At its Delhi session, while presiding over the session, he said:

> If an angel were to descend from the high heavens and proclaim from the heights of the Qutab Minar: "Discard Hindu-Muslim Unity and within 24 hours *Swaraj* is yours", I will refuse *Swaraj* but will not budge an inch from my stand. If *Swaraj* is delayed it will affect only India, while the end of our unity will be a loss to all mankind.[31]

I have been unable to find out if Azad and Jinnah ever met face-to-face and had a conversation, but even if they had there wouldn't have been much to talk about.[32] For one, Azad understood and wrote English, but only much later was he able to speak it tolerably well; his communication with the British was via interpreters. For another Azad was Jinnah's cultural opposite. In contrast to Jinnah's westernized mannerisms and upbringing, he had been an aspiring cleric in his earlier years, one strictly guided by the prophetic tradition and revealed text. He had once fantasized of becoming the imam of all India's Muslims.[33] From his autobiography one can picture a young boy standing on top of a large chest and preaching to an imagined audience the virtues of following the Holy Prophet. It is no wonder that protagonists of the Pakistan idea were appalled – and furiously angry – that a committed Muslim was insistent upon Hindu–Muslim unity. There were undoubtedly other Muslim scholars who belonged to this school of thought, Maulana Hussain Ahmad Madani and Maulana Shibli Nomani being examples. Azad, however, is the most prominent.

Born in Makkah to an Arab mother and a Bengali *maulana* father, Azad was clearly precocious. Home-schooled by private tutors, he was fluent in Arabic, Persian, Urdu, Hindi, and Bengali. Thereafter he soon became familiar with different schools of Islamic thought: Hanafi, Shafi'i, Maliki, as well as with the principles of sharia and the Hanbali *fiqh*. He was to author over 20 books in English and Bengali on philosophy, literature, politics, and general culture, as well as two novels and three volumes of verse.

The youthful Azad – who would teach Islam to men twice his age – followed and preached in the orthodox Deobandi and Wahhabi tradition, insisting that every act of a Muslim must be in accord with the rules set out by the Qur'an and Sunnah. His eloquent style in Urdu drew a huge audience of religious conservatives and his monthly magazine *Al-Hilal* began publication in 1912 drawing an unprecedented circulation of 26,000 subscribers. Azad, like other Muslim fundamentalists,[34] insisted that there is no true or significant knowledge to be found outside of the Qur'an. Like Iqbal, he too dismissed Golden Age Muslim achievements as mere extensions of Greek culture and knowledge:

> Muslims take great pride in the civilization, knowledges, and the arts of Baghdad. But those were mere decorations for the pleasure of the rulers. We deem them worthy of no pride. Rather, a single hadith of the prophet, which Imam Bukhari has collected by traveling a hundred miles, is a thousand times more precious than all those knowledges.[35]

Pakistani historian Dr. Mubarik Ali points out that Azad, in his book *Tazkira*, focuses on the contribution of the Indian *ulema* to the Muslim community and glorifies Sheikh Ahmad Sirhindi who had resisted and defended Islam against the alleged atheism of Mughal emperor Akbar. Azad was thus the first significant Muslim who promoted Sirhindi as a hero and criticized Akbar's religious policy.[36] Significantly, Azad remains fairly popular in Pakistan for his *Al-Hilal* days. His later politics is set aside as an aberration; in their eyes, his true accomplishment was to argue the case for ultraconservatism.

Then something changed.

Azad's voyage towards secularism begins with his encounter with Mohandas Gandhi during the course of a pan-Islamic movement (1919–1924) of which Azad was a leader together with the brothers Shaukat Ali and Mohammad Ali. Known as the Khilafat Movement, it sought restoration of the caliphate in Turkey. Gandhi supported the movement because he thought it would help weaken the British. Azad became impressed by Gandhi's philosophy that the British needed to be expelled through civil disobedience, not violence. The two men hit it off well.

182 Jinnah Trounces His Muslim Opponents

Azad's search for humanism and liberalism within the Islamic paradigm is in a sense similar to that of another peripatetic, Sir Syed Ahmad Khan. In fact, Azad devoured Sir Syed's essays in a similar effort to reinterpret Islam. The result is his magnum opus – a commentary on the Qur'an, *Tarjuman-ul-Qur'an* – published in four volumes. Influenced by Sir Syed, Azad's approach therein is eclectic: the unity of all religions is the starting point for his explanation of the Qur'an.[37]

Over time Azad developed a philosophy that was extremely unusual for one trained to be a cleric: he espoused Indian nationalism, organized against the British Raj, called for Hindu–Muslim unity, and insisted that the real problems of India were economic, not communal. Around his philosophy of *wahdat-i-deen* – or the essential oneness of all religions – he played with a variety of ideas on culture and religion. Imprisoned by the British for his views, he wrote his ornate, superbly crafted letters in Urdu, *Ghubar-i-Khatir*, wherein he dismisses the belief that music is forbidden in Islam and, instead, dwells at great length on Indian classical music as reflecting a composite culture of Muslims and Hindus. At age thirty-five, he served as president of the Indian National Congress and, following India's independence, became the country's first minister of education. His magnum opus, *India Wins Freedom – An Autobiographical Account*, is dedicated to "Jawaharlal Nehru, friend and comrade".

In the years after the Khilafat Movement crashed, Azad became a powerful proponent of secular nationalism and an implacable opponent of creating a new nation based upon religion. On 15 April 1946 – well into the height of the movement for Pakistan – he made his opposition known in strong terms: "It is one of the greatest frauds on the people to suggest that religious affinity can unite areas which are geographically, economically, linguistically and culturally different".[38] Azad objects to the very name Pakistan (Land of the Pure); the concept offends his religious sensibilities as a Muslim:

> I must confess that the very term Pakistan goes against my grain. It suggests that some portions of the world are pure while others are impure. Such a division of territories into pure and impure is un-Islamic and is more in keeping with orthodox Brahmanism which divides men and countries into holy and unholy – a division which is a repudiation of the very spirit of Islam. Islam recognizes no such division and the Prophet says, "God has made the whole world a mosque for me".... As a Muslim, I for one am not prepared for a moment to give up my right to treat the whole of India as my domain and to share in the shaping of its political and economic life.[39]

Jinnah's presidential address to the All-India Muslim League, delivered in Lahore before 50,000 people[40] on 22 March 1940, was the stark opposite. He insisted that Hindus and Muslims were fundamentally incapable of coexistence within a single national state because "[they] belong to two different religious philosophies, social customs, and literatures. They neither intermarry nor inter-dine together...To yoke together two such nations under a single state, one as a

Jinnah Trounces His Muslim Opponents **183**

numerical minority and the other as a majority, must lead to growing discontent, and final destruction of any fabric that may be so built up for the government of such a state".[41]

Jinnah used a broad brush because he wanted to be seen as the spokesman for all Muslims, not just those of north India. He dismissed the absence of commonalities that would join the language, literature, and customs of Bengal with those of Sind and Punjab. Nor, for that matter, were Sind and Punjab considered as being different in essence. Jinnah's speeches and letters made no reference to subnations. But Azad, referring to pre-British times when Muslim and Hindu had lived in equanimity, rejects Jinnah's position:

> Mr. Jinnah's Pakistan scheme is based on his two nation theory. His thesis is that India contains many nationalities based on religious differences. Of them the two major nations, the Hindus and Muslims, must as separate nations have separate states. When Dr. Edward Thompson once pointed out to Mr. Jinnah that Hindus and Muslims live side by side in thousands of Indian towns, villages and hamlets, Mr. Jinnah replied that this in no way affected their separate nationality. Two nations according to Mr. Jinnah confront one another in every hamlet, village and town, and he, therefore, desires that they should be separated into two states.[42]

As the time for Britain's exit approached, Azad's apprehensions grew. The Congress's top leadership had been jailed following their 1942 Quit India demand and, until their release, the Muslim League had full liberty to spread its communal message. If Pakistan was actually created, he feared there would be unending conflict between two states which were about to be born in hatred. Most importantly, what would happen to the Muslims left behind in India after Partition?

> Let us consider dispassionately the consequences which will follow if we give effect to the Pakistan scheme. India will be divided into two states, one with a majority of Muslims and the other of Hindus. In the Hindustan State there will remain 3.5 crores of Muslims scattered in small minorities all over the land. With 17 per cent in UP, 12 per cent in Bihar and 9 per cent in Madras, they will be weaker than they are today in the Hindu majority provinces. They have had their homelands in these regions for almost a thousand years and built up well-known centres of Muslim culture and civilization there.[43]

Azad passionately argues that the Muslims left behind would discover that they had just become aliens and foreigners in their own land. Backward industrially, educationally, and economically, they would surely be left at the mercy of what would become "an unadulterated Hindu Raj". And so Azad turned to proposing compromises that might keep India united. Although he wrote, "Jawaharlal is one of my dearest friends", yet he in his opinion Nehru's "fondness for abstract

184 Jinnah Trounces His Muslim Opponents

theory" had led him to commit a big blunder after the 1937 elections when the Muslim League had suffered a great setback except in Bombay and Uttar Pradesh (UP). At that point Azad had sought to bring into the fold of Congress the League's winning candidates in UP, Chaudhari Khaliquzzaman and Nawab Ismail Khan. This would have taken away the steam from the League's claim that Congress was a Hindu party. But Nehru agreed to have only one of the two winners, which both refused. Azad writes:

> This was a most unfortunate development. If the League's offer of coopera-
> tion had been accepted, the Muslim League party would for all practical
> purposes merge with the Congress. Jawaharlal's action gave the Muslim
> League in the UP a new lease of life. All students of Indian politics know
> that it was from the UP that the League was reorganized. Mr. Jinnah took
> full advantage of the situation and started an offensive which ultimately led
> to Pakistan.[44]

As things move towards their climax, he noted in his autobiography that, "Once states based on hatred came into existence, nobody knew where the situation would lead".[45] He pleaded with Patel and Nehru to accept the 1946 Cabinet Mission Plan – a power-sharing formula – and not to accept Partition. What about an agreement whereby a Hindu and a Muslim would alternate as head of the Indian federation? To Azad's dismay, Patel and Nehru's earlier rejection of Partition was rapidly changing as the law and order situation degenerated. At this point neither leader was prepared to listen to him. Both had arrived at the conclusion that partitioning was a lesser evil than living with each other in a state of constant strife:

> I was surprised and pained when Patel in reply said that whether we liked
> it or not, there were two nations in India…. I now turned to Jawaharlal.
> He did not speak in favor of partition in the way that Patel did. In fact,
> he admitted that partition was by nature wrong. He had however lost all
> hopes of joint action after his experience of the conduct of the League
> members of the Executive Council. They could not see eye to eye on any
> question. Every day they quarreled. Jawaharlal asked me in despair what
> other alternative there was to accepting partition…he was coming to the
> conclusion day by day that there was no alternative…. I told Jawaharlal
> that I could not possibly accept his views. I saw quite clearly that we were
> taking one wrong decision after another.[46]

Upon approaching Gandhi, his mentor, Azad felt reassured when Gandhi said he would never allow Partition to happen. It could happen only, "over my dead body", said Gandhi, promising to prevail upon Congress to reject the Partition plan. To Azad's deep dismay, after Gandhi went to see Mountbatten, this firm-ness evaporated:

Jinnah Trounces His Muslim Opponents   **185**

But when I met Gandhiji again, I received the greatest shock of my life, for I found that he too had changed. He was still not openly in favor of partition but he no longer spoke so vehemently against it. What surprised and shocked me even more was that he began to repeat the arguments which Sardar Patel had already used. For over two hours I pleaded with him but could make no impression on him.[47]

The trumpets sounded on 15 August 1947 as the first Prime Minister, Jawaharlal Nehru, raised the Indian national flag above the Lahori Gate of the Red Fort in Delhi. The night before had seen a vigil by members of the Legislative Assembly in New Delhi. All celebrated with abandon; it was soon to be midnight, when British rule would end and India would emerge a free country. But among those gathered there, one appeared dejected and despondent: "only the sad, sad face of Maulana Abul Kalam Azad, to whom the occasion was something of a tragedy, sticking out from the sea of happy faces like a gaunt and ravaged rock. The happy Congressmen ignored him".[48]

On 22 February 1988 – the 30th anniversary of Azad's death – the Delhi High Court broke open the seal to reveal 30 pages that Azad had sought to keep away from public knowledge. In his will, he had asked that they be revealed only thirty years after his death. And so, in this final piece of drama, the world came to know of his critical comments on his Congress colleagues. Actually, there was not much that was new in the released documents: Azad laid the blame for Partition on both Nehru and Sardar Patel for rejecting the UK Cabinet Mission Plan of 15 May 1946.[49] They shot down the notion of Muslim-majority provinces and a center whose role would be limited to defense, foreign affairs, and communications. Nehru wanted a strong center. Else, he reckoned, there would be countless insurgencies and revolts. Earlier on the Congress, as well as the Muslim League, had both accepted the Plan and to give such a statement in an atmosphere of mistrust and suspicion was certainly a mistake. That, said Azad, finally drove Jinnah to insist on Partition.

Azad also says Nehru erred by refusing to take two Muslim League members as cabinet ministers after provincial elections in 1937 in UP, making Jinnah distrustful of the Congress leaders whom he began to describe as "Hindu" leaders. Historians continue to debate whether the physical division of India would have actually occurred if Nehru had been more sensitive to Muslim needs, or had imagined the consequences of their actions. There were plenty of Patels around; Hindu nationalists were waiting for the day when they would be ruling India. Initially stunned and disappointed at Congress's U-turn, the Muslim League reacted by calling for Direct Action Day on 16 August 1946. In Azad's estimation, "The mistake in 1937 was bad enough. The mistake of 1946 proved even more costly".[50] The bloodbaths that expectedly followed, with 5000 killed in Bengal alone, put the final nail in the coffin of Hindu–Muslim unity.

Although Nehru does not specifically mention the Cabinet Mission Plan and his rejection of it, he lived to regret his hard line. In an interview published by

186 Jinnah Trounces His Muslim Opponents

The New York Times on 2 March 1957, he told C.L. Sulzberger: "Twenty years ago I would have said that certainly we should have some kind of confederation – not federation – of independent states with common defense and economic politics."

At the end of the day, it had made no difference that Azad was an Urdu-Persian-Arabic scholar of Islam, born in Makkah, and a practicing Muslim, whereas Jinnah was a westernized Muslim with little prospect of becoming a leader of consequence in a Hindu-majority state. The tide of history was too powerful, divisive forces too strong and unifying forces too weak. Partition was a resounding victory for Jinnah who was now surrounded by adoring crowds – an impossibility if India had stayed united. Equally it was a total defeat for Azad. Azad's later career as India's education minister was no more distinguished than Maulana Azad National Urdu University (MANUU), a university in Hyderabad which today bears his name but which, in fact, is no more than a glorified *mad-rassa*. Isolated and embittered by the twist of history that split India, he took to drinking secretly.[51] His end came three days after a fall in the bathroom in which he broke his hip. He died a sad man, defeated by the force of history.

Up against the Frontier Gandhi

Khan Abdul Ghaffar Khan (1890–1988), who earned the sobriquet "Frontier Gandhi" for his insistence on nonviolence, was an educator, pacifist, and revolutionary who led the Red Shirt Movement that, at its peak, had over 100,000 active members and many more supporters. After Partition, Jinnah promptly had him spirited off to prison. Ghaffar Khan remained there under house arrest from 1948 to 1954. By the time he died in Peshawar at the age of ninety-eight – still under house arrest – he had spent more than one out of every three days of his life in either British or Pakistani prisons. The total of thirty-seven years exceeds even the time that Nelson Mandela spent in South African jails. Jinnah, as we know, spent none.

As per his will, Ghaffar Khan wanted his burial to be in Jalalabad, Afghanistan. Tens of thousands of mourners carried his bier through the Khyber Pass. Despite the heavy fighting between the Soviet-backed Afghan government and the *muja-hideen* at the time, both sides declared a temporary cease-fire for the duration of the burial. There could not have been a more remarkable tribute from both sides of the divide.

In its obituary column, *The New York Times* describes Ghaffar Khan as,

> A tough Pathan tribesman from India's old northwest frontier, his martial beak of a nose and towering and powerful physique – at six and a half feet, he once weighed 220 pounds – made him look capable in earlier years of wrestling a bullock to the ground.[52]

Indeed, his very size had been a problem for his British jailers. As Ghaffar Khan notes in his autobiography, the fetters made for ordinary-sized prisoners had

Jinnah Trounces His Muslim Opponents **187**

to be forcibly squeezed to fit him.[53] For all that, he wrote, the time spent in Pakistani prisons was still worse.

The New York Times report continues, "A measure of the different feelings about Mr Ghaffar Khan in India and Pakistan was the immediate declaration of a five-day period of mourning for him in India and the lack of a similar declaration in Pakistan". This does not surprise. As a Pathan who sought a unified India for both Muslim and Hindu and autonomy for Pathans after the creation of Pakistan, Ghaffar Khan belonged to the "other side". To be called a follower of Gandhi – in fact as "Frontier Gandhi" – may well be a mark of honor and repute in India, but it brings an equal measure of opprobrium in Pakistan. Expectedly, Ghaffar Khan is unmentioned in today's Pakistani school textbooks and virtually erased from Pakistan's historiography.

Ignored by Pakistani academics, it has been left up to Indian scholars to tell us Ghaffar Khan's story. Rich in vignettes, Rajmohan Gandhi's[54] book on Ghaffar Khan, as well as that of Mukulika Banerjee,[55] are the most expansive to date. One learns of his obsessive devotion to educating his people; interpreting Islam as a religion of peace; stressing Pakhtun nationalism as a force for positive change; and being uncompromisingly opposed to British rule. This, together with a lifestyle that was quintessentially Gandhian in its frugality, earned him the honorific title Badshah Khan or Bacha Khan.

Pathans at the time placed little value on education, but Ghaffar Khan belonged to a tiny, privileged sliver of society that was both aware of its value and could afford it. The young boy was sent to the English-medium Edwardes College in Peshawar where he learned the Bible, mathematics, and history. Close to graduation, but already selected for the elite Guides Cavalry, he turned down the offer after witnessing an incident of haughty imperial behavior. Instead, as an idealistic young man of twenty, he decided to start his own village school. Pashto would be the medium of education here, not Urdu. This had a dual purpose: first, it made the task of teaching and learning easier and, second, it revived pride in Pakhtun culture.

Over the next few years, Ghaffar Khan walked to neighboring villages, persuading them to set up similar schools. His success made the British apprehensive, for they feared that these would turn into opposition hubs. Orders went out for the arrest of all responsible for setting up schools. An accusation was levelled that Ghaffar Khan was involved in cutting telephone wires, one he denied. A few violent encounters followed. He was identified as a dangerous man. Thereafter, he was put into fetters and then forced to walk 40 miles in scorching heat to Peshawar jail where he spent the next three years.

Earlier on, Ghaffar Khan had not been averse to using force for self-protection. But being jailed in the company of Akali Dal Sikhs, who were nonviolently protesting the control of Sikh gurdwaras by corrupt priests, led him to formulate his own response to British violence. Jihad against the colonial oppressors would not work, he reasoned, simply because they were too strong and prone to respond with extreme measures. The answer therefore lay in resolute resistance

188 Jinnah Trounces His Muslim Opponents

that would not allow violence to be answered with violence. The goal of community service should be supreme.

Ghaffar Khan's movement, the Khudai Khidmatgars (KK), recognizable by their red shirts, was dedicated to both community service and civil disobedience. Banerjee records that the following oath, taken on the Qur'an, was taken by members:

> In the name of God who is Present and Evident, I am a Khudai Khidmatgar.
> I will serve the nation without any self-interest.
> I will not take revenge (badla) and my actions will not be a burden for anyone.
> My actions will be non-violent.
> I will require every sacrifice required of me to stay on this path.
> I will serve people without regard to their religion or faith.
> I shall use nation-made goods.
> I shall not be tempted by any office.

One is tempted to compare the KK Movement with another uniformed movement, the Khaksar (humbleness). Both were roughly contemporaneous, sought freedom from the British, and opposed to the idea of Pakistan. Khaksar's founder, Inayatullah Khan al-Mashriqi was a Cambridge-educated mathematician and member of the Indian Educational Service who returned to India. He had been offered a knighthood which he refused. Al-Mashriqi was *Khaksar-e-Azam* (Great Leader of Khaksars) with supreme authority. Members wore khaki uniforms, carried *belchas* (shovels) on their shoulders, and proclaimed *khidmat-e-khalq* (social service). But the two movements could not have been more different. While Khaksar was organized tightly along military lines, the KK spoke of peace and coexistence.

For almost two decades, the KK cleaned village streets and built latrines, ran schools, and walked thousands of miles around India urging Hindu and Muslim alike to join the political struggle for freedom. Nevertheless, as Rajmohan Gandhi notes, there were also core weaknesses:

> The Pakhtun's admiration for him was stronger than their compliance. Although the Khudai Khidmatgars have been called "arguably the best organized" rural force in the freedom struggle in "the entire subcontinent", they did not remain as selfless in politics, or as dedicated in social service, or as strong in numbers, as Ghaffar Khan desired. His admonitions on their shortcomings shamed them but did not change them.[56]

The movement survived the massacre at Qissa Khwani Bazar in Peshawar where the British mowed down hundreds of peaceful demonstrators, including the KK. There was no sympathy to be had from the Muslim League or Jinnah. Arbab notes that:

Jinnah especially wanted to represent and safeguard the rights of this unified imagined nation at the colonial centre. From the outset then, the objectives of the Muslim League and the Khuda'i Khidmatgars were at cross-purposes. The former were fostering a homogenous identity dependent upon starkly distinct communal identities, one that later demanded distinct states as well, despite, quite paradoxically, also envisioning this future state as ahistorical and 'anti-territorial.' The other was a radical and nationalist call for decolonization that was materially embedded within a particular geographical space, historical context and linguistic ethos.[57]

Arrested multiple times, Ghaffar Khan refused to change his attitude. By 1930, the British estimated that were 50,000 KKs or more. The KK Movement was entirely centred around Ghaffar Khan: for them, he was a saint, *faqir*, holy man, and prophet. Deny as he would, people would even attribute miracles to him. A cult had been formed.

Rebuffed by the Muslim League which was uninterested in joining the anti-British movement, the KK ended up as an auxiliary to the Congress Party. The result was intensified repression with KK members having their property confiscated, crops burned, and entire villages blockaded. Although the civil disobedience movement was called off by Gandhi in April 1934, Ghaffar Khan remained under arrest until late 1935.

Because of the KK, the Congress had an overwhelming majority of seats in the North Western Frontier Province (NWFP) government. This was true even until 1946. But by now the Muslim League and its frankly communal message had gained traction; from here, it would be all the way to the grand finale. Seven weeks before Partition, KK participated in a loya jirga in Bannu that became known as the Pashtunistan Resolution. It demanded that the Pakhtuns be given a choice to have an independent state of Pashtunistan, composing all Pashtun territories of British India, instead of being made to join either India or Pakistan. Jinnah condemned Ghaffar Khan's resolution for a free Pathan state:

> The Khan brothers...have raised another poisonous cry that the PCA (Pakistan Constituent Assembly) will disregard the fundamental principles of the Shari'ah and Qur'anic laws. This, again, is absolutely untrue. More than thirteen centuries have gone by...we have not only been proud of our great and Holy Book, the Qur'an, but we have adhered to all these fundamentals all these ages, and now this cry has been raised...[that] we cannot be trusted...I want the Muslims of the Frontier Province clearly to understand that they are Muslims first and Pathans afterwards.[58]

In Delhi, Nehru had been told that the Congress had largely lost support in NWFP, but he did not want to believe it. Instead, he insisted upon visiting this predominantly Muslim province so that he could fairly judge the reports. Azad, in his autobiography, says he warned Nehru against visiting, while blaming the

Khan brothers for losing support through their "miserliness" and not effectively using the election funds put at their disposal by the Congress.[59] But Nehru still went ahead in October 1946. It was a huge mistake. Thousands of Pathans with black flags had amassed at the airport. Although Dr. Khan Sahib, Ghaffar Khan's brother, was then chief minister in the Congress-led government, there was nothing he could do to prevent it. The demonstrators turned violent and the cavalcade had to proceed under police escort. Weeks later, an orgy of communalist violence hit the NWFP. Ghaffar Khan's efforts to control matters proved futile. He was hospitalized in Peshawar after being hit by stones thrown by Muslim rioters.

Partition was now around the corner. Congress had reluctantly accepted this as inevitable and rejected the Cabinet Mission Plan. It also rejected Ghaffar Khan's plea that since the Congress government held the majority in NWFP, no referendum need be held to decide whether NWFP should join India or Pakistan. Nehru had not only gone back on his solemn pledge to Ghaffar Khan that there would be no partition, he was also smarting from his visit and had given up on the Pathans. Let there be a referendum – India did not want NWFP! In despair at this betrayal, Ghaffar Khan said his last words to Gandhi: You have thrown us to the wolves.

Ghaffar Khan did well to boycott the subsequent referendum. Even if the KK had participated, popular vote would likely have been against NWFP staying in India. In fact, to opt for India would surely have led to a full-scale bloodbath. As Hindus and Sikhs fled, and as armed attacks by the Muslim League followers on the KK increased in ferocity, Ghaffar Khan's son, Ghani Khan, defied his father by creating an armed defense youth wing called the *Zilme Pakhtun*. The two-decade-long, nonviolent movement was fast coming apart. Jinnah terminated the elected provincial NWFP ministry of Dr. Khan Sahib, appointing a Muslim League leader, Abdul Qayyum Khan, in his place. Protests were harshly quelled.

On 12 August 1948, the police and militia were ordered to open fire at a march of unarmed KK protesters going from Charsadda to Babra ground. Hundreds were killed; many dead bodies and the injured were thrown into the river.[60] Suhrawardy, President of the Awami League, told a large gathering in Dacca in July 1950 that the barbarous massacre of the Red Shirts committed at Charsadda in 1948 surpassed the massacre committed by the British in Jallianwala Bagh in 1919. So completely has the state erased memories that even nationalist Pushtoons today are only dimly aware of the Babra massacre. A patiently researched book by Muhammad Sohail published in 2022 is the first attempt to reconstruct a lost history.[61]

Who Won, Who Lost?

In conclusion, let's reflect upon the impact that each of Jinnah's opponents has had on the shaping of India's post-Partition history.

Maududi, the fiery ideologue, turns out to be a clear winner. True, he had been trounced by Jinnah in 1947 and his objections, as well those of other fundamentalists, had been overridden. Pakistan did come into existence – and that too with Jinnah, the man they so despised riding triumphantly at the new country's head. But a look at today's political landscape tells us that actually Maududi trumped Jinnah. A supposedly epic movie made on Jinnah by Akbar S. Ahmed and Jamil Dehlavi, though funded with millions of official and private dollars, flopped. There is much rah-rah on Jinnah's birthday – December 25 – and yet no student group or movement on a single Pakistani university or college campus derives inspiration or motivation from Jinnah's bland sermons or trite exhortations. On the other hand, Maududi's party through its militant student wing – the *Islami Jamiat-e-Talaba* (IJT) – has maintained a strong presence in most public universities[62] that shows no signs of fading. Building on Maududi's cultural resistance to westernism, the IJT zealously performs the duties of a vice-and-virtue squad that violently disrupts the playing of music, enforces physical separation of males and females, and forbids the celebration of Valentine's Day.

Still more significantly: Jinnah's thoughts – more rhetorical than substantive – have remained confined to Pakistan. However, Maududi's ideas have moved far out of the Indian subcontinent. According to Wikipedia, today's Jamaat has chapters in India, Bangladesh, Afghanistan, Sri Lanka, Mauritius, and the United Kingdom. Beginning in the late 1940s, Maududi's writings were translated into Arabic. They helped charge men like Hassan al-Banna, Sayyid Qutb, and Abdullah Azzam – the ideological founders of organizations such as Al-Qaida, Boko Haram, and Da'esh. In particular, Qutb borrowed and expanded Maududi's concept that Islam was fully modern and capable of meeting all challenges of the current age. He had no need for apologetic Muslims of the likes of Sir Syed Ahmad Khan, Syed Ameer Ali, Rashid Rida, or any of the past crop of Muslim modernists.

So who trumped whom? Jinnah got his Pakistan, even if he had to be content with what he once called a "maimed, mutilated, and moth-eaten Pakistan". As the *Quaid-e-Azam*, he stands immortalized and his mausoleum is Karachi's prominent landmark, another kind of Taj Mahal. And yet none listen to him anymore and he inspires nothing but routine tributes. As for Bengalis, their view of Jinnah is not salutary. On the other hand, while Maududi has no mausoleum, his followers are spread around the world, shaping discourses and fighting secularism tooth and nail. Maududi had gained power and influence much beyond what he could have aspired to in undivided India.

Azad never visited Pakistan but turned out to be hugely relevant. He was amazingly prescient in predicting that a united Pakistan could not last long. In a passionate speech delivered at Delhi's Jama Masjid,[63] and then developed further in an interview[64] given to the journalist Shorish Kashmiri in April 1946, he had warned that after dividing India, Pakistan would be at the mercy of the big powers, economically dependent, wracked by disputes between provinces, have hostile relations with its neighbors, ride roughshod on the country's poor,

192 Jinnah Trounces His Muslim Opponents

and its opportunistic political class would lead to a military takeover. He comes eerily close to what actually happened; as the Biharis will testify, the separation of East Pakistan in 1971 vindicated his stance that being Muslim does not endow nationality to an individual.

Azad, floored by Jinnah in the grand wrestling match that ultimately reshaped South Asia, lost out. He died sad and dejected but would have been still sadder were he alive today. His dreams of a secular, multicultural India are fast fading under the assault of Hindutva's ideologues. Many of his worst fears have come true now that Nehru's legacy of secularism is being ceaselessly attacked and India moves closer to being a Hindu *rashtra*. According to The New Indian Express, Muslims constitute 10.5% of the population but their representation in the Lok Sabha is presently just 4.4%. There is no Muslim member of the BJP. Muslims in India are feeling increasingly embattled and left out from the mainstream.

It is hard to predict how India's future will pan out. Will India become a Hindu version of Pakistan as Azad feared? So far, Allahabad has become Prayagraj, and Mughalsarai Junction Railway Station has officially been renamed Deen Dayal Upadhyaya Junction. Years earlier, the signs for Aurangzeb Road in Delhi were painted over to bear a new name – APJ Abdul Kalam Road. More name changes lie ahead. Renaming cities and roads is just one part of Hindutva's larger agenda to glorify the Vedic era and vilify Muslim rulers. Bit by bit India's cultural landscape and education system is being altered to exalt an imaginary past of a pure Bharat Mata undefiled by invaders. Prime Minister Narendra Modi, reelected in 2019 for another five years, says India is troubled by "1200 years of slave mentality" which he will change forever.

And what about Ghaffar Khan? I think his lasting legacy was to be a mythbreaker who showed cultural stereotyping can be broken. A people notorious for their culture of fratricidal violence and incessant war, and well known for blood feuds and vendettas, could be taught to use disciplined civil disobedience effectively against a much stronger occupying power. Pathans were not violent by intrinsic nature, as sometimes alleged, but could be converted to nonviolence and peaceful coexistence. For me, said Ghaffar Khan,

> My religion is truth, love, and service to God and humanity. Every religion that has come into the world has brought the message of love and brotherhood. And those who are indifferent to the welfare of their fellowmen, those whose hearts are empty of love, those who do not know the meaning of brotherhood, those who harbor hatred and resentment in their hearts, they do not know the meaning of Religion.[65]

In India, Ghaffar Khan is venerated as a Muslim who opposed Pakistan. However, the growth of anti-Muslim feelings in the BJP era has led to his demotion. In 2020 the Badshah Khan Hospital in Faridabad was renamed after Atal Bihari Vajpayee.

In Pakistan, Ghaffar Khan's spirit lives on in the peaceful protests of the Pakhtun Tahaffuz Mahaz (PTM), attended by tens of thousands. This movement was born in the aftermath of the US–Pakistan war on terror that used airpower and caused needless death and destruction across wide swaths of Pakistan's tribal areas. Initially spearheaded by eight young Pathan students of Gomal University, it demands an end to racial profiling, removal of land mines, elimination of military check posts that humiliate local residents, a return of the thousands abducted by Pakistan's security forces who are still unaccounted for, and establishment of a truth and reconciliation committee. These are goals that Ghaffar Khan would have fully supported. PTM's leaders have been elected to the National Assembly and are a visible political force that the military establishment fears and seeks to suppress. Some PTM leaders languish in jails. They stand in opposition to a state which seeks to crush the movement lest it grow still bigger. Even if PTM is suppressed by brute force or breaks up for internal reasons, Ghaffar Khan's message is likely to stay.

Notes

1 Abul Kalam Azad, *India Wins Freedom – An Autobiographical Narrative*, Orient Longman Limited (1959), p. 142.
2 *Muslims against the Muslim League – Critiques of the Idea of Pakistan*, edited by Ali Usman Qasmi and Megan Eaton Robb, Cambridge University Press (2017).
3 Ibid, p. 2.
4 Abul Ala Maudoodi, *Tarjuman-ul-Qur'an*, II, no. 6 (Jamadi-ul-Aakhir, 1352) [August 1933]: 19–20.
5 Many of Maududi's detractors believe he hurled at Jinnah the ultimate epithet, *Kafir-e-Azam* (the supreme infidel, a play upon the word *Quaid-e-Azam*, meaning the supreme leader). However, credible evidence for this is lacking.
6 Abul Ala Maudoodi, *minhaj al-inquilab al-islami* (Rawalpindi: n.d.), p. 10.
7 Seyyed Vali Reza Nasr, *The Vanguard of the Islamic Revolution: The Jama'at-i-Islami of Pakistan*, University of California Press (1994), p. 114.
8 Abul Ala Maudoodi, *Mussalman Aur Maujooda Syasi Kashmakash*, quoted in K. K. Aziz, *The Making of Pakistan*, p. 148.
9 A useful summary of positions taken by religious scholars can be found in: Fakhr-ul-Islam and M. Iqbal, *The Final Phase of the Freedom Struggle in India (1940–1947): The role of Religious Scholars*, University of Peshawar, https://www.pscpesh.org/PDFs/PJ/Volume52/9Muhammad%20Iqbal.pdf
10 A comprehensive account of the Ahmadi issue can be found in: Ali Usman Qasmi, *The Ahmadis and the Politics of Religious Exclusion in Pakistan*, Anthem Books (2014).
11 Nasr, op. cit.
12 Ibid, p. 23.
13 R. Jackson, *Mawlana Mawdudi and Political Islam: Authority and the Islamic state*, Routledge (2011).
14 Abul Ala Maudoodi, *Tarjuman-ul-Qur'an*, 4 (Jamadi-ul-Aakhir, 1352) [1933].
15 For a further discussion of this point, see: Ali Usman Qasmi, *Differentiating between Pakistan and Napak-istan, Maulana Abul Ala Maududi's Critique of the Muslim League and Muhammad Ali Jinnah*, in Qasmi and Robb, op. cit., pp. 109–141.
16 Abul Ala Maudoodi, *Purdah and the Status of Women in Islam*, Lahore, Taj Company Ltd (1991), p. 140.
17 Abul Ala Maudoodi, *Taalimat*, Lahore, Islamic Publishers.

18 *Single National Curriculum: Publishers Object to Textbook Review Fee, Ulema's Role*, Dawn, 4 June 2021.

19 Abul Ala Maudoodi, *Minhaj al-inqilab al-Islami* (The Method of Islamic Revolution), p. 19.

20 Sayyid Abul A'la Maudoodi, *Murtad ki Saza Islami Qanun Mein*, eighth edition, Lahore Islamic Publications Ltd, p. 32.

21 Maudoodi in *Murtad*, op. cit.

22 Ibid.

23 Abul Al Maudoodi, *Haqiqat-i-Jihad*, Lahore, Taj Company Ltd. (1964), p. 58.

24 A.A. Maudoodi, *Jihad in Islam* (Jihad Fi Sabillilah), Transl. Abdul Waheed Khan, Islamic Publications Ltd. (1970), p. 20.

25 Rewriting the History of Pakistan, Pervez Hoodbhoy and A.H. Nayyar in Asghar Khan, *The Pakistan Experience: State and Religion*, Lahore, Vanguard (1985).

26 *Education and the State: Fifty Years of Pakistan*, Oxford University Press (1998).

27 The interested reader is referred to Nasr (op. cit.) for details.

28 Ibid, p. 37.

29 Ibid, p. 37.

30 L. Gay, *Iqbal and Islamic Fundamentalism* (1990). Available at: http://www.samizdat.qc .ca/cosmos/sc_soc/histoire/iqbal_lg.htm

31 *Maulana Abul Kalam Azad – A Centenary Memorial Volume*, edited by Subhash C. Kasyap, Delhi, National Publishing House (1989), p. 10.

32 Jinnah, according to R.C. Mody, refused to shake hands with Azad at the first Simla Conference in June 1945. Azad had just been released from prison.

33 I.H. Douglas, Abul Kalam Azad and Pakistan, A Post-Bangladesh Reconsideration of an Indian Muslim's Opposition to Partition, *Journal of the American Academy of Religion*, 40, no. 4 (December 1972): 458–479.

34 The reader is referred back to the chapter in Iqbal and his denigration of Avicenna and Farabi, whom Iqbal considered afflicted by rationalist Greek thought.

35 Azad, quoted in Aijaz Ahmad, *Lineages of the Present: Ideology and Politics in Contemporary South Asia*, p. 68.

36 M. Ali, *Past Present: Understanding Azad*, 1 June 2014, Dawn.

37 Curiously, Azad did not openly repudiate his past even though he had set out in a very new direction.

38 Abul Kalam Azad, *India Wins Freedom – An Autobiographical Narrative*, Bombay, Asia Publishing House (1959), p. 227.

39 Samiullah Quraishi, *Qayam-e-Pakistan ka Tareekhi aur Tahzeebi Pasmanzar*, Lahore, Sang-e-Meel Publications (1977), p. 101.

40 One wonders how many of them understood English: 5% or 20%? Nonetheless, they probably knew history was being made.

41 Official website, Nazaria-e-Pakistan Foundation. *Excerpt from the Presidential Address Delivered Muhammad Ali Jinnah in Lahore on March 22, 1940.*

42 Azad, op. cit., p. 151.

43 Ibid, p. 143.

44 Ibid, p. 160.

45 Ibid, p. 185.

46 Ibid, pp.185–186.

47 Ibid, p. 187

48 L.O. Mosley, *The Last Days of the British Raj*, London, Weidenfeld (1961), p. 240.

49 Maulana Abul Kalam Azad, *India Wins Freedom: The Complete Version*, Bombay, Orient Longmans (1988).

50 Azad, op. cit., p. 162.

51 I.H. Douglas, *Abul Kalam Azad – An Intellectual and Religious Biography*, Delhi, Oxford University Press (1993), p. 252.

52 Abdul Ghaffar Khan, 98, Follower of Gandhi, obituary section, The New York Times, 21 January 1988.

53 Khan Abdul Ghaffar Khan, *My Life and Struggle; Autobiography of Badshah Khan*, Hind Pocket Books (1969).
54 R. Gandhi, *Ghaffar Khan – Non-Violent Badshah of the Pakhtuns*, Penguin Books (2004).
55 M. Banerjee, *The Pathan Unarmed: Opposition and Memory in the North West Frontier*, Oxford University Press (2001), p. 238.
56 Gandhi, op. cit.
57 Nonviolence, *Pukhtunwali* and Decolonization: Abdul Ghaffar Khan and the Khuda'i Khidmatgar – Politics of Friendship, Safoora Arbab, in Qasmi and Robb, op. cit., p. 224.
58 Jinnah Papers, Zawar Zaidi (ed), Vol II, doc# 299, p563 (quote on p. 565), Government of Pakistan, distributed and published by Oxford University Press, Pakistan, 1997.
59 Azad, op. cit., p. 170.
60 *ANP Terms Aug 12 Black Day for Pakhtuns*, Dawn, 13 August 2015.
61 M. Sohail, *Tareekh-e-Charsadda*, Peshawar, Mafkoora Books (2022).
62 Its stronghold is Punjab University in Lahore, Pakistan's largest university. IJT students have run a parallel administration for decades that restricts social behavior and decides on matters such as student and faculty selection.
63 http://www.pakpassion.net/ppforum/showthread.php?152243-Maulana-Abul-Kalam-Azad-The-Man-Who-Knew-The-Future-Of-Pakistan-Before-Its-Creation
64 Azad's interview by Kashmiri is in the journal Chattan whose original copy seems unavailable, but it is reproduced in https://dokumen.tips/documents/abul-kalam-azad-by-shorish-kashmiri-interview.html
65 My Life and Struggle, op. cit.m p. 195.

PART THREE

Postnatal Blues

Seven

STUBBORN ANGULARITIES I: EAST PAKISTAN

Angularity (dictionary definition): *Sharp corners, irregularities or deviations. In the context of Jinnah's speech of 11 August 1947, it means the humps and bumps of religion, language, and culture which Jinnah thought would simply disappear as Pakistan consolidated itself.*

> In course of time all these **angularities** of the majority and minority communities, the Hindu community and the Muslim community – because even as regards Muslims you have Pathans, Punjabis, Shias, Sunnis and so on, and among the Hindus you have Brahmins, Vashnavas, Khatris, also Bengalees, Madrasis and so on – will vanish. Indeed if you ask me, this has been the biggest hindrance in the way of India to attain the freedom and independence, and but for this we would have been free people long long ago.[1]
>
> Mohammad Ali Jinnah's Presidential Address to the First Constituent Assembly of Pakistan (11 August 1947)

Any country born with two parts separated by 1000 miles of a hostile country, formed solely because the two shared a common religion, would be considered to have a serious birth defect. It should not have expected to live very long – and it indeed did not. Yet the manner of death could have been far less cruel than it actually was. Argued here is that the seeds of destruction were thoughtlessly sown by West Pakistani leaders within a matter of weeks and months. Economic exploitation by West Pakistan, disrespect for Bengali culture, and the army being at the helm made catastrophe inevitable. Many are surprised that after a bloody separation West Pakistan's poor cousin has become less poor and more hopeful than the parent country. Explored here are reasons why Bangladesh is outpacing Pakistan

DOI: 10.4324/9781003379140-11

Jinnah's epic speech was delivered three days before independence. Its later part – which promises equal treatment for all citizens – has been committed to memory by Pakistan's anxious liberals and the country's embattled minorities. Every time the axe falls upon them, we hear it feverishly repeated. But the earlier part of the very same speech – excerpted above – has been overshadowed by events and thus is never referenced. Herein Jinnah is saying that in the new state Hindus and Muslims would somehow equalize, Shia and Sunni would agree to a cease-fire in war that began on the battlefield of Karbala in AD 680, and somehow regional identities and different ethnicities would meld together. It scorns the notion that such differences could ever lead to discord. All angularities, says Jinnah, would magically disappear and a unique Pakistani identity would reign supreme once the new state popped into existence. Jinnah hoped for a miracle. Unfortunately, miracles don't happen just because you want them to.

It was not only Jinnah who thought this way. His lieutenant, Liaquat Ali Khan, viewed the making of parties other than the Muslim League as treasonous and condemned demands for provincial autonomy as anti-Pakistan. He declared in March 1948 that "we must kill this provincialism for all times to come".[2] Indeed, from the very beginnings "provincialism" has been denounced by the Pakistani state as a dangerous, corrosive substance. That Pakistan was supposed to be a voluntary union of provinces each with a distinct history and age-old culture had overnight become a promise best forgotten.

Bengal was to be the acid test where religion would overpower cultural angularity. In 1946 large- scale Hindu–Muslim riots in Bihar had caused a million or so Urdu-speaking Muslims, largely Sunni, to migrate to East Bengal. Arrival of these Bihari *muhajirs* prompted Jinnah to exclaim: "I never dreamt that in my lifetime I shall see Pakistan in being, but the tragedy of Bihar has brought it about".[3] The Muslim League arranged for *muhajirs* to be transported overland to Karachi where they were paraded before gawking Sindhi locals – who would close doors for them down the line – as living proof of the Two Nation Theory. These refugees did look different and their spoken Urdu of the Bihari variety sounded strange to the Sindhi ear. Still, they drew sympathy. It took a decade for their presence to become overbearing. Thereafter, they would be much resented. Jinnah was oblivious to such matters, arguing that all cultural irritants would soon be ironed away once the *muhajirs* got absorbed into the wider Muslim milieu. True, nothing similar existed in human history, but he exuded confidence that the impossible would become possible:

> West Pakistan is separated from East Pakistan by about a thousand miles of the territory of India. The first question a student from abroad should ask himself is – how can this be? How can there be unity of government between areas so widely separated? I can answer this question in one word. It is "faith": faith in Almighty God, in ourselves and in our destiny.[4]

It turned out that Jinnah's optimism was unwarranted. The little humps and bumps not only stayed, they grew so overwhelmingly large that matters spun

Stubborn Angularities I: East Pakistan **201**

out of control. Hard systemic problems require careful and dedicated handling. But, preoccupied as he was with governance of the west wing, Jinnah had little time to spare for the east wing even though it was home to 56% of the country's population. It took him a full seven months to make his first brief visit to Dacca. Liaquat Ali Khan's priorities were similar. He had announced two visits a year but never quite managed to reach his own target.

Among all of India's Muslims, Bengalis had been the most vociferous and the earliest to demand Pakistan. It is therefore somewhat paradoxical that they were also the quickest to reject Pakistan. Now that Pakistan had arrived, it turned out that a country imagined by the Muslim *ashrafiyya* of north India and run by a largely Punjabi army was not what the Bengalis had bargained for. A big gap in expectations separated Bengali Muslims from north India's Muslims.

North India's Muslims had a very specific outlook. They subscribed to Sir Syed's loyalism to the British, had a large landed aristocracy and provided the bulk of recruits to the British Army. Their principal fear was that a joint electorate with Hindus would lead to their under-representation. There was genuine cause for worry. For example, in the United Province (UP) Muslims constituted 14% of the population but, under the new dispensation that relied on votes, they could not win a single seat under the joint electorate system.[5]

Bengal was different. There was no Muslim landed aristocracy there, and Bengali Muslims were conspicuous by their absence in the British Army and even the lower levels of the bureaucracy. As of 1947 Bengali Muslims had borne the brunt of Hindu violence – the carnage of Punjab was to come much later. One might therefore have expected that they would be in the forefront of separatist politics as well. But, as noted by Devji, apart from the Lahore-based lawyer Sir Muhammad Shafi during the Muslim League's early years, the top rankers had never included politicians from Muslim majority areas – including Bengal – except as wavering and suspect allies.[6] Even the Bengal premiers Fazlul Haq, Nazimuddin, and Suhrawardy were more or less ordinary members.

Jinnah's strategy of us-versus-them worked brilliantly in the 1946 elections with the Muslim League bagging 95% of the Muslim vote. Bengali enthusiasm for Pakistan is evident from movies of 14 August 1947 that can be viewed today with a Google search. Many are ones that today's Bangladeshis would rather not see. This wasn't the age of camera phones but that of 8- and 16-millimeter motion picture technology which had already been invented. Euphoric crowds in Dacca had gathered to celebrate with abandon the first Independence Day. Visible is a sea of green-colored Pakistani flags with crescent and star. Festivities included march-pasts and gun salutes. They show desperately poor people hugging each other, wiping tears from their eyes. Newly arrived refugees from India clambered by the hundreds onto the rooftops of railway carriages. Scenes in Calcutta, where Bengali Hindus had crossed over, were probably similar.

A Snapshot of History

Pakistan was born in Dacca, not Karachi or Lahore. A commonly forgotten fact is that most Pakistanis at the time were Bengali. But it didn't take long for the Bengali majority to realize that it was actually a minority and that the "real" Pakistan lay towards the West. *The Separation of East Pakistan* by Hasan Zaheer is a book which provides many insights.[7] A civil service officer from the West who was stationed in the East, Zaheer was captured by Indian forces and released in 1974. He identifies three principal areas of conflict during the first decade of independence: the status of the Bengali language, constitution-making, and economic centralization. In his opinion, the first left deep scars but it was partially resolved after a few years. The second and third proved irresolvable because they amounted to handing provincial autonomy over to the East, a demand that the West was not willing to entertain.

Bengali regionalist sentiment started rising within the first year of independence, taking twenty-five years in all to achieve final form. The Muslim League, which had midwifed the birth of Pakistan, was now perceived by Bengalis to be solidly aligned with the West's objectives. Jinnah had little familiarity with the political dynamics towards the east of Banaras. His political associates were *nawabs* from the north Indian elite because he had lived much of his life in Bombay and London. Liaquat Ali Khan, educated at Sir Syed's Aligarh Muslim University, was also thoroughly imbued with the spirit and ethos of his social class.

Opposition to ML came in the form of the United Front (UF), led by the Awami League and the Krishak Sramik Party. In legislative elections held 8–12 March 1954, the UF campaigned on a 21-point agenda that included making Bangla a state language, ending the zamindari system, and bringing the jute economy under the East Bengal government control.[8] The Muslim League was trounced, winning only 9 seats, while the UF won landslide victory with 223 of the 309 seats.[9] The West panicked. Even before the new legislature could meet for the first time, it was dismissed and Governor's Rule imposed from May 1954 until June 1955. The original Government of India Act of 1935 had been beefed up by the West to allow for the dismissal of provincial governments and so, legally empowered by Article 92-A, a "strong" Governor, Major-General Iskander Mirza, was flown in on 1 June 1955 from Karachi.[10] Within days, several hundred UF activists, including Sheikh Mujibur Rahman, were arrested. The Governor reportedly threatened to personally shoot opposition leader Maulana Bhashani.[11]

Meanwhile, for reasons entirely unrelated to matters in the East, political turbulence continued to wrack the West. Ahmadis, who had fully supported the Pakistan Movement, suddenly found themselves under attack. In 1953, violent riots broke out in Lahore which left hundreds dead and led to martial law being declared in the city for a period of three months. Political leaders played musical chairs. Hussain Shaheed Suhrawardy, a Bengali Oxford-educated politician, became the 5th prime minister of Pakistan in 1956. He was the only one ever from the East and lasted

Stubborn Angularities I: East Pakistan **203**

eleven months before falling victim to intrigues of the West Pakistani establishment. It is said he had a falling out with Iskander Mirza who, through a series of intrigues, eventually became president of Pakistan. Then, on 8 October 1958, Mirza announced Pakistan's first nationwide martial law and appointed General Ayub Khan as the country's Chief Martial Law Administrator. But barely three weeks later, Ayub Khan packed off his former boss for a one-way flight to the U.K. Martial law would continue until the end of the East–West union. Pakistan's second presidential elections, held on 2 January 1965, were massively rigged by Ayub to defeat his rival, Fatima Jinnah. Shaken by her clear win in East Pakistan and the support she had summoned in West Pakistan, Ayub was in need of means to shore up his sagging popularity.

This was why in 1965, advised by Bhutto, Ayub launched Operation Gibraltar in Kashmir. Pakistan's eastern flank was left virtually undefended, but Bengalis noted the fact that West Pakistan seemed unworried. In any case, with 1000 miles of hostile territory in between, the East had few Bengalis in the armed forces, and defense would have been impossible. It did not help when sometime after the war Foreign Minister Zulfikar Ali Bhutto made a statement in National Assembly that India did not attack East Pakistan because it feared Chinese intervention. Bhutto probably said so to express gratitude to China for its war support. At the same time it showed that the East and its defense were secondary.

The East had no trained bureaucracy. In 1947 it had received only one member of the former Indian Civil Service. This much vaunted "steel frame" had been erected by the British to run an entire half-continent. Bihari *muhajirs*, together with Punjabis, quickly acquired hegemonic control over it and put themselves in charge of East Pakistan's state administration:

> Of some 101 Muslim members of the Indian Civil Service and Indian Police Service at the time of partition, for example, only 18 had been from Bengal, and 35 had been from areas that became part of West Pakistan, with the others coming from areas that had remained part of India. A total of 95 of the 101 had opted for Pakistan, thus making the Bengali members of the successor national administrative service in Pakistan a distinct minority. Even by the mid-1950s, of 741 top civil servants, only 51 were Bengali, none of whom had the rank of secretary. Of 41 joint secretaries, only 3 were Bengali; of 133 deputy secretaries 10 were Bengali. With respect to the military, in 1955 there was only 1 Bengali brigadier, 1 colonel, and 2 lieutenant colonels out of 308 of equivalent or higher rank. As late as 1963 only 5 percent of the officer corps of the Pakistani army and 7 percent of the other ranks were Bengali. In the air force, Bengalis constituted 17 percent of commissioned officers and 30 percent of other ranks, and in the navy they constituted 10 percent of the commissioned officers and 29 percent of other ranks.[12]

An official document notes that in the Central Secretariat at Karachi, there was no Bengali secretary out of a total of 13; only one joint secretary out of 19; and

4 deputy secretaries out of 59.[13] Zaheer suggests that at the time a halfway solution did exist: a one-time relaxation of rules could have brought Bengali officers into the provincial bureaucracy, leading to a more responsive and representative government.[14] But there was little interest in pursuing such ideas. According to Dos Santos,[15] typically, 50–70% of Pakistan's total export earnings were earned by East Pakistan through its export of raw materials such as jute, hides, and skin. However, East Pakistan received only 25–30% of all foreign imports into Pakistan. East Pakistan's trade surplus was used to finance the industries of West Pakistan leading to a net transfer of resources of approximately $2.6 billion over the period 1948–1949 to 1968–1969. The per capita income in West Pakistan was 32 percent higher than in East Pakistan.

The lopsided distribution of wealth and administrative power worsened with time, especially since the East was governed from afar. Valuable irrigated land seized from fleeing Hindus became the property of Biharis and Punjabis. With a larger population in the East than West, power-sharing demanded that the federal capital should have been Dacca not Karachi. But the West easily laughed off this possibility. Choosing Karachi as the capital meant that wealthy businessmen, industrialists, and professionals fleeing India chose to settle in the West where their prospects would be brightest. They had relatively easy access to government jobs and the military. If you were a businessman, proximity to the capital was crucial for procuring export licenses and government facilities.

But it wasn't just the power differential, it was that West Pakistan never really understood why Bengali nationalism was entirely different from that of the Muslim renaissance movement of Sir Syed Ahmad Khan in northern India. Unlike the situation with Aligarh-inspired nationalists, Bengali Muslims did not have significant cultural and linguistic problems with Bengali Hindus with whom they shared greater cultural contiguity than Punjabis. A recent book by Rashiduzzaman addresses the social life of Muslims in rural Bengal, their feelings, relations with Hindus, and long struggle to advance administratively, politically, and educationally.[16] He relates that Muslim–Hindu relations in Bengal had all the patterns of closeness and distance between the two communities living side by side for centuries. The folk cultures of the two communities had many common elements: shared local legends, affinity for spiritualism, folk beliefs about ghosts, jinn, spirits, and music. Compared to north India, culturally there was much more mingling of Hindus and Muslims. Indeed, the pre-1947 Bengali Muslim separatist agenda was primarily focused on economic emancipation. Urban middle and upper-middle class Hindus dominated the professions, owned most of the urban real estate and agricultural lands, and held top administrative posts.

Mocking Bangla

Even as a school child in Karachi of the 1950s, my friends and I somewhat resented calling East Pakistan and West Pakistan by one name, Pakistan. As a thoughtless young boy, I had felt quite embarrassed about the few short and dark Bengali

Stubborn Angularities I: East Pakistan **205**

boys among my schoolmates. "Hey, hey, son of a rickshaw puller", we would taunt one boy, until he burst into tears and then we'd all run away laughing. We well "knew" that all good Muslims and Pakistanis are tall, fair, and speak chaste Urdu. Though I am Sindhi by ethnicity, my value system was thoroughly that of Urdu-speaking West Pakistanis. Bengalis were stereotyped as fish-eaters, which is a somewhat strange kind of slur because we Sindhis are also notoriously fond of fish. My friends and I would double up in laughter at the strange sounding Bangla news broadcasts from Radio Pakistan. In our macho world of 14-year-olds, they sounded so terribly feminine. And how we doubled up with laughter when a Bengali boy would pronounce a friend's name Zaleel instead of Jaleel!

As kids, we were not alone in deprecating a nonmartial race. One and a half centuries ago, Sir Syed Ahmad Khan feared that Bengalis would come out at the top. On 28 December 1887, he delivered a lecture in Lucknow warning against self-rule in India because,"the government will be in the hand of Bengalis, or other Hindus like Bengalis, and the Muslims will be in a miserable position".[17] In another speech, Sir Syed had denounced the British proposal for all civil service positions to be filled through open competition. Since Bengalis were better educated, they would likely surge ahead. He does not attempt to hide his racialism:

> Think for a moment what would be the result if all appointments were given by competitive examination. Over all races, not only over Mahomedans but over Rajas of high position and the brave Rajputs who have not forgotten the swords of their ancestors, would be placed as ruler a Bengali who at sight of a table knife would crawl under his chair. (*Uproarious cheers and laughter.*) There would remain no part of the country in which we should see at the tables of justice and authority any face except those of Bengalis. I am delighted to see the Bengalis making progress, but the question is – What would be the result on the administration of the country? Do you think that the Rajput and the fiery Pathan, who are not afraid of being hanged or of encountering the swords of the police or the bayonets of the army, could remain in peace under the Bengalis? (*Cheers.*) This would be the outcome of the proposal if accepted. Therefore if any of you – men of good position, raïses (rich men), men of the middle classes, men of noble family to whom God has given sentiments of honour – if you accept that the country should groan under the yoke of Bengali rule and its people lick the Bengali shoes, *then, in the name of God! jump into the train, sit down, and be off to Madras, be off to Madras! (Loud cheers and laughter.)* But if you think that the prosperity and honour of the country would be ruined, then, brothers, sit in your houses, inform Government of your circumstances, and bring your wants to its notice in a calm and courteous manner.[18]

This appalling depiction of Bengalis – cowards crawling under a chair – was also reflected in the attitudes of well-to-do Punjabis and Muhajirs who had settled in East Pakistan. They did not speak Bangla nor sought to learn it. Schools established by Urdu-speaking settlers in different parts of East Pakistan taught English, Urdu, Persian, and Arabic, but Bangla did not make the list.[19] Instead, they expected Bengalis to learn Urdu because this was considered a proper Islamic language built upon Arabic and Persian foundations, while Bangla rested upon Sanskrit. Other languages like Sindhi, Gujarati, and Kachhi were also regarded with suspicion because they were "contaminated" by Hindu idioms and beliefs. One proposed solution for Bangla was to develop a Roman script so that its "Hindu" character could be removed.[20] In 1951 the Aga Khan, Sultan Mohammed Shah, pleaded for an even more radical solution wherein Arabic should be the national language for Pakistan because, as he put it, "Arabic is the language of Islam. The Qur'an is in Arabic. The Prophet's hadith are in Arabic".[21]

There were also suggestions to create a new language – Pakistani – out of the mixture of Urdu and Persian and Arabized Bangla, to serve the needs of the country. Controversy erupted within Pakistan's first few months.[22] Which languages could be spoken in the Constituent Assembly? A resolution tabled by a representative from East Pakistan demanded that the Assembly's proceedings allow for Bangla, together with Urdu. But on 25 February 1948, Prime Minister Liaquat Ali Khan, an Urdu speaker, rose up to sternly reject the demand:

> Pakistan has been created because of the demand of a hundred million Muslims in this subcontinent and the language of a hundred million Muslims is Urdu... It is necessary for a nation to have one language and that language can only be Urdu and no other language.[23]

Civic unrest followed as Bengalis reacted, arguing that 56% of Pakistan's population spoke Bangla, while Urdu was not the mother tongue in any province of West Pakistan. The government appeared to waffle on the issue until Jinnah decided he would settle it once and for all. He was all-powerful now, holding simultaneously the positions of governor general, president of the constituent assembly, and president of the ruling Muslim League.

Three weeks after the disturbances, Jinnah flew out of Karachi, arriving in Dacca on 19 March 1948. It was his first – and last – visit to the East Wing. Over a total of nine days, he gave several speeches, the biggest one being on 21 March when he addressed a crowd of many thousands at the Racecourse Ground. Jinnah was fluent in only one language – English – but he had come to argue the case for Urdu, the Islamic language that would bind the East to the West. Warning that a fifth column was bent upon creating discord, he said that the Bengalis would be permitted to use their language for official matters in East Pakistan. However, on the state language, there could be no compromise:

> Let me make it very clear to you that the state language of Pakistan is going to be Urdu and no other language. Anyone who tries to mislead you is really the enemy of Pakistan. Without one state language, no nation can remain tied up solidly together and function. Look at the history of other

countries. Therefore, so far as the state language is concerned, Pakistan's language shall be Urdu. But as I have said, it will come in time.[24]

The crowd that had gathered was adulatory at first. Few could understand Jinnah's sophisticated English, spoken with his inimitable accent. They kept cheering until some of the educated ones finally deciphered his speech. The welcome turned to sullenness, and then to anger. There were reports that "people broke down a gate, destroyed a picture of the Quaid and protested against the Quaid's pronouncements".[25] Unfazed, he repeated his message on 24 March at Curzon Hall in Dacca University. Before he left Dacca on 28 March 1948, he delivered a speech on Radio Pakistan once again insisting on his Urdu-only position.

The normally shrewd Great Leader had bungled badly. In seeking to impose Urdu and calling opponents "enemies of Pakistan", he had accused an entire people of disloyalty and sealed Pakistan's fate. Maulana Azad's early recognition that religion was insufficient for nationhood turned out to be correct; Jinnah had been proved wrong. A rare government White Paper, written months before the final breakup, admitted that the "imposition of Urdu by the country's second prime minister, Khwaja Nazimuddin, himself a Bengali, in February 1952 resulted in language riots, police shootings, deaths, and the creation of the first martyrs for a Bengali movement".[26] How this admission managed to see the light of day during the martial law regime suggests that at least a part of the government had not entirely lost touch with reality.

The road to separation

The election of 7 December 1970 – Pakistan's freest and fairest in its entire history up to and including those of the present times – turned out to be so utterly polarizing that a united Pakistan acceptable to the country's ruling establishment became impossible thereafter. Since then, the Pakistani establishment has never forgotten how dangerous a nonmanipulated democracy could be. Mujib-ur-Rahman gained mass popularity on the basis of his Six Point Program that hovered somewhere between the East having full autonomy and total independence. GHQ in Rawalpindi had expected that no party could take a clear lead and elections would yield a coalition government weak enough to be manipulated at will. But Yahya Khan's regime was stunned when the results came in. The Awami League won all seats but two of the National Assembly seats in the East with zero seats in the West. This gave it a simple majority. Correspondingly, Bhutto's Pakistan People Party (PPP) won the most seats in Sind and Punjab but scored zero in East Pakistan. The Awami League's 162 seats versus the PPP's 81 seats gave it a parliamentary way to legally form the central government in Islamabad without having to share power with any West Pakistani party. Additionally, it could dictate the basis of the country's future constitution.

Within days of the result, it became clear that Bhutto would not allow his own prime ministerial ambitions to be frustrated by his Bengali rival's majority.

208 Stubborn Angularities I: East Pakistan

The National Assembly could not be summoned because Bhutto had declared in Lahore that he would not allow this to happen. Khalid Hasan, who was Bhutto's first press secretary, wrote, "I was present at that meeting and I reported it with Syed Amjad Hussain, my chief reporter, for the Pakistan Times – that he [Bhutto] would break the legs of those who went to Dhaka".[27] Bhutto had the majority vote of West Pakistan, home of the Armed Forces, and had been a minister in the military government for eight years. He enjoyed close friendships with the generals. By contrast, Mujib had no friends in the Army and the generals viewed him with suspicion because he opposed the military's role in politics and advocated decentralizing power.

Nevertheless, given how things had worked out, General Yahya met Sheikh Mujib in Dhaka after the elections and felt reassured enough by Mujib to describe him publicly as "the next prime minister of Pakistan".[28] However, upon returning from Dhaka he went straight on for "hunting" at Bhutto's estate in Sind where Bhutto succeeded in changing his mind. On 21 March, Bhutto in turn arrived in Dhaka and sent a message to Sheikh Mujib: "Tell him that I am the destiny." With the launch of Operation Search Light in the early hours of 26 March 1971, the fate of Jinnah's Pakistan was sealed. Yet when Bhutto returned to Karachi the next morning, he told a crowd at the airport: "By the grace of God, Pakistan has at last been saved".[29]

Akbar S. Ahmed, known for his film "Jinnah" among other things, essentially corroborates the above. Ahmed was then a young CSP officer posted in East Pakistan. Reminiscing about his encounters with Bhutto, he writes, "I next saw him on the PIA flight we had both taken from Dhaka in March 1971 ... He disembarked in Karachi, I was right behind him, and holding up his hands in benediction, he had said that God had 'saved' Pakistan."[30]

The events following Search Light have been documented in the recollections of Major General Khadim Hussain Raja who was sent by GHQ in East Pakistan to control the situation. Yahya had quietly left for Pakistan after appointing two senior Punjabi officers, Lieutenant General A.A.K. Niazi and Lieutenant General Tikka Khan. They had been flown in at short notice. Tikka Khan spoke of trying and publicly hanging Sheikh Mujib-ur-Rahman in Dacca. Niazi threatened mass rape of Bengali women:

> The last to enter was Niazi, who was wearing a pistol holster on his web belt. He announced that he had assumed command with immediate effect. He gave out some routine instructions for the future, including that all officers were to wear a pistol when in uniform. There was a sprinkling of Bengali officers in the gathering. To our consternation, Niazi became abusive and started raving. Breaking into Urdu, he said: "*Main is haramzadi qaum ki nasal badal doon ga. Yeh mujhe kiya samajhtey hain*" (They don't know me. I will change the race of this bastard nation.) He threatened that he would let his soldiers loose on their womenfolk. There was pin-drop silence at these remarks. Officers looked at each other in silence, taken

aback by his vulgarity. The meeting dispersed on this unhappy note with sullen faces.[31]

On 16 December 1971, in a televised ceremony at the Ramna Race Course garden in Dacca, Lieutenant General "Tiger" Niazi unstrapped his pistol (he later wrote that it was an old, nonworking one that he wanted to get rid of anyway), handed it over to the joint commander of the Indian Eastern Command and Bangladesh's Mukti Bahini, and signed the document of surrender. Just two days earlier the Tiger had preened himself before journalists and defiantly asserted that an Indian tank would roll into the city only over his dead body. It was all the more galling because, as Indian commentator Shashi Tharoor notes, the Indian Air Force in the northern sector was commanded by a Muslim (Air Marshal Idris Latif), the Army Commander was a Parsi (General Sam Manekshaw), the General Officer commanding the forces that marched into Bangladesh was a Sikh (Lieutenant General Jagjit Singh Aurora), and the officer flown in to negotiate the surrender of the Pakistani forces in East Bengal (Major-General Jack Jacob) was Jewish.[32]

In West Pakistan there was calm. It was assumed that the Americans wouldn't allow the Indians to move and, in contrast to Indira Gandhi, Yahya Khan was known to have a strong personal rapport with Richard Nixon.[33] State radio and television were still broadcasting patriotic songs and news of the surrender was dismissed as an Indian fabrication. Listeners had been assured for months that East Pakistan's defenses were impregnable, and so most rejected the news as no more true than the famous misreport of 1965 by BBC that Lahore had fallen to Indian forces. Incredulity soon turned to anger, then despair.

In Bangladesh that date – 16 December 1971 – is hailed as Victory Day. But why call it so? It was a pyrrhic victory. The mass insanity of the war resembled that of Partition, a quarter century earlier. Atrocities and pogroms were carried out against Bengalis by the Pakistani army and its Bihari collaborators. On the other side, the Mukti Bahini targeted Biharis, Urdu speakers, and suspected pro-Pakistan Bengalis. Of course, the exact numbers of dead, mutilated, and women raped can never be known for sure. But a holocaust-sized event had happened.

India, expectedly, also celebrates its victory over Pakistan. But, as Sumanta Banerjee reminds us, there was also an anti-India backlash. Anti-Pakistan leftists were actively discriminated against, while those organized by India's undercover agency, the Research and Analysis Wing (RAW), were steeply privileged. India's army and intelligence agencies had been very selective about which Bangladeshi freedom fighters were to be supported, and which to be used as cannon fodder.

This brings us to the complicated relationship between the liberators and the liberated. It involves the larger issue of national resistance/partisan struggles which achieve liberation from one foreign power, with the aid of another foreign power. We can recall the experience of Poland and other East European countries which freed themselves from Nazi German occupation with the help of the Soviet Red Army. Such foreign-aided

210 Stubborn Angularities I: East Pakistan

liberation often left a sense of humiliation among the liberated people. Whenever they had a chance, they always tried to assert their independence by shaking off memories of their past dependence on the foreign liberator. Manifestations of anti-Soviet dissent in Poland, and defiance of Soviet tanks in Czechoslovakia were expressions of such efforts to break away from that humiliating episode of the past.[34]

Punjab Still Doesn't Want to Know Why

Did Pakistan learn anything from the experiences of 1971? The speech on 23 November 2022 of outgoing army chief, General Javed Qamar Bajwa, suggests that if any, it was surely very little. Speaking at the National Security Workshop held at the National Defence University in Islamabad, he laid the blame elsewhere, "East Pakistan was a political failure, not military one" and went on to say that the number of soldiers fighting was not 92,000 but 34,000 who had "fought bravely and gave exemplary sacrifices which were acknowledged by Indian army chief Field Marshal Manekshaw".[35] Don't officers learn during training in cadet college or at the NDU that between 1958 and 1971 Pakistan had been under uninterrupted martial law? Or that the surrender of 93,000 Pakistani troops was the biggest surrender of any military post-World War Two? Even if Bhutto had been reluctant to share power with Shaikh Mujibur Rahman, the responsibility for initiating Operation Searchlight rests squarely with the army. One can safely assume that the good general has either never heard of the Hamood-ur-Rahman Report or has no interest in knowing.

Ten days after the fall of Dacca, the Government of Pakistan ordered a judicial inquiry headed by Chief Justice Hamood-ur-Rahman. It was constituted with the mandate "to prepare a full and complete account of the circumstances surrounding the atrocities and 1971 war", including the "circumstances in which the Commander of the Eastern Military Command, surrendered the Eastern contingent forces under his command laid down their arms". The commission's final report is said to be very lengthy, but it is hard to make a definitive statement. Reportedly there were 12 copies of the report. These were all destroyed; except the one that was handed over to the Government which disallowed its publication at the time. In 2000, parts of the commission report were leaked to Indian and Pakistani newspapers, but the authenticity could not be verified. This led popular columnist, the late M.B. Naqvi, to remark acerbically, "There are elements in the armed forces and some parts of the government that think that its publication would harm the national interests. Which national interests would they be, after 30 years of the 1971 war?"[36]

To this very day, with just a few exceptions, there has been no soul-searching. Punjab's ruling class remains uninterested in why 1971 happened. Pakistan Army officers were never punished for cowardice, tried for atrocities, or had their pensions taken away. The man on the street in Lahore is also likely satisfied with the story that General Yahya Khan's penchant for Black Label whisky and

Stubborn Angularities I: East Pakistan **211**

beautiful women had done Pakistan in. Even more worthy of blame are East Bengal's allegedly evil-minded, conspiracy-hatching Hindus. The India–Soviet nexus comes up next, together with atheistic communists who are assumed to always have sought the destruction of every Islamic state. And then, of course, there's America's betrayal: Nixon and Kissinger had promised to help Pakistan's embattled army, but then the Soviets calmly cut a deal with them. Shortly thereafter the nuclear-powered aircraft carrier USS Enterprise and Naval Task Force 94 steamed out of the Bay of Bengal to signal their retreat, leaving Pakistan high and dry.

One might have expected progressives on the Pakistani Left to support a struggle for national liberation, but the tiny left wing in Punjab was split 50-50 on whether to support the army action, or to support Bhutto and the army. A small group of left-wing professors at Islamabad University saw the Bengalis fighting against an army supported by imperialist America. Those who described themselves as hard-core Marxists and were known as the "Professors Group" of Punjab University said the insurrection owed to the Bengali national "comprador bourgeoisie" and not the working class. Thus they were unprepared to believe widely circulated reports at the time of the March 1971 massacre of students inside Dacca University's student hostel.[37] The power of ideology in suppressing human impulses should never be underestimated.

Those who think along with the Punjabi establishment would probably agree today with the late Dr. A.Q. Khan who said: "If we had had nuclear capability before 1971, we would not have lost half of our country – present-day Bangladesh – after disgraceful defeat".[38] But rationally speaking, it is hard to see how the bomb could have saved Pakistan from eventual dismemberment. Would the West have dropped it on the raging pro-independence mobs in Dhaka? Or used it to incinerate Calcutta and Delhi and have the favor duly returned to Lahore and Karachi? Or threatened India with nuclear attack to keep it out of the war so that Bengalis could be killed in still greater numbers?

Khalid Hasan, who was Bhutto's press secretary in 1971, in seeking to soften judgment on his boss's role, wrote: "What we need to remind ourselves, but don't, is that there was hardly a voice raised in West Pakistan against the army action in East Pakistan. In fact, the overwhelming opinion in the Punjab was that Yahya had done the right thing, his only mistake being just one: he had moved too late and let the situation deteriorate".[39] Unlike Bhutto – who rashly provoked the military establishment beyond breaking point – both military dictators went away peacefully. Ayub Khan died in his Islamabad villa of a heart attack on 19 April 1974. He never made any public comment on the loss of East Pakistan. His son, Gohar Ayub Khan, achieved notoriety for instigating ethnic riots in Karachi and for using his father's position to create a business empire. Yahya Khan died in Rawalpindi on 10 August 1980. Both Ayub and Yahya received state funerals. The Pakistani military establishment did not want to be seen punishing its own too harshly, irrespective of the harm they may have done to the country.

Fast forward fifty years. On the occasion of the 39th anniversary of the fall of Dhaka, a newspaper report simultaneously details what young Bangladeshis and young Pakistanis are being told about that part of their history.[40] Astonishingly, young Bangladeshis mention but do not emphasize the fact that East Pakistan was left vulnerable to Indian attacks after Ayub Khan initiated the 1965 war, or the West's indifference to the East's suffering after the 1970 Cyclone Bhola that killed a half million, or even the systemic economic exploitation of East by West. Instead they said that Bangladesh went to war "for our mother tongue".

On the Pakistani side, in the same survey, students largely repeated what is more or less the official narrative. In their textbooks written after 1971, the Hindu conspiracy narrative is promoted across the board. One says: "The same Bengali Hindu was responsible for the backwardness of East Pakistan. But, hiding the story of his two-century old sins, atrocities, and pillage, he used "Bengali nationalism" to punish innocent West Pakistanis for sins they had not committed".[41] An ex-chief justice of the Lahore High Court, Justice Shameem Hussain Kadri, wrote of "diabolical Hindus" and "Hindu conspiracies" in his officially circulated book.[42] Some more recent books repeat these themes.[43] But by and large there is only cursory mention of East Pakistan's separation. Having examined several, I have yet to see a school textbook published by an official Pakistani school textbook board that explains this momentous historical episode in a manner that would make sense to a student in Bangladesh today. Books that are objective by Pakistani standards also have warped accounts.[44] The memory that India took 90,000 Pakistani prisoners of war is lost; an ordinary student would be disinclined to believe that a valiant army could have been thus defeated. Just as the Afghan National Army collapsed in 2021 for lack of local support, so too had the West Pakistan army in 1971 – a full fifty years ago. Absolutely nowhere can one find the bald truth which is that the responsibility of the East Pakistan tragedy rests squarely upon West Pakistan and its arrogant military rulers who even today refuse to discuss this episode of history.

Bangladesh Overtakes Pakistan

Bangladesh, Bangladesh
Bangladesh, Bangladesh
When the sun sinks in the west
Die a million people of the Bangladesh

And so the story of Bangladesh
Is an ancient one again made fresh
By all who carry out commands
Which flow out of the laws upon which nations stand
Which say to sacrifice a people for a land

– Joan Baez, 1972

By the time Joan Baez sang Bangladesh, I had conquered my racism but, to my dismay, most of my compatriots had not. East Pakistan, the West's poor cousin, was always assumed to be a basket case. Many thought it could never survive economically and after a while would humbly request to rejoin Pakistan. It was a flight of fantasy that has finally landed but, as I have argued above, nobody in Pakistan today talks or cares much about where that landing point was. Few Pakistanis will want to recall TIME magazine's cover story on 17 January 1972, which tells us that, "Pakistan International Airlines left exactly Rs 117 (US$ 16) in its account at the port city of Chittagong".

Since that time, Bangladesh has certainly not become some Scandinavian heaven. Fifty years after birth it is poor and overpopulated, undereducated and corrupt, frequented by natural catastrophes, experiences occasional terrorism, and the farcical nature of its democracy is exposed in less-than-transparent elections and the so called battle of the begums. Its two major political parties, the Awami League and the Bangladesh Nationalist Party, have been at each other's throats almost from the time of mass uprisings against the dictatorial Ershad regime. It is at the front-line of climate change, and Islamism has aggressively asserted itself in public life with bombings and stifling of liberal voices. As in rapidly communalizing India, secularism hangs from a thread that is getting thinner.

In spite of these problems, the earlier caricature of a country on life support disappeared years ago. Today some economists say it shall be the next Asian tiger. Social indicators are positive. The health sector is, relatively speaking, impressive – far fewer babies die at birth in Bangladesh than in Pakistan. Immunization is common, and no one gets shot dead for administering polio drops. In contrast, Pakistan's religious extremists have killed dozens of health workers because they believe that these drops reduce fertility. Life expectancy (72.5 years) is higher than Pakistan's (66.5 years). According to the ILO, females in Bangladesh are well ahead in employment (33.2%) as compared to Pakistan (25.1%). A detailed comparison of Pakistan–Bangladesh quality of life indicators can be found in a paper by economics professor Mahmood Hasan Khan of Simon Fraser University.[45]

In 2020, the debt per capita for Bangladesh ($883) was significantly less than that for Pakistan ($1190) and its foreign exchange reserves ($32 billion) were four times Pakistan's ($8 billion). While these figures will change in the years to come, there is no question of Bangladesh having outpaced a Pakistan that once towered above it. Prior to the COVID-19 crisis, Bangladesh's growth rate in 2019 (8.15%) put it higher than India's (4.18%) and far above Pakistan (0.99%).

Year	Pakistan (%)	India (%)	Bangladesh (%)
2017	5.55	7.04	7.28
2018	5.84	6.12	7.86
2019	0.99	4.18	8.15

GDP Growth Rate before COVID-19 (World Bank)[46]

Much of Bangladesh's growth owed to exports which zoomed from zero in 1971 to $39.34 billion in 2018 (Pakistan's was then $23.33 billion).[47] Bangladesh produces no cotton but, to the chagrin of Pakistan's pampered textile industry, it has eaten savagely into its market share. Jute, which was East Pakistan's major export in the early days, is not even mentioned on the new and impressive list of exports. Bangladesh's GDP in 2022 was $461 billion whereas that of Pakistan was $320 billion. This means that the average Bangladeshi today is wealthier than the average Pakistani, with the Pakistan rupee having undergone a 30% devaluation in 2019 and a further steepfall in 2022. In 1971, Pakistan was 70% richer than Bangladesh; today, Bangladesh is 45% richer than Pakistan.[48]

Other indicators are equally stunning. East Pakistan's population in the 1951 census was 42 million, while West Pakistan's was 33.7 million. But today Bangladesh has far fewer people than Pakistan – 165 million versus 220 million. A sustained population planning campaign helped reduce fertility in Bangladesh. No such campaign – or even its beginnings – is visible today in Pakistan.

What made the once-poor cousin upstage its richer relative by so much, so fast? Nature has surely not been kind to Bangladesh with floods, cyclones, and arsenic-poisoned water. Bangladesh has no geostrategic assets saleable to America, China, or Saudi Arabia. It also has no nuclear weapons, no army of significance, no wise men in uniform running the country from the shadows, and no large pool of competent professionals. One can think of the following reasons:

- Bangladesh does not have a Kashmir-like problem, which means that there is no excuse for a massive army that dominates the country, consumes resources, and appropriates as much as it can. Simply put: Pakistan has a war economy, while Bangladesh has one geared for peace and development. Terrorism, which was a direct consequence of playing strategic games in Occupied Kashmir and Afghanistan, has not significantly impacted Bangladesh.
- Bangladesh is able to use the skills and resources of its minority population – with Hindus being the most significant component – far better than Pakistan where religious minorities have either fled the country or been marginalized. While Islam is nominally the state religion, Bangladesh has a secular constitution that does not formally recognize differences between its citizens.
- Bangladesh has a significantly lower population growth rate. In 2020 the estimated populations of Bangladesh and Pakistan are 165 million and 220 million. This puts Bangladesh at 43% and Pakistan at 57% – a reversal of the situation in 1947!
- Women in Bangladesh play a much larger role in public life than women in Pakistan. They are more visible in businesses, the garment industry, office jobs, the education sector, and in daily life. Bangladesh's growth rests on three pillars: exports, social progress, and fiscal prudence.

Stubborn Angularities I: East Pakistan **215**

- Large land owners in East Bengal were mostly Hindus prior to Partition, and so the agrarian reforms of 1951 were possible. In contrast, West Pakistan has not seen significant land reform to date. Instead, feudal families have invaded politics and assured their grip over the country.
- Greater investment in Bangladesh's civil society institutions, better education quality, and greater role for NGOs. Microfinance through the Grameen Bank has been important.

Final Reflections

Bangladesh and Pakistan are different countries today principally because they perceive their national interest differently. Bangladesh sees its future in human development and economic growth. Accordingly it sets its goal posts at increasing exports, reducing unemployment, improving health, reducing dependence upon loans and aid, and further extending microcredit. Water and boundary disputes with India are serious and Bangladesh suffers bullying by its bigger neighbor on matters of illegal immigration, drugs, etc. But its basic priorities have not wavered.

For Pakistan, human development comes second. The bulk of national energies remain focused on check-mating India and liberating Kashmir. Relations with Iran are therefore troubled, and relations with Saudi Arabia have cooled because Pakistan is unhappy with their closeness to India. But the most expensive consequence of the security state mindset was the nurturing of extra state actors in the 1990s. Ultimately they had to be crushed after the Army Public School massacre of 16 December 2014 by the Taliban. This, coincidentally, was the very day Dacca had fallen forty-three years earlier.

Bangladesh is also conflicted by internal rifts. From time to time, anti-Hindu groups have attacked temples and destroyed idols. Religious fervor is easily stoked up there – as elsewhere by allegations of blasphemy. The Durga Puja festival in 2021 turned out to be a particularly egregious example of that.[49] However, being more multicultural and liberal than Pakistan, its civil society and activist intelligentsia has stopped armed groups from grabbing the reins of power. Although elected or quasi-elected Bangladeshi leaders are often horribly corrupt and incompetent, they don't simply endorse decisions – they actually make them. Not having nuclear weapons is a blessing for the people of Bangladesh; having these weapons inspires wild megalomaniacal thoughts easily among those who possess them. Being held accountable by their electorate, Bangladesh's leaders are forced to invest in people instead of weapons or a massive military establishment.

Compare this with Pakistan's establishment which feels no such desire and which is so powerful that it does not feel threatened by popular insurrection except perhaps by religious extremists. After 1971 it could think of nothing beyond wounded honor and ways to settle scores with India. Thirsting for vengeance, Zulfikar Ali Bhutto's secret called for the nuclear bomb. This led to the famed Multan meeting just six weeks after the surrender. That centralization of

216 Stubborn Angularities I: East Pakistan

authority breeds local resentment remained an unlearned lesson. In 1973 Bhutto dismissed the National Awami Party (NAP) government in Balochistan and ordered military action, starting a series of local rebellions that has never gone away. In doing so, he reempowered those who ultimately hanged him.

After the fall of Dacca, some progressive people in the West imagined that the 1971 disaster had taught Pakistan a lesson so profound that change had now become inevitable. Responding enthusiastically to Bhutto's popular roti-kapra-makan slogan, they thought Pakistan would shift from pampering its hyperprivileged towards welfare for all. Equally, it was hoped that the rights of Pakistan's culturally diverse regions would be respected. But the leaders of Pakistan did not want to understand this matter then and do not want to understand it now. There was never a "Truth and Reconciliation Commission" as in South Africa, no soul-searching, and no court-martials for cowardice in one of the most stupendous debacles of recent military history.

The Pakistani nation-state continues to ignore secondary and tertiary identities, i.e., those that relate to region and language. Being a citizen does not automatically endow either equality of opportunity or equal treatment. Punjabi Sunni Muslims will disagree, but other Pakistanis will agree that citizenship in Pakistan comes swathed in multiple layers. Pakhtuns living around the Durand Line, the Baloch, Gilgit-Baltistanis, and Hazaras have discovered that state agencies enforce unwritten laws – those of the Pakistani deep state. Pending in the Supreme Court of Pakistan are the cases of many thousands who vanished. While a few hundred have emerged, they are too terrified to reveal who their captors were. Instead, a haunting fear of more partitions led to still greater suspicion of ethnic, linguistic, and religious diversity and an enduring belief that only an oversized military can keep the country from unraveling.

Notes

1 G. Allana, *Mohammad Ali Jinnah's Presidential Address to the First Constituent Assembly of Pakistan (August 11, 1947)*, Pakistan Movement Historical Documents, Karachi, Department of International Relations, University of Karachi (n.d.), pp. 407–411.
2 Constituent Assembly Debates (March 1, 1948), 82.
3 P. Ghosh, The Changing Discourse of Muhajirs, *India International Centre Quarterly*, 28, no. 3, Relocating Identities (Monsoon 2001), p. 58.
4 Mohammad Ali Jinnah, Speech at a public meeting in Dacca: 21 March 1948.
5 H.G. Rawlinson, *The British Achievement in India*, London, William Hodge (1948), p.188.
6 F. Devji, *Muslim Zion – Pakistan as a Political Idea*, Cambridge, Mass., Harvard University Press (2013), p. 45.
7 H. Zaheer, *The Separation of East Pakistan – The Rise and Realization of Bengali Muslim Nationalism*, Oxford University Press, 1994.
8 K. Callard, *Pakistan – A Political Study*, The Macmillan Company (1957), pp. 155–193.
9 A. Kamal Uddin, United Front in Islam, Sirajul, Jamal, Ahmed A. (eds.). *Banglapedia: National Encyclopedia of Bangladesh*, second edition, Asiatic Society of Bangladesh (2012).
10 K. Bin Sayeed, The Governor-General of Pakistan, *Pakistan Horizon*, 8, no. 2 (June 1955): 330–339.

Stubborn Angularities I: East Pakistan **217**

11 https://en.wikipedia.org/wiki/Iskander_Mirza
12 R. Sisson and L.E. Rose, *War and Secession: Pakistan, India, and the Creation of Bangladesh*, University of California Press, p. 10.
13 Proceedings of Constituent Assembly (Legislature) of Pakistan Debates (CALD), vol.1, no.18 (5 April 1952) 1063–1064, quoted in Zaheer, op. cit.
14 Ibid, p. 21.
15 A. Noronha Dos Santos, *Military Intervention and Secession in South Asia: The Cases of Bangladesh, Sri Lanka, Kashmir, and Punjab*, Greenwood Publishing Group (2007), p. 25.
16 M. Rashiduzzaman, *Identity of a Muslim Family in Colonial Bengal—Between Memories and History*, New York, Peter Lang (2021), reviewed by Mohammed Qadeer, The Friday Times, 21 May 2021.
17 *The Foundation of Pakistan: Vol. I*, edited by S.S. Pirzada, Karachi, National Publishing House (1969), p. XXV.
18 Speech of Sir Syed Ahmed at Lucknow [1887], Sir Syed Ahmed on the Present State of Indian Politics, Consisting of Speeches and Letters Reprinted from the "Pioneer", Allahabad, The Pioneer Press (1888), pp. 1–24 Lahore, Sang-e-Meel Publications (1982), http://www.columbia.edu/itc/mealac/pritchett/00islamlinks/txt_sir_sayyid _lucknow_1887.html
19 BBC interview of Ali Ahmad Khan, *Partition to Partition*, https://www.youtube.com /watch?v=sRZBn_SkYoE
20 Y. Bangash, *Jinnah, Culture, and Language-II*, The News on Sunday, 16 October 2016.
21 Sultan Mohammed Shah Aga Khan, the 48th Fatimid Imam Caliph and founder of Pakistan at a session of Motamer al-Alam-alIslamiyya on 9 February 1951 in Karachi.
22 P. Oldenburg, A Place Insufficiently Imagined: Language, Belief, and the Pakistan Crisis of 1971, *Journal of Asian Studies*, 44, no. 4 (August 1985): 711–733.
23 Constituent Assembly of Pakistan Debates vol II (25 February 1948), p. 15.
24 Jinnah Papers: Pakistan – Struggling for Survival, 1 January – 30 September 1948, vol. vi., Quaid-i-Azam Papers Project, Government of Pakistan, Karachi, Oxford University Press (2003), Z.H. Zaidi (ed.-in-chief); cf. Philip Oldenburg, A Place Insufficiently Imagined: Language, Belief and the Pakistan Crisis of 1971, *Journal of Asian Studies*, 44, no. 4 (1985): 711–733.
25 Y. Bangash, *Jinnah, Culture, and Language-I*, The News on Sunday, 9 October 2016.
26 White Paper on the Crisis in East Pakistan, Government of Pakistan, Islamabad, 5 August 1971.
27 Khalid Hasan, *QK Archives: Z.A Bhutto.*
28 A Riveting Account of Bhutto's Role in East Pakistan Is Given by Eqbal Ahmad in "I Am the Destiny", *London Review of Books*, 20, no. 12 (June 1998).
29 J. Sterba, *Bhutto Picks Up The Pieces of Pakistan*, New York Times, 25 June 1972.
30 Akbar S. Ahmed, *When News of Bhutto's Death Almost Killed Me in Waziristan*, The Friday Times, 24 November 2022.
31 K.H. Raja, *A Stranger in My Own Country: East Pakistan, 1969–1971.* Reproduced by Sani H. Panhwar.
32 S. Tharoor, *India: From Midnight to the Millennium and Beyond*, Arcade Publishing (2006), p. 53.
33 P. Oldenburg, *The Break-Up of Pakistan* (1974), republished in *Pakistaniaat: A Journal of Pakistan Studies*, 2, no. 3 (2010): 1–23.
34 S. Banerjee, Bangladesh Liberation War of 1971 – and a Hidden Episode of the Indian Government's Role, *Mainstream*, LIX, no. 49, New Delhi (November 20, 2021).
35 In his last public address, COAS Bajwa slams anti-army narrative, asks political stakeholders to move forward, Dawn, 23 November 2022.
36 Hamoodur Rahman Commission report surfaces again – Columnist M.B. Naqvi talks about the famous Report, http://www.defencejournal.com/2000/oct/hamoo-dur.htm
37 https://en.wikipedia.org/wiki/1971_Dhaka_University_massacre

38 Abdul Qadeer Khan, *I Saved My Country from Nuclear Blackmail*, Newsweek, 17 May 2011.
39 Ibid.
40 M. Husain (Dhaka) and H. Imtiaz (Karachi), *In-Depth: What Students Are Being Taught about the Separation of East Pakistan*, 16 December 2010.
41 A. Hamid et al., *Mutalliyah-i-Pakistan*, p. 32.
42 Justice Shameem Hussain Kadri, *The Creation of Pakistan*, Lahore, Army Book Club (1983).
43 *Pak Textbooks Still See '71 War as Conspiracy*, The Daily Star, 17 December 2010.
44 Pakistan Studies for Class IX–X, New College Publications Quetta, Balochistan Textbook Board, Quetta, both English and Urdu versions (2006).
45 M.H. Khan, *Bangladesh and Pakistan: The Great Divergence*, PIDE Knowledge Brief, 16 September 2020, https://www.pide.org.pk/pdf/PIDE-Knowledge-Brief-16.pdf
46 https://www.macrotrends.net/
47 https://www.statista.com/statistics/
48 M. Sharma, *South Asia Should Pay Attention to Its Standout Star*, Bloomberg, 31 May 2021.
49 *29 Hindu Homes Set on Fire in Bangladesh Amid Protests over Durga Puja Violence: Report*, ThePrint, 18 October 2021.

Eight

STUBBORN ANGULARITIES II: BALOCHISTAN

Injustice anywhere is a threat to justice everywhere.
— Dr. Martin Luther King (Birmingham jail, 1963)[1]

Viewed from Rawalpindi/Islamabad, Balochistan is a faraway land, too barren to be interesting but for one single fact — it is too rich to be left alone. While people from Punjab and north India have settled there since British times, they still remain culturally separated from the local population. In political terms, Balochistan has been in revolt since the birth of Pakistan. This remains such a sensitive issue for the ruling establishment that Pakistan's universities may not hold seminars or meetings, and Baloch students in Punjab and Sind are closely watched by the so-called "agencies". The mainstream media may not comment on Baloch matters. No journalist who reports accurately on events from Balochistan can expect to live too long. With the U.S. having largely pulled out of Pakistan, and with Afghanistan under Taliban rule, massive Chinese investments in power and transportation infrastructure have introduced a significant external element while assuring China's access to the warm waters of the Persian Gulf. In the murky world of geopolitics, the competing national interests of China, India, the U.S., Arab states, and Iran operate through their proxies in Balochistan with the Pakistani establishment declaring that it has become a battleground for so-called 5G warfare. How did this come to be? What makes the Baloch dissatisfied and angry with Punjab and Pakistan? And what could be the way forward?

Today the flag is saluted with great fervor in Punjab and the national anthem dutifully sung in school assemblies. But this does not happen in Balochistan's schools except for those watched over by army spies. In June 2013 the Ziarat Residency in Balochistan, where Mr. Jinnah had spent the last days of his life, was attacked by militants wielding hand grenades who, to avoid army check

DOI: 10.4324/9781003379140-12

220 Stubborn Angularities II: Balochistan

posts, had walked well over 100 miles from Afghanistan. Built in 1892 as a scenic resort for colonial rulers, together with memorabilia associated with Jinnah, this iconic two-storey wooden structure that decorates the cover of schoolbooks was reduced to cinders. As Pakistan reeled in shock, the Balochistan Liberation Army (BLA), one of several insurgent groups fighting for Baloch independence, claimed responsibility. In a terse statement, its spokesman declared that, "We, the Baloch, do not recognize Pakistan or any Pakistani monument". As if to underscore that point, in September 2021 the Baloch Liberation Front – yet another ethnic organization – blew up a statue of Jinnah placed in the strategic port of Gwadar.[2]

Baloch insurgencies have ebbed and flowed with time. After the capitulation of the Khan of Kalat in 1948, insurgencies by Baloch nationalists were fought in 1958–1959, 1962–1963, and 1973–1978. The last-mentioned started after Zulfikar Ali Bhutto who sought absolute authority and dismissed the elected provincial government of Balochistan. A cache of arms had allegedly been discovered in the Iraqi embassy on 10 February 1973 and the crates, opened in the presence of newsmen and the Iraqi ambassador, contained Soviet manufactured weapons allegedly for use by Baloch nationalist insurgents. The authorities in Islamabad had been tipped off by Nawab Akbar Bugti who was then out of power. Bhutto subsequently appointed Bugti as the Governor of Balochistan.[3] Khan Abdul Wali Khan and Mir Ghaus Bakhsh Bizenjo, both liberal and secular opposition leaders, were imprisoned in 1974.

Soon after the Iraqi embassy's discovery, the Pakistan Army swung into action. It was led by General Tikka Khan, earlier nicknamed the Butcher of Bengal. Bhutto's order to uproot the insurgency was a godsend for an army despondent after its surrender to Indian forces in 1971. The final cost of suppressing this insurgency stood at 3000–3500 soldiers, over 5000 Baloch fighters, and many thousand civilians. When Bhutto was overthrown in 1977, this ended the military action but in 2006 General Pervez Musharraf ordered the killing of Nawab Akbar Bugti who, then 79, had turned into a leader of Baloch nationalists.[4] Smoldering resentments blazed up again. Bugti is now a Baloch national hero and symbol of resistance.

This time around the crackdown by the military establishment was brutal but different. Like the dreaded generals of Latin America, Pakistan's generals too had learned how to quell insurgencies. Dead bodies appeared on the roadsides with marks of torture and many thousand young Baloch men went missing, some forever.[5] The Supreme Court of Pakistan expressed helplessness in face of numerous petitions.[6]

A Pakistani scholar notes that in Balochistan's post-independence history:

> Peace has rarely been a part of the lexicon used by the state or by the nationalists. The state speaks in terms of "national integrity," "development," and "securing itself from external forces seeking to destabilize and dismember the country." The nationalists speak of Punjabi

Stubborn Angularities II: Balochistan **221**

occupation, the revival of Baloch independence (referring to the Kalat State) and the reunification of the historical Baloch territory now spread between three states and among numerous provinces within them.[7]

Although a 2012 poll run by a local affiliate of Gallup claims only 37% of Baloch and 12% of Pakhtuns want independence from Pakistan, one does not reliably know either the questions or the manner and circumstances in which they were asked. Is Balochistan peaceful now or is violence lurking just below the surface? To draw firm conclusions on the basis of anecdotal experiences could well be misleading. But certainly, all is not well. In April 2022, Pakistan's first female suicide bomber killed three Chinese teachers and the driver of the minibus they were travelling in as she blew herself up in front of the Confucius Institute at the University of Karachi. Thereafter, all Chinese teachers working at cultural and educational institutions left Pakistan. The attack was claimed by the BLA.[8]

Although insurgency levels were relatively low in 2022, the Pakistani state was fully determined to suppress discussion and information. Balochistan remained blacked out from investigations by the national press and television. All news media in the province operate under the watchful eye of the Director General of Public Relations (DGPR). Journalism is limited to reporting events in ways deemed appropriate, covering press releases, and conducting harmless interviews.[9] Social media is also an unreliable indicator since ISPR, the information wing of the Pakistan Army, considers Balochistan a battleground for 5G warfare.[10]

Baloch alienation and the total blackout of news from Balochistan in the rest of Pakistan is articulated powerfully by a rising star of local Baloch politics, Maulana Hidayat-ur-Rahman.[11] A fisherman's son, he has garnered a mass following by emphasizing the deprivation of Gwadar's population. In December 2021, protests in Gwadar were so visible and loud that it became impossible for the establishment to hide or suppress the fact. These drew tens of thousands of people, including women and children, day after day for three weeks from nearby areas of Gwadar including Turbat, Pishkan, Zamran, Buleda, Ormara, and Pasni. The movement called *Gwadar Ko Huqooq Do Tehreek* (Give Rights to Gwadar Movement) focuses on fishing by foreign trawlers, lack of water and electricity, and the humiliation suffered by local residents at security checkpoints.[12]

A Shotgun Wedding

Baloch nationalism was problematic for Pakistan from day one.[13] Contrary to the official narrative, Balochistan did not become a part of Pakistan on Independence Day. Among the Baloch there was open skepticism of Jinnah's Two Nation Theory and little appetite for pan-Islamism. Muslim identity in Balochistan was much less well formed as compared to northern India. This is logical since there were far too few Hindus, Sikhs, or other non-Muslims for significant religious conflict, and therefore less need for separate identity markers. In 1947, Ghaus Bux Bizenjo gave a speech in the *Dar-ul-Awam* (Baloch Parliament):

> We are Muslims but this fact does not mean it is necessary to lose our independence and to merge with other [nations] because of the Muslim [faith]. If our accession to Pakistan is necessary, being Muslim, then the Muslim states of Afghanistan and Iran should also merge with Pakistan.[14]

Readers will find a fairly up-to-date account of the Balochistan issue in Jaffrelot, including details of the four wars referred to earlier.[15]

In earlier times Balochistan had been ruled by the Mughals from Delhi, and later by the British. Of Balochistan's four princely states – Makran, Lasbela, Kharan, and Kalat – the Khanate of Kalat was the most powerful. With the British exit from India now only a matter of time, the Baloch middle class also started dreaming of independence and in 1931 had formed a nationalist organization *Anjuman-e-Ittehad-e-Balochistan*. While campaigning for the Pakistan idea in the Muslim majority areas of India, Jinnah was well aware of the lack of enthusiasm within Balochistan. He therefore promised to respect the sovereignty of the Kalat state, and so a communiqué was issued on 11 August 1947 (the day of his famed speech delivered before the Constituent Assembly) from his office stating that: "The Government of Pakistan recognizes Kalat as an independent sovereign state in treaty relations with the British Government with a status different from that of Indian States". On 12 August 1947, Mir Ahmad Yar Khan, the Khan of Kalat, formally declared Balochistan as an independent state.

But Jinnah was uncomfortable with his earlier promise: upon further reflection, having an independent Balochistan was problematic. Mountbatten – who saw the usefulness of Balochistan in future British efforts to stop Soviet expansion into the warm waters of the Persian Gulf – had cautioned Jinnah, arguing that an independent Balochistan might well become a security threat on Pakistan's western border. Jinnah agreed and therefore now demanded that all four princely states accede to Pakistan. The Baloch parliament, however, repeatedly rejected the merger. Instead it insisted upon an independent federation of Baloch feudatory states under Kalat.

Where persuasion failed, coercion succeeded. In 1948, Jinnah sent in his army. Mir Ahmad Yar Khan, the Khan of Kalat, briefly hesitated. In the 1940s the Khan had employed Jinnah as his legal adviser and hoped to exercise some leverage.[16] But, seeing the writing on the wall, he signed over Balochistan to Pakistan and thereafter lived to enjoy all his privileges. Baloch nationalists today consider him a sellout. However, his brother, Abdul Karim, resisted and led a Baloch coalition of forces until he was arrested by the Pakistan Army and sentenced in 1949. The sovereign Baloch state after British withdrawal had lasted only two hundred twenty-seven days. The pro-Congress *Anjuman-e-Watan* party was declared unlawful and various tribal leaders were arrested. Pro-independence demonstrations were quickly suppressed.

Without Jinnah's arm-twisting, the princely states of Balochistan would not have voluntarily surrendered their independence. He had to use force because the Baloch indicated they would resist being ruled by outsiders even

Stubborn Angularities II: Balochistan **223**

if they happened to be Muslims rather than British Christians. Today's Baloch nationalists eulogize the fall of the Kalat state as their national tragedy. In the words of an unnamed scholar of Baloch history:

> One of the reasons why Pakistani intellectuals are unable to understand the national movement is that they do not recognize something which is deeply embedded in the Baloch psyche: their obsession with the Kalat State. The Baloch have still not gotten over the fact that they had their own State for centuries and lost it – for the first time – to Pakistan.[17]

Baloch Identity Emerges

Sparsely populated and with little water, but with area almost equal to that of the other three provinces, Balochistan was viewed by Pakistan's early political leadership as having marginal significance other than purely territorial. Its largely pastoral and nomadic people are a mixture of various ethnic groups such as Aryans, Arabs, Persians, Turks, Kurds, Dravidians, Sewais (Hindu), and the black African people.[18] One source establishes their original home as the Aleppo valley in Iraq. The Baloch have their own myths of origin: "the Baloch are the native inhabitants of Balochistan and have been living in Baloch land for 11000 years with a rich civilization (Mehrgarh) and language…Mehrgarh is one of the ancient civilizations on planet earth".[19] Anthropologists do not agree with this. Surely the debate over nationhood is more a political one than a sociological or anthropological one.

Baloch nationalism didn't suddenly wake up to some self-realization of its existence. Like every other nationalism on earth, it too is the inevitable result of social evolution over long periods of history. And, like every other nationalism, Baloch nationalism imagines a Baloch community – one which has no existence beyond the belief that such a community exists. Communal rules can, of course, be highly iniquitous, hierarchical, and exploitative. All tribal systems – the Baloch included – are generally cruel. Baloch women are frequent victims of honor killings and acid attacks. Their literacy levels and deaths during maternity are the poorest in Pakistan. But normative values are irrelevant here. In identity formation, the hierarchical and exploitative nature of the tribal system is secondary. Instead, internal differences are overridden by the perceived distinction between us-versus-them. Thus the *sardar* and the ordinary tribe member share a commonality whether he is cruel or kind by a tribe's standards.

Balochistan, by virtue of its proximity to Oman, is known to have been connected to the Omani Empire from pre-Islamic times (roughly 4 BC). According to the official Omani website,[20] remnants such as ceramic dishes engraved with Harappan writing (circa 2600 BC) have been found in Ras Al Hadd and Ras Al Jinz in Oman. Large communities of the Baloch exist in Oman. Makran, the coastal strip of Balochistan that runs along the Persian Gulf, provided soldiers defending Omani rulers. In 1792 the governor of Balochistan,

Stubborn Angularities II: Balochistan

Mir Naseer Khan, awarded Sayyid Sultan bin Ahmed, then ruler of Oman, the port city of Gwadar on the Makran coast. During the rule of Sultan Said bin Taimur (1932–1970), some Makrani Baloch served as his bodyguards. After being ruled for two hundred years by Oman, Gwadar was purchased by Pakistan in 1958 for a negotiated price of £4 million.

British rule over India did not create Baloch identity, but it helped in solidifying it because efficient administration required accurate categorization of those it ruled over. From an administrative viewpoint, it was convenient to lump together the disparate tribes of Balochistan into a single category, putting them as a pre-modern people to be governed by Frontier Crimes Regulation (FCR). Until formally abolished in 1976, FCR was part of the governance system first introduced in 1871 that relied upon *jirgas* and tribal chiefs with final approval resting on the centrally appointed Political Agent.

During the Raj, the Baloch could not be admitted into the colonial administrative apparatus because they lacked formal education. Instead, peoples from northern parts of India were encouraged to migrate to the then-small trading town of Quetta, the nominal administrative capital of Balochistan. Punjabis, Hindus, Sikhs, and Urdu speakers from northern parts of India came here in large numbers to occupy positions of power. Curiously, after 1947, both Bengali and Baloch nationalists would refer to these "foreign occupiers" as Punjabis rather than Pakistanis when, in fact, the foreigners included Urdu-speaking migrants and some Sindhis as well.

Changes since 1947

Post-1947 Balochistan has changed a great deal politically, culturally, and even topographically. Pakistan's first two constitutions did not recognize the Baloch people as a distinct national group; it was the Bhutto era 1973 constitution that gave Balochistan the status of a province. Baloch culture and the way of life were deeply affected by effects arising from the 1973 Arab–Israeli war. The oil embargo imposed by oil-producing states caused the price of oil to skyrocket. With their newfound wealth, Arab countries found they could purchase labor and expertise from across the world, including Pakistan. The migration of Baloch labor to the Middle East brought back wealth and, together with it, changes in politics and culture.

Contact with Arab Islam helped to propagate conservative values in a culture that was Muslim but still largely secular. Because of geographical proximity, there exist well-formed communities of Baloch *Bedoons* in Oman and UAE. In fact, of every seven Baloch, one lives in the UAE and Oman with many serving in their armed forces. Baloch workers returning from Gulf countries, and the ready availability of Saudi petrodollars have changed the provinces' political ethos and fueled the separatist drive. Some returned to become vigorous proselytizers. Aided by generous Saudi grants, they created *madrassas* propagating Salafi and Deobandi Islam. As Amir Rana points out, the changes are very visible today:

Along the major highways across the country, madressahs, mosques and other big and small structures of various religious denominations are a common sight. From Karachi to Torkham, Islamabad to Gilgit and Peshawar to Kotri, the spread of religious institutions is a visible indication of the religious ethos in the country. But the architectural symmetry of madrassahs, mosques and religious centers also points to the presence of religious forces that are at work to create a kind of national cohesion.[21]

Although militant religious organizations like *Sipah-e-Sahaba*, are formally banned by Pakistan, they continue to thrive in Balochistan. Islamabad's authorities calculate that they will provide an antidote to the kind of nationalism that was once Marxist-inspired as had been the case for the 1973 uprising. Social engineering from outside has led to massive changes:

> There are more than 10,000 small and big madrassahs in Balochistan, which roughly translates into availability of one madrassah for every 1,200 to 1,300 people in the province. In Sindh and Khyber Pakhtunkhwa provinces, by contrast, there is one madrassah for about 45,000 to 50,000, and 10,000 to 12,000 inhabitants, respectively.[22]

A nationalist Baloch scholar, Naseer Dashti acknowledges that Baloch society has undergone profound change during the last few decades.[23] The traditional social and tribal structures have changed, nomadism has vanished and, with the development of numerous townships throughout Balochistan, a middle class has emerged on the Baloch sociopolitical horizon. With this change in society, claims the scholar, the essence of nationalist leadership is also transforming; instead of tribal elders, the urban Baloch middle class is taking up the leadership role.

How this will pan out far into the future remains to be seen. The formerly dominant tribal system is being challenged by those educated in *madrassas* as well as in formal schools. But, apart from those political–religious organizations directly supported by the Pakistani establishment, the sense of Baloch grievance has not dissipated. It has, in fact, been exacerbated by the presence of the Chinese and the tens of thousands of security personnel brought from Punjab to protect them.

Amir Rana comments that: "The process of religious cohesion is slow and complicated. The ultimate outcome of this process is anybody's guess. Whether or not it will dilute the nationalist tendencies among Baloch remains to be seen. But as has been proven time and again, an ideological dose cannot be an alternative to a cohesive social contract and an equitable distribution of resources." Clearly the jury is out on this question.

Too Rich to Be Left Alone

The process of state-building was guided in the years after Partition primarily by the Punjab- dominated establishment with sizeable participation by *muhajirs*.

226 Stubborn Angularities II: Balochistan

Initially it saw Balochistan only through the security lens. But systematic exploration of Balochistan's fabulous underground wealth of minerals and oil began in the 1950s. Resource extraction became important with the discovery of natural gas in the Sui area in 1952. Although the gas was promptly used for industries and homes in Sind and Punjab, the first supply to Balochistan was not to come until thirty years later.

An assessment by Kaiser Bengali, a development economist who was consulted by various provincial government departments from 2013 to 2016, lays bare the situation in the numbers below:[24]

- Balochistan produced the bulk of natural gas, but its consumption has been minimal, as can be seen below.

Year	Production	Consumption
1955–1969	91.3	0
1970–1982	84.2	0
1983–1993	68.2	2.2
1994–2000	48.7	2.2
2001–2004	37.5	7.5
2005–2014	20.8	7.1

- As a result of pricing policies, the amount of resource transfer from gas-producing to gas-consuming provinces resulted in Balochistan paying 7.69 trillion rupees to other provinces where the gas was used for fertilizer production, power, transport (CNG), and commercial/domestic uses. Relative to other provinces, the lowest rate of growth in Pakistan is in Balochistan. Most of the economy is centered on subsistence farming, livestock, fishing, mining and quarrying, manufacturing, construction, electricity and gas generation, etc. The table below is for 2000–2011.

Province	Growth
Punjab	4.5
Sind	4.7
KPK	5.5
Balochistan	2.8

- Persistent underdevelopment is because of grossly inadequate federal investment in basic infrastructure. The federal government allocates a part of the annual budget for the Public Sector Development Program (PSDP) for schemes in various physical and social sectors. The average PSDP allocations for Balochistan from 1989–1990 to 2015–2016 constitute less than 6% of total federal PSDP allocations and a mere 0.19% of national GDP.

Pakistan's Punjabi-dominated establishment cannot conceive a situation where the Baloch would have more than nominal control over what they consider to be Baloch resources. Viewed from General Headquarters in Rawalpindi, Balochistan is far too rich to be left alone. But, then, who should properly be the guardians of its vast natural wealth? The answer is not simple. Central governments have always found it much easier to deal with tribal leaders on one-to-one basis. But these leaders are naturally inclined to enrich themselves leaving little to filter down below. Although there are examples of caring and concerned Baloch *sardars*, far too many lead luxurious lives while their tribesmen suffer poverty and deprivation. Where democracy has yet to take root, and where corruption coexists with a tribal culture, elections are also not a panacea. Incompetence is fairly evenly distributed across provinces, as is the acceptance of bribery as a tool to extract concessions.

Examples of bad governance notwithstanding, equitably distributing benefits from natural resources to the widest possible net of recipients can only be done through some form of representative government that is accountable to the people. The current insurgency draws its strength from a sense of deprivation felt by young educated Baloch men who point to the total control exercised by the center.

A nominally elected provincial government can be terrible when it deals with astronomical sums of money.[25] The Reko Diq disaster shows just how bad things can get.

In 1993 an agreement was negotiated by the Balochistan government with Tethyan Copper Company, a huge international mining company. Rekodiq is believed to be the largest undeveloped gold-copper deposit in the world. For nearly twenty years, Tethyan spent large amounts of money in mapping out mineral resources. Believing it had been shortchanged, Pakistan unilaterally abrogated the contract in 2013. Thereafter, international litigation slapped Pakistan with a staggering fine of·$5.7 billion. Reko Diq was supposed to change the fortunes of Balochistan but, unless an out-of-court settlement is reached, the fine could well bankrupt future Balochistan governments for years to come! For now, the government has obtained a stay order but Pakistan is required to furnish an irrevocable bank guarantee amounting to 25% of the penalty.[26] Assets of Pakistan International Airlines, including the Roosevelt Hotel in Manhattan and Scribe Hotel in Paris, were reportedly provisionally seized by a court order in the British Virgin Islands as settlement of the liability to Tethyan.[27] Although the mining site is theoretically out of bounds, Baloch nationalists claim that secret mining is in progress with China-bound trucks laden with high-grade ores leaving the site during nighttime. Verification, of course, is problematic. In March 2022 the federal and Balochistan governments reached a deal with Barrick Gold Corporation that would give it a 50% share.[28] This, it was said, would enable Pakistan to avoid an $11 billion penalty. In October 2022, another settlement was reached wherein Reko Diq will be owned 50% by Barrick, 25% by Balochistan province, and 25% by major Pakistani state-owned enterprises. Expectedly, Baloch nationalists have decried the deal.

CPEC and Balochistan

Theoretically the Balochistan government is empowered by the 18th Amendment to the Constitution – a measure passed in 2010 by the government under President Asif Ali Zardari – in matters that relate to natural wealth, taxations, and resource conservation. But Islamabad's czars have made sure that the Balochistan assembly and various chief ministers have almost no say in matters related to the $62 billion China–Pakistan Economic Corridor (CPEC) project of which Gwadar is the linchpin. In 1974, Zulfikar Ali Bhutto, who met with Nixon twice in the White House, had reportedly offered Gwadar to the U.S. with the view that the U.S. could use Gwadar as a naval base.[29] The U.S., however, rejected the proposal because it already had ships in Chabahar under the Shah of Iran's pro-American government; the Shah is said to have been deeply upset by Bhutto's attempt to reach out independently to the Americans. Ambassador Dennis Kux notes:

> The prime minister (Bhutto) also sought U.S. help to construct a new port at Gwadar, on the Arabian Sea coast of thinly populated Baluchistan, and said that the U.S. Navy could use the facility. Although Nixon responded that he would have the proposal examined carefully, his NSC briefing paper indicated no "great interest in having a naval facility in Baluchistan," which would stir up the Soviets, the Indians, and the Afghans "without greatly contributing to US interests".[30]

In 1979, following the Soviet invasion of Afghanistan, the U.S. mobilized opposition on the claim that the strategic imperative for the invasion was to access the warm waters of the Persian Gulf. What the Soviets could not achieve with hard power, the Chinese succeeded using soft power.

Initiated in 2013, CPEC is centered upon Gwadar and is the largest investment Pakistan has attracted since independence and is the largest by China in any foreign country. Although frequently referred to as a game changer by the civil and military establishment, only a meager $400 million has been allocated to Balochistan as of 2020. To quote from press reports, leaders in Balochistan say that out of a total 15 energy projects worth $33 billion, only one was slotted for Balochistan, while the rest went to Punjab and Sind.[31] Of the 13 electricity grid stations for 500-kilovolt transmission lines, Balochistan got none. The energy projects have started producing and distributing 7000 megawatts into the system. As part of CPEC, two 500-kilovolt transmission lines, each 1000 kilometers long, worth $4 billion were approved. One line goes from Matiari district in southern Sind to Punjab's capital, Lahore, while another goes to the nearby industrial hub of Faisalabad. Not a single kilometer provides electricity to Balochistan.

Baloch sentiment has opposed CPEC deals made by the federal government, and so these have had to be endorsed by a rubber stamp provincial government. China is therefore viewed as an accomplice of Islamabad and Chinese

Stubborn Angularities II: Balochistan **229**

businessmen, engineers, and technicians are seen as fair game for assassination and kidnapping. The 2018 attack on the Chinese consulate in Karachi, and on the Pearl Continental Hotel in Gwadar in 2019, were claimed by the Baloch Liberation Army and sent shockwaves down the CPEC corridor. In April 2021, a suicide attack at a luxury hotel hosting the Chinese ambassador in Quetta killed four people and injured dozens. In April 2022, a well-educated Baloch female suicide bomber killed three Chinese teachers in Karachi along with their local driver.[32] On every occasion, security forces have blamed India. The capture of Kulbhushan Yadhav in 2017, an Indian national with a fake passport, was held as solid proof of Indian involvement in seeking to subvert CPEC. Could this allegation be correct?

India has certainly not been unaware of Pakistan's difficulties in Balochistan. As a general rule, whenever a population is angry with those who they see as an occupying power, it is not hard for enemies of that power to find domestic allies. This is exactly why Pakistan was able to successfully recruit Kashmiris on the Indian side of the Line of Control (LOC). And this is also why Balochistan is now an arrow in India's quiver against Pakistan. Vikram Sood, a perceptive commentator on India–Pakistan affairs and a former head of RAW, wrote in 2009:

> The Baloch are a secular people, they have been our friends and we must retain their friendship. While Balochistan remains Pakistan's internal problem, we cannot be seen to be helpless if there is injustice in our neighborhood. At the same time, what is happening in Balochistan is not India sponsored terrorism unlike what is happening in India where Pakistan sponsored terrorism by the Lashkar-e-Tayyaba and others continues unabated...War is an ugly option but it is an option that one would not exercise but before that there several intermediate options – economic, political, para-military/covert that can be considered.[33]

Prime Minister Modi has openly played around with this idea of tit-for-tat. In 2016, drawing outrage from Pakistan, on India's independence day he said, "People of Balochistan, Gilgit and PoK (Pakistan Occupied Kashmir) have thanked me a lot a lot in past few days, I am grateful to them".[34] National Security Advisor Ajit Doval argues that India should play the Balochistan card while some Indian strategists openly call for subversion. In "How India Can Play the Balochistan Card Against Pakistan," Pramit Pal Chaudhuri deliberates on possible Indian strategies.[35] Since Kashmir is in ferment again, he says it will be difficult for India to make a moral case over Balochistan. Weapons and material help should be given to the Baloch, but he concedes that not having a common border means India cannot really make a difference. Following other Indian strategists, Chaudhuri says the best way to put a thorn in Pakistan's side is by fanning Pakistan's exaggerated fears. This could be done by providing an Indian home to Baloch nationalist leaders or by encouraging Baloch émigré groups in the West to harass Pakistan in the halls

230 Stubborn Angularities II: Balochistan

of the U.S. Congress or the European Parliament. India should hope, he says, that the Pakistan Army's angry overreaction will keep Balochistan aflame.

The Secession Question

Balochistan and Kashmir have similarities in that a substantial section of the population resents being ruled from outside. What could be a rational and humane way to look at the problem? To get a broader perspective that goes beyond India and Pakistan, let us make a triumvirate that includes Scotland as well. This gives a common thread: these are three geographical regions having large numbers of people – and possibly a majority – who want to secede from the country they are currently a part of. Defined by a common history, culture, and language, these groups constitute distinct and separate nations and hence insist they have a right to self-rule and to form their own nation-state with definite borders.

So when is secession justifiable? Allen Buchanan, late professor of Political and Moral Philosophy at Duke University, has extensively studied this question. He says that some will dismiss it with the smug, world-weary sigh that naked power alone decides. Indeed, today's world map was largely made by conquest, colonialism, conflict, and cleansing of ethnic minorities. Nevertheless, moral justifications for their actions are sought by even the most ruthless perpetrators of injustices. Buchanan's answer: one part of an existing national state has a right to secede from the rest only if it is suffering systematic abuse. He endorses the view invoked in the world's most famous secessionist document, the U.S. Declaration of Independence.

According to the Declaration, "Governments long established should not be changed for light and transient causes". Secession can only be justified in light of "a long train of abuses", such as suppression of minorities or undue extraction of wealth. Britain's mistreatment of its American colonies morally justified the treason of American secessionists – who later became known as revolutionary heroes.

Scotland's bid for secession therefore fails to carry moral weight. It cannot claim to be the victim of a "long train of abuses" by the U.K. Whether a free Scotland is a good thing or a bad thing is not for you or me to decide. British nationalists are alarmed, but they have not sent in their army to blind protesting secessionists with pellet guns. Nor have British security forces launched a systematic campaign of abduction, torture, killing, and then dumping the dead bodies of secessionists. Scotland has no cases of "missing persons". At least in internal matters, Britain behaves in a civilized manner.

There are other, perhaps even better, examples of civilized behavior. After a plebiscite in 1905, Norway seceded from Sweden. Initially there was some tension and fear of war, but secession was not viewed as something catastrophic. Good sense prevailed, and within months the two countries were trading and behaving normally. Of course, all secessions are not desirable or worthy of moral support. Imagine the chaos it would bring to Japan if its 47 prefectures, based on

Stubborn Angularities II: Balochistan **231**

somewhat different cultures, insisted on becoming separate nation-states. This could bring limitless upheaval, disrupt commerce, and possibly create refugee populations.

On the other hand, the Muslims of Kashmir can certainly make this case against India. So can the ethnic Baloch against Pakistan. The peculiar circumstances of Partition, and the subsequent behavior of governments at the center, meant that some regions were never truly part of India or Pakistan. A moral sanction for struggle does not, of course, necessarily mean that Kashmir or Balochistan will ever succeed in seceding. Regional separatists are reviled by large majorities in the respective countries. Deemed as traitors in the pay of some enemy, they are targeted with massive military might and repression.

The Way Forward

Extreme positions on Balochistan are well known: separatist-nationalists see the center as imposing its colonial *diktat* and exploiting Balochistan's natural resources. They want total separation from Pakistan in the form of a sovereign Baloch state. But this is unlikely in the foreseeable future both because of the overwhelming strength of the Pakistani state's military power and, equally, because secession is not favored by a majority of the Pashtun population.

On the other side is Pakistan's military, which identifies the interests of its senior officers as equal to those of Pakistan's. Its position is unequivocal: Baloch nationalist forces will be subdued however much the human cost. Human rights do not figure in the Army's calculations. When questioned during a press conference about thousands of those who have gone missing, Maj. Gen. Asif Ghafoor, then the Director General of ISPR, was frank: "We don't want anyone to be missing, but war is ruthless. Everything is fair in love and war".[36] General Ghafoor's immediate predecessor, Lt. Gen. Asim Saleem Bajwa, held similar views. He was appointed chairman of the CPEC Authority in November 2019 and a special adviser to the prime minister. He remained in his position in spite of evidence that he had an undeclared pizza empire in the U.S. and the matter was quickly hushed up.[37]

Baloch nationalists are a loud, noisy, and argumentative lot. Spread between moderates, radicals, and guerillas (details may be found in Amirali[38]), some equate self-determination with secession, while some do not. Some see the Baloch tribal system as oppressive, but others claim it is democratic because leaders can be changed by consensus. Groups have formed and then split on questions such as transcending tribal identities and building an inclusive, democratic national movement. Marxists have collided amongst themselves, as well as with other more social democratic groups. Progressives have asked whether women can get a fair deal in a patriarchic Baloch society. Some ask: can the tribal foundations of Baloch society be democratized and people liberated without destroying the bonds and the cultural markers of the indigenous system? In short, an outsider stands quite dizzied by the internal debates and differences.

232 Stubborn Angularities II: Balochistan

Differences notwithstanding, a strong sense of Baloch unity persists. Relatively few Baloch think that armed struggle will succeed. Hence, for many years moderate Baloch nationalists have called for progress towards ending the Baloch insurgency. In 2009 Senator Sanaullah Baloch was indignant at the Pakistan military's refusal to negotiate with the Baloch while noting its ready embrace of Sufi Mohammed's Taliban. In 2009 he wrote: "Islamabad's recent move to grant religious self-rule to the Taliban in Swat and the denial of political autonomy to the people of Balochistan are obviously beyond comprehension".[39] The senator asked the government to restore peace to Balochistan through a series of steps: (a) Ending military operations and halting the construction of military and paramilitary cantonments, (b) withdrawing security forces, (c) repatriating and rehabilitating displaced persons, (d) cancelling civil/military land allotments in Balochistan, (e) demilitarizing the area, (f) assuring equal wellhead prices for Balochistan's gas, and (h) abandoning torture camps and establishing a "truth and reconciliation commission" for the trial of those involved in killing veteran Baloch leaders Nawab Akbar Bugti and Balach Marri, and other human rights violations.

With the 2008 elections and the rejection of General Musharraf's hardline policies, it seemed that Balochistan would finally get a break from violence. Baloch nationalist parties cautiously welcomed the apology from the new President of Pakistan, Asif Ali Zardari: "The PPP, on behalf of the people of Pakistan, apologises to the people of the province of Balochistan for the atrocities and injustices committed against them and pledges to embark on a new highway of healing and mutual respect". Zardari also called for an immediate halt to the ongoing military operation there and release of all political prisoners, including former chief minister Akhtar Mengal.[40]

The 18th Amendment to the Constitution passed in 2010 during the PPP's tenure was, from the Baloch nationalist point of view, insufficient but still a step in the right direction. Balochistan's share in the provincial pool jumped from 5 to 9.09%.[41] In addition, the 7th NFC Award also revised the formula for the computation of the gas development surcharge (GDS) and provided for the retroactive payment of GDS arrears to Balochistan on the basis of the new formula. Moreover, the 18th Amendment gave the provinces 50% ownership of natural resources within their territorial boundaries and, thus, addressed a long-standing demand of the people of Balochistan. On the other hand, critics of the 18th Amendment argue that it has weakened the center without necessarily strengthening the provinces, leading to a tug of war between federal and provincial governments and thereby creating confusion and duplication of authority.[42] The PPP's determined advocacy of 18th Amendment is not for any selfless reason or with Balochistan in mind: now that it has been reduced from a federal party to a Sind-only party, the 18th Amendment ensures the PPP's access to resources and its legislative power.

Ten years later, one can ask: has the Federation been weakened or strengthened by the 18th Amendment? Rafiullah Kakar gives a strongly positive

Stubborn Angularities II: Balochistan **233**

balance sheet[43] while noting that all major Baloch and Pashtun ethno-nationalist parties that had boycotted the 2008 general elections participated in the 2013 general elections; national parties like the PPP and PMLN were forced to develop local bases; and devolution encouraged smaller ethnic parties to use parliamentary means rather than violence. Significantly, secular and religious parties in Balochistan are on the same page when it comes to the question of provincial autonomy.[44] However, the military establishment, both directly and through the PTI government, pushed back against the 18th Amendment with a demand to establish a new National Finance Commission with a view to devising a new formula for the distribution of financial resources, with more deployed towards the center than the provinces.[45] The military, of course, would like to keep getting the lion's share of resources without hindrance from the provinces.

To conclude: Pakistan's Punjab-centered civil and military establishment could have spared the country much agony and blood had it been sensitive to the fact that Pakistan is actually an ethno-federation. The diversity of its various peoples means that ethno-nationalism will always to be a challenge to the center. But this, by itself, is not a bad thing. India with far greater diversity could nevertheless succeed in evolving a stable political dispensation. The devastation of Pakistan in 1971 showed decisively that religion alone cannot cement disparate peoples together. Nor will raw force work forever. The key to Pakistan's stability does not lie in making the Army's fist yet harder or peddling hard varieties of religion in an attempt to contain nationalist discontent. Instead, it must be found in sharply limiting the power of the federation, sharing power between provinces, equitably distributing resources, and giving Pakistan's various cultures and languages their due. In the long run, only a system where all have a stake can survive and prosper.

Notes

1 https://www.africa.upenn.edu/Articles_Gen/Letter_Birmingham.html
2 B. Baloch, *Quaid's Statue Destroyed in Gwadar*, Dawn, 27 September 2021. https://www.dawn.com/news/1648664
3 For other versions of the Iraqi embassy story, see: Hamid Zafar, Arms Cache Discovery, *Pakistan Forum* (February 1973), https://www.jstor.org/stable/2568993
4 S.M. Baloch, *Akbar Bugti's Death and the Revival of the Baloch Insurgency*, Herald, 16 September 2017. https://herald.dawn.com/news/1153862
5 *Balochistan War: Pakistan Accused over 1,000 Dumped Bodies*, BBC News, 28 December 2016. https://www.bbc.com/news/world-asia-38454483
6 *Agencies Told to Produce Balochistan's 'Missing' in Next Hearing*, Dawn, 20 June 2012. https://www.dawn.com/news/728041/balochistan-case-sc-resumes-hearing
7 A. Amirali, *Balochistan, SAGE Series in Human Rights Audits of Peace Processes*, Volume III, Rita Manchanda (ed.), New Delhi, Sage Publishers (2015).
8 *Pakistan Attack: China Condemns Killing of Tutors in Pakistan Blast*, BBC News, 27 April 2022. https://www.bbc.com/news/world-asia-61225678
9 A. Aamir, *Covering the Periphery – Balochistan as a Blind Spot in the Mainstream Newspapers of Pakistan, From Terrorism to Television – Dynamics of Media, State, and Society in Pakistan*, eds. Qaisar Abbas and Farooq Sulehria, Routledge (2020).

234 Stubborn Angularities II: Balochistan

10 General Asif Ghafoor reported on Naya Daur-TV, 16 January 2020. https://nayadaur .tv/2020/01/gen-asif-ghafoor-praised-by-many-controversial-to-some/

11 Adnaan Amir, *Developing Gwadar IV*, The News, 3 July 2022.

12 G. Nihad, *Gwadar Residents' Protest for Rights Enters Day 17*, Dawn, 1 December 2021. https://www.dawn.com/news/1661313

13 Mir Gul Khan Naseer, *A Widely accepted Narrative among the Baloch Is Tarikh-e-Balochistan* (two volumes), Kalat Publishers (1952).

14 For a point of view that reflects the official Pakistani narrative, see: D.H. Saiyid, The Accession of Kalat: Myth and Reality, Strategic Studies, 26, no. 3 (Autumn 2006): 26–45.

15 C. Jaffrelot, *The Pakistan Paradox – Instability and Resilience*, Oxford University Press (USA), Translated by Cynthia Schoch (2015), pp. 135–152.

16 F.H. Siddiqi, *The Politics of Ethnicity in Pakistan: The Baloch, Sindhi and Mohajir Ethnic Movements*, Routledge (2012), pp. 56–58.

17 Interview conducted by Alia Amirali on 5 August 2008 in Quetta as part of her MPhil research project at Quaid-e-Azam University.

18 M. Ahmed and G. Khan, The History of Baloch and Balochistan: A Critical Appraisal, *South Asian Studies*, 32, no. 1 (January–June 2017): 39–52.

19 Ibid.

20 Brief History of the Relationship between Oman and Balochistan: https:// www.atheer.om/en/7162/brief-history-of-the-relationship-between-oman-and -Balochistan/#ixzz6mEatFFwj

21 M.H. Rana, *Religion, Nationalism and Insurgency in Balochistan*, Dawn, 14 July 2019. https://www.dawn.com/news/1493929

22 Ibid.

23 Naseer Dashti as quoted in *Religion, Nationalism, and Insurgency in Balochistan*, Muhammad Amir Rana, Dawn, 14 July 2019. https://www.dawn.com/news /1493929

24 K. Bengali, *A Cry for Justice – Empirical Insights from Balochistan*, Karachi, Oxford University Press (2018).

25 A. Amir, *Bearing the Burden: The Cost of Reko Diq (Balochistan) Disaster*, The Friday Times, 2 August 2019. https://www.thefridaytimes.com/2019/08/02/bearing-the -burden-the-cost-of-reko-diq-disaster/

26 N. Iqbal, *Reko Diq Stay Comes with Bank Guarantee Condition*, Dawn, 19 September 2020. https://www.dawn.com/news/1580453

27 *Reko Diq Case: Roosevelt and Scribe Hotels Seized by Court*, News Pakistan, 23 January 2021.

28 S.I. Raza, *Pakistan Signs Deal to Avoid $11bn Penalty in Reko Diq Case*, Dawn, 21 March 2022. https://www.dawn.com/news/1681071

29 A. Vatanka, *Iran and Pakistan – Security, Diplomacy and American Influence*, London and New York, I.B. Tauris (2015), pp. 101–102.

30 Dennis Kux, *The United States and Pakistan, 1947–2000: Disenchanted Allies*, Washington DC, Woodrow Wilson Press (2001), p. 209.

31 M. Zubair, *Balochistan Deserves Justice in Chinese Projects*, Gandhara, 14 January 2019. https://gandhara.rferl.org/a/pakistan-balochistan-deserves-justice-in-chinese -projects-cpec/29708813.html

32 *Alarmed by Suicide Attack, China and Pakistan Work Together on Probe*, Reuters, 31 October 2022.

33 V. Sood, *Balochistan-Pakistan's Other Colony*, 23 August 2009. http://soodvikram.blogspot.com/2009/09/balochistan-pakistans-other-colony.html

34 *People of Balochistan, Kashmir Thanked Me: Modi on India's Independence Day*, Dawn, 15 August 2016. https://www.dawn.com/news/1277670

35 P.P. Chaudhuri, *How India Can Play the Balochistan Card against Pakistan*, Hindustan Times, 7 Oct 2016. https://www.hindustantimes.com/analysis/how-best-can-india

-play-the-balochistan-card-against-pakistan/story-vOq6IkRKSdlzgGYKkI7pjK
.html

36 *Army Shares Pain of Missing Persons' Families: DG ISPR*, Daily Times, 11 May 2019. See also Asif Ghafoor interview: https://www.youtube.com/watch?v=xIOhjM9PaAE &feature=youtu.be&t=3904

37 *Asim Saleem Bajwa Quits as SAPM after PM Finally Accepts Resignation*, Dawn, 12 October 2020. https://www.dawn.com/news/1584668

38 Amirali, op. cit.

39 *Baloch Demands Still Unmet*, Dawn, 19 February 2009. https://www.dawn.com/news/940332/baloch-demands-still-unmet

40 R. Asghar, *PPP Apologises to Balochistan for 'Excesses': Pledge of Maximum Provincial Autonomy*, Dawn, 25 February 2008. https://www.dawn.com/news/290904/ppp-apologises-to-balochistan-for-excesses-pledge-of-maximum-provincial-autonomy

41 R. Kakar, *A Matter of Federal Integrity*, The News, 5 April 2018. https://www.thenews.com.pk/print/300676-a-matter-of-federal-integrity

42 F. Batool, *Why the PPP Fears the End of Pakistan's 18th Amendment*, South Asian Voices, 16 May 2019. https://southasianvoices.org/why-ppp-fears-end-18th-amendment/

43 Kakar, op. cit.

44 S. Shahid, *Balochistan Opposition Vows to Resist Move against 18th Amendment*, Dawn, 17 May 2020. https://www.dawn.com/news/1557681

45 S.R. Sheikh, *Military Creep – Pakistan's Federal System Is Being Undermined by Militarization*, Himal, 4 August 2021. https://www.himalmag.com/military-creep-pakistan-2021/

PART FOUR
Five Big Questions

Nine

WAS PARTITION WORTH THE PRICE?

Little cheer does this wine bring	ابھرے تو جوشِ بادہ گساراں نہیں رہا
Spring comes without its bright colors	بادل گھرے تو رنگِ بہاراں نہیں رہا
Conversations are limp and lifeless	باتیں کھلیں تو رقصِ نگاراں نہیں رہا
Even the wine brings not us together	بو حِل کھلی تو مجمعِ یاراں نہیں رہا
Drink as much as you want but it does so little	کوئی سبیل بادہ پرستی نہیں رہی
The night of our celebration is dark and joyless	مستی کی رات آئی تو مستی نہیں رہی

— *Josh Malihabadi, Matam-e-Azadi (Mourning Independence)*[1]

Winds from the communal storm of 1947 blew millions across borders drawn by the hastily retreating British. Unresolved were multiple issues. Whom was this new country for? Well, obviously for Muslims – that's what the Two Nation Theory said. But that does not answer the question because different Muslims were situated differently. Who would gain or lose? Landlord or peasant, Sunni or Shia? Punjabis would gain but what about others? An attempt is made in this chapter to create a balance sheet. Many gained: of the millions who crossed over, some became rich from properties abandoned by fleeing Hindus, jobs were now plentiful in the civil service, and the army was desperate to recruit officers who had served in the Royal Indian Army. Feudal families ruling vast territories in Sindh and Punjab were able to consolidate their rule. They made sure the land reforms promised by later Pakistani leaders from time to time would never happen. But there were plenty of losers as well. Before the movement for Pakistan caught on in the Muslim-majority states, the most enthusiastic among Muslims had been those from Muslim minority states in pre-Partition India. Ahmadis and Shias had also pitched in their lot with Jinnah. How did it pan out for them? Did Muslims of the subcontinent as a whole win or lose?

DOI: 10.4324/9781003379140-14

240 Was Partition Worth the Price?

A utilitarian like Jeremy Bentham or John Stuart Mill would use the principle of greatest good for the greatest number and so might have tried to estimate the sum total of human happiness if India had not been divided versus the same otherwise. This is easier said than done because defining the quantity of "good" is ambiguous. Should one include Muslims only? Just Hindus? Or those Muslims now split into three different countries – India, Pakistan, Bangladesh? If India had remained united, would Muslims and Hindus have fought tooth and nail or would they have eventually reached some kind of mutual accommodation? Over time would an Indian identity have become primary and all other factors – caste, ethnicity, sect, and religion – become secondary? Muslims had ruled India for centuries, and now the ballot box was threatening to take away from them what little was left. Could they now submit to the idea of one man, one vote?

To keep the discussion focused, I shall view the balance sheet of Partition strictly from the Muslim perspective. This still leaves open the question of a net positive versus a net negative. Before religious identity became the all-in-all of politics, and before hatreds rose to pathological heights in the 1930s and 1940s, the Muslims of undivided India lived side-by-side with each other. Partition was supposed to "clean up" India. As it turned out, only a small fraction of the total Muslim population actually moved across borders. That's why today's Muslims live in three separate, unfriendly, and noncommunicating blocks of territory with roughly equal numbers in each: Pakistan, India, and Bangladesh. Arguably, being together would have made the Muslims of South Asia a powerful bloc with higher levels of achievement in science and education than presently. Again, strictly from the Muslim point of view, was the partitioning of India worth the cost of having two nearly equal Muslim populations forever separated into two heavily militarized antagonistic nuclear states?

Amid strong disagreement on this question (and much else), there is complete agreement that a terrible cataclysm happened in 1947. An estimated 1 million people from all sides were killed, about 14 million desperate refugees crossed the new borders, organized gangs of young thugs roamed the streets burning shops and buildings, corpses floated down rivers and canals, pregnant women were hacked to death, and enduring bitterness was created. This did not end after 1947. East Pakistan had to undergo a second holocaust in 1971, the issue of Kashmir remains unresolved, and now the threat of mutual nuclear annihilation hangs heavy over the subcontinent.

As subsequent history shows, drawing hard borders based on the Two Nation Theory did not do away with religious divisions. Pakistan was to see the first violent manifestations in the anti-Ahmadi riots of 1953. Ahmadis were expelled from Islam by a decision of the Pakistani parliament in 1974. This decision was firmly supported by Shias, but after General Zia's attempt to redefine Pakistan as an Islamic state, anti-Shia sectarianism grew steadily. After Iran, Pakistan has the world's second largest Shia community. Extremist Sunni organizations demand the expulsion of Shias from Islam. However, the Pakistani establishment does have some Shia representation. The issue of whether Shias as a whole won or

Was Partition Worth the Price? **241**

lost from the making of Pakistan is a complex one that will not receive a definite answer here because it lies in a gray area. Instead, I refer the reader to a recent book, *The Shias of Pakistan: An Assertive and Beleaguered Minority* by German scholar, Andreas Rieck.[2] His description of Pakistani Shias as an assertive minority is appropriate: during Muharram they insist on public processions – *Azadari* and *Tazia*. This angers many Sunnis and so frequently invites planned or spontaneous violence. But even at quieter times of the year their townships, hospitals, doctors, and *Imambargahs* have been attacked often since the 1980s. Da'esh and the Taliban relentlessly target the Hazara community who are not just Shia, but also ethnically identifiable by distinctive facial features. Notwithstanding the growth of anti-Shia sentiment in a sizeable section of the population, Rieck still sees Shias as well integrated into the power structure. This, in my opinion, is a semi-plausible conclusion but needs a more careful and broad-based study. However, there can be no doubt that as Pakistani politics moves into the realm of hyper-religiosity, the Shia–Sunni schism in Pakistan has widened over the last few decades.

India under Nehru was initially relatively successful at keeping religious conflict within bounds but received its first major challenge after Operation Blue Star and the subsequent assassination of Nehru's daughter, Indira Gandhi, by her Sikh bodyguard in 1984. Sikhs in Delhi became victims of organized pogroms with deaths estimated in the range of 4000–16,000. Still more impactful was the destruction of the Babri Mosque in 1992 by Hindu mobs. The forces of religious extremism could not be tamed there either. Once religious fanaticism and ethnic hatreds spilled over, carnage resulted. In both Pakistan and India, these forces have disrupted internal peace and sabotaged the process of creating a modern nation-state committed to pluralism, human rights, and rapid economic development.

Still, one can argue that things could have been even worse for Muslims without Partition. An undivided India with the Sangh Parivar gaining over Nehru, and with Jinnah being edged out by Muslim fanatics, would have been the ultimate nightmare. The reemergence of the extremist Rashtriya Swayamsevak Sangh (RSS) in Modi's India and a splurge of killings of Muslims suspected of cow slaughter is a grim reminder. One cannot rule out the possibility that a still bloodier Partition would have happened if the British had left some years or decades later. It is therefore important to keep our minds open as we explore possibilities.

The No-Pakistan Option

For whatever it's worth, let us speculate on what might have happened if Congress had accepted the 1946 Cabinet Mission Plan. This was the last chance to avert Partition. It visualized a weak center with provinces grouped on the basis of religious majorities. Unified India would then have been ruled by a coalition government of Hindus and Muslims with the issue of princely states left for future

242 Was Partition Worth the Price?

discussion. The Muslim League had reluctantly accepted the proposal since there seemed to be no other option. But the Congress, after deliberating on the implications, went back on its initial acceptance. Why it did – and the correctness of this decision – remains hotly debated. One hypothesis is that it was losing control over events. The party's infrastructure had been much weakened because the Congress leadership has been imprisoned for opposing the war against the Axis powers. Jinnah thereafter seized the opportunity, calling for Direct Action Day on 16 August 1946. This led to the infamous Week of the Long Knives. With this, the League's street power was amply demonstrated; the rioting that left thousands dead clinched the case for Jinnah being the sole spokesman for Muslims. After the riots the creation of Pakistan was, to use a popular American expression, a slam dunk. Seeking to justify their acquiescence to the division of India, the Congress took the position that

> without Partition there might have been no transfer of power at all, or the whole of India might have been involved in civil war the consequences of which would have been infinitely more tragic than the sad events of the latter half of 1947.[3]

But a decade later, Nehru admitted – with reluctance and in a roundabout way – that he had made a mistake by pulling out of the Plan and thus allowing India to be divided.[4] But what if it had been otherwise and power had been shared as stipulated?

Pessimistic possibilities abound. Chaos could have continued indefinitely and a dysfunctional government would have been unable to make progress on any front – infrastructural development, economic planning, science and technology, education, etc. Perhaps Muslims would have been squeezed out of jobs and positions of power. A coalition government may soon have fallen apart and communal tensions could have flared up again, this time blazing on for still longer. One needs only to look at the hate-filled violence of Serbs, Croats, and Bosnian Muslims that followed the breakup of Yugoslavia. They had lived together and intermarried for centuries before turning savagely upon each other in a final divorce.

A dedicated optimist, on the other hand, can see flexibility developing over time as Hindus and Muslims realized the need to live together in peace. One could have hoped for a steady de-politicization of religion and greater toleration for diverse strands of belief; absence of territorial disputes such as over Kashmir and the division of waters; a greater acceptance of modernity among Muslims; and use of resources for economic development rather than weapons to fight wars. Faced with a more competitive environment, Muslims would have improved their educational and skill levels. They could have had real universities to go to rather than the sham ones that litter Pakistan today. Meritocracies could have developed, caste and creed deemphasized, and the intrinsic worth of individuals far better recognized.

Such transformations have occurred elsewhere. After all, there are multireligious countries that have gone through teething troubles but which eventually have managed to create a secular dispensation respecting the rights of the minority and majority. The religious wars in Europe were far bloodier than even Partition and had lasted centuries, and yet today a European Union – though smitten by Brexit and COVID-19 – still functions reasonably well. Maybe Maulana Azad's belief that the "chapter of communal differences was a transient phase of Indian life" would have turned out to be correct. Who knows?

Before doing a final tally of gains and losses of Partition as it actually transpired, I will first ask what mobilized Muslims to seek a separate state and what their expectations had been. We must therefore discover what brought ordinary people out into the streets. What did they want or, perhaps more importantly, what were they told that they should want? Was it the pursuit of some Islamic utopia or, instead, safety from Hindu domination?

Answering these questions will allow us to properly compare expectations and results. Every mass movement has millions who move together like a herd. To get it moving needs either a strong pull (an attractive ideology) or a big push (racialism, discrimination). We know that in the socialist revolutions, such as those of Russia and China, achieving high ideals of social justice was the mobilizing force. So what positive ideals did the Muslim League hold out that could enthuse the Muslim masses of India? Whatever they were, egalitarianism was not among them.

Socialist Utopia Rejected

By the late 1940s Jinnah and the All-India Muslim League (AIML) had successfully brought to the center of Indian politics the landowning groups of the Muslim majority provinces. All the movers and shakers of AIML – i.e., the men who wanted India divided along religious lines – nominally represented Muslim interests but virtually all came from the landed gentry who recognized the importance of politics to protect their interest. There was only a sprinkling of industrialists and businessmen; by and large the Muslim trading community of Bombay and Calcutta was not enthusiastic.

Socialism and communism were anathema to the rich, politically conservative men who held top positions in the Muslim League. Jinnah, a fabulously successful lawyer in the 1920s, had briefly considered running for the British Conservative Party.[3] As a political leader, his goal was not to fight for the end of imperial rule or for a stricter Islamic society but, instead, to get a better deal from the ruling British for upper-class Muslims. Since the departure of the British would place Muslims in a minority, he resolutely resisted every such move against the imperial power. This became the cause of his differences with the Congress. Once the movement for Pakistan got underway, he was unequivocal in stating his aversion to communism and advised students at Aligarh Muslim University to stay away from progressive politics:

Another party which has become very active of late is the Communist party. Their propaganda is insidious and I warn you not to fall into their clutches. Their propaganda is a snare and a trap. What is it that you want? All this talk of socialism, communism, national-socialism and every other *ism* is out of place.[6]

Shortly before his epic 1940 speech in Lahore which led to the Pakistan Resolution, he addressed the Punjab Students Federation in Lahore with a stern admonition: "I warn the Communists to keep their hands off Muslims. Islam is our guide and a complete code of our life…We do not want any 'ism'".[7] On more than one occasion, Jinnah accused the Congress of siding with socialism, communism, and anti-imperialism and – somewhat strangely and counter-factually – also accused socialists and communists of aiding the rise of Hitlerism:

> The Congress is struggling to achieve independence and to establish a communistic and socialist government…This has been constantly dinned into the ears of the youth. When you think you will be able to destroy the British Government, the zamindars, the capitalists with one stroke, refer to the conditions of Europe. In Germany Hitlerism came into existence because of socialistic and communistic movements. So did Fascism rise in Italy.[8]

Congress had taken the socialist path, a fact that the late Mushirul Hasan of Jamia Millia credits to Gandhi rather than Nehru. He contrasts Gandhi's beliefs and actions with those of Jinnah, who "stayed clear of the dusty roads, the villages inhabited by millions of hungry, oppressed and physically emaciated peasants, and the British prison where so many of his countrymen were incarcerated for defying the colonial government". He notes that:

> While Gandhi walked barefoot to break the Salt Law and to galvanize the masses by culturally resonant and action-oriented symbols, a pensive and restless Jinnah waited in London to occupy the commanding heights of political leadership in Delhi. While Gandhi treaded the path fouled by Hindu and Muslim zealots in the riot-stricken areas of Bihar and Bengal, Jinnah was being crowned as the Governor-General of Pakistan.[9]

Ironically, as noted by Oldenburg, by the time Jinnah took power, Gandhi had lost his position as the unquestioned leader of the Congress.[10]

Unlike Jinnah who remained consistently opposed to socialism, Allama Iqbal started out with left-wing credentials. In his youth he had written laudatory poems in praise of Lenin and Mussolini. Left-wingers cited his stridently revolutionary verses:

Lush fields that give not to the tiller his daily bread	جس کھیت سے دہقاں کو میسر نہیں روزی
Burn down every ear of wheat that grows thereupon	اُس کھیت کے ہر خوشۂ گندم کو جلا دو

Was Partition Worth the Price? **245**

But Iqbal's earlier romance with socialism and universalism had evaporated by the 1930s. In his letter of 28 May 1937, he asked Jinnah to demand redistribution of India's population as a counter to what he called Nehru's "atheistic socialism".

> in order to make it possible for Muslim India to solve the problems it is necessary to redistribute the country and to provide one or more Muslim states with absolute majorities. Don't you think that the time for such a demand has already arrived? Perhaps this is the best reply you can give to the *atheistic socialism* of Jawahar Lal Nehru.[11]

The rejection of socialism by the Muslim League and its refusal to address the question of land distribution left the dilemma: how to attract the peasant and worker who is supposed to value his economic welfare over all else? In a country that was almost totally agrarian a century ago, what could be a pulling force? Jinnah never gave a clear answer to this except for the vague promise of creating a system based on Islam. Since Islam was supposed to be the solution for every kind of problem, this is as far as he was willing to go on the specifics of wealth redistribution. It was more fruitful to dwell upon feelings of Muslim victimhood – that they were being punished for their faith. Poverty among Muslims could always be blamed on other factors such as black marketers, corruption, wrong choice of leaders, or a biased distribution of goods. However, taking wealth away from the rich was not on Jinnah's agenda. Muslim League leaders were to become part of the rapacious elite that would devour Pakistan's wealth in the decades ahead while keeping the majority of Muslims in permanent poverty.

This appeal for Pakistan sans socialism by Jinnah resonated with an important section of Muslim society. Hamza Alavi, a Marxist academic sociologist, identified that social class – the so-called *salariat* – provided the real force behind the social and political impetus for the Pakistan idea.[12] Peasants and workers (in the rather few industries that then existed) had no political clout. Instead, the push came from the class of salaried Muslim professionals from northern India especially that of UP, Bihar, and Punjab. Alavi called this salaried class *salariat*. These were the urban, educated Muslims employed by the colonial state. Associated with them were lawyers, journalists, teachers, and other urban professionals. It is they, or their forebears, who were ruined when Hindus steadily took over land ownership, and then jobs in the colonial army and administration.

Alavi asserts that Hindu–Muslim differences can be traced back to a conflict between the Muslim *ashrafiyya* versus the Hindu service castes such as the *khatris*, *kayasthas*, and Kashmiri *brahmins* in northern India or the *kayasthas*, *brahmins*, and *baidyas* in Bengal. Indeed, as emphasized in Chapter Two, there had been a big decrease in the number of employed Muslim professionals after 1857. This led to Muslim grievances against the British but even more against the better educated Hindus with whom they were in direct competition. The figures and tables shown in Chapter Two demonstrate the enormous size of the Hindu *salariat* as compared to the Muslim *salariat*. With Hindus leading so massively, the *ashrafiyya*

246 Was Partition Worth the Price?

demanded safeguards and quotas in jobs for the Muslims of North India. Wider support came through their organic links with the landlords and rich peasants. The Pakistan Movement was barren ground for progressive thought. Liberal-left sensibilities were near absent from the Muslim League with the exception of Mian Iftikharuddin, a former Congress leader who was a large landowner as well but happened to be a progressive who had joined the Muslim League in 1946 on orders of the Communist Party of India (CPI). The CPI, under Stalin's instruction, had accepted the Two Nation Theory as a legitimate demand for national self-determination. The workers' paradise could wait. Hindu members of CPI living in Sindh were ordered to leave for India, Muslim members living in India told to move to Pakistan.

The case of Bengal was different from that of north India. Bengali Muslims were virtually absent from among the salaried classes. Instead, the Pakistan Movement in Bengal drew upon resentment against Hindu money lenders and landlords. But by and large the Indian Muslim capitalist class stayed aloof. About 90% of the subcontinent's industry and taxable income base remained in India, including the largest cities of Delhi, Bombay, and Calcutta. Hamza Alavi emphasizes that, notwithstanding Jinnah's central role and his Gujrati roots, the Gujarati-speaking business community of Bombay were not particularly enamored by the Pakistan idea. More concerned with protecting their commercial interests than ideological politics, they were inclined towards Hindu–Muslim coexistence.

So far the urban Muslims in Muslim-majority Punjab had been dormant and had voted for the status quo landlord dominated Unionist Party. Mobilizing Muslims in Balochistan and the North West Frontier Province (NWFP) was also a special challenge because the Muslim League had been routed over there in the 1937 elections. The social and economic situation in the two areas was significantly different from that in the fertile plains. Largely tribal and pastoral, their chieftains wanted continuity not change. Sikhs and Hindus had lived there for centuries more or less peacefully with the Muslim majority. But once things got stirred up, most were forced to leave.

How then were Muslims of Muslim-majority provinces to be enthused into the Pakistan idea? Until the communal temperature could be made to go up, there would be little enthusiasm. However, once the movement got going, they were quite happy at the thought of wiping out debts to Hindu money lenders and seizing abandoned properties. The dormant Muslim majority areas finally came into action; no longer was the movement for Pakistan solely *salariat*-driven.

Mobilizing the Muslim Masses

In the past, the Muslim peasant in Muslim-majority areas had not been particularly affected by political developments. There appears to be no history of mass peasant uprisings in these areas (the Moplah uprising was in Kerala, a Hindu-majority area) in British India. As a tiller of the soil, the peasant did not benefit much when Muslims were in power and did not lose much when non–Muslims took over after Mughal power declined. Jinnah could therefore afford to ignore the peasants who formed the bulk of the population in areas where Muslims were in the minority. But those in Muslim-majority areas had to be taken seriously.

Working through the feudal lords in the Punjab and Sind was useful but not enough. Though powerful, they were not leaders of the Muslim masses. Until the point that the Congress vowed to abolish the feudal system, there was not much enthusiasm among them for national politics, but thereafter it became an existential issue. Still, what force set their serfs, servants, and ordinary peasants into motion? For this we must study the elections of 1946, particularly those in Punjab.

The provincial elections of January 1946 spelled the doom of united India and virtually guaranteed the birth of Pakistan. Held to elect members of the legislative councils of British Indian provinces, the provincial assemblies thus formed would elect a new Constituent Assembly that would begin formulating a constitution for an independent India. As minor political parties were eliminated, the political scene became restricted to the Congress and Muslim League. What gave the Muslim League such importance was the system of separate electorates. Muslim contestants could compete only with other Muslim candidates instead of facing non–Muslim contestants. The Congress won 90% of the general non–Muslim seats, while the Muslim League won the majority of Muslim seats (87%) in the provinces. This established the AIML claim to being the sole representative of Muslim India, and Jinnah to be its sole spokesman.

Once could argue that the 1946 elections were based on the Sixth Schedule of the Government of India Act of 1935 and thus had a limited franchise. A relatively small percentage of adults – those with money and property – were eligible to vote. By one count only 3% of the population could vote for the central assembly and, on average, only 13% could vote for the provincial assemblies. Thus the large mass of people – Hindu, Muslim, and Sikh – did not have a voice. However, this argument is not fully convincing because the opinion makers and influential people from these communities did vote and would most likely have taken most others along with them. Once the communal fire had spread, the Muslim League became a mass movement to which thronged those who tilled the fields, worked the factories and offices, or were rickshawalas, tongawalas, small shopkeepers, mechanics, and other small-time urban dwellers.

How exactly did the League win? And how did it upstage the Unionist Party of rich landlords in Punjab, that which had badly defeated the League in 1937? This question has been studied by many historians.

Ian Talbot emphasizes that AIML exploited wartime economic discontent. It alleged that rationing favored Hindus over Muslims and often used mosques to convey this message.[13] Medical supplies had become scarce and AIML workers – some of whom had come from Aligarh and were personally lauded by Jinnah – distributed clothes and medicines to peasants in Central Punjab villages. As such they were reaching out to the masses much as the Chinese Communist

248 Was Partition Worth the Price?

Party and Vietnamese NLF had. Notwithstanding his aversion to socialism, Jinnah understood well that ordinary people wanted ordinary things and so he released money from the AIML account to workers who journeyed out to villages. But the outreach was not to all the needy, just to Muslims. The Qur'an was frequently paraded during the elections as the League's symbol: a vote for the Qur'an would be a vote for Pakistan. Much later in the game, the Unionists latched on to similar messages, but unlike the AIML they did not even try to solve ordinary people's problems.

Moving the peasant masses also required critical help from the local *pir* who was much more influential in villages than the *mullah*, then a low-level cleric. Under the influence of the League's religious rhetoric, landlords and *pirs* moved rapidly away from Unionists to embrace the Pakistan idea. Appeal was made directly to *pir-mureed* loyalty. For example, Syed Fazal Ahmed Shah, the *sajjada nashin* (hereditary administrator) of the shrine of Hazrat Shah Nur Jamal published in the newspaper *Nawa-e-Waqt* the following announcement:

> *An announcement from the Dargarh of Hazrat Shah Nur Jamal:* I command all those people who are in my *silsilah* to do everything possible to help the Muslim League and give their votes to it. All those people who do not act according to this announcement should consider themselves no longer members of my *silsilah*. (Signed: Fazal Ahmad Shah, *sajjada nashin* Hazrat Shah Nur Jamal.)[14]

The *sajjada nashins* saw Pakistan as a *shariat*-based state in the making.[15] As the traditional leaders of rural society, they saw their future lighting up. Influential *pirs* raised "personal identification with Pakistan to a level that transcended politics," with the *pir* of Golrah Sharif warning his *murid*, Prime Minister Malik Khizr Hayat Tivanah, "not to separate himself from the Islamic movement lest he become 'fuel for the fires of Hell'".[16]

Other *pirs* appealed to the glories of Muslim history, as for example in the *fatwa* issued from the Qadiri Dargah of Hazrat Shah Muqim Mujravi at Hujra:

> I'm not only making an announcement but a compassionate appeal to my brothers in unity that they should give every vote to the nominated candidates of the Muslim League and prove their solidarity....God's promise that He made in the Sura-e-Nur in the Qur'an will be fulfilled. If you are in love with Islam you should do things the way Iqbal asked you to do it. (Signed: *Sayed Imdad Ali Shah Gilani, sajjada nashin Dargarh Hazrat Shah Muqim Nujravi, 1-1-1946.*)[17]

Note the reference above to Allama Iqbal in this command by the *sajjada nashin*. Iqbal had died seven to eight years before the elections, but militant verses of his poetry reminiscing about past glories and wars of conquest were particularly popular and were recalled at public meetings:

Was Partition Worth the Price? **249**

O'Muslims have you even imagined how

That sword of steel could cut its way through?

سوچا بھی ہے اے مردِ مسلماں کبھی تُو نے

کیا چیز ہے فولاد کی شمشیر جگر دار

Iqbal provided the ideological foundation of the Pakistan Movement in a way that the anglicized and culturally aloof Jinnah could never have. As a scholar fully familiar with Islamic teachings, exemplars, and history, his poetic recreations of the past served to fire the popular imagination. The *mard-e-momin* and *shaheen* became emblematic of how one could once again reach greatness. The man on horseback with sword in hand would show the way.

Gilmartin has examined the 1946 election to see how religious and national visions of community led to images of the new nation, one that was now around the corner.[18] During his research he accessed a collection of 40 different flyers, almost all in Urdu, that were used by the parties contesting the 1946 elections. Generally speaking, the posters simply equated Pakistan with the glory, triumph, and unity of the Muslim community in India having the fortunes of the Muslim League. The exhortation on one flyer reads: *Musalman votaron ka farz; paidal chal kar bhi vot den* (Muslim voters should walk to vote if need be). Another slogan: *Islami riyasat qa'in hokar rahegi* (We must and will establish an Islamic state). There were even appeals to the broader movement of Muslim opposition colonialism in the world at large: "Do the Muslims of Punjab ... understand that the independence of the Muslim world is connected to Pakistan."

Bengal was different from Punjab, although here too the Muslim League won massively, bagging 83.7% of Muslim votes. The campaign for Pakistan used popular slogans like "Land to the Tiller" and for abolition of *zamindari* (most *zamindars* were Hindu). These populist slogans had been taken over from Krishak Praja Party (KPP), which ended up being wiped out in the elections. However, Omar Ali notes that the Pakistan campaign in Bengal was not about peasant populism. Rather while the KPP promised pro-peasant state action, the League promised a utopia. Pakistan was to be the "land of eternal Eid," where "speech and food were pure," where the nightingale calls the *azaan* and the flowers say their *namaaz* after doing their ablutions with the morning dew.[19]

Fears are generally more effective than dreams. Once communal temperatures went up, those ordinary Muslims who lived in proximity to Hindus often became victims of violence but, perhaps equally, were also its perpetrators. As neighbour turned against neighbour, Pakistan eventually became a haven for those who lost relatives or property to Hindus and Sikhs – or perhaps feared that they would be next. Local activists on all sides fomented violence and so inflamed emotions; the more there was of it the more vociferous became the demand for separating communities. With communal passions at a boil and the evident desperation of the British to get out as fast as possible, there was confusion all around. On the question of Pakistan, even the communists who believed only in class solidarity were split.[20]

Three-quarters of a century later, it is important to reflect upon who the winners of Partition were.

250 Was Partition Worth the Price?

The Winners

- *Large Landlords*: The grand winners were feudal families to whom the British had gifted large tracts of lands in Sind, Punjab, and NWFP. In return for these land gifts, *nawabs* and *khan bahadurs* helped the British in collecting taxes from the peasantry. About 70% of those in the Second Constituent Assembly (1954–1956) were feudal lords. Partition allowed them to consolidate their power. Many grabbed the opportunity to seize evacuee property left behind by fleeing Hindus and Sikhs. Nawab Iftikhar Hussain Mamdot, a powerful member of the landed élite who became Punjab's chief minister, had to be removed by Jinnah in 1946 upon advice by Punjab's Governor, Sir Francis Mudie.[21] He had allegedly added 17,000 acres to his holdings in Montgomery district. A nominal agriculture reform committee of the Muslim League was headed by Mumtaz Daultana, the Oxford educated scion of a large landlord clan. Nevertheless, even according to this landlord-friendly committee's report,[22] more than 80% of the land in Sind, over 50% in Punjab, and slightly less in NWFP was owned by big landlords. One owned a staggering 300,000 acres, while the more usual holdings in Sind and Punjab were around 3000–5000 acres.

Prior to the 1946 elections to the constituent assembly, some younger members of the Muslim League had been hopeful their party leaders would pay attention to the plight of poor *haris* (peasants). They insisted that land reform be taken up by the League's leadership without which, they said, the League would lose the popular vote in Sind. Jinnah put his lieutenants Liaquat Ali Khan and Chaudhry Khaliquzzaman to head an investigating body known as the Sind Hari Committee. But, after the landslide victory, the Committee felt no need for reforms and in its final report of early 1948 it chose to describe landlordism as benevolent and in the best interest of the peasant. A strong but solitary note of dissent was written by Mohammed Masud (aka Masud Khaddarposh) who was then a young and energetic pro-reform civil service officer. In spite of some public pressure the Sind government, now fully controlled by feudal lords, forbade publication of Khaddarposh's dissenting note. Jinnah stayed aloof.

A thorough discussion of Pakistan's agrarian structure from British times until around 1980 concludes that the land systems of Punjab and Sind remained totally dominated by predatory landlordism.[23] According to the Human Rights Commission of Pakistan, bonded and slave labor is still common in parts of Sind.[24] A 2004 study by the International Labour Office (ILO) estimated that there are up to a million *hari* families in Sind alone, the majority living in conditions of debt bondage, which the UN defines as modern-day slavery.[25]

A United Nations Development Programme (UNDP) report released in April 2021 reveals that Pakistan's feudal land-owning class, which constitutes 1.1% of the population, owns 22% of all arable farmland. This figure is the present figure; in between, land has been divided and subdivided between three generations.

Elite privilege consumes $17.4 billion of Pakistan's economy.[26] "Powerful groups use their privilege to capture more than their fair share, people perpetuate structural discrimination through prejudice against others based on social characteristics, and policies are often unsuccessful at addressing the resulting inequity, or may even contribute to it", says the report.

On the Indian side, the Congress had vowed to abolish the feudal system, and it did so promptly after Partition. A socialist Nehru quickly eliminated large land holdings in East Punjab. But, as pointed out above, anything smelling of communism and socialism was anathema for Muslim League stalwarts. After Partition, even nominal land reforms in West Punjab and Sind took a long time in coming. Scholars agree that those announced by Ayub Khan in 1959 were bare tokenism. Steps promised by Zulfikar Ali Bhutto in 1972 were selective, aimed against political opponents. Whatever little did change at the time was finally overturned by a landmark 1989 decision of the Federal Shariat Court which declared land reform to be un-Islamic.

A recent monograph by Nicholas Martin[27] copiously documents how 21st-century rural politics in Punjab remains intensely parochial and kinship-based. Rural elites continue to keep an impoverished rural workforce under their thumb by mediating between the state's resources and the intended recipients. In return, they are expected to provide votes during election times. An exploitative system of extraction and abuse persists, permitting only moral critiques of individual elites and their behavior instead of allowing systemic exploitation to be uncovered. In spite of a perpetual financial crisis that has forced Pakistan to approach the IMF 22 times so far, no government has been able to summon the strength or will for taxing agricultural revenue. Imran Khan's promised Islamic utopia, *Riyasat-e-Madina*, was silent on land reform. It proved to be just as status quo as earlier governments.

In 2020 a widely circulated internet video shows peasants lining up to reverentially kiss the feet of Shah Mahmood Qureshi, their landlord-spiritual master as well as Pakistan's foreign minister in Imran Khan's cabinet. Academic investigators, since they must concentrate upon what is considered scholarly, can only hint at the power differential between landlord and peasant. The landlord's loutish son, under the protection of his armed guards, who rapes a 14-year-old peasant girl in front of her parents, knows well that they will never dare report it to the police.

- *Pakistan's Military*: Events subsequent to Partition made the army and bureaucracy the twin pillars of power in Pakistan. They took charge of Pakistan's political affairs, foreign policy, and economic affairs. The army was largely Punjabi with some Pakhtuns and Muhajirs, while the bureaucracy was a mixture of Punjabis and Muhajirs. In time, the Muhajir element in the Army became less important. The sinking fortunes of the Muttahida Qaumi Movement (MQM) reduced Muhajir influence across the board. That the future of Pakistan would be Punjabi-dominated had

252 Was Partition Worth the Price?

already been featured in the 1930 Allahabad address of Allama Iqbal. He argued that after the amalgamation of Punjab, NWFP, Sind, and Balochistan into a single Muslim state, India would be secure against further invasions from Central Asia and Afghanistan. The defenders would be largely Punjabis:

> Punjab with 56 percent Muslim population supplies 54 percent of the total combatant troops to the Indian Army, and if the 19,000 Gurkhas recruited from the independent State of Nepal are excluded, the Punjab contingent amounts to 62 percent of the whole Indian Army. This percentage does not take into account nearly 6,000 combatants supplied to the Indian Army by the North-West Frontier Province and Baluchistan.[28]

The largely Punjabi military has been a big winner. Although civilian governments have nominally been in charge since the early days, Pakistan's warrior class was never tamed by civilians. Today, apart from political power exercised either overtly or from behind the shadows, it also controls vast commercial and industrial assets. A look at Pakistan's economic landscape tells the real story. Ayesha Siddiqa in her path-breaking book,[29] *Military Inc.: Inside Pakistan's Military Economy*, details just how "milbus" has become an independent class that owns massive rural and urban properties. Retiring officers receive massive large land grants and defense housing societies exist in all Pakistani societies with houses and plots sold to rich civilians. The CEOs of many, if not most corporations, public and private, are retired military officers – many fairly young. The military owns airlines and freight companies, banks, petrochemical factories, power generation plants, sugar mills, cement and fertilizer plants, road construction, banks, insurance and advertising companies, and more. All business dealings are beyond the scrutiny of the citizenry. It is a criminal offense to "criticize the armed forces of Pakistan or to bring them into disaffection".[30]

The UNDP report referred to above, as well as a related Al-Jazeera interview,[31] go on to state that Pakistan's military is also "the largest conglomerate of business entities in Pakistan, besides being the country's biggest urban real estate developer and manager, with wide-ranging involvement in the construction of public projects". The UNDP country chief Kanni Wignaraja says that: "you almost get a double privilege by the military. The minute in a country the military is a part of big business, it obviously doubles the issue and the problem". She warned that it would take "almost a social movement" to displace structures of power that were so entrenched.

- *Salaried Classes*: Muslims had been hugely under-represented in the civil bureaucracy and academia. But after Partition members of this class benefited much by filling positions formerly occupied by Hindus. The numbers are revealing: in 1947 Europeans (468) had formed the bulk of the Indian Civil Service, followed by Hindus (352) and Muslims (101) of whom only

18 were Bengali.[32] After Partition less-qualified Muslim officers filled the posts abandoned by Europeans and Hindus. Urdu speakers who migrated to Pakistan and were largely concentrated in Karachi or Hyderabad did very well in earlier decades. Relatively more educated, they claimed they deserved a special deal since they had felt the pain of Partition much more than local inhabitants and expected the new state to recognize that. The MQM was built around the idea of Muhajir grievance. For two decades, it commanded the allegiance of Muhajirs before it eventually disintegrated. That – and time – have corroded Muhajir dominance over Karachi. Now in the process of mainstreaming, they find themselves outnumbered by Karachi's growing Pathan population.

The situation in colleges and universities just after Partition was quite dramatic in favoring Muslim teachers and professors. Numbers cannot reflect the true situation since there is no proper measure by which quality can be measured in teaching institutions. There was only one university at the time, the University of Punjab. Its best faculty was almost exclusively Hindu, almost all of whom had to flee. Muslim professors who subsequently took their positions were of lower academic caliber. Over time they could have improved academically or have allowed better teachers to replace them, but most took the soft way and simply rose in the ranks without doing so. In a united India, they would have had to struggle much harder.

- *Middle-Level Peasants*: The middle-level Muslim peasant in Punjab, Sind, and NWFP gained land from Hindus who had large land holdings. Their debts came to an end as well. By one estimate, about 40% of the total land in these provinces was held by Hindu landlords.[33] Some was seized by Muslim middle-level peasants although larger holdings were appropriated by more powerful landlords. For poorer peasants such as sharecroppers there was little gained. In fact with the protective shadow of the British now gone, expectations that the law would provide justice decreased further. In contrast with large-scale peasant uprisings in India as well as other parts of the world, Pakistan has seen only sporadic attempts such as in Hashtnagar and Okara.

Now let's do a tally for losers. Again, for specificity, I shall consider Muslims only:

The Losers

- *Muslims of Bengal*: Some were local to East Bengal, while others moved there from West Bengal after communal temperatures rose. They had been uprooted from their ancestral homes by rising Hindu intolerance. After 1947 the yoke of Hindu money lenders and landlords was overthrown, but little did they know that a second holocaust at the hands of their fair-skinned Muslim brothers was just twenty-five years down the line.

- *Biharis of East Pakistan*: These Muslims took Jinnah's Two Nation Theory to be the gospel truth but, to their horror, found themselves abandoned in 1971. Tens of thousands were left in the lurch by their misplaced belief that an ideological Pakistan would save them. In their last-ditch attempt to keep East and West united, they had fought alongside the Punjabi-dominated West Pakistani army killing thousands of Hindus and nationalist Muslim Bengalis. In turn, they were also killed in the thousands. Formally, the Biharis remained Pakistani citizens, but after Pakistan recognized the implications of opening its doors to Biharis, it shut them firmly. Their fate was now sealed. Until they died of old age or moved out somewhere in desperation, Biharis remained stranded in crowded refugee camps for decades. Culture and pragmatic necessity had trumped religion.

- *Muslims Who Stayed in India*: Taunted after 1947 by Hindutva ideologues as closet Pakistanis who should now migrate, they are considered naturally disloyal to India since that might be their motherland but is not their holy land. The expected had happened: vulnerable to accusations of being Pakistani rather than Indian, the Muslims left behind retreated from many senior positions. In his book, *Legacy of a Divided Nation – India's Muslims since Independence*, Mushirul Hasan gives a wide ranging summary of the Muslims who chose to stay behind in India.[34] Those in UP – who had been at the forefront in demanding Pakistan – had in effect committed political suicide and were left hanging high and dry. They would face taunts such as: "you got your own country so why are you hanging around here and complaining?", "You are lucky to be here at all!" Indeed back in 1947 some might have chosen Pakistan on ideological grounds, but they stood to lose property and family ties. In one fell swoop, a powerful elite group had been reduced to a helpless, complaining minority. With the rise to power of Narendra Modi's Muslim-phobic politics, their worst nightmares are coming true as never before. A recent book has examined the condition of Muslims in Indian cities:

> The lost children of India's Partition, Indian Muslims bear the stigma of the past. Their forefathers are often—unfairly for certain analysts—perceived as the main culprits in the "vivisection of India", and their loyalty has been continuously questioned by sections of the state, of the media and of the political class. Moreover, they are suspected of Pan-Islamist leanings by Hindu nationalists, particularly since the 1980s, which saw the rise of a new fear of "Gulf money" flooding Indian Muslim localities and religious institutions. And unlike other religious minorities such as the Sikhs, Indian Muslims cannot claim and take comfort in a territorial bastion. Lastly, Muslims largely evade the general rise in their standards of living witnessed by other Indian minorities such as the Sikhs, the Christians or the Buddhists.[35]

Was Partition Worth the Price? **255**

Some religious scholars like Maulana Abul Kalam Azad had anticipated what would befall those left behind, passionately arguing that they would become aliens and foreigners in their own land. Backward industrially, educationally, and economically, they would surely be left at the mercy of what he predicted would become "an unadulterated Hindu raj". As 1947 drew closer, Azad spoke ever more frequently about this but he had no mass following. A few months before Partition, he had been derided by Aligarh Muslim University (AMU) students at Aligarh station during a train journey from Shimla to Calcutta.[36] They had brought along a garland of shoes for him.

Jinnah, on the other hand, did have a mass following but had little to say to those Indian Muslims who either did not want to migrate to Pakistan or who felt they could not uproot themselves for family reasons, fixed properties, etc. According to the *Civil Military Gazette*, in his address on 30 March 1941 to the Cawnpore Muslim Students Federation Conference, "Mr. Jinnah said that in order to liberate 7 crores of Muslims where they were in a majority he was willing to perform the last ceremony of martyrdom if necessary and let two crores of Muslims be smashed".[37] In 1942 a young electrical engineering student at AMU – Abdul Hafeez Siddique, also known as Hafeez Khan – rose up to ask Jinnah a simple question: what shall be the fate of Muslims left in India after partition? Jinnah replied: sacrifice, sacrifice, sacrifice! Other students shouted Siddique down.[38] However, two weeks before the announcement of independence, Jinnah advised them to become loyal citizens of India, learn Hindi if that was necessary, and not expect help from Pakistan.[39]

In these circumstances it is easy to forget that while there was an aggressive demand – especially in northern India – for a separate Muslim state, there was never a plebiscite prior to independence. Millions of Indian Muslims only wanted to continue living as they and their forefathers had done. They felt (as time was to show) as much Bengali as Muslim and as grounded as Christians, Buddhists, Sikhs, or Jains were in Kerala, Punjab, Gujarat, Andhra, or Assam. At the time they felt themselves as much of the soil as their Hindu neighbors.[40]

After three-quarters of a century, Muslims on both sides of the India–Pakistan border have become essentially indifferent and unknowledgeable about each other. Public discourse in Pakistan today rarely mentions Indian Muslims unless they are Kashmiris. The discriminatory Citizenship Amendment Act of 2020, while mentioned in Pakistani newspapers, drew only a flicker of concern. Marriages between Muslim families separated by Partition had continued into the first few decades after Partition, but these have petered out to near zero now. Urdu inside India went into sharp decline in areas which had been steeped in Urdu and Persian culture – street signs in Delhi once used to be Urdu but are now rarely so. In India there is a sustained attempt to criminalize marriages of Muslim men with Hindu women, now referred to as love jihad. Pakistan uses this violation of basic human rights in international forums as proof of India's mistreatment of minorities. Hemmed in at both ends, Muslims in India are becoming ghettoized.

256 Was Partition Worth the Price?

- *The Muslims of Kashmir*: Four wars later, the status of this disputed territory remains just as settled as in 1947. Massive repression by the Indian state, and incessant meddling by Pakistan through extra-state actors, has not changed this fact. Insurgencies have grown and ebbed with the toll around 100,000 deaths. More will be said about Kashmir later.
- *The Muslims of Balochistan*: Most Baloch think they are ruled from Punjab. Tens of thousands have died in insurgencies and thousands have gone missing. Too rich in gas and mineral resources and too important strategically to be left alone, Islamabad thinks it has a natural right over Balochistan and cannot conceive a situation where the Baloch would have more than nominal control over what they consider to be their resources. Every Pakistani leader from Jinnah to Bhutto, and Zia-ul-Haq to Imran Khan has subscribed to this belief. Deals under the Chinese Pakistan Economic Corridor, which terminates at the port of Gwadar, have been made in opposition to popular Baloch sentiment and endorsed by a rubber stamp provincial government. A majority of the Baloch believe that they are an occupied people, although it appears that a majority would prefer to seek rights within the union with Pakistan rather than out of it. Bloody insurgencies began with the birth of Pakistan and have since ebbed and flowed. There seems no sign that they will disappear.
- *Ahmadis – Now Expelled from Islam*: The followers of Mirza Ghulam Ahmad were unreservedly enthusiastic about Pakistan. They had been criticized by mainstream Muslims, both Sunni and Shia, but Jinnah assured them they had nothing to worry about. Indeed, he kept his word by appointing Chaudhry Zafarullah Khan, an Ahmadi, as Pakistan's first foreign minister. Exceptionally articulate and intelligent, Zafarullah had vociferously supported the Objectives Resolution of 1949 that segregated the population according to Muslim and non-Muslim. This decision was to prove fatal to his community. More educated than most other Punjabis, Ahmadis occupied high profile posts in the bureaucracy and military out of proportion with their tiny numbers. Ultimately this visibility went against them when Zulfikar Ali Bhutto's government declared them to be non-Muslims in 1974. They have since been Pakistan's most persecuted minority, far more so than even Hindus or Christians. In his detailed monograph, Ali Usman Qasmi has recently explored the exclusion of Ahmadis.[41]
- *Communists and Leftists:* The sophisticated Marxists of the Communist Part of India were the first to regret Partition although, to be fair, some had accepted a division of India on religious grounds only half-heartedly. Party discipline, with orders coming from Josef Stalin, had left them with little choice. Even as Jinnah spoke against communism as an evil, the Communist Party of India (CPI) issued orders to Muslim communists to join the Muslim League because that would weaken the Hindu bourgeoisie which was far stronger than the Muslim bourgeoisie. Sajjad Zaheer, a member of the Central Committee of CPI recommended that, "the Party should assist League to enroll Muslims in large numbers in order to make it a mass

organization which would eventually pass out of the control of its present reactionary leadership".[42] By 1944–1945 the Muslim League's publicity and information department was energized, English and Urdu language newspapers were pressed into service, and books and pamphlets endorsing Jinnah's blueprint for a Muslim state, including some written by left-wing activists, came to be circulated widely.[43] After Partition, a crackdown on the Left by Pakistan's pro-West governments soon made them wonder if they had acted wisely. The left-wing poet Faiz Ahmad Faiz's regret-filled soliloquy, *Subh-e-Azadi* (Dawn of Independence), has turned out to be one of the most enduring pieces of writing on Partition.

The Cobra Effect

Sanjeev Kulkarni has a parable on what emphasizing communal identities in politics can do to a society. It involves the "cobra effect", the story of which goes something like this: there was once a menace of poisonous cobras in Delhi, so the British offered a reward for dead cobras. But then people started breeding cobras for rewards. When the British realized this, they discontinued rewards. Thereafter, the breeders realized that nothing more was to be gained and set free their entire crop of cobras. At the end there were more cobras than before. Moral: a bad solution can easily worsen a problem.

In the above parable, the "problem" was the differential development of two communities and their access to resources and privileges. The "solution" that was offered by the respective community leaders was to emphasize and amplify religious identification and hence the differences between the two, i.e., to promote religious communalism. Breeding this kind of cobra brought rewards to the breeders, in this case the Muslim League and the Hindu Mahasabha. For the former, it led to Pakistan being created, while for the latter and its Hindutva descendants, it is the way towards eventually making a Hindu *rashtra* (state) – one that could be a mirror image of Pakistan but with a Hindu agenda.

Pakistan's cobras became problematic for its people and even for its all-powerful establishment, which has lost more soldiers to the bullets of religious fanatics than in all its wars with India. How the country's founders would cope with the religious forces they unleashed is not difficult to guess. Sir Syed Ahmad Khan continues to inspire hate-filled books by the orthodox and would be no safer than other modernist Muslim scholars who are now forced to live abroad. Allama Iqbal would surely be mortified to see his verses routinely used by those Muslims who happily slaughter other Muslims, thinking their actions will buy heavenly rewards. As for Jinnah: we can only imagine what might happen to him as a Shia Muslim, was he somehow brought back to life today. Would he have to live in a fortified palace and would he be safer than Governor Salman Taseer, killed by a personal guard who thought that modifying a blasphemy law was itself blasphemy?

258 Was Partition Worth the Price?

Notes

1 Author's original voice recording at: https://www.youtube.com/watch?v =RRn6p2umPws
2 A. Rieck, *The Shias of Pakistan: An Assertive and Beleaguered Minority*, Oxford University Press (2015).
3 M. Hasan, *Vote Congress – Congress and the Welfare State*, New Delhi, Central Publicity Board (n.d.), quoted in *Islam in the Subcontinent*, Manohar Books (2002), pp. 213–214.
4 Jawaharlal Nehru interview to C.L. Sulzberger of The New York Times on 2 March 2 1957 wherein he told Sulzberger: "Twenty years ago I would have said that certainly we should have some kind of confederation – not federation – of independent states with common defense and economic politics".
5 S. Wolpert, *Jinnah of Pakistan*, Oxford University Press (1984), pp. 129–130.
6 Mohammed Ali Jinnah, Speech at a meeting of the Aligarh Muslim University Union, Aligarh, 9 March 1944.
7 *Sayings of Quaid-i-Azam Mohammad Ali Jinnah*, Karachi, Quaid Foundation and Pakistan Movement Centre (1993), p. 153.
8 Jamiludin Ahmad, *Some Recent Speeches and Writings of Mr. Jinnah*, p. 68, https://archive .org/details/SomeRecentSpeechesAndWritingsOfMr.Jinnah-JamiluddinAhmad/ page/n25/mode/2up
9 P. Oldenburg, Mushir-ul-Hasan, quoted in *India, Pakistan, and Democracy - Solving the Puzzle of Divergent Paths*, Routledge (2010).
10 Ibid, p. 27.
11 G. Allana, *Pakistan Movement Historical Documents*, Karachi, Department of International Relations, University of Karachi (n.d.), pp. 129–133.
12 H. Alavi, Pakistan and Islam: Ethnicity and Ideology, in *State and Ideology in the Middle East and Pakistan*, edited by Fred Halliday and Hamza Alavi, Macmillan Education Ltd. (1988), pp. 64–111.
13 I.A. Talbot, The 1946 Punjab Elections, *Modern Asian Studies*, 14, no. 1 (1980): 65–91.
14 Nawa-e-Waqt (Lahore), 19 January 1946.
15 D. Gilmartin, Religious Leadership and the Pakistan Movement in the Punjab, *Modern Asian Studies*, 13, no. 3 (1979): 485–517. http://www.jstor.org/stable/312311
16 S.W. Fuchs, *In a Pure Muslim Land – Shi'ism between Pakistan and the Middle East*, The University of North Carolina Press (2019), p. 47.
17 Nawa-e-Waqt (Lahore), 3 January 1946.
18 D. Gilmartin, A Magnificent Gift: Muslim Nationalism and the Election Process in Colonial Punjab, *Comparative Studies in Society and History*, 40, no. 3 (July 1998): 415–436.
19 T.O. Ali, *Pakistan and Partition: Peasant Utopia and Disillusion, in A Local History of Global Capital: Jute and Peasant Life in the Bengal Delta*, Princeton University Press (2018), pp. 168–193, 169.
20 M. Hasan, *Left Wing Confusions over the Movement for Pakistan Are Explored in "Communism's Love-Hate Relationship with Pakistan"*, The Express Tribune, 2 December 2019.
21 I. Chattha, Refugee Resettlement and Centre—Province Relations in Pakistan, 1947–49, *Journal of the Punjab University Historical Society*, 32, no. 2 (July–December 2019).
22 Report of Agrarian Reforms Committee, Muslim League (1949).
23 M.H. Khan, *Underdevelopment and Agrarian Structure in Pakistan*, Boulder, Colorado, Westview Press (1981).
24 *Slave Labour Still Common in Sindh*, The New Humanitarian, 3 November 2015. https://www.thenewhumanitarian.org/feature/2006/11/28/slave-labour-still-common-sindh
25 E.B. Skinner, *Pakistan's Forgotten Plight: Modern-Day Slavery*, Time, 27 October 2009.

Was Partition Worth the Price? **259**

26 Al Jazeera interview of assistant secretary-general and regional chief of the UNDP, Kanni Wignaraja, https://www.aljazeera.com/news/2021/4/13/elite-privilege-consumes-17-4bn-of-pakistans-economy-undp

27 N. Martin, *Politics, Landlords and Islam in Pakistan*, Routledge India (2016).

28 Sir Muhammad Iqbal's Presidential address to the 25th Session of the All-India Muslim League Allahabad on 29 December 1930 Iqbal Academy (Lahore), 1977 [1944], 2nd ed., revised and enlarged.

29 A. Siddiqa, *Military Inc.: Inside Pakistan's Military Economy*, Random House Publishers (2017).

30 Pakistanis warned to stop criticising armed forces, BBC News, 15 May 2017. https://www.bbc.com/news/world-asia-39919354

31 Al-Jazeera, op. cit.

32 R. Sisson and L.E. Rose, *War and Secession: Pakistan, India, and the Creation of Bangladesh*, University of California Press, p. 10.

33 G. Husain and A. Mohyuddin, Historical Sketch of Peasant Activism: Tracing Emancipatory Political Strategies of Peasant Activists of Sindh, *International Journal Humanities and Social Sciences*, 3, no. 5 (September 2014): 23–42.

34 M. Hasan, *Legacy of a Divided Nation – India's Muslims since Independence*, Westview Press (1997).

35 L. Gayer and C. Jaffrelot, eds., *Muslims of Indian Cities – Trajectories of Marginalisation*, Columbia University Press (2011), p. 2.

36 A. Maheshwari, *Aligarh Muslim University: Institution of Learning or Identity, (Centenary Year) 1920–2020*, to be published.

37 The Civil Military Gazette, 1 April 1941 and The Star of India, 1 April 1941.

38 Related to the author by Hafiz Saad, son of AHS, who says that his father repeated this episode before he died in 1988 many times in front of his former AMU colleagues with none contradicting him.

39 The Eastern Times, 2 August 1947.

40 L. Tyabji, *Why I Will Never 'Go to Pakistan'*, The Wire, 7 February 2020.

41 A.U. Qasmi, *The Ahmadis and the Politics of Religious Exclusion in Pakistan*, Anthem Press (2014).

42 S. Zaheer, *Muslim League and Freedom*, People's War, 19 March 1944.

43 M. Habib, Communists in the Muslim League, *Proceedings of the Indian History Congress* 69 (2008): 563–573. Accessed 8 May 2021. http://www.jstor.org/stable/44147220

Ten

WHAT IS THE IDEOLOGY OF PAKISTAN – AND DOES IT MATTER?

> Whoever, within or without Pakistan, with intent to influence, or knowing it to be likely that he will influence, any person or the whole or any section of the public, in a manner likely to be prejudicial to the safety or *ideology of Pakistan*...shall be punished with rigorous imprisonment which may extend to ten years and shall also be liable to fine.
>
> – Section 123-A, Pakistan Penal Code[1]

Contesting the ideology of Pakistan is punishable by law. But what does that ideology mean? After eight decades rightfully there should not have been any ambiguity left. But, in fact, a formal definition of this term does not exist in any official document. Jinnah's utterances made no reference to any Pakistan ideology. It is therefore an open question as to whether such a quantity exists or was ever defined and by whom. One might have expected the ideology question to be no more than an arcane historical dispute, but this is not so. Therefore, to further investigate this vexing issue, in this chapter I first explore what could possibly be an appropriate academic definition of ideology in this specific historical context and how it took root in the minds of north India's Muslims. The ubiquitous slogan: *Pakistan ka matlab kya? la ilaha illallah* is worth reflecting upon for this reason and multiple others as well. This drives us to a key question: what makes the Pakistani establishment so nervous about discussions of the country's foundations? Left to this book's very last chapter is a still more important question: does Pakistan need an ideology to move forward?

Equilibrium is a concept of physics that cannot be used exactly for societies or politics because here change is incessant and unstoppable. People make things change all the time, and so there's never stillness except perhaps momentarily. Citizens of the former Soviet Union know that and, after the 2021 siege of the Capitol, Americans know it too. Those changes happened whether or not they

DOI: 10.4324/9781003379140-15

What Is the Ideology of Pakistan – and Does It Matter? **261**

were desired. But the men who run Pakistan today are desperate to freeze time lest something terrible happen. Therefore, questioning the Ideology of Pakistan remains strictly off limits even as Pakistan enters its eighth decade. This is quite curious because even if one looks hard to see what this ideology is – or what it may have been – it has not been put down anywhere in the books. There was never a formal enunciation of its meaning at any time in the past. Founders of the movement for Pakistan – Iqbal and Jinnah most particularly – did not refer to it nor sought to define it. Liaquat Ali Khan, who was Jinnah's right-hand man (but lacked his authority), similarly stayed silent. So why has today's Pakistan military and civil establishment chosen to criminalize deviations from something to which no legal definition has ever been provided? We shall reflect upon this in a while.

To assert that Islam is the ideology of Pakistan is, of course, heard often and with great force. And yet, while this clearly rules out the consumption of liquor and pork, it is not clear what else it could mean. Ideology, if understood in the popular sense, is supposed to be all-encompassing and capable of giving clear answers to big questions; smaller ones can be left for the country's courts to adjudicate upon. Therefore, assuming that Pakistan had an ideology, we should have clear answers to questions such as these:

- Does Islamic ideology permit or forbid dictatorship?
- Can a woman be head of state or army chief?
- Can a non-Muslim be a judge and part of the superior judiciary?
- Is bank interest forbidden?
- Can the required payment of *jizya* (tax on non-Muslims) be waived?
- Is it permissible to ignore the Qur'anic injunctions on amputation of limbs or soften the prescribed punishment for adultery?
- Are new churches and temples of worship permitted on Pakistani soil?

Islamic religious scholars have given conflicting opinions on the above, suggesting that ideology remains a fluid concept. And yet, even without an official definition, the Ideology of Pakistan hangs heavy over the present. Today no Pakistani student can hope to matriculate from high school, and no candidate for the military or civil services can hope to pass qualifying examinations, without memorizing officially prescribed texts. All school textbooks are required by law to devote large sections towards teaching the topic.

Despite the present emphasis, in textbooks written prior to 1977 one finds no mention of ideology. But a sea change happened following General Zia-ul-Haq's coup. Vowing to change Pakistan from a Muslim state into an Islamic state, in 1981 Zia asserted that: "Pakistan is like Israel, an ideological state. Take the Judaism out of Israel and it will fall like a house of cards. Take religion out of Pakistan and make it a secular state; it would collapse".[2] This was also the year when Zia made mandatory the teaching of Pakistan Studies to all degree students, including those at engineering and medical colleges. Shortly

262 What Is the Ideology of Pakistan – and Does It Matter?

thereafter, the University Grants Commission – then responsible for school-book content as well as managing universities – issued a directive to prospective textbook authors. They were given specific instructions on the writing of history books:[3]

> To demonstrate that the basis of Pakistan is not to be founded in racial, linguistic, or geographical factors, but, rather, in the shared experience of a common religion. To get students to know and appreciate the Ideology of Pakistan, and to popularize it with slogans. To guide students towards the ultimate goal of Pakistan – the creation of a completely Islamised State.[4]

Thereafter the Ideology of Pakistan became ubiquitous and was extended to the present; to question it is treasonous. A notification issued by the Ministry of Federal Education Ministry and Professional training, dated 12 March 2021, warns that in the printing and publication of textbooks the supervisory boards must ensure, "that the textbooks do not contain any hate material against any community, faith, the Ideology of Pakistan and there is nothing against Islamic injunctions of life". The phrase Ideology of Pakistan makes its appearance on, or near, page one of all textbooks. The definitions vary. One book has: "As citizens of an ideological state it is necessary to first know the basis upon which Pakistan was founded, the ideology of Pakistan".[5] A virtually identical beginning is found elsewhere: "Pakistan is an ideological state. The Ideology of Pakistan was the inspiration and the basis of the Movement for Pakistan".[6] Another book merely states that "the Ideology of Pakistan is Islam".[7] In yet another, there is a slightly more explicit definition: "that guiding principle which has been accepted by the Muslims of the majority regions of the South Asian subcontinent and which allows them to lead their lives individually and collectively according to the principles of Islam".[8] Subsequent education policies have maintained the emphasis. The National Education Policy (2017–2025) document says that the goal of achieving "Pakistani Nationhood and National Integration" requires that education should "promote and foster Ideology of Pakistan creating a sense of Pakistani nationhood on the principles of the founder of Pakistan, i.e., Unity, Faith and Discipline".[9]

Pakistan's Constitution, as modified up to 28 February 2012, carefully defines all other legal terms but also stops short here. However, it declares that no person may become a member of parliament if he has opposed the Ideology of Pakistan at any point. Dismissal from employment can happen for the same reason in any number of government and private institutions. For example, service regulations of the Civil Aviation Authority are explicit in this regard.[10] But again the definition of Ideology of Pakistan is absent.

Whatever the precise definition, in a 2010 paper a former Chief Secretary of the Khyber Pakhtunkhwa province issues a stern warning:

De-ideologization of Pakistan must be treated as intellectual subversion. Physical subversion can heal but intellectual subversion is like a cancer that goes undiscovered until it is too late. Such intellectual subversion was allowed in the universities and colleges of East Pakistan with tragic consequences. The phenomenon is again on the rise; it should be understood and guarded against. Textbooks should be reinforced, and not diluted, in their ideological and normative content. There should be absolutely no disconnection of Pakistan and Islam. They should occur together in memory, system, conduct, planning, individual steps and national policies. The moment such division and disconnection begins, cracks appear in the foundations of the country, and they can become very large.[11]

The foundations of Pakistan will crack! If this senior ex-bureaucrat really thinks so – and there certainly are a large number who think similarly – then the matter of ideology surely calls for a serious discussion. Hopefully I shall not be wasting precious pages and the readers' time in what follows.

Ideology Defined

Ideology as a concept is frequently misunderstood. It is not some comprehensive system of ideas, about values that we should pursue, or about epistemology and ethics. Ideology is also not Weltanschauung, which is the fundamental all-encompassing cognitive orientation of an individual or a society built upon normative postulates. In short, people have it wrong when they confuse ideology with worldview. So what is ideology?

Every concept in politics – fascism, democracy, communism, anarchy, neoliberalism – can be understood in multiple ways. Ideology too can be. In fact it may even be fruitful to define the same word differently for different historical epochs and different political or social circumstances. Take, for example, communism. As understood in formally communist North Korea today, it bears no resemblance to the communism of the 1871 Paris Commune or that of today's Vietnam. So, while multiple definitions of ideology can legitimately exist in scholarly discourse, the acid test of a definition is its aptness for a particular situation.

I think a definition of ideology particularly appropriate for discussing the ideas and forces prior to the partition of India is that of Mostafa Rejai, professor of Political Science at Miami University, Ohio. He describes political ideology as "an emotion-laden, myth-saturated, action-related system of beliefs and values about people and society, legitimacy and authority, acquired to a large extent as a matter of faith and habit".[12] Consistent with Rejai's definition is that proposed by Harvard sociologist Daniel Bell (1919–2011). Bell pithily defines ideology as that which converts grand ideas and beliefs into social levers. It does so by inspiring dreams of utopias and paradises to be achieved by men of faith:

> Ideology, then, as I have used the term, deals with social movements that seek to mobilize men for the realization of such beliefs, and in this fusion of political formulas and passions, ideology provides a faith and a set of moral certitudes...Ideology is a reification, a frozen mimicry of reality, a hypostatization of terms that gives false life to categories. And that is also its fatal flaw, its Achilles heel, which leaves it vulnerable in the end to other forms of cognition and faith.[13]

Because ideology is faith and belief, it does not ask for or receive scientific validation. In fact its expression may even violate formal rules of grammar while keeping intact the message.

Hindutva Ideology

The purifiers of Islam – outraged at how Muslims had adapted to India – had sought to reverse what they called corrupt Hindu practices. Hindus, with equal enthusiasm, responded by seeking to distance themselves from those who they said had invaded their pristine civilization. Both Hindu and Muslim communalists appealed to history to vindicate their positions. With two entirely different and mutually antagonistic teleologies, each sought to establish its correctness and superiority over the other, deleting entire chunks of history or glossing over them. Each tried to push its narrative of being a separate nation that had existed from ancient times. This gave rise to theories of separate nationhood. But what really is a theory?

Theory in science has a very definite meaning, one that all practitioners of science agree upon. It is a well-substantiated explanation of some aspect of the physical world that is based upon a body of facts, each of which is verifiable through repeated observation and experiment. Such fact-supported theories are not opinions or guesses; they actually account for and explain reality. In this sense, the use of "theory" as in Two Nation Theory (TNT) is inappropriate since it expresses a political opinion or position. TNT could arguably have some merit if physical characteristics of the nation's members were distinguishable. This is not the case for north Indians of different religions where even DNA testing fails in finding clear genetic differences between Hindus and Muslims.[14] TNT should therefore be understood as in its original Urdu expression *do qaumi nazariyya* where *nazariyya* is used strictly in the sense of opinion. Thus it is an ideological and mobilization tool, not a sociological or anthropological one. As will be dwelt upon below, Hindu and Muslim ideologues developed their own respective TNTs.

We now focus on the Hindu version of two nations. It surprises many Pakistanis that there is a Hindu version because they have always assumed a single version – that originating from the observations of Sir Syed Ahmad Khan and his followers. Thus a typical candidate swotting away for his civil service exams does not encounter the names of Savarkar, Golwalkar, or Lala Lajpat Rai. He

What Is the Ideology of Pakistan – and Does It Matter? **265**

would, for example, be unaware that a partitioned India had been suggested by Lala Lajpat Rai (1865–1928) of the Arya Samaj. This had been published six years before Allama Iqbal's famous 1930 Allahabad address, and a full sixteen years before Jinnah's 1940 Lahore speech where he made his demand for Pakistan.

Rai was strongly anti-British and had earlier allied with Gandhi but split after Gandhi called off the Non-Cooperation Movement. He supported TNT arguing that while Hindus and Muslims needed to unite to overthrow the British Raj, a separate nation for each would solve the greater purpose of peaceful coexistence. In 1924 he published his detailed scheme for partitioning India. Therein Muslims would be confined to four separate Indian states (including Bengal):

> Under my scheme the Muslims will have four Muslim States: (1) The Pathan Province or the North-West Frontier; (2) Western Punjab; (3) Sindh; and (4) Eastern Bengal. If there are compact Muslim communities in any other part of India, sufficiently large to form a province, they should be similarly constituted. But it should be distinctly understood that this is not a united India. It means a clear partition of India into a Muslim India and a non-Muslim India.[15]

Rai's scheme drew some negative commentary but, given Congress's hegemony over politics, also went relatively unnoticed.

Jaffrelot has extensively discussed two-nation theories enunciated by Hindu ideologues.[16] This dates from about a century ago, a time when Mahatma Gandhi had transformed the Indian National Congress into a mass organization inclusive of Hindus and Muslims. Consequently few paid attention when Vinayak Damodar Savarkar, then supreme leader of the Hindu Mahasabha, published in 1923 his seminal work, *Hindutva – Who Is a Hindu?*[17] This is the first recorded instance where the word Hindutva was used. Savarkar – who considered himself an atheist – gives the following answer (with bold emphasis and full capitalization) upon the title page: "A HINDU means a person who regards this land of BHARATVARSHA, from the Indus to the Seas as his father-land as well as his Holy-Land that is the cradle land of his religion".

For Savarkar, Hindus are direct descendants of the original inhabitants of India, unadulterated by outside influences. Mother India was credited with cradling civilization within her bosom and thereafter protecting it from the very beginnings of time. Then, goes the lore, about 1400 years ago Arab Muslims from across the seas invaded her privacy in search of loot and plunder, leaving a trail of destruction. To reclaim Mother India's purity called for combating the invaders and their progeny. India therefore belongs to Hindus, and they should rule it as their majority pleases. Hindus, he said, constituted a 'race', and while that certainly had something to do with Hinduism as a religion, it wasn't very much. Instead, Hinduism should be understood as an ethno-cultural category purporting to bring Hindus of all castes within the ambit of a communitarian fold, Hindutva. This, he said is a concept:

266 What Is the Ideology of Pakistan – and Does It Matter?

> So varied and so rich, so powerful and so subtle, so elusive and yet so vivid that it defied such definition....Hindutva is not a word but a history. Not only the spiritual or religious history of our people, but a history in full.[18]

The implication is that Hindutva is beyond logic and rational analysis. It is defined only by ancestry and legacy of Hindus, a permanent category that must forever exclude outsiders like Muslims and Christians. During his 1937 presidential address at the All India Hindu Mahasabha convention in Karnavati (Ahmedabad), Savarkar was unequivocal: "India cannot be assumed today to be a unitarian and homogeneous nation, but on the contrary *there are two nations in the main*; the Hindus and the Moslems, in India".[19]

In Savarkar's vision, India belongs to Hindus, and they should rule it as their majority pleases. While minorities would be allowed to live in India, they could not ask for rights, political representation, or protection. In particular Hindus and Muslims could not coexist as equals because Muslims don't possess "the unity of thought, language and religion". Savarkar rejected the partition of India; Muslims must live in undivided India as subordinates or leave for elsewhere. This became the philosophy of Rashtriya Swayamsevak Sangh (RSS), founded in 1925. Savarkar wished this to be the ideology of the new Indian political disposition once the British left India.

> We are Indian because we are Hindus and vice versa...India must be a Hindu land, reserved for the Hindus...[who] are not only a *Rashtra* (Nation), a *Jati* (Race) but in consequence of being both, own a common *Sanskriti* (Civilization), expressed, preserved chiefly and originally through Sanskrit, the real mother tongue of our race. [20]

On 30 January 1948 Savarkar's follower, Nathuram Godse, assassinated Mahatma Gandhi after which Savarkar was charged as a co-conspirator. Savarkar was also a man of contradictions. This inventor of Hindutva as a political movement was also against Hindu superstition, the caste system, and cow worship. Sentenced by the British to the Andaman Islands, he spent nearly a third of his life in some form of confinement before he died in 1966 at age eighty-three.

Savarkar's contemporary was M.S. Golwalkar, an ideologue who was clear about the impossibility of Hindus and Muslims living together. In a book published in 1939 – the very year Hitler invaded Poland and started his Jewish pogroms – Golwalkar wrote:

> To keep up the purity of the nation and its culture, Germany shocked the world by her purging the country of Semitic races – the Jews. National pride at its highest has been manifested here. Germany has also shown how well-nigh impossible it is for Races and Cultures, having differences going to the root, to be assimilated into one united whole, a good lesson for us in Hindusthan to learn and profit by.[21]

In *We or Our Nationhood Defined*, Golwalkar ridicules the idea that "the Nation is composed of all those who live in one country". Instead, he says, "Ever since that evil day, when Moslems first landed in Hindusthan, right up to the present moment, the Hindu Nation, has been gallantly fighting on to shake off the despoilers".[22] Golwalkar defined a Hindu as one who lives within the boundaries of British India presently and is descended from the Aryan race. This separates the "true inhabitants" of India from those who imposed themselves from the outside. All other "foreign elements" residing in India cannot be accorded any rights or privileges:

> From this standpoint, sanctioned by the experience of shrewd old nations, the foreign races in Hindusthan must either adopt the Hindu culture and language, must learn to respect and hold in reverence Hindu religion, must entertain no idea but those of the glorification of the Hindu race and culture, i.e., of the Hindu nation and must lose their separate existence to merge in the Hindu race, or may stay in the country, wholly subordinated to the Hindu Nation, claiming nothing, deserving no privileges, far less any preferential treatment – not even citizen's rights. There is, at least should be, no other course for them to adopt. We are an old nation; let us deal, as old nations ought to and do deal, with the foreign races, who have chosen to live in our country.[23]

It was a chilling message: Muslims, Christians, Sikhs, and Parsis must be treated for what they are – a minority at the mercy of the majority. Numbers began to matter more and more – the bigger the majority and smaller the minority the better. Throughout the 20th century, high-caste Hindu organizations were haunted by the fear that their religious majority would be destroyed if low-caste groups were to convert to Islam or, less importantly, to Christianity, a fear that was never too far from the many efforts undertaken by such organizations to "uplift" Dalits and cleanse Hinduism itself of caste discrimination. And indeed, starting in the 1920s, both Hindu and Muslim missionaries began imitating their Christian predecessors, so as to convert communities of indeterminate religious affiliation and thus augment their respective numbers.

Today, to complete Savarkar's and Golwalkar's civilizational project has become the mission goal to which Narendra Modi and the Bharatiya Janata Party (BJP) are committed. Many, if not most, Indians today have bought into the notion that a thousand years have been lost because of foreign occupation; it is time for Mother India to rise. This means building the Ram temple and claiming other holy sites, banning beef, and privileging Hindus over others. For this goal to be achieved, the decades-old post-Partition official ideology of India – secularism – had to be overthrown. Even if there was some mumbling about being formally secular, henceforth India would be a Hindu-first nation.

The Two Nation Theory, from the Muslim side, shared the principle of exclusivism. It had two parts. The first was a sociological premise: Hindus and

268 What Is the Ideology of Pakistan – and Does It Matter?

Muslims living on the Indian subcontinent form two separate nations defined by their distinct values, practices, and beliefs. Moreover, each nation could be comfortable only with its own kind, irrespective of variations in ethnicity, language, and culture within it. The second premise came later and called for political action because it was assumed that the two different religions could not cohabit upon the same piece of land. Hence a new nation state had to be created on the basis of religious identity. Once these two premises were accepted sufficiently widely, it became difficult – if not impossible – for neighbor to continue living with neighbor. An unstoppable force would soon split India asunder and create for the very first time in history an ab initio Muslim majority state.

I turn now to a proto-ideology in the sense that it contains all the elements referred to in the first section of this chapter where, given the absence of an existing definition, I tried to find a definition of ideology appropriate to the case at hand. But, more potent and relevant than any academic discourse is a certain political slogan. Coined in pre-Partition days, all Pakistani schoolchildren know it even today.

Pakistan ka Matlab Kya?

The popular slogan *Pakistan ka matlab kya? la ilaha illallah* (What is the meaning of Pakistan? There is only one God) is best characterized as a proto-ideology. Although it violates rules of Urdu grammar, this bagatelle from 1944 became famously popular. Coined by a minor Urdu poet, Asghar Saudai, it has since been used in rallies and by right-wing political parties.[24] Although it became a battle cry of the All-India Muslim League (AIML), Jinnah himself did not use this slogan. However, he was certainly aware of it and never forbade its use. The cultural historian Alyssa Ayres devotes her book's conclusion to a discussion of the slogan's impact upon the psyche of Muslims in pre-Partition India.[25] I am inspired by Ayres's observation to delve below into *Shahabnama*, the title that the well-known Urdu writer and civil servant, Qudratullah Shahab (1920–1986) gave to his memoirs. One of *Shahabnama*'s chapters is titled, "*Pakistan Ka Matlab Kya*".

A staunch Muslim nationalist, Shahab is an authentic voice who fully reflects the communal hatreds of his times. While he had a coveted position working with the British government, he saw his own patriotism as siding with fellow Muslims, of whatever linguistic and ethnic type, and saving them from Hindu majority rule. As a north Indian Urdu-speaking Muslim of the *ashrafiyya*, he feels himself a foreigner. He cannot let go of the idea that they had ruled for centuries a land where Hindus formed the majority. As he and his cohorts saw it, the British had snatched from them their right to rule and made the Hindu majority more powerful. His book is replete with how Hindus have deceived and outwitted Muslims over the ages and he is fond of repeating Urdu adages against Hindus such as *moo'n say ram ram aur bagl main churi* (Hindus chant peace-peace citing Ram, but hide a knife under their armpits). It is therefore instructive to

What Is the Ideology of Pakistan – and Does It Matter? **269**

see how this class of people perceived the world around them in the first part of the 20th century.

The chapter begins with the author – then a deputy secretary in the Orissa secretariat responsible for authorizing passports – receiving a secret request from Hussain Shaheed Suhrawardy who was then the chief minister of Bengal and an AIML stalwart. Suhrawardy asked Shahab to issue a passport for an individual who was at the time blacklisted by the government (the reader is not told why this was so). Shahab instantly complies with this manifestly illegal request, moves into AIML high circles, and eventually travels to meet Jinnah in Bombay where he hands over some stolen confidential document. A stickler for the law, Jinnah is nevertheless pleased. He mildly reprimands Shahab and tells him to be careful in the future since this page was ripped out of a numbered book.

Fast forward: by this time the All India Congress had rejected the Cabinet Mission Plan. Jinnah's subsequent call for Direct Action Day on 16 August 1946 sparked riots leaving thousands dead. Partition had become inevitable. On 3 June 1947 Prime Minister Clement Attlee announces Partition and Shahab is listening on All India Radio to Lord Mountbatten, Jawaharlal Nehru, and Mohammed Ali Jinnah as they respond to the Partition Plan. In the same room is Shahab's Kashmiri cook, Ramzan, and Bengali driver, Roz Mohammed. Both are transfixed although neither understands English. They are aware that history is being made. Ramzan lovingly caresses the radio and thanks Allah for all these *baray baray sahib loag* who are helping bring Pakistan into existence. Shahab is taken aback: here is an ignorant Ramzan, overcome with gratitude, thanking Mountbatten and Nehru along with Jinnah for making Pakistan! He asks Ramzan if he knows what the meaning of Pakistan is, to which Ramzan promptly shoots back: yes, sir! He then reverentially recites: *Pakistan ka matlab kya? La ilaha illallah.*

Shahab doesn't scold Ramzan. On the contrary, he is so inspired by this simpleton's faith that his mind now begins to focus upon the meaning of Pakistan. Picking up his thick official secretariat notebook, he jots down 19 items about what Pakistan means. He starts with Pakistan being the distillate of Muslim aspirations that began with the 1857 War of Independence, the Aligarh Movement of Sir Syed Ahmad Khan, Allama Iqbal's sermon in Allahabad, the absolute incompatibility of Muslims and Hindus, a declaration of freedom from Hindu capitalists and money lenders seeking to entrap Muslims in perpetual slavery, an expression decrying the conniving British who insisted on a hasty departure so that Pakistan would face insuperable problems, and the destined victory of a nation which embodies Muslim faith, unity, and discipline. That night Shahab goes to sleep dreaming the sweetest of dreams, softly singing to himself *Pakistan ka matlab kya? La ilaha illallah.* For him the Ideology of Pakistan is what's now in his notebook.

Across the length and breadth of India, there were millions of Ramzans who craved ideas simple enough to be captured in a phrase or a sentence. So, yes, Pakistan did have an ideology for them even if it was an inchoate one and meant different things to different people. For men like Ramzan and his boss, ideology would establish a claim to truth, and from the union of simplicity with truth would spring a commitment to action. This is what gave the Muslim League (ML) its muscle power. Boss and servant shared the same ideology, and this inspired them to act in their own respective ways. Neither was thinking much beyond 14 August 1947 and each was dreaming of the land of milk and honey that lay ahead. Some would later identify themselves as *muhajirs*, a word used for those who migrated to Pakistan that derives from *hijrat*, the journey of Prophet Muhammad (PBUH) and his followers in AD 622 from Mecca to Yathrib (later renamed by him as Medina). Shahab died in 1986 and is buried in Islamabad.

Armed with the meaning of ideology, let us proceed to examine the particularities of the Two Nation Theory whose Muslim version formed the raison d'être for Pakistan.

The Weaponization of Ideology

Muhammad Munir, former chief justice of Pakistan, wrote in his 1980 monograph, *From Jinnah to Zia*,[26] that the Ideology of Pakistan was absent from the political lexicon until 1962. He says that just as discussion on the Political Parties Bill had started, these words were then used for the first time. At that point the sole member of the Jamaat-e-Islami injected them during his intervention. Upon this, Chaudhry Fazal Elahi, who later became president of Pakistan, rose from his seat and objected that the Ideology of Pakistan shall have to be defined. The member who had proposed the original amendment replied that the "Ideology of Pakistan was Islam". However, no member present asked him the further question, "What is Islam?" The amendment to the bill was therefore passed.[27]

While the AIML campaigned on a frankly communal platform, there is no record of the key architects of the Pakistan Movement – either Iqbal or Jinnah – ever having used the phrase Ideology of Pakistan or its Urdu equivalent, Nazariyya-e-Pakistan. This phrase made its entry into the political lexicon much later.

With the coming to power of General Zia-ul-Haq, the Ideology of Pakistan became so foundational that Zia repeatedly underscored its importance, vowing that "the armed forces bear the sacred responsibility for safeguarding Pakistan's ideological frontiers".[28] But why did the Army have to take upon itself this responsibility? And why did ideology suddenly become so important into Pakistan's fourth decade with children being taught *Pakistan ka matlab kya*? The immediate reason was the crisis of legitimacy. Zia had deposed an elected leader; he simply had to have a good reason for that. But the utility of religious ideology was not limited to him or that moment in time. It was useful then – and remains useful now – for three reasons:

First, Islam is used as a weaponized ideology for combatting Baloch, Pashtun, Sindhi, and Gilgit-Baltistani nationalisms. The clearest articulation of this was

What Is the Ideology of Pakistan – and Does It Matter? **271**

given by Zia's law minister, A.K. Brohi, who launched a blistering attack on the very notion that Pakistan has nationalities. In October 1978, he wrote in *Dawn*:

> Pakistan was founded on the basis of religion and religion alone. It can be kept together only by the cementing force of Ikhwan. There are no nationalities in Pakistan or, for that matter, anywhere else; and the idea of nationalities is subversive.[29]

Post-Partition, Jinnah had mostly dropped the Two Nation Theory from his speeches and began preaching pure Pakistani nationalism, hoping it would submerge both cultural and religious identity. Although nascent Pakistani nationalism had piggybacked on the furious passion of Hindu–Muslim divisions, Jinnah hoped it could now survive without that. As such he was following a well-trodden path. Before the French and American Revolutions, raising religious passions had been the only way to bring people out into the streets. But, as Napoleon and Bismarck had discovered, full-blown nationalism could also mobilize people through singing national anthems, devotion to the flag, celebration of the Fatherland – and going to war against another state.

Jinnah's successors did not have the mettle of Bismarck, Napoleon, or Mazzini. They therefore reverted to the primordial notion of the Islamic *ummah* as protection against ethnic nationalism. In East Pakistan, the Jamaat-e-Islami organizations Al-Badr and Al-Shams operated under the control of General "Tiger" Niazi. To counter Baloch nationalism, Pakistan's military establishment continues to promote religious and sectarian organizations some of which, like Sipah-e-Sahaba, are formally banned but continue to thrive.

A narrative vigorously promoted today is that Pakistan can be kept together in its present form only through the threat of military force or its actual application against Baloch nationalists, dissenters such as those of Pashtun Tahafuz Movement, and nascent movements in Gilgit-Baltistan. Unlike Bangladesh which was comfortable with a mixed identity of culture and religion, a Pakistan cut in half has insisted with ever increasing vigor that it must be an ideological Islamic state. This makes Kashmir as much a religious cause as a nationalist one. Jihadist groups sponsored and armed by military and secret agencies fought Indian forces for decades until finally strong limits were imposed through a coercive financial international instrument, the Financial Action Task Force (FATF).

Second, like all totalitarian ideologies, the Ideology of Pakistan is a vital instrument for social control because sovereignty arguably lies with Allah and not the people. Hence it is a means for manipulating and controlling people by the so-called interpreters of Allah's will who insist upon creating and enforcing conformity. In his book, *Pakistan: Between Mosque and Military*, ex-ambassador Husain Haqqani notes that,

> Belief in a national ideology based on Islam had nothing to do with personal piety or lack of it. It was a strategy for national integrity, and the

272 What Is the Ideology of Pakistan – and Does It Matter?

military – as an institution – had adopted it. The military's adoption of Islamic ideology conferred legitimacy on its right to rule Pakistan and was seen by Yahya Khan and his colleagues as the key to continued military preeminence in the country's political life.[30]

Those who conform are rewarded, while dissenting attitudes eventually wither from lack of nourishment. In the name of ideology as a superior principle, religious minorities can be denied equal status, women can awarded an inferior status, the Universal Declaration of Human Rights can be set aside, and freedoms can be snuffed out.

Third, ideology helps Pakistan's warrior class legitimize its holding on to the helm of affairs. Army rule has been upfront, as during four periods of martial law, or from a clearly visible backstage as with the Imran Khan government. From the time of General Zia-ul-Haq, the Army considers itself the guardian of not just Pakistan's geographical frontiers but also the protector of its ideological basis. General Zia's Islamization drive was to shore up the notion that Pakistan is an Islamic state rather than just a Muslim state. Prayers in government departments were deemed compulsory, punishments were meted out to those who did not fast in Ramadan, selection for academic posts required that the candidate demonstrate knowledge of Islamic teachings, and jihad was propagated through schoolbooks.

In the years after 911, General Musharraf's call for "enlightened moderation" was a tacit admission that a theocratic Pakistan cannot work. But his call conflicted with his other, more important, responsibility as chief of the Pakistan Army which had consciously nurtured radicalism in previous decades. The relationship between the army and religious radicals is today no longer as simple as in the 1980s. To maintain a positive image in the West and China, the Pakistani establishment must continue to decry Islamic radicalism while maintaining it as a reserve force. Hard actions are taken only when Islamists threatened the army's corporate and political interests, or when senior army commanders are targeted for assassination. Islamists in the army still hope for action by zealous officers to bring back the glory days of the military–mullah alliance led by General Zia-ul-Haq. Cadet colleges and army training institutions continue to emphasize that Pakistan is an ideological state.

Resolving the Ideology Conundrum

In the above I have dwelt upon the three principal reasons why Pakistan's current leadership remains fixated upon giving Pakistan an ideology. But the remaining puzzle remains unsolved: if Justice Munir's account is to be believed, the Ideology of Pakistan was an unknown phrase until 1962. So why did leaders starting from Jinnah and Liaquat and all the way down to Bhutto never talk about Pakistan's ideology? Why did it have to start with Zia?

The answer: until Zia came along there never was a game plan for the nascent state or, in modern parlance, no business model. For Jinnah or Liaquat to have

What Is the Ideology of Pakistan – and Does It Matter? **273**

stated that Pakistan's ideology was Islam would have cut no ice anywhere because there were plenty of Muslim states with no similarity between their political or cultural systems. Some were as far as Egypt and Indonesia, and others as near as Afghanistan and Iran. On the other hand, by the end of the Second World War, there were only two powerful and well-defined ideologies in town: the capitalist ideology of the United States and the communist ideology of the USSR. The first emphasized private property, individualism, democracy, and a world safe for American businesses. The second stressed collective ownership, state control, a one-party system, and commitment to spreading communism globally. Jinnah would have had to define Pakistan's ideology, which would have required him to set down specifics such as those mentioned at the beginning of this chapter. That he was not willing to do, because massive infighting would have followed over which he would have had no control.

The disillusion of individuals with political movements ultimately causes all ideologies to dissipate. American capitalist ideology rallied its citizens to fighting communism, but its appeal to most Americans has hugely diminished today. Under neoliberalism – which involved privatization of public enterprises and reduced the state's role to a bare minimum – The U.S.'s global outreach has shrunk, the quality of its health and education system is barely first world, and the condition of its poor is wretched. So pervasive was American neoliberalism – until it collapsed – that it was often not even recognized as an ideology. Rather, it was thought to be a neutral force and a kind of law like Newton's except that it applied to societies. But surely it was a conscious effort to change the locus of power within a society.

As for communism as an ideology, the USSR was born in 1922 and died in 1991 burying with it a host of USSR-supported movements around the world. All watched in amazement when on 25 December 1991 the hammer and sickle flag was lowered for the last time and the former Communist monolith peacefully separated into multiple separate nations.

Pakistan was not so lucky. As reality began to bite in the days after independence, it became clear that the force of ideology had separated Muslims from Hindus in parts of what was once United India. But that force was insufficiently strong to keep Muslims together. After Partition, Muslims were spread out in roughly equal numbers between East Pakistan, West Pakistan, and India. Where should Pakistan head towards now that it had been established? There had been no deep thinking on this matter – or any thinking at all, it seems.

Lacking direction and riven by internal rivalries, it took barely thirteen months for the Muslim League to fall apart after Jinnah's death. Reading between the lines, one learns from the memoirs of Pakistan's fourth prime minister, Chaudhry Muhammad Ali, that Jinnah had lost his grip to the extent that he was unable to command authority over ML stalwarts like Mamdot, Daultana, and Shaukat Hayat Khan.[31] By 1953 the ML had disappeared from view.

In 1957 the political scientist Keith Callard wrote that "Pakistanis are a people united by a common will to be a nation, but they do not yet know what kind of a

274 What Is the Ideology of Pakistan – and Does It Matter?

nation they want to be".[32] This, in my opinion, captures the essence of Pakistan's dilemma. Pakistan's rulers continue to bewilder the people of Pakistan by dismissing their organic ties to the cultures of the historically formed nations that comprise the country. Instead, they continue to insist that the straightjacket of religious ideology alone can hold the country together.

Notes

1 https://www.pakistani.org/pakistan/legislation/1860/actXLVof1860.html
2 The Economist, 12 December 1981, p. 48. Quoted in F. Devji, *Muslim Zion – Pakistan as a Political Idea*,
   Harvard University Press (2013), p. 4.
3 P. Hoodbhoy and A.H. Nayyar, Rewriting the History of Pakistan, in *Islam, Politics, and the State*, ed. Asghar Khan, London, Zed Press (1985).
4 University Grants Commission directive, quoted in A. Hamid et al. *Mutalliyah-i-Pakistan*, Islamabad, Allama Iqbal Open University (1983), pp. xii–xiii.
5 S. Mahmood et al., *Government of Pakistan, Federal Ministry of Education, Pakistan Studies (Compulsory) for Intermediate Classes*, Islamabad, Government of Pakistan. Approved for the Departments of Education of the Punjab, Sind, NWFP, Baluchistan, Federal Areas, and liberated Kashmir vide notification number F.11-16/81-HST, dated 2 November 1981, as the sole textbook for intermediate classes.
6 S. Husain and M.A. Hasan, *Mukhzun Mutalliyah-i-Pakistan*, Lahore, Kitab Khana Danishwuran (1981), p. 1.
7 Ibid, p. 2.
8 M.D. Zafar, *Pakistan Studies for Medical Students*, Lahore, Aziz Publishers (1982), p. 20.
9 National Education Policy 2017–2025, Government of Pakistan, Ministry of Federal Education and Professional Training, Islamabad.
10 Civil Aviation Authority Service Regulations, 15 January 2000, p. 37.
11 Ideology and State, Abdullah, *Policy Perspectives*, 7, no. 2 (July–December 2010): 75–103. https://www.jstor.org/stable/42909277#metadata_info_tab_contents
12 For an extensive discussion on the nature of ideologies in modern and ancient discourse, see: M. Rejai, Political *Ideologies: A Comparative Approach*, M.E. Sharpe, Inc. (1995), p. 11.
13 D. Bell, *The End of Ideology – On the Exhaustion of Political Ideas in the Fifties*, Cambridge, Harvard University Press (1965), p. 437.
14 R. Gutala et al., A Shared Y-chromosomal Heritage between Muslims and Hindus in India, *Human Genetics*, 120, no. 4 (November 2006): 543–551. doi:10.1007/s00439-006-0234-x.
15 The Tribune, 14 December 1924.
16 A useful compendium of documents on early Hindutva can be found in *Hindu Nationalism – a Reader*, Ed. Christophe Jaffrelot, Princeton University Press (2007).
17 V.D. Savarkar, *Hindutva – Who Is a Hindu?*, (1923). https://archive.org/details/hindutva-vinayak-damodar-savarkar-pdf/
18 V.D. Savarkar, *Essentials of Hindutva* (1923). http://www.savarkar.org/en/hindutva-hindu-nationalism/essentials-hindutva
19 S.S. Vadmay, *Maharashtra Prantik Hindusabha Publication*, vol. 6 (1963–1965): 296.
20 Hindu Rashtra Darshan, a collection of Savarkar's Presidential Addresses to the Hindu Mahasabha.
21 M.S. Gowalkar, *We or Our Nation Defined*, Nagpur, Bharat Publications (1939), E-book, pp. 87–88. http://hinduebooks.blogspot.com/
22 Ibid, p. 52.
23 Ibid, pp. 104–105.

24 One sometimes hears that this slogan was invented by the Jamaat-e-Islami after Partition. This is untrue.
25 A. Ayres, *Speaking Like a State – Language and Nationalism in Pakistan*, Cambridge University Press (2009).
26 M. Munir, *From Jinnah to Zia*, Lahore, Vanguard Books Ltd. (1980).
27 Ibid, p. 26.
28 Nawa-i-Waqt (Karachi), 14 August 1984.
29 A.K. Brohi, Dawn, February 1978.
30 Hussain Haqqani, *Between Mosque and Military*, Carnegie Endowment, epub (2005).
31 C.M. Ali, *The Emergence of Pakistan*, Columbia University Press (1967), pp. 366–367.
32 K. Callard, *Pakistan – A Political Study*, Macmillan (1957), p. 6.

Eleven

WHY COULDN'T PAKISTAN BECOME AN ISLAMIC STATE?

بتان رنگ وخوں کو توڑ کر ملت میں گم ہو جا

نہ تُورانی رہے باقی، نہ ایرانی نہ افغانی

Smash the idols of blood and color – become Muslim
Be not Turani nor Iranian nor Afghan – just be Muslim

– Allama Iqbal

This chapter chases myths surrounding the Islamic state. My hope here is to create some measure of clarity on a matter that has vexed Pakistan since its very inception. To be explored are certain key questions:

1. Is an Islamic state religiously mandated in Islam?
2. Has any Islamic state actually existed in history?
3. What are some competing visions of an Islamic state?
4. What fuels multiple present struggles for creating Islamic states?
5. Why do so many Muslims support the idea of a caliphate?
6. What gave birth to political Islam?
7. What might happen if Pakistan actually became an Islamic state?
8. Is a liberal sharia state possible?

If Iqbal's above call is taken as a measure of pan-Islamism, today's Pakistan is not even halfway from an Islamic state. Prejudice against Afghans fleeing post-2021 Taliban terror is rampant in the Pakistani media and public. As such it is evidence of ethnicity and language trumping religion and a negation of pan-Islamism. Nevertheless, Pakistan has never stopped trying to become an Islamic state and the calls have gotten louder with time. The name immediately after 1947 was Dominion of Pakistan which changed into the Republic of Pakistan. The word

DOI: 10.4324/9781003379140-16

Why Couldn't Pakistan Become an Islamic State? **277**

"republic" notionally indicates adherence to a secular, constitutional government rather than a monarchy. Then in March 1956 this changed again when it formally became the Islamic Republic of Pakistan. But the addition of "Islamic" was formal only and not particularly consequential in terms of how people then lived.

Seventy-five years down the road, Pakistan may not be a secular state, but it is still not an Islamic one either. For the most part, it is ruled by secular law and not the sharia; alcohol is banned but interest is not (although a modern banking system has been nominally adjusted to make it "Islamic" in appearance); none of its leaders so far has been a cleric (unlike the Islamic Republics of Iran and Afghanistan); its penal system does not allow for amputation of limbs or stoning to death; many persons convicted of blasphemy are on the death row, but as of 2022 none has yet been executed as required by law; it has had a female head of state and a ban forbidding women has not been announced; and the country's political system is structured along modern lines rather than any Islamic system in the past.

The rhetoric from political leaders has been at variance with this. Beginning with Muhammed Ali Jinnah, from time to time and with varying levels of urgency, they have called for a state where Islam would be the supreme law of the land. However, the notion of an Islamic state has been understood quite differently by each leader or left vague.

- Jinnah flip-flopped between Islamic and secular notions of governance in the years before Partition; this has been covered in detail in Chapter Five. Back in the 1940s, he was quite casual in referring to the new state-to-be; it was interchangeably a "Muslim state" one day and an "Islamic state" another. That ambivalence did not go away after 1947. Addressing the Karachi Bar Association on 25 January 1948, Jinnah said: "Why this feeling of nervousness that the future constitution of Pakistan is going to be in conflict with Shariat Laws?...Islamic principles today are as applicable to life as they were 1,300 years ago".[1]
- Zulfikar Ali Bhutto's initial populism derived from his appeals for socialism and a just social order which would eliminate feudalism and capitalism. But as reality set in, he backtracked on his promises. As his popularity waned, he began leaning on Islam. In place of his promised socialism came "Islamic socialism". The end of his regime was marked by concession after concession to the nine political parties that had banded together demanding a return to Nizam-e-Mustafa, the political system of the Holy Prophet. As Bhutto retreated, he banned alcohol, declared Friday as a holiday instead of Sunday, and expelled the Ahmadiyya community from the ranks of Muslims. These steps did not suffice in saving him from the hangman's noose.
- General Muhammad Zia-ul-Haq was by far the most explicit and determined, pinning the legitimacy of his government (1977–1988) upon

redefining Pakistan as an Islamic state run by Islamic law. Supported by the Council of Islamic Ideology, he banned political parties as well as labor and student unions, instituted Islamic punishments, and took important steps towards incorporation of sharia. This turned out to be the most visible use of Islam in Pakistan's history.

- Mian Muhammad Nawaz Sharif, in his second term as prime minister, was preparing in September 1998 to move a bill in parliament for introduction of sharia law. The economy at the time was suffering from international sanctions imposed after the nuclear tests four months earlier. Although he was visibly clutching at straws in a desperate bid to save himself, it is likely that the bill could have made it through parliament where his party held the absolute majority. For technical reasons, it was deferred but meanwhile Sharif was ousted by General Pervez Musharraf in the coup of 12 October 1999. Thereafter, Sharif lived in exile in Saudi Arabia before returning and becoming prime minister for the third time. He made no mention of his earlier efforts to impose sharia. On the contrary, to the surprise of many, he started espousing liberal and secular ideals with ever greater vigor until he was ousted again in 2018 and, as of early 2023, lives in London. This is a story still in progress.

- Imran Khan, upon his election in August 2018 as prime minister, vowed in his inaugural speech to make the 7th century *Riyasat-e-Medina* (state of Medina) the template upon which Pakistan would reconstruct its social, educational, political, and judicial system. He repeated his vows several times. Midway into his five-year term, his government made the teaching of Arabic mandatory from primary classes onward, *madrassa* and regular schools were conjoined with identical books and examinations for all, and it was deemed that no university degree in Punjab can be awarded without passing a Qur'an-based examination. In October 2021, an ordinance was signed to create the National Rahmatul-lil-Alameen Authority for creating Islamic values and "building character" in the younger generation.[2]

It can be argued that Zia-ul-Haq and Imran Khan have been the only Pakistani leaders who introduced significant changes bringing Pakistan closer to becoming an Islamic state. Others have not brought any clarity into what an Islamic state is, nor shown how to approach that goal in matters of governance. However, neither leader was able to effect changes as deep as those in Iran; at best these were incremental rather than revolutionary.

To be fair, the question of what an Islamic state is can be asked not just of Pakistan but of all other Muslim states too. Iran calls itself the Islamic Republic of Iran just as Pakistan declares itself the Islamic Republic of Pakistan. Being sovereign states they are at liberty to do so, and if their people so want. Absent, however, is the source of authority or historical precedence which can justify the term "Islamic". Every use of this term has been challenged, often by physical violence, by other Muslims. Shias have fared better in this regard. Although

Why Couldn't Pakistan Become an Islamic State? **279**

there is some dispute over proper authority, for Shias the concept of *vilayat-e-faqih* (Rule of the Clergy) has been agreed to at the highest level of the Shiite hierarchy. However, as we shall see later, this too is a late 20th century development.

For Sunnis there is absolutely no such agreement, even in principle. After Osama bin Laden's Al-Qaida flew airliners into the twin towers of the World Trade Center on 11 September 2001, the hottest question in town was: what exactly is the "Islamic state" for which they had killed themselves and so many others? Militant Islamic groups have fought for this entity – and some are still fighting – in Afghanistan, Syria, Iraq, Sudan, Nigeria, and, of course, Pakistan. This sent academics scrambling to history textbooks looking for practices within early Islamic empires, investigating theories of governance, and revisiting the works of 20th century Muslim ideologues like Khomeini, Shariati, Qutb, Maududi, and others.

Twenty years later, some key militant groups have been defeated, but others are thriving. Al-Qaida is much weakened, but its clones operate across the world. The caliphate of Abu Bakr al-Baghdadi has crumbled in Iraq and Syria, but ISIS (Da'esh) is expanding in Afghanistan and Pakistan, and is also operational in 17 other countries. All continue their fight to establish an Islamic state in some shape and form. Their methods may be disliked, but their dictum that Islam is a complete code of life – and hence that religion and state cannot be separated – is popularly believed by large numbers, if not majorities, in many Muslim countries. This makes it all the more important for us to seek clarification on the nature of an Islamic state.

Warmup: A Christian State

Let's first go for the low-hanging fruit and examine the far simpler notion of a Christian state. The hope is that this will give us some clarity of what a religious state could mean in modern times. By definition, a Christian nation-state is that in which the majority of its citizens are Christians. This makes the United States a Christian nation-state. In fact its majority is that of believing Christians – a recent Gallup poll found that more than 8 in 10 Americans say they are affiliated with some Christian denomination. This is unlike some countries in the western part of Europe where entire populations are largely atheistic.

Nevertheless, the U.S.'s ideological construction is secular. "In God We Trust" is printed on all dollar bills, but the U.S. recognizes only laws made by man, not God. Its constitution famously asserts that: "All men are created equal, that they are endowed by their Creator with certain unalienable Rights, that among these are Life, Liberty and the Pursuit of Happiness". Despite abundant recognition of the Christian God in the Declaration of Independence, the Constitution was carefully crafted to avoid any hint of a theocracy. It would therefore be correct to say the U.S. is Christian-secular and Norway, for example, is atheist-secular.

What of a Christian theocratic state? In present times, there actually exists one – the Holy See. This absolute monarchy dates back to early Christian times.

280 Why Couldn't Pakistan Become an Islamic State?

Today it is a relatively benign entity, deriving income from the sale of Vatican postage stamps and memorabilia sold to tourists who gawk at past splendors. Legally, the Holy See is a state in the Vatican spread over 110 acres inside the city of Rome. It exercises jurisdiction over a mere one thousand citizens, but the government has its own money, its own laws, and a permanent diplomatic mission in the United Nations as well as in over 170 countries. It also has state-run tribunals, congregations, pontifical counsels, and numerous other bureaucratic entities. According to Wikipedia, citizenship is not based on birth but granted only to those who reside in the Vatican because of their work or office. Cardinals living in Vatican City or Rome, as well as diplomats of the Holy See, are also considered citizens. Technically no one can be born in the Vatican, as there are no hospitals. All wishing to move to the Vatican must have their citizenship approved by the pope or papal authority.

The Holy See of old times is a far cry from the harmless tourist attraction it is today. In the age when the Roman Catholic Church ruled over the Papal States (756–1870), it was known for trafficking in ecclesiastical appointments, deceit, scandals, immorality, aggression, frauds, murder, and cruelty. Its religious tyranny was breathtaking; torture was freely used as standard operating procedure in its infamous inquisitions. From a biblical standpoint, and particularly a Protestant viewpoint, the very existence of the Holy See is challengeable on two counts:

> First, the concept of a "holy chair" in which resides the head of the church is unscriptural. The true church is never to consider one man as its head, no matter his title. The exalted Head of the true Body of Christ is Jesus Christ, the living Head of the living church. How can the living church be headed by a mortal man who dies? Second, the Bible nowhere gives credence to the idea of the church forming its own city-state or its own government. The church as a political or diplomatic kingdom is unknown in Scripture. In fact, Jesus made it clear that His kingdom is not of this world (John 8:23; 18:36). The Bible never condones or encourages the establishment of earthly kingdoms or diplomatic entities because these things, by their very nature, focus attention on the world, which is passing away (1 Corinthians 7:31; 1 John 2:17). Christians are to be focused on the heavenly kingdom and our only diplomatic efforts are to be spreading the gospel of Jesus Christ and warning others of the wrath to come.[3]

The above openly challenges the Holy See's legitimacy, whether that of ancient or modern times. Nevertheless, it can easily be warded off because the state derives authority from the pope who, "as shepherd and teacher of all Christians" is officially protected from error and can therefore define a doctrine of faith and morals for the entire Church. So, yes, there is such a thing as a Christian state. It exists because it has the authority of a supreme leader. But what about Islam and the Islamic state? This begs the critical question: who speaks for Muslims?

Who Speaks for Islam?

There is no clergy in Islam and, in fact, no word in Arabic that captures its meaning. Unlike Christianity, Sunni Islam does not have the equivalent of a pope – a supreme religious authority. The Qur'an does not speak of intermediaries and so, at least in principle, Islam is between man and God. Hence there is no church, cardinals, bishops, or priests. The concept of Confession is absent. In this sense, Islam is a more democratic and less hierarchical religion than Christianity. In practice this has led to a medley of individual Muslims claiming they understand Islam better than other Muslims and so can speak for God.

The hierarchy of Sunni interlocutors does not have clear nomenclature and is confusing even to Muslims. Perched at various levels are the *mufti*, *aalim* (plural, *ulema*), *sheikh-ul-islam*, *sheikh*, *khatib*, and *mullah*. Rankings are defined differently from region to region, and from time to time. There was never a unified clerical Sunni establishment in the past, and there does not exist one presently. In Pakistan, the word "mullah" is used in a derogatory sense for a small-time cleric, but in Afghanistan the Taliban supremo was Mullah Omar. He was chosen by the Taliban council to be the *amir-ul-mo'mineen* (leader of all the faithful), a term that the King of Morocco still uses and which was used by the first four successors of the Holy Prophet. On the other hand, Abu Bakr al-Baghdadi of ISIS, who also claimed to be the religious and temporal leader of all Muslims, chose to be called caliph (*khalifah*). Apart from the confusion over nomenclature, the ascent of al-Baghdadi as caliph vexed those of Pakistan's clergy who were drawn towards him. How could he be accepted as supreme leader when Mullah Omar was already in charge? Some were puzzled but Mufti Tahir Jami, a teacher at Madressah Ali Murtaza in Karachi said there was no problem:

> However, what is not permissible is to have more than one *khalifah* (caliph) at the same time. When that happens, you have to get rid of the person who was the second to declare himself. This problem does not arise at the moment. Al-Baghdadi has declared himself a *khalifah* while Mullah Omar has kept himself restricted to an emirate.[4]

The Shia *ulema*, on the other hand, are much more organized. Vali Nasr in *The Shia Revival* notes that they enjoy a privileged spiritual status that their Sunni counterparts have never had because they are considered repositories of knowledge linked to the Twelfth Imam, the Mahdi.[5] Last seen in the Islamic year 260 Hijri (AD 874) when he was five years old, the Mahdi is expected to reappear at the end of time. Shia clergy are tasked to look for signs of his reemergence and suggest ways to speed it up. A rigorous, standardized curriculum decided upon in the seminaries of Qom (Iran) creates a competition leading to a religious hierarchy. As in the world of peer-reviewed academia, Shia clergy also judge one another on the quality of their scholarship and publications. At the very top are ayatollahs with a particularly deep knowledge of history, law, and theology. Shiism has no pope, but ayatollahs are very much like Catholic cardinals.

282 Why Couldn't Pakistan Become an Islamic State?

Contrary to popular notions, Iran as an Islamic state is actually a new development. Prior to the 1979 Revolution, Shia clerics had agreed to what historians call the "Safavid Contract". As the last of the "Gunpowder Empires", the Safavid dynasty had ruled over Iran for five hundred years. In anticipation of the Mahdi's return, the clergy had supported secular rulers while protecting and propagating Shi'ism. The famed Contract was abrogated when the secular, autocratic regime of the last Shah was overthrown by popular revolution. Thereafter, Ayatollah Khomeini imposed the theocratic doctrine of *velayat-e-faqih* (guardianship of the Islamic jurist) upon Iran. A long Iranian tradition was finally broken in 1979 when the notion of clerical dominance over politics achieved ascendancy. It was opposed by some of even the most learned of Iran's *Ulema* and Khomeini's peers:

> Not all Shia ulama were persuaded by Khomeini's argument. Some found his line of reasoning and the sources on which it relied weak. Others saw it as a violation of Shia historical tradition and even theology. No one among Khomeini's peers was more vocal in his criticism than the grand ayatollah Abol-Qasem al-Khoi, Ayatollah Sistani's mentor. Khoi and Khomeini did not like each other. During Khomeini's Najaf years (1964–78), the two had kept their distance and often exchanged barbs through their students. In fact, Khomeini's lectures on Islamic government were a response to a provocation from one of Khoi's students. Khoi saw *velayat-e-faqih* as an innovation with no support in Shia theology or law.[6]

Ahlul Bayt, a Shiite Iran–based Islamic organization, has this to say about nationalism:

> In Islam, there is no room for one to be a loyal and genuine nationalist. The goal of nationalism is to create national units, whereas the goal of Islam is universal unity. To nationalism what matters the most is loyalty and attachment to the homeland, whereas to Islam, it is God and religion.[7]

We see therefore that even in Shia Islam, there has been no unanimity on the role of the clergy in politics. That Khomeini succeeded in creating a theocratic state only means that the clergy's search for power was successful; the mullah and ayatollah had finally triumphed over secular rulers.

Qur'an and Islamic State

The highest authority in Islam is the literal Word of God, the Qur'an. While explicit on many matters of faith, personal law, and rituals, it is totally silent on matters of the state, political system, and governance of the state. Among the many Islamic scholars who have forcefully made this point are Maulana Wahiduddin Khan of India and Egypt's Al-Ashmawy, a former judge. Al-Ashmawy argues that the state and Islam are entirely separate entities else, "it [state] would have been… sketched out in general outlines in the Qur'an".[8] During the time of the Prophet, classical Arabic had no word for state. Of course, modern Arabic does; today the word that comes closest is *dawlah*, but this would have carried no meaning at the time.

Why, in the absence of crucial support from the Qur'an and hadith, do Islamists insist upon an Islamic government? Their logic is that Islam has to be everywhere, not just in the mosque. Islam must govern lifestyle and even daily routine; its grip must be total over all aspects of a person's life. It cannot stop at just prayer and fasting, nor just at *zakat* (alms) and *Haj*. Instead, it is a complete code of life that tells you what to wear and what not to wear, what you may or may not eat, personal hygiene, laws of inheritances, family relationships, laws of marriage and divorce, laws of buying and selling, laws of war and peace, etc. The orthodox warn that Islam must not be thought of as just another religion like Christianity, Judaism, or Hinduism. Other religions, they say, have their own theologies but are insufficiently comprehensive. The "complete code" argument translates rapidly into calling for a state that possesses executive power and executors who would enforce the "Islamic way of life".

In this narrative, the Islamic way of life is governed by Qur'an and hadith. While none dispute the authenticity of the Qur'an or challenge its contents, the authenticity of the thousands of different hadiths has been a subject of perennial disagreement and contention. These sayings and practices of the Holy Prophet had been collected decades after the Prophet's death. But even on matters specified by the Qur'an, there is no agreement on how to interpret it. The possibilities of disagreement are endless.

Take, for example, the question of how much a Muslim woman needs to cover herself. For some, the simple Malaysian headscarf and Iranian-style *hijab*, which leave the face uncovered, will do. Liberal Muslims go further and contend that almost any (modest) clothing is sufficiently Islamic, and the Qur'an merely enjoins men and women to avoid gazing at each other lustfully. But the revitalized orthodoxy finds the headscarf and *hijab* excessively promiscuous. The Saudi *burqa*, with even the eyes covered, is finding increasing favor in much of the Sunni world. An energetic British-born proselytizer, Farhat Hashmi, chooses to reside in Canada but makes frequent forays to Pakistan, India, Bangladesh, Britain, and various African countries. She, like others, has weighed in on the orthodoxy's side and made deep inroads into the Muslim urban middle and upper classes. Her message: "Cover up", "stay at home", and "obey your man", was – and continues to be broadcast – from hundreds of *Al-Huda* centers across the world. Millions of housewives have bought into this.[9]

On technical issues such as economics, consensus on Islamic grounds has even less chance. It was once the opinion of Muslim scholars that banking is forbidden in Islam. During the 19th century, interest was conflated with *riba* and rejected by the bulk of Muslims. Muslim modernists had to fight against this rejection and advance arguments why fixed interest did not constitute *haram* (forbidden). Since inflation is a fact of life for all modern economies, every depositor has to be assured some level of guarantee that his money will not lose value.

Over time fixed interest, renamed as profit, became acceptable in Muslim countries and banking began to grow. But how correctly Islamic – or otherwise – are bonds, commodities, currencies, interest rates, market indexes, stocks, and derivatives? And what is the correct "Islamic" way of determining international currency exchange rates. So, for example, Pakistani banks today advertise "sharia-compliant" debit and credit cards as though the Holy Prophet had somehow endorsed electronic banking and wire transactions. Would an Islamic bank credit card be somehow morally superior to the credit card of, say, that issued by Bank of America? If that isn't enough, bitcoin and various cryptocurrencies pose ethical and moral problems that can send anyone's head spinning.

There is an additional problem – one that has engaged religious scholars for centuries. It is called *naskh*, or the abrogation of one divine Qur'anic ruling by a later divine Qur'anic ruling. In *Interpretations of Jihad in South Asia*, Rahman has extensively dealt with the different positions taken by scholars on *naskh* in the context of jihad.[10] However, the scope of naskh can be widened to include much more. Examples: the question of *iddah* (the waiting period for a widow or divorced woman), women's apparel, and even the consumption of alcohol can be similarly examined. Again, many different conclusions would emerge.

The "complete code" argument demands a huge leap of faith across centuries of societal development and not many Muslims engage with it. This is good strategy else they would have a hard time justifying photography, television, allopathic medicines, vaccines, plastic surgery, blood transfusions, organ transplants, x-ray and ultrasound machines, modern banking practices, etc. Indeed most Muslims are pragmatic, perfectly willing to let these vexing matters go unexamined. They prefer a simpler formula: prayer, fasting, charity, and pilgrimage.

Islamic Scholars on the Islamic State

Lacking specific guidance from the Holy Book, or even those derived from the Prophet's sayings and deeds, Islamic scholars have had to invent their own concepts of an Islamic state. Islam's first political theorist was Abul Hasan al-Mawardi (974–1058), a scholar who served the Abbasid Caliphs at a time when they were seriously weakened by Buyid Emirs.[11] Al-Mawardi's task was to ideologically protect the caliphate against the insurgent Emirs. He did this by giving justification to the notion of the caliph as the religious leader. His famous political handbook *Al-Ahkām As-Sulṭāniyyah wal Wilāyāt Ad-Diniya* (The Ordinance of Government and Religious Leadership) is a standard reference and key document in the evolution of Sunni Islamic political thought. Al-Mawardi posits the caliph as a vicegerent to Prophet Muhammad rather than vicegerent to God directly, identifying seven key requirements to be a caliph. He also compiled the different opinions of jurists in the matter of caliph's succession and on crucial matters such as heirdom, elections, and designation.

But other Islamic scholars refute al-Mawardi's connection between state and religion. The greatest Muslim historian and social anthropologist of all times, Ibn Khaldun, argued that the Holy Prophet had deliberately sought to separate the temporal from the religious:

> Some wrongly assume the imamate to be the pillars of the state. It is one of the general public interests. The people are delegated to take care of

it. If it were one of the pillars of faith, it would be something like prayer, and Muhammad would have appointed a representative, exactly as he appointed Abu Bakr to represent him in prayer.[12]

The Qur'an is clear that the leader of the *ummah* is to be obeyed: *O You who believe, obey Allah, His Messenger and the Ulul Amr (those in charge of rule over you)* (Surah Nisa, verse: 59). But it does not specify the manner and procedure by which the *Ulul Amr* are to be chosen. This vexing problem has found no resolution over the centuries. Instead, says Ibn Khaldun, humans can live civilized lives without the need for prophets. Political laws govern this world; religion is for the afterworld. He rejects the doctrine of scholars who argue that chaos would result if there was no religion:

> One of its premises is that the restraining influence comes into being only through a religious law from God, to which the mass submits as a matter of belief and religious creed. This premise is not acceptable. The restraining influence comes into being as the result of the impetus of royal authority and the forcefulness of the mighty, even if there is no religious law.[13]

To state it bluntly: if it is too hard to get rid of the usurper who has intrigued his way to power, become his humble subject and serve him well. True, the caliph is supposed to embody high ideals of piety and truth, but that's only in principle and not in practice. The great theologian al-Ghazali frankly confesses that facts on the ground are what one must accept:

> An evil-doing and barbarous sultan, so long as he is supported by military force, so that he can only with difficulty be deposed and that attempt to depose him would cause unendurable strife, must of necessity be left in possession and obedience must be rendered to him, exactly as obedience must be rendered to emirs Government in these days is a consequence solely of military power, and whoever he may be to whom the holder of military power gives his allegiance, that person is the caliph.[14]

If some time machine could transport us back into earlier centuries, what would they look like to modern eyes? Let us now investigate three presumed models for the Islamic state.

Model I: The Medina "State"

> I came to politics 22 years ago inspired by the dream of Allama Iqbal to make an Islamic welfare state in Pakistan like the state of Medina. Those disparate tribes were welded together to become the leaders of the world.
> — *Prime Minister Imran Khan's inaugural speech, 19 August 2018*

It is widely believed among Muslims that in AD 622 the Prophet of Islam had created a state in Medina which combined the religious with the temporal. After

286 Why Couldn't Pakistan Become an Islamic State?

his migration from Makkah to Medina, he had successfully negotiated an accord with various Jewish and pagan tribes known as the *Misaq-e-Medina*. This was a landmark deal serving imminent needs. Through a process of consultations, the Prophet apportioned various rights and responsibilities upon Muslims, Jews, Christians, and pagans. Thereafter, the bitter intertribal fighting between *Aws* and *Khazraj* of Medina came to an end. While the original document has long been lost, bits and pieces of the *Misaq* have survived in the works of early scholars such as *Sirat-al-Rasool-Allah* by Ibn Ishaq (704–770).[15]

The entity headed by the Prophet had no geographical boundaries. Borders were irrelevant and so where you lived did not matter. Built around a tribal accord, *Misaq-e-Medina*, citizenship required only that an individual submit to the authority of the Holy Prophet (PBUH). Perhaps anticipating that his followers would someday spread beyond the oases of Makkah and Medina, he very wisely left unspecified which territories constitute *dar-ul-Islam*. The modern national state assumes defined boundaries. This raises the vexing question: how then can one use the term Medina "state"? Momentarily setting aside this question, how was this entity run and what rules defined it?

Dr. Tahir-ul-Qadri, a Canadian-Pakistani cleric and politician who sporadically engaged in street agitations to overthrow elected governments in Pakistan, and who is a popular Islamic preacher in western countries, wrote his PhD dissertation on the *Misaq*. He claims that the 63 items of this document make it the first written constitution of human history.[16] Qadri's thesis lists and discusses the clauses. They concern the following issues:

1. Settling various blood feuds between tribes; payment of ransoms.
2. Restrictions on killing of believers at the instigation of non-believers.
3. Guaranteeing of life protection for Muslims and Jews.
4. Rules for sanctioning revenge killings.
5. Rules for apportioning of war expenses between Muslims and Jews.
6. Declarations of equality between different Jewish tribes.
7. Prohibition of treachery.
8. Denial of shelter for women (unless agreed to by their families).

Viewed through the prism of history, the accord negotiated by the Holy Prophet was perfectly logical at a time of bitter intertribal wars. On the Arabian peninsula, such issues were then the most important ones of the times and the Holy Prophet's wisdom led him towards the most expeditious solution of local disputes. However, it dealt exclusively with those issues important for the particular tribes involved. The *Misaq* did not go beyond that or attempt to anticipate what the future might bring.

The *Misaq* is silent on issues concerning a modern state. It contains nary a hint of any taxation system or police or army, nor mentions administrative units or jails. It does not offer any concept of territorial governance or defense. Each tribe was expected to follow its customs and traditions. In those days it was assumed

Why Couldn't Pakistan Become an Islamic State? **287**

that intertribal wars would continue forever, and all adult tribal men would take part in defending their tribal interests. The only law prevalent was that of *qisas*, i.e., retaliation. Tribal societies were simple; patronage and family relations were the source of authority, not government. With rules being set into final form when Islam was in its tribal stage, extending these to cover large empires was always fraught with ambiguities and gaping holes.

Although Dr. Qadri would have us believe that the *Misaq* is the first constitution in history, there are big holes in his argument. The obvious one is the total silence on how the state's ruler is to be chosen and what might be legitimate cause for his removal. It does not specify the limits of the ruler's powers or that of the *shura* (consultative body). Did the *shura* have the necessary power to choose a caliph? To overrule or dismiss him? Would there be an executive, judiciary, or government ministries, and what would their functions be? How would the *shura* be chosen? It is therefore hard to accept that the *Misaq* is a document relevant to the running of a state, particularly in modern times. At best, Medina was only a proto-state and the *Misaq* covered only matters that were immediately important to establishing the Holy Prophet's rule.

The absence of guidelines meant that the death of the Holy Prophet – who, according to Sunni doctrine, did not specify either his successor or even a procedure for determining one – created an enduring schism on the question of who would succeed him as the next leader of the faithful. The first four caliphs were companions of the Holy Prophet: Abu Bakr (632–634), Omar (634–644), Osman (644–656), and lastly, Ali (656–661), the Prophet's son-in-law and a first cousin. The selection of the second and third caliphs was done largely by their dying predecessors according to tribal law. Only the first – Abu Bakr – died a natural death. Three of the four rightly guided caliphs were assassinated, including one (Osman) who was brutally lynched by a mob while he was reading the Qur'an. This suggests the lack of internal consensus even among those who had been close to the Holy Prophet and an unstable political order.

The procedural vacuum led to bitter power struggle within – the political establishment of the time had come apart. Thousands of Muslims were killed at the hands of fellow Muslims in two bloody civil wars of Jamal and Siffin within twenty-five years of the death of the Prophet. The tragedy of Karbala, which followed the succession by Yazid, created the enduring division between Sunni and Shia Islam, responsible for much of the blood that flows in internecine wars today. Yazid was elected by a tribal dynastic tradition, rather than consensus. For Sunnis, Yazid was just another caliph. But for the Shia, the very mention of his name invites angry (and sometimes extreme) reaction.

The *Misaq* is quoted by Qadri as the basis of an Islamic system of justice. But justice is an ever-evolving concept in every culture and religion. What it contains is no longer relevant to the modern world of jurisprudence.

Take slavery. Two thousand years ago Aristotle argued that some individuals and races are "natural slaves" better enslaved than left free. In fact until two hundred years ago, socially respectable Americans were slave owners with the kinder ones treating their slaves better. But slave owning is now viewed everywhere as utterly abhorrent. Among today's Muslims, apart from Da'esh and Boko Haram and a few others, no one defends slavery. Countries legally forbid it even if slaves are to be treated extremely well. In Pakistan too, owning slaves is a criminal offense. Pakistani law also makes it illegal to barter women as goods or as booty. Owning another human being was considered okay once, but today it is not acceptable anymore, anywhere, and under any circumstance.

The notion of egalitarianism has evolved as well. Nearly all societies now accept or at least give lip service to the idea that all people are equal before the law. Limited to men at first, it was extended later to include women as well. In 2009, Pakistan legally recognized transgender as a separate category; in 2018 some transgender candidates ran for elections, albeit unsuccessfully.

Blood money, common in earlier times, also takes on a very different flavor. Pakistanis were outraged when a grinning young man Sharukh Jatoi emerged from jail and gave a thumbs-up after murdering 20-year-old Shahzeb Khan in cold blood after a fight. Jatoi's wealthy parents had purchased his pardon through *diyyat*, most likely by pressuring Khan's family. Months earlier, CIA contractor Raymond Davis had been released after the families of the two men he had killed were paid $2.4 million as blood money.[17] In present times, it has become fairly common for the rich and influential to purchase pardons – including for heinous crimes – since under Islamic law those committing them have harmed the families but not the state. This has opened the doors to arm-twisting the survivors into an agreement.

The world of yesterday and the world of today bear no comparison. One marvels at the Holy Prophet's sagacity in negotiating a better deal for all warring Arabian tribes. Still, we should appreciate just how different the world has become from those times. The combined population of Makkah and Medina was less than Kharadar's, a typical Karachi neighborhood. The state was not under a loan of $180 billion, did not have a burgeoning population, there were no electrical power shortages or compelling issues of joblessness, urban development, housing, transport, water, sanitation, money-laundering, or health and education that we face today. Joblessness and lack of housing were nonissues; air pollution hadn't yet been conceived and white-collar crime was awaiting invention centuries later. No police or standing army existed in the Medina state. There were no jails.

Model II: Maududi's Islamic State

Maulana Abul Ala Maududi (1903–1979), whose life trajectory and political role as an ideologue we have already encountered earlier, was perhaps the most influential among 20th century Islamic scholars in creating the notion of an Islamic state.[18] Paradoxically, in the years before Partition, he had argued against a state with defined borders but, threatened by isolation and irrelevance, he eventually threw his lot in with those who chose to migrate to Pakistan. After that he did

Why Couldn't Pakistan Become an Islamic State? **289**

not again question the need for Pakistan but contended that Muslims throughout the world were one single nation, and they would have to seize political power if they were to lead lives of piety.[19] This explains why after his works were translated into Arabic, his insistence that Islam demands a single global Islamic state resonated across the Middle East.

Maududi's is a major theoretical attempt to unite state with religion in which there can be no separation between *deen* (faith) and *dunya* (worldly matters). Islam, he says, cannot be practiced only through prayer, contemplation, and fasting alone. He was, in fact, openly contemptuous of those who regarded piety as a goal in itself. This, he said, amounts to mere self-gratification. Instead, his goal was to fuse religion with politics; to create the scaffoldings of a state that would enforce Islamic principles as he saw them. Irfan Ahmad argues that for Maududi,

> The state became central to Islamism not because of theology. Rather, the configuration of modern political formations – particularly the unprecedented interventionist role of the modern state in everyday life – catalysed the state to become central in Islamist thought. In a context where the colonial Indian state had begun to impact deeply on individual and collective lives, Maududi interpreted Islam to equate it with the state.[20]

Maududi says political power is what really matters. The only credible means of making Muslims lead Islamic lives is to have religious authority lie with the state. This would therefore have to be a cultural and ethical entity as well as political and administrative, and would enforce that which is enjoined by Islam. It would stand in opposition to western cultural values. Rahman points to the frequent use of the word *taghut* by Maududi: "any form of rule, whether Western democracy, communism, fascism, or kingship, is a revolt against this principle and is called *taghut*".[21] Maududi heaps contempt upon those who have surrendered to western supremacy: "those Muslims who pride themselves as modern. They are breathless in their praise of every new fad of the *farangis* (foreigners). They ape their dress, mannerisms, food and drink, salutations, and even copy their names. They hate anything to do with the faith and run after western ideas".[22]

Maududi defines carefully what the ideal state should be. In particular, how *zimmis* (non-Muslims) would fare. They may, he says, continue to live in an Islamic state, but they would be subject to restrictions:

> In their own towns and cities zimmis are allowed to do so (practice their religion) with the fullest freedom. In purely Muslim areas, however, an Islamic government has full discretion to put such restrictions on their practices as it deems necessary.[23]

The non-Muslim would have to pay *jizya*, literally meaning penalty. This is a protection tax levied on *zimmis* living under Islamic regimes affirming that their

290   Why Couldn't Pakistan Become an Islamic State?

legal status is not that of a full citizen. Maududi states that "acceptance of the jizya establishes the sanctity of their lives and property, and thereafter neither the Islamic state, nor the Muslim public have any right to violate their property, honor or liberty".[24] Maududi emphasizes that *jizya* is a symbol of humiliation and submission because *zimmis* should not be regarded as full-fledged citizens of the Islamic state even if they are natives to the country. In support of his exegesis, he cites Qur'anic verses:

> Qur'an 9.05: When the sacred months are past [in which a truce had been in force between the Muslims and their enemies], kill the idolaters wherever you find them, and seize them, besiege them and lie in wait for them in every place of ambush; but if they repent, pray regularly and give the alms tax, then let them go their way, for God is forgiving, merciful.

He also quotes:

> Qur'an 9.29: Fight those who do not believe in God or the Last Day, and who do not forbid what has been forbidden by God and His Messenger [Muhammad], and those among the People of the Book who do not acknowledge the religion of truth until they pay tribute [jizya], after they have been brought low.

Zimmis, says Maududi, may not build new churches, temples, or synagogues. However, they are allowed to renovate old churches or houses of worship provided they do not add any new construction. "Old churches" are those which existed prior to Islamic conquests and are included in a peace accord by Muslims. Construction of any church, temple, or synagogue in the Arab Peninsula (Saudi Arabia) is prohibited. It is the land of the Prophet and only Islam should prevail there. Yet, Muslims, if they wish, are permitted to demolish all non-Muslim houses of worship in any land they conquer.

To be fair to Maududi, one must note that he calls for every state to be ruled by a religion even if that religion is the wrong one. Summoned before the 1954 Justice Munir Commission on the anti-Ahmadi riots of Punjab in 1953, Maududi was questioned about his advocacy of an Islamic state in Pakistan:[25]

> Q.—Will you have any objection if the Muslims are treated under that form of Government as *malishes* or *shudras* under the law of Manu?
> A.—No.
> Q.—If we have this form of Islamic Government in Pakistan, will you permit Hindus to base their Constitution on the basis of their own religion?
> A.—Certainly. I should have no objection even if the Muslims of India are treated in that form of Government as *shudras* and *malishes* and Manu's laws are applied to them, depriving them of all share in the Government and the rights of a citizen. In fact such a state of affairs already exists in India.

Why Couldn't Pakistan Become an Islamic State?   **291**

It is of interest to note that Maudui supported democracy as a concept. Indeed, the Jamaat-e-Islami boasts of being the only party in Pakistani that actually votes its leaders into power. But no more than a single political party would be allowed, and only that which swears to enhance the Islamic way of life. Sharia would be the law of the land. Dissent would be permitted against the government but not against the state. This would be a democracy very different from that generally understood. Vali Nasr comments:

> In Mawdudi's writings, therefore, democracy was merely an adjective used to define the otherwise undefinable virtues of the Islamic state. The state was defined as democratic because it was an ideal state. Mawdudi used the term democratic to express the virtues of the Islamic state and embellish it because in Western political thought the term had positive connotations. Mawdudi later featured democracy in his discussions as a concern he had to contend with before the Islamic state was established…he had to deal with democratic rights because Muslims were concerned with them, especially once critics began to point to the authoritarian tendencies that were implicit in Mawdudi's views on social organization.[26]

Maududi's Islamic state does not permit birth control, bank interest, and mixing of men and women. No room is left for human volition and legislation since all legislative functions vest in God. Lack of choice is logical because, in this worldview, Islam is about everything: economics, science, politics, health, psychology, and sociology. The only function left for Muslims lies in their observance of God-given edicts and laws. In effect, Allah purchases the believer's life for which he will be reimbursed once he enters paradise.

Socialism and communism are greater threats than Christianity or the capitalist West, as Maududi saw it. In fact the horror of socialism – which he interpreted as equivalent to godlessness – shaped his attitudes towards economic issues. Using the logic he had used to defend the hugely wealthy Nizam of Hyderabad against the Hindu insurgent poor, he felt that God had sanctioned inequality on earth. This would be made up for in the afterlife. Private property was sanctioned in Islam and attempts at land reform in Punjab, he argued, were un-Islamic. He also reacted against the mobilization of workers against capitalism. In the 1970s, the Jamaat was therefore aligned against labor unions until it became clear that this strategy was a self-defeating one; thereafter, it did its best to seize the leadership of unions for its own members.

In electoral terms, Maududi's Jamaat has never done well in Pakistani politics. It has therefore had to ally itself with those who actually wield political power and influence. As a member of the anti-Bhutto alliance in 1977, it was welcomed by General Zia-ul-Haq as a close ally and was given the most valuable opportunity in its history of furthering its agenda. Then, following 9/11, it gained influence by joining an alliance of extreme right-wing parties, the Muttahid Majlis-e-Amal (MMA). After the 2013 elections, it allied itself with

292 Why Couldn't Pakistan Become an Islamic State?

Imran Khan's Pakistan Tehreek-e-Insaf (PTI) in the KPK province. But in the 2018 elections, the Jamaat was completely routed, winning not a single seat in the National Assembly. Islamic parties even further to its right made huge gains, while the Jamaat actually regressed.

Is it then a waste of time to spend time understanding Maududi's ideology when, in fact, his political party has never had mass appeal? The answer is, no. Pakistan's steady march towards greater religiosity owes much to the Jamaat and its influence upon the public's mind. It is through the power of Maududi's systematic exposition of ideas – and their dissemination through an education system captured by the Jamaat during the Zia-ul-Haq years – that the Jamaat's success ought to be measured. Other right-wing Islamic parties may garner more votes by appealing to particular constituencies. But they lack a coherent system of thought. In contrast, Maududi was able to plant seeds that formed the worldview of his party's members which they now propagate everywhere. This is what makes a real difference. As Gramsci said, the real battleground is inside the mind:

> Ideas and opinions are not spontaneously "born" in each individual brain: they have had a centre of formation, or irradiation, of dissemination, of persuasion – a group of men, or a single individual even, which has developed them and presented them in the political form of current reality.[27]

Model III: Taliban Islamic State

By faith, the Taliban are Deobandis, a strand of Islam that originates from a Hanafi *madrassa* founded in 1866 in the town of Deoband, India. After 1947, two strands emerged from just one. The Indian version accommodates secularism, while Pakistani Deobandis fiercely oppose it. Following the 1979 Soviet invasion, petrodollars harnessed the latter in the service of the United States, Saudi Arabia, and Pakistan. *Madrassas* in Pakistan churned out the *mujahideen* who ultimately defeated the Soviets.

Officially, under the U.S.-backed government of Ashraf Ghani, Afghanistan was called the Islamic Republic of Afghanistan. The Taliban captured Kabul on 15 August 2021 but waited another four days before renaming it the Islamic Emirate of Afghanistan; 19 August was the date when Britain withdrew from Afghanistan in 1919.

What is the vision for Afghanistan? Even though much time has gone by, only a little has been decided. The victors have specified only that it will be governed by a ruling council. The movement's supreme leader, Hibatullah Akhundzada, remains in overall charge but only rarely makes a public appearance. In the days after taking over, a Taliban spokesman ruled out an electoral democracy:

> There will be no democratic system at all because it does not have any base in our country. We will not discuss what type of political system we will apply in Afghanistan because it is clear. It is Sharia law and that is it.[28]

The earlier way of ruling through the traditional council, known as the loya jirga, has been rejected.

Reflecting the tribal nature of Afghan society, the Taliban version of the Islamic state is insufficiently imagined and the least theorized. Its central premise seems to reside in the Qur'anic injunction: *amr bil ma'roof wa nahi 'anil munkar* (promote that which is good and approved, and forbid that which is evil and disapproved). The promised Islamic state was little more than a revival in some slightly softened form of the older Islamic Emirate of Afghanistan, such as had existed for five years, 1996–2001. Headed by Mullah Omar, the Taliban emphasized a strongly tribal version of Islam with emphasis upon its punitive aspects. This included stoning adulterers to death, amputation of limbs for theft, public floggings, closure of girls schools, restriction of hospitals to men only, extreme limitations on the mobility of women, and destruction of the 2000-year-old Bamiyan Buddhas. Such actions had never been experienced in the living memory of Afghans.

A rare glimpse into the Taliban mindset before their final victory in 2021 came from a study[29] in which members of the Taliban's political commission were interviewed, both directly and indirectly through intermediaries, by the Center for International Cooperation at New York University. At the outset, the study recommends caution:

> the views in this paper should not be seen as representative of "the Taliban"—the movement is too disparate and fragmented (both horizontally and vertically) for there to be any unity of thought beyond foundational issues like the presence of foreign troops.

Indeed, going through the Q&A, one sees commonality on only two issues: that the United States must leave immediately and that the new state should be based around Islam. The latter says little because even under the current constitution, no law may contradict sharia. So why was the Ashraf Ghani government insufficiently Islamic? No coherent answers were given. The Taliban's emphasis was entirely cultural: opposition to western dress, education, and language; insistence on "morality" and importance of the kameez and turban; regularity of prayers and fasting; etc.

Although the pre-victory Taliban had declared that Afghanistan state would be sharia-based, shortly after the takeover optimists predicted that it would be less repressive this time around. This speculation turned out to be unjustified. In many places women are banned from bazars without a male escort. The beard requirement has been re-imposed in captured areas during the war years.[30] Barber shops are closed down or closely monitored. Even more seriously, education for girls has ground to a near halt. Armed men are often sent into girls' classrooms to force staff into inspecting girls' bodies for signs of puberty. If found, they would be disqualified from further schooling. In December 2022, the Taliban announced a blanket ban on women in higher education. The Taliban have been encouraged by similar assaults on women's rights in Iran and Turkey. Pakistan, which has also seen a slide

294 Why Couldn't Pakistan Become an Islamic State?

downward, has resolutely refused to condemn such actions. Unable to see beyond tribal horizons, the hope of a modern economy is receding. Hunger is widespread with nine out of ten households having insufficient food. Desperate Afghans are reported to have sold their children or their children's organs.

Presently there are still some unanswered questions: how will the Taliban government organize its future administrative functions? Is narcotics production to be regularized into the economy or forbidden? How will valuable mineral deposits be handled and regulated? Will the rank and file obey the Taliban high command?

Perhaps the most difficult question – one that may eventually split the movement – is the question of succession. There is no procedure by which the *emir* of the Taliban is selected, only the requirement that he should be a pious Muslim man belonging to the Hanafi school of thought. Mullah Omar's death in 2013 and the killing of his successor Mullah Mansour in a U.S. drone strike in 2016, sparked off power struggles within. Nevertheless, faced with an external enemy, the Taliban restitched themselves together. What will happen now that the external adversary has been vanquished cannot be foretold.

Forty years ago the United States worked hard to bring down the Soviet Union in Afghanistan. After losing much blood and treasure, it withdrew, leaving behind a country in utter chaos and its reputation in tatters. Over the next few years we shall get to see whether Islamic Emirate 2.0 will result in Da'esh, Al-Qaida, or other such groups getting a second chance. The assassination in August 2022 of Al-Qaeda leader Ayman al-Zawahri in Kabul by an American drone suggests that the romance of the Taliban with Al-Qaida is not yet over.[31]

The Caliphate's Undying Appeal

On 3 March 1924 Turkey's Kemal Atatürk abolished the Ottoman caliphate. This ended a structure of Islamic governance that combined religious as well as political authority that had emerged and evolved over the previous 1300 years. India's Muslims, helped along by Mahatma Gandhi, protested. They were unsuccessful. One scholar of the time regretfully described what happened subsequently as the "cutting up of Muslim lands into measly little pieces called nations". Dorsey[32] notes that Jordanian ruler Abdullah I bin al-Hussein gloated,

> The Turks have committed suicide. They had in the Caliphate one of the greatest political forces, and have thrown it away... I feel like sending a telegram thanking Mustapha Kemal. The Caliphate is an Arab institution. The Prophet was an Arab, the Koran is in Arabic, the Holy Places are in Arabia and the Khalif should be an Arab of the tribe of Khoreish...Now the Khaliphate has come back to Arabia.[33]

But Arab states showed little enthusiasm for reviving the caliphate. Though a staunch Islamist who is seeking to expand Turkish influence across the Middle East, Tayyip Erdogan has not proposed any such idea either. In 2014, Abu Bakr al-Baghdadi, the leader of the militant group Islamic State of Iraq (ISI), also known as *Dawlat al Islami fil Iraq wa Shaam*, commonly referred to as *Da'esh*, declared himself caliph. The experiment ended tragically, but Da'esh lives on.

Although the caliphate does not have a Qur'anic basis, historically Muslims have generally associated it with a political and religious community without national borders, ruled by a male Sunni caliph who would command the allegiance of the entire *ummah*. However, such unity is unrooted in history and long precedes the advent of western imperialism. It can be seen from the fact that soon after the birth of Islam two Muslim dynasties – the Umayyads and Abbasids – claimed legitimacy and leadership of the Muslims at the same time. Later, the Safavids of Persia fought the Ottomans of Turkey for the caliphate. Theoretically, as the head of state, the caliph would govern as prescribed by the sharia and would command allegiance from all living Muslims as their supreme religious and political authority. Al-Mawardi described a caliph as God's viceregent on earth, and, "a leader through whom he [Allah] provided for the deputyship of the Prophet".[34]

In an unexpected turn at the start of the 21st century, the idea of the caliphate caught the imagination of millions of Muslims the world over. According to a 2006 Gallup survey of Muslims living in Egypt, Morocco, Indonesia, and Pakistan, two-thirds of respondents said they supported the goal of "unifying all Islamic countries" into a new caliphate.[35]

Why a 21st-century caliphate? Nostalgia for past glories and wonderful achievements, both real and imagined, lies at the heart of this fascination. Most wonders of Muslim glory are associated with one or the other caliph. Muslim achievements over the last several hundred years having become ever sparser, the appeal of the past is vastly magnified. Cherished both as memory and ideal, the caliphate is seen through the prism of centuries with all rough edges smoothed over. Movements such as the *Hizb-ut-Tahrir* (HUT), or the Liberation Party, which agitate for a global caliphate, draw strength from the fact that most Muslims across the world think of themselves as Muslims first, and then as citizens of their respective countries. A Pew Global Attitudes Survey found that even in Turkey – an officially secular Muslim country – 43% of Turks consider themselves Muslim first and only 29% as Turks first. A majority of Muslims in six countries want Islam to be part of political life.[36] While contemplating Muslim political opinion about a caliphate, one is confronted by a bewildering range of facts:

- Many Islamically motivated movements across the world today seek the creation of an Islamic state out of the conviction that they can truly practice their faith only in such a state. Among them are Da'esh, Taliban, Boko Haram, Al-Shabab, the Muslim Brotherhood, etc. Syed Ali Shah Geelani, a recently deceased Kashmiri leader and member of the Jamaat-e-Islami, put it succinctly: it's as difficult for a Muslim to live in a non-Muslim society as it is for a fish to live out of the water.

- Most Muslims think that a modern caliphate uniting all Muslims would be a good thing, will embody within it justice and fair play, and think it is sanctioned by the Qur'an and Sunnah. However, they see little chance of it becoming reality. Even those who strongly support a sharia-based state would not like to be judged by those presently in charge of the state.[37]
- Most Muslims are deeply upset when Westerners and other non-Muslims criticize the politics of global Islam or the goal of a modern caliphate.
- Most Muslims have little idea of what a caliphate might mean in practical terms. In today's world, the state and society are expected to provide a wide range of public goods – public education, healthcare, etc. But there is no discussion of what would be involved in trying to govern 1.6 billion Muslims today in a caliphate.
- Most Sunni Muslims do not support Taliban, Da'esh, Boko Haram, Al-Shabab, Hamas, and other extremist organizations. Shias, of course, are prime targets for elimination by these organizations. And yet there is no sign that Sunnis are willing to cast militant extremists out of their fold and term them non-Muslims, although they have done so for other "deviant" groups like the Ahmadis.
- In an ideal world, Muslims would be ruled by an Islamic government headed by the caliph in accordance with the sharia. Some newly emerged political groupings, such as the HUT, are indeed trying to bring the Muslim world under one umbrella. However, apart from Britain, HUT has not made much progress elsewhere.

How is one to imagine a modern caliphate? Regardless of who becomes caliph, there is the question of what kind of rules will prevail. How would the legislation impact upon the Muslim population, which is made up of diverse Muslim sects? And, since modern Muslim states have sizeable non-Muslim populations, what could they expect? The only organization that seems to have addressed these questions is the HUT. It calls for imposing *jizya* on non-Muslims and barring them from holding political office, emphasizes unification of all Muslim countries through jihad, and wants Arabic to be the official language of the caliphate. Once having established the caliphate, it will expand into non-Muslim states through "invitation" and military force. For having instigated coups and rebellions, HUT is banned in many Muslim countries as well as in the West.

The *Ummah* and Pan-Islamism

The *ummah* is a concept that refers to the Muslim religious community and is as old as Islam itself. Most Muslims appear willing to believe that this entity is real and somehow encompasses all 1.6 billion Muslims throughout the world. This is in spite of most having to live in 46 Muslim-majority nation-states with western-styled constitutions, each with defined borders that may be crossed

Why Couldn't Pakistan Become an Islamic State? **297**

only by individuals bearing valid passports and visas. For the ordinary unskilled Pakistani and Bangladeshi worker who is seeking a visa to Saudi Arabia or a Gulf State this is no small problem. The difficult process of going to another Muslim country is a tedious and difficult process that may involve risking one's life savings and even one's life. It is also likely that the worker will be exploited and abused by his Arab Muslim employers, but he will take more abuse from them than if they were non-Muslim. Yet this severely exploited worker, if asked, is still likely to believe that there exists a unified *ummah* and some form of a global Muslim community – the Muslim world.

A recent book, *The Idea of the Muslim World – A Global Intellectual History* by an author of Turkish origin, Cemil Aydin, makes the case that although the concept of *ummah* is old, the idea of the "Muslim world" is actually a colonial construct which began to develop in the 19th century and achieved full flower in the 1870s.[38] The geopolitical idea of the Muslim world is not because Muslims have had a shared history in past centuries or because of some immutable ideology. Rather, it developed when Muslim societies encountered European empires. At that moment, about thirty dynasties ruled Muslim societies. Pan-Islamic thought grew out of new transportation and communication technologies such as steamships and the telegraph. These fostered unprecedented levels of connection among Muslims, creating the concept of a Muslim world which, through sheer numbers, could confront European racialism. Aydin remarks that Muslim leaders and thinkers of the 19th and early 20th centuries were not, for the most part, anti-imperialists. Instead they sought fair treatment from the four major European empires: British, Dutch, French, and Russian. Muslim solidarity emerged as a political response, not a religious one.

Aydin's claim tallies well with our earlier discussions in the context of British India. In Chapter Three we had encountered the archetypical modernist, Sir Syed Ahmad Khan, and studied his political and theological ideas in some detail. He, like several others – Syed Ameer Ali, Muhammad Abduh, Rashid Rida, and Muhammad Asad – sought to create a response to modernity brought in by colonial rule, not to fight it. In doing so, these modernists sought to create political unity among Muslims and so created ab initio the notion of a Muslim world that was united from Morocco to Indonesia through common values and a distinct civilization. This was intended to reject European discourses of Muslim inferiority. Pan-Islamism, it was hoped, would empower Muslims against racist imperialist discourses that held them to be inferior.

In colonial India, the man who lit the fire for pan-Islamism was Allama Iqbal, covered extensively in Chapter Four. His poetry put "warmth in the Muslim's blood, a raging tempest in his soul". Iqbal is at his best when he calls for a unity that Islam had so far never seen. He had to omit or gloss over the bitter internecine battles from the early days of Islam, through the Umayyad and Abbasid periods, among Muslim rulers in India, blood feuds between Mughal brothers, and all that might discolor a seraphic past. In verse after verse, flaying the divisions he sees as spurious, Iqbal repeats his message of oneness:

298 Why Couldn't Pakistan Become an Islamic State?

You are Syed, Mirza, and perhaps Afghan too
یوں تو سید بھی ہو، مرزا بھی ہو، افغان بھی ہو

Shall you not say that you are Mussulman too
تم سبھی کچھ ہو، بتاؤ تو مسلمان بھی ہو

Curiously, the darkish Bengali gets no mention. Nor are the Javanese, Malays, or Sudanese mentioned anywhere in his poetry. Islam is Arab Islam for Iqbal, no other. He says one must be aware of the white man's impositions of language, culture, and dress – and reject them:[39]

You look like a Christian and behave like a Hindu
وضع میں تم ہو نصاریٰ تو تمدن میں ہنود

Mussulman sunk so low – even a Jew would be ashamed
یہ مسلماں ہیں جنہیں دیکھ کے شرمائیں یہود

Clearly, as we can see, Iqbal was a pan-Islamist. But let us also note that he did not join the Khilafat Movement and, in fact, derided the Ottomans for "being a shame to the Muslims" while expressing his admiration for Mustafa Kamal (that changed later). His lack of enthusiasm for the caliphate is probably shared by the majority of Muslims today as well. Unification efforts are widely feared; nationalism trumps pan-Islamism.

While Muslims are politically fractured, events have shown that they come together when there is a perceived insult to Islam – as in the Charlie Hebdo case in France. The level of outrage when Muslims are hurt, if it occurs at all, is far less. So, for example, the persecution of Muslims – as with the Uyghurs of China or the U.S. invasion of Iraq – has failed in getting Muslims to agree with each other. Worse, the *ummah* has been at war with itself. What other way is there to describe the brutal bloodletting by Muslims of Muslims in Syria, Iraq, Libya, Yemen, Afghanistan, Turkey, and, of course, Pakistan. To be fair, the *ummah* has not mattered for a long time to the governments or peoples of Muslim lands. State-to-state relations among Muslim states have been astonishingly independent of religious identity. They have depended instead upon perceived self-interest, domestic politics, and the whims of rulers. This is not a new phenomenon.

We need only look at the evidence from the 19th century onwards. In the 1840s and 1850s the Ottomans, despite being sworn enemies of Russians, did not help Caucasian Muslims against Russian imperial expansion. In fact the Ottomans and the British cooperated with each other in the Crimean War, 1853–1856. Nor did they support the 1857 uprising of Muslims in India against the British. More to the point: Pakistan was created on a religious premise. But, in the days of the Suez Crisis of 1956, its position was ambiguous. It refused to side with Gamal Abdul Nasser after he nationalized the Suez Canal and threw out the British. On the other hand, India was active in the Non-Aligned Movement, fully pro-Arab, and loud in support of liberating Palestine. To show gratitude, King Saud bin Abdulaziz paid a state visit to India and declared that Indian Muslims were being treated well.

There was outrage across Pakistan. Newspapers exploded in anger when Jawaharlal Nehru, on his return visit to Riyadh, was greeted by the King and

Why Couldn't Pakistan Become an Islamic State? **299**

with street banners in Riyadh bearing the slogan *Rasul-ul-Salam* (messenger of peace). Karachi-based *Dawn* had an editorial on 1 December 1956 that bitterly criticized the Arabs and "Nasser's hatred of Pakistan, and love of Bharat and its Nehru". It went on to suggest that such sensate bias and blind prejudice "may well be examined by psychiatrists". In other words, the Arab world's greatest hero of the moment was denounced as crazy.

Today, Pakistan has disputes with both its Muslim neighbors, Afghanistan and Iran. The borders are presently in the process of being fenced and electrified. Iran and Pakistan occasionally lob artillery shells over to the other. Pakistan Air Force jets brought down an Iranian drone in 2019.[40] Ironically, Pakistan has excellent relations with one of its neighbors – China, a communist state that is "reeducating" Muslims and has banned the beard and burqa in its only Muslim-dominated province. On the other hand, India has good relations with both Iran and Afghanistan. And, India's trade with China far exceeds Pakistan's trade with China.

It is not just Pakistan. The Muslim monarchies of Saudi Arabia and Qatar, both Wahhabi, were practically at war with each other. Tiny Qatar, said the Saudis, is acting too big for its boots and cannot conduct its own foreign policy. Qatar dismissed the Saudi–UAE demand to close down Al-Jazeera, the Arab world's only independent news source. In response, all Qataris and their families, as well as 15,000 dancing Qatari camels, were expelled from Saudi Arabia.[41] A conference held in 2021 may have decreased tensions between Gulf Cooperation Council states but equally increased their tension with Iran.

What was especially galling to Pakistan was that in 2017, Saudi Arabia's highest civilian award was conferred upon Hindu fundamentalist Narendra Modi by King Salman. The Saudi King left Kashmir and pellet guns used on young protesters unmentioned. Saudi Arabia's war on Yemen, which was once headed by Pakistan's retired General Raheel Sharif, showcased the emptiness of the *ummah* notion.[42] Directed against one of the world's poorest Muslim countries, so far it has killed around 20,000 Muslims and wounded over 60,000. Most casualties have resulted from air strikes of the Saudi-led multinational coalition. Pakistan has shown little concern. No TV news report or evening talk show in Pakistan discussed the Yemen war.

Ending Israeli occupation of Palestine was once the *ummah*'s grandest cause that cut through the Shia–Sunni divide. But now Saudi Arabia is fast nearing rapprochement with Israel, while UAE has already recognized it. Both countries see Iran as the greater enemy. After the failed Arab Spring, General Sisi's Egypt and the Gulf's monarchies fear Iran as an insurrectionary power and prefer working with Israel. Palestine is not mentioned; Israel's savage attacks on Gaza are suppressed by Arab media. To complicate everything, Arab states have increased pressure upon Pakistan to recognize Israel and threatened to cut off visas for Pakistanis. Yet, in seeking to please powerful Arabs who hunt an endangered species of bird, the Houbara Bustard, Pakistan's officials bend over backward and flout the country's environmental laws with impunity.[43]

300 Why Couldn't Pakistan Become an Islamic State?

Where does this leave the Organization of Islamic Cooperation (OIC), whose job is to bring together and represent the *ummah*? Based in Saudi Arabia, it has 57 member states and calls itself "the collective voice of the Muslim world". But the world's powerful Muslim states are fighting for geopolitical influence, not for Islam or Muslims. The OIC has had nothing to say about wars that have consumed Syria, Iraq, Libya, or Yemen. Nor is it relevant to any other conflict between Muslim states or that within them. It has yet to give a single cent to desperate refugees who, instead, must rely on the West. Pakistan bought into the OIC fantasy early on, but the euphoria of the 1974 Lahore meeting organized by Zulfikar Ali Bhutto has gone with the wind. What's left is the magnificent flag-adorned building on Constitution Avenue in Islamabad that serves as the headquarters of COMSTECH, the highest scientific body of the OIC, for which Pakistan pays the lion's share of its operating expenses.

If Muslim states have paid no attention to the *ummah*, non-state actors have paid even less. They have slaughtered tens of thousands of co-religionists. The Afghan Taliban and the Pakistani Taliban are like two wings of the same bird. One kills Afghan Muslims, the other kills Pakistani Muslims. One found shelter in Pakistan, the other in Afghanistan. Da'esh seems to be everywhere and kills with even less concern. There is no sign any of them will fade away soon.

Bitter fratricidal wars rage in many Muslim countries such as Pakistan, Iraq, Syria, and Afghanistan where the ordinary Muslim lives in fear from day to day, anticipating attacks from Muslims belonging to a different sect. Mosques and imambargahs have therefore to be protected from attacks by co-religionists. Nonetheless, when myths achieve control over minds, objective realities become secondary and the notion of *ummah* remains intact. Most Muslims still feel emotionally connected to each other.

What Created Political Islam?

Political Islam does not owe to one single reason. Certainly, there was a time when it did not exist. Looking back to the mid-20th century, one cannot see a single Muslim nationalist leader who was a fundamentalist. Turkey's Kemal Atatürk, Algeria's Ahmed Ben Bella, Indonesia's Sukarno, Pakistan's Muhammad Ali Jinnah, Egypt's Gamal Abdel Nasser, and Iran's Mohammed Mosaddeq – all sought to organize their societies on the basis of secular values. They were part of the larger anticolonial nationalist current across the Third World. With Muslims and Arabs included, a nascent nationalism sought to control and use national resources for domestic benefit. The conflict with the West's greed was inevitable. The imperial interests of Britain, and later that of the United States, feared independent nationalism. Anyone willing to collaborate was preferred, even the ultraconservative Islamic regime of Saudi Arabia. In time, as the Cold War pressed in, nationalism became intolerable. In 1953, Mosaddeq of Iran was overthrown in a CIA coup, replaced by Mohammad Reza Shah Pahlavi. Britain

Why Couldn't Pakistan Become an Islamic State? **301**

targeted Abdel Nasser. Sukarno was replaced by Suharto after a bloody coup that left more than half a million dead.

The failure of the nationalist regimes was not solely because of imperial machinations. Many secular rulers had inherited the mantle from their former colonial masters. Adopting shallow Westernized ways, they failed massively to fulfill the expectations of populations just released from the yoke of colonial rule. Corruption, cronyism, disconnection with the masses, denial of social justice, and extreme income inequalities led to unstable political systems in many countries.

Faced with internal failure, manifest decline from a peak of greatness many centuries ago, afflicted by cultural dislocation in the age of globalisation, and the defeat of nationalist forces, many Muslim societies started to turn inwards. Failure after failure left a vacuum that Islamic religious movements quickly filled. These spread from Algeria to Indonesia with the Jamaat-e-Islami (Indian subcontinent), Ikhwan-ul-Muslimeen (Egypt), and Hamas (Gaza) being examples. But they achieved limited traction in an environment that preferred modernity to tradition, progress to history.

It was the simultaneous coupling of internal failure and imperial interests that gave birth to political Islam. Had the U.S. not cultivated Islamists as allies against communism during the Cold War, history could have been very different. But things came to a head with the Soviet invasion of Afghanistan in 1979. The American strategy for defeating the 'Evil Empire' required marshalling the forces of Islam from every part of the world. With General Zia-ul-Haq as America's foremost ally, and Saudi Arabia as the principal source of funds, the CIA openly recruited Islamic holy warriors from Egypt, Saudi Arabia, Sudan, and Algeria. Radical Islam went into overdrive as its superpower ally and mentor funnelled support to the *mujahideen*. It worked. In 1988, Soviet troops withdrew unconditionally, and the U.S.–Pakistan–Saudi–Egypt alliance emerged victorious. A chapter of history seemed complete, and hubris defined U.S. policy for another two decades. But the true costs of this victory did not take long to become known. Even in the mid-1990s – long before the 9/11 attack on the U.S. – it was clear that the victorious alliance had unwittingly created a genie suddenly beyond its control.

What if Pakistan Becomes an Islamic Sharia State?

Though it is unlikely that Pakistan will fall completely to religious forces, the possibility cannot be ruled out. The Tehrik Labaik Pakistan (TLP) and Tehrik-e-Taliban Pakistan (TTP) are two violent organizations, one Barelvi and the other Deobandi. At daggers drawn, both have mass followings; that of TTP is expected to skyrocket now that the Taliban rule Afghanistan. It has, in fact, accelerated attacks upon Pakistani security forces in 2022–2023. Both TLP and TTP want a sharia state but with their respective versions of sharia. At the very least they will push politics strongly to the right. One therefore needs to ask: what would happen if sharia became the law of the land in Pakistan?

302 Why Couldn't Pakistan Become an Islamic State?

At the very outset, in creating an Islamic sharia state in Pakistan, one would be confronted with the deceptively simple question of who is a Muslim and who is not. I say deceptively because it could not be answered by the exhaustive investigations of a court of inquiry constituted shortly after the anti-Ahmadi riots of Lahore in 1953. Headed by Muhammad Munir, who went on to become Chief Justice of Pakistan, it led to one of the most famous public documents in Pakistan's history, the *Munir Report*.[44] Comprising 387 pages, it was presented in 1954. Referring to the *ulama*'s call for Pakistan to be run as an official Islamic state, and their demand that Ahmadis be declared non-Muslims, the Report sought answers from all parties involved in the riots:

> The question, therefore, whether a person is or is not a Muslim will be of fundamental importance, and it was for this reason that we asked most of the leading *ulama* to give their definition of a Muslim, the point being that if the *ulama* of the various sects believed the Ahmadis to be *kafirs*, they must have been quite clear in their minds not only about the grounds of such belief but also about the definition of a Muslim because the claim that a certain person or community is not within the pale of Islam implies on the part of the claimant an exact conception of what a Muslim is. The result of this part of the inquiry, however, has been anything but satisfactory, and if considerable confusion exists in the minds of our *ulama* on such a simple matter.[45]

Thereafter, the Report records the answers given by various *ulama* to the question posed by the court: What is the definition of a Muslim? At the very end of the answers, the Report draws the following conclusion:

> Keeping in view the several definitions given by the *ulama*, need we make any comment except that no two learned divines are agreed on this fundamental. If we attempt our own definition as each learned divine has done and that definition differs from that given by all others, we unanimously go out of the fold of Islam. And if we adopt the definition given by any one of the *ulama*, we remain Muslims according to the view of that *alim* but *kafirs* according to the definition of everyone else...no two *ulama* have agreed before us as to the definition of a Muslim.[46]

The Munir Report has been extensively discussed by Qasmi who also records the objections of conservatives claiming that the court was biased against religious scholars.[47] They alleged that the government had unfairly used and circulated earlier writings by Allama Iqbal and thus that there was no level playing field. In conservative opinion, Pakistan's modernizing elites had employed state influence to depict the mullah as savage and barbaric, and, "This cultural construct of the mullah – conjuring up images of violence, bigotry and intolerance – was further ideologically appended to writings which discredited mullahism as irrelevant to

Why Couldn't Pakistan Become an Islamic State? **303**

the state and society of Pakistan".[48] The reader can form his own opinion on the matter, but one fact stands out: seven decades after the *Munir Report*, Pakistan still has not formalized the definition of Muslim.

Nevertheless, let us hypothesize what might transpire if Pakistan becomes an Islamic sharia state headed by a caliph.

- For Pakistan's Sunni majority, the choice would be between any one of the four brands of sharia – *Hanafi, Sha'fi, Maliki*, and *Hanbali*. Since there is no pope in Islam, there is just no way of answering which sharia is the right one. If one Sunni faction succeeded in imposing one form of sharia, competing factions could accuse it of heresy or apostasy. Assassinations in Pakistan of *Deobandis* by *Barelvis*, and *Barelvis* by *Deobandis* suggest that this is not mere hypothesis. Will all, or most, Pakistanis ever accept any *amir-ul-mo'mineen* or a caliph? What of the Shias, who reject the very notion of a caliphate and who reject the very notion of sharia? If pressed to the wall, they will likely react as they did in the 1980s by creating militant outfits such as *Sipah-e-Muhammad* and *Sipah-e-Abbas*. Targeted killing of sectarian leaders, bombings of *Imambargahs*, and Sunni mosques had followed subsequently.
- Women would lose all gains made in the last two centuries. Pakistan's Council of Islamic Ideology (CII) has made clear what women should expect under the sharia dispensation.[49] These have included the abolition of an age limit for a girl's marriageability, making child marriages permissible. A man would not need his wife's permission for another marriage, whether that is to be the second, third, or fourth one. The CII declared that Islam had given the woman the right to separate from her husband, but another marriage could not be a valid ground for doing so. It also ruled that DNA is insufficient evidence for a rape. The Pakistani Taliban, who subscribe to a Wahhabi–Deobandi–Salafi understanding of *sharia*, call for forbidding females to leave their houses, be educated, or hold jobs.
- The Islamic penal code will be made mandatory, a part of which includes public decapitation, amputation of limbs, and floggings. Indeed, after every gruesome crime there is no lack of those who demand as deterrence such exemplary punishments and blame the crime onto the present system of justice.
- Non-Muslim minorities would be marginalized, silenced, forced to emigrate, or physically eliminated. Several communities that are currently considered Muslim would see themselves characterized as non-Muslims. The destruction of precious human capital would take many decades to recover from.
- Education would be supervised by the clergy. Giving a foretaste of things to come, religious scholars appointed as members of Imran Khan's committee to implement a new curriculum supervised the content of schoolbooks in all subjects including science.[50] In the name of Islamic morality, they have warned textbook publishers not to print any diagram or sketch in biology textbooks that show human figures "sans clothes".

304 Why Couldn't Pakistan Become an Islamic State?

So far it has been impossible to achieve wide consensus on any significant matter related to governance, taxes, penal code, banking, or economy. In November 2022, the finance minister announced that Pakistan will move towards interest-free banking in accordance with the demand of the Islamic Ideology Council.[51] How this would be done was not explicated. Even sighting of the new moon is contentious.

At best, the caliphate would be a brief, bloody moment in Pakistan's history before some cataclysmic implosion. Any serious move in the direction of a sharia state could lead to civil war. Of course, sharia could be understood very differently as, for example, shown by recent developments in the United Arab Emirates.

Is a Liberal Sharia State Possible?

In the Kingdom of Saudi Arabia, there is no penal or civil code and so judges rule on the basis of sharia, applying their own interpretation to it. The Qur'an and the Sunnah are declared to be the country's constitution. Interpretations are based upon the Hanbali school. Criminal law punishments include public beheading, stoning, amputation, and lashing. Serious criminal offenses can include adultery, apostasy as well as, somewhat curiously, witchcraft, and sorcery.

But some changes to a medieval system are on the horizon. Although the legitimacy of sharia cannot be challenged, the heir apparent to the present king is a reformer who seeks a more uniform interpretation of sharia. Prince Mohammed bin Salman has specified that in the Kingdom "a punishment must be applied only in the presence of a clear Qur'anic stipulation or a *mutawātir hadīth*", i.e., a saying of the Prophet of Islam, transmitted over the centuries through an uninterrupted and numerically significant chain of transmitters.[52] These *hadīths* would be binding, unlike *ahādī hadīths* (i.e., transmitted by single narrators), which become binding only when they are corroborated by Qur'anic verse, and *khabar hadīths* (stories whose core is identical across different versions but that vary in their details and formulation), whose authenticity is doubtful and which therefore cannot be invoked as sources of law, even if they can be useful for personal edification. The truth of a *hadīth* is to be judged by how widespread it is. Significantly, this principle would permit the abolition of stoning to death for adultery since in the Sunnah this punishment is technically based on a saying that is *ahādī* and is therefore not binding. However, the problem of flogging remains. Saudi Arabia may abolish the death penalty for apostasy. There is, however, no scope in the Saudi constitution for any legal system except sharia. How much further liberalization can go is unclear.

Formally, the United Arab Emirates (UAE) is also a country whose socio-political matters are declaredly driven by sharia law. But radical changes have nevertheless been effected. According to an official decree that took effect in November 2020, unmarried men and women may now live together, alcohol restrictions are gone, and honor killings will be judged a crime just as any other.[53]

Why Couldn't Pakistan Become an Islamic State? **305**

These new rules apply equally to expatriates (88%) and UAE citizens (12%), the latter being mostly Sunni Muslims.

Islamic morality interpreted in the usual way has apparently been ripped to shreds in the UAE. In a frankly patriarchal desert culture where local women wear *niqab*, what was unthinkable happened. Still, no internal protest was reported and neighboring countries seemed indifferent. Other Gulf Cooperation Council countries – and even normally hostile Turkey – did not comment. Theocratic Iran, which has killed hundreds of young women and men for fighting against the imposition of hijab, semi-officially admits its alcohol problem and seems resigned. Billboards in Teheran warn against drinking and driving. Saudi Arabia, once a bastion of Sunni conservatism, is following a similar path:

> The public delight is visible everywhere from the capital city to remote rural provinces like Jizan in the south and Tabuk in the north. Teenage Saudi girls scream hysterically at a performance here by the Korean boy band BTS. Young Saudi women with bared faces run a 5K through city streets clad only in short-sleeved T-shirts and tight leggings. Groups of young men and women relax together in Starbucks. Hotels are no longer permitted to ask Saudi couples for proof of marriage at check-in. All this change and more in a society where until very recently women, uniformly clad in floor-length abayas, couldn't exercise, drive or appear in public with men other than close relatives.[54]

As with child-marriage, widow-remarriage, and polygamy, cohabitation will doubtless lead to furious disputes. But no Arab Spring movement is driving cultural liberalization nor is popular democracy on the cards. Unless something happens, dynastic rulers and clerics will continue to rule. Various new top-down changes simply aim at making Arab countries more western tourist- and business-friendly. The opening up to Israel by the UAE undoubtedly plays some part. Such legislative changes freeing cultural behavior are likely to impact society far more than political changes. They bring with them many key questions: what is sinful and improper and what does Islam forbid or permit? Which values are truly permanent and absolute and which must inevitably change with time?

Notions of right and wrong are being turned upside down everywhere. There is, for example, complete acceptance now of television across the Muslim world. Even in Pakistan – a more conservative Islamic country than most – families spend evenings glued to the drawing room TV set. Men with beards and women from Al-Huda casually snap selfies and WhatsApp them around. Yet older citizens cannot forget admonitions that Islam prohibits photography and the strident denunciations of TV as a "shaitani ala" (devil's tool).

Aniconism, or a prohibition in religion of depicting images of all living beings, was considered immutable and absolute by almost all early Islamic religious authorities. Scholars and clerics took as axiomatic that the creation and depiction of living forms is God's prerogative, not to be trespassed upon by artists and painters. So,

306 Why Couldn't Pakistan Become an Islamic State?

although Muslims can rightfully boast of magnificent Islamic architecture such as Taj Mahal and Dome of the Rock, Islamic art was narrowly restricted to decorative figural designs. Mosques and holy places are completely empty of figurative imagery. Aniconism was taken so seriously that – although he later relented – a thoroughly liberal and scientific-minded man like Sir Syed refused to be photographed. Taliban's founder, Mullah Omar, also never relented and so no photo of him exists. The introduction of television in 1965 offended some ultraconservative Saudis, and one of King Faisal's nephews, Prince Khalid ibn Musa'id ibn 'Abd al-'Aziz, was killed in a police shootout in August 1965 after he led an assault on one of the new television stations.[55] The 2005 earthquake in Pakistan's northern areas was widely attributed to watching television and, two days later, local clerics organized a mass smashing of TV sets in the town of Kaghan.

And yet, in spite of the literalists who were strict aniconists, drawings and paintings of human figures steadily crept into parts of Islamic culture. Finely detailed Mughal miniature paintings depicted both men and women. In Iran, it is common to find prayer rugs woven with visualizations of the Prophet and Hazrat Ali. This, of course, would be unthinkable in a Sunni country. But it was the march of technology, however, that made clerics realize they were missing a huge opportunity. Thus began the age of religious TV channels. Although limited initially to audio recitations and images of floating clouds and heavens, talking heads followed. Thereafter, televised sermons and religious gatherings became popular and today's clerical screen personalities have millions of devotees. Asked about earlier restrictions, one such megastar replied, in a complicated way, that although Islam does indeed prohibit drawings and photos, videos with motion are allowed provided they are not for purposes of worship.

Such adaptive changes are not unique to Islam or Pakistan. Fundamental transformations of thought and action have happened everywhere. Take slavery, for example. From the 15th century onwards European colonialists stole manpower for developing Europe by depopulating Africa. But slavery began phasing out after the European Enlightenment. The British Empire formally outlawed it in 1833. For the United States to follow suit took a civil war and an additional thirty-two years. Banning slavery from Muslim countries took much longer. Since the Qur'an discourages but does not forbid slavery, for nearly 13 centuries the possession of slaves was never condemned as sinful or illegal by any religious authority. In 1909 antislave Young Turks inspired by the westernized Kemal Atatürk forced Sultan Abdul Hamid II to free his personal slaves. Atatürk dismissed the last caliph in 1924 and so ended slavery. Turkey formally ratified the 1926 League of Nations convention abolishing slavery in 1933. Though western-driven, it was surely a good thing. One notes that there was no movement anywhere in the Muslim world comparable to Western abolitionism; the West led the way and Muslims followed.

The changes in the UAE's laws are clearly western-driven. How the country's authorities will explain them to the world and their people remains to be seen. Quite possibly no explanation will be forthcoming since the UAE is a sovereign

Why Couldn't Pakistan Become an Islamic State? **307**

country where ruling dynasties exercise total control. Its people don't have a voice. On the other hand, the UAE could try to get endorsements for the new dispensation from pliant muftis and *shaikh-ul-Islam*s. This won't be the first time. Muslim rulers are thoroughly familiar with using friendly clerics for blessing bank interest disguised to avoid its condemnation as *riba*. The UAE has supported various militant Salafist groups overseas and is said to have considerable control over the authorities of Egypt's Jamia al-Azhar. This wide outreach could be useful for suppressing possible criticism.

Arab rulers could also try a more straightforward explanation. The West thrives and prospers in spite of having values that continuously evolve. In other words what was immoral yesterday can now simply be the new normal. For example, until the 1960s, cohabitation and gay unions were fiercely frowned upon in much of Europe and the U.S. But religious opposition has since softened and, in fact, most religions are following the trend. Arab rulers might try arguing that Islam suitably interpreted, can do so as well. Whether for good or for bad, the arrow of time is unidirectional and irreversible.

The Taliban have yet to understand this. After the takeover of Kabul in August 2021, their spokesmen had initially been defensive, seeking to avoid the question of whether they will impose punishments such as amputation of limbs and *rajm* (stoning to death). This was understandable. Accustomed to the comfort of Doha's luxury hotels, and of their bungalows in Quetta and Peshawar, they were returning to the mountain villages from where they fought against an invader. However under orders from Taliban supremo Haibutallah, Islamic *tazeerat* (punishments) have become the law of the land.

In time the Taliban, or maybe the generation that succeeds them, may want the good life the invader has invented. Perhaps some day they will send their children to regular schools instead of Pakistani or Afghan *madressah*s. For this to happen, the spigot of international aid must be turned on again. However, given the insularity of Afghan rural culture, one must not expect rapid change. The burqa, for example, was once again made mandatory by the Taliban in 2022.

For Muslim states and peoples to move forward and become part of the normal world is possible. But it requires that they dispense with craving a return to the 7th century and stop imagining that an Islamic state or a caliphate can ever exist. The *ummah* has a symbolic existence but no more. The delusions of political Islam must be dispensed with. Instead, the way out is to create strong democratic institutions based upon equal rights for all citizens, encourage the participation of women in public life, respect all Muslim sects equally as well as other religions, provide space and freedom to individuals, and base their education systems upon the foundations of science and reason.

Notes

1 S.M. Burke, *Jinnah: Speeches and Statements 1947–1948, Introduction*, Karachi, Oxford University Press (2000), pp. 97–98.

308 Why Couldn't Pakistan Become an Islamic State?

2 *Rehmatul lil Alameen Authority Ordinance Promulgated*, The Express Tribune, 15 October 2021. https://tribune.com.pk/story/2324860/rehmatul-lil-alameen-authority-ordinance-promulgated

3 J.G. McCarthy, *The Gospel According to Rome: Comparing Catholic Tradition and the Word of God*, Harvest House Publishers (1995).

4 H. Abdullah, *Analysis: Battle for 'Ameer-ul-Momineen'*, Dawn, 6 December 2014. https://www.dawn.com/news/1149112

5 V. Nasr, *The Shia Revival – How Conflicts within Islam Will Shape the Future*, W.W. Norton & Company (2006).

6 Ibid, chap 4.

7 A.M. Naqvi, *Islam and Nationalism, Part Seven*, Ahlul Bayt Digital Islamic Library Project (1995–2022), http://www.al-islam.org/islamandnationalism/9.htm

8 M.S.Al-Ashmawy, *Against Islamic Extremism:The Writings of Muhammad Said Al-Ashmawy* (ed. C. Fluehr-Lobban), Gainesville, University Press of Florida (1998).

9 S. Ahmad, *Transforming Faith – The Story of Al-Huda and Islamic Revivalism Among Urban Pakistani Women*, Syracuse University Press (2009).

10 T. Rahman, *Interpretations of Jihad in South Asia – An Intellectual History*, Pakistan, Oxford University Press, (2019).

11 Abu Hasan al-Maward, *The First Islamic Political Scientist, Wan Naim Wan Mansor*, unpublished. http://www.iais.org.my/e/attach/AlMawardi_The%20First%20Islamic%20Political%20Scientist.pdf

12 Ibn Khaldun, *The Muqaddimah*, translated by Franz Rosenthal, Princeton University Press (1969), p. 169.

13 Ibid, p. 145.

14 Al-Ghazzali quoted in *Law in the Middle East*, edited by Majid Khadduri and Herbert J. Liebesny, Vol.1, Origin and Development of Islamic Law, The Lawbook Exchange, Clark, New Jersey (2008), p. 13.

15 WikiIslam, *Sirat Rasul Allah*, https://wikiislam.net/wiki/Sirat_Rasul_Allah, accessed on

16 Constitutional Analysis of the Constitution of Medina, Dr. Muhammad Tahir-ul-Qadri, Islamic Library.

17 Wikipedia, *Raymond Allen Davis Incident*, https://en.wikipedia.org/wiki/Raymond_Allen_Davis_incident#Aftermath.

18 A valuable reference is: V. Nasr, *Mawdudi and the Making of Islamic Revivalism*, New York, Oxford University Press (1996).

19 O. Khalidi, *Between Muslim Nationalists and Nationalist Muslims: Mawdudi's Thoughts on Indian Muslims*, New Delhi, Institute of Objective Studies (2004).

20 I. Ahmad, Genealogy of the Islamic State: Reflections on Maududi's Political Thought and Islamism, *The Journal of the Royal Anthropological Institute*, 15 (2009): S145–S162.

21 Rahman, op. cit., p. 177.

22 Syed Abul Ala Maudoodi, *Musalman aur maujudah seyasi kasmakash* (Muslims and the Present Political Predicament), Islamic Publishers, Vol. 1, Pathankot, Maktaba Jamaat-e-Islami (1937).

23 Ibid.

24 Syed Abul Ala Mawdoodi, *The Rights of Non-Muslims in Islamic State*, Islamic Publications, Ltd. Lahore, Pakistan (1982).

25 The 1954 Justice Munir Commission Report on the Anti-Ahmadi Riots of Punjab in 1953. https://archive.org/stream/The1954JusticeMunirCommissionReportOnTheAntiAhmadiRiotsOfPunjabIn1953/The-1954-Justice-Munir-Commission-Report-on-the-anti-Ahmadi-Riots-of-Punjab-in-1953_djvu.txt

26 Nasr, op. cit., p. 86.

27 *Selections from the Prison Notebooks of Antonio Gramsci*, edited and translated by Quintin Hoare and Geoffrey Nowell Smith, New York, International Publishers (1971), p. 192.

Why Couldn't Pakistan Become an Islamic State? **309**

28 *Taliban Announce Creation of Islamic Emirate of Afghanistan, Will Rule Country through Council*, Dawn, 19 August 2021. https://www.dawn.com/news/1641540
29 B. Osman, A. Gopal, and B. Rubin, *Taliban Views on a Future State*, New York University Center for International Cooperation (July 2016).
30 *'No Smoking, No Shaving': Taliban Restore Old Rules in Newly Seized Afghan Territory*, AFP, Dawn, 14 July 2021. https://www.dawn.com/news/1635051
31 Ayman al-Zawahiri, *Who Was al-Qaeda Leader Killed by US*, BBC News, 2 August 2022.
32 J.M. Dorsey, *The Battle for the Soul of Islam*, Hudson Institute, 28 October 2020. https://www.hudson.org/research/16463-the-battle-for-the-soul-of-islam
33 The Manchester Guardian, *Hussein the New Khalif: Special Interview in His CAMP in Trans Jordania. Arab Claims to Moslem Leadership. Dangers to Hedjaz from Arabia: Reproach For the Allies.* Emir Abdullah Confident, 13 March 1924, ProQuest Historical Newspapers: The Guardian and The Observer.
34 al-Mawardi, op. cit.
35 *Return of the Caliphate*, http://www.bbc.com/news/magazine-29761018
36 Most Muslims want democracy, personal freedoms, and Islam in political life, Pew Research Global Attitudes Project, 10 July 2012.
37 An example of confused thinking about the sharia was related to me by a colleague who teaches political science at Quaid-e-Azam University, Islamabad. He had lectured his class on legal systems in a secular, democratic society and then compared them to those in Saudi Arabia and Iran. Subsequently he asked the students: what would you rather have, a state run by sharia or a state that is secular? With no exception, all replied: Islamic state. Suppose you were accused of a crime, in which country would you prefer to be tried? Saudi Arabia, Iran, or the UK? No one put up their hand for Iran, one went up for SA and the rest for UK. He then asked why don't the rest want to be tried in Saudi Arabia? Answer: we believe in Islam, but we don't believe there is real Islam in Saudi Arabia.
38 C. Aydin, *The Idea of the Muslim World – A Global Intellectual History*, Harvard University Press (2017).
39 Iqbal was smartly dressed in western clothes during his student days in Cambridge and Heidelberg, and wore a suit to receive his knighthood in 1923 long after he found western civilization odious. This poem must therefore be regarded as expiatory.
40 https://tribune.com.pk/story/1440748/iranian-drone-shot-paf-fighter-jet-balochistan-report
41 B. Allen-Ebrahimian, *Saudi Arabia Deports 15,000 Qatari Camels*, Foreign Policy, 20 June 2017. https://foreignpolicy.com/2017/06/20/saudi-arabia-deports-qatari-camels-gulf-diplomacy/
42 S. Masood and B. Hubbard, *Pakistan Approves Military Hero to Head Tricky Saudi-Led Alliance*, The New York Times, 2 April 2017. https://www.nytimes.com/2017/04/02/world/asia/pakistan-general-saudi-alliance-raheel-sharif.html
43 *Tabuk Governor Arrives in Dalbandin to Hunt Houbara Bustard*, Dawn, 28 January 2021. https://www.dawn.com/news/1604044
44 *Report of the Court of Inquiry Constituted under Punjab Act II of 1954 to Enquire into the Punjab Disturbances of 1953*, Lahore. Government Printing Press (1953).
45 Ibid, p. 215.
46 Ibid, p. 219.
47 A.U. Qasmi, *The Ahmadis and the Politics of Religious Exclusion in Pakistan*, Anthem Books (2015).
48 Ibid, p. 23.
49 K. Ali, *Muslim Women Cannot Object to Husbands' Marriages*, Dawn, 22 October 2014. https://www.dawn.com/news/1139597
50 Pervez Hoodbhoy, *Cost of Enforced Modesty*, Dawn, 19 June 2021. https://www.dawn.com/news/1630231

310 Why Couldn't Pakistan Become an Islamic State?

51 Radio Pakistan, *Committee Constituted to Prepare Road Map for Interest-Free Banking System: Finance Minister,* 26 November, 2022.
52 C. Pellegrino, *Saudi Vision2030 and Mutawātir Hadīth: An Unexpected Combination,* Oasis Center, 15 June 2021.
53 W. Cole, *Drinking Alcohol and Living Together without Marriage Become Legal in the UAE while Honour Killings Are Criminalised in Relaxation of Islamic laws,* MailOnline, 8 November 2020. https://www.dailymail.co.uk/news/article-8927849/Drinking -alcohol-living-without-marriage-legal-UAE.html
54 K.E. House, *Saudi Arabia Is Changing Fast: Social Liberalization Has Outpaced Economic Reform, but There Doesn't Seem to Be Any Turning Back,* Wall Street Journal, 4 November 2019. https://www.wsj.com/articles/saudi-arabia-is-changing-fast-11572909143
55 H. Dekmejian, *Islam in Revolution: Fundamentalism in the Arab World,* Syracuse University Press (1995), p. 133 (referenced in Wikipedia https://en.wikipedia.org/wiki/Aniconism_in_Islam#cite_note-22).

Twelve

WHY IS PAKISTAN A PRAETORIAN STATE?

A word for the disruptionists, political opportunists, smugglers, black marketeers and other such social vermin, sharks, and leeches. The soldiers and the people are sick of the sight of you. So it will be good for yourself to turn a new leaf and begin to behave, otherwise retribution will be swift and sure.

> – Broadcast to the nation by General Ayub Khan,
> 8 October 1958[1]

Pakistan, together with North Korea, is the world's most heavily militarized praetorian state. In theory the armed forces of Pakistan function under the federal government as per Article 245 of the 1973 Pakistani Constitution. But in actual fact key decisions on nuclear weapons, foreign policy, internal security, infrastructure contracts, and major economic matters are made by the military, not by elected governments. Military finances, including personal wealth of military officers, are beyond the purview of civilian authority. This chapter explores why Pakistan's warrior class was never tamed by civilians. Reasons lie both in the bankruptcy of the early civilian leadership and a clear vision of Pakistan, as well as the calculated use of Pakistan by the United States during the Cold War. A civilian-military oligarchy – the code word for which is the Establishment – continues to set goals and priorities and to define the national interest. Among the consequences of giving this oligarchy a free hand was the separation of East Pakistan. Decades later, the country suffered a further blow when the military prepared jihadist forces for cross-border operations but then failed to anticipate a disastrous blowback. Finally, in this chapter I make a comparison is made with India and a key question is investigated: what has kept the military under a tight leash on the Indian side of the border?

DOI: 10.4324/9781003379140-17

312   Why Is Pakistan a Praetorian State?

I was eight years old and a tad scared but also fascinated by Ayub Khan's stern admonition. It was Pakistan's first day under martial law and my first introduction to politics and politicians. Knowing that a major announcement was to be made, we had all gathered around the family's almirah-sized Philips radio to hear Ayub lash out at politicians. I anxiously looked at my elder sister, Naseem, for confirmation: could there actually be human-like leeches that suck people's blood? She looked somewhat uncertain, but my father nodded emphatically, filling me with a vague dread. I wondered what these human vampires called politicians might look like.

The Pakistan Army had taken over Pakistan. The first couple of months went as promised: food prices came down, streets were regularly cleaned, the trains ran on time, government employees could actually be found in their offices, and land reforms were announced. How long before things normalized? Some would say six months, others a year – take your pick. What can be said for sure is that army rule had come to stay. Thereafter, civilians have been periodically tolerated, but only if they understand the limits of their authority.

Praetorian is a somewhat uncommon word but apt for Pakistan. Daniel R. Headrick, professor of History and Social Sciences at Roosevelt University, describes praetorianism as,

> a type of militarism oriented to the interior life of a nation that does not aspire to fight or win international wars, but instead to maintain its influence in the domestic political system, controlling decisions that could affect the interests of the military as a corporation, or supporting some particular political faction or party.[2]

Wherever civilian political structures are weak, the political culture undeveloped or viewed as illegitimate and in the hands of venal leaders, the military seeks to control the political process.

According to the political scientist Samuel Finer, as of 31 December 1974, the number of praetorian states was 38, representing about a quarter of all independent states.[3] That number is far fewer today, as countries have moved away from direct military rule. Today, apart from Pakistan, one should include Egypt, Thailand, Myanmar, Libya, and Sudan.

For most of Pakistan's history, military rule has been upfront either through martial law or with an army general as the country's chief executive. But even when the country is nominally ruled by civilians, voices hidden in the shadows give instructions to the media, universities, and to political leaders. The persons issuing these instructions do not reveal their identity – sometimes it will be some Major Khalid, at another time a Colonel Omar. In 2018 opposition leader Maryam Nawaz humorously dubbed these mysterious creatures *khalaee makhlooq* – creatures from outer space. Nevertheless these otherworldly creatures have strong desires for land, property, and seek post-retirement migration to America, Australia, or Europe.

Apart from political power exercised either overtly or from under the covers, the military also controls vast commercial and industrial assets. Ayesha Siddiqa's work on documenting parts of this has become a canonical reference.[4] How the military has usurped agricultural lands from Punjabi peasants is covered in the monograph, *The Military and Denied Development in the Pakistani Punjab – An Eroding Social Consensus*, which details the military's systematic land-grabbing.[5] This can be traced back to the colonial period when the British made extensive land grants to retired military personnel in order to secure their loyalty. Since Punjab provided the bulk of soldiers and officers, this became institutionalized. The authors of *Denied Development* detail how that land-grab has morphed into a social welfare retirement program for senior military officers. I can bear testimony to the Pak Army's land-grab in Okara district, where I had personally witnessed scenes of violence against villagers whose lands had been seized by the Army Welfare Trust.[6]

The most desirable – and expensive – real estate in the country is either owned or operated by the army. Prime among these are Defence Housing Authorities. These are residential neighborhoods for the urban rich in Karachi, Lahore, Islamabad, Multan, Gujranwala, Quetta, Bahawalpur, and Peshawar. Their head is a corps commander. But curiously, there is little legal justification for the military to acquire land for commercial purposes. As pointed out in the recent naval farms case[7] the only "enumerated function" of the armed forces is to "defend Pakistan against external aggression or threat of war, and, subject to law, act in aid of civil power when called upon to do so." If the armed forces want land for achieving these purposes, they have to ask the federal government for it, which can provide the same using powers conferred upon it by the Cantonments Act, 1924. Under Article 173(2) of the constitution, such land, even if it is being used for defence purposes, will continue to vest in the federal government and not be transferred in the name of any other force or institution. If the forces want money, they cannot raise it through business; they have to ask the federal government for it, which can provide the same through the next Finance Act. The forces can do no such thing on their own. That, of course, is how it should theoretically be but not how it actually is.

How rich are Pakistan's generals? This is a tabooed topic but intrepid journalists have chipped away. According to the investigative news website FactFocus, the tax records of freshly retired COAS Bajwa's extended family amounted to Rs 12.7 billion. These showed massive gains by the general's wife, daughter, her father-in-law, and others. Were these tax records fudged? While the Inter Services Public Relations denounced the "false propaganda", the government implicitly affirmed that they were correct by announcing that the Federal Board of Revenue (FBR) has traced the identities of the individuals who had leaked the tax records.[8] In 2020, FactFocus had published a report that former China-Pakistan Economic Corridor Authority chairman Lt-Gen retired Asim Saleem Bajwa and his family had been running a multi-million dollar Papa John pizza franchise in four countries with 133 restaurants worth an estimated $39.9 million.

314 Why Is Pakistan a Praetorian State?

Aqil Shah, a specialist on the Pakistan military, has extensively explored attitudes of Pakistani army officers towards politicians.[9] His research was based on 100 military interviews conducted between 2007 and 2013, the Pakistan Army Green Book (1991–2011), the training curriculum, as well as journal and strategy papers of the National Defence University (NDU). The main results of his work are:

- Three-fourths of military informants viewed a coup being a legitimate form of regime change under "crisis" conditions.
- Three-fourths believed civilian politicians were incapable of managing national security.
- Two-thirds considered politicians as unfit to rule.
- Without exception, officers advocated a permanent "watchdog" role for the military in governance.

The-then serving Inter-Services Intelligence (ISI) chief, Lt. General Ahmed Shuja Pasha, put his view on civilians in government in his characteristic blunt way: "The political leadership lacks the aptitude to read basic defense policy documents, and *even the ability to think*...they cannot formulate any policy".[10] Officers are frequently known to refer to "bloody civilians", a reflection of their disdain for the non-soldier. And yet, as Oldenburg observed,

> The military has never been explicitly disloyal to the democratic system, even when it has taken over in a coup and implemented laws that seek to transform the country. It always has claimed a dual-aspect guardian role: guardian of the nation and the country; guardian of its ward – the political system – until it can be revived, once purged of its faults.[11]

Celebrations of the army's valor are lavish. The annual 23 March parade in Islamabad is preceded by several days of preparation with fighter jets screeching across the sky and road traffic diverted along side streets. Since 1998, this tightly choreographed showcasing of military manpower has been accompanied by trucks bearing nuclear-capable missiles – the Shaheen, Ghauri, and Hatf. City streets are named after war heroes and public squares are named Missile Chowk, Tank Chowk, Tayyara Chowk, Submarine Chowk, etc. Perhaps absurdly, the last named *chowk* had an actual decommissioned submarine placed at a busy intersection of Karachi roads. Elsewhere, discarded tanks, artillery pieces, and fighter aircraft guard the entrances to universities and military institutes. These serve to remind one that India is an enemy into perpetuity.

The army's centrality in national affairs is evident. Whereas appointments of air force and navy chiefs stir little public discussion or interest, those of the Chief of Army Staff and ISI chief are followed with bated breath. Media commentary on who will gain or lose takes away attention from all else. To an extent this is understandable: the creation of the opposition party Islami Jamhoori Ittihad

Why Is Pakistan a Praetorian State? **315**

(IJI) is now proudly accepted by the ISI as its handiwork.[12] The role played by the intelligence agencies in ousting Nawaz Sharif, as well as the role played by the ISI in the extension given to former Army Chief Raheel Sharif, was quite transparent.

More recently, in 2018 Khan was catapulted into power through a combination of tactics: the serving prime minister, Nawaz Sharif, was banned from holding political office on charges of financial corruption. This was followed by a systematic dismantling of his party. Mysterious desertions from Pakistan Muslim League (N) party ranks, the sudden appearance of "Jeep" candidates across the country, opposition by extremists and militants newly mainstreamed into political parties, and whispers that PMLN candidates will run afoul of the *khalaee makhlooq* sapped PMLN's strength. But Khan's nearly four years as prime minister ended when he insisted that Gen. Faiz Hameed – who was a known Khan supporter – be chosen as ISI head. This went against what the army's leadership had in mind. The subsequent souring of relations led to the army's withdrawal of support and, soon thereafter, the collapse of Khan's government in April 2022. Khan protested that it was the army's newfound neutrality that had empowered the political opposition to displace him. He called upon the army's rank and file to disobey its top leadership, and that families of military personnel should join his 'million-man' rallies.[13] How this challenge plays out and whether the army is indeed split remains to be seen. The chances are, however, that the army's supremacy will only be lightly dented; the inability or unwillingness of political parties to assert themselves has not changed.

The Pakistan Army is largely Sunni Punjabi, perhaps to the order of 80%, with a large base of power in Punjab that it can manipulate through invoking the dangers of separatism and presenting the specter of disintegration. It can readily persuade the ordinary Punjabi soldier that the Baloch, although Muslim, have played into India's hands. Stoking these fears has helped the army establish hegemonic control over the population. In 2006 a survey on the State of Democracy in South Asia found that Pakistanis were far more accepting of army rule than other peoples of the region:

> 84% of the citizens of Pakistan consider that democracy is suitable for their country. However, Pakistan has the highest levels of identified non-democrats of any country in the region and 50% of the respondents are indifferent to democratic rule. The survey also indicates that in Pakistan, almost 60% of the population supported army rule when this study was conducted and over 50% of the surveyed population demonstrated preference for major decisions being taken by religious leaders.[14]

However, a symbiotic relationship exists between the military establishment and the civilian establishment, there being a mutual recognition that one cannot do without the other. The relationship, however, is not symmetrical. Dirt can be

316 Why Is Pakistan a Praetorian State?

thrown at politicians but not at military officers. Exposing corruption within the army allegedly plays into the hands of the enemy and so can lead to somebody's mysterious sudden disappearance. Several journalists in Islamabad, once thought to be a relatively safe city, have been violently assaulted in recent years.[15] Curiously, the army is rarely named – one reads in the Urdu press that so-and-so was punished by unknown assailants for having spoken out against the *idaras*, a vague illusion to institutions consisting of the army and ISI. They are assumed above reproach.

The Imran Khan government did not seek to hide the fact that it was visibly taking orders from its benefactor, the army. This was sanctified by the name "hybrid government" with all parties "on the same page". Apart from steering national security and foreign policy, military presence was visible in developmental planning, finance, commerce, internal security, railways, highway building, and the China–Pakistan Economic Corridor (CPEC). The army's corporate entities lie beyond the control of civilians: the Planning Commission of Pakistan made some waves by expressing its resentment publicly after it declared itself unable to "rein in" the National Logistics Cell (NLC) because, "they do not share details even about audit-related paras in meetings of the departmental accounts committee (DAC)".[16] The NLC had made massive overpayments to subcontractors for carrying out work on Karachi's Green Line Bus Rapid Transit System from Surjani Town to Saddar.

Access to information is controlled by Inter-Services Public Relations (ISPR) which runs a network of over 70 FM commercial stations, makes documentaries and feature films, and overtly instructs what is considered acceptable content for television audiences. Its message: democracy needs to be disciplined by a concentration of power. Another repeated message is to do away with the 18th Amendment to the Constitution. This amendment gives, in the army's view, too much power to the provinces. A more centralized presidential form of government is preferable. Under Imran Khan's government the Army Chief, General Qamar Javed Bajwa, received from Imran Khan's government a three-year extension beyond retirement. This allowed him to sit on all committees of high national importance until his retirement in November 2022. Lest the amateurish Imran Khan make serious mistakes, the general saw to it that key decisions on India, Afghanistan, China, and the United States would be made in his presence. When meeting with business leaders, he would sit at the head of the table.[17] Large public sector organizations for housing, disaster management, water supply, and electricity are headed by active-duty officers. This had been the quid pro quo for placing Khan in the prime minister's seat.

Until things went awry, the investment in bringing Imran Khan to power paid off in shielding the army from public criticism. In April 2021 – under Khan's government – the Ministry of Interior sent a working paper to parliament upon which Pakistan Tehreek-e-Insaf (PTI) members moved a bill to make amendments to the Pakistan Penal Code and Code of Criminal Procedure. The amendment labelled as Section 500-A reads:

Punishment for intentional ridiculing of the Armed Forces etc.: Whosoever intentionally ridicules, brings into disrepute or defames the Armed Forces of Pakistan or a member thereof, he shall be guilty of an offence punishable with imprisonment for a term which may extend to two years, or fine which may extend to five hundred thousand rupees, or with both.[18]

Ironically, after relations with the army soured a year later, these lawmakers – and Khan in particular – were charged with having insulted the military using the very same bill they had passed. In earlier years, following the tradition of western military institutions, the Pakistan Army had once allowed critical voices from outside the military as well as within. This no longer exists. In 2021 when it gave itself a whopping 25% across-the-board increase in salaries – duly approved by parliament – there was no visible protest from any quarter.[19] In recent years it has become much less willing to reflect on its own weaknesses. The NDU and other military academies are correspondingly less capable of installing a critical mindset among officers. That the institution has turned into its own echo chamber is suggested by the strong reaction within the army against former ISI Chief Gen. Asad Durrani – once a full-fledged member of the ruling establishment – after he published a frank tell-all book. His pension was stopped, security clearances revoked, and – quite absurdly – he was accused by the Ministry of Defence of being an Indian RAW agent.[20] Nevertheless, the treatment he received must be considered as gentle compared to the methods used by ISI against civilian dissidents.

The Establishment Defined

Gone are the days when the sole role of an army was limited, either to invade or beat back the invaders…Geopolitical and geo-strategic regional compulsions of South Asia have made the revision and redefinition of Pakistan Army's role a necessity.

– Army Green Book, 2007

The Green Book expresses upfront what everyone knows, but most will dare not say – that it falls upon the army to rule Pakistan. Still, one must not go too far in thinking this. In fact it is a still wider entity – the Establishment – that runs Pakistan. An equally good name could be the Oligarchy. The late Stephen Cohen, an astute observer of Pakistani politics over the decades, defined the Establishment as "an informal political system that ties together the senior ranks of the military, the civil service, key members of the judiciary, and other elites".[21]

Arguably, most forms of government anywhere are reducible to the rule of a few. In Pakistan's case, how few is few? In 1996 Syed Mushahid Hussain, long an Establishment insider and survivor under multiple regimes, had sized it at around 500 persons plus a list of wannabes many times this number. Establishment members are serving and retired generals, politicians in office as well as some in the

318 Why Is Pakistan a Praetorian State?

opposition, ex-ambassadors and diplomats, civil servants, and selected business-men. The overwhelming majority is Punjabi with a few Muhajirs and Pushtuns. There is just a sprinkling of Sindhi and Baloch members. Boundaries are fluid – as some members move in, others move out. In earlier decades, English was the preferred language of communication, but this morphed into Urdu as the elite indigenized, becoming less cosmopolitan and more religious. Without sacrific-ing any of his privileges, the brown *sahib* had shed his pant and shirt in favor of the *shalwar kameez*. Although the British accent disappeared, attitudes towards those they rule remained unchanged.

Like the Russian *siloviki*, Establishment members are naturally attached to the idea of public order, an order that guarantees their own power and property, but which they also believe is essential to prevent India from swallowing up Pakistan. The corruption of Pakistani *siloviki* has certain special features. Patriotism is their ideology and the self-justification for their immense wealth. Club membership rules say anti-Indianism has to be worn on the sleeve. There can be no deviation from a common set of beliefs: that India must be countered at every turn; that nuclear weapons are Pakistan's greatest assets; that Kashmir is the unfinished business of Partition and the fight must go on indefinitely; that large-scale social reforms such as land distribution are out of bounds; that the uneducated and illiterate masses are to be held in contempt; that vociferous Muslim nationalism is desirable, but true Islamism is dangerous; and that Washington is to be despised but fully taken advantage of.

While some civilians have been important members of the Establishment, it is the military that really matters. The Establishment has a long history of engineering the rise and fall of political governments, a fact that it only half-denies. Interference is considered necessary because politicians cannot be trusted to run the country. Ex-spy master Asad Durrani, who fell out of favor with the Establishment, says this belief is deeply held:

> Every now and then, we get a junta that crosses the redline in the naïve belief that the state was created by the Almighty to serve as a lab, and the khaki leadership had divine sanction to experiment to its heart's content. One catalyst that all these scientists found useful was a civilian façade to cover their flanks and to do the heavy lifting. In vernacular this exercise is called political engineering – and it has bombed always and every time.[22]

The notion of army-guided rule – the so-called hybrid regime – has gained traction among soldiers, bureaucrats, engineers, teachers, and doctors thanks to a hugely simplified narrative that goes like this: Pakistan is extremely well endowed with both highly qualified people and abundant natural resources, but it is poor and eternally in debt because of a corrupt political class made of looters. These looters have stashed away billions of ill-gotten gains in offshore companies and Swiss banks. If brought to task, Pakistan can then bask in riches and never have to go to the IMF again. The natural guardian of the nation's values and real interests is the military, whose selflessness and sacrifice makes possible Pakistan's continued existence.

We now turn to how the Establishment defines Pakistan's national interest. This normative term is hugely meaning-laden. For comparison, let us look at how other countries have perceived their respective national interests at different points of their history.

National interest for the post-War American establishment meant the export of American culture and values, and free trade in particular. As such, the United States was an ideologically driven state, one which became less so after the end of the Cold War. On the other side of the ideological spectrum, national interest in the days of Stalin's Russia and Mao's China was understood as the overseas implantation of their respective brands of communist ideology. Since those times much has changed. The United States, China, and Russia have powerful militaries that project power all over the globe. However, they all are frankly driven by pragmatic objectives. National interest is now defined as having a high standard of living, a contented populace, and some degree of influence in world affairs. As such, they are not mission-driven and their national interests can be called normal (even though Russia–Ukraine and China–Taiwan borders on the abnormal).

In Pakistan's case, national interest has never been put down formally in any official document. Instead, one must search for its possible meaning in speeches and statements by leaders, in theses and articles in various university departments, and particularly publications of the National Defence University in Islamabad. The result of a lengthy internet browse yields the expected: Pakistan's national interest is understood almost exclusively in relation to India. More specifically, this means resolving Kashmir on Pakistan's terms, ensuring strategic depth against India via an Afghanistan with a Taliban government (now achieved), nurturing the Pakistan–China relationship to neutralize Indian power, etc. It is for the Establishment to decide what may or may not be discussed in the public media and whether Balochistan or Sind – and now the nascent Pashtun Tahafuz Movement in Khyber Pakhtunkhwa – is to be handled with a velvet glove or an iron fist.

The fall of Kabul was a great victory for Pakistan's generals, the result of an institutional decision of the army starting from General Musharraf and then onwards. Pakistan would finally have its western border protected from India. Although Imran Khan had greeted the Taliban victory as "having broken the shackles of slavery",[23] celebrations turned out less boisterous than expected. There was anxiety that the West has perceived this victory as a result of logistical support provided by Pakistan, and also some concern that extreme forces in Pakistan will want to emulate the Taliban Emirate. The post-victory rise of the terrorist sharia-seeking *Tehrik-e-Taliban-e-Pakistan* (TTP) is now resulting in almost daily killings of Pakistan's security forces near the Afghan border. The country's education system has produced fertile grounds for militant messianic groups to induct young people into their folds.

320 Why Is Pakistan a Praetorian State?

The Establishment sees its ultimate protection lying with nuclear weapons. They are portrayed as Pakistan's greatest national asset. On the one hand, they offer protection against India and, on the other, allow for some limited military initiatives that would otherwise be impossible. To maximize their numbers and make ever more effective nuclear delivery systems is therefore held as the highest national interest. As early as 1966, just after Operation Gibraltar had failed to reach its objectives, Bhutto had wanted the Bomb as a deterrent that would work even if Pakistan became proactive again in Kashmir. He had correctly anticipated Kargil.

The Establishment's perception of national interest is a strongly limited one. Missing is a positive vision for Pakistan's future. I could not find any sustained, enthusiastic call for Pakistan to explore space, become a world leader in science, have excellent universities, develop literature and the arts, deal with critical environmental issues, achieve high standards of justice and financial integrity, and create a poverty-free society embodying equalitarian principles. Instead the unstated principle is: what's good for the army is good for Pakistan.

To the extent that the military sets national policies to favor its institutional interests, Pakistan loses. Political analyst Mosharraf Zaidi puts it succinctly:

> Pakistan is an economic outlier. India and China have grown at phenomenal rates over the last two decades. So too have Indonesia, Vietnam and Bangladesh. So too have a dozen other countries in Asia and even the wider MENA region. Pakistan's lack of growth makes it an exception to the rule. There are a lot of technocratic answers to the question of why there is low or no growth here – but the most important one is hard for economists to deal with in any serious manner: national security.[24]

Bankrupt Political Class

> Military intervention in politics definitively ends only when the civilian polity has tamed the warrior class. That happens when the legitimacy of the civilian system of power is established over a period of time; when the principles of governance as embedded in the constitution, laws, and conventions of contemporary statehood are observed by governments and politicians; and when the civilian system of power is regarded by citizens normatively as just, appropriate, and authoritative.
>
> *– Eqbal Ahmad (1995)[25]*

Pakistan's praetorian past dates back to the Cold War. Its insecure and self-aggrandizing civilian founders and the overdeveloped military it inherited from the British meant that all parties were perfectly happy and willing to serve as sepoys of the United States and become a frontline state. The absence of a long-term vision, ideological confusion, and lack of a moral framework showed up at every point. What should be the relationship between state and religion, executive and

Why Is Pakistan a Praetorian State? **321**

judiciary, or authority and accountability? In a world that had come to be defined by Soviet–U.S. confrontation, what should be Pakistan's position in international affairs? These questions received no clear answers.

Until the disintegration of the Soviet Union in 1991 took away its role as a Cold War frontline state, Pakistan had successfully petitioned the United States for weapons and assistance. Conscious that Pakistan had once been America's "most allied ally", U.S. policy until that point had been to treat both India and Pakistan at par. But with India's growing economic and military might, the time came for a decisive shift. Under the Clinton administration, the tilt towards India became explicit. Once this de-hyphenation policy was implemented, the Establishment had to determine the extent to which America was to be challenged and confronted and, instead, China wooed. That China must not be displeased morphed into a core principle. To "borrow" power through military alliances against India is seen as natural. Hence switching from America's protection to China's tutelage happened effortlessly.

While foreign patronage contributed to weakening a democratic polity, the real cause was internal weakness and an insufficiently imagined Pakistan. Once Jinnah died, the moral and intellectual bankruptcy of those who had led the Pakistan Movement became starkly evident. The Muslim League, made of feudal lords and powerful members of the north Indian *ashrafiyya*, was adrift now that its anchor was gone. Only the inherited colonial framework of governance remained, not a positive vision of the future. Power seekers scurried up and down the corridors of power, plotting and scheming against each other with every individual seeking to maximize personal gain. In a feudal culture, factionalization happened almost instantaneously on purely personal grounds. Honor, status, insult, and revenge determined the drift of politics. The absence of a culture of debate and discussion led to anarchy. Post-1948, meetings of the Constituent Assembly were sparsely attended and in later meetings there was often a total loss of decorum with members hurling abuse, insult, silverware, and even furniture at each other. That these scenes are witnessed in parliament even today is a reflection of what happened long ago.

Evacuee property was on the minds of many politicians, the majority of whom were large landlords. In 1949 the governments of India and Pakistan had agreed on modalities for the transfer of properties and assets because at the time of Partition millions on both sides were expected to return to their ancestral homes.[26] But looters, assisted by those in power, moved in quickly and the losses had to be written off on both sides. Many politicians on the Pakistani side were far too busy grabbing properties left behind by the Hindus and Sikhs who had fled. When Ayub declared martial law in 1958, much of the population bought into his emphatic narrative that politicians are scum. This was reinforced by the visible behavior of Muslim League politicians.

The political mess after Jinnah's death gave rise to multiple putschist dreams. In 1951, discontent on various grounds – including the botched First Kashmir War – led to the Rawalpindi Conspiracy Case. This failed coup d'état was

322 Why Is Pakistan a Praetorian State?

inspired by resentment against the Kashmir ceasefire. Attempted by Major-General Akbar Khan against Liaquat Ali Khan's government, it was amateurish and the army high command was alerted in time. Nevertheless, the army had just begun to assert itself. The weakness of political structures meant that it would become stronger with time.

In 1980 Eqbal Ahmad (1933–1999) gave a lengthy interview on Pakistani politics to Arab journalist Nubar Hovsepian.[27] He sketched the manner and method by which the military establishment evolved from being merely strong to becoming a total hegemon. I will paraphrase his arguments as follows: for the first few years, the Establishment milked the ideological cow of Islam. Then for the next ten years, it milked the development cow that had been born during the Cold War in Harvard Yard to parents who were staunch anti-communist ideologues.[28] Their offspring was shipped off to Ayub Khan for pursuing developmental nationalism and opposing communism. The hope was that countries with impatient populations could be weaned away from communism – then an attractive possibility for developing countries – through accelerated development. Dependence upon external benefactors rather than reliance on internal strength thus became etched into the country's DNA. Each subsequent ruler looked outside rather than inside for strength. Over decades, Pakistan adapted to its changing strategic circumstances by renting itself out to powerful states. Territory and men were part of the services provided. Payment came not just from the U.S., but Arab countries as well. Today the Pakistan Army, supported by China rather than the Americans, sees itself as a permanent part of Pakistan's political establishment.

A Once Apolitical Army

A retired brigadier – one of the many who have come to dominate television talk shows in recent years – described the Pakistan Army as Pakistan's largest political party. Why not, he asked rhetorically, aren't we military people stakeholders in the country's future? It was a bold, in-your-face statement that the fig leaf of civilian control was no longer needed. Decades ago, Dewey had perceptively observed that,

> In the long term, retaining the confidence of the army is far more important than winning elections. Political parties in Pakistan are temporary expedients which pick up the pieces after the generals fail to reconcile internal conflicts. Their main function is to pave the way for restoration of military rule.[29]

Although Muslims are said to be a martial people, in fact this is only selectively true. Bangladesh is not known for military prowess, but even majorities in Sind, Gilgit-Baltistan, Balochistan, and some parts of Punjab are not unduly anxious for military careers. As noted by Fair and Nawaz, this is a fact which

Why Is Pakistan a Praetorian State? **323**

the army appears to be conscious of and has made some attempts, even if not wholeheartedly, to change.[30] But in areas that are the abode of the so-called martial races – Punjabis and Pathans – militarism and Islam go hand in hand. Dewey notes that, "Studies of militarism in countries as diverse as Germany and Japan suggest that 'dominant armies' are respected and civilian regimes are despised if large sections of the population admire the macho qualities – courage, strength, belligerence – which make men successful soldiers".[31] This is indeed very true. Martial castes have value systems celebrating heroism and honor, propagating them into their generations through folklore, songs, and poems. Dewey proposes that the roots of miliarism in Pakistan are to be sought in certain catchment areas:

> The deep and enduring roots which the military have sunk into thousands of Punjabi villages may be the key to military dominance in Pakistan…The heavily enlisted castes in the great recruiting grounds derive far greater economic benefits than civilian ministries can ever hope to provide, and their martial ethic, their admiration for the virtues of the warrior, prejudices them in favor of everything the army represents. This combination – pay and pensions on the one hand, primordial values on the other – produces a bond so strong that the "most-martial" families and tribes identify their honor – their *izzat* – with the honor of the regiment they serve.[32]

The military mindset is created at the outset in military academies which expressly seek to instill primordial values of valor and patriotism. But, in her recent book, *Dying to Serve – Militarism, Affect, and the Politics of Sacrifice in the Pakistan Army*, Maria Rashid suggests that half of the army's work is done within the societies from where recruits are derived. But, at a second stage, a distance is created between the recruit and the milieu from which they derive:

> The manufacture of the soldier-subject requires the establishment of distance from former objects of affection and ways of living and the continuous control of sadness, fear, and shame. It involves the destabilization of stubborn familial attachments seen as feminine and as threats to the soldier's ability to stay in service. In place of such attachments, the military pulls in feelings of mastery, of masculine and rational superiority, and of attachment to one's army battalion and comrades.[33]

Grief is carefully choreographed by the ISPR for broadcast on television at such occasions as *Yaum-e-Shuhada* (Day of the Martyr).[34] The fighting image of the army, and every attack made upon it in the social media, is countered by thousands of keyboard warriors recruited from college graduates and paid for by the ISPR. Before hiring, they are first checked to see if they have the correct attitudes, particularly if they carry the belief that the army must dominate over civilian institutions.

324 Why Is Pakistan a Praetorian State?

To make sense of this, one needs a bit of history.

Just before Partition, what became the Pakistan Army was thoroughly apolitical. It was, in fact, a mere rump of the British Army with its entire high command being British. Its members had not fought against colonialism; on the contrary, they had been a bulwark against nationalist forces. Ethnically, the newly formed Pakistan Army was largely Punjabi, a consequence of martial races being considered more suited for the British Army. In 1939 about 29% of soldiers were Punjabi Muslims, most being from Pakistani Punjab.[35] Punjabis had not participated in the Great Mutiny of 1857 and so, in British eyes, were preferable to the more nostalgic Muslims of northern India. But Pathans, originating from a rugged terrain, were thought to be natural fighters. Together with Muhajirs, they too had considerable representation in the nascent Pakistan Army. However, the Baloch and Sindhi were almost completely absent. This fact has barely changed over eight decades. Those whose mother tongues are Balochi, Brahui, and Sindhi are few and far between.

Post-Partition, the army's size was modest. The division of assets between India and Pakistan, including military personnel and hardware, was to be in proportion with the population size. But India did its best to shortchange Pakistan. In his classic work on the Pakistan Army, Shuja Nawaz notes that "Out of the 46 training establishments that existed in pre-partition India, only 7 were in Pakistan", and that of 40 ordnance depots only 5 retail depots were located inside Pakistan and these too had depleted stocks.[36] As part of the agreed upon division of assets, Pakistan would get one-third of the military stores and equipment but this did not happen.[37] The Government of India was determined to give as little as possible to Pakistan, while the Government of Pakistan wanted to have as much as possible. Trained officers on the Pakistani side were few. Many were promoted to higher ranks without properly completing the requirements. Equipment too was in short supply. In 1951, when India rattled sabers, Prime Minister Liaquat Ali Khan suggested to General Ayub Khan that "It was time to fight it out" with the Indians to which Ayub Khan responded: "I submitted to him that before making up his mind he should take into account the views of those whose profession it was to fight. We had only thirteen tanks with about forty to fifty hours engine life in them".[38]

Nonetheless, though outgunned and outnumbered, the army had established its public credibility by fighting India to a standstill in the 1947 war over Kashmir. In contrast to dithering civilians, the military was projected to be hard-nosed and above the fray, single-mindedly dedicated to defending the country. That we must cultivate this image was the advice given in 1969 by Maj. Gen. Sher Ali Khan Pataudi to Gen. Yahya Khan. The army must be seen by people as "a mythical entity, a magical force, that would succour them in times of need when all else failed...the army was the final guarantor of Pakistan and its well-being".[39]

The army was now poised to grow by leaps and bounds. Ayub Khan, then Commander-in-Chief of the Pakistan Army, was frankly dismissive of sharing power with civilians, evincing the thought that democracy could work only in

Why Is Pakistan a Praetorian State? **325**

cooler climes. "We are not like the people of the temperate zones....We are too hot-blooded and undisciplined to run an orderly parliamentary democracy".[40] Decades later, General Musharraf would echo these thoughts.

America's Junior Partner

On the international stage, from the 1950s Pakistan willingly became a client state of the United States and served America's Cold War needs by turning itself into a bastion against communism. Pakistan demanded – and received – vast amounts of military aid from the United States. Ayub became a frequent visitor to Washington and entered into direct negotiations with top officials. The Pakistan Army was well on its way to making decisions on foreign policy; the Government of Pakistan was merely to be informed of what it had decided. However, in 1953 a declassified memo from the Assistant Secretary of State for South Asia recommended that while Ayub should be assisted in his aid-seeking meetings, caution should be exercised because: "It is also important to consider that General Ayub is not officially commissioned by his Government to discuss military assistance".[41]

Ayub Khan's "Friends, Not Masters" was published in 1967 and titled to reflect Ayub's view that Pakistan would be a faithful junior partner in alliance with the United States in its competition with the Soviet Union. The West adored him. Samuel Huntington, who served the Pentagon establishment during the Cold War, compared the unfriendly nationalistic Gamal Abdul Nasser of Egypt with the friendly Ayub of Pakistan. Nasser was a dictator, said Huntington, but Ayub was a supremely wise man who, "in the subsequent coup of October 1958 simply transferred the leadership from inefficient civilian bureaucrats to efficient military ones".[42] Huntington's praise was lavish and breathtaking: "more than any other political leader in a modernizing country after World War II, Ayub came close to filling the role of a Solon or Lycurgus, or 'Great Legislator' on the Platonic or Rousseauean model".[43] Conservative historian Niall Ferguson was no less enthusiastic, declaring that Ayub was the ultimate ally: "his English perfect, his regime secular albeit undemocratic, his commitment to the alliance demonstrated by his willingness to let American U-2s fly from Pakistani airbases".[44] The 1950s was a decade of messy coups all over the world; Ayub was seen as a "clean", model usurper.

There was no large-scale movement at the time that demanded democracy. That the road to power lay through Washington was clear to Ayub. His fledgling steps as Commander-in-Chief ended with the Pakistan Army taking charge of foreign policy and eventually becoming a pawn in America's hands. This trend became stronger after his 1958 coup when the U.S. was keen to cultivate allies against communism during the Cold War. Pakistan was invited into the SEATO and CENTO alliances and, to quote arch anti-communist John Foster Dulles, became America's "most allied ally". When China eventually displaced the United States as the center of gravitational attraction, little effort

326 Why Is Pakistan a Praetorian State?

was required in shifting focus from one benefactor to another. Claiming that security reasons demand it, a fresh lieutenant general was put in charge of all affairs to oversee the China–Pakistan Economic Corridor. One wonders whether his soldiering background has prepared him for a technical task of this magnitude.

Decades after Partition, Washington loomed large over the consciousness of Pakistani politicians who sought to curry favor in Washington. In her years out of power, Benazir Bhutto spent her energies wooing editors of *The Washington Post* and *The New York Times*. Compared to other Pakistani politicians, she had a relatively easier time: the Americans were inclined to look upon her favorably since she was western educated, desperate for power, and thus considered pliable. But the army was suspicious. So in the summer of 1990, just after Kashmir heated up again, she repeated her father's famous promise to fight a 1000-year war with India hoping this would endear her to the army. She also made overt her enthusiasm for nuclear weapons, famously throwing down her bangles before a large public gathering where she taunted a reluctant Nawaz Sharif into testing nuclear weapons.[45]

Nevertheless, the army's trust could not be bought so easily. Having a woman prime minister is hard for an organization steeped in macho culture. Notwithstanding the closeness of the Pakistani and U.S. militaries, she was also seen as too close to the Americans. This suspicion is why the nuclear establishment kept her at arm's-length from its innermost circle.[46]

Unfortunately, Benazir Bhutto was no Jacinda Ardern either in terms of vision or uprightness. Her personal corruption, as well as that of husband Asif Ali Zardari, became legendary. Administrative incompetence was leading to a countrywide financial meltdown. Even those who believed in democracy heaved a sigh of relief when, after less than two years in office, she was dismissed and new elections were eventually scheduled.[47] Years later, Lt. Gen. Asad Durrani, a former director-general of the ISI, admitted he had taken personal responsibility for "distributing money to the alliance against Benazir Bhutto" during the 1993 election. "After seeing the period that she had ruled, I thought it would be better if the lady did not come to power", he said.[48] It was a matter-of-fact statement, made without a hint of embarrassment or wrongdoing.

Strong Men Make Weak Countries

> Whatever be the constitutional position, one thing is clear that in the final analysis, political sovereignty in Pakistan resides where the coercive power resides. They decide when to abrogate the Constitution; when it should be held in abeyance; when elected governments should be sacked; and when democracy should be given a chance. Behind the scenes, they also decide whether an elected prime minister shall live or die.[49]
>
> *– Roedad Khan (1923–present), former Interior*
> *Secretary*

Why Is Pakistan a Praetorian State? **327**

A worn-out adage – yet no less true for being that – is that power corrupts, but absolute power corrupts absolutely. It frees individuals and institutions to act wantonly and without constraint, pursuing a selfish interest or even a whim. This is why a system of checks and balances, even one with major faults, works better in the long run than a system where power cannot be challenged. At the end of the World War II, powerful militaries of the western world were flush with victory. Adoring publics showered rose petals upon hero generals who, at some point, could have asserted themselves and become dangerous. One such example is that of General Douglas MacArthur, sacked by President Harry Truman when he became too big for his boots. The U.S. establishment had set direction by insisting that civilian control is crucial and requires professionalizing the military by setting it apart from the rest of society while teaching it to execute but not formulate policy. This, in fact, worked well in preventing bloodshed at the Capitol in Washington, DC after Donald Trump refused to accept his defeat in the 2020 elections. But how much support would there have been for a military coup, and what led to Americans being somewhat ambivalent? This question had been earlier explored in considerable detail by Reynolds.[50]

Men of steel are good for fighting wars and some can easily be tempted into believing that they are capable of everything, including becoming their country's saviors. Military academies train their students in a very specific way. Physical drill discipline comes first and foremost. At Sandhurst, where many a military officer from British India was trained, one senior British officer wrote that drill would ensure that:

> the cadet has a graceful carriage, stands easy and erect, and shows by his bearing that he is manly and self-reliant...The contrast between Hyperion and a Satyr is scarcely more striking than that which exists between the loutish bearing of a Lancashire lad and the firm, respectful, and self-respecting carriage of the same person after he has been disciplined and polished by the drill.[51]

Hyperion (a deity who holds the cosmos in place) rather than Satyr (a goat-like man) was how the handsome young Sandhurst-trained Ayub Khan – Pakistan's first military dictator – thought himself to be. Upon leaving office, he installed in his place Pakistan's second military dictator, General Yahya Khan. A generation later Ayub was also a role model for General Pervez Musharraf. Although Ayub never won any war, a strong self-image gave him sufficient confidence to launch the coup of 1958, dismiss President Iskander Mirza from office, and spend the next decade steering a whole country. He is the world's first self-declared Field Marshal.

Ayub Khan typified the military mind of the postcolonial subcontinent, one which persists into present times. His solutions to complex issues were breathtakingly simple. In his autobiography, written while in office, he complains that student indiscipline is rampant because "there are far too many students

328 Why Is Pakistan a Praetorian State?

and not enough buildings, laboratories, and libraries". His suggested fix: "One instructor on a platform with a loudspeaker can take a very large body of students at one time, and just half an hour a day should build up their bodies and minds, and take the devil out of them".[52]

Actually the business of purging devils is called exorcism, not education, and sending PT masters to colleges or universities is just about as cockeyed as it can get. But Ayub Khan's charming modesty buys him reprieve. He readily admits that: "I was not a very bright student, nor did I find studies a particularly absorbing occupation". In 1926 his father, a Risaldar-Major in the British Army, paid his fees for the Royal Military Academy Sandhurst where "life was spartan" and there was much rough-and-tumble among cadets. In keeping with the Academy's tradition to create a privileged officer class, he was duly assigned a British soldier as orderly. Fortunately, British military academies have produced very few Ayub-like putschists. Certainly several British officers must have had Ayub-sized egos. Many an officer must have preened himself before a mirror and seen Hyperion there. But a military coup in the British system was and remains unthinkable. Why?

Successful societies know that those who fight wars well are not always best suited for running industries, academia, or government. Therefore, British military officers, whether serving or retired, are not given preferential treatment outside of their specific skills. It is broadly realized that men in uniform can be heroic fighters in wartime but in other situations they can be dimwits, bureaucratic, obstinate, slow, disorganized, inflexible, and just as clueless as their civilian counterparts.

What might have worked in simpler times has little chance of working in modern times where problems have become more technical and complex. Imagine for a moment that the British military ran present-day Britain or had a big hand in running it. Would British Airways survive cut-throat competition if its CEO was a retired RAF air marshal rather some tech-savvy, hi-fi business type? In working out complicated Brexit policy options, would a retired lieutenant-general negotiate British interests better than a PhD in economics from Cambridge? Should the British Electricity Authority look for some distinguished electrical engineer or for a British army colonel instead? And would a Royal Navy admiral – serving or retired – be best placed to protect Britain's interests in North Sea oil?

Fortunately for Britain, such an experiment has never been tried and military officers are not automatically made heads of organizations upon retirement. Else the result would be a graveyard of failing or flailing institutions similar to chronically sick organizations such as Pakistan Steel Mills, Pakistan International Airlines, SUPARCO, WAPDA, PCSIR, and countless others. In these places merit is regularly superseded not just at the very top but inside departments as well.

Pakistan, on the other hand, lost civilian control over its military early on. Today many, if not most, diplomatic assignments and positions of top

Why Is Pakistan a Praetorian State? **329**

management are occupied by retired military men or, if not, they are approved by the Establishment. The three lists below, put together by the Lok Sujag organization in 2020, gives a glimpse of how power is distributed.

A priori, some minds are better suited for some jobs than others. Military mindsets undeniably contain some exceptional qualities. The testing conditions of war require that militaries develop a spectrum of capabilities stretching from command and control to logistics and materiel management. Many develop their own engineering and medical facilities that are very useful when a natural or man-made disaster strikes. In fact most countries have legislation requiring armed forces to support civilian authorities during emergencies and war.

Although military men in the age of electronic warfare have to be smarter and better informed than their predecessors, a jack-of-all-trades from some military

TABLE 12.1 Military Officers in High Executive Positions

Name	Division	Post
Lieutenant General (Ret) Ikram-ul-Haq	Defense	Secretary Defense
Rear Admiral Mirza Foad Amin Baig	Defense	Additional Secretary – III
Major General Muhammad Ahsan Khattak	Defense	Additional Secretary – I
Air Vice-Marshal Muhammad Nadeem Sabir	Defense	Additional Secretary – II
Lieutenant General (Ret) Sadiq Ali	Ministry of Defense Production	Secretary
Major General Akif Iqbal	Ministry of Defense Production	Additional Secretary
Rear Admiral Javaid Iqbal	Directorate General Defense Purchase	Director General
Brigadier Shehryar Anwar	Directorate General Defense Purchase	Deputy Director General
Brigadier Tahir Rashid	Cabinet	Joint Secretary
Brigadier Sajjad Salim	Cabinet	Joint Secretary
Squadron Leader (Ret) Shahrukh Nusrat	National Security	Secretary
Major (Ret) Qaiser Majeed Malik	Science and Technology	Additional Secretary
Captain (Ret) Abid Husain	National Security	Additional Secretary
Captain (Ret) Munir Azam	Power	Special Secretary
Captain (Ret) Naseem Nawaz	Science and Technology	Secretary
Captain (Ret) Javed Akbar	Commerce	Additional Secretary
Captain (Ret) Saeed Ahmad Nawaz	Industries and Production	Additional Secretary
Lieutenant (Ret) Ejaz Ahmad Khan	Kashmir Affairs and Gilgit-Baltistan	Additional Secretary

330 Why Is Pakistan a Praetorian State?

TABLE 12.2 Military Officers in Top Administrative Positions

Name	Appointing Organization	Post
Lieutenant General Hamood-uz-Zaman Khan	National Command and Control Center (NCOC)	Head
Lieutenant General Muhammad Afzal	National Disaster Management Authority (NDMA)	Chairman
Lieutenant General Asim Saleem Bajwa	China–Pakistan Economic Corridor Authority (CPEC)	Chairman
Lieutenant General Asim (Ret) Muzammil Husain	Water and Power Development Authority (WAPDA)	Chairman
Air Marshal (Ret) Arshad Mahmood Malik	Pakistan International Airlines (PIA)	CEO
Major General Aamer Ikram	National Institute of Health (NIH)	Exec Dir
Major General M. Arif Malik	Anti Narcotics Forces (ANF)	Dir Gen
Major General Shahid Pervaiz	Survey of Pakistan	Head
Major General Ali Farhan	Special Communication Organization	Dir Gen
Major General Amer Azeem Bajwa	Pakistan Telecommunication Authority (PTA)	Chairman
Major General Amer Aslam Khan	Naya Pakistan Housing Development Authority	D-Chairman
Brigadier Nasir Manzur Malik	Naya Pakistan Housing Development Authority	ED of Admin
Brigadier Tofique Ahmed	National Radio and Telecommunications Authority	Managing Dir.
Colonel (Ret) Dr Amirullah Marwat	National Commission for Human Development	Chairman
Squadron Leader (Ret) Aniqa Waseem Bajwa	National Education Assessment System	D-Director
Lieutenant Colonel (Ret) Asif Mahmood	Pakistan Cricket Board	Director Sec.
Captain (Ret) Fazeel Asghar	Sui Southern Gas Company	Board of Dir
Captain (Ret) Sikandar Qayyum	National Highway Authority	Chairman

TABLE 12.3 Military Officers in Ambassadorial Positions

Ambassador	Country
Major General (Ret) Abdul Aziz Tariq	Brunei
Captain Sahebzada Ahmed Khan	Cuba
Major General (Ret) Junaid Rehmat	Jordan
Major General (Ret) Sajid Iqbal	Libya
Major General (Ret) M. Saad Khattak	Sri Lanka
Vice Admiral (Ret) Ather Mukhtar	Maldives
Major General (Ret) Waqar Ahmad Kingravi	Nigeria
Air Marshal (Ret) Rashid Kamal	Syria
Major General (Ret) M. Khalid Rao	Bosnia and Herzegovina
Major General (Ret) Zahid Mubashir Shaikh	Ukraine

Why Is Pakistan a Praetorian State? **331**

academy cannot take the place of those who have spent their lives honing specific skills in academia, diplomacy, industry, commerce, and a plethora of technical fields. All Pakistani institutions are desperately short of competence and sorely need the right people in the right places. Ayub Khan's drillmasters when put at the head of organizations may superficially improve institutional discipline but can do little else. Soldiers should stick to what they are good at and paid for – fighting wars rather than running businesses, making movies, or manipulating social media. Statecraft is not part of their job description.

Wars of Choice

War and conflict are what sustain armies – armies lose importance when they disappear or are defeated. Pakistan has fought four wars with India. Three were wars of choice. The First Kashmir War, initiated by Jinnah in 1947, was relatively successful since it gained for Pakistan the part that is called Azad Kashmir. Aided by Pathan tribesmen, the war lasted fourteen months. The fronts gradually solidified and led to what is known today as the Line of Control (LOC). The second was in 1965. Flush with weapons that he had persuaded the Americans to give to Pakistan, Ayub launched Operation Gibraltar. This started the war but, after all options were gone, he had to end it with a whimper. The third war was one that Pakistan did not either want or initiate: thirteen years of army rule over East Pakistan had created conditions that had irreversibly alienated the Bengalis. The ensuing civil war is one that India took advantage of, thoroughly and completely. Pakistan split in two.

The fourth war, waged in the mountains of Kargil, was also a war of choice. It was the very first war in world history to have been caused by nuclear weapons – Pakistan assumed that its nuclear weapons would deter an incursion across the LOC. Of course, these very weapons also limited the level of hostilities. The nuclear genie cannot now be made to return to the bottle and will determine the military relationship between Pakistan and India.

Let us examine in more detail what led up to this fourth war. Long before nuclear weapons, there was a kind of rough military balance that became evident in the no-defeat no-victory 1965 war. This balance disappeared after 1971. At that point, another conventional war with India would have had disastrous consequences for Pakistan. Nevertheless, the Soviet withdrawal from Afghanistan in 1988 and the euphoria of victory over a mighty superpower gave hope to the army high command that the *mujahideen* nurtured by Pakistan would balance out India's advantage in conventional arms. They would not only help liberate Kashmir but also give strategic depth to Pakistan on the Afghan side. But the *mujahideen* and their offshoots could easily be targeted by Indian air power and incursions from across the border unless, of course, Pakistan had a big enough deterrent.

In 1974 India tested a nuclear device in the Pokhran desert. While it was not a deliverable weapon, it was a big step towards making one. Bhutto had made no secret of his desire for nuclear weapons after the fall of Dacca and the quest for the bomb now became serious. With crucial Chinese assistance, Pakistan needed only a little more than a decade to catch up.[53] By 1986 it already had a F-16 deliverable nuclear warhead available to it. India made a second strategic blunder by testing its nuclear weapons in May 1998. Just eighteen days later, Pakistan followed suit. After these tit-for-tat tests were successful, Pakistani generals believed that the calculus of power had changed forever in their favor. The NATO-Warsaw Pact experience had already established that parity could be obtained even with a much larger conventional force on the other side. So the fact that India had 1.3 million personnel in military uniforms, and Pakistan had only 0.6 million, did not matter all that much anymore. Nuclear weapons could now be used for more than just a stand-off with India. Convinced of an impregnable defense, Pakistani military planners embarked on what they thought was a brilliant covert operation in Kashmir, the Kargil adventure of 1999. It proved disastrous, but the faith in nuclear weapons remains undiminished.

Cross-Border Jihad – A Failed Experiment

An ill-thought out undercover adventure was started in 1987 by General Headquarters (GHQ) with the goal of attacking India surreptitiously. It was to exact a heavy toll upon Pakistan and a still higher toll on Kashmiris. Unconstrained by civilians, it relied upon the use of extra-state actors. This decades-long experiment ultimately had to be abandoned both because border fencing along the LOC has made it difficult for Pakistan-based militants to cross over into Indian controlled Kashmir but, even more importantly, because Pakistan's economic survival would be threatened were it to be blacklisted by the Paris-based Financial Action Task Force.[54] In 2022 it finally succeeded in getting off the list after showing credible progress on several dozen demands aimed at cutting off funds to terrorist entities. That there is seriousness now is suggested by the fact that a Pakistani court sentenced Hafiz Saeed, founder of *Lashkar-e-Taiba* (LeT), the armed group blamed by the United States and India for the deadly 2008 Mumbai siege, to thirty-one years in prison in two cases of terrorism financing.[55]

Background: in 1987, New Delhi's unconscionable manipulation of Kashmiri politics had led to a popular uprising. Pakistan was quick to translate India's losses into its gains. The Afghan war was over, fighters were aplenty, and large numbers of Kashmiri refugees flowed onto the Pakistani side. Pakistan's military establishment hit upon the bleed-India-through-jihad policy, to be simultaneously accompanied by denials of involvement. It was imagined as a low-cost option leading to eventual victory, a means to change an otherwise unchangeable stalemate.

Militants – such as Hafiz Saeed's LeT and Masood Azhar's JeM – suited the Pakistani military's agenda well. Others, such as *Sipah-e-Sahaba* and *Lashkar-e-Omar*, were sectarian and for use only against nationalists in Balochistan. Yet

Why Is Pakistan a Praetorian State? **333**

others – the most important being TTP – were unintended by-products that had made the Pakistan Army its primary target. All jihadist groups were products of a deliberate, officially encouraged culture of jihad that, prior to 11 September 2001, was visible through collection boxes placed in markets and shops, as well as prominently placed street banners. Gradually, Pakistan morphed into Jihadistan, attracting a multitude of Islamists from Europe to the Middle East and Central Asia to Indonesia. By 2002 there were already enough jihadist groups in Pakistan for one to need a guidebook.[56] So deeply anarchic had the situation become that ISI operatives would thumb through it, not knowing which branch of their organization had set up and was maintaining a particular group.

In 2002, on Washington's insistence, the Pakistan Army had established military bases in South Waziristan. This rugged area had become a refuge for Taliban and Al Qaeda fighters fleeing Afghanistan from America's post-911 attacks. Combat soon followed, with the Pakistan Army making extensive use of artillery and U.S.-supplied Cobra gunships. But the Pakistani state was ultimately expelled from this ferociously conservative area. An Islamic emirate, governed by particularly regressive interpretations of religious law, took its place.

Also in 2002, a militant jihadist movement emerged in Swat. It started its violent campaign in 2006. In 2007 Mullah Fazlullah, also known as Mullah Radio, had inspired the population of Swat Valley through his mobile transmitter broadcasts supporting the Pakistani Taliban (TTP). His fiery sermons led to the cessation of such "un-Islamic" activities as shaving beards, women leaving their houses without a guardian, singing, and education for girls. Soon the Valley was drenched in blood. For the next three years, the whole region saw dogfighting between the armed forces of Pakistan and the Taliban. The militancy of Mullah Radio was particularly deadly because right in the middle of "mainstream" Pakistan he was able to work with tools of modern-day destruction that ranged from media outreach to different kinds of weaponry and professional militants trained by the Pakistani state for its projects in Afghanistan and Kashmir.[57] After the military operation finally crushed the TTP, Swat was portrayed to the world as a success story for counter-insurgency operations.

By 2005, Taliban influence had spread from South to North Waziristan. Even though soldiers rarely ventured out from guard posts and heavy fortifications, the army was taking losses whose extent has never been revealed. The stock phrase used by the senior army leadership was that the enemy amounted to just a few hundred foreign militants and terrorists. But morale continued to sink, with junior army men wondering why they were being asked to attack their ideological comrades – the Taliban. Local village clerics flatly refused to conduct funeral prayers for soldiers killed in action.[58]

The half-hearted war failed, leading to the signing of a "peace treaty" on 1 September 2006 in the North Waziristan town of Miramshah.[59] By now the town was firmly in the grip of the Pakistani Taliban. To save face, army officers hugged the militants they had fought for four years while heavily armed Taliban stood guard. Although the military governor of the province, Lt. Gen. Ali Muhammad

334 Why Is Pakistan a Praetorian State?

Aurakzai, praised the peace agreement as "unprecedented in tribal history", in fact it was reminiscent of earlier Shakai agreement in South Waziristan, which too had ended up making the militants stronger.[60] The Miramshah treaty met all demands made by the jihadists: the release of all jailed militants, dismantling of army checkpoints, return of seized weapons and vehicles, the right of the Taliban to display weapons (except heavy ones), and residence rights for fellow fighters from other Islamic countries. As for "foreign militants", whom General Musharraf had blamed exclusively for the resistance, the militants were nonchalant: we will let you know if we find any! The financial compensation demanded by the Taliban for loss of property and life has not been revealed, but some officials remarked that it was "astronomical". In turn the jihadists promised to cease their attacks on civil and military installations and give the army a safe passage out. The Pakistan Army had surrendered.

The organization of jihadists by the Pakistani state had to be clandestine lest there be trouble with the United States. Not all could be centrally directed and handlers were semi-autonomous because they handled militants of different hues and kinds. In the confusion that followed, the military ended up killing its former protégés even as it supported others. Conspiracy theories were rife: the dynamiting of schools and suicide attacks on shrines were ascribed to Blackwater, an American security company.

The empire of jihad with multiple centers of power had by now become a complete mess. In 2007 a full-blown insurrection in the heart of Pakistan's capital Islamabad was launched by the Lal Masjid clergy, which had expected payback for having long been a source for supplying hardened jihadist fighters. It got out of hand and a military operation led to over 150 dead, including 12 Special Services Group commandos. And yet fourteen years later the central figure, Maulana Abdul Aziz, has not been charged with their killing and moves around Islamabad a free man heavily protected by armed men. After the Lal Masjid operation flushed out the militants, the scale of violence shot upwards. On 10 October 2009, Taliban militants stormed the apparently impregnable GHQ of the Pakistan Army in Rawalpindi. The twenty-hour siege, followed diligently by private television channels, left nine insurgents, nine soldiers, and three hostages killed. The meticulous planning, culminating in hostage-taking and killing, bore an eerie resemblance to the Mumbai attacks a year earlier.

As of 2023, Maulana Aziz retains his presence in Islamabad, threatening the government with dire consequences if action is taken against him. From time to time, he makes his presence felt as when celebrating his ties with the Afghan Taliban. He made the news when he set on fire the sofas of the *madrassa* that he heads, arguing that Islam forbids sitting on a couch particularly for those training to be *mujahids*.[61] Never, he said, had the Holy Prophet (PBUH) or his companions sat on sofas. The Taliban flag flew from his stronghold, Jamia Hafsa, after the Taliban captured Kabul.

But what must count as the most catastrophic failure of army policy in sanctioning independent groups to function is the episode of Osama bin Laden.[62]

Why Is Pakistan a Praetorian State? **335**

The most intensive manhunt in history ended on 2 May 2011 with his killing. When helicopter-borne U.S. Navy Seals slipped into Pakistan from Afghanistan, they returned with the body of al-Qaida's founder-king. It was the mother of all embarrassments. For years the country's military and civilian leaders had flatly denied bin Laden's presence in the country. Some had slyly suggested he might be in Sudan or Somalia. Did the Pakistan Army leadership know that the world's most famous and recognizable terrorist's abode was within easy walking distance of the famed Pakistan Military Academy at Kakul? There is no clear answer either way. Just days earlier, General Pervez Ashraf Kayani had declared that "The terrorist backbone has been broken and Inshaallah we will soon prevail".

For multiple reasons, bin Laden's killing became a bone stuck in the throat of Pakistan's establishment, which despised the Americans but was then formally aligned with them. It could neither be swallowed nor spat out. To approve would infuriate the Islamists who were already fighting the state. To protest too loudly, however, would suggest that Pakistan had willingly hosted the king of terrorists.

One clear consequence of the U.S. operation was to put into stark relief the humble subservience of Pakistan's civilians to their military masters. As the story broke on Pakistani news channels, the elected government of Asif Ali Zardari quaked. It was too weak, corrupt, and inept to take initiatives. Thus there was no official Pakistani reaction for hours after President Obama had announced the success of the U.S. mission. A stunned silence was finally broken when the Foreign Office declared that "Osama bin Laden's death illustrates the resolve of the international community including Pakistan to fight and eliminate terrorism". Hours later, Prime Minister Gilani described the killing as a "great victory".[63] Thereupon Pakistan's high commissioner to the U.K., Wajid Shamsul Hasan, rushed to claim credit: "Pakistan's government was cooperating with American intelligence throughout and they had been monitoring (Osama's) activities with the Americans and they kept track of him from Afghanistan, Waziristan to Afghanistan and again to North Waziristan".[64]

This welcoming stance was reversed almost instantly. A stern look from the military, which had finally decided to condemn the raid, took a few hours in coming. Praising the killing of the world's most wanted terrorist was now out of the question. In its moment of shame, the government furiously twisted and turned. Official spokesmen babbled on, becoming increasingly incoherent and contradictory. Tongue-tied for thirty-six hours, the president and prime minister awaited pointers from the army, following them dutifully after they were received. But simple obedience could not satisfy the army. General Kayani announced his unhappiness with the government: "Incomplete information and lack of technical details have resulted in speculations and misreporting. Public dismay and despondency has also been aggravated due to an insufficient formal response". The threat was barely veiled: government must proactively defend the army and ISI or else....

Thus prodded, a full eight days after the incident, Prime Minister Gilani broke his eerie silence. Losing the opportunity to take the army to task, he absolved

336 Why Is Pakistan a Praetorian State?

the ISI and army of "either complicity or incompetence". Before an incredulous world, he claimed both allegations were "absurd". Attempting to spread the blame, he declared in Paris that "This is an intelligence failure of the whole world, not Pakistan alone." Gilani, more loyal than the king, had somewhat overstretched himself. *The Express Tribune* quotes an unnamed young military officer who made a stinging comment before the army chief: "Sir, I am ashamed of what happened in Abbottabad." replied General Kayani, "So am I".[65] He promptly went on to hold the government responsible for allowing Pakistan to get a bad press. Even the head of the ISI, Lt. Gen. Ahmad Shuja Pasha, was not confident that he had done a good job. In appearing before an in-camera session of the parliament, Pasha broke a long tradition of overt military dominance by offering to resign for his institution's monumental intelligence failure. But, it is said, dead silence met his offer. None dared to accept what they privately wanted to.

The militancy was finally confronted with the power of the Pakistan Army on 15 June 2014 with 30,000 soldiers marching under Operation *Zarb-e-Azb* and then followed up on 22 February 2017 with Operation *Radd-ul-Fasaad*. The threshold of pain had been crossed as suicide bombers had targeted cities, attacked Karachi airport, and military installations. Lieutenant General Sanaullah Niazi, a three-star general, had become the fourth general to be assassinated by militants.[66] The beheading of 23 captured soldiers from Pakistan's Frontier Corps in February 2014, followed by their severed heads being kicked around like footballs, was recorded by the TTP on video as part of its propaganda campaign.[67] By one estimate, in the War on Terror about 49,000 Pakistanis were killed between 2001 and 2013.[68] More deaths happened subsequently with the storming of the Army Public School by TTP militants killing 149 people including 132 schoolchildren, ranging between eight and eighteen years of age.

Much remains unexplained about Pakistan's ambiguous relationship with terrorism and terrorists. The ones who eventually turned against the Pakistan Army were fiercely excoriated as proxies for some foreign hand and most certainly could not be Muslim since they were fighting a Muslim army. But finally the fact could no longer be denied that they were Muslim. General Hamid Gul – whom I frequently debated on television in those times – lost his temper at me during one session when he claimed that terrorists could not be Muslim since they were uncircumcised, to which I responded by asking if he had checked the fact himself.

The delusionary bubble had finally burst, as indeed it had to someday. The cost of this self-deception was high. It was paid for much more by the ordinary soldier than anyone else, and much less by their commanding officers. Trained to believe that India was the only enemy he would ever be called upon to fight, the *jawan* was psychologically and emotionally unprepared for the battles ahead. More were killed in counterterrorism operations than in all the wars fought against India. Thousands were wounded and maimed for life. But what hurt morale even more was that instead of being appreciated as *shaheed*s (martyrs), those slain in combat were refused proper burial rites by village imams. Things came to a head in 2013 after a U.S. drone strike that killed the Taliban supremo Hakimullah Mehsud. The *Jamaat-e-Islami*, under the leadership of Syed Munawar Hasan, declared the dead leader as *shaheed* while stating that Pakistani soldiers fighting the Taliban were actually fighting against Islam at the behest of the United States.[69]

Nawaz Sharif's government, sidelined by the deep state, had recognized that the use of covert jihad as an instrument of state policy had isolated Pakistan from the world community of nations. Diplomats tasked to improve the national image found themselves powerless when confronted by the force of facts. It therefore attempted – albeit only feebly – to make a break and concentrate on national development. Apart from the disagreement over jihadist groups, Nawaz Sharif's engineered removal in 2017 owed to his other disagreements with the army. His personal corruption and that of his family as revealed in the Panama Papers was a godsend for his enemies who exploited it to the hilt.[70]

Power corrupts, but absolute power corrupts absolutely. The costliest experiment in Pakistan's history appears to be over. But will there ever be an inquiry into those who conceived it and the others who executed it? You should not hold your breath because yet another experiment has been conducted, this time with followers of Barelvi Islam.

Courting the Blasphemy-Busters

Jihadist groups that were armed and funded by the Pakistani establishment as instruments of foreign policy belonged to the Deobandi sect of Islam. Excluded were Barelvi groups whose claimed love for the Holy Prophet results leads to a non-negotiable demand: death to all blasphemers. Since 2017, the Establishment's support has rocketed Barelvis into prominence and, in the years ahead, they will undoubtedly play a greater role in the country's political calculus.

Earlier, Deobandi groups had immediate utility in terms of hard, armed militancy for use across borders. Their more literalist form of Islam lent itself easily for liberating Kashmir or for establishing strategic depth in Afghanistan. But the point of diminishing returns was reached shortly after Swat nearly fell into the hands of the TTP in 2009 and the Army Public School slaughter in 2014. The realization started creeping in that even the other Deobandi groups – including the *Lashkar-e-Taiba*, *Jaish-e-Muhammad*, and *Lashkar-e-Janghvi* – were a bad investment. Confronted with better interception tactics across the Pak–India border, with time these groups became less militarily effective against Indian forces. Worse, others turned against the army and had to be militarily suppressed. This gradual realization did not, however, end the army's appropriation of Islam. The political engineering department of the Pakistan Army continued to add to its toolkit. Even as Saudi-supported Deobandis were phased out for jihad across borders, the long-marginalized Barelvis were phased in for domestic use.

Barelvis are associated with the name of Ahmad Reza Khan (d.1921) of Bareilly, a town in north India. They form the bulk of Pakistan's Sunni population and

338 Why Is Pakistan a Praetorian State?

are often perceived as following a Sufi, shrine-based Islamic mysticism that seeks a spiritual connection to God through extreme devotion to the Holy Prophet. This form of Islam is partly syncretic, having absorbed Hindu beliefs and colorful traditions over a thousand-year existence in India. Earlier they had been seen as too soft and remained confined to the periphery of the state's interests. In fact, because of their opposition to suicide bombings, they had been the targets of violent attacks from the Pakistani Taliban as well as other militant Deobandi groups.[71] The military establishment's decision to bring in the Barelvi groups was, however, to use them for goals internal to the country rather than on external ones.

The sudden emergence of Barelvi power in a radicalized form came as a surprise to most. It was spearheaded by the extreme right-wing sectarian party, *Tehrik-Labaik-Pakistan* (TLP) under the leadership of Khadim Husain Rizvi (1966–2020). This charismatic, foul-mouthed, wheelchair-bound cleric derived his popularity from having *Khatm-e-Nabuwat* (End of Prophethood) demonstrations across Pakistan. As a political movement, TLP burst upon the scene in the form of a popular movement to support Mumtaz Qadri, the bodyguard who had assassinated Punjab Governor Salman Taseer in 2011. Taseer had advocated a fair trial for a village Christian woman, Asia Bibi, who was accused of drinking water out of a cup meant for Muslims and for subsequently making blasphemous remarks regarding the Holy Prophet. The governor's killer was a follower of Barelvi clerics. His arrest and subsequent trial saw the killer instantly turn into hero. Upon being hanged to death in 2016, he was transformed into a martyr and mobs chanting anti-government slogans rampaged through cities across Pakistan. Tens of thousands seeking the killer's blessings every year throng to his shrine, located close to Quaid-e-Azam University in Islamabad.

Even as the TLP was rising for reasons of its own, developments were happening in the political sphere. By 2016–2017 the army establishment had decided to do away with Nawaz Sharif's government. One instrument used to remove him was the mobilization of religious forces. Towards this end, some experience has already been gained when the largely Deobandi LeT/JuD militant organizations had been reoriented away from cross-border affairs towards local political affairs. They had been encouraged to launch a new political party, the Milli Muslim League (MML). This hitherto unknown party rocketed its way up to the fourth position in August 2017 during the Lahore NA-120 by-elections, splitting the vote before disappearing from view. MML election posters denounced Nawaz Sharif as a traitor for seeking peace with India. Its candidates carried aloft pictures of LeT's supremo, Hafiz Saeed.[72] However, this use of existing jihadist power came at the cost of international sanctions and grey-listing by Financial Action Task Force.

Meanwhile the TLP was cautiously welcomed into the anti-Nawaz camp by Imran Khan. However, the army establishment was even more enthusiastic in wanting Nawaz defeated, and so it went a step further in encouraging the siege of Islamabad that began at Faizabad in November 2017. Calls from the civilian government to disperse the rioters were dismissed by GHQ.[73] Claims of impartiality were laid to rest when a video recorded by spectators showed the disbursement of cash to TLP rioters by the director general of the Rangers Force, Major-General Naveed Azhar.[74] The video went viral and was not refuted – in fact the cash was justified as payment for the rioters bus ride back to their homes. This ended residual doubts of the army's role.

Relying on extremists is never straightforward and risks blowback. This became clear the very next year. In 2018 the Supreme Court of Pakistan acquitted Asia Bibi, after which the TLP took to the streets once again. It then released an inflammatory video[75] that received well over 5 million views. Therein the TLP leadership called for the murder of the three Supreme Court judges who had dismissed blasphemy charges against Asia Bibi, demanded that soldiers of the Pakistan Army revolt against COAS General Qamar Bajwa, condemned Imran Khan as a "yehudi bacha" (Jewish child); and called for overthrowing the PTI government. Confronted with this strident challenge, the establishment tried to bluster but then quickly caved in. The Supreme Court did not dock TLP leaders for contempt of court, nor did the ISPR remark upon the call for mutiny. Instead, it pleaded for "an amicable and peaceful resolution" of the Asia Bibi matter because it "does not want the Army dragged into the matter".[76] TLP's flaccid half-apology was accepted, ignoring the lives lost and property damaged by the rioters.

Upon the death of Khadim Husain Rizvi, a crowd of 500,000 turned out in Lahore to pay homage. For a while the issue of succession was debated, but it became clear that his son, Saad Rizvi, would now take on his father's mantle. The mass popularity of this extremist group is not in doubt. In the 2018 elections it became the sixth largest vote-getter. The 2021 elections provincial assembly elections in Karachi placed it as the third most dominant party after the PTI and PMLN.[77] Given its huge gains in electoral politics, at least for now the TLP does not need to pick up the gun. However, this may not last. It was reported that TLP cadres had used submachine guns against the policemen who had tried to stop their march onto Islamabad in October 2021.

Blasphemy politics has driven Pakistan's mainstream politics in the direction of extremism; the future is likely to see still more of it. In the name of protecting the Holy Prophet's honor, the TLP has succeeded in fetishizing politics to a point where no politician or member of the national assembly dares to challenge any blasphemy-related stance or statement. This became startlingly evident in September 2020 after the French satirical magazine *Charlie Hebdo* republished caricatures of the Holy Prophet to commemorate the attack on its staffers five years earlier. In the name of freedom of expression, President Emmanuel Macron had supported *Charlie Hebdo*'s decision. Macron's statement immediately led to an explosion of resentment among Muslims globally, but nowhere was it as strong as in Pakistan. Faizabad Interchange, a central junction in Islamabad was taken over by the TTP once again. The militants ended their demonstration after the government agreed to present a resolution to parliament by 20 April 2021 calling

340 Why Is Pakistan a Praetorian State?

for the French ambassador to be expelled. To pressurize the government, violent protests were staged in the days before the deadline. In response, Prime Minister Imran Khan declared that TLP and his government share the same objective but the only difference was one of approach.[78] Not to be outdone or to be seen as soft on blasphemy, members of the political opposition joined the TLP's call for severing ties with France. Privately, however, they conceded that this would be an economic disaster because the European Union would retaliate strongly.

The TLP has broken taboos holding back extremism. Some parts of the establishment see bringing extremists into the mainstream as a sign of success. In part this was because there seemed to be no alternative: urban-based Punjabi militant groups are based in conservative areas where the mullah has multiplied his power over the decades. But these areas are also where the army draws most of its rank and file from. But Khan's sympathies were with the militants, not with those whom they attacked. Subsequent to the takeover of Kabul, even as the TTP ramped up its attacks on Pakistani forces, Imran Khan insisted that the TTP should be negotiated with.[79] While refusing ever to condemn Taliban atrocities, he argued that huge costs would be incurred if the path of confrontation is chosen. However, as with jihadist militancy, they choose to overlook that dedicated military operations were needed to contain the fanatical backlash from previously favored militants.

Political commentator Fahd Husain notes the irony of the situation when the National Security Committee – chaired by Imran Khan with the army's top brass in attendance – met in Islamabad in October 2021 to chalk out a plan for thwarting a march by thousands of TLP militants demanding the removal of the French ambassador:[80]

> Here was the highest security forum of the nation deliberating not on the evolving difficulties in Afghanistan, or the fresh provocations from India, or even the deep stratagems of nuclear deterrence – not so at all, the august forum was embroiled in dealing with a threat that should, in fact, have not been a threat had it not been made into one for reasons that had little to do with national security...Here were gentlemen who were only a few years back egging on the TLP to pile pressure on the then government; people who had milked the situation back then for partisan brinkmanship knowing full well the damage it would do to – yes, irony galore – the writ of the state. Unless this writ has mutated into something alien in the last few years, it was the same one then that they were willing to barter for, that today they are dying to uphold.

The real lesson from surrendering to religious extremism and injecting them into the political mix remains to be learned. When large masses of people react unthinkingly to emotive slogans, an explosive, unstable configuration is ultimately dangerous for everyone. Such groups gain the ability to paralyze life and terrorize all who disagree with their specific understanding of Islam.

Why Is Pakistan a Praetorian State? **341**

Ultimately political leaders – and those who secretly engineer political outcomes – also become unsafe. This should have been evident from the early years of the Pakistan–Saudi–American supported jihad. Instead Pakistan should aspire towards becoming part of a civilized, cosmopolitan world society. To let religiously charged mobs set policy is extremely dangerous. The state's reluctance to confront clerical power makes its earlier promises ring hollow. Forgotten is the anti-terrorism National Action Plan that called for financial audits of *madrassas*, uncovering funding sources, curriculum expansion and revision, and monitoring of activities. Auditing *madrassa* income or regulating their curricula is beyond what the state – or even the army – can accomplish. This particular praetorian state cannot afford to dispense with a pillar from which it derives its strength.

India under Martial Law?

In his book, *The Army and Democracy – Military Politics in Pakistan*, Aqil Shah notes that the Indian and Pakistani militaries inherited the same organizational structure, bureaucratic norms, fighting doctrines, training regimes, and, above all, a belief that the military and civilians had separate jurisdictions of responsibility that neither should breach. Headed by senior British military officers, both militaries were apolitical at birth. A common military culture kept alive a sense of camaraderie even when they were pitched against each other in the 1947 and 1965 wars. And yet, in spite of their identical beginnings, their paths soon diverged. Starting with the acquisition of military hardware, by 1951 the Pakistan Army was taking major initiatives of its own. While he held the dual portfolio of Commander-in-Chief as well as the Minister of Defense (1953–1958), Ayub Khan was empowered to veto virtually any government policy that he felt was inimical to the interests of the armed forces.

The Indian situation has been different from Pakistan's. From the time of Jawaharlal Nehru to the time of Narendra Modi, India's civilian leadership has exercised full control over even those issues which directly affect national security. This includes relations with China and Pakistan, alliances with the United States and Israel, command and control of nuclear weapons, and purchases of weapon systems from overseas vendors. Even though the Indian Army may be informed about major construction projects such as dams or highways, it plays no role in their implementation. Officers have been court-martialed for offloading highly subsidized defense rations and liquor on the open market at great profit, and the Indian Army still manages to operate about 100 golf courses and clubs which became the focus of a corruption inquiry by auditors.[81] When General Bipin Rawat waded into politics just days before his retirement as army chief, he was strongly criticized for having overstepped the limits of civilian supremacy.[82]

Martial law in India appears difficult, if not impossible. What explains the difference with Pakistan? This million-dollar question is exhaustively explored by Philip Oldenburg in his book, *India, Pakistan, and Democracy - Solving the Puzzle of Divergent Paths.*[83] I have paraphrased below the reasons he proffers:

342 Why Is Pakistan a Praetorian State?

- India's nationalist movement was much older than the Pakistan movement; reached a mass public much earlier; and was directed democratically (by and large). It valorized non-violence and a respect for the rule of law. The Pakistan movement was a generation younger than the Congress; it became a mass movement twenty-five years after the Congress did; it was directed in a less democratic fashion; and at a critical point in 1946 it resorted to mob violence to make its political point.[84]

- Gandhi was vital to making the Congress a mass movement and hence endowing its leaders with credibility even after independence. Miraculously perhaps, the movement put itself under Gandhi's direction even when its leaders did not seriously share his most important beliefs.[85] Oldenburg quotes the late Mushirul Hasan who argued that it was Gandhi who made the difference in setting India's course: "While Gandhi walked barefoot to break the Salt Law and to galvanize the masses by culturally resonant and action-oriented symbols, a pensive and restless Jinnah waited in London to occupy the commanding heights of political leadership in Delhi. While Gandhi trod the path fouled by Hindu and Muslim zealots in the riot-stricken areas of Bihar and Bengal, Jinnah was being crowned as the Governor-General of Pakistan".[86]

- India was able to develop a political society with a thick layer of institutions and leaders who could forge their identities and capacities in some sort of struggle for democracy, and were thus able to maintain and develop the citizen–politician link, typically through a vigorous party system. Politicians with that base of legitimacy can win the critical battles for authority with the state apparatus, in its bureaucratic and military form.[87]

Pakistan's generals have turned out to be able tacticians some of the time. But they are poor at strategic planning. The country remains adrift for want of that. Bad political engineering ended in creating the mother of all crises in 2022. Will the army's former pick, Imran Khan, be allowed back into power? Will the politics of vengeance and retribution continue indefinitely? How this will play out in 2023 and beyond is being watched with bated breath.

Notes

1. M.A. Kundi, Militarism in Politics: A Case Study of Pakistan, *Pakistan Horizon*, 56, no. 1 (2003): 19–34. http://www.jstor.org/stable/41394010
2. https://dbpedia.org/page/Praetorianism
3. S. Finer, *The Man on Horseback – The Role of the Military in Politics*, Harmondsworth-Middlesex, Penguin Books (1975), pp. 269–273.
4. A. Siddiqa, *Military Inc.: Inside Pakistan's Military Economy*, Random House Publishers (2017).
5. S.R. Khan and A.S. Akhtar with S. Bodla, *The Military and Denied Development in the Pakistani Punjab – An Eroding Social Consensus*, Anthem Press (2014).
6. *Okara Tenants Being Forced to Sign Lease Deeds: Hoodbhoy*, Dawn, 13 September 2002. https://www.dawn.com/news/57011/okara-tenants-being-forced-to-sign-lease -deeds-hoodbhoy

Why Is Pakistan a Praetorian State? **343**

7 Umer Gilani, *Beyond Naval Farms*, The News, 15 January 2022.

8 *Identities of Those Behind Leak of COAS Bajwa's Family's Tax Records Traced: Dar*, Dawn, 22 November 2022.

9 A. Shah, *The Army and Democracy – Military Politics in Pakistan*, Dartmouth College, 12 September 2014. http://media.hudson.org.s3.amazonaws.com/files/publications/2014.11.14ArmyandDemocracyNDUData.pdf

10 Ibid.

11 P. Oldenburg, Loyalty, Disloyalty, and Semi-Loyalty in Pakistan's Hybrid Regime, in *Commonwealth & Comparative Politics* (2016). DOI: 10.1080/14662043.2017.1261650.

12 *Hamid Gul Accepts Responsibility for Creating IJI*, Dawn, 30 October 2012. https://www.dawn.com/news/760219/hamidgul-accepts-responsibilty-for-creating-igi

13 *Imran Says Families of Army Personnel Will March with Him to Islamabad*, Dawn, 18 May 2022. https://www.dawn.com/news/1690304

14 State of Democracy in South Asia: Pakistan, SDSA Team Editor: Harsh Sethi. Principal investigators: Peter R. de Souza, Suhas Palshikar, Yogendra Yadav. Country Coordinator: Mohammad Waseem, Oxford University Press, New Delhi, 2008.

15 M. Asad, *Missing SECP Official Sajid Gondal Returns Home after 5 Days, Is 'Safe'*, Dawn, 3 September 2020. https://www.dawn.com/news/1578597

16 M. Asad, *Planning Commission Washes Its Hands of National Logistics Cell*, Dawn, 16 July 2021. https://www.dawn.com/news/1635291

17 N. Siddiqui, *Army Chief Assures Business Community of Complete Support for Economic Uplift*, Dawn, 9 June 2021. https://www.dawn.com/news/1628447

18 K. Abbasi, *NA Panel Approves Bill against Intentional Disrespect for Forces*, Dawn, 8 April 2021. https://www.dawn.com/news/1617040

19 S. Khan, *Cabinet Approves 15pc Increment in Military Personnel Salaries in Addition to Earlier 10pc Raise*, Dawn, 13 July 2021. https://www.dawn.com/news/1634869

20 Z. Gishkori, *Asad Durrani Was Affiliated with RAW Since 2008: MOD*, The News, 28 January 2021. https://www.thenews.com.pk/print/780797-asad-durrani-was-affiliated-with-raw-since-20018-mod

21 S.P. Cohen, *The Idea of Pakistan*, Washington DC, Brookings Institution Press (2004), p. 68.

22 A. Durrani, *Of monsters and Genies*, Pakistan Today, 23 May 2022.

23 https://www.business-standard.com/article/international/afghans-have-broken-shackles-of-slavery-pakistan-pm-imran-khan-121081601134_1.html

24 M. Zaidi, *Notes on Pakistan's Strategic Autonomy*, The News, 12 October 2021. https://www.thenews.com.pk/print/899585-notes-on-pakistan-s-strategic-autonomy

25 E. Ahmad, *The Signals Soldiers Pick*, Dawn, 12 November 1995.

26 M.A. Chaudri, Evacuee Property in India and Pakistan, *Pakistan Horizon* 10, no. 2 (1957): 96–109. Accessed 11 October 2020. http://www.jstor.org/stable/41393804.

27 N. Housepian, Pakistan in Crisis: An Interview with Eqbal Ahmad, *Race & Class*, XXII, no. 2 (1980).

28 This is a reference to the Harvard Advisory Group composed of trickle-down theory development economists headed by Gustav and Hanna Papanek.

29 C. Dewey, The Rural Roots of Pakistani Militarism, in *The Political Inheritance of Pakistan*, edited by D.A. Low, Cambridge Commonwealth Series, London, Palgrave Macmillan (1991), p. 256.

30 C.C. Fair and S. Nawaz, The Changing Pakistan Army Officer Corps, *Journal of Strategic Studies*, 34, no. 1 (July 2010), DOI: 10.1080/01402390.2011.541765

31 Dewey, op. cit., p. 257.

32 Ibid, p. 261.

33 M. Rashid, *Dying to Serve - Militarism, Affect, and the Politics of Sacrifice in the Pakistan Army*, Stanford University Press (2020), p. 14.

34 Ibid.

344 Why Is Pakistan a Praetorian State?

35 S.A. Khatlani, *In fact: Punjabis Dominate the Pakistan Army — But Only Just*, The Indian Express, 7 December 2016. https://indianexpress.com/article/explained/pakistan-army-general-qamar-javed-bajwa-4412295/

36 S. Nawaz, *Crossed Swords – Pakistan, Its Army, and the Wars Within*, Oxford University Press (2008), p. 32.

37 H.A. Rizvi, *The Military and Politics in Pakistan 1947–1997*, Lahore, Sang-e-Meel Publications (2013), p. 44.

38 M. Ayub Khan, *Friends Not Masters – A Political Autobiography*, Oxford University Press (1967), p. 40.

39 R. Khan, *The Role of the Military-Bureaucratic Oligarchy*, Dawn, 25 August 2001, cited in *Pakistan Between Mosque and Military*, Lahore, Vanguard Books (2005), p. 54.

40 Quoted in: A.R. Khan, *Ayub the First*, Dawn, 16 January 2020.

41 TOP SECRET: *Memorandum by the Assistant Secretary of State for Near Eastern, South Asian, and African Affairs (Byroade) to the Assistant Secretary of Defense (Nash) [WASHINGTON,] October 15, 1953.* https://history.state.gov/historicaldocuments/frus1952-54v09p1/d155

42 S.P. Huntington, *Political Order in Changing Societies*, Yale University Press (1969), p. 250.

43 Ibid, p. 251.

44 Quoted in: A. R. Khan, op. cit..

45 *Economy and Benazir Bhutto*, The Nation, 11 August 2011.

46 Pakistan had the bomb in 1989, Benazir Bhutto interviewed by Shyam Bhatia, Rediff, 9 March 2004.

47 Among Benazir Bhutto's many financial crimes against Pakistan during her second term, one was to distribute the land of Quaid-e-Azam University, a public university, to her political cronies in 1996. I initiated the resistance and became deeply involved in trying to stop this theft of public land. Using public litigation, my colleague Dr. A.H. Nayyar and I were ultimately successful, but over 10 years later another major PPP leader, Nayyar Bukhari, managed to steal a hefty chunk and build his palatial residence on QAU land. It signifies how Pakistan's corrupt win ultimately.

48 O. Waraich, *Pakistan's Spies Elude Its Government, Time*, July 31, 2008. http://content.time.com/time/world/article/0,8599,1828207,00.html

49 R. Khan, *Pakistan: A Dream Gone Sour*, Karachi, Oxford University Press (1997), p. 179.

50 G. H. Reynolds, Of Coups and the Constitution, *Colum Hum. Rts. L. Rev.* 48, no. 111 (2017).

51 T.B. Bronson, *The Value of Military Training and Discipline in Schools, The School Review, 1893–1979*, Vol. 1, No. 1–Vol. 87, No. 4, The University of Chicago Press.

52 Ayub Khan, op. cit., p. 101.

53 P. Hoodbhoy, *Confronting the Bomb: Pakistani and Indian Scientists Speak Out*, Pakistan, Oxford University Press (2013).

54 K. Yousaf, *Pakistan Reaches out to FATF Members for Support*, Express Tribune, 12 October 2020. https://tribune.com.pk/story/2268002/pakistan-reaches-out-to-fatf-members-for-support

55 M. Bukhari, *Pakistani Court Jails Islamist Hafiz Saeed for an Extra 31 Years*, Reuters, 9 April 2022. https://www.reuters.com/world/asia-pacific/pakistani-court-finds-hafiz-saeed-guilty-two-more-charges-terrorism-financing-2022-04-08/

56 M.A. Rana, *A to Z of Jehadi Organizations in Pakistan*, (Translated by: Saba Ansari), Lahore, Mashal Books (2002).

57 H.A. Shah, *Silence in Swat – Memory, militancy and the military in Swat Valley, Hurmat Ali Shah*, Himal, 28 September, 2020.

58 R. Yusufzai, *Pakistan Army Ventures into Tribal Areas*, The Central Asia Caucasus, 8 October 2003.

59 Peace Agreement in North Waziristan (Miranshah Peace Accord), Peace Agreements Database, The University of Edinburgh. https://www.peaceagreements.org/wview/1530/

60 Shakai Peace Agreement, Peace Agreements Database, The University of Edinburgh. https://www.peaceagreements.org/view/1531

61 P. Hoodbhoy, *Burning Sofas in Islamabad*, Dawn, 27 March 2020. https://www.dawn .com/news/1614871

62 For a roundup 10 years after the event, see Z. Hussain, *After the Raid*, Dawn, 2 May 2021. https://www.dawn.com/news/1621439

63 *Death of Osama bin Ladin, Ministry of Foreign Affairs*, Government of Pakistan, 2 May 2011.

64 S. Unnithan and Q. Abbas, *Osama Killed: Pakistan's Duplicity in Fight against Terror Unveiled*, India Today, 7 May 2011. https://www.indiatoday.in/magazine/world/ neighbours/story/20110516-osama-bin-laden-killed-by-us-forces-pak-trapped-in -web-of-deceit-745963-2011-05-07

65 *The Express Tribune, 13 May 2011.*

66 *Gen Sanaullah the 4th general to Die Fighting Militants*, The News, 16 September 2013.

67 S. Kakakhel, *TTP Tries to Justify Ruthless Killing of 23 FC Soldiers*, Dawn, 18 February 2014. https://www.dawn.com/news/1087719

68 *49,000 Pakistanis Have Been Killed Since the War on Terror began in 2001*, Express Tribune, 29 April 2013. https://tribune.com.pk/story/542287/49000-pakistanis -have-been-killed-since-the-war-on-terror-began-in-2001

69 *Petition Filed against Munawar Hasan on Martyr Remarks*, Dawn, 12 November 2013. https://www.dawn.com/news/1055872

70 *Panama Papers: Pakistan PM Nawaz Sharif to Face Investigators*, BBC Report, 20 April 2017. https://www.bbc.com/news/world-asia-36092356

71 *Naeemi among Several Dead after Suicide Bomber Attacks Mosque*, Business Recorder, 13 June 2009. https://fp.brecorder.com/2009/06/20090613923569/

72 *Hafiz Saeed Opens MML Office in NA-120*, Dawn, 25 December 2017. https://www .dawn.com/news/1378682

73 *Pakistan Army Called on to Stop 'Blasphemy' Clashes in Islamabad*, BBC, 25 November 2017. https://www.bbc.com/news/world-asia-42124446

74 YouTube, *DG Punjab Rangers Distributes Cash among Tehreek e Labaik Members*. https:// www.youtube.com/watch?v=woFaE5rIJZ8

75 Dailymotion.com, https://www.dailymotion.com/video/x7smoix

76 *DG ISPR Says Army Has Nothing to Do with Aasia Case, Urges Protesters to Take Legal Route*, Dawn, 2 November 2018. https://www.dawn.com/news/1443073

77 Zia Ur Rehman, *TLP Rift May split Barelvi Votes in NA-249 By-Election*, The News, 3 April 2021. https://www.thenews.com.pk/print/813839-tlp-rift-may-split-barelvi -votes-in-na-249-by-election

78 *TLP and Govt Have the Same Objective but Our Methods Are Different: PM Imran*, Dawn, 19 April 2021. https://www.dawn.com/news/1619131

79 *Pakistan in Talks with Taliban Militants even as Attacks Ramp Up*, The New York Times, 1 November 2021. https://www.nytimes.com/2021/10/02/world/asia/pakistan -taliban-talks.html

80 F. Husain, *Irony on the March*, Dawn, 30 October 2021. https://www.dawn.com/news /1654851

81 R. Bedi, *Armies That Create Their own Lucrative Empires*, The Irish Times, 27 September 2011. https://www.irishtimes.com/news/armies-that-create-their-own -lucrative-empires-1.610298

82 '*Unconstitutional Outburst': Sharp Response to Army Chief's Criticism of Anti-CAA Protests*, The Wire, 26 December 2019. https://thewire.in/politics/army-chief-gen- eral-bipin-rawat-caa-protests

83 P. Oldenburg, *India, Pakistan, and Democracy – Solving the Puzzle of Divergent Paths*, Routledge (2010).

84 Ibid, p. 21.

85 Ibid, p. 226.

86 Ibid, p. 27.

87 Ibid, p. 226.

Thirteen

IDENTITY

I'm Pakistani, but What Am I?

Bulleh: how should I know who am I ?	بلھا کیہ جاناں میں کون
Not from Arabia nor from Lahore	نہ میں عربی نہ لاہوری
Not am I an Indian from Nagore	نہ میں ہندی شہر نگوری
Not Hindu nor Turk from Peshawar	نہ ہندو نہ ترک پشوری
Bulleh: how should I know what I am?	بلھا کیہ جاناں میں کون

— Bulleh Shah (1680–1757), Sufi mystic and poet

Now that Hindu hegemony is gone and the Two Nation Theory is irrelevant, anxious Pakistanis ask what defines them as a people. The more worried ones are seeking ancestral roots in Arabia, Afghanistan, and Central Asia hoping to find a closer connection with Arab invaders of centuries past. They would like to be known as Syed, Qureshi, Baqri, Usmani, Mir, Turani, Khurasani, Hashimi, etc. In recent years there has also appeared a strong yearning for finding Turkish roots. All this is driven by the Pakistani official narrative, hammered into young ones from school onward which contends that Pakistan is the culmination of a natural process beginning with Muslims coming to India as foreigners and invaders but then convincing the locals to voluntarily convert to Islam. Suffering discrimination at the hands of the Hindu majority, those who converted sought their own identity and finally win the land where they can freely be Muslim. Many Muhajirs seem content with this simplistic narrative and disinclined to think beyond. Punjab is also largely unworried. But does it work well enough for Sindhis, Pushtuns, the Baloch, or the people of Pakistan's newest province, Gilgit-Baltistan? We must confront the question: Pakistan is certainly a reality, but how should all those who inhabit its geographical confines conceive of themselves? What about those who live abroad or were born to Pakistani parents and now desperately seek identity? After options are considered, the best answer to

DOI: 10.4324/9781003379140-18

Identity **347**

these anxieties is: colloquially speaking, chill out! We're all pretty much the same, the progeny of an African mother with similarities far exceeding differences.

The standard, official narrative of Pakistan's identity says the new nation born in 1947 was merely the culmination of a natural historical process that actually began in AD 712 with the arrival of Muslims in Sind. Driven by virtuosity and the need to spread their faith, the visitors eventually became conquerors who convinced the locals to abandon the caste system and voluntarily convert to Islam. Centuries later, Pakistan emerged because there had always been only two nations – Hindu and Muslim – who could not live together in peace.

While this "natural" explanation works for some Pakistanis, it does not work for all. When told that he is Muslim with Arab or Turkish roots, a Punjabi or Muhajir will likely nod his head in vigorous agreement. But a Pathan might stay impassive, a Sindhi would likely wince, while a Baloch – provided no one was watching – might vigorously shake his head in denial. Speakers of the Shina, Balti, Wakhi, Domaki, Khowar, Burushaski, and Gojri languages in Gilgit-Baltistan would likely not bother to respond. They are so visibly indigenous and genetically different that it would be fruitless to even pretend they have a connection with Arab Muslim migrants or invaders. Among a majority of those with strong tribal roots, it is common belief that their tribal connections stretched into the limitless past. In fact most find it hard to conceive that some ancestor long ago did not belong to the same tribe. How could someone so venerated have broken the family line? A father of someone belonging to the Gujjar tribe simply had to be a Gujjar, just as his father had to be one, and so on indefinitely. That marriage had occurred within a much broader set of people and that tribes had crystallized much later will not be admitted by many, if not most. It is no different elsewhere: Hindu castes such as Brahmins believe they belong to a chain that had never been broken and stretches into the infinite past.

In seeking to understand who a Pakistani really is – and whether he is an alien arrival from Arabia or belongs to his soil – let us begin by recognizing that in the 21st century everyone lives in some nation-state to which are usually attached powerful feelings and emotions of loyalty very similar to the tribal emotions felt by our ancestors. People identify with a nation, their "own nation". Many people are therefore quite shocked when told that the very idea of a nation is purely subjective, derived from some myth devoid of real existence. How can something so sacred be a mere figment of the imagination? On the other hand, no one can doubt that nation-states are very real and physical; India and Pakistan bristle with nuclear weapons that serve as grim reminders.

But wait! Almost by definition a nation is something nonmaterial, an abstraction existing only in your mind and nowhere else. You cannot ever *discover* an abstraction, you must invent it! This is just like in pure mathematics – ordinary numbers or perfectly straight lines or noncommuting numbers don't exist anywhere; your mind is what gives them life. Or take physics where every beginning student is told to first deal with a particle that is free from every kind of push or

348 Identity

pull. No such situation exists, and so it must necessarily be imagined. Similarly, nationalism doesn't exist or suddenly wake up to some self-realization of its existence – it too has to be imagined.

Because it is so fundamental, we need to take a short theoretical detour before returning to the issue: what is it that makes a nation in the context of Pakistan and Pakistani identity?

Imagined Communities

One of the most influential books written on the birth of nations and nationalism is Benedict Anderson's *Imagined Communities: Reflections on the Origin and Spread of Nationalism*. In his magisterial work, Anderson comes up with a succinct definition:

> In an anthropological spirit, then, I propose the following definition of the nation: it is an imagined political community – and imagined as both inherently limited and sovereign. It is *imagined* because the members of even the smallest nation will never know most of their fellow-members, meet them, or even hear of them, yet in the minds of each lives the image of their communion.... In fact, all communities larger than primordial villages of face-to-face contact (and perhaps even these) are imagined. Communities are to be distinguished, not by their falsity/genuineness, but by the style in which they are imagined.[1]

A nation, Anderson goes on to say, is a *community* because, "regardless of the actual inequality and exploitation that may prevail in each, the nation is always conceived as a deep, horizontal comradeship".[2] Here I think we can get additional insight into the nature of nationalism from Plato's classical theory of forms, so let's imagine looking at the natural landscape. We see there many different trees where some are short, others tall, some leafy, and yet others coniferous. Our brains nevertheless abstract a kind of "treeness". This creation of the mind simplifies communication by creating a category, hence allowing us to use symbols and a common language. Intriguingly, that's how the neural networks used in computer artificial intelligence programs can be made to work. It's most probably neural networks within our minds that enable us to have a sense of nationhood and nation.

Nations can be as old as a few thousand years ago, but the nation-state with defined geographical boundaries came much later. The ones that we might be able to recognize date to the 1648 Treaty of Westphalia, i.e., barely five centuries ago. And yet, "the nations to which they give political expression always loom out of an immemorial past, and, still more important, glide into a limitless future. It is the magic of nationalism to turn chance into destiny".[3] Crosscutting allowed individuals to have multiple identities: you can belong to a different tribe, ethnic or linguistic group, or religion and yet identify with a particular nationality. The process is open-ended. If a few centuries later Mars is colonized and develops a significant population, we might become comfortable with still broader identities as Martians and Earthlings while still retaining some subidentities.

Being capable of retaining more than one identity has profound political ramifications. As we saw in Chapter Two, after the failed uprising of 1857, upper-class Muslims in British India formed an economic and political class that was fighting to preserve and enhance its interests. There was little or no regard to the general welfare of lower-class Muslims. And yet the ordinary Muslim peasant or manual laborer – once he was convinced into believing that he belonged to the Muslim nation – could readily be made to fantasize that Muslim political leaders were actually fighting for his independence.

What about Hindus? Once he convinces himself that his dominant identity is Hindu and all others are peripherally important, he becomes a subscriber to Hindutva and the BJP, regards the Muslims around him are descendants of those who forcibly entered his country, subdued his forefathers, divided his country, and now demand pseudo-privileges like the right to Muslim person law. A 2021 Pew Global Survey concludes that:

> Indians live religiously segregated lives. Most form friendship circles within their own religious community and marry someone of the same faith; interreligious marriages are very uncommon. Indeed, a majority of Indians say it is very important to stop both women and men in their community from marrying outside their religion…Among Hindus in particular, attitudes toward interreligious marriages and neighborhoods are closely tied to views on politics and national identity. Hindus who strongly favor religious segregation – those who say that all their close friends are Hindus, that it is very important to stop Hindus from marrying outside the faith and that they would not accept people of some other faiths as neighbors – are much more likely than other Hindus to take the position that it is very important to be a Hindu to be "truly" Indian. They are also more likely to have voted for the Bharatiya Janata Party (BJP) in the 2019 parliamentary elections.[4]

The point is that once nationalism captures the imagination, all barriers are crossed and it stands ready for transplantation across a great variety of social terrains. At some point, it becomes so fundamental that people are willing to die and kill for their nation. The Dalit in today's India is oppressed by the Hindu majority but can still be made to believe he is part of the Indian nation and will therefore willingly pick up the gun to fight against Pakistan.

Manufacturing Cultural Nostalgia

Given sufficient tools and time, the power brokers within every nation can persuade it to reimagine its past and to place there what never existed. In previous chapters we have encountered countless examples where history in Pakistan has

350 Identity

been deliberately modified according to the state's changing needs. But it is not just history that is under relentless attack, so is culture. This has to be re-manufactured so as to suit the state's ideological needs. Those who hold the reins of power believe that an Islamic monoculture alone can keep Pakistan united. Film maker and critic Hasan Zaidi reminds us that this way of thinking goes back to the first decades of Pakistan. He writes that a committee on culture headed by poet Faiz Ahmad Faiz issued a report – one that never saw the light of day – which stated that

> Art … has an important dual political role. Internally, it holds up the mirror to a nation or society and helps it to discover its own image and its own personality. The consciousness of this personality helps a nation to bring about a closer and harmonious integration among its component elements. It is thus a powerful agent for national integration.[5]

Zaidi points out that in the early 1980s Pakistan produced over 100 feature films in a year. Today, despite a small revival post-2013, it produces fewer than 25. From about 1200 cinemas in 1980, there are fewer than 125 left today. Since the time of Gen Zia-ul-Haq's regime, stringent censorship and religious disapproval have throttled Pakistan's nascent film industry. The only acceptable entertainment themes permitted were those involving unbridled violence, jingoism, and so-called patriotism, and coarse misogyny. The travails of *Joyland* typify the reaction that depictions of social realism face. An internationally acclaimed movie that explores the world of transgenders, *Joyland* unleashed a storm of invective from Islamic conservatives.[6] Although an initial ban imposed upon it was lifted by the federal government, the provincial government in Punjab banned it once again.

While Pakistan represents an extreme case of willful cultural distortion, these are universal and becoming more common rather than less. Wave after wave of collective narcissism is crashing across the globe, helped along by the machinery of nation-states with populists at their helms. Across Pakistan's eastern border, Indian nationalism is dying and resurgent saffronized Hindu nationalism claiming a mythical past is replacing it. Shivaji sword replicas are now popular in India. This warlord is lionized as the perfect heroic leader – brave, wise, and just. Under every old mosque, remnants of some old Hindu temple or the birthplace of some deity is being "discovered". In the United States – the world's most scientifically advanced country – revivalism and revanchism went on the backfoot with Trump's defeat. But this may not last long. His black-hating, Muslim-hating, foreigner-hating Republican base is already rallying alongside him, urging him to fight the presidential elections for 2024 and win back a "rigged election". Like Trump, they want to make America great again – and white.

How odd! Country after country is placing its spacecraft on or around Mars, and helicopters are flying on a distant planet. To the mind of every thinking person comes the question of why political cultures are regressing towards primal values even as we leap from one achievement to the next. What in the human condition makes possible the conjoining of space-age science with stone-age politics?

It appears to me that this phenomenon might be usefully described as cultural nostalgia. The word "nostalgia" originated from the medical literature and was first seen in the 17th century as a psychological condition found among certain Swiss soldiers who had become inordinately attached to past memories because of long absences from home. In modern times, psychologists have observed that individuals suffering from dementia and Alzheimer's disease suddenly burst into tears, applause, or expressions of pleasure upon encountering some blast from the past – a picture, song, or even a smell.

For a more precise description, let us define cultural nostalgia as collective, societal nostalgia and, in excess, also a disease. In her book, *The Future of Nostalgia*, Svetlana Boym lays out two main plots – the return to origins, and conspiracy.[7] So, on the one hand, there is deep longing for a pure unsullied past which lies in the twilight zone between history and memory. On the other, that utopia is thought to be spoiled by schemers and plotters who conspire because of their own selfish motives. Scientific progress hasn't cured nostalgia, it has exacerbated it. Boym says that nostalgia "inevitably reappears as a defense mechanism in a time of accelerated rhythms and historical upheavals". So, even though it was initially understood as a longing for a lost place, she proposes that nostalgia should instead be seen as "a longing for a different time" that results from being unable to cope with progress. And so we are led to reinvent a past. It may be one that was never actually there but might still make us sigh and wish for those days again.

Inventing an Ancient Pakistan

> The Indus region, comprising the northwestern part of the Indian subcontinent (now Pakistan), has always had its distinct identity – racially, ethnically, linguistically and culturally. In the last five thousand years, this region has been a part of India, politically, for only five hundred years. Pakistan, then, is no "artificial" state conjured up by the disaffected Muslim elite of British India.
>
> – The Indus Saga: From Pataliputra to Partition,
> *Aitzaz Ahsan*[8]

A newly opened museum in Lahore has a section on ancient and pre-colonial history. It is titled "Ancient Pakistan".[9] The exhibit refers to the Indus Valley civilization, the Mauryan Empire, the Kushan dynasty and even the Khalsa Empire of Ranjit Singh. There is no reference to ancient India. One infers that Pakistan had existed forever.

An interesting – but ultimately unconvincing – narrative that belongs to the same genre has been invented by one of Pakistan's better known liberals. Senator

352 Identity

Aitzaz Ahsan, a prominent Punjabi member of the Pakistan People's Party and a former minister in the federal government, has produced a teleological argument purporting to give meaning to Pakistan other than it being simply not-India. He hopes to somehow explain the subcontinent's divide in 1947 and make an argument for Pakistan's "naturalness". His 600-page book, *The Indus Saga – From Pataliputra to Partition*, begins with the frank admission: "The Pakistani is still in search of an answer to the question: what, in essence, is the Pakistani's identity? This question still confounds the minds of many".[10] Jailed for opposing General Zia-ul-Haq's anti-democratic regime, he tells how he came to discover his theory:

> I began my journey to discover Pakistan in the New Central Jail, Multan. This journey continued in later years, in the Sahiwal, Faisalabad and Mianwali jails. As I journeyed into the distant past, it dawned upon me that 'Pakistan' had existed for almost five and a half of the last six thousand years. Indus had seldom been a part of India. This gave me a newfound vision of myself as a part of an old and continuous tradition.[11]

Ahsan's effort is remarkable in some ways. First, he centers his arguments on the archaeological sites of Mohenjo Daro and Harappa. These have long been considered irrelevant to Pakistani civilization by religious parties such as Jamaat-i-Islami who term them as relics of *daur-e-jahiliyya* – the time before Islam when the human race struggled in darkness and savagery. From time to time, there have been suggestions to do away with these ancient ruins, much as the Taliban did away with the Bamiyan Buddhas. Remarkably, Ahsan also admits to inspiration received from Jawaharlal Nehru's book *Glimpses of World History*, written from his prison cell in the form of letters to his daughter Indira and, later, the more comprehensive Discovery of India. Like Nehru – or perhaps like Shankaracharya (788–82) and Vivekananda (1863–1902) – he hopes to find the oneness of Pakistan among the diversity of its peoples – a unity that is, "so powerful that no political division, no disaster or catastrophe, had been able to overcome it".[12] Pakistan, he contends, preceded even the advent of Islam in the subcontinent and has still deeper, more ancient foundations to be found in its culture and geography. That culture is the Indus culture as opposed to Indian culture. Hence today's India–Pakistan border – or the "Gurdaspur-Kathiawar salient", as he calls it – is that which has been sanctioned by history.

The arguments given by Ahsan – which are quite breathtaking – can be summarized as follows:

The Indian subcontinent has two large widely separated river systems, Indus and Ganga (Ganges), with each giving birth to distinct and mostly separate cultures and histories. The Ganga-Yamuna (or Ganga-Jamuna) valley is the region lying between south Bihar in the east and the eastern-most tributaries of the Indus and east Rajasthan in the west. As such it is the great hinterland of the

Indian subcontinent. From north to south, it extends roughly from the foothills of the Himalayas to the forests and uplands of the Vindhyas, that is, up to the Narmada river. Ahsan contends that of the last 6000 years of civilizational history, for nearly 5500 years the Indus led a separate life from the Indian mainstream. For only five hundred years had it been a political unit under the Mauryan, Mughal, and the British empires. A watershed in the plains between the Indus and Gangetic drainage systems is the palpable divide between two lands, two peoples, and two civilizations: Indus and India. He claims that since the Indus system never really became a part of India, Indian history is really about central India, Deccan, and the South whereas Indus civilizational history is linked to the peoples of Central Asia and Iran. As for the Arab world, there was only perfunctory contact with it. The Arabian Sea and the monsoons were a natural boundary separating the Indus civilization and the Arabian peninsula, the contact extending only from 711 to 854, a mere one hundred forty-four years.

As the astronomer Carl Sagan used to say, extraordinary claims demand extraordinary evidence. But here the proof given is sparse, disconnected, and anecdotal. For example, Ahsan says the Arabs consistently referred to Indus as "al-Sind" and to India as "al-Hind", showing they knew the difference between the Indus peoples and the Ganga-Jumna peoples. But couldn't the names have been simply for convenience, custom, or convention? Were all Arabs making that distinction in the same way and were they sufficiently knowledgeable to tell differences between people, languages, etc.? He dwells upon how various materials have influenced riverine civilizations: the size and strength of bricks, availability of iron and bronze for implements, problems of horse and cattle breeding, soil erosion, etc. But in response one can ask: these are two only somewhat geographically separated regions – no great mountain ranges separate the Indus and Ganges river systems. Nor is the climate so very different. So why should moderate differences lead to two recognizably distinct, well-formed civilizations?

Many statements made in the book are sweeping: the "Indus person had a liberal and tolerant frame of mind", the Guptas were "a rich, fair-minded and brave dynasty", etc. These might be more appropriate for a high school history book than one setting out a grand civilizational hypothesis. The anecdotes and stories are entertaining and bespeak a well-read author attuned to culture: there are stories of Chandragupta and Chanakya, charming recounts of pre-Islamic folk heroes like Raja Rasalu and Prithviraj, and Punjabi heroes such as Dulla Bhatti and the revolutionary Bhagat Singh. Anything pulled out of the air, no matter how tenuous the connection, is okay if it somehow supports the author's two-civilization thesis. But critical issues are missing: how Bengal fitted into the Muslim League's demand for Pakistan is sluffed over, as is the separation of East Pakistan.

Although the argumentation in Indus Saga is unpersuasive, from it one still takes away some important lessons. First, the quest for Pakistani identity is ongoing and has not been quenched by the Pakistani state's strident official identification with Arab Islam. Second, even the Punjabi nationalist – the author being

354 Identity

a strong voice among them – yearns for a rationale for Pakistan as a natural, organic entity rather than being merely non-India. Third, a strong ideological tension continues to persist between the "locals" of what were Muslim-majority states in pre-Partition India and the Urdu-speaking Muhajirs hailing from Agra, Lucknow, and Allahabad.

Telling Hindu from Muslim

> First we are born to man and wife,
> Then they give us our names,
> Those names then our prison make
> Of inflexible religious frames.
> But I that a "Hindu" am
> Might well have a "Muslim" been,
> Had the sperm and egg that wrought me
> Come from an Aslam and Nasreen.
>
> – *Badri Raina*

Rewind to 1947. To tell Muslim from Hindu was once a matter of life and death as desperate populations fled their homes to reach the other side. Roaming gangs of Hindus and Sikhs massacred Muslims, and Muslims equally slaughtered Hindus and Sikhs. But how was anyone to know whom to kill and whom to spare? Appearance, language, mannerisms, and local knowledge sometimes sufficed. At other times, you couldn't tell if some individual was posing to be of the other religion. Here's where the "lungi" test was applied: males were forced to disrobe and their state of circumcision revealed. Females were problematic, and sometimes the wrong ones got raped and killed – the novelist Saadat Hasan Manto was creative but surely didn't invent the history of Partition when he dwelt on its horrors. Everything could have been so much simpler if facial features, height, and build had been sufficient to tell Muslim apart from Hindu. But it was not, and sometimes people mistakenly killed or raped their co-religionists.

Now fast-forward to Watson and Crick's discovery of the double helix. Just imagine that killer gangs had a computerized DNA testing kit at their disposal with all available genetic data stashed into flash memory. Would a pinch of tissue from a captive identify his or her religion and race? Hitler would have been delighted by this invention and would have sent everyone with more than 1% Jewish genes to Auschwitz. But the magic kit would be useless in India because Hindus and subcontinental Muslims are quite often too closely linked genetically to disentangle. Modern laboratory tools are dispensing with dearly held myths of racial purity. A study published in 2006 concluded that a Pakistani Muslim and a North Indian Hindu are not just indistinguishable in appearance but also genetically:

We find that the Muslim populations in general are genetically closer to their non-Muslim geographical neighbors than to other Muslims in India, and that there is a highly significant correlation between genetics and geography (but not religion). Our findings indicate that, despite the documented practice of marriage between Muslim men and Hindu women, Islamization in India did not involve large-scale replacement of Hindu Y chromosomes. The Muslim expansion in India was predominantly a cultural change and was not accompanied by significant gene flow, as seen in other places, such as China and Central Asia.[13]

Said more plainly, run-of-the-mill commercial gene testing companies can tell a lot about an Indian or Pakistani's ancestry, but none can determine your religion if you send to them a piece of your genetic material. At best they can make an educated guess. Presently, genetic marker studies suggest that most Indian Muslims are descended primarily from local Hindu converts. Studies using the Y chromosome are particularly significant since this is passed only from father to son. North Indian Muslims exhibit the highest affinity to local Indian regional populations. There are also studies that have detected genetic signatures characteristic of populations of the Middle East in some of the contemporary Indian Muslim populations. This is unsurprising because the Indian subcontinent has been exposed to several waves of human migrations from the Arabian Peninsula and Iran, the homelands of Indian Muslim rulers.

Another study also finds that most of the Indian Muslim populations received their major genetic input from geographically close non-Muslim populations. However, admixtures were also present in those surveyed:

> Low levels of likely sub-Saharan African, Arabian and West Asian admixture were also observed among Indian Muslims...Overall, our results support a model according to which the spread of Islam in India was predominantly cultural conversion associated with minor but still detectable levels of gene flow from outside, primarily from Iran and Central Asia, rather than directly from the Arabian Peninsula.[14]

Religious conversion characterized the last few centuries of expansion of Muslim populations into India. Cultural diffusion of Muslim traditions among the ethnic Indian populations was a consequence of sharing the same land for a sufficiently long time. Muslim immigrants from Iran and Central Asia married local Hindu females, generating a new admixed genetic pool. For both Muslim and Hindu nationalists – particularly the latter – lack of racial purity is a surely a bitter pill to swallow. It has inspired programs such as *ghar wapsi*, a call for India's Muslims to return to their Hindu roots.[15] The difficulty of separating populations on the basis of race and religion is leading the state machinery in both India and Pakistan to seek other means as each attempts to build a nation on the basis of religious identity.

356 Identity

State-Imposed Identity

> Identity is a subjective sense as well as an observable quality of personal sameness and continuity, paired with some belief in the sameness and continuity of some shared world image. As a quality of unself-conscious living, this can be gloriously obvious in a young person who has found himself as he has found his communality.[16]
>
> *— Erik Erikson, developmental psychologist*

National identity doesn't come from the mother's womb. As argued earlier, it is a social construct. Nation-states deliberately create this identity using national paraphernalia such as national insignia, cricket teams, national holidays, anthems and music, flag-carrying airlines, drama and fiction, and, of course, the display of military might. Success means achieving a clear separation of "us" from "them". This is what schooling in many countries seeks to achieve. While Pakistani Punjab may have found what it wants to teach in its schools, for other provinces the choice is less clear.

Keep Erikson in mind as quoted above – "a young person who has found himself as he has found his communality" – if some day at the usual time of morning assembly you happen to walk by a school in a middle-class or lower middle-class neighborhood anywhere in Punjab. After the national anthem is played, you will likely hear chanting which goes like this:

Teacher: *hum kon hain*? (who are we?)
Children: *hum sub Pakistani hain*! (we are all Pakistani!)
Teacher: *hum kya hain*? (what are we?)
Children: *hum sub mussulman hain*! (we are all Muslims!)
Teacher *(repeats)*: *hum kya hain*?
Children: *hum sub mussulman hain*!

The message: your national identity is Pakistani *and* Muslim. Khaled Ahmed, a journalist who hosted a TV series in Islamabad in 2006, recalled in one such program a large interactive audience of students was confronted with this very question: are you Pakistani first or Muslim first. Those saying they were Muslim first won by 90% in a hand-count.[17] Said one student, we've been Pakistanis for seventy years but Muslims for a thousand. A survey conducted by *The Express Tribune* found that a majority of Pakistan's internet users say they consider themselves "Muslim first" (49%), "Pakistani second" (28%), while 23% voted "Other".[18] A Pew Global Survey in 2013 found that most Pakistanis believe sharia is the revealed word of God rather than a body of law developed by men based on the word of God, and 82% want it to be the law of the land.[19] Drawing conclusions from a British Council survey conducted in 2009, *The Telegraph* says:

> The report found that three-quarters of respondents identified themselves foremost as Muslims, with just 14 per cent describing themselves primarily

as a citizen of Pakistan. Only 10 per cent have a great deal of confidence in national or local government, the courts or the police and just one third advocate democracy for the country.[20]

How different is it in India? Reportedly about two-thirds of Hindus (64%) said it was very important to be Hindu in order to be "truly Indian".[21] Several Indian states have introduced laws criminalizing interfaith love and interfaith marriages. Indian religious nationalism, deepened and widened by deliberate state intervention, is producing generations reared on the basis of otherness. However, it would be out of place to dwell here on this phenomenon, and we limit our discussion to Pakistan here.

Punjab, the power center, is the spearhead of Pakistan's religious nationalism. The revolutionary Punjab-born Bhagat Singh, executed by the British in Lahore, is an Indian hero but not a Pakistan hero – efforts by the left-wing activists to rename a road in Lahore after him received a fierce pushback from the religious right-wing. But perhaps paradoxically this religious nationalism has come at the cost of the Punjabi language. Urban Pakistani Punjabis have largely abandoned their mother tongue in favor of Urdu, telling their children that speaking Punjabi marks one as belonging to the lower classes and that it is a low-level *gunwaar* language suitable for coarse talk only. The language is not taught in schools, no Punjabi newspaper is published, and there is no satisfactory script for writing Punjabi. This also helps increase further the distance from Sikhs, a stone's throw from the Wagah border where the commitment to the Punjabi language is intense.

Sikhism came to Punjab in the 16th century. This was a synthesis of Islam and Hinduism, drawing upon both the Sufi tradition of Islam and the reformist Bhakti movement of Hinduism. As a result, the body of Guru Nanak, founder of Sikhism, was claimed by both Hindu and Muslims after his death. Even today, the rallying cry chanted at his birth anniversary celebrations in Nankana Sahib, is "Guru Nanak Shah Faqir/ Hindu ka Guru, Musalman ka Pir". This invokes him as "Guru Nanak, King of Faqirs/ A guru to Hindus and a pir to Muslims". The rise of Ranjit Singh at the start of the 19th century created Punjabi nationalism. His administration employed Hindus and Muslims, evicted foreigners, and extended Punjab's frontiers to Tibet, Afghanistan, Sind, and Baluchistan. However, Ranjit was ultimately defeated and the British annexed Punjab in 1849, thereby ending the Sikh kingdom.

This bit of history informs us of the reluctance of the Pakistani state to encourage a secular basis for Punjabi nationalism. Using the Gurmukhi script, Indian Punjabi is vibrant and alive with newspapers and books. It is unusual for Sikhs to speak to their children in Hindi; Punjabi is their preferred choice. But, as we have noted earlier, on the Pakistani side the state actively discourages Punjabi. And yet there can be no doubt that this language is intensely alive. When temperatures rise during a TV discussion, guests and hosts speaking in Urdu freely break out into Punjabi and appear as though they were released from a prison.

358 Identity

As for the quality of Urdu spoken by most Punjabis: this brings an involuntarily groan from those who speak proper Urdu, i.e., that which was once spoken in Delhi, Lucknow, or Hyderabad.

Seeing a loss of the collective self, many stalwarts have sallied off into the battle seeking to reclaim the Punjabi language. During the 1950s the late Masood Khadarposh sought to have the *namaz* in Punjabi instead of Arabic but ran into strong religious opposition. Alyssa Ayres describes several ethno-literary efforts in the 1980s and 1990s.[22] In 1986 the World Punjabi Congress, spearheaded by Fakhar Zaman, convened its first World Congress. There was a recognition that the center had dictated a similar loss of identity to Pakistan's other nationalities as well with tragic consequences there. In *Panjābī Zabān Nahīṉ Maregi*, the Punjabi nationalist Farani wrote:

> For the sake of murderous Urdu, first they slit the throat of our Punjab and murdered hundreds of thousands of Punjabis. Then, for this man-eating language, [they] wanted to make the Bengalis slaves. They tried to rob them of their freedom. And having become the spokesmen of the other brothers, they spilled the blood of Bengalis… And not just Bengalis, but for this murderous language they also fired bullets upon Sindhis, the next door neighbors for thousands of years.[23]

The romance with Punjabi revivalism, however, has been sporadic and limited. The choice of Urdu over Punjabi is ideologically based. Governments in Punjab have done far more to promote religious nationalism than governments in Sind and Balochistan. A recent example: although recitation of the Qur'an had been declared compulsory in schools since the 1980s, the Punjab Government enforced this in 2020 at the college and university level as well.[24] Henceforth without passing the required examination no student will be able to get a BA, BSc, BE, ME, MA, MSc, MPhil, PhD, or MD degree. Conflating nationalism with religion had earlier been vigorously pursued by General Zia-ul-Haq's, regime but in some ways that of Imran Khan's military-backed regime was more proactive. In earlier times, to get a university teaching job in the 1980s, one had to name all the Holy Prophet's wives and recite some difficult religious passages such as *Dua-e-Qunoot*. Still, students could get degrees without that. But in the new dispensation Punjab (and so far Punjab only), it was deemed that all university degrees would henceforth be contingent upon passing Qur'anic recitation together with translation. Significantly, no other province has passed such a law.

To discuss the change, weeks after its announcement, I was fortunate in soliciting a meeting with the Governor of Punjab, Ghulam Sarwar, on 23 July 2020 at the Governor's House in Lahore. As I walked into his office, I could visualize Mountbatten around me and imagine the end days of the Raj. It was an interesting experience, but not much was achieved because the Governor soon became defensive. He rejected my plea that Qur'an teaching should remain limited to schools, adding that in the new dispensation our university students will have to learn Arabic which is the best of languages. They would become better Muslims and Pakistanis now since they would also have to know the meaning of what they read. He could not elaborate on how this would help Pakistan produce better doctors, economists, engineers, or scientists.

Cultural Orphans

Egyptians are Egyptians, Turks are Turks, Iranians are Iranians, and Afghans are Afghans. Each is joined to the other by a common history, ethnicity, language, and ways of thought. It is therefore fair and accurate to call them nations. While Islam is the religion of almost all those within these countries, it is not the fountainhead of their national identity. Instead that source is ethnic, territorial, and historical. So, for example, Sunni Turks and Sunni Egyptians share the same Muslim sect and yet are comfortable with having separate national identities.

To call a Turkish-speaking Sunni an Arab, or a Farsi-speaking Shia an Arab, would be unwise and could place your otherwise good personal relationship with either in serious jeopardy. Religion is no longer an important organizing principle in Arab countries. Arabs fight each other on the basis of a national identity, not a religious one. An Egyptian will bristle at being identified as Arab – this in spite of the fact that an earlier name for Egypt was the United Arab Republic. But those heady days of pan-Arabism under Gamal Abdul Nasser have long since passed. Most modern Egyptians will likely tell you that ancient Egypt preceded Islam by thousands of years and that just 17% of Egyptians are Arabs, while 68% of the indigenous population is from North Africa, 4% are from Jewish ancestry, 3% have East African origins, another 3% are from Asia Minor, and 3% are South European.[25] The shoddy treatment given to Egyptian Muslims by wealthy Gulf Cooperation Council Arabs has created resentments that earlier were expressed only by Egyptian Copts. Egyptians don't want to be known as Arabs. But, of course, lots of Pakistanis would love to have this association.

What is the ancestry of those who hold a green passport? In pre-Partition times subcontinental Muslims belonging to Muslim-majority areas – my Muslim Sindhi parents included – had generally faced the question of their origins in good cheer. They recognized that some unknown number of generations ago someone along the line had converted from Hindu to Muslim and had accepted that as being in the normal course of things. But other Pakistanis – those of Punjab and those who migrated from India – generally do not like to accept that they became Muslim through conversion from Hinduism and so their search for Arab roots is unlikely to end.

360 Identity

The First Pakistani

> The Pakistan Movement started when the first Muslim put his foot on the soil of Sindh, the gateway of Islam in India.
>
> — *Class VI — Pakistan Studies textbook, Sind Textbook Board (2006)*

Beginning in 1979, the above view of Pakistan's origin was inserted into school textbooks. This was done in various subjects, and in all provinces. For example, in another Class VI Social Studies textbook there is a chapter titled "First Citizen" from which one learns that "Yusuf sent Muhammad bin Qasim to conquer Sind. This was the foundation of Pakistan".[26]

By this account the righteous 17-year-old Mohammed bin Qasim (AD 695–715), an Arab general who barely lived to be twenty, was the very first Pakistani. Somehow this pious young man had heard the distress calls of Muslim girls who were accosted by pirates near the port of Debal (near modern Karachi) while on the way from Ceylon to Arabia. In AD 712 he rescued them after defeating the cruel, psychotic Hindu ruler Raja Dahir. The story is derived from the *Chachnama*, the story of the Brahmin King Chach and his death at the hands of bin Qasim.

Authored about four hundred years after bin Qasim's death, *Chachnama* was suitably embellished with tales of bravery and cowardice as per popular tradition in times where documentation and authentication counted for little. Nevertheless, parts of it were presented as solid fact by Urdu novelist Nasim Hijazi (1914–1996) who turned it into a cartoon version of history. Hijazi's books are available in bus-stop bookstores today, sharing the shelves with a smattering of other books on epical religious figures. His novels were relatively unknown in the 1950s but were subsequently seized upon by Pakistan's Jamaat-e-Islami and eventually became part of the standard school curriculum in the Zia-ul-Haq era (1977–1988). Hijazi's strength lay in creating imagery unconstrained by facts.

If there had existed substantial other historical evidence of bin Qasim's times, *Chachnama* would have been tossed away by historians. It is, after all, a 13th-century narration of 8th-century history. But since there is no other preserved detailed historical account, it remains important. Depending on who you are, you use it differently. The Muslim narrative uses them to show the benevolence and fairmindedness of the early conquerors, while a resurgent Hindu revivalist movement uses the war and violence related in it as proof of the conquest's perfidious beginnings. The British seized upon *Chachnama* as authentic history to show how benevolent their colonialism was in relation to the bloody conquests by the Muslims of earlier times.

An important recent book by Manan Ahmed Asif, professor of history at Columbia University, challenges these instrumental narratives. The author argues that *Chachnama* is not a work of history or a book of conquest although,

Identity **361**

ironically perhaps, he titles it: *A Book of Conquest – the Chachnama and Muslim Origins in South Asia*. He warns that:

> *Chachnama* had already inherited from the colonial historians a marked valence as a politically sensitive text unveiling the destruction of the golden age of India (pre-Muslim classical period) by the invading Muslims, and the subsequent ushering in of India's dark ages (the medieval period).[27]

The book's central (and controversial) point is that *Chachnama* is not a translation of some Arabic manuscript as is claimed. Also, that this Persian volume was written for political purposes that must be viewed in the context of how that part of the world had become four hundred years after bin Qasim. The author contends that the purpose might have been not to produce a true historical account but instead a template for the good governance of Uch, the city where *Chachnama*'s author Ali Kufi had lived after his migration in the 12th century from somewhere in Arabia.

The notion of bin Qasim as the first Pakistani may fit the Pakistani state's ideological need, but it leaves countless questions hanging. Why does the Pakistan founded by bin Qasim not include Afghanistan and Iran, as well as the geographically contiguous Central Asian Republics of Uzbekistan and Turkmenistan, etc.? If Islam is the real glue, then why does Pakistan's establishment not welcome staunch Muslims on both sides of the so-called Durand Line uniting them with each other? Should Bangladesh, once East Pakistan, also pay homage to bin Qasim?

The notion of a damsel-in-distress bringing bin Qasim to Sind is hugely attractive for those who contend that Islam was spread not through the sword but by its manifest righteousness. That the valorous Muslim is one who protects his womenfolk has never lost its appeal. "Where is our Muhammad bin Qasim?",[28] asked an anguished Fouzia Siddiqui, sister of Aafia Siddiqui, the MIT- and Brandeis-educated neuroscientist who joined Al-Qaida and is now serving an 86-year sentence in a Texas jail. In a clear reference to General Musharraf, the incarcerated woman's sister bitterly criticized him for having had her arrested: "from the very soil where General Muhammad Bin Qasim liberated our sisters and declared dignity and honor for all, another general started selling our brothers and sister to a foreign master".[29]

Arab Wannabe Syndrome

One irritated Pakistani writer has called Pakistan's desire to seek Arab roots by emulating Arab culture its Arab Wannabe Syndrome (AWS). He defines this affliction to be "an uncontrollable urge to pretend to be, or to behave like, an Arab, when in fact the patient is not an Arab".[30] Indeed, a good number of Muslims of the Indian subcontinent revere the invaders as their forefathers. They cling to the notion of foreign roots because admitting local origins would

362 Identity

cause them to lose self-esteem and perhaps make them feel inauthentic and impure. Islam, as they see it, is fundamentally Arabian and hence geographically foreign to India. Some claim descent from Iranian or Central Asian stock. This outsider origin of the faith makes its adherents outsiders as well and makes people dig under family trees, hoping to discover Arab roots. Names beginning with Syed, Sayyid, or Sayyed are status marks because these are implicit claims of descent from Prophet Mohammed through his grandsons. Whether such a connection exists, the extent to which it has been diluted or weakened by marriages, or has been invented must be left unexamined. Cultural critic Nadeem Paracha humorously relates how awe of Arabs can mislead the naive among Pakistanis.[31]

The desire to be Arab is reflected in the names being given to newborns. Back in the 1950s many more children than today had names such as Pervez, Jamshed, Rustam, Sohrab, Firoz, Nayyar, Shameem, Firoza, Jugnu, Chanda, etc. From such names one could not tell religion: Pervez or Jamshed could be as easily Parsi names or Muslim ones, Nayyar could be either Hindu or Muslim, etc. Ambiguity helped assimilation into a wider South Asian community. But as Pakistan's religious identity firmed up, such names gave way to more local Arabic ones like Talha, Firas, Mudrik, Wael, Farafisa, Hajjah, etc.

The yearning for Arab roots was hugely heightened once General Zia-ul-Haq embarked upon his mission to convert Pakistan from a Muslim state into an Islamic state. This meant connecting it more closely with Saudi Arabia while distancing it from Iran. The earliest sign of the cultural Arabization of Pakistan was heralded in the 1980s by a subtle but significant linguistic shift. Television and radio announcers, and flight announcers for Pakistan International Airlines, were instructed to drop the customary parting salutation *khuda hafiz* (God be with you, *khuda* is Persian for God) in favor of the Arabic-sounding *allah hafiz*. Although the latter is not used in Arab countries, it somehow seemed more "Islamic" to use the Arabic god than the Persian one. Hindi and Farsi words were expunged from Urdu wherever possible. The month of fasting, written as *Ramzan* in Urdu morphed into the Arabic-sounding *Ramadan* or *Ramadan Kareem*. Similarly, *sehri* (the beginning time of fasting) became *suhoor*, *namaz* (prayer) became *salat*, etc.

Absurdities multiplied: "Al-Bakistan" and "Al-Bunjab" appeared on the number plates of cars in Lahore and Karachi. In earlier times these could have been objects of ridicule because, unlike Urdu, the Arabic language has no sound for "p" and so instead uses "b". In effect this phoneme deficiency led to renaming Pakistan and Punjab! A worried Pakistan wondered if "the land of five rivers is slowly giving way to sand dunes, camels and date trees".[32] There were also efforts to recreate an Arab desert environment within Pakistan: at a cost of 25 thousand rupees each, thousands of date palms were imported by Nawaz Sharif's government in the mid-1990s from the United Arab Emirates to line Islamabad's avenues and streets. Few survived the very different climes; hardly any can be seen today.

Dress and outward appearances also changed. Only a few Pakistani men took to the traditional Arab dress of *thawb, ghutrah*, and *agal*. These words are still unfamiliar to Pakistanis. But for women it was different. In the 1990s, *abaya* was a word unknown to speakers of Urdu. The shapeless gown, usually black, is of Arab origin. But now countless shops in every city of Pakistan specialize in abayas, hijabs, and burqas. Some are at the high-end, frequented by rich housewives and their daughters. Those in burqa sometimes also wear black socks and gloves, covering every inch of the body except for two slits around the eyes. While some women are not allowed to step outside their house, others are veiled even inside their house because of hired male domestic help.

Up until the late 1980s, the fully veiled student was a rarity on Pakistani university and college campuses. But in colleges and universities across Pakistan today, the female student is increasingly seeking the anonymity of the burqa. And in some parts of the country, she seems to outnumber her sisters who still "dare" to show their faces. The success of dedicated efforts to promote the separation of the sexes, and to radically change women's apparel, is particularly noticeable among educated Pakistani women, including those who live in the elite Defense Housing Societies of Karachi, Lahore, and other big cities. Proselytizers, such as Farhat Hashmi, became immensely popular there.

A personal observation: middle-class female students in hijab and burqa are far less engaged and interactive in a classroom environment when compared to their counterparts of the 1970s or 1980s. This was when the hijab and burqa were a rarity on campuses: back then in the entire Quaid-e-Azam University, there were no more than one or two burqa-clad women, although hijab was not so uncommon. Today, female students frequently outnumber male students, and yet they rarely ask questions in class. Most are silent note-takers, satisfied at merely recording what has happened in class.

The ethnography of the expanding Pakistani middle classes and its visible Arabization has recently being explored by Ammara Maqsood in her book, *The New Pakistani Middle Class*.[33] She distinguishes between the "old" middle class – which is liberal and secular in outlook – and the new, which wears religiosity on its sleeve. Maqsood apologetically claims that the "new" middle-class women wearing headscarves or burqas do so entirely by choice and, in doing so, are making a statement that this derives from their knowledge and understanding of Islam as conveyed to them by organizations such as Al-Huda. This is an elephant-sized lie: It certainly would not cut much ice with Iranian girls and women who despise the chadar and must wear it literally at gunpoint; hundreds have died and been raped in demonstrations that followed the killing of anti-hijab activist Mahsa Amini in September 2022. Many Pakistani women simply do not have the option of appearing bare-faced in public. In that case, the "new" is a misnomer since it is actually going back to traditional values. However, the "new" categorization is justified in describing a religiously conservative class that has become hooked on to specious consumerism and consumption.

364 Identity

Pakistan's new middle class, while despising the West for its immorality, is enamored with buying the products of western technology and industry. It is therefore the target of aggressive advertising. Across the country men with beards and women wearing veils can be seen snapping up mobile phones and electronic gadgets while scouting around for attractive deals at western-style shopping malls and mega-stores. Lacking the full means to buy them, most prefer cheap bazaars or wholesale markets. As in oil-rich Arab countries, gross commercialization, with advertising and marketing as its handmaidens, has created artificial wants. Increasingly, the middle classes – both old and new – live in a throwaway culture associated with the greed, wastage, and frivolous desires that are characteristics of capitalism. Noteworthy is the slick marketing of designer apparel under MTJ branding. This is the brainchild of a *Tableeghi Jamaat* preacher, Maulana Tariq Jameel, who preaches austerity to the masses but has a lifestyle that is marked by conspicuous consumption. Other pop-idol preachers such as the recently deceased Junaid Jamshed and Amer Liaquat Husain also had million strong followings.

My Name Is Ertugrul

In 2020 a Turkish drama series brimming with tribal intrigues, blood, murder, and conquest – all wrapped in pious religious idiom – took Pakistan by storm. Filmed in Anatolia and produced by Turkish Radio and Television Corporation (TRT), "Dirilis Ertugrul" is a 150-episode fictional extravaganza of Ertugrul Ghazi, father of the Ottoman Empire's founder. This brave 13th-century warrior faces vicious infidels in the form of Byzantines, Crusaders, and Mongols all of whom he manages to defeat with courage and intelligence and thus clearly shows the superiority of Islam over others.

Here's a typical scene of what the drama series has inspired. Using the internet you will easily find videos made using a smartphone such as the following: 7- to 10-year-old kids are playing in some dusty, Seraiki-speaking village of South Punjab. Each boy has fashioned for himself a crude wood and tin sword, ensconced in a scabbard tied to his shalwar's *narra*. "What's it for?", asks the off-camera interviewer, who seems to be enjoying himself. "I'm a Muslim", says one proudly, pulling out his sword and waving it in the air, "It's for cutting off the heads of *kafirs*". "Your name?", inquires the interviewer. "Ertugrul", the boy replies. Many such videos can be found by the reader using Google. A Pashto version[34] of Ertugrul has been produced by a group of young men in Swat, once the hotbed of Taliban insurgency.

The first scene of the first (Turkish original) episode begins with sword-making and sword-sharpening in the background of nomadic tents. The tribe's adversaries are Christians and Byzantines whose bloodied bodies lie scattered here and there after every fight. The hero, Ertugrul Ghazi, not only beheads several Knight Templars but also former associates from his tribe, such as Kurdoglu Bey, whom he suspects of disloyalty. "Dirilis Ertugrul" seeks both to idealize Islam and to vent Turkish nostalgia for a long-lost empire. It feeds into the naïve belief that victory comes from the Muslim warrior's unflinching faith and brave arm, with intrigue and betrayal explaining away any setback. The sound of galloping horses brings back the glory days of Salahuddin Ayyubi, and a tear drops from many an eye. In many ways Ertugrul brings to memory King Richard I, who led the third crusade against the Muslim defenders of Jerusalem. One thousand years ago, every boy and man in England had dreamed of following their valiant king into battle and cutting off a Muslim's head. Although Richard I ultimately failed in his crusade, he too was mythologized and earned the title, Richard the Lionheart. Like Ertugrul, he was the ultimate leader: brave, wise, and just.

Production of this intricate drama series demanded massive funding by the Turkish state. A horse farm was created, together with a special zoo-like area for the sheep, goats, nightingales, and partridges that appear on the show. A Hollywood stunt team was hired to train actors for the movie's staged fights. President Erdogan and his family are reported to have repeatedly visited the filming site.

That this drama reflects authentic Islamic history is doubtful. Rather, this is a freewheeling caricature of 13th-century Anatolia of which we know next to nothing. Facts are not important, says Mehmet Bozdag, the man who wrote and produced the series. To quote:

> There is very little information about the period we are presenting – not exceeding 4-5 pages. Even the names are different in every source. The first works written about the establishment of the Ottoman State were about 100-150 years later. There is no certainty in this historical data...we are shaping a story by dreaming.[35]

Nevertheless, Prime Minister Imran Khan publicly urged the youth to watch the show and learn about the 'true' Islamic culture, values, and history. In a Tweet that made historians roll their eyes, he proudly said that Turks had ruled India for six hundred years. Depending on how charitable one feels, this is no more than between quarter-true to half-true only. But it must be rare for a prime minister to hail imperial rule over his country. Upon the prime minister's orders, the state-run Pakistan Television aired a continuous dubbed translation of the series in Urdu that left Dirilis's makers astonished and thrilled at its tumultuous welcome. Some Pakistanis were appalled that the prime minister chose to meet with the Dirilis team in Islamabad instead of being with the survivors and families of a dozen coal miners belonging to the embattled Hazara community who had had their throats slit by Da'esh militants in Mach, Balochistan.[36]

One might not expect tribal Turkmen fighting for a homeland to capture the imagination of millions in some far-off country. But Pakistan is different. Transfixed, entire families spent evenings watching it together, thinking it to be wholesome entertainment and imagining this to be genuine Islamic history. So deep is the nostalgia that Ertugrul statues have been erected in Punjab's cities.[37] For some he is Pakistan's newly dreamed messiah, a leader who will restore

366 Identity

Islam's glories and liberate Kashmir and Palestine from infidels. Reportedly some newborns are being named after characters in the drama series. I wonder what the little boys with little swords that I saw will grow up to be.

It is unclear whether the shift away from Arabism towards Turkism will be long-lasting or deep. One can readily discern the political reasons behind it. Saudi Arabia is disinclined to support Pakistan on Kashmir, and because of its business interests it is leaning more towards India. The tendency toward social liberalization under Crown Prince Mohammed bin Salman creates uneasiness. But because of Pakistan's dependence on Saudi Arabia as employment for its manpower and for financial assistance, it cannot voice its disappointment except in carefully couched words. On the other hand, Turkey under Erdogan has been proactive on both Kashmir and Palestine, and his Islamist agenda – including his decision to turn the iconic Hagia Sophia cathedral-museum into a mosque – has received huge plaudits in Pakistan.[38]

The Turks being a more modern people than Pakistanis do not attract to themselves the conservative elements of Pakistani society. So, for example, in spite of the adulation showered upon the Ertugrul series, there was much heart-burning at the role played by the actresses. The actress Esra Bilgiç who plays Halima Sultan, dresses as a modern Turkish woman and has for that reason drawn remarks like, "For what reason are some Turkish and Pakistani on-screen characters following Western culture?" and "I loathe you in the wake of seeing this image Halima Sultan".[39]

Citizens and Subjects

If you are Muslim, you can be a full citizen of Pakistan. It does not matter if you or your parents were born here or somewhere on the Indian side – Bihar, UP, or Hyderabad. But what if you are not Muslim and your family has lived on this land for as far back as can be traced? In that case, you simply happen to live in Pakistan.

In Volume II of Mein Kampf, Adolf Hitler declared the future Third Reich would classify its population into three groups: citizens, subjects of the state, and aliens. Citizens would enjoy all the legal rights and privileges granted by the state; the subject must obey the law but could not enjoy rights or privileges unless granted citizenship; and the alien – citizen of another state – would also have no rights. Citizenship was open only to those whose racial origins were purely Germanic. Women were subjects at birth, but those of proper race could become citizens by marrying a true German.

With the defeat of Germany a revulsion against racial politics occurred world-wide together with a consensus on the ideal of universal citizenship. This meant that citizen and subject should be inseparable and that citizenship, and national-ity implied equality before the law. Correspondingly the law must guarantee that no individual or group of individuals be privileged or discriminated against by the government. This core principle of liberalism is enshrined in Article 7 of the UN's Universal Declaration of Human Rights (UDHR) which states: "All are equal before the law and are entitled without any discrimination to equal protection of the law".

A non-Muslim living in Pakistan is a subject, not a citizen. Formally, as per Pakistan's Constitution, a non-Muslim citizen of Pakistan can be half-Pakistani or two-thirds Pakistani but never a full Pakistani. But in reality, the price is in terms of constant fear, denied employment opportunities, discrimination at the workplace and socially, and restricted mobility. Non-Muslims hope to be less noticeable and name their children appropriately, but back in the 1950s the names of Karachi's Christians were usually biblically derived. Boys could be Jacob, Joseph, Michael, Paul, Peter, Robert, etc. Girls were often Mary, Pauline, Rachel, Rita, Ruth, etc. Changed circumstances have led to safer names: Emaan, Hina, Iqbal, Maryum, Naveed, Saima, Shafqat, Shahbaz, etc. Survival in a hostile milieu demands camouflaging. Today even a 13-year-old (or younger) Hindu or Christian girl can be kidnapped and legally converted to Islam. A parliamentary committee rejected the anti-forced conversion bill.[40]

Religious minorities did not expect to get a good deal once Partition took place, and that expectation was borne out. The number of Hindus and Sikhs left behind in Pakistani Punjab is minuscule, and the only sizeable Hindu population is in Sind. Many are anxious to leave.[41] At the instant of Pakistan's birth, one could have argued that pluralism would arrive by slow degrees. Well into the early 1960s the English-speaking native elite from the Raj days was still firmly in command. Religious right-wing parties in Pakistan that opposed equal citizenship rights, in particular Jamaat-e-Islami and Deobandis, did not as yet have enough members with sufficient education or skills to be significant players in governing the new country. This fact allowed many non-Muslims to continue with their pre-Partition positions in the civil service and armed forces.

Although a movement centered on Muslim identity had created Pakistan, non-Muslims took heart from Jinnah's celebrated 11 August 1947 speech assuring them that they "may belong to any religion or caste or creed; that has nothing to do with the business of the State". Jinnah's appointment of Jogendra Nath Mandal as Pakistan's first law minister made it seem serious. Mandal, a scheduled caste leader from Kolkata, was instrumental in getting Dr B.R. Ambedkar elected to India's Constituent Assembly. Like Ambedkar himself, Mandal believed that the Dalits or Untouchables did not belong to mainstream Hinduism.[42] By choosing Chaudhry Zafarullah Khan, an Ahmadi, as the first foreign minister of Pakistan, Jinnah sent a strong message of reassurance to Ahmadis. They were then, of course, legally Muslims and many were well placed in official positions. Only a few of Jinnah's close associates disagreed, and that too in private.

The unraveling of pluralism happened in slow motion. The first hint that Pakistan would be not just a Muslim state but a Sunni Muslim state came when Jinnah's state funeral was not led by a Shia *alim*, as is the Shia custom. Instead a Sunni Deobandi *alim*, Shabbir Ahmed Usmani, was selected for the task. The Objectives Resolution, passed by the Constituent Assembly in 1949, was a sure indication that pluralism

368 Identity

was headed for the rocks. This legislation introduced the term "religious minority" into the constitutional lexicon, making explicit that Pakistan would henceforth officially differentiate between its citizens on the basis of their held religion. It was supported by Shia members of the Assembly, as well as those who were Ahmadis. Rather strangely, Mandal also supported the resolution but, faced by hostile attitudes of his colleagues, he resigned his position and migrated back to India after violence against Dalits broke out in East Pakistan in 1950.

The first large-scale religious violence happened in 1953 when Lahore was engulfed in anti-Ahmadi riots leaving hundreds dead. The Ahmadis had supported Jinnah's Two Nation Theory believing that they would be better off in an Islamic Pakistan than a secular India. In 1956 Pakistan underwent a name change and became the Islamic Republic of Pakistan with Islam now formally the religion of the state. Minorities could practice their religions but only if the practices were allowed by the principles of "democracy, freedom, equality, tolerance and social justice as enunciated by Islam". Constitutionally, no non-Muslim could become head of state or army chief.

Although these changes had occurred at a high political level, society remained open and liberal. Karachi, Lahore, and Quetta were culturally diverse metropolises with wine shops, women in fashionable clothes, and cinema houses showing the latest movies. Several Christians, like Flight Commander Cecil Chaudhury and Wing Commander Mervyn Leslie Middlecoat, were prominent in the list of war heroes of the 1965 war. It was sometime in the 1970s that this relative open-mindedness began to fade. Large sections of Pakistan's Christian, Hindu, and Parsi communities saw the writing on the wall. Many chose to emigrate rather than continue living their lives on the margins. The West had an open immigration policy at the time. Since non-Muslims were among the best educated and skilled, the loss of human capital was large. One talked about "brain drain" in those days.

In earlier years the definition of religious minority encompassed Hindus, Christians, and Parsis. But in 1974 there was an addition – the Ahmadis. By an act of parliament, they were formally declared non-Muslims. Emboldened, elements in the religious establishment demanded that smaller Muslim communities, such as the Ismailis and Zikris, should also be expelled from Islam. Shias and Ahmadis had both been enthusiastic about Pakistan but were now being forced to reassess. Chaudhry Zafarullah Khan, commended by Jinnah for eloquently arguing the Two Nation Theory, lived long enough to see disillusionment. So did the physics Nobel Prize winner, Professor Abdus Salam, who was also a vociferous supporter of the idea of Pakistan. Ahmadis held senior positions in the armed forces, and some were celebrated as war heroes for having fought against India in the 1947 and 1965 wars.

Nevertheless, the inevitable happened: once religion was placed at the very center of state and governance, the question of which version of Islam was correct became bitterly contentious. The Two Nation Theory was falling victim to its own contradictions. Ironically, Ahmadis were among the strongest proponents

Identity **369**

of the division of India. But today they are undoubtedly the most fearful, and the most strongly discriminated against. Those who remain are fearful, conscious that any dispute with "real" Muslims could instantly result in their being falsely accused of blasphemy.

Until Zia-ul-Haq's Islamization, Pakistan's Shias did not have the self-image of a religious minority. In fact they had joined Sunnis in supporting Mr. Bhutto's 1974 decision to declare Ahmadis as non-Muslim. They too paid a price. In the years after 9/11, tribal areas were convulsed in sectarian warfare: Kurram, Parachinar, and Hangu became killing grounds for both Sunni and Shia, but with most casualties being Shia. The Taliban have an openly anti-Shia agenda. Suicide bombings laid to waste bazaars and mosques. An estimated 60% of people in Parachinar were said to be suffering from post-traumatic stress disorder in the wake of frequent terror attacks.[43] City life also became increasingly insecure and segregated. The target killing of Shia doctors in Karachi, followed by a suicide attack[44] upon Abbas Town in 2013 led to Karachi's Shia neighborhoods being barricaded and fortified. Shia Hazaras, a significant minority community in Pakistan, have facial features that make them readily identifiable. Targeted by Sunni extremists, they fled Pakistan by the thousands with many losing their lives in an attempt to reach Australia by sea. The majority lives a ghettoized existence in Quetta.

That Shias are deviants from the Islamic faith was certainly whispered in pre-Partition days, although this was never broadcast from minarets as is done today.[45] In 2020, huge crowds estimated at 100,000 or more gathered in Karachi chanting the slogan *Shia-kafir*, and 42 cases of blasphemy were recorded against Shias for allegedly slandering the companions of the Holy Prophet.[46] Government representatives such as the chairman of the Ruet-e-Hilal Committee, Mufti Muneebur Rahman, were present in the crowd that held aloft banners with "Long live Ameer Yazid Zindabad" – the ultimate provocation for Shias.[47] This mufti was the key mediator that restored the extremist TLP into Pakistan's political mainstream in 2021.[48]

Every applicant for a Pakistani passport must declare his faith. Choosing the non-Muslim option comes with a cost. The only Pakistani government that sought to remove the religion entry in passports was that of General Pervez Musharraf. In October 2004, as a new system for issuing machine-readable passports was being installed, the word was let out that passports would be issued without applicants having to specify their religion. The reaction was fierce. Islamic parties denounced this as a grand conspiracy aimed at secularizing Pakistan and destroying its Islamic character. But even before they actually took to the streets, the government lost nerve and the volte-face was announced on 24 March 2005 by Information Minister Sheikh Rashid who said the decision to revive the religion column was made else, "Qadianis and other apostates would be able to pose as Muslims and perform pilgrimage in Saudi Arabia".[49]

As Pakistan careens from "Al-Bakistan" to "Turko-Pakistan" in search of identity, its minorities live in the shadow of fear. They know that their departure

370 Identity

would be welcomed by the country's majority but, should they insist on staying, they will have to agree to behave as the majority wants them to. The demands of survival require that the non-Muslim be as unobtrusive as possible and conceal his identity. Unequal treatment is to be expected, and they should not look for support from more than a handful of Muslims. In 2020, when religious zealots blocked the construction of the officially sanctioned Shri Krishna Mandir in Islamabad, most citizens applauded. This would have been the first new place of worship for the 3000 Hindus residing in the country's capital.[50] The year 2020 ended with a mob looting and then setting fire to a Hindu temple in Karak, KPK.[51]

Price of Prejudice

As discussed in Chapter One, Hindu revivalists get upset at scientific evidence that points at an Aryan invasion which brought foreigners to Indian soil and even more upset that the liturgical language of the Vedas has come from outside. But on the whole, the Hindus of India are happy with their identity because they like to think they are people of the soil. Soon after Partition, India under Nehru had rapidly embraced its racially and ethnically diverse population. With 22 constitutionally recognized different languages and 800 dialects, what could be the basis of unity? In his book, *The Discovery of India*, which was written while in jail, Nehru saw India emerging from a teleological principle – multiculturalism and an abstract national spirit. He fired a warning shot at Hindutva – then a weak force – which sought to create an identity around India as a mother:

> It was absurd, of course, to think of India or any country as a kind of anthropomorphic entity. I did not do so. I was also fully aware of the diversities and divisions of Indian life, of classes, castes, religions, races, different degrees of cultural development. Yet I think that a country with a long cultural background and a common outlook on life develops a spirit that is peculiar to it and that is impressed on all its children, however much they may differ among themselves. Can anyone fail to see this in China, whether he meets an old-fashioned mandarin or a Communist who has apparently broken with the past? It was this spirit of India that I was after, not through idle curiosity, though I was curious enough, but because I felt that it might give me some key to the understanding of my country and people, some guidance to thought and action. Politics and elections were day to day affairs when we grew excited over trumpery matters. But if we were going to build the house of India's future, strong and secure and beautiful, we would have to dig deep for the foundations.[52]

Nehru overtly privileged cultural diversity and tolerance. And so until Hindutva emerged as the dominant political force, Muslims, Sikhs, and Christians were proud to declare themselves Indian.

For Pakistanis, cultural identification worked differently. Jinnah and the Muslim League, fearing diversity and difference, insisted a Pakistani identity could only be achieved through Islam. Centralization and ideologically driven unity was the principal tenet of nationhood. The insistence then – as today – was that Islam would provide a broad set of values acceptable to all citizens. That broad set of values has yet to be agreed upon. With the exception of Punjab, cultural identification has not happened. Excluding non-Muslims from full citizenship has come at great cost to Pakistan, a cost that it does not want to acknowledge or recognize but which makes entering the competitive modern world difficult. Here's why:

Among other things, every country needs proficient engineers who can design and build efficient electricity distribution grids, architects and town planners, people who can build and maintain water works, forecast requirements for edibles and fuel, negotiate international treaties, understand and deal with issues of economic planning, and run complex systems such as airlines and railways. In a nutshell, to succeed, a country needs multiple skills properly integrated within multiple systems that, in order to function well, must place merit and competence above other considerations. To function well, a country needs meritocracies where persons in an institution are evaluated by what they do and not by who someone is. Merit is precisely defined by a simple formula: IQ + effort = merit. A well-designed society nurtures and rewards talent, a badly conceived one will ignore and waste it. Most people accept that a performance-based system amounts to fair play; your work is what you should be judged upon and paid for. Countries that have been able to create layered meritocracies in government, industry, and academia are successful. Conversely if a group is given unfair advantage, or if race and religion are important for positions and promotions, failure is never very far away.

The United States is perhaps the best example of how this principle has played out. After the Second World War, and for over half a century before countries like China caught up, it was the world's most prolific generator of knowledge and ideas, spawning revolutionary science and technology that had incredibly important consequences. A combination of three innovations: the computer, the microchip, and the internet fueled its economy for fifty years and changed the world. A fierce dedication to meritocratic principles lies behind the success. In contrast Soviet Russia, where party loyalty had to be written on your sleeve, was unable to make things work – except in the making of better and more destructive weapons – and so finally collapsed.

At the core of America's success is its academia and universities. Without them America's prosperity would be as likely as a snowstorm in the Sahara desert. And so, knowing that their success hinges upon it, universities jealously guard academic freedom and the meritocratic principle. Strict professionalism was why they could produce the world's lion's share of high achievers as measured by any metric – the number of Nobel Prizes, Fields Medals, or owners of hi-tech businesses worth over $100 billion. To be sure, the U.S. has plenty of "cow colleges"

372 Identity

and educational institutions that are de facto racially segregated. Moreover, access to college education is less than in welfare-state European economies, and student debt requires many years of full employment to be paid back. These are indeed strong negative attributes, but they do not take away from the fact that the best and brightest across the world make a beeline for America's top universities. They know they cannot get better.

Pakistan's elite, on the other hand, chose to deprive itself of its best and brightest. Disowning sons and daughters of the soil because they are not Muslim has had a devastating effect on institutional and organizational culture. Although very few non-Muslims were left after Partition, the psychological consequence of excluding the remaining ones from high positions was huge. Once it is accepted that merit is insufficient to land you the position or job that you are suited for, cracks widen until the structure starts creaking and ultimately collapses. Over the decades its universities have been reduced to academic wastelands. Except perhaps for agricultural and biotechnology laboratories, closing down the rest would go unnoticed by the world of science. Because no real skills are imparted except by a few universities for the super-rich, the economy would not notice the change.

Religious prejudice led to Pakistan's most famous scientist and sole Nobel Prize in Physics winner – Abdus Salam – being an outcast in the land of his birth. From the mid-1960s he had been very influential in creating scientific infrastructure in a country which had barely any at the time. But in 1974 his Ahmadiyya community was declared non-Muslim after which his acceptability and influence vanished. No road in any city bears his name, and the sole institution in Pakistan that bears his name – the Abdus Salam School for Mathematical Studies (Lahore) – is too afraid to either display his name on the signboard or on official stationery. Others of the same city who have accomplished magnificent feats also remain unrecognized. Har Gobind Khorana (1922–2011) was born in Multan, earned his MSc degree from Government College Lahore in 1946 and went on to earn the Nobel Prize in Physiology in 1968 for his work in protein synthesis via nucleotides. In 1983 another son of Lahore, Subrahmanyan Chandrasekhar (1910–1995), became a Nobel Laureate in Physics after his definitive work on the death of stars. NASA's satellite, named Chandra, searches the skies for black holes and other unusual astronomical objects. As with Salam, no signboard in Lahore acknowledges the existence of either Khorana or Chandrasekhar. Nevertheless, they must still be considered fortunate at being spared the vilification that Salam must endure.

The Overseas Pakistani

dhobi ka kutta, na ghar ka na ghat ka

– Urdu/Hindi proverb: The washerman's dog has no hearth nor home

ABCD is an acronym for American Born Confused Desi. Since millions of South Asians live in traditionally white countries, its inventor could have been either Indian or Pakistani. Distinct by color of skin and facial features, their search for identity and social meaning – collective or individual, ascribed or constructed – is intense for many. The tension between religious, national, and ethno-linguistic identities is sometimes wrenching. Perhaps more than other Muslims, immigrants from Pakistan to the West feel at sea when asked by their children: What is our culture? Where do we really belong to? A few parents respond by identifying themselves through their ethnic origins. Most simply say: we are Muslims.

Of course, people have been crossing borders and settling in distant lands for thousands of years, but there is something distinct and unique about the present globalized era where people, goods, and ideas freely move from one area to another. Television, followed by the internet, have made instant communication possible and allowed many different kinds of imagined communities to coexist.

Unlike many Pakistanis born in Pakistan, second-generation Pakistanis born in western societies do not ache for Arab or Turkish roots. They search for their identity in the country to which their parents belong. In that sense they are similar to Indians born overseas. But, when compared to Indian second-generationers, Pakistanis belonging to the same cohort have done far less well in academia, business, and the professions. Most Pakistani communities, particularly in Britain and Canada, are tightly bound and introverted. They emphasize clan loyalty, give jobs to family members and friends, marriage within the family is strongly encouraged, and honor killings happen from time to time. Urdu is spoken at home, with family evenings spent watching television programs broadcast from Pakistan. Calls are made from time to time by various groups that western societies would be better off having sharia and that, at least for Muslims, should become the law of the land.

Palpable fear of losing or diluting one's original identity has become still more evident in recent times because religion has trumped nationalism as a marker of identity. In western cities such as Toronto, Sunnis and Shias live in separate communities while Ahmadis – who have a large presence – are shunned by both. Imams who have never lived in a western society and who do not approve of its norms are imported from abroad, either Pakistan or Saudi Arabia. Religious education and homeschooling causes Pakistanis in cities such as Bradford, Birmingham, and Manchester to underachieve. Much of this comes from an insistence on children learning Arabic verses by rote and through deliberately dulling the child's natural propensity to ask questions.

The embrace of Islam as their identity marker, and a rejection of values espoused by the host society, has led to migration becoming the biggest political issue within Europe in recent times. It has also led to a deep alienation of the Muslim youth. On the one hand, they do not fit into western society but, on the other, they cannot relate to life back in Pakistan. Some visit relatives only to find Pakistani society too ridden with problems of lawlessness and corruption

374 Identity

to be attractive. Disaffected ones take a third route – political Islam. Da'esh has benefited from the angst and frustration of such individuals.

Folks: Here's What I Really Am

> I am the universe
> I am the Milky Way Galaxy
> I am the Earth
> I am the Flora and Fauna
> I am a Homo Sapien
> I am a Global Citizen
> I am an Asian
> I am a South Asian
> I am a Pakistani
> I am a Sunni, Shia, Ahmedi, Hindu, Buddhist, Christian, Parsi Atheist
> I am a Man, Woman, Transgender
> I am a Son, Daughter, Brother, Sister, Father, Mother, Friend
> I am All of Above and None of Above
>
> *– Shaheryar Azhar (Karachi)*

Pretending to be what you are not can result in strange, bizarre behavior. As with other types of disorders, this kind of delusion can be passed on from parents to their children, which makes it more dangerous. It is surely time for the peoples of Pakistan to come to terms with what they really are. In the age of globalization and of the ever-accelerating intermingling of elements in which we are all caught up, a new concept of identity is needed, and needed urgently. This is as true for Pakistanis within Pakistan as for those who were born outside its border and living outside but who still have a vicarious relationship.

In a nutshell: we must accept our principal identity as global, not national. There can be any number of other subsidiary identities – religious, ethnic, linguistic, national, or gender – but a rationalist sees them as add-ons.

Inside Pakistan, the ruling establishment has goaded society into inventing nostalgia for cultures that it never knew and which have never been its own. An infatuation first with Arab culture, and now increasingly with Turkish culture, is being encouraged. More worrying is the evident desire of culture managers to form a self-image of Pakistan as a warrior nation besieged by hostile forces. Only war is admired – not music, art, or science. So, even though Arab or Turkish culture are considered superior and worthy of emulation, nothing is being copied from their scholarly and intellectual traditions. This has led to enormous confusion and nervousness: what am I, and where do I come from?

Here is a simple proposition for every Muslim Pakistani: instead of imagining India arbitrarily divided into Indus and Ganga civilizations some arbitrary number of millennia ago, or thrilling to the clatter of hooves bringing your ancestors here from Central Asia or Turkey, simply try accepting that it was the force of history and circumstance that brought you to South Asia or wherever you were born. You could have been born in Birmingham or New York to parents from Mirpur or Sukkur. Study after study has established the scientific fact that your genes are no different from that of a Hindu, Sikh, or Christian. That's because somewhere along your family tree when someone changed religion, his or her genes stayed put.

The evolutionary needs of humans have changed and will continue to change beyond what you and I can presently imagine. Just a century or two ago it made a lot of sense to identify with those from your village and to be able to tell the difference between them and those from the next village. We know that this kind of identification made possible the emergence of a species that ended up controlling the earth and all that live upon it.

Bewildered human beings are being forced by national governments towards an excessive assertion of their identity. But the earlier close identification with village and nation is no longer necessary – or even possible – in a world of instant communication and constant movement of people, ideas, and goods across the globe. Culturally we are becoming transnational and, even more, transitional. Ideas and viruses are sweeping the planet. COVID-19 floored the entire planet, but it also showed the feasibility of online education, Zoom and Skype conferences, and even high-level meetings with participants scattered across different countries. Scientific collaborations had already functioned in this way for two decades.

Surely it is time to deemphasize our differences and to take greater pride in the collective achievements of humankind. On 11 February 2016 there was a stunning announcement: it had just been confirmed that certain signals detected on Earth had originated from a collision of two black holes some 1300 million years ago. A wonderfully ingenious experiment had verified a prediction from Einstein's 1906 theory of General Relativity. For a few brief moments my eyes watered up. I felt thrilled and proud although I had played absolutely no role; my field of specialization is a little different. But pride at what? Those engaged in the gravitational wave project were physicists and engineers from probably 50 different countries with the equipment spread between the United States and Europe. So clearly there could be no question of national pride. But what I felt was just what my community – that of physicists – must also surely have felt. It was a vindication of the astonishingly simple assumptions underlying the General Theory of Relativity, and the immense power of mathematics built from the time of Ancient Egypt to the age of Euclid and then taken a step further by Riemann. Instead of groveling on earth and looking at our feet like wild dogs, we physicists were gazing at the skies and were awestruck that we could know so much.

So there you have it! There was no thought of Jinnah or Nehru or my one-time Pakistani militarism. I was but one of those who had pondered on the nature of things, in other words a simple member of the Homo sapien community with no particular claims to success. To be joyous at the success of others

376 Identity

who do not belong to our clan is a step towards becoming a citizen of the world which someday I hope to be. Global citizenship is around the corner, unless it is perversely opposed by forces that benefit from conflict – armies and politicians.

And yet one should proceed cautiously. To get rid of boundaries and divisions carries dangers because one universal culture would not only be terribly dull and boring, it could also kill creativity and destroy precious experiences gained by humanity over eons. To know, appreciate, and preserve the best that we humans have conceived and practiced – whether literature, fiction, music, poem, painting or sculpture – is no less important than the General Theory of Relativity.

Notes

1 B. Anderson, *Imagined Communities – Reflections on the Origin and Spread of Nationalism*, Verso Books (2006), pp. 5–6.
2 Ibid, p. 7.
3 Ibid, p. 12.
4 *Religion in India: Tolerance and Segregation*, Pew Global Survey, 29 June 2021.
5 Hasan Zaidi, *The Cultural Confusions of Pakistan*, Dawn, 20 February, 2022
6 *Lawyers Move Peshawar High Court for Ban on 'un-Islamic' Movie Joyland*, Dawn, 22 November 2022.
7 S. Boym, *The Future of Nostalgia*, Basic Books (2001).
8 A. Ahsan, *The Indus Saga – From Pataliputra to Partition*, Delhi, Roli Books (2005).
9 H. Khalid, *If Pakistan Shuns the Term 'Ancient India' in Its History Books, Is It Entirely to Blame?*, Dawn, 6 September 2018. https://www.dawn.com/news/1431314
10 Ahsan, op. cit.
11 Ibid.
12 Ibid, Nehru, quoted in Ahsan.
13 A Shared Y-Chromosomal Heritage between Muslims and Hindus in India, *Human Genetics*, 120, no. 4 (November 2006): 543–551. doi:10.1007/s00439-006-0234-x.
14 *European Journal of Human Genetics*, 18 (2010): 354–363; doi:10.1038/ejhg.2009.168; published online 7 October 2009.
15 M. Katju, The Politics of "Ghar Wapsi", *Economic and Political Weekly*, 50, no. 1 (2015): 21–24. https://www.jstor.org/stable/24481234
16 E.H. Erikson, Autobiographic Notes on the Identity Crisis, *Daedalus*, 99, no. 4 (1970): 730–759. http://www.jstor.org/stable/20023973.
17 K. Ahmed, *Muslim First or Pakistani First?*, The Express Tribune, 17 September 2011. https://tribune.com.pk/story/254426/muslim-first-or-pakistani-first
18 *Tribune Survey: Online Pakistanis 'Muslim' First, 'Pakistani' Second*, The Express Tribune, 16 February 2012. https://tribune.com.pk/story/337202/tribune-survey -online-pakistanis-'muslim'-first-'pakistani'-second?amp=1
19 *Chapter 1: Beliefs about Sharia*, Pew Research Center, 30 April 2013. https://www .pewresearch.org/religion/2013/04/30/the-worlds-muslims-religion-politics-soci ety-beliefs-about-sharia/
20 S. Shah, *British Council: Pakistan Facing 'Frightening' Demographic Disaster*, The Telegraph, 20 November 2009. https://www.telegraph.co.uk/news/worldnews/asia /pakistan/6616402/British-Council-Pakistan-facing-frightening-demographic-dis aster.html
21 L. Diseko, *Most Indians Oppose Interfaith Marriage, Survey Shows*, BBC Report, 29 June 2021. https://www.bbc.com/news/world-asia-india-57647931
22 A. Ayres, *Speaking Like a State – Language and Nationalism in Pakistan*, Cambridge University Press (2009).

Identity **377**

23 *Panjābī Zabān Nahīn Maregi*, Saeed Ahmad Farani, quoted in Ayres, op. cit., p. 78.
24 *Holy Quran Teaching Made Compulsory in Universities*, Daily Times, 15 June 2020. https://dailytimes.com.pk/626641/holy-quran-teaching-made-compulsory-in-universities/
25 H. El-Behary, *DNA Analysis Proves that Egyptians Are not Arabs*, Egypt Independent, 17 January 2017. https://egyptindependent.com/dna-analysis-proves-egyptians-are-not-arabs/
26 *Social Studies for Class 6*, Lahore, Punjab Textbook Board (2003), p. 72. Quoted in: M.A. Asif, *A Book of Conquest – The Chachnama and Muslim Origins in South Asia*, Cambridge, Mass., Harvard University Press (2016), p. 7.
27 Asif, op. cit., p. 11.
28 *Where Is Our Muhammad bin Qasim, Asks Fouzia*, Aafia Movement, 31 July 2012. http://aafiamovement.com/where-is-our-muhammad-bin-qasim-asks-fouzia/
29 Ibid.
30 H.A. Syed, *Arab-Wannabe Syndrome (AWS)*, Pakistan Today, 26 November 2015, http://www.pakistantoday.com.pk/2015/11/26/comment/arab-wannabe-syndrome-aws/
31 N.F. Paracha, *My Name Is Pakistan and I'm not Arab*, Dawn, 28 July 2013. https://www.dawn.com/news/1032519
32 S. Rizwan, *Ahlan Wasahlan, Al Bakistan!*, Dawn, 23 March 2014. https://www.dawn.com/news/1094959
33 A. Maqsood, *The New Pakistani Middle Class*, Harvard University Press (2017).
34 F. Khaliq, *Young Swat Residents to Release Their own Pashto Version of Ertugrul after Eid*, Dawn, 19 April 2021. https://images.dawn.com/news/1187031/young-swat-residents-to-release-their-own-pashto-version-of-ertugrul-after-eid
35 C. Polat, (10 May 2016). *Diriliş Ertuğrul'un Yapımcısı Mehmet Bozdağ: Her şey bir rüya ile başladı!* (in Turkish). https://www.cuneytpolat.com/mehmet-bozdag-her-sey-bir-ruya-ile-basladi/
36 *Ertugrul's Celal Al Can't Get Enough of Islamabad*, Dawn, 10 Jan 2021. https://images.dawn.com/news/1186371
37 X. Jalil, *Ertugrul Gets a Statue in Lahore*, Dawn, 7 June 2020. https://images.dawn.com/news/1185375
38 Hagia Sophia, *Turkey Turns Iconic Istanbul Museum into Mosque*, BBC, 10 July 2020. https://www.bbc.com/news/world-europe-53366307
39 S. Malik, *Why do Pakistanis Criticize Stars of Turkish Drama 'Ertugul Ghazi'?* Global Village Space, 21 May 2020. https://www.globalvillagespace.com/why-do-pakistanis-criticize-stars-of-turkish-drama-ertugul-ghazi/
40 N. Gurmani, *Parliamentary Panel Rejects Anti-Forced Conversion Bill Amid Protest by Minorities' Lawmakers*, Dawn, 13 October 2021. https://www.dawn.com/news/1651813
41 *Why Pakistani Hindus Leave Their Homes for India*, BBC Report, 28 October 2015. https://www.bbc.com/news/world-asia-india-34645370
42 *Dalit Hindu in Pakistan Cabinet – A Secular Story to Remember as Imran Khan Is Set to Form Government*, Jijo Jacob, International Business Times, 27 July 2018.
43 *60 Percent of People of Parachinar Suffer from Post-Traumatic Stress Disorder*, Dawn, 30 July 2017. https://www.dawn.com/news/1348525
44 I. Shah, *Bomb at Shi'ite Mosque Kills 45 in Pakistan*, Reuters, 3 March 2013. https://www.reuters.com/article/uk-pakistan-violence-karachi/bomb-at-shiite-mosque-kills-45-in-pakistan-idUKBRE9220AP20130303
45 The anti-Shia content of current sermons can be gauged from the approximately 200 Friday sermons delivered recently in Punjabi villages and towns that have been recorded, translated, and categorized at www.mashalbooks.org.
46 *Several Shia Speakers Arrested on Blasphemy Charges after Ashura*, Naya Daur TV, 4 September 2020. https://nayadaur.tv/2020/09/several-shia-speakers-arrested-on-blasphemy-charges-after-ashura/
47 *Slogans Eulogising Yazeed by Sunni Muslims in Pakistan Evoke Protests by Indian Muslims in Delhi*, New Age Islam News Bureau, 4 October 2020. https://www.newageislam

378 Identity

.com/islam-sectarianism/new-age-islam-news-bureau/slogans-eulogising-yazeed-sunni-muslims-pakistan-evoke-protests-indian-muslims-delhi/d/123035

48 *We Will Return with Full Force if Govt Fails to Implement Agreement with Proscribed TLP: Mufti Muneeb*, The News, 1 November 2021. https://www.thenews.com.pk/latest/905006-tlp-to-return-with-full-force-if-govt-fails-to-implement-agreement-mufti-muneeb

49 Dawn, October 12, 2006.

50 K. Ali, *Construction of Hindu Temple Opposed*, Dawn, 2 July 2020. https://www.dawn.com/news/1566418

51 H. Bhatti, *SC Orders EPTB to Start Reconstruction of Damaged Hindu Shrine in Karak*, Dawn, 5 January 2021, https://www.dawn.com/news/1599843

52 J. Nehru, *The Discovery of India*, Oxford University Press (1946), p. 59.

PART FIVE

Looking Ahead

Fourteen

THREE PHYSICAL PERILS UP AHEAD

Be realistic: plan for a miracle.

— source unknown

When prayer becomes your habit, miracles become your lifestyle.

— source unknown

Whichever form its political dispensation takes in the times to come, Pakistan cannot avoid three urgent, immediate existential threats. First: in common with many other countries, global climate change threatens to disrupt Pakistan's environment, economy, and make parts of the country unlivable within the next decade. Second: the furious rise of population remains unchecked, accelerating the degradation not just of the physical environment but also the quality of education, availability of health services, and employment. Third: nuclear war, in spite of it having receded from public consciousness and blanket reassurances from the military, remains an ever-present possibility. The quality of life for Pakistan's citizens — and even the country's continued existence — will depend upon how the state handles these perils.

Imagine seeing from the Titanic's bridge a field of icebergs. Not all were avoidable but had the crew been up and alert with binoculars in hand, with some clever navigation their ship could have sustained some limited damage and still stayed afloat. For Pakistan, we do not need binoculars to see three looming dangers up ahead: the impact of climate change arising from greenhouse gas (GHG) emissions, an exploding population bomb, and a possible war with India — one that which would almost certainly turn nuclear unless somehow contained at an early stage.

Each of these perils needs examination and reflection upon what it might take to survive the next several years ahead. For definiteness, consider the time frame

DOI: 10.4324/9781003379140-20

from now to the year 2047, when Pakistan will turn one hundred. That may be as far as one can usefully go. Beyond this time, matters will likely have moved into an altogether different realm.

Climate Change

> Anyone who believes in indefinite growth in anything physical, on a physically finite planet, is either mad or an economist.
> – *Kenneth E. Boulding (1910–1993)*

There is a well-known story of two frogs loitering near the kitchen stove.[1] One frog fell into a pot of hot water and was so jolted that he jumped out instantly. He was saved. The other one fell into a pot wherein the water was only slowly warming up. He swam around and around but did not summon the energy to make a sudden jump. Ultimately he was boiled to death. The obvious moral: instant shocks are better survived than long-term threats.

Think of what this means for Pakistan. Like water on the stove, the Earth's air, land, and seas are slowly getting hotter and hotter by the year. Climate change models depend upon certain details (like deep ocean currents) that are not accurately known, and so there is some variation among them. However, they all predict beyond doubt that by 2050 anthropogenic activity will have produced a planet Earth that is different from what it was in 2000 or even 2020. The tipping point may already have been crossed. It is therefore certain that ice at the polar caps will have mostly melted, deserts will have spread globally, and forests will have greatly thinned.[2] From melting polar ice to wildfires to hurricanes, the backlash from nature is visible all around us.

The monster floods in summer 2022 have left no uncertainty in what lies ahead. After UN secretary general Antonio Guterres toured the flood-devastated areas, he said Pakistan was facing "a level of climate carnage beyond imagination" and that it was paying a "supersized price for man-made climate change". The 2022 climate disaster was even worse than that in 2010 when extreme rainfall during the monsoons had left 20% of the country under water.

At the core of the climate crisis is the rapacious consumption aided and abetted by capitalism, a system that is highly exploitative of both people and planet. Driven by a desperate need for profit and accumulation, oil companies have been notorious for relentlessly adding pollutants to the atmosphere while branding themselves with green flower logos in a shallow pretense to be seen as environmentally friendly. Jason Moore describes humanity's predicament as being at a "geohistorical moment that systemically combines greenhouse gas pollution with the climate class divide, class patriarchy, and climate apartheid" and makes the case that it is not the human species that has failed. Rather, he says, it is the failure of a specific economic system.[3] That system is centered around the belief – whose most articulate spokesman was Adam Smith – that individual self-interest is, and ought to be, the main motivating force of human economic activity, and that this, when realized by the free market, serves the wider social interest. The free market has indeed turned out to be the optimum prescription for economic growth. However, history has also shown that there is something horribly wrong or incomplete about the idea that individual self-interest alone, uninfluenced by ethical and ecological considerations, and totally free from governmental intervention, can be the main motivating force of a happy and just society.[4]

John Avery in his book, *Madmen and Economists*, makes the point that a completely isolated human being would find it as difficult to survive for a long period of time as would an isolated ant or bee or termite and so, "it seems correct to regard human society as a superorganism. In the case of humans, the analog of the social insects' nest is the enormous and complex material structure of civilization. It is, in fact, what we call the human economy. It consists of functioning factories, farms, homes, transportation links, water supplies, electrical networks, computer networks and much more".[5] The problem with this superorganism is that it has not realized to a sufficient degree that economies that keep growing will very soon lead to global asphyxiation and heat death.

Asphyxiation is indeed literally what is felt by the residents of Lahore, which stood at the world's number-one city for the filthiest air in the world, exceeding even that of Delhi.[6] This is a foretaste of what lies ahead as pollutants are relentlessly pumped into the atmosphere. Pakistan will be among the countries hit most severely by global climate change. According to a report[7] commissioned by the Asian Development Bank, the annual mean temperature in Pakistan has increased by roughly 0.5°C over the past fifty years, while the number of heat wave days per year has increased nearly fivefold in the last thirty years. By the end of the present century, the annual mean temperature in Pakistan is expected to rise by 3–5°C. Recent studies predict melting of Himalayan glaciers at unprecedented speed, unpredictable drought and flooding, large temperature fluctuations, and more intense heat waves. In 2019 the city of Jacobabad was listed as the hottest city in the world (52.8°C). This borders close to where life may become impossible to sustain.

According to the mentioned report, the sea level along the Karachi coast has risen approximately 10 centimeters in the last century and will rise a further 60 centimeters by the 21st century's end. Flooding and progressive loss of land awaits those living in low-lying coastal areas south of Karachi toward Keti Bunder and the Indus River delta. Water availability will become erratic, demand for irrigation water may increase due to higher evaporation rates, yields of wheat and basmati rice will decline and will be driven northward. Cities will become hotter and air conditioning requirements will increase. This will create local heat traps. Urban drainage systems in mega-cities are already unable to deal with normal rainfall and will undergo catastrophic damage from high rainfall and flash floods.

To be sure, Pakistan's economy is no more than a tiny fraction of the world's larger economies. It therefore cannot be faulted excessively for global climate

384 Three Physical Perils up Ahead

changes – its contribution to GHG emissions is small and estimated at around 0.8%.[8] However, were it richer, there is no doubt that its economic system would have worked in the same way and contributed just as much – or perhaps even more – than the global average. But the local environmental degradation is certainly of its own making and a result of poor governance. The World Wildlife Fund has recently revealed that Pakistan has the second highest deforestation rate in Asia.[9] Barely 5.7% of its land is under forest cover against the recommended 25%. Timber mafias operate freely with the open connivance of state officials. Fewer trees lead to rapid silting of waterways and dams. Stub burning, lack of control over industrial pollution and auto emissions, and dumping of untreated wastes into waterways and reservoirs have resulted in a steady rise of air and water pollution levels.

Looking at the future, one must bear in mind that what were regarded as ultra-luxuries in earlier decades will become essential for survival in hot urban areas and perhaps rural areas as well: air-conditioning, instant communication, fast transportation, etc. In earlier times, one could assume the existence of clean air, clean drinking water, and free public spaces. With time, these will become scarcer with the rich having privileged access to them and the poor most afflicted by environmental changes.

To mitigate some effects, technology offers a growing number of options. Energy can be generated with much less negative environmental impact by harnessing solar and wind energy, building small-scale dams, more efficient devices, and using massive conservation strategies. Water can be used more efficiently through drip irrigation, laser field leveling, lining canals, water harvesting and recycling, and integrated watershed management. Drought- and pest-resistant as well as more heat-tolerant crops are now possible to design. Coastal areas can be protected through extensive mangrove plantation. Food processing and preservation can contain wastage, etc. The list of existing and future technologies is long.

There is also much to be learned by looking around at models of success. Pakistan can study how Germany has used alternate energy to solve its power problem, how Turkey has developed sewage treatment plants to treat 100% of its sewage, how Finland provides the finest education to its children, how Holland promotes bicycles to overcome its traffic problem, how the U.K. government uses only 83 pool cars for all its ministries as against 20,000 cars used by the Sindh Government alone, how the Canadian government provides proactive 'access to information', and how Japan runs railways. These models exist in real life and can be seen, studied, modified, and adapted to the needs and conditions of Pakistan.

The choice is between the proverbial frog who jumped out of the pot and the one who simply accepted a hotter and hotter environment. Although climate change is inevitable, its impact will vary from country to country and may not be apocalyptic for everyone. Countries can reduce their vulnerability through better governance, resource reallocation, and implementing well-thought plans.

In Pakistan quite a few reports have been written, and some thought has been given to mitigation strategies.[10] But without an efficient system of governance – which a responsive political system alone can produce – implementation of these plans is unlikely.

An Exploding Population

Western leftists and liberals, conscious of being politically correct, are afraid to open their mouths when it comes to addressing the issue of rising populations in poorer countries such as Pakistan. Even a mention of it can have such people accused of racism, colonialism, or misanthropy. This is unfortunate because one sees important environmental thinkers like George Monbiot, Jared Diamond, and Fred Pearce argue that the real problem is excessive consumption under capitalism. But the uncontestable fact is that consumption, large or small, gets directly multiplied by the number of people. With the world's population having crossed eight billion, the impact on the environment is easily visible from space.

An old Persian story helps understand how populations grow. Once upon a time, a clever courtier presented an elaborate ivory chess set to his king. In return he asked for only one grain of rice for the first square, two for the second, four for the third, etc. Now, kings in those times did not have degrees in mathematics and did not know about the law of exponential growth. This one was no exception. He foolishly agreed and ordered the rice be brought out from the storage. Working on the agreed upon terms, the 10th square had 512 grains, the 14th weighed around 1 kilograms, and the 20th around 128 kilograms. Long before reaching the last square (64th), the kingdom's entire rice stock was exhausted. The moral: if something doubles, and doubles again and again, then even the sky is not high enough.

Let us put the above in the context of Pakistan's population. At the present moment, every two years its population increase is enough to create one more Israel. In 1947 Pakistan had 27 million people, but in 2020 it had over 220 million. This gives a doubling time of roughly twenty-five years. For the sake of argument only, assume that the doubling time remains unchanged. Then twenty-five years later, there will be 400 million Pakistani NIC holders. Wait another one hundred years, and that number will comfortably exceed the world's current population of 7.2 billion. The effects will be much more dramatic after yet another twenty-five years, i.e., one hundred and fifty years from today.

The demand for living space has accelerated vastly. Even now green areas are vanishing as villages become towns, and one city spills over into the next. Karachi and Hyderabad are approaching their eventual merger, just as Islamabad and Rawalpindi have become practically one city and Islamabad is furiously racing towards Taxila. Imagine that all 800,000 square kilometers of Pakistani territory is somehow leveled. Even so, there will be only room for standing shoulder-to-shoulder. In such circumstances it is hard to imagine how further reproduction will be physically possible. Pakistan Army generals who receive

386 Three Physical Perils up Ahead

retirement gifts of 93 acres of land today will be lucky if they get 93 square feet after some decades.

The impact of the population explosion has been documented as follows by economist Hafiz Pasha: availability of agricultural land has decreased from 2.5 hectares to 0.2 hectares per capita of rural population; water availability has decreased by 49% between 1990–1991 and 2020–2021; the number of persons served per hospital bed has increased from 1440 in 1998 to 1566 in 2020; unemployment has risen from 1.7% in 1961 to 3.1% in 1981 to 5.8% in 2018; the quality of life in Karachi has been downgraded to 201 out of 231 cities in the world; etc. The reader will find more details in Charter of the Economy.[11]

Nevertheless, believing that more is better, many religious conservatives continue to oppose contraception. Every newborn, they say, comes with a guaranteed *rizq* (provision) stamped on their forehead. Now let's assume that this is correct and food and water were to drop miraculously from the skies for every Pakistani man, woman, and child. Fact: The law of exponential growth says that Pakistan will eventually run out of physical space. One can only imagine the amount of human waste generated. Yet, fearing the wrath of the religious orthodox, Pakistan abolished the ministry for population planning many years ago. Upon Googling, I came across the website of the Population Welfare Department (PWD). This ridiculous name suggests that PWD will seek, and succeed, in delivering welfare to Pakistanis irrespective of their number. I could not find an Urdu version of the website. Apart from giving advertisements in English language newspapers – where it matters little – I am unaware if the PWD does anything else.

Of course it's good news that birthrates are declining. The bad news is that this decline is among the slowest in the world and a Malthusian nightmare is only a small step ahead. Short of nuclear war or a miracle, nothing can now prevent Pakistan, with 220 million people in 2021, from reaching 340 million by 2050. This figure is based on United Nations estimates that the current 3.4 births per woman in 2020 will decrease to 2.3 by 2050.[12] This is far from being good enough.

With 340 million people, and even if one assumes that the water supply will not decrease because of global warming, there will be only two-thirds the amount of fresh water relative to today. The air will become yet filthier, pollutants will poison the land and sea, and road traffic will vastly increase. As poverty skyrockets, hordes of beggars will roam the streets, *madrassas* will swell in size and number, and the unemployed and unemployable will chafe in anger and frustration. They will be easily persuaded that their predicament comes from some international conspiracy. More needed than the military operation *zarb-e-azb* is operation *zarb-e-tauleed* (hit against reproduction) if Pakistan is to avoid the second frog's fate.

Averting catastrophe because of overbreeding does not need rocket science, but it does need common sense. It also needs courage, which the country's leaders – both civil and military – have so far failed to muster. To avoid doom, as a first step Pakistan must declassify its best kept national secret – knowing how babies are made. Only then can contraception be discussed in the public media, and in schools and colleges. Phenomenal ignorance on these matters has led to extremely low rates of contraceptive usage by Pakistani women. This also reflects their disempowerment in deciding the number of children. The contraceptive prevalence rate (CPR) for Pakistan is 34.5%. Compare this against Iran (77.4%), Turkey (73.5%), and Bangladesh (62.4%). Pakistan's CPR of 34.5% means that 65.5% of women of reproductive age or their husbands are not using any contraceptive method.[13]

Birth and fertility rates in Pakistan exceed those in Bangladesh, India, Sri Lanka, and the rest of South Asia. Unfortunately, with discussion suppressed because of prudery (*sharm-o-haya*) all kinds of nonsensical belief are going unchallenged today. Should we be surprised that dozens of workers administering polio shots – which are falsely alleged to decrease fertility – have been shot and killed? A proper diagram of the mammalian reproductive system – even for rabbits – cannot be found in any Pakistani school textbook. Of course, books produced by local textbook boards do not stray even near the subject of human reproduction.[14] By introducing the Single National Curriculum, Imran Khan's government has made understanding human biology next to impossible. His removal from power made no difference in this regard. Religious scholars, who have been invited on to committees that determine the curriculum, have told publishers not to print any diagrams or sketches in the biology textbooks showing human figures "sans clothes".[15]

Well before Pakistan reaches 300 million people, it will face economic catastrophe. Presently, every year about 3 million young people are entering the job market in Pakistan. Unemployment among them has been variously estimated at 10–15%. Even the few with college degrees are largely without skills. Substandard education makes most unfit for any kind of high-quality job and yet all expect that a college degree will entitle them to a career that rapidly points upward. Frustration comes at not being able to find jobs at home and the lessening of possibilities overseas. Earlier, a sizeable fraction could be absorbed into government jobs – the much cherished *pakki naukri* – that were relatively low-paying but secure. This took off some of the pressure but hugely increased public sector costs and is unsustainable. It was also possible to escape to some Western country, but the borders there are becoming increasingly harder to penetrate. The Middle East is also increasingly more inclined to give jobs to the Arab youth rather than foreigners. The rapidly increasing mass of discontented young people constitutes dangerous, flammable material. Its quantity will increase dramatically with time.

Nuclear War

Nuclear weapons have fixed Pakistan's geographical boundaries into the foreseeable future. Both India and Pakistan know that a conventional war aimed at capturing territory, or damaging the other beyond a certain point, will rapidly escalate into a nuclear war that neither can survive. This means that whatever internal developments occur within Pakistan, the Line of Control (LOC) in Kashmir as determined in the 1947 First Kashmir War will remain the effective border with India. Balochistan, Gilgit-Baltistan, and Azad Kashmir will continue to remain part of Pakistan whether or not the last two are formally absorbed or given a temporary status. Likewise, India's boundaries will not change with China and, if at all, only with Bangladesh.

That was the good news. It should not be underestimated because it gives to Pakistan an unprecedented degree of security. In principle it means that the fear of India walking into Pakistan should disappear or be much reduced, Pakistan and India could begin to have some kind of a normal relationship, fewer troops and tanks would be needed, and monies taken away for defense could now be used for meeting the urgent needs of the population.

Now for the bad news: we cannot be sure that nuclear war will not happen. In fact the phrase "conventional war under a nuclear overhang" has made its way into the military lexicon. Pakistan has on multiple occasions explicitly rejected the No First Use (NFU) of nuclear weapons, arguing that this would put it at the mercy of an aggressor with superior weaponry. India, in earlier days, had much of its NFU policy, but of late its top political leaders have suggested that India might revoke its earlier attitude. In August 2019, Defence Minister Rajnath Singh made headlines when he appeared to walk back on India's earlier commitment: "Till today, our nuclear policy is no first use. What happens in future depends on the circumstances".[16] His line was consistent with Prime Minister Narendra Modi's efforts to promote a more muscular image of India. In 2014 the incumbent party, the BJP, had threatened to revisit India's declared nuclear policy.

The defence minister's statement that continuation of India's NFU policy depends on "circumstances" says little of substance since the nature of those circumstances was left unspecified. Moreover, as is well known, NFU is purely declaratory, impossible to verify and impossible to enforce. Nevertheless, the statement was significant. India's hint at moving away from NFU towards counterforce owes to its increased military advantage over Pakistan. The reaction from Pakistan's political leaders was, as expected, strongly negative. Responding on Twitter, Foreign Minister Shah Mehmood Qureshi termed the statement over a possible change in NFU as a "damning reminder of India's unbridled thirst for violence". Prime Minster Imran Khan, speaking at the UN General Assembly on 27 September 2019, warned that nuclear war was no longer impossible. For once, the army's response was relatively muted – the official Inter-Services Public Relations official spokesperson merely warned against Indian "misadventures" and threatened a "befitting response".

To an already tense state of affairs, various nuclear strategists have added their own contribution. The highflying ones belong to various think tanks and universities – including prestigious ones in the United States. Some have repeatedly hinted that NFU has run its course and needs a replacement. A few

Indian strategists have been openly advocating a so-called counterforce doctrine – i.e., the possibility of knocking out Pakistan's nuclear forces before they are activated.

Such attitudes raise the question: just how much do nuclear strategists employed in universities and think tanks actually know? Can they reliably comment on nuclear matters and should they be taken seriously? Many write densely referenced and annotated papers that are published in academic journals. They are daunting to read, and one fears challenging experts. Nevertheless, there is every reason to be cautious.

Innovations in weapons technology are making possible cheaper and better killing machines, warhead and delivery systems are increasing in number, global arms control mechanisms have all but disappeared, and the human element remains as capricious as ever. In a detailed analysis, Toon et al. make a grim prognosis of the consequences following a nuclear war between India and Pakistan:

> Pakistan and India may have 400 to 500 nuclear weapons by 2025 with yields from tested 12-kt to 45-kt values to a few hundred kilotons. If India uses 100 strategic weapons to attack urban centers and Pakistan uses 150, fatalities could reach 50 to 125 million people, and nuclear-ignited fires could release 16 to 36 Tg of black carbon in smoke, depending on yield. The smoke will rise into the upper troposphere, be self-lofted into the stratosphere, and spread globally within weeks. Surface sunlight will decline by 20 to 35%, cooling the global surface by 2° to 5°C and reducing precipitation by 15 to 30%, with larger regional impacts. Recovery takes more than 10 years. Net primary productivity declines 15 to 30% on land and 5 to 15% in oceans threatening mass starvation and additional worldwide collateral fatalities.[17]

This and other such dire predictions have had little impact on present nuclear postures across the world, including on South Asia.

A relatively long period of peace should not deaden us to what may lie around the corner. Hubris often paves the way to overconfidence and disaster. As every military commander worth his salt knows, all plans look fine until the battle begins. In September 2019 a ragtag Houthi militia took out 50% of Saudi Arabia's oil-producing capacity underscoring how even a relatively ill-equipped force can wreck an adversary bristling with the most advanced weapons that limitless oil dollars could buy.[18]

With nuclear weapons, uncertainties get multiplied. All nuclear nations confine their deepest secrets to an extremely tight inner circle. Outsiders – meaning civilians who are nuclear analysts – are excluded from what is absolutely critical for arriving at an informed opinion. They cannot know such crucial details as the chain of nuclear command, geographical dispersal of warheads and delivery vehicles, intelligence on how well the adversary has concealed its nukes, whether warheads are mated or de-mated from delivery vehicles, integrity of communication channels, efficacy of decoys and countermeasures, and much other vital information that would determine whether a first strike would achieve its objective.

Fact: no nuclear strategist knows the threshold of a nuclear war, can predict the sequence of events following a first strike, or persuasively argue whether nuclear hostilities could somehow be wound down. Of course he can guess – just as every one of us can. But guesses are only guesses. Could it perhaps be better inside a military organization? War gaming is certainly a compulsory part of an officer's training in every modern military. One can feed parameters into a computer set up for simulating the onset and subsequent trajectory of a nuclear conflict. If properly programmed and proper probabilities are inputted, it will output the probabilities of various possible outcomes. But, as in tossing coins, probabilities make sense only when something can be repeated a large number of times. The problem is that nuclear war can happen only once.

That's bad enough but, in fact, it's even worse than that. You can give probabilities for missiles to be intercepted or for getting through, and for mechanical and electrical systems to work or fail. But you cannot assign probabilities for humans to act in a particular way during a crisis because that depends on mood, perception, personality, and circumstance. Nuclear strategy pretends to be a science but is by no means one. Where has the other party drawn its nuclear red line (the real, not stated, one)? No one really knows.

In the India–Pakistan nuclear situation, consider whether one tactical nuclear weapon fired at invading Indian tanks from a Pakistani Nasr missile battery would elicit by way of retaliation zero, one, three, or thirty Indian nukes. The Indians say that a single nuke used against them, whether on Pakistani or Indian soil, constitutes a full blown nuclear attack upon India. Should one believe them? Would panic ensue and cause one or both sides to descend into a totalistic use-them-or-lose-them mode? No one knows. One recalls what President General Zia-ul-Haq famously said in 1986 at a time of high tension: "Neither India nor Pakistan wanted to go to war but we could have easily gone to war".

Where perceptions could make all the difference, it is stupid to assume the rational actor model – such as used in game theory applied to financial systems. Nuclear conflict situations could work by very different rules with fear and aggression being important factors that cannot be written into operating manuals.

Take a recent example: in 2019 a suicide attack on Indian troops in Kashmir killed 40 Indian security personnel near the town of Pulwama. The attack was immediately claimed by the Pakistan-based jihadist organization Jaish-e-Muhammad but multiple investigations traced the attacker to a radicalized young Kashmiri who seems to have had no contact with Pakistan.[19] In retaliation, Indian warplanes crossed into Pakistan and sought to target what the Indian leadership described as a terrorist training camp. Although success was claimed, available evidence suggests that the attacking aircraft missed their target. Nevertheless, to show that it has the capacity to respond, Pakistan retaliated with an air attack on targets inside India. In the subsequent dogfight, an Indian Mig-21 was shot down over Pakistani territory and its pilot was captured. Quickly releasing the pilot led to de-escalation. No nuclear threats were issued by either side and the crisis wound down. A happy ending!

But will all future skirmishes end equally well? As with the Pulwama incident, one anticipates that a sequentially escalatory process is more likely than a "bolt from the blue" attack. During a crisis, launch authority and codes will likely be provided to local commanders since decapitation strikes are a real possibility. In this chaotic environment, information, misinformation, and deliberate disinformation will compete. Mood, perception, personality, circumstance, and general atmospherics will determine the outcome. So will big-power diplomacy – earlier Pak-India nuclear crises had been defused with help from the United States. With the U.S.'s much reduced role in South Asian affairs, it is unclear whether this will be important in a future nuclear crisis.

To conclude, given their nuclear weapons, South Asia's two opponents could strictly eliminate each other. In addition their war would seriously devastate neighboring countries and poison much of the globe. To reduce the chances, more and better safeguards are always to be welcomed: Permissive Action Links (PALs), de-alerting, separating cores from missiles, hot lines, signaling protocols, confidence-building measures, etc. are all good things. Nuclear war-gaming can be improved with additional inputs, but there are still far too many imponderables for nuclear strategic decision making to be called a science. Luck, more than anything else, will determine the outcome in any crisis.

Some years after the Kargil episode, General Pervez Musharraf realized that nuclear weapons had brought Pakistan and India to an impasse. He is so far the only leader courageous enough to explicitly acknowledge this and – most importantly – to say out aloud that, for better or for worse, mutual fear of nuclear annihilation has etched the LOC in stone. It remains to be seen if other Pakistani and Indian leaders can dare to follow his example. Only then might peace get half a chance.

Prognosis up to 2047

To imagine Pakistan when it turns one hundred, let us assume that the present can extrapolated smoothly into the future, i.e. let's assume there are no catastrophic events. The following scenario results:

High-to-medium probability: population crosses 380 million (UN estimate for 2047), serious water and air quality crises, physical separation enforced between those who have water, electricity, and jobs and those who don't. Religious and ethnic communities are at daggers drawn with all the well-off living in gated communities. Afghanistan under Taliban has a love–hate relationship with Pakistan and low-intensity conflict continues indefinitely in spite of Pakistan drawing socially closer to Afghanistan. Travel across provincial borders very

392 Three Physical Perils up Ahead

risky, vigilante groups replace police in many areas, crime syndicates proliferate. Pakistani graduates unable to secure any but low-level employment overseas.

Medium-to-low probability: population stabilizes at around 300 million, water conservation measures enforced, understanding arrived at with India, defense spending sharply reduced, terrorism is defeated both militarily and morally, provinces agree to share resources and responsibilities, education system brought to level of surrounding countries.

Low probability: Sind vs. Punjab water crisis erupts, Balochistan seeks separation from Punjab, army intervenes massively and creates East Pakistan situation. Borders get redefined.

Possible but improbable: series of Mumbai-style attacks, jihadis hijack nuclear materials or steal bombs along with codes and use against India. Nuclear war breaks out between India and Pakistan. The subcontinent's cities become radioactive ruins.

Notes

1 This is a parable, not to be taken too seriously. Actual experiments done with frogs have yielded varying results depending upon initial and final temperatures as well as rates of change.
2 D. Carrington, *Climate Emergency: World 'May Have Crossed Tipping Points'*, The Guardian, 27 Nov. 2019. https://www.theguardian.com/environment/2019/nov/27/climate-emergency-world-may-have-crossed-tipping-points
3 J. Moore, *Who Is Responsible for the Climate Crisis?*, Maize, 4 November 2019. https://www.maize.io/magazine/what-is-capitalocene/
4 J.S. Avery, *Adam Smith's Invisible Hand Is at Our Throats*, EACPE, 14 December 2020. https://eacpe.org/adam-smiths-invisible-hand-is-at-our-throats/
5 J. Avery, *Madmen and Economists*, 2020, p. 22. http://eacpe.org/app/wp-content/uploads/2020/12/Madmen-and-Economists-by-John-Scales-Avery.pdf
6 *Lahore again Tops List of World's Most Polluted Cities*, Dawn, 10 Dec 2021. https://www.dawn.com/news/1662926
7 *Climate Change Profile of Pakistan*, Asia Development Bank (2017), http://dx.doi.org/10.22617/TCS178761
8 N. Abas et al., Review of GHG Emissions in Pakistan Compared to SAARC Countries, *Renewable and Sustainable Energy Reviews*, 80 (December 2017): 990–1016. See also, M. Hussain et al. A Comprehensive Review of Climate Change Impacts, Adaptation, and Mitigation on Environmental and Natural Calamities in Pakistan, *Environ. Monit. Assess.*, 192, no. 48 (2020). https://doi.org/10.1007/s10661-019-7956-4
9 *Perils of Deforestation*, Dawn editorial, 16 Aug 2020. https://www.dawn.com/news/1574643
10 *Pakistan's Options for Climate Change Mitigation & Adaptation*, LEAD Pakistan, http://www.lead.org.pk/lead/Publications/Pakistan
11 H.A. Pasha, *Charter of the Economy – Agenda for Economic Reforms in Pakistan, publication of Friedrich Ebert Stiftung*, Islamabad (2021).
12 *Pakistan Population Growth Rate (1950–2022)*, macrotrends, https://www.macrotrends.net/countries/PAK/pakistan/population-growth-rate
13 Z. Mirza, *Pakistan Needs Contraception*, Dawn, 27 August 2021. https://www.dawn.com/news/1642890
14 P. Hoodbhoy, *Promoting Anti-Science Via Textbooks*, Dawn, 3 December 2016. https://www.dawn.com/news/1300118

15 *Single National Curriculum: Publishers Object to Textbook Review Fee, Ulema's Role,* Dawn, 4 June 2021. https://www.dawn.com/news/1627392
16 P. Chakraborty, *No First Use Nuclear Policy: Explained,* Times of India, 29 August 2019. https://timesofindia.indiatimes.com/india/no-first-use-nuclear-policy-explained/articleshow/70844818.cms
17 O. Toon et al., Rapidly Expanding Nuclear Arsenals in Pakistan and India Portend Regional and Global Catastrophe, *Science Advances,* 5, no. 10 (2 October 2019). https://doi.org/10.1126/sciadv.aay5478
18 *Two Major Saudi Oil Installations Hit by Drone Strike, and U.S. Blames Iran,* The New York Times, 15 September 2019. https://www.nytimes.com/2019/09/14/world/middleeast/saudi-arabia-refineries-drone-attack.html
19 *Kashmir Attack: Tracing the Path That Led to Pulwama,* BBC report, 1 May 2019. https://www.bbc.com/news/world-asia-india-47302467

Fifteen

THE PATHS TRAVELLED POST-1971

From the flower's broken stem
جہاں سے پھول ٹوٹا تھا وہیں سے

Emerges now a fresh new bud
کلی سی اک نمایاں ہو رہی ہے

If there's will to move forward
اگر ہے جذبۂ تعمیر زندہ

Then nothing is it that we lack
تو پھر کس چیز کی ہم میں کمی ہے

— *Ahmad Nadeem Qasmi, 1972*

With the fall of Dacca and the breakdown of the Two Nation Theory, Pakistan needed a new raison d'être and a new direction. Measured by population size, most of Pakistan was now gone. But, as it turned out, this was only a big blow not a fatal one. The alacrity with which the "real" Pakistan reasserted itself proved that it had always been the center and was intact; only its periphery – a colony – had been lost. Nevertheless it raised the question: what could now be sufficient reason for a religiously homogeneous but culturally heterogeneous Pakistan to continue existing as a unit? This chapter discusses four experiments that sought to repurpose and redirect Pakistan: Bhutto called for vengeance against India, Zia-ul-Haq for full-blown Islamization, Musharraf sought to ameliorate Zia's excesses and called for enlightened moderation, and Imran Khan was the nominal head of a hybrid civil–military government that swore to make Pakistan a replica of the Medina state. Common to all four is reliance upon the military for protecting the state from its own people. This chapter serves as a prelude to the next where we explore the road not yet taken.

In 1971 a cyclone of angry and awakened Bengali nationalism swept the Two Nation Theory into the Bay of Bengal. This put an end to the original idea of Pakistan. It was hugely paradoxical because the original impetus to seek a

DOI: 10.4324/9781003379140-21

The Paths Travelled Post-1971 **395**

homeland for all Muslims had come from the unrelenting enthusiasm of Bengali Muslims. Many in West Pakistan had assumed that Bengalis would soon realize their mistake and humbly seek their return to the fold. But half a century later Bangladesh is doggedly unrepentant. Instead it routinely repeats its demand that Pakistan apologize for mass killings during its struggle for independence. Just as routinely, Islamabad rejects the demand.

How did West Pakistan adapt to the loss of 56% of the country? There were dire predictions that everything would fall apart. But soon after it got over the shock, like the proverbial phoenix, it rose from the ashes and simply dusted them off. The poet Ahmad Nadeem Qasmi optimistically wrote of buds on twigs getting ready to bloom into flowers. State organizations and institutions quietly changed their names to reflect the new reality. Fifty years later one can still occasionally see "Pakistan Western Railways" visible under the peeling paint of old railway bogies with all newer ones having Pakistan Railways on them. On official documents, West Pakistan literally scrubbed away "West" everywhere. Without ever having officially admitted the fact, the West always knew that a united Pakistan had been a geographical and cultural absurdity. The breakup had allowed it to get rid of some unwanted baggage.

And yet there was an existential dilemma that would not go away. The movement for Pakistan had been solely rooted in separate religious identities for Muslims and Hindus. That idea had had its day and now stood negated. What to do now? Before 1947 it had been politically profitable to harp upon Hindu–Muslim differences and their fundamental incompatibility. But this made no sense now. Hindus from Muslim-majority provinces had mostly fled to India during the Partition riots and so had been reduced to an insignificant minority in West Pakistan. Moreover, the Baloch, Sindhis, and even the once-privileged Muhajirs were chafing at Punjabi domination. So how could a religiously homogeneous but culturally heterogeneous West Pakistan continue existing as a unit? Where should it seek direction, purpose, and create for itself a vision of its future?

These questions have been around now for about half a century. While a consistent answer is still lacking, different options have been explored. In the following I shall evaluate four significant experiments to repurpose Pakistan after the fall of Dacca. These are associated with the names of Zulfikar Ali Bhutto, Zia-ul-Haq, Pervez Musharraf, and Imran Khan. Each derided and rejected the preceding attempt, and each was conditioned by different regional situations and geopolitical environments. And yet, at the end, what stands out is continuity rather than change. Whether in the forefront or just a little removed, as the direct beneficiary of the existing order, the Army establishment has closely watched – or directed – these political experiments.

Experiment I – Vengeance

Zulfikar Ali Bhutto was a political genius who not only succeeded in bringing back 93,000 Pakistani troops who had surrendered to India but did so by

396 The Paths Travelled Post-1971

driving a hard bargain with Indira Gandhi allowing Pakistan to retain its claim on Kashmir. Bhutto came from a family of Sindhi landlords and was influential. His hatred for India and Hindus was almost pathological, a fact that some have attempted to explain using Freudian theory.[1] In 1965 Bhutto had advised and encouraged General Ayub Khan into launching Operation Gibraltar. This involved sending infiltrators across to Indian held Kashmir in the hope of inspiring a local insurrection.[2] After Gibraltar flamed out, he blamed the fiasco on Ayub, claiming that he had needlessly surrendered. Resigning as foreign minister made him enormously popular, a calculated move that appealed to outraged national sentiment. Anti-Indianism seemed the best way both to boost his political fortunes and build national cohesion.

Bhutto was possessed with a Nietzschean will to power. In a letter to his daughter, Benazir Bhutto, he advised her to read of Napoleon Bonaparte (whom he described as the "most complete man of modern history") and Bismarck among others.[3] Salman Taseer, who later on went to become governor of Punjab tells us that Metternich and Talleyrand were also his favorites.[4] All were unsurpassed egotists, believing in the primacy of power and determined to have it at any cost.

As the Pakistani establishment lay bleeding and wounded after 1971, Bhutto shrewdly assessed that its loss of power was temporary only. His prospects for rising to the very top lay in buying it over with a call for revenge against India. Declaring the pursuit of nuclear weapons as Pakistan's priority and purpose had already earned him much credit in those quarters. As far back as 1968 he had made the very first appeal by a Pakistani for the Bomb: "It would be dangerous to plan for less and our plans should, therefore, include the nuclear deterrent".[5] Promising a "war of a thousand years" after the fall of Dacca, he called a meeting on 20 January 1972 in the city of Multan to which senior scientists and engineers were invited. Bhutto exhorted them to build the bomb, fired the-then chairman of the Pakistan Atomic Energy Commission, Dr. Ishrat Hussain Usmani, and hired an ambitious new one, Munir Ahmad Khan. Pakistan's quest for nuclear weapons began just six weeks after the fall of Dacca.

At the same time, Bhutto was smart enough to realize that harping upon India alone would never get him power in a nation that yearned for social justice and economic opportunity. On 30 November 1967, Bhutto formally launched the Pakistan People's Party manifesto in Lahore. This brought to Pakistan the era of mass socialist politics for the very first time. Pakistan's earlier history, with feudal lords at the helm of affairs, had no such precedent of progressive politics. Socialist politics had been frowned upon from Jinnah to Ayub. However, in the early 1950s, as a student of political science at Berkeley (University of California), Bhutto had no such aversion to socialism and he quickly latched on to the political possibilities. His academic study would serve him well politically in the coming decades.

The late 1950s and 1960s were times of enormous hope for colonized peoples around the world. The colonizers had reluctantly recognized that they could no

The Paths Travelled Post-1971 **397**

longer rule. Patrice Lumumba's defiant speech upon the recognition of the independence of the Congo stands as a landmark.[6] Argentine journalist Adolfo Gilly observed in his 1965 introduction to political philosopher Frantz Fanon's studies in *A Dying Colonialism* that, "The whole of humanity has erupted violently, tumultuously onto the state of history, taking its own destiny in its hands... Liberation does not come as a gift from anybody".[7] All of a sudden recently decolonized peoples across the world were taking on their government, standing up to American imperialism and articulating a belief that the world needed to become more equal. Political imaginations opened wide open. Although at birth, Pakistan's Left had been feeble, it gained strength from happenings around the world. Anushay Malik notes that:

> This does not mean that a revolution in which workers took over the factories and maintained hold of them was ever really on the cards in Pakistan, but workers, students and activists all believed it was. Their actions, their political demands, the organizations they formed were guided by this belief. It was this belief, this faith in the inevitability of revolution that fueled the conspicuous absence of despair.[8]

In diametrical opposition to mainstream parties, the Pakistan People Party (PPP) manifesto demanded social justice and the establishment of a classless society with commitments to a constitutional democratic order based on universal adult franchise; civil rights and liberties; full remuneration to peasants and workers for their labor; further elimination of feudalism and landlordism; encouragement of self-help projects and voluntary cooperative farming; development of nationwide unions in certain industries; minimum wages and the workers' right to strike; free health care for peasants and workers; reorganization of education to bring about a classless society; encouragement of regional languages expressing the people's cultural personality. The manifesto came out strongly for the freedoms of belief and expression, press, organization, and assembly.

The PPP manifesto and Bhutto's rhetoric galvanized society in Pakistan as never before. In the years after the 1965 war, they gave it hope for a better future. It did not matter that Bhutto was one of Sind's richer landlords and had never submitted to land reform. The cry of *roti-kapra-makan* rang across West Pakistan, as did the cry to free Pakistan from American influence. Bhutto had unwittingly discovered just the right political buttons to be pushed. Hitherto ensconced in the elite upper class of society, for him traveling around the country was a voyage of discovery. With dry wit, journalist and writer I.A. Rahman recalled how Bhutto converted in 1966 to the Left:

> Thousands of students were at the Lahore railway station to receive him. They were shouting anti-Ayub, pro-Bhutto slogans but most of all: "*surkh hai, surkh hai. Asia surkh hai*" (Red it is, red it is. Asia is red). Mr. Bhutto

was upset. "What is this nonsense? Stop this nonsense," he said several times as he got into the car. But who could stop the students? When the slow cavalcade reached the YMCA and Bhutto got out of his car, he was vigorously shouting "*surkh hai, surkh hai, Asia surkh hai*". People around him said: "There is a leader who follows the masses".[9]

Defeating religious right-wing parties ideologically opposed to socialism and communism had seemed impossible in Pakistan's religious milieu. Pakistan's founders had also been vehemently against these non-Islamic ideologies. But, in spite of his profligate, ultra-rich lifestyle Bhutto easily persuaded voters that 22 super-wealthy families ruled over Pakistan. Feudal families, recognizing that he belonged to their social class and would not compromise his personal wealth, were annoyed but not excessively perturbed. Many, after an adjustment period, became comfortable with his rhetoric and he gradually chose to depend upon them.

Industrialists, however, found their factories taken over with the power to run them handed over to state functionaries. This was to open the doors to nepotism and corruption. One particularly egregious example was that of the Batala Engineering Company; what could have been Pakistan's equivalent of Tata Industries in India was destroyed by a thoughtless – or perhaps malicious – takeover.[10] The shipping industry was likewise nationalized and rendered inefficient and uncompetitive.[11]

Bhutto had calculated that once firmly in the saddle he could dispense with the working class and the left-wingers who had made that possible. On 7 June 1972, the Karachi police opened fire on workers killing several. The next day the police fired again on the funeral procession of one of the workers. Kamran Asdar Ali notes that these killings marked the end of Bhutto's progressivism.[12] Days later as a student at MIT, at a meeting of Pakistanis at Ashdown Hall (MIT) I recall challenging Benazir Bhutto, then a student at Radcliffe College, on the killing of workers and the role of her father. Her answer remains stuck in my memory: those workers were enemies of the state!

In earlier years Bhutto's dynamism as a leader setting new, independent foreign policy for Pakistan and seeking the development of heavy industry was enormously inspirational to his followers. Trade unions and student unions sprouted, creating a generation of left-wing activists. That he thumbed his nose at Washington and made friends with left-wing nationalists like Sukarno and Nasser added to his popular appeal. Developing an *entente cordiale* with China initially brought frowns from the Nixon–Kissinger team until the United States realized the potential of using Pakistan as a diplomatic bridge to China. This, in fact, was why the United States was hesitant to condemn Pakistan's excesses in the 1971 war.[13] The Second Islamic Summit held in Lahore in 1974, attended by 24 heads of state, was a triumph for Bhutto and his greatest foreign policy success. It also provided an occasion for Pakistan to recognize Bangladesh as an independent sovereign state, an astute move that won him many plaudits.

The Paths Travelled Post-1971   **399**

With his rhetoric of perpetual war with India lighting the fires of nuclear nationalism, and rising ambitions of leading the *ummah*, Bhutto created excitement in what had earlier been a dejected Pakistan. Although known more for his love of whisky and beautiful women rather than devoutness, Bhutto knew well the power of Islam as a rallying tool. Could Pakistan lead the entire Muslim world with him playing an essential role? There were enormous strategic and political dividends to be had because of the newfound Arab unity following the humiliating defeat of Arab armies at Israel's hands in the 1973 war. Bhutto correctly calculated that Muslim countries would rally behind him and also fund his ambitions for the Bomb. Indeed, suitcases stuffed with dollars were reportedly flown in on Pakistan International Airline flights from Libya, Saudi Arabia, and Gulf countries.[14] It was whispered that relief monies sent for helping December 1974 earthquake victims was diverted to the burgeoning nuclear program.

But those leftists who had brought him into power and had been the mainstay of the PPP were in for a disappointment. In the year after becoming the president, and then prime minister, he had moved away from delivering on his earlier promises. By now he had even stopped talking about land reform and a socialist economy. Factory workers who had been aroused to action by his promises showed their resentment with public demonstrations but were met with armed force from Bhutto's specially created goon squad, the paramilitary Federal Security Force (FSF). Dozens died in clashes.

Provincial autonomy was another direction where Bhutto's election rhetoric had promised hope. According to the 1973 Constitution, representatives of the Council of Common Interests from all four provinces would sit side by side to oversee river water distribution, a critical resource for an agricultural economy. Sindhi grievances at under-representation in the bureaucracy and army would be redressed, and the Sindhi language would be taught side by side with Urdu in Sindh. A discussion around these points may be found in Jaffrelot.[15] While Sindhis identified ethnically with Bhutto, nationalists were soon to feel the force of his authoritarianism. The nationalist leader G.M. Syed was promptly hauled off to jail.

By 1974 Pakistan was now well on its way to becoming a police state, a fact first recognized and written about by Eqbal Ahmad.[16] Dissent within the party was crushed, its founding leaders beaten to a pulp. I well remember that morning in 1974 when, two streets down from where I was living in Islamabad, FSF hoodlums had surrounded the house of J.A. Rahim. He was one of Bhutto's cabinet ministers and a one-time confidante. It was whispered that he had been sodomized, physically brutalized, and his ribs broken. Political opponents were harassed, thousands were jailed, and the state bureaucracy became his instrument of personal power. The elected state governments of North-West Frontier Province and Balochistan were dismissed. In contrast, although Ayub was undemocratic, his regime was not as repressive as Bhutto's. At the time, the armed forces and bureaucracy – the inherited steel frame – had worked out a power-sharing agreement. Bureaucrats had no problem in serving their new masters and this helped civilianize army rule. But in 1972 the professionalism of

400 The Paths Travelled Post-1971

the bureaucracy received a big hit under Bhutto's so-called lateral entry program, a way of smuggling in PPP supporters into positions of power.

As it turned out, Bhutto's greatest mistake was to rehabilitate and re-empower an army that finally had been brought under civilian rule. In 1973, headed by Gen. Tikka Khan who had achieved notoriety as the Butcher of Bengal, he sent off the army to fight Baloch nationalists. Once again the Pakistan Army was at war with the people of Pakistan. Bhutto's popularity plummeted and he became unsure of winning the forthcoming 1977 elections. He still had a cult following but his left-wing supporters were now suspicious of him. In making concessions to established elites, he had lost their trust as well. By most accounts, the 1977 elections were massively rigged, inspiring the Pakistan National Alliance (PNA) protest movement. This ultimately became his undoing. His base was still intact and, in retrospect, had Bhutto not dealt with the elections so ham-handedly, it is possible that he might actually have won.

After a few months of debilitating street agitation by nine opposition parties, General Zia-ul-Haq, whom Bhutto had appointed over the heads of other senior generals as chief of army staff, was ordered by Bhutto to use the military to restore order. This worked perfectly for Zia. To his genuine surprise, Bhutto soon found himself behind bars, accused of murdering a political opponent. How could the military who owed so much to him have done that?

Bhutto had overstepped by too much. For all his seeming deference, Zia had scores to settle, insults to avenge, and ambitions to realize. Bhutto had been overheard at meetings referring to Zia as his "pet monkey". Bhutto is said to have devised a test for his leading generals. He dropped his silken handkerchief and put his foot on it. General Zia-ul-Haq reportedly bent down and attempted to tug at the hanky in order to retrieve it. Bhutto continued to press his foot on the hanky, thus embarrassing the kneeling general.[17] The seemingly servile general, he thought, was so awed by him that disobedience was impossible. This was a fatal miscalculation. The army establishment indeed owed a great deal to Bhutto, but now that his personal ambitions had run wild he could expect no mercy and, as it turned out, received none.

Addressing posterity from his death cell in Rawalpindi jail, Bhutto became the very first Muslim leader to introduce the term "Islamic Bomb" into the nuclear lexicon. In his book, *If I am Assassinated*, he wrote: "We know that Israel and South Africa have full nuclear capability. The Christian, Jewish, and Hindu civilizations have this capability. The communist powers also possess it. Only the Islamic civilization was without it, but that position was about to change".[18] In doing so, he tried to give Pakistan's atomic bomb a civilizational basis rather than a strictly national one. Although appending "Islamic" to "bomb"—and thus associating destruction with a religion—did cause some Muslims to take umbrage, most welcomed the bomb as a sign of Muslim prowess and power.[19]

On 2 April 1979, the authorities of Rawalpindi jail flew in Tara Masih from Bahawalpur by official plane. This was the first and only time this officially deputed hangman had traveled by air. The official fee fixed for the execution was

The Paths Travelled Post-1971   **401**

25 rupees. On the early morning of 4 April 1979, Zia settled his personal scores with Bhutto once and for all. Revenge ended the life of a man who had espoused revenge as his country's top priority. It was supreme irony.

Experiment II – Nizam-e-Mustafa

General Zia-ul-Haq, because he had put a noose around Bhutto's neck, was desperate for legitimacy. By conviction a religious man with messianic zeal, he put his faith to good use soon after the 1977 coup but ran into a patch of bad luck. On 21 November 1979 the United States Embassy in Islamabad was burned down by a mob incited by Ayatollah Khomeini's pronouncement that the Americans had engineered a takeover of the Masjid al-Haram in Mecca. At the head of the mob were students from Quaid-e-Azam University which is just down the road from the embassy. I cannot forget that day because half of my physics class immediately got up to join the protesters and my lecture stood cancelled. For two days, a cloud of thick smoke hung over the city as the embassy burned. Zia had botched it – that day for the very first time he had tried to put on a populist hat and show off his cycling skills in Rawalpindi's Raja Bazar.

Zia may not have lasted if the Americans had stayed angry, but fate was exceptionally kind to him. In December 1979, just four weeks later, the Soviets walked into Afghanistan. History may well have taken a different course if the year of this invasion had not also been the year for presidential elections in the U.S. But with Ronald Reagan as the rival candidate, President Jimmy Carter could not afford to appear soft on the Soviets. Angrily condemning Soviet expansionism, Carter withdrew the SALT II treaty from consideration by the Senate, announced that the United States would boycott the Moscow Olympics, and prepared a major military buildup which included a Rapid Deployment Force intended primarily for the Persian Gulf. The U.S. administration requested approval for a CIA covert operation in Afghanistan and offered Pakistan $400 million in aid. Zia famously dismissed this as "peanuts", correctly grasping that Afghanistan had become the focal point of American global strategy.[20] This led to setting up the complex machinery for the world's first international jihad. Over his eleven years in office, Zia milked the Americans for all he could.

The rest is history: from the early 1980s onwards, Pakistan became the hub of a thriving global jihad industry financed and assisted by the U.S. and Saudi Arabia.[21] American strategy was to drive what President Ronald Reagan called the "evil empire" out of Afghanistan. This required marshalling the forces of Islam from Algeria and Morocco to Egypt and Saudi Arabia. The Pakistan Army participated enthusiastically – "Islam, Pakistan, Jihad" was emblazoned on banners at recruitment centers, beards proliferated, promotions went with piety, and few soldiers and officers could afford not being seen at Friday prayers. A new ethos different from the colonial one was being created; this was to be an army not just for Pakistan, but to fight the enemies of Islam everywhere. Henceforth, it would defend Pakistan's geographical borders as well as its ideological borders.

Zia began a massive decade-long, state-sponsored project to give Pakistan new meaning. Democracy was demonised and declared un-Islamic. Following the warnings of Shah Waliullah some three hundred years earlier, official doctrine was now to ensure that Pakistani culture be purified of Hindu "contamination". Urdu was systematically cleansed of Hindi words to the extent possible, dress codes were introduced, university teachers had their faith examined under a microscope, capital punishment was freely used, and religion was introduced into every aspect of public and private life. Nizam-e-Mustafa – which would bring to Pakistan the glorious state of Islam under the Prophet – was now to be Pakistan's goal and destiny.

Education was the key weapon for Zia's strategy. In 1981, he ordered the education authorities to rewrite the history of Pakistan. The University Grants Commission instructed that all new school textbooks would now "induce pride for the nation's past, enthusiasm for the present and unshakeable faith in the stability and longevity of Pakistan". Jinnah and other icons of the Pakistan Movement had to be henceforth portrayed as pious fundamentalists whether or not they carried beards. Lest the truth leak out, their lifestyles had to be hidden from public view.

Zia's strategy was showing signs of working well in Punjab and NWFP. But, even as overall religiosity increased, the paradoxes of religious nationalism also became starker. Sindhis, Baloch, and Muhajirs were becoming restive and upset about rule from the center. Besieged nationalists were attacked by A.K. Brohi, the law minister in Zia-ul-Haq's military regime who launched a blistering attack on politicians belonging to the political parties of Pakistan's nationalities. In October 1978, he wrote in Dawn:

> Pakistan is a successor state to British India, which had a unitary, rather than a federal form of Government First there was a Centre, which extended to peripheral parts (now forming Pakistan) and it was this Centre, which delegated powers to the provinces for the sake of administrative convenience. Thus, when Pakistan was founded, it retained its unitary character. Subsequent federalization was merely a result of Center's progressive decentralization rather than a product of voluntary surrendering of partial sovereignty by the constituent parts of Pakistan. Furthermore, Pakistan was founded on the basis of religion and religion alone. It can be kept together only by the cementing force of *Ikhwan*. There are no nationalities in Pakistan or, for that matter, anywhere else; and the idea of nationalities is subversive.

Zia's major "achievements": instituting the death penalty for blasphemy; creating a hand-picked *Majlis-e-Shoora* in lieu of a federal parliament; mandatory deduction of 2.5% from all bank accounts for *zakat*; and exacerbation of Shia–Sunni divisions. Some laws enacted in his time must count among the most regressive and grotesquely cruel in modern history, in particular those that concerned the rights of Pakistani women. Enacted into the law in 1979, a presidential ordinance was moved for converting Pakistan into a theocracy governed by sharia. Under the Hudood Ordinance, Pakistani law prescribes death by stoning for married Muslims who are found guilty of extramarital sex (for unmarried couples or non-Muslims, the penalty is 100 lashes). The law is exact in stating how the death penalty is to be administered: "Such of the witnesses who deposed against the convict as may be available shall start stoning him and, while stoning is being carried on, he may be shot dead, whereupon stoning and shooting shall be stopped".[22]

Rape was still more problematic. A woman who failed to prove that she has been raped was automatically charged with fornication and adultery. Under the Hudood Law, she is considered guilty unless she can prove her innocence. Proof of innocence requires that the rape victim must produce "at least four Muslim adult male witnesses, about whom the Court is satisfied" who saw the actual act of penetration. Inability to do so may result in her being jailed, or perhaps even sentenced to death for adultery. The case of Safia Bibi, an unmarried blind woman, became iconic. Her rapist was acquitted, leading to outrage by Pakistani women.[23]

Prayers in government departments were deemed compulsory, punishments were meted out to those who did not fast in Ramadan, selection for academic posts required that the candidate demonstrate knowledge of Islamic teachings, and jihad was propagated through schoolbooks. Across the country there was a spectacular increase in the power and prestige of the clerics, attendance in mosques shot up, people organized home prayer meetings (*dars* and *zikr*), and special religious festivals were observed with fervor. Religion was now the currency of power – if you wanted to get somewhere, you had better be religious or at least appear religious.

Zia's death in a mysterious air crash brought some relief but not much. Elections were held in 1988, 1990, 1993, 1997, 2002, 2008, 2013, and 2018. No candidate for office came up with an agenda that could fire up a popular reformist movement that could roll back Zia's initiatives. Zia's immediate successors, Benazir Bhutto and Nawaz Sharif, were mainstream leaders and both were content to live with the status quo, accepting without question the army's primacy. They were told – and reluctantly accepted – that they would have no role in nuclear policy or the management of nuclear weapons, that relations with India and the United States did not fall within their purview, and that the Kashmir jihad would be controlled by the army only. Their role would be to support the national position as determined by the army but lesser decisions related to agriculture, railways, communications, construction, etc. would rest with the government. Unsurprisingly, they also did not dare to make a serious attempt at education reform by overturning Zia's remolding of the curriculum. They left no outstanding imprint upon Pakistani culture and society. Before he finally gave up, the army general who followed them at least tried to loosen up Zia's extremism – unsuccessfully.

404 The Paths Travelled Post-1971

Experiment III – Enlightened Moderation

General Pervez Musharraf, like General Ayub Khan, was a man infatuated by his own wisdom. Again, like Ayub he was not pathologically anti-Indian, at least no more than the ordinary officer. A *muhajir* rather than Punjabi and one whispered to be a closet Shia, he must be considered the next significant national leader after Zia. Twenty years after Musharraf overthrew Nawaz Sharif's government on 12 October 1999, political columnist Zahid Husain assessed each of the following seven promises made by Musharraf in his speech five days later: rebuild national confidence and morale; strengthen the federation, remove interprovincial disharmony and restore national cohesion; revive the economy and restore investor confidence; ensure law and order and dispense speedy justice; depoliticize state institutions; devolve power to the grass-roots level; and ensure swift and across the board accountability.[24] While the reader is referred to this useful summary of Musharraf's impact on governance, in this section I shall deal with his handling of foreign policy, militancy, and attempts to steer the state away from religious fundamentalism.

The earlier years were not promising. Seeing opportunity, in the early months of 1999 Musharraf launched his secret Kargil war in Kashmir. Unguided by any larger strategic vision, he was merely acting out his army instincts that if you can somehow hurt India without destroying yourself, do it! General Headquarters (GHQ) quickly conned Nawaz Sharif – then in his second term in office as prime minister – into believing that this short incursion into Indian-occupied Kashmir would lead to a quick, decisive victory for Pakistan. Thereafter, like a plum ripened by decades of waiting, Kashmir would fall into Pakistan's lap. Once that happened, both Nawaz and Musharraf would be able to claim credit.

An excellent exposition of the events leading up to Kargil and officers involved is given in the recent book by Nasim Zehra.[25] One learns that Musharraf, like Ayub Khan in 1965, had badly miscalculated India's reaction – there was no plan B. Once the Indians counterattacked, Nawaz was adrift and lost nerve after Pakistan faced both military defeat and international isolation. On 4 July 1999 Nawaz met with President Bill Clinton in Washington. Bruce Riedel, who was present at the meeting as Clinton's senior adviser on South Asian issues, wrote that Clinton warned Nawaz that Pakistani forces would have to retreat unconditionally. Being told that nuclear war was around the corner, Nawaz meekly agreed to the American demand.[26]

Upon return to Pakistan, Nawaz was in the Army's bad books. He had failed to sell Pakistan's case to the Americans and had made the Pakistan Army look bad. Musharraf's coup followed on 12 October 1999. This was a vindictive action that came from personal pique and not for any larger ideological reason. Nawaz was a Sunni Punjabi steeped into the Establishment's ethos with political support from right-wing Islamist parties. He was, however, resentful of being led up the garden path – it had turned out that Kashmir was a prickly pear and he had been tricked by the army. Musharraf's convoluted autobiography, written while he was still head of state (as was Ayub's!), details the drama coup with his plane being refused permission to land upon his return from an official visit to Sri Lanka.[27] Therein he also suggests that had Saudi Arabia not intervened, Nawaz, like Bhutto, would have met the gallows.

Video footage of the time shows that Musharraf had been feted by the United Jihad Council during and after the Kargil war. This may suggest that jihadists thought of him as being one from among them. But he was by no means a religious man and found their beliefs appallingly irrational. Following the tradition of desi officers during British rule, he enjoyed his evening pegs of whisky (some of his post-retirement drunken bawdies can be found on Facebook videos). Shortly after taking over as chief martial law administrator, he appeared in photos holding two Pekingese, Dot and Buddy, under his arms.[28] In a country where dogs are held to be *na-pak* (unclean), the faithful were appalled and the two dogs were never seen again in public. Curiously, just as the secular Jinnah ruled over a religiously charged Muslim League, the secular Musharraf headed an Islamized army. In the larger scheme of things, personal choices and preferences of leaders did not make a significant difference.

Initially, the Americans were unimpressed by Musharraf and his army colleagues. President Bill Clinton, who had spent a normal official week in India and Bangladesh together with sightseeing at the Taj Mahal, flew to Islamabad on 25 March 2000 amid extraordinary security precautions to spend a total of six hours there during which he sternly lectured Pakistan on state television against the use of terrorism as an instrument of foreign policy. But, as it turned out, fate in the form of 9/11 gave to Musharraf the chance to head the Islamic Republic of Pakistan for nearly nine years. Just as the Soviet invasion had been a windfall for Zia, the World Trade Center destruction was a bonanza for Musharraf. Faced with George W. Bush's ultimatum "you are with us or against us", Musharraf acted swiftly to declare Pakistan was indeed on America's side and officially sought distance from the Taliban but without declaring them as terrorists.

"Enlightened moderation" became the new mantra. Would Musharraf now become the Kamal Ataturk of Pakistan? Or was this mere optics? Musharraf loved playing to the gallery. His speech before the Council of Foreign Relations in New York drew a standing ovation.[29] In his new role as a world leader, he spoke charmingly to the international media about a modernized and moderate Islam that would displace the legacy of an orthodox, militant, and violent version of Zia-era Islam.

If one excludes his misogyny,[30] Musharraf's personal instincts were undeniably liberal at the level of lifestyle. Pakistan saw some significant relaxation of draconian laws passed in the Zia era. Initially there was a perceptible shift in institutional practices and inclinations. Heads of government organizations were no longer required to lead noon prayers as in the 1980s; female announcers with undraped heads could now freely appear on Pakistan Television; passengers on PIA flights noted that thickly bearded stewards had been replaced by stewardesses; and the first women fighter pilots were inducted into the Pakistan

406 The Paths Travelled Post-1971

Air Force. Then, in early July 2006, Musharraf directed the Council of Islamic Ideology to draft an amendment to the controversial Hudood Ordinance, put in place by Zia and not repealed by any of the civilian governments that ruled from 1988 to 1999. This law gave women a lower legal status and punished the victims of rape. Repeal of these anti-women laws had been a long-standing demand of Pakistani women's groups. Hundreds of women prisoners arrested under the Hudood Ordinance, many of whom had spent years awaiting their trial, were released shortly thereafter. Musharraf proposed amending the Ordinance and opened it for parliamentary discussion in early September 2006.

Some suspected that a part of the gain would be political: he might be seeking to split the parliamentary opposition to government policies in Balochistan, where the insurgency has pitted that province against the Punjab. Musharraf did expect opposition to his liberalism from some of his allies who were fundamentalists of the Muttahida Majlis-e-Amal (MMA), the main Islamic parliamentary group that commanded majorities in the provincial assemblies of the Frontier and Baluchistan. But their reaction to the initiative was far more violent than he had anticipated. MMA members tore up copies of the proposed amendments on the floor of the National Assembly and threatened to resign en masse. And so, long before any threats by the Islamic opposition were actually carried out, Musharraf's government scuttled its own initiative. This retreat doomed the bill to obscurity.

Musharraf had retreated earlier as well. On 21 April 2000 – well before 9/11 and hence not an action designed to woo America – he had announced a new administrative procedure for registration of cases under the Blasphemy Law 295-C. This law prescribes death as the minimum penalty and has frequently been used to harass religious minorities as well as personal opponents. To reduce such occurrences, Musharraf's modified procedure would have required authorization from the local district magistrate for registration of a blasphemy case. A modest improvement at best, it could have ameliorated some of the worst excesses. But this commitment too was less than firm. Twenty-five days later – under the watchful glare of the mullahs, Musharraf hastily climbed down saying: "As it was the unanimous demand of the *ulema*, *mashaikh* and the people, therefore, I have decided to do away with the procedural change in the registration of FIR under the Blasphemy Law".[31]

As though to compensate for Musharraf's liberal image, others in his government rushed to establish their religious credentials. The federal minister for religious affairs Ijaz-ul-Haq (Zia-ul-Haq's son), speaking at the launch of a book authored by a leading Islamic extremist leader on "Christian Terrorism and The Muslim World," argued that anyone who did not believe in jihad could not be either a Muslim or a Pakistani. He then declared that given the situation facing Muslims today, he was prepared to be a suicide bomber. Shaukat Aziz, a former Citibank employee who was chosen to be prime minister, made a call for nationwide prayers for rain in a year of drought. At an education conference in Islamabad that I had personally attended, he rejected the suggestion of a moderate Islamic scholar, Javed Ghamidi, that only after their fifth year and above should schoolchildren be given formal Islamic education. Instead, Aziz proposed that Islamic religious education must start as soon as children enter school. Henceforth, the government's education policy would require Islamic studies to begin in the third year of school, a year earlier than in the previous policy.

Many of Musharraf's other ministers felt even less need to show a liberal face. The health minister, Mohammad Nasir Khan, assured the upper house of parliament that the government could consider banning female nurses looking after male patients at hospitals. This move arose from a motion moved by female parliamentary members of the MMA. Maulana Gul Naseeb Khan, provincial secretary of the MMA, was among those holy men to whom women's bodies are of particular concern. He said, "We think that men could derive sexual pleasure from women's bodies while conducting ECG or ultrasound".[32] In his opinion women would be able to lure men under the pretext of these medical procedures. Therefore, he said, "to save the supreme values of Islam and the message of the Holy Prophet (PBUH), the MMA has decided to impose the ban". Destroyed or damaged billboards with women's faces could be seen in several cities of the NWFP (now renamed at KPK) province because the MMA deemed the exhibition of unveiled women as un-Islamic.

Why did the army, a conservative institution, not revolt against a lifestyle liberal who was defying their cultural values? To be sure, there were disgruntled elements that repeatedly attacked him. But Musharraf's other life was to head the Establishment. He remained thoroughly committed to its goals of countering India in Kashmir through the use of extra state actors. The Pakistani state was running with hares and hunting with hounds. After the October 2005 earthquake that killed more than 90,000 in northern Pakistan, I was personally witness to powerful jihadist groups showing off their impressive capabilities by rescuing soldiers and treating them in their own special hospitals. Many national and international relief organizations were left insecure by their overwhelming presence. Banners of so-called banned organizations could be seen in all major towns of Azad Kashmir. Some obtained relief materials from government stocks to pass off as their own, and used heavy vehicles that could only have been provided by the authorities.[33]

American pressure led to Musharraf formally banning some of many jihadist groups that the Pakistan Army had helped train and arm for over two decades. Nevertheless, they operated quite freely, leading to American accusations of hypocrisy. A mass of junior officers and low-ranking soldiers – whose world view is similar to that of the Taliban in most respects – felt resentful at being used as cannon fodder for fighting America's war. Those killed were denied the status of *shaheed* by their village elders and *moulvis*, and their funeral prayers are sparsely attended. Army discipline had to be forcefully used to squelch dissent. This forced the radicalized ones underground, and some defected to the enemy.

Nevertheless, the relationship between the army and religious radicals was no longer as simple as it had been in the 1980s. To maintain a positive image in the

408 The Paths Travelled Post-1971

West was important – as yet China had not stepped in as America's replacement. The Pakistani Establishment depended on both weapons and aid from the U.S. So it could conveniently decry Islamic radicalism as excessive and claim it had broken with the Taliban, but no hard actions had to be taken unless Islamists threatened the army's corporate and political interests or when senior army commanders were targeted for assassination. Musharraf, in particular, was twice targeted by suicide attacks. Presumably the attackers saw what everyone else also saw – duplicity.

More generally, duplicity became the military's de facto foreign policy: even as it formally withdrew its support for the Taliban, it continued to actively support and train anti-India extremist groups on Pakistani soil. The membership of these jihadist groups largely subscribed to the Deobandi/Salafi/Wahhabi schools. Most were bitterly anti-Shia, while some considered worship at shrines, practiced by Barelvi Muslims and others, as heretical. Shrines became their targets, preferred by their proximity over distant and dangerous India.

In 2006, Musharraf reignited Baloch anger by ordering the killing of 79-year-old Akbar Bugti and thus revived an insurgency that has since smoldered. Before the action, he issued a chilling warning: "Don't push us. It is not the 1970s when you can hit and run and hide in the mountains. This time you won't even know what hit you".[34]

In 2007 the mood in Pakistan's mosques and *madrassas* turned insurrectionary with open calls for jihad.[35] Islamabad's Red Mosque's challenge to the Pakistani state had to be quelled with the loss of well over 200 lives, including a dozen elite Special Service Commandos. Students of the associated *madrassa*, Jamia Hafsa, formed morality squads that terrorized city residents, kidnaped alleged prostitutes, and then tried them in an Islamic court. Musharraf's government badly botched the response. The military action of 4 July 2007 to rid the Lal Masjid of militants started near-daily suicide attacks on public places, market, mosques, and shrines across the country. The sound of ambulances carrying victims to hospitals could be heard in most cities and towns. The war on terror had brought to Pakistan near-daily suicide bombings and the widespread destruction of lives, limbs, and property.

For all his inconsistencies, Musharraf must be credited with the longest peaceful period that Pakistan has enjoyed with India. In doing so he acted idiosyncratically, and without attempting to take along with him either the rest of the Establishment or popular opinion. To their astonishment, Musharraf reversed Pakistan's insistence upon a plebiscite being the only solution of the Kashmir problem. In his good moments – which came four to five years after he planned and executed the Kargil operation – Musharraf had envisaged a settlement over Kashmir that was realistic and in which Pakistan would not be the loser. Open borders, allowing divided Kashmiri families to reunite, trade with India, etc. was in the works.

None of Musharraf's thinking on Kashmir was put into practice. By insisting on absolute power, he had badly miscalculated on two counts: first, peremptorily

The Paths Travelled Post-1971 **409**

dismissing the Chief Justice of Pakistan and, second, acting much too late on the Red Mosque challenge. Weakened, he struggled, but by mid-2007 he was a lame duck. In 2016 he traveled to Dubai and has since remained there. In 2019 he was sentenced to death for high treason on a charge initiated by Nawaz Sharif in 2013. The army immediately rallied around its former chief and four weeks later the Lahore High Court exonerated him of the charge.

In summary: Musharraf's call for "enlightened moderation" was an admission by him – and a sizeable part of the Establishment he represented – that a jihad-directed theocratic Pakistan was too socially regressive, closed the doors for economic progress, and invited fear and dislike by the world community. It was an embarrassment and a hurdle to be overcome. Musharraf's attempts resemble those of Ayub Khan who had gone some way to change family laws and had quietly sought to take the "Islamic" out of Pakistan's formal name – Islamic Republic of Pakistan – but retreated when faced by opposition. In different circumstances, Musharraf could have gone further to change Pakistan's direction and become a better approximation to Turkey's Ataturk. But his other, more important, responsibility was that of chief of the Pakistan Army. Therefore, he remained committed to pursuing its institutional agenda – one that cannot include peace with India in the foreseeable future – and so could take no decisive action against the jihadists who drew their strength by claiming to be Kashmir's liberators.

Experiment IV – Hybrid Regime

Imran Khan assumed office of the prime minister of Pakistan on 18 August 2018. Finally he had the prize for which he had campaigned with inexhaustible, messianic zeal. Repeating earlier promises, in his inaugural speech Khan promised a new Riyasat-e-Medina (state of Medina as headed by the Holy Prophet). It would be a concrete realization of Allama Iqbal's dream and a replication of Islam's perfect past, free from injustice and exploitation.

Khan first burst upon Pakistan's political scene in 2011 with his mammoth Lahore *jalsa* at the Minar-e-Pakistan. Cavorting on the stage under floodlights, he loudly prayed towards Makkah for success. The reformed and cleansed Khan, with his lavish lifestyle and raunchy past neatly tucked away somewhere, promised to steer the country out of its myriad problems ranging from economic mismanagement to corruption, terrorism, and a darkened international image. Allama Iqbal's vision for Pakistan and the tireless *shaheen* was the way forward, he said.

The entrance of Khan, and the engineered removal of Nawaz Sharif, is not without irony. Sharif too had been eased into politics by the army and was known to have been General Zia-ul-Haq's protégé with whose help he had begun his political career. After Zia's mysterious air crash, he returned to the political arena as a right-wing leader. In the second of his three terms in office, and just before the post-Kargil coup of 12 October 1999, he had been poised to introduce sharia

410 The Paths Travelled Post-1971

as the law in Pakistan. But strangely enough, a decade of exile in Saudi Arabia changed his outlook substantially. Thus, to the surprise of many, Sharif's third term (2013–2017) turned out to be very different from his first two. He had begun to think in ways that were strange and different from before – sending out peace feelers to India, shutting down support to Pakistan-supported jihadist groups operating in Kashmir, and reaching out to reassure Pakistan's religious minorities. An invitation to Narendra Modi, who arrived for a surprise personal visit to Jatti Umra, was an effort to create a détente with India. This initiative had been taken without the army's permission. For the first time in Pakistan's history, a Punjabi leader with popular support was making decisions independent of the Punjabi military establishment.

For Imran Khan to seize power from Sharif – who was now unpopular with the army – took a long struggle. For one, it had taken a while for the Establishment to fully endorse Imran Khan. His entry into politics and becoming prime minister are separated by twenty-three years. Initially there was skepticism – Khan was charismatic but he had no mass base, no experience in politics, and was prone to intemperate outbursts. On the positive side, his right-wing credentials were impeccable and, unlike Sharif, he clearly understood that he must faithfully follow instructions "from above". Thus, in the years after 9/11, one cannot find a single instance where he condemned any Taliban atrocity on Pakistanis, seeking to shift the blame onto the United States. This included the blowing up of schools and the attempted killing of Malala Yusafzai. On 22 September 2013, a twin suicide bombing was carried out by the *Tehrik-e-Taliban Pakistan* (TTP) at the All Saints Church in Peshawar leaving 127 worshippers dead and over 250 injured. It was the deadliest attack on the Christian minority in the history of Pakistan. Imran Khan briefly visited the Church, but his remarks were less than sensitive and seemed to obliquely justify the attack. Subsequently, columnist Saroop Ijaz wrote:

> Hearing [Imran] talk after the Church attack, it is clear that Mr Khan is no "apologist". An apologist makes excuses, often in an oblique manner for the acts of another, after the commission of the act. Mr. Khan does no such thing. He is crystal clear in his absolute defense of the terrorists. And more importantly, he pre-approves of all future murderers. Mr. Khan is no "apologist", he is an "advocate", an "ally". Whether he does it out of fear or a single digit IQ no longer matters, he is for murder in the name of faith. His vision of 'Naya Pakistan' has the PTI as a political wing of the non-corrupt Tehreek-e-Taliban Pakistan (TTP).[36]

Khan harshly condemned the killing of Osama bin Laden in 2011 and thereafter declared him a martyr,[37] a statement that he repeated ten years later.[38] After an American drone killed the organization's supremo Hakimullah Mehsud in 2013, he appeared on television, livid in anger and made it clear that he would rather shoot at drones than terrorists and led massive "peace" marches against the killers from the sky.[39] Even as the Taliban spokesmen claimed certain terrorist acts

The Paths Travelled Post-1971   **411**

as their work, Khan would seek to shift the blame on the U.S. This consistent and tenacious defense of Taliban terrorism led to Khan being nominated by the TTP in 2014 as their representative to peace talks with the government.[40] He repaid the favor by demanding from the Nawaz Sharif government that TTP be allowed to open offices in Pakistan's cities and function as a normal political party. This cozy relationship ended when the TTP went a bit too far. On 16 December 2014, in retaliation to the army operation *Zarb-e-Azb*, the TTP carried out a gut-wrenching massacre at the Army Public School in Peshawar leaving 138 students and teachers dead.

Remarkably, even before the Army began to own him, Khan was managing to extend his support base well beyond the Taliban and their supporters. It now encompassed overseas Pakistanis, college-educated youth, and brigades of bejeweled begums. To all he promised the moon: ending corruption in ninety days, bringing back $100 billions of looted money from overseas, ending loans taken from the IMF, and more. Personal charisma was at work: worshipful followers love aggressive leaders who proclaim to be self-made, and Khan certainly fitted the bill. As Zulfikar Ali Bhutto had shown fifty years earlier, exceptionally vain and self-absorbed men, who see themselves as deserving attention and power, are often the winners in political contests. Explaining this phenomenon is a challenge for those who study group psychology.

The decisive step which installed Imran Khan in power was the siege of Islamabad, the so-called Great Dharna. Lasting one hundred twenty-six days, the siege disrupted business and government, the state visit of China's president was postponed, and normal life was suspended in parts of the city. Khan, together with the Canada-based cleric Tahir-ul-Qadri, claimed that the national elections held fifteen months ago were rigged and must be redone. The Khan–Qadri duo brought a new level of instability to Pakistan. From atop his *dharna* container, he hurled abuse upon the government of Nawaz Sharif and his political opponents, promising to put his political opponents in jail (most promises were ultimately not kept although this one was).

A sensationalist media – possibly instructed by a "higher power" than the government – gave 24/7 coverage for months on end, creating national trauma. Hapless citizens, glued to their television sets, watched Pakistan's heavily fortified capital fall to protesters. Privately hired cranes tossed aside concrete barriers and shipping containers, while razor wire was cut through by professionals. A demoralized police was initially too afraid to follow attack orders. The siege ended a day after the TTP massacre of schoolchildren by the TTP (referenced above).

From the shadows, the Pakistan Army watched the violent takeover of Pakistan's state institutions with uncharacteristic calm. But rather than restore law-and-order, it chose to confer legitimacy on the insurgents by advocating negotiations. The brief takeover of Pakistan Television by agitators did not result in any subsequent punitive action; the occupiers left shouting "Pak Fauj Zindabad". Even as Khan paralyzed life in Islamabad, the army resolutely refused

412 The Paths Travelled Post-1971

the civil administration's request for supporting law and order. In a major faux pas, the head of the Rangers, Major-General Azhar Naveed, allowed himself to be recorded on video while handing out 1000 rupee notes to the rioters blocking the Faizabad entrance road to Islamabad. He was heard saying that the agitators were fully in the right.[41] Qazi Faez Isa, a senior Supreme Court judge who noted this fact, had to face a long and debilitating series of corruption accusations initiated against him as revenge.

By now the game plan was clear enough: create enough chaos so that the elected government can be forcibly overthrown. But chaos itself may not have sufficed. Help came from an unexpected quarter. The Panama Leaks – beginning April 2016 – turned out to be an unexpected gift to Imran Khan. Nawaz Sharif was confronted with allegations of corruption and possessing eight offshore companies. Petitioned by Imran Khan, the Supreme Court gave a 3–2 split decision on 20 April 2017, concluding there was insufficient evidence to order Sharif's removal from office. However, it ordered further investigation into corruption allegations. On 27 July 2017 the Court unanimously decided that the sitting prime minister, Nawaz Sharif, was disqualified from holding public office, forcing him to resign. His brother Shahbaz Sharif, chief minister of Punjab, would now be the Pakistan Muslim League–Nawaz (PMLN)'s candidate in the July 2018 elections.

The banning of third-term Nawaz Sharif turned out to be the first step towards a systematic dismantling of Sharif's party, the PMLN. The government saw mysterious desertions from its ranks, a coup in the Balochistan assembly, and the sudden appearance of "Jeep" (indicating army sponsorship) candidates across the country. There was a whispering campaign that PMLN election candidates would run afoul of the "khalai makhlooq" (hidden powers from outer space), a euphemism for the Inter-Services Intelligence. With the electronic media controlled by the army, Nawaz and his party did not stand a chance in a "landslide victory" for Imran Khan and his Pakistan Tehreek-e-Insaf (PTI) party. After winning, Khan lost no opportunity to declare that PTI and the army are "on the same page".

That Nawaz Sharif, once a scion of the Punjabi Establishment, should have broken with it so dramatically shocked his party members. That he identified generals Qamar Bajwa and Faiz Hameed as having worked to remove him, and as direct beneficiaries of corruption, was unprecedented. The sacred cow has finally been named, its hitherto unnamed persons brought into public view. But this is not without irony. Those who had dipped their fingers into the public till – and had quietly watched others do it as well – were hailed as heroes for standing up to the Establishment. Even so, public trust in political parties is low – they say the right things only when their own interests are in danger.

Under the so-called hybrid system of governance before the installation of Imran Khan, the army chief and his corps commanders continued to decide upon defense, nuclear weapons, and Pakistan's foreign policy. However, immediately after Khan took charge, the army expanded its role further to encompass

The Paths Travelled Post-1971 **413**

every area of importance. To assure that these changes would happen as directed, the Army chief, General Qamar Javed Bajwa, demanded – and was granted – a three- year extension after his retirement date had passed. He formally became part of economic decision making as well.[42] Delegations of businessmen with gripes about taxes and duties thereafter directly interacted with him.[43]

Owen Bennett-Jones, a frequent commentator on Pakistani politics, noted that of all other Pakistani civilian leaders, Imran Khan had the easiest deal. With him being on the "same page" as the army, he has never had reason to fear that his government was about to be overthrown.

> The fact that he has not had these concerns means he should have been able to devote himself to delivering his many ambitious policy objectives. And there is another factor to consider. The best-resourced and best-run organisation in the country, the army, has been willing to support the Khan government with technical expertise in a way that it may have been reluctant to do for the other civilian governments.[44]

Bennett-Jones comments on Khan's relationship with Washington as more or less the same as that of many other Pakistanis who often liken Washington's relationship with Islamabad to that of a virile man and his vulnerable mistress. Often with a sense of shame, they admit to being passionately wooed and courted but at other times – such as presently – being cruelly spurned and ignored:

> Prime Minister Imran Khan is a living embodiment of all these contradictions. Virtually every speech he makes now contains some bitter criticism of the West and its various hypocrisies. And it is likely he will forever be identified with his declaration that the Afghan Taliban – whose personal values are so utterly removed from his own – should be seen as liberation fighters who have broken the shackles of slavery. And yet Imran Khan has been the most famous man in Pakistan for most of his life because of his very Western pursuits of an Oxford education, a playboy lifestyle and his brilliant performances as a great player in the most English of games, cricket.[45]

Notwithstanding the fullest support that the army has given to any civilian government, there is no evidence that Khan's dispensation was superior in terms of better governance, lesser corruption, increased ability to collect taxes, decreased dependence upon external aid, or improvements in health and education.

Hussain Haqqani, former Pakistani ambassador to the United States, noted that, "The politicians who pushed for greater control over policy-making in the last decade now seem to have accepted that they cannot have that control".[46] Najam Sethi, known for his sharp commentaries and a deep understanding of Pakistani politics, saw Nawaz Sharif's removal as coming from the Establishment's inability to digest threats to its power: peace with India, passage

414 The Paths Travelled Post-1971

of the 18th Constitutional Amendment which devolves some important powers to the provinces, and a vibrant media.

> We – people and institutions – are all drinking from a poisoned chalice. Imran Khan is guzzling from the poisoned chalice of a rigged election. The people are choking on the poisoned chalice of the IMF. The opposition parties and leaders are swallowing from the poisoned chalice of their corruptions and commissions. The Establishment is gulping from the poisoned chalice of its regional adventures and internal interventions.[47]

Three years into Khan's regime, things had not worked out well. Among others, Ahmed Faruqui, a U.S.-based Pakistani political analyst noted that Khan has done everything which he said he would never do.[48] He had borrowed heavily from the Gulf Arab states and the dreaded IMF, bonded with dictators and tyrants around the world, and his political associates, including the finance minister were named in the Pandora Papers. One recalls that the Supreme Court had dismissed Khan's predecessor because he was named in the Panama Papers. The dreams of a robust, thriving economy that Khan had peddled to the electorate turned out to be illusions. When the Pakistani rupee became one of the worst performing currencies in the world and inflation rates soared to squeeze millions into poverty, Khan went on record to say that he didn't enter politics to "keep a lid on the prices of potatoes and tomatoes".[49]

Economic indicators told a story of woe:

> What is the reality? Based on the Trading Economics website, virtually all economic indicators are trending in the wrong direction. External debt stands at $122 billion, up by 20% from the time Imran assumed office. The deficit in the balance of trade is Rs. 691 billion, up by 70%. The consumer price index has risen by 50%. The Rupee, at 0.6 cents to a dollar, has lost a third of its value. GDP per capita, a widely used measure of economic well-being, has stagnated. At $1168, it is just 9% of the world average.[50]

Khan had few foreign policy successes to show: the world (including China) has paid scant attention to his demand for implementing plebiscite in Kashmir. Although Pakistan tried hard to get the world's attention after Modi's formal annexation of Indian-held Kashmir in August 2019, nothing worked. The UN Security Council declined Pakistan's request for a formal meeting and Pakistan's Arab allies seemed unperturbed. Khan's calls for ending Islamophobia have not been accompanied by any letup in the persecution of Pakistan's non-Muslim minorities, and his statements such as the Taliban had "broken the shackles of slavery" showed that, in calling for resuming U.S. aid to Afghanistan, he had more than humanitarian reasons in mind.

At the end of his third year, as skepticism about Khan kept increasing, he pushed back with greater energy by mashing together religion and politics. At

The Paths Travelled Post-1971   **415**

a preparatory meeting ahead of the Prophet's birthday, Khan announced creation of the Rehmatul-lil-Alameen Authority (RAA) and appointed himself its patron-in-chief. The RAA would monitor school curricula, check social media content, ferret out blasphemers, and organize research in universities for spreading the true message of Islam. But the endgame was now being played out: the Army turned neutral and made it clear that it would no longer be his protector. This prompted a furious Khan to famously declare that, "Humans either side with good or evil. Only animals remain neutral".[51] Later, his supporters were booked for spreading cartoons depicting General Bajwa as half-human, half-animal. The National Assembly, now dominated by the former opposition, condemned Khan for hinting that the army had betrayed the country through his allusions to "the Mir Jafars and Mir Sadiqs of today".[52] Mir Jafar had been the commander-in-chief of Siraj-ud-Daula, the governor of Bengal, who joined hands with the British to fight the governor and seize his throne. There was little doubt about who Khan was pointing toward! Nevertheless, Establishment insiders say that Khan enjoys considerable support in the ranks of officers and soldiers.

Why did the Imran Khan's sponsors eventually dump him? Why did this particular political engineering project run aground? There was no ideological rift at the level of policy. Instead, there appear to be three reasons why the relationship soured. First, Khan sought to perpetuate his rule by appointing an ISI director general, Faiz Hameed, who he would elevate to the status of army chief upon the retirement of General Bajwa. This created a mud fight within an otherwise highly disciplined institution, the very thing that it fears most. The rifts created by Khan's insistence were papered down in official statements, but the damage had been done. Second, Khan's capacity for governance turned out to be much below expectations. Influenced by his séance and wife, he appointed as the governor of all-important Punjab a hitherto unknown man of little capability. Khan's relations with the political opposition were deeply hostile because he sought to prosecute rivals through corruption cases while overlooking corruption in his own party members, and his frequent changes of key officials disoriented the system while turning off allies. To their embarrassment, Khan's sponsors were now being blamed by the public for the rapid downslide of the economy and the crashing rupee. Third, Khan's open hostility to the United States was seen as dangerous by the military. Voices within the Establishment understood that burning bridges with a superpower while placing all eggs in the Chinese basket was poor strategy. Nevertheless, Khan's cult followers happily nodded their heads when he alleged that the U.S. was responsible for his removal from power.

The bottom line: Imran Khan's promises to create a Riyasat-e-Medina were for the naïve only. As skeptics had predicted long before it actually happened, the sheen soon wore off in a matter of months – well before the onset of COVID-19 and the global slowdown of economies. The promised Naya Pakistan was simply old wine in a new bottle – military rule with a civilian face with a consolidation of army control over hitherto purely civilian areas. Just how disastrous the

416   The Paths Travelled Post-1971

fourth experiment will turn out is uncertain at the time of writing. What is fairly certain, however, is that Pakistan is in for a long period of instability. Khan played deftly to a public brought up on Islam and anti-Americanism. Now a cult figure, he has divided even the Establishment. There is no other such precedent in Pakistan's history.

Why the Experiments Failed

Four experiments sought to repurpose and redirect Pakistan after the 1971 cataclysm, but none succeeded. Each started from the wrong premise, misunderstood the country, and sacrificed long-term interests to expediency. Each experiment left the country divided and polarized and fell far short of hammering the country into a nation. The last one is so far the most polarizing one in Pakistan's history. There is widespread fear that Khan will bring the country to a stop if he is not reelected and perhaps ignite a civil war between his followers and the rest.

People across the world hunger for political leaders who can do miracles, but Pakistanis are hungrier than most. Although the country's founders gave it the Two Nation Theory, they provided no roadmaps or further directions. After rough weather and stormy seas battered the country for three-quarters of a century, a nation adrift saw two miracle men arise. Separated by fifty years, and endowed with magical personalities, Zulfikar Ali Bhutto and Imran Khan set the public imagination on fire by challenging the established order. Bhutto's rule proved disastrous to the country and to him personally. We have yet to see the end of the Imran Khan story.

Unlike Bangladesh which was comfortable with a mixed identity of culture and religion, a Pakistan cut in half insisted with ever-increasing vigor that it had to find meaning by either fighting India or becoming an ideological Islamic state or perhaps both. For this it sought to flog a dead horse – the Two Nation Theory – in the hope that it would miraculously come to life and bring about national cohesion. That did not happen and cannot happen. Emphasizing religious exclusion can further marginalize Ahmadis, Christians, Hindus, and Shias but cannot lead to anything much beyond that.

There is a road not taken, the subject of the next and final chapter. In fact the prescription offered is the straightest and most obvious one for creating a viable nation. This simply requires acknowledging that Pakistan become a normal country with its diverse peoples held together only by their mutual needs and interdependence. A normal country is not possessed by an ideological mission; it exists for the bulk of its people and not some minority. A normal country has a military; it is abnormal for a military to own and run a country.

Examples of near-normal nations are plentiful: Norway, Denmark, Switzerland, the Netherlands, Canada, United Kingdom, Germany, Costa Rica, Ireland, Indonesia, Morocco, Australia, New Zealand, Japan, etc. I say "near-normal" because one can find deviations from normalcy: 16 European countries have declared Holocaust denial as illegal, Canada does not permit organizations

The Paths Travelled Post-1971 **417**

calling for a boycott of Israel, etc. However, within these countries such foreign policy alignments can (and have) been challenged in court by their citizens. Much more importantly, their stability does not owe to powerful militaries or the pursuit of some religious or ideological agenda; instead, it comes as natural consequence of a national goal to seek prosperity and general well-being. A citizen of these countries would be dumbfound by the question: what is your country's ideology? Their goal is down-to-earth, not lofty: a higher quality of life for citizens. Unsurprisingly, such countries count among the world's happiest, most prosperous, and stable countries.

Just a little bit of thinking and some plain common sense can tell us what needs to be done to successfully repurpose Pakistan and steer it towards peace and prosperity. We now turn to this.

Notes

1 S. Ahmad, Zulfikar Ali Bhutto: the psychodynamics of his rise and fall, Paramount Books, (2018).
2 Altaf Gauhar who was Secretary of the Ministry for Information and Broadcasting (1963–1969) was close to Ayub Khan and has chronicled Bhutto's role in detail in *Ayub Khan – Pakistan's First Military Ruler*, Sang-e-Meel Publications (1993).
3 A.H. Syed, *The Discourse and Politics of Zulfikar Ali Bhutto*, London, Macmillan Press (1992), p. 12.
4 S. Taseer, *Bhutto: A Political Biography*, New Delhi, Vikas Books (1980), p. 143.
5 Z.A. Bhutto, *Myth of Independence*, Karachi, Oxford University Press (1969), p. 54.
6 Patrice Lumumba speech, https://en.wikipedia.org/wiki/Congolese_Independence _Speech#The_speech
7 T. Mantan, *Africa in the Colonial Ages of Empire: Slavery, Capitalism, Racism, Colonialism, Decolonization, Independence as Recolonization*, Bamenda, Langaa RPCIG (2018), p. 13. doi:10.2307/j.ctvh9vtjn.
8 A. Malik, *Radical Demands of the 1960s and Lessons for Our Present*, Pakistan Left Review, 14 May 2020.
9 I.A. Rahman quoted in "I am the destiny", Eqbal Ahmad, *London Review of Books*, 20, no 12, (18 June 1998).
10 The Legend – C.M. Latif: Origin, Growth and Destruction of a Great Emerging Industrial Complex, (The Story of BECO), Manzar Latif, (2009), private distribution.
11 An exception was my friend and shipping magnate, the late Ardeshir Cowasjee, who never forgave Bhutto for nationalizing shipping and destroying him financially. Cowasjee was one of the few Parsis I know who fully believed in Jinnah, a point that we always discussed with great vigor.
12 K.A. Ali, The Strength of the Street Meets the Strength of the State: The 1972 Labor Struggle in Karachi, *International Journal of Middle East Studies*, 37, no. 1 (2005): 83–107. http://www.jstor.org/stable/3880083
13 P. Oldenburg, *The Break-Up of Pakistan* (1974), republished in *Pakistaniaat: A Journal of Pakistan Studies*, 2, no. 3 (2010): pp. 1–23.
14 S. Weisman and H. Krosney, *The Islamic Bomb*, Times Books (1981).
15 C. Jaffrelot, *The Pakistan Paradox – Instability and Resilience*, Oxford University Press (USA), Translated by Cynthia Schoch (2015).
16 E. Ahmad, Pakistan—Signposts to a Police State, *Journal of Contemporary Asia*, 4, no. 4 (1974): 423–438. DOI: 10.1080/00472337485390601.
17 Akbar S. Ahmed, *When News Of Bhutto's Death Almost Killed Me In Waziristan*,The Friday Times, 24 November 2022

418 The Paths Travelled Post-1971

18 Zulfikar Ali Bhutto, *If I Am Assassinated*, 1979, p21. http://www.bhutto.org/Acrobat/If-I-am-assassinated-by-Shaheed-Bhutto.pdf
19 P. Hoodbhoy, *Myth Building – the Islamic Bomb*, The Bulletin of the Atomic Scientists, 1993.
20 F.J. Prial, *Pakistan Reaction to Hijacking Shows Zia's Strength*, The New York Times, 8 April 1981. https://www.nytimes.com/1981/04/08/world/pakistan-reaction-to-hijacking-shows-zia-s-strength.html
21 P. Hoodbhoy, The Genesis of Global Jihad in Afghanistan, *Peace Research*, 37, no. 1 (2005): 15–30.
22 The Offence of Zina (Enforcement of Hudood) Ordinance, 1979. Ordinance No. VII of 1979, February 9th, 1979.
23 C.H. Kennedy, Islamic Legal Reform and the Status of Women in Pakistan, *Journal of Islamic Studies*, 2, no. 1 (1991): 45–55.
24 Z. Hussain, *The Last Coup – Musharraf's Agenda: What Did He Achieve?*, Dawn, 13 October 2019. https://www.dawn.com/news/1510606
25 N. Zehra, *From Kargil to the Coup: Events That shook Pakistan*, first edition, Sang-e-Meel Publications (May 17, 2018).
26 B. Riedel, *American Diplomacy and the 1999 Kargil Summit at Blair House*, publication of the Center for the Advanced Study of India, University of Pennsylvania (2002).
27 P. Musharraf, *In the Line of Fire: A Memoir*, Free Press (2008).
28 P. Aroon, *Where, Oh Where, Have Musharraf's Little Dogs Gone?*, Foreign Policy, 20 December 2007. https://foreignpolicy.com/2007/12/20/where-oh-where-have-musharrafs-little-dogs-gone/
29 *A Conversation with Pervez Musharraf*, 25 September 2006, https://www.cfr.org/event/conversation-pervez-musharraf
30 *Musharraf's Rape Remarks Condemned*, Dawn, 17 September 2005. https://www.dawn.com/news/156984/musharraf-s-remarks-condemned-rape-victims
31 *General Pervez Musharraf*, Dawn, 17 May 2000.
32 M. Shehzad, *MMA Bans Ultrasound, ECG Scanning of Women by Male Technicians*, 21 September 2003, The Friday Times, Lahore.
33 When I mentioned this to President Musharraf at a formal meeting held in his office in 2005 at the behest of the Pugwash Council, he was furious at my bringing it up and ordered a halt on my promotion to the next level of professorship at Quaid-e-Azam University. As ex-officio chancellor of QAU, he approved 11 of 12 names sent to him leaving out just one – mine.
34 S. Shams, *Bugti's Killing – Has Islamabad Learnt Anything?*, DW, 26 August 2016. https://www.dw.com/en/traitors-and-villains-has-islamabad-learnt-anything-from-bugtis-killing/a-19505075
35 The video documentary *Among the Believers* by Hemal Trivedi and Mohammed Ali Naqvi is largely based on interviews of Maulana Abdul Aziz in the aftermath of the Lal Masjid operation and chronicles the events leading up to and beyond the military operation.
36 S. Ijaz, *From Apologist to Ally*, The Express Tribune, 23 September 2013. https://tribune.com.pk/story/608148/from-apologist-to-ally
37 Osama bin Laden is a Martyr, Pakistan Today, 16 May 2011.
38 N. Gurmani, *Opposition Lambastes PM Imran for sAying Osama bin Laden Was Martyred*, Dawn, 25 June 2020. https://www.dawn.com/news/1565160
39 *Pakistan Taliban Name Imran Khan for Talks*, BBC News, 2 February 2014. https://www.bbc.com/news/world-asia-26008815
40 Z.S. Sherazi, *Taliban Nominate Imran, Sami among Others to Mediate Peace Talks*, Dawn, 1 February 2014. https://www.dawn.com/news/1084259
41 *Why Was Pakistan General Giving Money to Protesters?*, BBC News, 29 November 2017. https://www.bbc.com/news/world-asia-42149535
42 *PM, Army Chief Part of Body Formed for Economic Revival*, The Express Tribune, 18 June 2019. https://tribune.com.pk/story/1995131/coas-part-national-development-council

43 *Business Tycoons Call on Gen Bajwa as Economy Nosedives*, Pakistan Today, 3 October 2019.
44 O. Bennett-Jones, *Power Games*, Dawn, 6 April 2021. https://www.dawn.com/news/1616677/power-games
45 O. Bennett-Jones, *No Clear Direction*, Dawn, 2 November 2021. https://www.dawn.com/news/1655453/no-clear-direction
46 H. Haqqani, *All That Remains for Pakistan Now Is to Hope Gen Bajwa Doesn't Turn Out to Be Gen Ayub Khan*, Hudson.org, 11 January 2020. https://www.hudson.org/foreign-policy/all-that-remains-for-pakistan-now-is-to-hope-gen-bajwa-doesn-t-turn-out-to-be-gen-ayub-khan
47 N. Sethi, *Poisoned Chalices*, The Friday Times, 25 October 2019. https://www.thefridaytimes.com/2019/10/25/poisoned-chalice/
48 A. Faruqui, *Three Years on, PM Imran Khan Has Yet to Deliver on His Promises*, The Friday Times, 16 October 2021. https://www.thefridaytimes.com/2021/10/16/three-years-on-pm-imran-khan-has-yet-to-deliver-on-his-promises/
49 *Didn't Enter Politics to Keep a Lid on Potato Prices: PM*, The Express Tribune, 13 March, 2022. https://tribune.com.pk/story/2347766/didnt-enter-politics-to-keep-a-lid-on-potato-prices-pm
50 Faruqui, op. cit.
51 H. Asad, *Profanity-Laden Outburst by PM Imran Adds to Quagmire*, Dawn, 12 March 2022. https://www.dawn.com/news/1679538
52 A. Wasim, *NA Condemns Imran for 'Maligning' Armed Forces*, Dawn, 10 May 2022. https://www.dawn.com/news/1688917

Sixteen

REPLACING THE TWO NATION THEORY

> There is one thing stronger than all the armies in the world, and that is an idea whose time has come.
>
> – Victor Hugo[1]

The Two Nation Theory gave birth to Pakistan in 1947. Now, three-quarters of a century later, it is time to abandon it in favor of a Single Nation Theory. The movement for Pakistan was built upon exclusion and the assertion that just one group of inhabitants is the rightful possessor of certain territories. Carried further, that movement provided justification for an economy of perpetual war and infusions of hyper-religiosity into Pakistan's body politic. This made it difficult to build a single nation where people could be joined together by common bonds in a caring relationship. And so, after the four unsuccessful experiments detailed in the previous chapter, Pakistan now needs to chart a path toward viable nationhood and, in the process, surrender some old assumptions. This final chapter contends that Pakistan needs new priorities, a new vision, and a new definition. In fact the very idea of Pakistan must be rethought if the country is to ever become viable as a state. What could be a reasonable manifesto for change towards a better Pakistan? An outline, open to modification and discussion, is sketched here.

Pakistan is heading for a shipwreck averting which will require a change of course as well as good luck. The army's experiment in bringing Imran Khan to power went awry with consequences that will stretch into the far future. The damage this has done to the morale of the warrior class is more than India could have inflicted through subversion or war. For the first time ever, the consensus within Punjab's establishment has broken down. Many in the ranks of colonel and lower are with Khan while senior officers supported the army chief General Qamar Javed Bajwa all through until his retirement in November 2022.

DOI: 10.4324/9781003379140-22

Senior members of Khan's political party have been imprisoned for stirring mutinous sentiments within the army.[2] For Bajwa, retirement was a mea culpa moment: while criticizing political parties for being intolerant towards rivals, he admitted days before relinquishing power that for seven decades the army had "unconstitutionally interfered in politics".[3] But this will not be enough.

Each successive government has routinely blamed its predecessor for all that's gone wrong. Whichever party wins the next elections – whenever it is held – will be equally powerless to reverse the downslide but will surely continue this childish charade. In so passing the buck, Pakistan seeks to avoid recognizing that it is the sick man of South Asia. This denial means it will resist seeking the right medicines. Today Pakistan lags behind Bangladesh and India in every indicator of consequence: economy, political stability, and human development. Surely it is time to reflect why this happened and chart out a new course.

Pakistan, like Israel, was formed through a historical process that emphasized religious identity. One can forever debate whether the modern world should have states that segregate citizens according to accidents of birth such as religion, race, ethnicity, or language. These obviously privilege one section of the population over another and hence violate fundamental principles of equality of their citizens. But it is pointless to debate now whether Pakistan or Israel deserve to exist. In fact no country that has been around for long enough needs such a justification. If we were to go back far enough into history looking for rights and wrongs as the raison d'être for creating a new country, we would find that not even a single one properly deserves to be born. All were formed through processes involving violence, conquest, and injustice inflicted upon some subdominant group. Pakistan, now seventy-five years old at the time of writing, has nearly a quarter billion of its citizens living – mostly voluntarily – within the geographical confines of a country recognized by the United Nations. It has its own police, army, and systems for education, tax collection, building roads, supplying electricity, coping with natural disasters, etc. While it is manifestly unfair to millions of its own citizens, it is not the only country on Earth that violates fundamental rights.

But unlike Israel – which made the Jewish diaspora formidably strong and able to dominate the Middle East – the creation of Pakistan brought, at best, only mixed benefits to the subcontinent's Muslims. Non-Muslims, of course, did not stand a chance and most have left or desperately seek to leave the country. But even among Muslim citizens of Pakistan there are profound inequalities of wealth and opportunity with large-scale unemployment, absence of effective democracy, the legal system barely functions, health care is inadequate, a substantial fraction of children are malnourished and stunted, education quality ranks among the lowest in the world, and citizens feel insecure. In 2020, Pakistan was ranked 154th among 189 countries on the United Nations Human Development Index (HDI). Elite privilege accorded to Pakistan's elite groups – the corporate sector, feudal landlords, the political class, and the military – consumes $17.4 billion of Pakistan's economy.[4] Kanni Wignaraja, assistant secretary-general and regional chief of the UNDP, held meetings in April 2021 with the government

422 Replacing the Two Nation Theory

and informed the prime minister and his cabinet of stark income disparities and the report's finding:

> Powerful groups use their privilege to capture more than their fair share, people perpetuate structural discrimination through prejudice against others based on social characteristics, and policies are often unsuccessful at addressing the resulting inequity, or may even contribute to it.[5]

None of this is likely to be even slightly surprising to those she spoke to, nor can one expect any meaningful action from them. In fact the political ruling class is heavily invested in the corporate sector, both private and military owned. It is a direct beneficiary of extraordinary privileges in the form of tax breaks including agricultural tax, cheap input prices, higher output prices, or preferential access to capital, land, and services. Pakistan's military and political leaders are certainly aware of these inequities. In fact, with very few exceptions, they have had their fingers in the public till.

This is nothing new; corruption was endemic to the system from the very beginning. After 1948 all governments have been unstable, out for quick bonanzas, and military dominated. Whether the Army rules upfront or from behind the scenes, it remains insulated from the people as it pursues its own institutional interests and agendas while operating massive business and commercial interests. Most Pakistanis do not view the state as a moral actor, and hence disrespect its laws when they can. On the international stage, from the 1950s onward, Pakistan chose to become a client state of the United States and served its Cold War needs. In the process, the state stifled trade unions, reneged on promises of land redistribution, and imposed its tyranny on the press. Under General Ayub Khan and then General Yahya Khan, East Pakistan felt colonized by Punjab and sought total divorce. Sindhis and the Baloch turned rebellious after the first two decades and had to be put down periodically. Tribal Waziristan, where the Pakistani deep state had helped the Taliban to establish their base after 9/11, was alienated once the Taliban turned against their deep-state Army sponsors. Today there are thousands of "disappeared" persons among the Baloch and Pakhtuns, abducted by security forces. Their families do not know if they are dead or alive.

Some therefore call Pakistan a failed state. This, however, means little. Unlike in school examinations, no universal examination board is authorized to decide upon which countries can be deemed to have passed or failed. Therefore, it is to the future that one must look. This has to begin from the premise that the Partition of India can never be undone and Pakistan will never be part of India again. Apart from a tiny minority of "Akhand Bharat" Hindutva extremists, few would disagree.

The earlier chapters of this book established beyond reasonable doubt that neither Jinnah nor anybody else in the movement for Pakistan had a post-Partition game plan, and the subsequent lack of direction has confirmed this over and over again. The Two Nation Theory has finally been wrung dry, its emptiness fully revealed. Although the ideology behind it clearly failed with the catastrophic events of 1971, the Pakistani establishment has so far resolutely refused to reevaluate or revise it, or to derive any lesson from this tragic period of Pakistan's history. Instead it withholds facts, feeds misinformation through doctored history books in schools, and continues to harp upon the need for more weaponry to fight India.

It is therefore time for adopting a Single Nation Theory – one that has a logical basis and that officially espouses equality before the law for all citizens of Pakistan. Much can flow from this simple principle. It does not mean the end of Pakistan, just a new beginning. Although religion will necessarily be an integral part of the country's existence, the need is for developing new roots that lie within the country's social reality. Nation-building is the need of the time, and building a nation lies well within the realm of possibilities. In fact Pakistan will almost certainly become a nation with a definable national culture if it manages to stay around for long enough.

Look at it this way: rain inevitably grinds down stony mountains over centuries and ultimately creates fertile soil. Similarly, nations are inevitably formed when people experience a common environment and live together for long enough. How long is long enough? In Pakistan's case, the time scale could be fairly short and technology is helping. Its people are diverse, but almost all understand Urdu. They watch the same television programs, hear the same radio stations, deal with the same irritating and inefficient bureaucracy, use the same badly written textbooks, buy similar products, and despise the same set of rulers. Slowly but surely a composite, but genuine, Pakistani culture is emerging. The real question comes back to whether it can exist long enough for enough to emerge and crystallize. Both the Soviet Union and Yugoslavia broke apart after seven decades. If Pakistan is to stay together and chart a path to viable nationhood, it must identify its most pressing problems and seek their amelioration.

Change – howsoever it comes – will eventually come simply because that lies in the nature of things. But what should be its direction? Like a diabetic patient fixated in his belief that cure lies in a diet of honey and sugar, the religiously orthodox see only one way ahead – that of inserting Islam still more vigorously into society and politics. And, although few in numbers, orthodox Marxists in Pakistan have yet to abandon their traditional belief in some imagined working class revolution ushering in a classless society which would be the result of the inevitable victory of labor over capital. Both are dead ends. As one looks around, one sees that the active agents of change in Pakistani society are those who clamor for the rights of religious minorities, economic justice for the lower sections of society, democracy and genuine civilian control, the right of provinces to their fair share of resources, the rights of women and children, education reform, and environmental causes. These are the very issues of concern to enlightened sections of the Left worldwide.

Pakistan needs a manifesto of change. It is not difficult to create one. For example, the late senior journalist Ziauddin penned his program of change for the economy.[6] My wish list is below and probably shares common points with the dozens of manifestos that many others may have invented.

End Legalized Discrimination

Pakistan legally discriminates between its citizens who belong to different religious faiths; this is written into the Pakistan Constitution which defines non-Muslims as minorities and endows them with lesser rights. This is at variance with civilized countries where, at least legally and formally, the life and property of all citizens are valued equally. In such countries, access to jobs is determined by aptitude and track record rather than an individual's religious affiliation. This is not true in Pakistan.

What constitutes a religious minority in Pakistan? In earlier years, these were Hindus, Christians, and Parsis. Ahmadis followed in 1974. But if Pakistan ever becomes a Sunni Islamic state, the Shias will join the list. The very concept of a religious minority written into law is discriminatory and discouraging to those identified as such. The failure to integrate the country's diverse and plural set of peoples has led to minority groups withdrawing from public life. Many have migrated overseas, taking with them precious human and non-human resources. The list of undesirables has expanded much further as religious belief is becoming more central to the Pakistani state. Many mainstream Muslims now fear other mainstream Muslims. Today, if you are known to be Shia or Barelvi, you could be endangered in many parts of the country. Pakistani Muslims now offer Friday prayers under the shadow of vigilant gun-wielding guards.

As Pakistan's problems have become deeper, the call to return to the faith has become louder. Attempts to make Pakistan a *mamlikat-e-khudadad* (theocracy) have lighted fires of religious intolerance. There is evidence of active connivance by the state in secretly promoting dangerous, militant extremists. Movements demanding imposition of sharia were initially welcomed by the public. Considering education outside *madrassa*s to be *haram*, sharia-seeking Taliban have blown up well over a thousand schools for girls and boys in the last two decades. Although many Pakistanis found this distasteful, a survey conducted at that time by WorldPublicOpinion.org discovered that 54% of Pakistanis still wanted strict application of sharia, while 25% wanted it in some more dilute form. Totaling 79%, this was the largest pro-sharia percentage in the four countries then surveyed (Morocco, Egypt, Pakistan, Indonesia).

To become viable, Pakistan must eventually become a secular state that treats all citizens alike irrespective of faith. Religion could remain important but not central. One notes that the founders of modern secularism were religious men who did not think that secularism was a threat to religion. Secularism made its debut in Europe through the 1648 Treaty of Westphalia. Without it, religious wars would have consumed European societies and states. Yet, As George Jacob Holyoake put it in 1648, "Secularism is not an argument against Christianity, it is one independent of it. Secular knowledge is manifestly that kind of knowledge which is founded in this life, which relates to the conduct of this life, conduces to the welfare of this life, and is capable of being tested by the experience of this life".

Replacing the Two Nation Theory **425**

It is false that Muslims can practice their religion only in an Islamic state. One has to only look at Muslims in the West where a majority of visibly practicing Muslims lead lives free of persecution. Of course, some complain of discrimination – as they rightly should. Islamophobia is a fact, just as racism or homophobia is discriminatory. But only a slim minority of migrants in the West is willing to return home and an overwhelming majority believes that they are treated equally before the law. On the other hand, extremist groups like the Taliban, Da'esh, al-Qaida, Boko Haram, Sipah-e-Sahaba, and many others that promise to establish Islamic governance and caliphates have transformed Muslim countries into hell holes from which millions have sought to escape or have already escaped. With 7th-century minds and 21st-century weapons, it is they who pose an existential threat to Muslims.

Secularism is possible in South Asia. It survived in India for some decades and, although injured, is still breathing. Pakistan, too, bordered on being secular in its first few years; it can happen again. Even those who are devoutly religious people can be persuaded that genuine faith flourishes only when individuals are free to choose, without having religion imposed upon them by their government. Surely, the church, mosque, synagogue, and temple all inform humans in some way. But peace and progress lie in giving Reason stewardship in matters of science, technology, economics, commerce, trade, industry, finance, public affairs, warfare, education, research, public discourse and debate, arts, and literature. Laws (personal, family, civil, corporate, criminal, international) and social ethics (including sexuality and morality) must be made by humans for humans. The rightful domain of religion is in personal conduct, beliefs, worship, and conscience.

Spread the Wealth

The statistics on wealth concentration in Pakistan are damning. The gross national income (GNI) is estimated by the World Bank at $314.4 billion in 2018–2019.[7] According to the Pakistan National Human Development Report 2020, of this wealth the poorest 1% held just 0.15%. Overall, the richest 20% of Pakistanis hold 49.6% of the national income, compared with the poorest 20%, who hold just 7%. Pakistan's elite – the top 1% of its population – has 9% of the country's total personal income. In her 2020 book, *Big Capital in an Unequal World: The Micropolitics of Wealth in Pakistan,* Rosita Armytage has meticulously researched how laws and regulatory mechanism are mere formalities when, in fact, this elite works through a "complex network of familial and social structures through which economic and political competition, deals, alliances and agreements were pre-negotiated in living rooms and private social forums".[8] Like other global elites, Pakistan's super-rich have become adept at navigating – and exploiting – laws and regulations to their advantage.

The military establishment, which represents the largest conglomerate of business entities in the country, was found to receive $1.7 billion in privileges

426 Replacing the Two Nation Theory

annually. This was mainly in the form of preferential access to land, capital and infrastructure, as well as tax exemptions. The military is the country's biggest urban real estate developer and manager, with wide-ranging involvement in the construction of public projects. The report said that Pakistan's military enjoyed 257 billion rupees in privileges in 2017–2018. The military's business activities are essentially run through two entities, the Fauji Foundation (FF) and the Army Welfare Trust (AWT), with high net profits and rapid growth. The military's Defence Housing Authorities (DHAs) also enjoy significant privileges in terms of federal sales tax exemptions and the earmarking of property tax, which goes solely to cantonment boards.

The feudal land-owning class, which constitutes 1.1% of the population, in 2017–2018 owns 22% of all arable farmland. According to the quoted UNDP report, Pakistan's feudal class enjoyed privileges totaling 370 billion rupees annually. This must be contrasted with India which had abolished feudalism upon attaining independence. Pakistan did not. The huge pre-Partition land holdings of Pakistan's feudal lords remained safe and sound, protected by the authority of the state. Land reforms announced by Ayub Khan and Zulfikar Ali Bhutto were in name only. In later years, with the consolidation of military rule in national politics, the army turned itself into a landlord and capitalist class. It owns land assets that have no relation to national defense. The cruelties of an old feudal structure of land ownership have been magnified by the steady mechanization of agriculture. Sweeping land reforms are long overdue.

The poverty of urban slums where rag-picking children have only just learned to walk is worse than that in rural areas. Pushed off from ancestral lands, migrants from rural to urban centers live lives of extreme poverty. Critically needed for them are economic justice and the working machinery of a welfare state. But economic justice should not be understood as flinging coins at a beggar. Rather, it requires creating an organizational infrastructure that prevents the capture of natural resources and land by military, civilian, and corporate elites. The fundamental right of local communities to their water and mineral resources must be written into the law.

To create a prosperous welfare state is a universal objective. Such a start provides employment but also rewards appropriately according to ability and hard work. Incomes should be neither exorbitantly high nor miserably low. To be sure, "high" and "low" are not easily quantifiable, but an inner moral sense tells us that something is desperately wrong when rich Pakistanis fly off to vacation in Dubai while a mother commits suicide because she cannot feed her children.

Serving the needs of their citizens without prejudice is the hallmark of social justice. A few modern secular states already have operational systems in place. In Pakistan it is easy to see why certain religious slogans appeal to the popular imagination. In a situation that is deeply unequal and plagued by huge class asymmetry, people yearn for an unblemished past when everything was perfect in a utopic Islamic welfare state. Ambitious political leaders have been quick to

Replacing the Two Nation Theory **427**

recognize this. This is how Imran Khan could sell his *Riyasat-e-Madina* to his followers.

Nearly three centuries earlier, philosopher Jean-Jacques Rousseau observed that each citizen of a state voluntarily places his person under the supreme direction of the "general will". An unwritten compact between the individual and society requires that a citizen accept the rule of law and acknowledge certain basic responsibilities. In return the citizen receives certain rights from the larger entity. Without this voluntary submission by individuals, said Rousseau, humans would be no better than beasts.

This notion of a social contract – a commitment that citizens will be treated fairly and equally and, in turn, they will fulfill certain basic responsibilities – is now being articulated in Pakistan somewhat more often than earlier but much less frequently than it needs to be. Only a small fraction of Pakistanis pays their fair share of income tax. This leads to an abysmally small 10% tax-to-GDP ratio. Few respect basic environmental rules, heed traffic laws, dispose of garbage as they should, or respect their neighbor's rights. Seeing a state that cannot fulfill its basic obligations, most citizens, rich and poor, feel no urgency to fulfill their civic responsibilities. Most Pakistanis are currently denied their basic entitlements as citizens, including the most fundamental rights and even the truncated ones defined in the Constitution. The poor suffer the denial of their rights, while the rich are compelled to buy them. Irresponsible social behavior is rampant. Law-breaking occurs because ordinary people see the nation's leaders openly flouting the very rules they were empowered to protect. Law enforcement is often little more than a token. The problem is compounded by Pakistan's fundamental confusion: is the citizen obligated to obey secular (or common) law or one of the many interpretations of Islamic law, or even the tribal law of *jirgas*? Surely a modern state has to set uniform rules for its citizens or else risk losing its legitimacy.

Pakistan not Punjabistan

Punjab's ruling elite has a tendency to mistake Punjab for Pakistan. This is a consequence of being the most populous and richest of four provinces. Quite naturally this invites resentment elsewhere. Even in logistical terms a giant centralized government machine sitting in Islamabad and mostly managed by Punjabis cannot effectively and fairly manage a large and diverse country. After 2008, all five elected prime ministers and three army chiefs have been Punjabi. What made matters worse was that this governmental apparatus is both inefficient and ethnically partisan, drawing its roots from the powerful landed and feudal class. The army leadership and the economic elite had joined forces after Partition to claim authority, but they were transparently self-serving and therefore lacked legitimacy. Coercion through the largely Punjabi army followed.

Dividing Punjab into two or three provinces has sometimes been discussed. Haneef Ramay, a chief minister of Punjab, who argued for a united Punjab in

428 Replacing the Two Nation Theory

his book *Punjab ka Muqadama*, came around to advocating a division of Punjab both because this would improve administrative efficiency as well as address grievances of smaller provinces against a single large province. However, Seraiki nationalism seeking a Seraiki province made out of Punjab has yet to organize itself politically. A more radical proposal by Haroon Khwaja is to dispense with Punjab's majoritarianism by converting the country's existing 123 districts into new provinces.[9] Social scientist Anjum Altaf has a similar take: instead of having just four second-tier units, Pakistan's existing 38 administrative divisions should be declared as the second tier of government, each with their own legislatures and executives.[10] This would divide the country's problems into manageable pieces and make the divisions comparable with those in Malaysia (13), Iran (25), Brazil (27), India (36), and the Philippines (76). This would deflate calls from separatists and make governance easier. So far, no serious discussion on these proposals has taken place.

A natural resistance against melding into some larger entity is the reflexive response of historically constituted groups that seek to preserve their distinctiveness as expressed in terms of diverse forms of dress, food, folklore, and shared history. This force, like gravity, always acts in one direction and seeks to avoid assimilation into a homogenized national culture. It is not to be unduly applauded because it can lead to a dangerous expression of differences. Ethnonationalism is, of course, vulnerable and can be overcome by integrative forces, which arise from the natural advantage of being part of a larger economy with correspondingly greater opportunities. But for these forces to be effective, it is essential that the state machinery provides effective governance, demonstrates fairness, and shows indifference to ethnic origins. Decentralization is the key.

A partial recognition of the need for provincial autonomy emerged in the form of the 18th Amendment to the Constitution. It was a break from past practices such as Ayub Khan's infamous One Unit. Passed in 2010, it came with the exit of Gen. Musharraf's military regime. This was a compromise between advocates of a federation and those of a strong center. It did not challenge the budget, priorities, policies, and perks of the all-powerful military. Nevertheless, because it emphasized devolution of authority and a strengthened role for the Council on Common Interests in apportioning resources and tax revenues, it was generally acknowledged as a good step forward in limiting presidential powers and empowering parliament. No longer could the president dismiss parliament on vague grounds.

Even this limited concession had been under relentless attack by the military and Imran Khan's government, which acted as its proxy. This is primarily because the center wants a greater share of taxes and revenues, claiming that the provinces lack capacity to deliver in multiple areas. This includes resource extraction, education, and health. The dismal performance of the Pakistan People Party government in Sind in matters of governance provides ammunition to opponents of the 18th Amendment. Whether the Amendment will ultimately survive, be repealed, or rendered toothless is unclear at the moment.

Balochistan presents by far the greatest challenge to the federation. Military force has been used to deal with it rather than political sagacity and persuasion. A sharp break with that is needed. Pakistan's rulers must respect diversity and hand important powers over to the provinces while reconceiving Pakistan as a federation of autonomous states with defense and foreign affairs held in common. India's decentralized state structure – at least as conceived in the Nehru era – serves as model. While the spirit of federalism has been violated in Kashmir, Assam, Manipur, and Nagaland, India is run largely by its constituent states rather than by the center. Pakistan needs a similar level of self-management if its peoples are to be taken as equal parts of the same nation.

Uncage the Women

Pakistan currently ranks 153 out of 156 countries on the World Economic Forum's Global Gender Gap Index, with 32% of primary school-aged girls out of school. The resistance is culturally based, but religious forces are even stronger. They have fiercely resisted the notion that a woman can marry out of choice, be seen out of a burqa, deserves education, or be the family's breadwinner. This is equally true for Muslims in India, as elsewhere. The vice-chancellor of Aligarh Muslim University, Zameeruddin Shah, put it as the main reason for the Muslim world's backwardness:

> You have not utilized half of your population. Women remained enslaved. They remained inside home. Muslims have no one else to blame. You enslaved women and the result is you are enslaved.... I stayed in Saudi Arabia, the situation remains the same. Women are confined. Except Turkey and Iran, women remained enslaved in all Muslim world. That is the reason they are backward.[11]

In parts of Pakistan, a woman is likely to be spat upon, beaten, or killed for being friendly to a man or even showing to him her face. Newspaper readers expect – and get – a steady daily diet of stories about women raped, mutilated, or strangled to death by their fathers, husbands, and brothers. As the old order disintegrates and traditional arguments become manifestly unreasonable, the misogynist stocks up his arsenal with abuse and vilification against *mera jism mairee marzee*, a feminist slogan maliciously misrepresented as women demanding permission to sell their bodies for material and sensual gain.

So low is the status of women in Pakistani society that when a mosque announces a death, the introductory words never change: *hazraat: aik zaroori ailaan sunyeh* (respectable sirs, hear now an important announcement). It's always men – and only men – who need to be informed of any significant happening. Lest *haya* (modesty or propriety) be violated, women cannot be addressed directly. The rest follows a well-established pattern. Had the deceased been a man, one would learn his name. But *haya* requires the woman to remain unnamed. If married, she

430 Replacing the Two Nation Theory

would be identified as somebody's wife. If unmarried, it wouldn't be different, except that she would be joined to either her father or a brother. Mothers and sisters don't count. In ultraconservative parts of the tribal areas, it is said that a woman needs to leave her house only twice: once for Haj, and the second time for her burial.

To see where women stand in the pecking order, tour any graveyard. One walks past hundreds, perhaps thousands, of stories now silenced. In these somber environs, every tombstone marks the final resting place of some individual. Their inscriptions record the passage of someone who shall never stir again. Though six feet under, all males hold on to the name they used along their life's journey. The male's identity has been literally etched into stone – a stone that's expected to stay. Sometimes the father's name appears as well but, of course, never the mother's. And the female? Some tombstones do carry her name but many do not. Whether the end of the woman's journey shall be marked or remain unmarked is not for her to decide. That too is up to some man, or possibly men. Even if named, she is invariably identified as somebody's wife or as her father's daughter.

Not all women lament their marginalization or resent loss of control over their bodies. On the contrary, many accept it either stoically or gladly. But some, such as the female militants of Lal Masjid's *Haya Brigade*, actually celebrate their inferiority. They believe that men and women have separate, nonoverlapping role and have willingly surrendered freedom of movement, freedom of dress, freedom of association, and freedom to seek employment. This lack of freedom is evident across society but even more starkly in poorer sections. The majority of Pakistan's young women cannot choose their life partners and, instead, are "given away" by their parents. Divorce and child custody overwhelmingly favor the man over the woman. Nor is marital rape recognized as an offense. Inheritance laws are sharply skewed against women, as are employment opportunities. Nevertheless, for the Haya Brigade and supporters, restricting a woman's freedom is both natural and divinely ordained – and hence to be welcomed.

Those who value freedom find the Haya Brigade's position unacceptable, but it has many parallels. Countless examples exist where individuals have voluntarily traded their freedom for security. Notably, prisoners released from jails have sometimes pleaded to be taken back. Or, as another example, after slavery was declared illegal in America, many black slaves petitioned their white owners to keep them on the plantations. So, if jailors and slave owners can provide more security than the wilderness, then why not? More to the point: whenever a woman accepts patriarchy in exchange for lessened freedoms, she buys security for herself and her children.

The erudite Yuval Noah Harari asks in *Sapiens: A Brief History of Humankind* why patriarchy has tenaciously weathered political upheavals, social revolutions, and economic transformations. Over thousands of years, why have there been so few alpha-women like Cleopatra, Indira Gandhi, or Golda Meir? Is the reason lesser muscle power, lack of male aggressive genes, lesser social networking skills? After much discussion, Harari concludes: we don't really know.

Replacing the Two Nation Theory **431**

But, wait! We do know something very important – modernity is corroding patriarchy, laws of the old world are sliding into irrelevancy. For example, the Book of Deuteronomy instructs Christian soldiers that if they "find a beautiful woman" among captives taken in battle, then if "you desire to take her, you may". Notwithstanding this sanction, even staunch Jews and Christians today recoil in horror at the idea of sexual slavery. Instead, gender equality is now the West's new mantra; even CEOs and presidents dread accusations of gender discrimination.

Islamic countries are also rushing to catch up. Even if some decry gender equality as a Western imposition, fewer and fewer women remain shuttered in their homes. In spite of deadly opposition from Taliban-like forces, education for girls is expanding in Afghanistan and Pakistan. Although the Pakistan government has pledged to uphold Islamic values, it refuses passports unless a burqa-clad woman agrees to a mugshot. Just as significantly, though generally banned from visiting cemeteries, you can see more and more women grieving over their loved ones. Whether in the graveyard or out in the living world, Pakistan's women are denied dignity and equality by those who claim to know God's will. In the struggle for justice, they have a long road ahead – longer than in most countries. But time is on the woman's side. It is for men to march alongside them. Pakistan must adjust to the age of female emancipation.

Give Skills, Don't Brainwash

Muslims lost out to Hindus in science and modern learning, a major reason for why differences between the communities began snowballing under British rule. In support of this argument a considerable part of Chapter Two laid out statistics that showed the growing learning distance between the two groups. Unwilling to adapt their philosophy of education to fit the modern age, Muslims chose solace in past greatness rather than seek a forward-looking, adaptive system. Allama Iqbal, discussed in great detail in Chapter Five, soothed wounded egos and promised a revival of greatness by becoming truly religious again. Partition has by no means ended the quest for what it means to be truly religious nor led to a viable system of education. Employers are now well aware that certificates and degrees handed out by Pakistani institutions are worthless pieces of paper.

One key purpose of any country's education system is to create skills required by a modern economy. This generates employment, both within the country and outside of it. In Pakistan's case, ever since the oil boom of 1973, labor export has been the mainstay of its foreign exchange earnings and remittances have steadily increased with the years. The figures are impressive: in FY-2020, $21.1 billion was remitted from Saudi Arabia, GCC, U.S., U.K., Europe, etc. This should be compared against $20.8 billion for exports (textiles, clothing, cotton, cereals, leather, copper, minerals, fish, medical, etc.). Export of labor is eagerly sought by less-developed countries because it lowers unemployment and brings

432 Replacing the Two Nation Theory

in remittances and skills. It is a win for migrants who can earn more income and escape poverty.

However, one needs to reflect upon the following: Pakistan has the world's tenth largest workforce, but only 1% of migrant workers are classified as highly qualified (engineer, doctor, accountant, computer analyst, pharmacist) and 2% highly skilled (nurse, teacher, manager).[12] The remaining 97% belong to different categories ranging from skilled (welder, painter, carpenter, etc.) to low-skilled (agriculture worker and laborer). Of the estimated migrant labor demand from GCC countries, an average of 85% is for low-skilled labor, predominantly in the construction and service sectors.[13] All are Muslim. The 2015 ILO-GIZ report noted that employers in the popular destination countries have certain positive perceptions of Pakistani workers in a few occupations; for example, drivers are regarded as tough and construction workers will accept low wages.

Export of semi-skilled and low-skilled labor, though highly lucrative, is a poor way for any country to go. Apart from the indignity of being a provider of menial services to others, it means that millions of Pakistanis are freely exploited by those who either export or import labor. Many live in dreadful circumstances, saving as much as they can to send back home. All are insecure knowing that everything could be wiped out by some combination of political events, reduction in oil revenues, and replacement of human labor by machines. When COVID-19 struck, planeloads of Pakistani laborers and skilled workers were sent back from the Middle East and elsewhere. Many returned, but the long-term forecast for semi-skilled and low-skilled labor is definitely negative.

Dealing with this issue of labor export in theory is a no-brainer – go for skill development! In principle, expanding and improving programs like TVET (Technical and Vocational Education and Training) should take care of it. These can be further supplemented by the employing countries to move towards some kind of local certification of skills. All this requires some education but not very much. Strong reading and comprehension skills at the high school level is adequate for training to become certified auto mechanics, electricians, accountants and cashiers, sales and marketing people, etc. Pakistani high school education is so poor that it does not provide adequate skills even for a basic understanding of manuals and written instructions, except for the very simplest ones. Former finance minister Miftah Ismail notes that "half of all school-age children aren't even in school, and of those who matriculate from government schools, most can't solve a simple sum involving percentages, or write a decent paragraph."[14]

As one moves up the ladder of professions – data processing, system analysts, medical technicians, nurses, doctors, and various engineering areas – more than just basic comprehension skills are required. Producing high-quality pro-fessionals requires not just more years of formal education but also acquisition of critical thinking skills. It is here that the inadequacy of the Pakistani educa-tion system becomes starkly clear. Because socialization into an Islamic society is seen to be of primary importance and skill learning secondary, Pakistani

Replacing the Two Nation Theory **433**

education emphasizes rote memorization and religious indoctrination. This puts Pakistanis at a clear disadvantage relative to Indians or even Bangladeshis in higher level professions. Religious conservatism also translates into the exported labor being almost exclusively male; rare is the female who can go by herself to a foreign country to earn a living for herself and her family.

While skill creation is an important part of education, evolved countries use it to create a modern mindset wherein students are taught to be inquiring and open-minded, to be creative and scientific in solving problems, to value social responsibility, to look forward and to cherish diversity. But Pakistani schools aim for different objectives. Children are taught to obey authority without ever challenging it, to look to the past for solutions to today's problems, and to be intolerant of the religion, culture, and language of others. With the aim of creating a "patriotic spirit", schools fill young minds with suspicion and hatred of other religions and countries. Reform efforts speak of improvements to school infrastructure, books, teacher salaries, etc. But this is far from enough. The very notion of education and its contents cries out for revision.

These presently appear to be impossible dreams. In 2021 implementation of the Single National Curriculum (SNC), Imran Khan's brainchild, was started in Islamabad's schools. Learning the Arabic language has been made compulsory.[15] This has continued even after Khan's removal; reversing it will prove difficult even for a government that is not sympathetic to it. The volume of religious material contained in Khan's curriculum exceeds that in all earlier curriculums in Pakistan's history. So heavy is the religious burden that some schools in Islamabad have dropped the teaching of computer essentials and reduced/eliminated time spent in the lab. A column-by-column comparison with two major *madrassa* systems – *Tanzeem-ul-Madaris* and *Rabitat-ul-Madaris* – tells us that ordinary schools will henceforth impose more rote learning than even these *madrassas*.[16] Normal schoolteachers being underequipped religiously, SNC calls for summoning an army of *madrassa*-educated holy men – *hafiz*'s and *qari*'s – as paid teachers inside schools. Discrimination between students of different religions is automatic. Since non-Muslim students cannot be allowed to study from the Holy Book, they must be separated out.

Pakistan's universities need many changes. But most of all they need a revitalized youth movement that is idealistic and hopeful that things can be made to change. The present state of apathy among young people has an explanation. You cannot persuade people to take to the streets to protest against earthquakes or raging storms, polio and cancer, birth defects, or aging. These are understood to be givens, outside our control, and street activism is meaningless. Most young people think that the world is naturally cruel and will remain so. They think vague hopes for a better world are like wanting a piece of the moon or eternal youth, and hence a waste of time. But this damning state of mind is recent – it was brought about by the deliberate policy of leaders to cripple our will so that we stop fighting them. This is why General Zia-ul-Haq banned student unions and no subsequent government restored them. A generation of left-wing activists

434 Replacing the Two Nation Theory

has gone missing from the heady optimism of the late 1960s and early 1970s – when revolution seemed around the corner. The despair of the present owes to a lack of large popular progressive movements.

Cool Down Kashmir

For over seventy-five years, the Establishment has sought to build a core national identity based upon fear, loathing, and hatred of India. Correspondingly, at least for the last two decades now, India has reciprocated with its version of xenophobia. Two nationalisms are colliding in the nuclear age. Nothing can be more dangerous.

This fierce animosity has made the problem of Kashmir doubly difficult. On the one hand, Kashmiris are oppressed and brutalized by India's forcible occupation. On the other hand, attempts by Pakistan to liberate Kashmir have achieved nothing beyond creating a militarized Pakistani security state which uses the excuse of Kashmir, as well as the need for strategic depth in Afghanistan, to justify its hold over Pakistani society.

Narendra Modi's annexation of Kashmir in August 2019 shows Pakistan's helplessness in the face of superior military might. Changing Kashmir's status was the culmination of India's efforts to forcibly resolve the Kashmir problem. The annexation changed Kashmir's formal status, stripping it of its earlier special autonomous status and making it a normal Indian state. Under Congress governments, the plan had been somewhat different: Delhi created clients among the Valley's leaders and political parties. However, they turned out to be useless in combating popular Muslim sentiment. Elections and inducements also failed to produce a decisive outcome. In 1989 India's unconscionable manipulation of Kashmiri politics led to a popular uprising that sparked an insurgency lasting into the early 2000s. When it ended, 90,000 civilians, militants, police, and soldiers had been killed.

Pakistan has long tried to translate India's losses into its gains. It hijacked the indigenous uprising, but the excesses committed by Pakistan-based mujahideen eclipsed those of Indian security forces. The massacres of Kashmiri Pundits, targeting of civilians accused of collaborating with India, destruction of cinema houses and liquor shops, forcing of women into the veil, and revival of Shia–Sunni disputes, severely undermined the legitimacy of the Kashmiri freedom movement. Three Pakistan–India wars initiated by Pakistan have failed to provide Pakistan a positive outcome. By now it is a hackneyed truth that the Pakistan Army has conquered Pakistan multiple times but never won any other war.

Much has changed in the last ten to fifteen years. Pakistan's "bleed India with a thousand cuts" policy is in shambles today and jihad is an ugly word in the world's political lexicon. Apart from taking legitimacy away from those fighting Indian rule, Kashmir-oriented militant groups operating from Pakistani soil turned out to be a menace to Pakistan's society and armed forces. Financial Action Task Force has led to the defanging of Lashkar-e-Tayyaba, Jaish-e-Muhammad, etc.

Consequently Pakistan's options are now more limited than at any earlier time. Imran Khan's military-backed government huffed and puffed at Modi's annexation but could do little more than rouse Pakistani domestic sentiment through state-sponsored protests, changing the name of some highways in Islamabad, and redrawing maps to which the world pays no attention. It failed to get support from Organization of Islamic Cooperation and is bitter at being abandoned by Saudi Arabia, a close ally.

If Kashmir is ever to have a solution, then all three contenders – Pakistan, India, and the Muslims belonging to the Kashmir valley – will need to rethink their present positions.

- Thoughtful Pakistanis must understand that their country's military-made Kashmir policy has led nowhere. The Line of Control is here to stay. Technology in the form of smart sensors, drones, and physical impediments has made crossing to the other side more and more perilous by the day.
- Thoughtful Indians must understand that cooling down Kashmir lies in India's hands, not Pakistan's. India needs to formally acknowledge Kashmir as a problem that can only have a political solution, not a military one. It could move towards that through a series of graduated steps aimed at lessening internal tensions.
- Thoughtful Kashmiri nationalists must recognize the grave dangers of giving more space to religious extremists. They must not demand an exclusivist Islamic state and instead work for some form of pluralistic entity, whether independent or under nominal Indian or Pakistani control. That entity must assure personal and religious freedoms. An ISIS-type state with its cruel practices makes mockery of the very idea of *azadi* and would pave the way for Kashmir's descent into hell.

The advantages that would accrue to Pakistan as a result of peace with India go well beyond avoiding a destructive war and waste of resources in buying or manufacturing weaponry. At the moment, Pakistan does not trade with India at all except through third parties. Regional economic integration would hugely benefit Pakistan. In fact the benefits would be for both countries but, because of its size, more for Pakistan than India. It would also allow civilians to take charge of Pakistan.

Send Army to the Barracks

The year 2022 sees the Pakistan Army ruling Pakistan through a thin façade of civilian rule. A prime minister was installed through elections in 2018 that were manifestly manipulated and grossly unfair. Called hybrid civilian–military rule, it was military rule with all important levers securely held by the General Headquarters in Rawalpindi. The military helped create the TLP, using its fanatical hordes to subdue the civilian leadership. With the treasury running empty,

436 Replacing the Two Nation Theory

it speaks of Pakistan becoming part of the global economic system. But a state cannot be both an economic and extremism hub.

The army could not have had it better. The army chief personally oversaw relations with all important countries (China, U.S., Saudi Arabia), held court with businessmen who flocked to apprise him of their problems, had important foreign dignitaries meeting him in his office, decided upon strategies to combat COVID-19, and regulated other purely civilian functions. Military men continue to make all key decisions related to CPEC and negotiate contracts for infrastructure such as roads and railways; civilians are required to sign on the dotted line. This is in addition to the military setting nuclear policy and having control over the nuclear button, determining the temperature of India–Pak relations and the level of border clashes, as well as matters of the defense budget and weapons procurement.

The hope was that a civilian front would permit failures of planning and execution to be readily attributed to those without uniforms. Politicians could be tried in open court for corruption, but generals could continue to enjoy protection under the law and the Army placed above reproach. This did not exactly happen; Khan proved too mercurial and had his own agenda. Still, the basics remain unchanged. Under the pretext of national security, civilians may not audit how funds earmarked for national defense are spent. Therefore, although eye-popping stories are rife, how much wealth resides in the hands of soldiers and how much ends up leaving the country cannot be known. Senior army officials and their families move out of Pakistan upon retirement but, again, none may comment on this in the public media.

While the army has not won any war against India, it congratulates itself for having subdued the monster of terrorism. Indeed, Pakistan is far more peaceful today in 2023 than it was ten to twenty years ago. Since that time it has managed to clamber out of a self-created hell hole. Earlier, no one was safe. Bits of suicide bombers could be found scattered over mosques, churches, shrines, markets, schools, police stations, intelligence headquarters, and army barracks. The army takes credit for two dedicated military operations – *zarb-e-azb* and *radd-ul-fasaad* – that ultimately restored peace and broke down terrorist structures in FATA, Swat, and in major cities. But what cannot be said openly even today is the secret known to all: that the army created the terrorism monster with the aim of wresting Kashmir from India and creating "strategic depth" in Afghanistan. The architect of the latter was General Mirza Aslam Beg, then army chief. Yet, because dissent and opposition are curbed, none in the army have been held responsible for creating a situation that brought suffering to the institution itself, its children, and the country as a whole. Pandering to far-right groups has become a hallmark of the military-intelligence establishment's appropriation of Islam. It seems to believe that Pakistan would cease to exist without the use of religion in maintaining internal security and defense of external borders.

For the first time in Pakistan's history, some of the country's politicians and senior members of the judiciary have spoken out at the military's role in

Replacing the Two Nation Theory **437**

fomenting violent religious groups, manipulating elections, and abducting opponents – some of whom were brutally murdered. Civil society is well aware of heavy censorship of the media. In 2020, for a brief moment, the military was openly challenged by the Pakistan Democratic Movement. However, it was rendered impotent once the establishment pulled enough levers. What is certain, however, is that this was not the last challenge to army rule.

Epilogue

> Freedom of thought is the only guarantee against an infection of mankind by mass myths, which, in the hands of treacherous hypocrites and demagogues, can be transformed into bloody dictatorships.
>
> *– Andrei Sakharov (1968)*

The path to creating a Pakistani nation is doubtlessly difficult. As the population explodes, oceans of poverty and misery deepen, limbless beggars in the streets multiply in numbers, water and clean air become scarce, education is stalemated, true democracy remains elusive, and the distance from a rapidly developing world increases. There is a strong temptation for one to step aside, give up, and admit helplessness. But no, surely that is wrong, for what we fear will then actually come to pass. We must heed Antonio Gramsci, the great Italian philosopher, who spoke of "pessimism of the intellect, optimism of the will". With the pessimism of the intellect, we must calmly contemplate the yawning abyss up ahead. But then, after a period of reflection, one should move to prevent falling into it.

The Two Nation Theory cannot continue to be the basis for Pakistan. But a nation convinced into wrong beliefs does not change these easily. In fact no nation wedded to a deeply dysfunctional philosophy has ever voluntarily surrendered what it holds to be its founding principle. Nazism would have survived but for its decisive defeat at the hands of the Allied Powers. Pan-Arabism under Nasser ended after Egypt lost to Israel in the 1967 war. Soviet communism evaporated and the Soviet Union fell apart after economic collapse and defeat in the Cold War. Neoliberalism – which embraces individuals and rejects the idea of social responsibility – is now visibly collapsing in its very heartland, the United States.

Empowerment and people's participation can come to Pakistan even without a major wand if we are so determined. Labor must organize again, the ban on student unions must go, minorities must feel that their lives and property are secure, and the political parties must organize on real issues and be allowed to freely campaign without fear of arrest and persecution. We need to dream our dreams once again.

Howard Zinn – whom I first heard speak at an anti-Vietnam war rally in Boston in 1970 – has a powerful message of hope for all who want to change their societies:

438 Replacing the Two Nation Theory

> To be hopeful in bad times is not just foolishly romantic. It is based on the fact that human history is a history not only of cruelty but also of compassion, sacrifice, courage, kindness…. If we see only the worst, it destroys our capacity to do something. If we remember those times and places – and there are so many – where people have behaved magnificently, this gives us the energy to act, and at least the possibility of sending this spinning top of a world in a different direction. And if we do act, in however small a way, we don't have to wait for some grand utopian future. The future is an infinite succession of presents, and to live now as we think human beings should live, in defiance of all that is bad around us, is itself a marvelous victory.

Let us hope, with Rabindranath Tagore, for a Pakistan:

> Where the mind is without fear and the head is held high;
> Where knowledge is free;
> Where the world has not been broken up into fragments by narrow domestic walls;
> Where words come out from the depth of truth;
> Where tireless striving stretches its arms towards perfection;
> Where the clear stream of reason has not lost its way into the dreary desert sand of dead habit;
> Where the mind is led forward by thee into ever-widening thought and action
> Into that heaven of freedom, my Father, let my country awake.

Wisdom indeed. Let my country awake, thought roam free, false myths be shattered. It's ours to grab the chance or to squander it. Nothing is written.

Notes

1 https://en.wikiversity.org/wiki/Talk:Victor_Hugo_quote
2 *Swati Held again for Tweets against Military High-Ups*, The Express Tribune, 27 November 2022.
3 *Army Has Resolved to shun Politics*, Assures Bajwa, Dawn, 24 November 2022.
4 *Elite Privilege Consumes $17.4bn of Pakistan's Economy: UNDP – In an Exclusive Interview with Al Jazeera, UNDP's Kanni Wignaraja Says Pakistani Leaders Have Promised Action over the Damning UN Report*, 13 April 2021. https://www.aljazeera.com/news/2021/4/13/elite-privilege-consumes-17-4bn-of-pakistans-economy-undp
5 Ibid.
6 M. Ziauddin, *A Nationally-Owned Charter of Economy*, Business Recorder, 13 January 2021.
7 World Bank data, https://data.worldbank.org/indicator/NY.GNP.ATLS.CD?locations=PK
8 R. Armytage, *Big Capital in an Unequal World: The Micropolitics of Wealth in Pakistan*, Berghahn Books (2020), p. 3.
9 H. Khawaja, *Presidential Form of Government?*, The Express Tribune, 1 February 2022.

Replacing the Two Nation Theory **439**

10 Anjum Altaf, *Getting Out of This Mess*, Dawn, 20 November 2022.
11 http://indianexpress.com/article/cities/lucknow/muslims-lagged-behind-because
-they-kept-women-enslaved-amu-v-c/
12 *From Pakistan to the Gulf Region: An Analysis of Links between Labour Markets, Skills and the Migration Cycle*, Deutsche Gesellschaft für Internationale Zusammenarbeit (GIZ) GmbH and International Labour Organization (2016).
13 International Labour Organization and Deutsche Gesellschaft für Internationale Zusammenarbeit, 2015 reports.
14 M. Ismail, *Failure of Governance*, Dawn, 19 November 2022.
15 P. Hoodbhoy, *Making Arabic Compulsory*, Dawn, 13 February 2021. https://www.dawn.com/news/1607107
16 A.H. Nayyar, *Dissecting the Single National Curriculum*, Dawn, 31 July 2020. https://www.dawn.com/news/1572130

INDEX

1857 uprising 52, 88, 94, 95, 298
1871 Paris Commune 263
18th Amendment 228, 232, 233, 235, 316, 428
18th Constitutional Amendment 414
1965 war 31, 38, 39, 124, 212, 331, 368, 397
1971 war 210, 398
1979 Revolution 282
2008 general elections 233
2013 general elections 233

aalim 281
abaya 363
Abbasid Caliphs 284
Abbasids 295
Abd al-'Aziz, Prince Khalid ibn Musa'id ibn 306
Abd-al-Rahman 113
Abdul Aziz 9, 88, 330, 334, 418
Abdul Qadir 133
Abdullah Shah Changal 32
Abu Bakr 287
Abu Bakr al-Baghdadi 279, 281
Abul Ala Maududi 13, 38, 171–173, 193, 288
Abul Fazl 83
Abul Kalam Azad 13, 126, 149, 171, 172, 185, 193, 194, 255
Adam and Eve 85, 87
Adil Shah II, 49
adl-e-jehangiri 37
Adolf Hitler 366
Aeschylus 118

Afghanistan 30, 35, 37, 39, 69, 73, 117, 132, 148, 176, 179, 186, 191, 214, 219, 220, 222, 228, 252, 273, 277, 279, 281, 292–294, 298–301, 316, 319, 331, 333, 335, 337, 340, 346, 357, 361, 391, 401, 414, 418, 431, 434, 436
agal 363
ahādī hadīths 304
Ahlul Bayt 282, 308
Ahmad, Eqbal 33, 154, 217, 320, 322, 343, 399, 417
Aḥmad Shah Abdali 39
Ahmad Shah Durrani 39
Ahmadi xi, 4, 15, 104, 110, 117, 166, 174, 180, 193, 202, 239, 240, 256, 259, 277, 290, 296, 302, 308, 309, 367, 368, 369, 373, 424
Ahmadiyya 110, 116, 138, 277, 372
Ahmadiyyat 116
Ahmed, Akbar S. 208, 217
Ahmed, Ishtiaq 143, 144, 161, 168
Ahmed, Khaled 356
Ahsan, Aitzaz 352
Ain-e-Akbari 83, 84
Akali Dal Sikhs 187
Akbar 9, 36–39, 60, 65, 80, 81, 83, 85, 160, 181, 191, 208, 217, 220, 232, 233, 322, 329, 408, 417
Akbar Allahabadi 65
Al Jihad f'il Islam 175
Al-Ahkām As-Ṣulṭāniyyah wal Wilāyāt Ad-Diniya 284
alams 166
Al-Ashmawy 282, 308

442 Index

Al-Badr 271
Al-Bakistan 362, 369
al-Banna, Hassan 191
Albert Einstein 118–121, 375
al-Biruni 25
Al-Bunjab 362
Alexander the Great 30
Al-Farabi 114
Alfred Lyall 53
Al-Hilal 181
Al-Huda 283, 305, 308, 363
al-Hussein, Abdullah I bin 294
Ali, Choudhry Rehmat 158
Ali, Kamran Asdar 398
Ali, Mubarik 181
Ali Abbas Jalalpuri 103
Ali Usman Qasmi 41, 138, 169, 193, 256
Aligarh Muslim University 78, 85, 92, 94, 97, 98, 101, 144, 169, 202, 243, 255, 258, 259, 429
Aligarh Scientific Society 85
Alighieri Dante 118
al-Khoi, Abol-Qasem 282
All India Muslim League 109, 162, 173
All Saints Church 410
allah hafiz 362
Allahabad address 130, 252, 265
Allama Iqbal 65, 102–104, 137, 138, 153, 175, 244, 248, 251, 257, 265, 269, 274, 276, 285, 297, 302, 409, 431
All-India Azad Conference 172
All-India Jamhur Muslim League 172
All-India Momin Conference 172
All-India Muslim Majlis 172
All-India Shia Political Conference 166, 172
Al-Mamun 113
al-Mawardi, Abul Hasan 284, 309
Al-Qaida 191, 279, 294, 361
Al-Shabab 295, 296
Al-Shams 271
Al-Tabari 163
Altaf, Anjum 428
Altaf Hussain Hali 78, 80, 94
alternate energy 384
Ambedkar, Dr. B.R. 162, 170, 367
Amirali, Alia 234
Ancestral North Indians 28
Ancestral South Indians 28, 29
Andaman Islands 266
Anderson, B. 348, 376
angeethees 77
Anglican-Catholic law 132
Anjuman-e-Himayat-e-Islam 106
Anjuman-e-Ittehad-e-Balochistan 222

Anjuman-e-Watan party 222
Anjuman-i-Watan Baluchistan 172
anthropogenic 382
Arab Wannabe Syndrome 361
Arab-Israeli war 224
Ardern, Jacinda 326
Army Public School 215, 336, 337, 411
Army Welfare Trust 313, 426
Armytage, Rosita 425
Article 92-A 202
Arya Samaj 73, 93, 96, 265
Aryan invasion 370
Aryan migration 28, 29
Aryans 27, 28, 31, 223
Aryavarta 58
Asad, Muhammad 297
Asbab-e-Baghawat-e-Hind 89
Asharites 114
Ashraf Ali Thanawi 70
ashrafiyya 10, 11, 52, 58–60, 62, 65, 66, 68, 80, 91, 92, 94, 201, 245, 268, 321
Asian Development Bank 383
Asian tiger 213
asphyxiation 383
Ata Muhammad 116
Atiya Faizee 102, 103, 128, 136
Aurakzai, Lt. Gen. 334
Aurangzeb 9, 37–39, 83, 192
Aurora, Lieutenant General Jagjit Singh 209
Auschwitz 354
Avery, John Scales 23, 41, 383, 392
Avicenna 114, 194
Awami League 190, 202, 207, 213
Aws 286
ayatollah 282
Ayatollah Khamenei 106, 132, 137
Ayatollah Khomeini 282, 401
Ayatollah Sistani 282
Aydin, Cemil 297
Ayesha Siddiqa 21, 41, 252, 313
Ayman al-Zawahri 294
Ayres, Alyssa 268, 358
Ayyaz 131
Ayyubi, Salahuddin 365
azaan 249
Azad Muslim Conference 172
azadari 165
azadi 435
Azhar, Major-General Naveed 339
Azhar, Masood 332
Aziz, K.K 34, 155
Aziz, Shaukat 406
Azzam, Abdullah 191

Bacha Khan 115, 187
Baconian scientific method 120
Baez, Joan 212, 213
Baghdad 85, 181
Bahadur Shah Zafar 53
baithaks 77
Bajwa, General Qamar Javed 316, 413, 420
Bajwa, Lt. Gen. Asim Saleem 231
Baloch, Sanaullah 232
Baloch nationalism 23, 221, 223, 271
Balochistan Liberation Army 220
Bamiyan Buddhas 293, 352
Banerjee, Sumanta 209
Bangladesh Nationalist 213
Barelvi 16, 34, 69, 87, 301, 337, 338, 345, 408, 424
Barveli Islam 337
Batala Engineering Company 398
Bay of Bengal 211, 394
bayat 80, 116
Beg, General Mirza Aslam 436
Bell, Daniel 263
Bella, Ahmed Ben 300
Bengal Krishak Praja Party 172
Bengali, Kaiser 41, 226
Bengali Muslims 201, 204, 246, 395
Bengali nationalism 204, 212, 394
Ben-Gurion, David 141
Bennett-Jones, Owen 413
Benthall, E.J. 146
Bertrand Russell 36, 118
Bhagat Singh 134, 353, 357
Bhakti movement 26, 27, 357
Bharat Mata 192
Bharatvarsh 27
Bhatti, Dulla 126, 353, 378
Bhitai, Shah Abdul Latif 145
Bhutto, Benazir 326, 344, 396, 398, 403
Bhutto, Zulfiqar Ali 30, 31, 38, 168, 203, 215, 220, 228, 251, 256, 277, 300, 395, 411, 416–418, 426
Bibi, Asia 338, 339
Bibi, Safia 403
bid'ah 69, 82
bid'at 69, 70
Bilgiç, Esra 366
Bismarck, O.V. 271, 396
Bizenjo, Ghaus Bux 221
Bizenjo, Mir Ghaus Bakhsh 220
BJP 2, 94, 98, 192, 267, 349, 388
Blasphemy Law 406
Boer War 88
Boko Haram 35, 117, 191, 288, 295, 296, 425

Bolitho, Herbert 154
Bolshevik 109
Bolshevik Roos 109
Bombay Presidency 153
Book of Deuteronomy 431
Book of Joshua 30
Bourke-White, Margaret 147
Boym, S. 351, 376
Bozdag, M. 365
Brahmanical *smrti* 47
Brahmo Samaj 11, 67, 73, 79
Brigadier John Coke 52
British East India Company 10, 24, 44, 46
British Raj 43, 182, 194, 265
Brohi, A.K. 271, 275, 402
Buchanan, Allen 230
Bugti, Nawab Akbar 220, 232
Bukhari, MaulanaAttaullah Shah 172
burqa 66, 283, 299, 307, 363, 429, 431
Bush, G.W. 117
Butcher of Bengal 220, 400
Buxar 46
Buyid Emirs 284

Cabinet Mission Plan 149, 184, 185, 190, 241, 269
Calcutta High Court 62
Caliph 157, 217
caliphate 90, 91, 105, 132, 181, 276, 279, 284, 294–296, 298, 303, 304, 307
Callard, Keith 141, 273
Cambridge University 72, 73, 100, 106, 107, 168, 170, 193, 275, 376
Canaanites 30
Cantor sets 120
Cardinals 280
Carter, Jimmy 401
Caste distinctions 67
CENTO 325
Central Secretariat 203
Chabahar 228
Chachnama 360, 361, 377
Chakravarty, J.C. 94
Chanakya 353
Chandragupta 2–3, 353
Chandrasekhar, S. 372
Changez Khan 130
changezi 130
Charles Alfred Elliot 48
Charlie Hebdo 298, 339
Charter of the Economy 386, 392
Chaudhry Rehmat Ali 43, 126
Chaudhuri, Pramit Pal 229
Chishtia 174
Christian Troll 80

444 Index

Christophe Jaffrelot 29, 32, 274
Churchill, Winston 38, 151
CIA 288, 300, 301, 401
Citizenship Amendment Act of 2020 255
Civil Aviation Authority 262, 274
civilian control 322, 327, 328, 423
classless society 397, 423
Cleopatra 430
climate change 17, 118, 213, 381–384
climate crisis 382
Clinton, Bill 404, 405
Code of Criminal Procedure 316
Cold War 147, 148, 300, 301, 311,
    319–322, 325, 422, 437
colonialism 36, 40, 45, 70, 105, 176, 230,
    249, 324, 360, 385
Commander of the Eastern Military
    Command 210
communalism 12, 97, 106, 122, 136,
    180, 257
communism 108, 109, 167, 243, 244, 251,
    256, 263, 273, 289, 291, 301, 322, 325,
    398, 437
communist ideology 5, 273, 319
Constituent Assembly 29, 141, 144, 147,
    155, 199, 206, 216, 217, 222, 247, 250,
    321, 367
contraceptive prevalence rate 387
Cornwallis–Shore reforms 67
Council of Common Interests 399
Council of Foreign Relations 405
Council of Islamic Ideology 278, 303, 406
COVID-19, 213, 243, 375, 415, 432, 436
Cowasjee, A. 417
CPEC 148, 228, 229, 231, 316, 330, 436
Crick, F. 354
cultural evolution 23

Da'esh 35, 117, 191, 241, 279, 288,
    294–296, 300, 365, 374, 425
Dalit 162, 349, 377
Dara Shukoh 38
Dar-ul-Awam 221
Dar-ul-Harb 69
Dashti, Naseer 225, 234
Daultana, Mumtaz 148, 250
David Gilmartin 41
Davis, Raymond 288
dawlah 282
Debal 360
Debendranath Tagore 67
Declaration of Independence 230, 279
deen 289
Deen Dayal Upadhyaya Junction 192
Defence Housing Authorities 313, 426

deforestation rate 384
democracy 5, 15, 23, 30, 33, 40, 108,
    122, 129–132, 134, 155, 156, 161, 163,
    164, 175, 207, 213, 227, 258, 263, 273,
    291, 292, 305, 309, 315, 316, 324–326,
    341–343, 357, 368, 402, 421, 423, 437
Deobandi 16, 34, 70, 87, 165, 181, 224,
    301, 303, 337, 338, 367, 408
departmental accounts committee 316
Devji, Faisal 168–170, 201, 216, 274
Dewey, C. 322, 323, 343
Dharmasastra 47
Diamond, J. 385
dictatorship 16, 30, 130, 261
Dilip Singh 133
din-e-ilahi 37
Direct Action Day 151, 185, 242, 269
Director General of Public Relations 221
Dirilis Ertugrul 364, 365
Divide et impera 52
diyyat 288
DNA 23, 264, 303, 322, 354, 377
do qaumi nazariyya 96, 264
document of surrender 209
Dominion of Pakistan 276
Dorsey, J.M. 309
Dowson, John 32
Doval, Ajit 229
drip irrigation 384
Dua-e-Qunoot 358
Duke University 230
Dulles, J.F. 325
duniya-darana 128
dunya 289
Durand Line 216, 361
Duriya Hashmi 106
A Dying Colonialism 397

economic justice 423, 426
economic system 167, 382, 384, 436
education reform 403, 423
Edmond, Reverend E. 51
Edward Said 5
Elahi, Chaudhry Fazal 270
Elliot, Henry M. 32
Emma Wegenast 128
Emperor Jehangir 37, 60
English education 11, 62, 63, 67, 71
English language 10, 59, 62, 63, 81, 85,
    135, 386
Enlightenment 5, 86, 114, 156, 306
entente cordiale 398
environmental causes 423
Erdogan, T. 294, 365, 366
Erikson, E. 356, 376

Index 445

establishment 16, 26, 31, 55, 67, 146, 151, 193, 211, 215, 219–221, 225, 226, 228, 233, 257, 261, 271, 280, 281, 287, 315, 317, 319, 322, 323, 325–327, 332, 335, 338–340, 361, 365, 368, 374, 395, 397, 400, 410, 420, 425, 436, 437
European capitalism 10, 43, 109
Express Tribune 72, 258, 308, 336, 344, 345, 356, 376, 418, 419, 438

failed state 422
Faisal Devji 22, 41, 141, 158
Faiz Ahmad Faiz 15, 180, 257, 350
fall of Dacca 17, 210, 216, 332, 394–396
Fanon, F. 397
Faraizi Movement 70
farangis 24, 289
Farani, S.A. 358, 377
Faruqui, A. 414, 419
fascism 108, 263, 289
Fatwas 38
Fauji Foundation 426
Federal Security Force 399
Ferguson, N. 325
feudalism 277, 397, 426
Financial Action Task Force 271, 332, 338, 434
Finer, S. 312, 342
fiqh 166, 181
First Kashmir War 321, 331, 388
First World War 88, 107
Fisher, R.A. 23
Francis Robinson 21, 33, 41
free market 383
Freudian theory 396
Frontier Crimes Regulation 224
Fuchs, Simon 165

Galileo Galilei 118
Gamal Abdel Nasser 108, 300
Gandhi, Indira 209, 241, 396, 430
Ganga-Yamuna 352
Gaya Muslim League Conference 159
GDP 213, 214, 226, 414, 427
Geelani, Syed Ali Shah 295
General Headquarters 227, 332, 404, 435
general relativity 119, 120, 121, 375
General Theory of Relativity 119, 120, 375, 376
General Zia-ul-Haq 16, 103, 152, 162, 168, 174, 178, 270, 272, 291, 301, 352, 390, 400, 401, 409, 433
genetic 16, 23, 28, 29, 41, 264, 274, 347, 354, 355, 376
George Cantor 119

Ghafoor, Maj. Gen. Asif 231
Ghalib, Mirza Asadullah 50, 51, 83–85
Ghani, Ashraf 292, 293
ghar wapsi 355
Ghauri 314
Ghazi, Maulana Abdul Aziz 334
GHG emissions 384
Ghubar-i-Khatir 182
Ghulam Ahmad 116
Ghulam Ahmad Pervez 99
Ghulam Ishaq Khan Institute of Engineering Sciences and Technology 39
ghutrah 363
Gilani, Yousaf Raza 335
Glancy, Bertrand 160
Global Gender Gap Index 429
Godse, Nathuram 266
Golwalkar, M.S. 30, 266
Gopal, Krishna Gokhale 73, 100, 157, 309
Government College 39, 106, 111, 123, 372
Government of India Act of 1935 202, 247
Gramsci, A. 292, 308, 437
Great Dharna 411
Great Flood 85, 87
Great Mutiny 10, 50, 52, 68, 324
Green Book 314, 317
Green Line Bus Rapid Transit System 316
gross national income 425
Gul, General Hamid 336
Gunpowder Empires 45, 282
gunwaar 357
Guru Nanak 27, 357

hadīths 304
Hafeez Malik 80, 100
Hagia Sophia 366, 377
Haji Shariatullah 70
Hajj 34
hakeem-ul-Ummat 103
Haldane, J.B.S. 23
Hamas 296, 301
Hameed, General Faiz 315, 412, 415
Hamid II, 80, 306
Hamood-ur-Rahman 210
Hamood-ur-Rahman Report 210
Hanafi 36, 166, 181, 292, 294, 303
Hanbali 181, 303, 304
Hanbali *fiqh* 181
Haq, Fazlul 201
Haqqani, Hussain 275, 413
haram 283
Harappa 352
Harari, Yuval Noah 43, 430
Haroon-ul-Rashid 113
Hasan, Syed Munawar 337

446 Index

Hasan, Wajid Shamsul 335
Hashmi, Farhat 283, 363
Hasrat Mohani 134
Hatf 314
havelis 77
Haya Brigade 430
Hebrew Bible 30
Hibatullah Akhundzada 292
hijab 283, 305, 363
Hijazi, Nasim 360
hijrat 270
Himalayan glaciers 383
Himalayas 353
Hindu-Muslim 49, 100, 180
Hindustani 31, 36
Hindutva 27, 29, 31, 39, 124, 151, 192,
    254, 257, 264–266, 274, 349, 370
Histadrut 141
Hizb-ut-Tahrir 295
Holy Prophet (PBUH) 111, 286, 334, 407
Holy See 279, 280
Holy-Land 265
Holyoake, G.J. 424
Homer 118
Hommel 107
honor killings 223, 304, 373
hoors 86
Houbara Bustard 299, 309
Housepian, N. 322, 343
Hudood Ordinance 403, 406
Human Development Index 421
Huntington, S. 5, 124, 325, 344
Husain, Fahd 340
Husain, Zahid 404
Hussain, Syed Amjad 208
Hussain, Syed Mushahid 317
Hussain Ahmad Madani 38, 126, 144,
    172, 181
Hyder Ali 46
Hyperion 327, 328

Ibn Ishaq 286
Ibn Khaldun 284, 285, 308
Ibn-e-Rushd 86, 114
Ibn-Khaldun 163
Ibrahim Lodhi 36
Iconoclasm 30
idaras 316
iddah 284
ideology of Pakistan 15, 260–262
If I am Assassinated 400
ihtijaj aur qurbani 166
Ijaz, Saroop 410
Ijaz-ul-Haq, Muhammad 406
ijma 108

ijtihad 86, 105, 108, 131
Ikhwan-ul-Muslimeen 301
Imam Al-Ghazali 60, 85
Imam Mahdi 101, 281, 282
Imambargahs 241, 303
Immanuel Kant 110, 113
imperialism 6, 41, 61, 92, 130, 135, 244,
    295, 397
imperialist historiography 27
Imran Khan 16, 17, 30, 104, 162, 251,
    256, 272, 278, 285, 292, 303, 315, 316,
    319, 338–340, 342, 358, 365, 377, 387,
    388, 394, 395, 409–416, 419, 420, 427,
    428, 433, 435
Indian Air Force 209
Indian Civil Service 47, 203, 252
Indian Eastern Command 209
Indian Education Commission 62
Indian Mig-21 391
Indian National Congress 3, 88, 94, 140,
    152, 153, 156, 171, 180, 182, 265
Indian Parliament 95
Indian Subcontinent 2–4, 41, 42
Indigenous Aryanism 27, 29
Indo-Aryan Migration Debate 27, 41
Indus Valley Civilization 28, 29
Industrial Revolution 41, 59, 117
integrated watershed management 384
Inter Services Public Relations 313
International Labor Organization (ILO)
    213, 250, 432
International Monetary Fund (IMF) 251,
    318, 411, 414
Iqbaliat 103
Iran 2, 28, 31, 33, 106, 107, 113, 132,
    167, 215, 219, 222, 228, 234, 240, 273,
    276–278, 281, 282, 299, 300, 305, 306,
    309, 353, 355, 359, 361, 362, 387, 393,
    428, 429
Irfan Habib 8, 52
Isa, Qazi Faez 412
ishq 115, 137
Ishwari Prasad 94
ISIS 279, 281, 435
Islam 9, 11–16, 21, 24, 29–31, 34–40, 42,
    49, 60, 63, 65, 66, 69–73, 77, 78, 80,
    82, 85–87, 90, 98–101, 105, 106, 108,
    111–114, 116–118, 124–126, 129–131,
    134, 136–138, 140, 143, 146, 148, 151,
    155–162, 165, 166, 169–172, 174–179,
    181, 182, 186, 187, 191, 193, 194, 206,
    214, 216, 224, 240, 244, 245, 248, 256–
    258, 261–264, 267, 270, 271, 273, 274,
    276–287, 289–293, 295–298, 300–310,
    322, 323, 334, 337, 338, 340, 346, 347,

352, 353, 355, 357, 359–364, 366–368, 371, 373, 374, 377, 399, 401, 402, 405, 407, 409, 415, 416, 423, 436
Islam ka Qanun-i-Jang 175
Islami Jamhoori Ittihad 314
Islami Jamiat-e-Talaba 191
Islamic Bomb 400, 417, 418
Islamic conservatives 44, 350
Islamic Emirate of Afghanistan 292, 293, 309
Islamic Golden Age 113, 167
Islamic Golden Era 60
Islamic law 82, 176, 179, 278, 288, 427
Islamic modernists 44
Islamic socialism 277
Islamic state 13, 16, 31, 139, 151, 153, 155, 162–165, 171, 173, 176, 178, 179, 193, 211, 240, 249, 261, 271, 272, 276–280, 282, 284, 285, 288–291, 293, 295, 302, 307, 309, 362, 416, 424, 425, 435
Islamic Summit 398
Islamic theology 80, 99, 111, 177
Islamic welfare state 285, 426
Islamised State 262
Israel 6, 13, 31, 135, 141, 142, 261, 299, 305, 341, 385, 399, 400, 417, 421, 437
izzat 323

Jackson, Roy 175
Jacob, Major-General Jack 209
Jacobabad 383
jagir system 60
jagirdar 61
Jahanara Begum 38
jahilyah 177
Jaish-e-Muhammad 337, 434
Jallianwala Bagh 71, 134, 135, 157, 190
jalsa 409
Jamaat-e-Islami 173, 178, 270, 271, 275, 291, 295, 301, 308, 337, 367
Jamaluddin Afghani 80, 87
Jameel, Maulana Tariq 364
James Mill 48
James Watt 118
Jami, Mufti Tahir 281
Jamia Hafsa 334, 408
Jamiat Ahl-e-Hadith 172
Jamiat Ulema-e-Hind 38
Jati 266
Jatoi, Sharukh 288
Jauhar, Mohammad Ali 181
Jauhar, Shaukat Ali 181
Javaid Iqbal 124, 127, 128, 133, 329
Javed Ahmad Ghamidi 99
jawab-e-shikwa 125

jawan 336
Jayaprakash, MS 32
Jefferson, Thomas 153
Jericho 117
Jerusalem 365
Jha, D.N. 23, 41, 73
Jihadistan 333
jinns 86, 87
jizya 9, 37, 261, 289, 290, 296
Jodha Bai 36
Joyland 350
Judaism 30, 142, 261, 283
Jung, Salar 175

kabootar baazi 87
Kadri, Justice Shameem Hussain 212, 218
Kakar, Rafiullah 232
Kalat state 14, 222, 223
Kalim Siddiqui 97
Karachi Bar Association 277
Karbala 77, 157, 200, 287
Kargil 40, 320, 331, 332, 391, 404, 405, 408, 409, 418
Karim, Abdul 222
Karim Bibi 127
Karin Deutsch 66
Karl Marx Ki Awaz 109
Karnavati 266
Kashmiri, Shorish 191
Kate Brittlebank 49
Kayani, General Ashfaq Pervez 335, 336
Kayani, General Pervez Ashraf 335
Kemal Atatürk 294, 300, 306
Keti Bunder 383
khabar hadīths 304
Khaddarposh, Masud 250, 358
Khadim Hussain Rizvi 105
Khaksar-e-Azam 188
khalaee makhlooq 312, 315
Khalid bin Sayeed 145, 152
Khaliquzzaman, Chaudhari 184
Khan, Abdul Wali Khan 220
Khan, Ahmad Reza 337
Khan, Danish 153
Khan, General Ayub 14, 36–38, 145, 174, 203, 211, 212, 251, 311, 312, 322, 324, 325, 327, 328, 331, 341, 344, 396, 404, 409, 417, 419, 422, 426, 428
Khan, General Yahya 14, 207, 209–211, 272, 324, 327, 422
Khan, Ghaffar 13, 30, 172, 186–190, 192–195
Khan, Ismail Nawab 184
Khan, Liaquat Ali 141, 145, 148, 162, 200–202, 206, 261, 322, 324

448 Index

Khan, Lieutenant General Tikka 208
Khan, Mahmood Hasan 213
Khan, Maulana Gul Naseeb 407
Khan, Maulana Wahiduddin 282
Khan, Mir Ahmad Yar 222
Khan, Mohammad Nasir 407
Khan, Nawabzada Nasrullah 172
Khan, Qayyum 148, 172, 190
Khan, Roedad 326
Khan, Shahzeb 288
Khan, Shaukat Hayat 273
Khan, Zafarullah 174, 256, 367, 368
Khan of Kalat 14, 220, 222
khatib 281
Khazraj 286
Kheer Bhawani 117
khilafa bi-la-fasl 166
Khilafat Movement 135, 157, 175, 181,
   182, 298
Khizr-i-Rah 109
Khoja Ismaili Shia 151
Khoja Isna-Ashari 151
Khorana, Har Gobind 372
khuda ka saya 106
khuda mard 126
Khudai Khidmatgars (NWFP) 172, 188
khudi 126, 135, 136
Khuhro, M.A. 148
Khwaja, Haroon 428
King, Martin Luther 153, 219
King Chach 360
King George III, 49
King George V, 135
King Richard 365
King Saud bin Abdulaziz 298
Kissinger, H. 211, 398
Kosambi, D.D. 8, 40, 42
Krishak Sramik Party 202
Kufi, A. 361
Kulkarni, Sanjeev 257
Kurt Gödel 119

Lal Masjid 334, 408, 418, 430
Lala Amarnath 94
Lala Lajpat Rai 95, 101, 264, 265
laser field leveling 384
Lashkar-e-Janghvi 337
Lashkar-e-Omar 332
Lashkar-e-Taiba 332, 337
Lashkar-e-Tayyaba 229, 434
Latif, Air Marshal Idris 209
Lenin Khuda Ke Huzoor Mein 109
Line of Control 229, 331, 388, 435
Lord Canning 51
Lord Elphinstone 52

Lord Linlithgow 140
Lord Lytton 82
Lord Mountbatten 7, 140, 184, 222,
   269, 358
Lord Palmerston 51
Lord Shiva 117
Lord Wavell 140, 160
Loyal Mohamedans of India 89
Lt. Col. Alexander Dow 49
Lucknow Pact 152, 157
Lumumba, P. 397
Lux, Dennis 228

ma'aqulat 38, 85
MacArthur, General D. 327
Macron, Emmanuel 339
madhe-sahaba 165
Madras Muslim Association 111
Madrassa-i-Ramiyya 69
madrassas 63, 65, 79, 82, 98, 224, 225,
   292, 341, 386, 408, 424, 433
Madressah Ali Murtaza 281
Mahabharata 49
Mahatma Gandhi 265, 266, 294
Mahboob Tabish 103
Mahmud Ghazni 49
Mahmud of Ghazni 25
Mahomedans 54, 205
Majlis-e-Shoora 402
Majlis-i-Ahrar 172, 173
Makrani Baloch 224
maktabs 63, 65
Malala Yusafzai 127, 410
maleech 26
Malihabadi, Josh 239
Malik, Anushay 397
Malik Firoz Khan Noon 145
Malik Mumtaz Qadri 133
Maliki 181, 303
Malthusian nightmare 386
mamlikat-e-khudadad 424
Manan Asif 45
Mandela, Nelson 186
Manekshaw, General Sam 209
manqulat 38, 85
mansabdars 91
Manto, Saadat Hasan 354
Manu Smriti 47
MAO College 82, 87, 92, 94, 96, 98
Maqsood, Ammara 363
mard-e-momin 105, 129, 249
Marshall Hodgson 45
marsiyas 77
Martial law 174, 203, 341
Martin, O.M. 49

Index 449

Marxism 8, 115
Marxist 225, 245
mashaikh 406
masih maw'ud 116
Masih, Tara 400
Massachusetts Institute of Technology 23
Maulana Bhashani 202
Maulana Hidayat-ur-Rahman 221
Maulana Yaqoob of Deoband 87
Maynard, H. J. 70
Mazzini, G. 271
Mecca 34, 69, 94, 157, 270, 401
Mehsud, Hakimullah 337, 410
Mein Kampf 366
Meir, Golda 430
mellat 33
mera jism mairee marzee 429
Metternich, K.V. 396
Mian, Zia 41
Mian Mumtaz Mohammed Khan
    Daultana 145
Michael O'Dwyer 71
Michelson–Morley experiment 121
millah 33
millet 33
Minar-e-Pakistan 409
Ministry of Federal Education Ministry
    and Professional training 262
Mir Jafar 46, 415
Mir Muttaqi 80
Miramshah 333, 334
Mirza, Iskander 148, 202, 203, 327
Misaq 286, 287
mission civilisatrice 44
mleccchas 24
modernity 9, 12, 60, 66, 69, 70, 84, 85,
    91, 118, 168, 242, 297, 301, 431
Modi, Narendra 3, 192, 229, 234, 241, 254,
    267, 299, 341, 388, 410, 414, 434, 435
Mohammed, Ghulam 148
Mohan Bhagwat 93
Mohandas Gandhi 88, 157, 181
Mohenjo Daro 352
Mohsin-ul-Mulk, Nawab 157
Monbiot, G. 385
Monier-Williams M. 46, 71
Moore, J. 382
Moore, J.J. 84
Moradabad Panchayat Madrasa 98
Mosaddeq, Mohammed 300
Moscow Olympics 401
Mother India 2, 3, 21, 29, 93, 140, 265, 267
Mua'tizila 86
Mubarak Ali 103
Mudie, Francis 145, 250

mufakkir-e-Pakistan 103
mufti 281, 369, 378
muftis 91, 307
Mughalsarai Junction Railway Station 192
Muhajir/Muhajirs 14, 17, 30, 145, 205,
    216, 225, 251, 253, 270, 318, 324, 346,
    347, 354, 395, 402, 404
Muhammad Abduh 80, 297
Muhammad Ali Jinnah 4, 6, 7, 12–16, 27,
    29–31, 71, 78, 98, 101, 103, 109, 115,
    137, 139–174, 176, 178, 180, 182–186,
    188–195, 199–203, 206–208, 216, 217,
    219–222, 239, 241–250, 254–257, 260,
    261, 265, 268–273, 275, 277, 300, 307,
    321, 331, 342, 367, 368, 371, 375, 396,
    402, 405, 417, 422
Muhammad bin Qasim 21, 360, 361, 377
Muhammad ibn Abdul Wahhab 69
Muhammad Qasim Firishta 49
mujaddid 177
mujaddid alf-i-thani 37
mujahideen-e-Pakistan 98
mujahidins 36
mujras 87
Mukti Bahini 209
mullah 38, 104, 126, 134, 157, 179, 248,
    272, 281, 282, 302, 340
Mullah Fazlullah 333
Mullah Mansour 294
Mullah Omar 281, 293, 294, 306
Munir, Justice M. 31, 72, 169, 270, 272,
    275, 290, 302, 303, 308, 329, 396
Munir, Mohammed 148
Munsif 55
musalmans 24
mushairas 77
Musharraf, General Pervez 220, 278, 327,
    369, 391, 395, 404, 418
Mushirul Hasan 36, 48, 99, 157, 244,
    254, 342
Muslim Brotherhood 295
Muslim Nationalists 308
Muslim separatism 58, 78
Muslim state 43, 44, 126, 134, 139, 161,
    163, 171, 172, 176, 252, 255, 257, 261,
    272, 277, 362, 367
Muslim Zion 141, 168, 169, 216, 274
Musulman 56, 105
Mu'tazila 113, 135
Muttahida Majlis-e-Amal 406

namaz 362
namaaz 249
Napak-istan 173, 193
Napoleon, B. 44, 271, 396

450 Index

Naqvi, M.B. 210, 217
Narmada river 353
naskh 284
Nasr, Vali 175, 281, 291
Nasr missile 382, 390
Nathaniel Brassey Halhed 47
National Action Plan 341
National Finance Commission 233
nationhood 21, 92, 141, 207, 223, 262, 264, 348, 371, 420, 423
natural-selection 23
Naval Task Force 211
Naveed, Major-General Azhar 412
Nawab Abdul Latif 79
Nawab Iftikhar Hussain Khan 145
Nawab of Mamdot 109
Nawa-i Waqt 116
Nawaz, Maryam 312
Nawaz, Shuja 324
Nawaz Sharif 105, 278, 315, 326, 337, 338, 345, 362, 403, 404, 409, 411–413
Naya Pakistan 104, 330, 410, 415
Nazi German 209
Nazimuddin, Khwaja 201, 207
nechari 80
Nehru, Jawaharlal 138, 142, 149, 156, 168, 182, 185, 258, 269, 298, 341, 352
neoliberalism 273
New York University 293, 309
Newtonian gravity 120
Niazi, Lieutenant General A.A.K. 208
Niazi, Lieutenant General Sanaullah 336
Nietzsche, F. 177, 179
Nietzschean 105, 396
Nixon, R. 209, 211, 228, 398
Nizami, K. A. 59, 71, 72, 87
Nizam-e-Mustafa 16, 277, 401, 402
Nizam-ul-Mulk 175
No First Use 388, 393
Noam Chomsky 21, 41
Nomani, Shibli 181
Non-Aligned Movement 298
Non-Cooperation Movement 157, 265
nuclear nationalism 23, 399
Nur Jehan 124
NWFP 145, 160, 161, 165, 172, 189, 190, 246, 250, 252, 253, 274, 402, 407

Obama, Barack H. 335
Oldenburg, Philip K. 22, 41
Olivier Roy 69
One Unit 428
Operation Gibraltar 38, 39, 203, 320, 331, 396
Operation *Radd-ul-Fasaad* 336

Operation *Zarb-e-Azb* 336
Organization of Islamic Cooperation 300, 435
Orissa secretariat 269
orthodox 12, 13, 37, 39, 77, 80, 87, 92, 112, 125, 171, 180–182, 257, 283, 405, 423
Osama bin Laden 40, 108, 279, 334, 335, 410, 418
Osman 287, 309
Ottoman caliphate 294

Pahlavi, Mohammad Reza Shah 300
Pak Fauj Zindabad 411
Pakhtun Tahaffuz Mahaz (PTM) 193
Pakistan Air Force 37, 38, 299
Pakistan Atomic Energy Commission 396
Pakistan Constituent Assembly 139, 143, 144, 161, 189
Pakistan Constitution 424
Pakistan Democratic Movement 437
Pakistan International Airlines 213, 227, 328, 330, 362
Pakistan ka matlab kya? la ilaha illallah 260, 268
Pakistan Movement 73, 87, 137, 151, 156, 162, 166, 174, 202, 216, 246, 249, 258, 270, 321, 360, 402
Pakistan National Alliance 400
Pakistan National Human Development Report 425
Pakistan Occupied Kashmir 229
Pakistan Penal Code 316
Pakistan People Party 30, 207, 397, 428
Pakistan Television 152, 365, 405, 411
Pakistani establishment 34, 207, 219, 225, 240, 260, 272, 337, 396, 423
Pakistani nationalism 104, 271
pakki naukri 387
Paleedistan 173
Panama Leaks 412
Pandits 38, 47, 116
Pandora Papers 414
Panipat 36, 39
Pan-Islamism 296, 297
Papal States 280
Paracha, Nadeem Farroq 362, 377
Pasha, Hafiz 386
Pasha, Lt. General Ahmed Shuja 314
Pasha, Usman Ali 175
Pashtunistan Resolution 189
Pataudi, Major General Sher Ali Khan 324
Patel, Sardar Vallabhbhai 157
Paul Brass 58
Payam-i-Mashriq 109
Pearce, F. 385

Permissive Action Links 391
Persian Gulf 219, 222, 223, 228, 401
Petit, Dinshaw 176
Petit, Rattanbai 176
Pew Global Survey 349, 356, 376
Philosopher of the East 110
Pir, Amn-ul-Hasanat 161, 170
Planning Commission of Pakistan 316
Plassey 46
Political Parties Bill 270
Polk, William R. 33
pope 53, 280, 281, 303
population dynamics 23
population genetics 23
Population Welfare Department 386
Prasad, Rajendra 157
Prayagraj 192
Prince Mohammed bin Salman 304, 366
Prithviraj 353
Prophet Muhammad (PBUH) 30, 87,
  108, 132, 133, 270, 284
Prophet of Muslim Renaissance 103
Public Sector Development Program 226
Pulwama 390, 391, 393
Punjab ka Muqadama 428
Punjab Legislative Assembly 109
Punjab University 119, 195, 211, 258
Pythagoras 118

qari 433
qasidas 77
Qasim Nanautvi 87
Qasim Zaman 70
Qasmi, A.Q. 394, 395
qaum 92, 93, 96, 97, 176, 208
qazis 91
qisas 287
Qissa Khwani Bazar 188
Qom 281
Quaid-e-Azam 23, 39, 140, 143, 154, 170,
  191, 193, 234, 309, 338, 344, 363,
  401, 413
Queen Victoria 106
Quit India 183
Qureshi, Shah Mahmood 251
Qutab Minar 180

Rabindranath Tagore 110, 438
Rabitat-ul-Madaris 433
Radcliffe College 398
radioactive ruins 392
Rahim, J.A. 399
Rahman, I.A. 397, 417
Rahman, Mufti Muneebur 369
Rahman, Shaikh Mujibur 210

Raja, Major General Khadim Hussain 208
Raja Dahir 31, 145, 360
Raja of Mahmudabad 163, 165, 170
Raja Radhakanta Deb 67
Raja Ram Mohan Roy 67, 79
Raja Rasalu 353
rajm 307
Rajmohan Gandhi 21, 41, 80, 95, 187
Rajpal 133, 134
Ramadan 272, 362, 403
Ramay, Haneef 427
Ramayana 35
Ramna Race Course garden 209
ramuz-e-beykhudi 127
Ramzan 269, 270, 362
Rana, Amir 41, 224, 225
Rangeela Rasool 133
Rapid Deployment Force 401
Ras Al Hadd 223
Ras Al Jinz 223
Rashid, Maria 323
Rashid, Sheikh 369
Rashid Ahmad Gangohi 63
Rashid Rida 80, 191, 297
Rashidun 30
Rashiduzzaman, M. 204, 217
rashtra 27, 31, 150, 192, 257, 266, 274
Rashtrakutas 30
Rashtriya Swayamsevak Sangh 241, 266
Rasul-ul-Salam 299
Rawalpindi jail 400
Rawat, General B. 341
Reagan, Ronald 401
recycling 384
red shirts 188
Rehmatul-lil-Alameen Authority 415
Rejai, Mostafa 263
Reko Diq 227, 234
religio-political 38
religious identity 16, 23, 24, 34, 50, 141,
  153, 240, 268, 271, 298, 355, 362, 421
religious minorities 104, 139, 214, 254,
  406, 410, 423
religious orthodox 386
Rene Descartes 120
Republican 350
Reynolds, G.H. 327, 344
riba 283, 307
Richard 22, 31, 41, 209, 365
Richard Dawkins 22
Richard Eaton 31, 32, 34, 42, 71, 193
Richards, Martin P. 28
Riedel, B. 404, 418
Rigveda 29
Risalah Jihaddiyah 69

452 Index

Riyasat-e-Medina 16, 278, 409, 415
rizq 386
Rizv, Saad 339
Rizvi, Khadim Husain 338, 339
Robert Clive 44, 46
Robert Orme 36, 44
Romila Thapar 8, 24, 41, 42
roti-kapra-makan 397
Rousseau, Jean-Jacques 427
Roy, Shankar 144
Rudyard Kipling 43

sadr-e-amin 81
Sadruddin Azurda 82
Saeed, Hafiz 332, 338, 344, 345
Safavid Contract 282
Safavid dynasty 282
Safavids of Persia 295
Sagan, Carl 149, 353
Sahib, Dr. Khan 190
Sajjada nashins 71
Sakharov, A. 437
Salafi 87, 224, 303, 408
Salafism 69
Salam, Abdus 368, 372
salat 362
Salman Taseer 133, 257, 338, 396
SALT II treaty 401
Salt Law 244, 342
Samuel 5, 67, 124, 312, 325
Sangathan 175
Sanskrit 3, 21, 23, 25–29, 38, 42, 47, 48,
    67, 79, 83, 206, 266
Sanskriti 266
Santos, A. Noronha Dos 217
sardar 223
Sardar Begum 128
Sarfaraz 166, 169
Sarmaya-o-Mehnat 109
Sarwar, G. 358
Satyr 327
Saudai, Asghar 268
Savarkar, Vinayak Damodar 265
Sayyid Ahmad Dehlawi 39
scientific modernity 80
SEATO 325
Second World War 147, 180, 273, 371
secular 11, 13, 30, 36, 37, 60, 64, 65, 80,
    85, 98, 108, 125, 130, 132, 142, 150,
    152–156, 159, 162, 174, 176, 180, 182,
    192, 214, 220, 224, 229, 233, 243, 261,
    267, 277–279, 282, 295, 300, 301, 309,
    325, 357, 363, 368, 405, 424–427
secularism 102, 130, 154, 156, 176, 181,
    191, 192, 213, 267, 292, 424

selfish genes 22
Seraiki 364, 428
Sethi, Najam 413
Sewall Wright 23
Shafi, Mian Muhammad 179
Shafi, Muhammad 201
Shafi'i, 181
Shah, A. 314, 341
Shah, Sultan Mohammed 152, 206, 217
Shah, Zameeruddin 429
Shah Abdul Aziz 39, 69
Shah Alam II, 47, 53
Shah Ghulam Ali. 80–81
Shah Nur Jamal 248
Shah of Iran 228
Shah Waliullah 9, 38, 39, 69, 88, 402
Shahab, Qudratullah 268
Shahabnama's 268
shaheen 105, 106, 129, 249, 409
Shahjehan 36, 37
Shaikh Ahmad Sirhindi 9, 37, 177
sha'ir-e-Mashriq 103
shaitani ala 305
Shakai agreement 334
Shamsuddin Hasan 109
Shankaracharya, A. 352
sharia 69, 125, 143, 161–163, 179, 181,
    276–278, 291–293, 295, 296, 301–304,
    309, 319, 373, 376, 403, 409, 424
Shariat Laws 277
Sharif, Raheel 299, 315
Sharif, Shahbaz 412
sharm-o-haya 387
Shashi Tharoor 44, 209
Shaykh Nur Muhammad 116
sheikh 281
Sheikh Ahmed Sirhindi 85
sheikh-ul-islam 281
Shia 4, 6, 69, 87, 90, 116, 131, 132, 139,
    151, 163–166, 168, 170, 172, 200,
    239–241, 256, 257, 281, 282, 287, 299,
    308, 359, 367–369, 374, 377, 402, 404,
    408, 424, 434
The Shia Revival 281, 308
shikinee 30
shikwa 105, 112, 124
shirk 30, 69
Shri Krishna Mandir 370
Shuddhi 175
shuhada 177, 178
Sibi Darbar 163
Sibte Hasan 103
Siddiqui, Aafia 361
Siddiqui, Fouzia 361
Siffin 287

Sindhi, Obaidullah 172
Singh, Rajnath 388
Singh, Ranjit 69, 351, 357
Single Nation Theory 420, 423
Sipah-e-Abbas 303
Sipah-e-Muhammad 303
Sipah-e-Sahaba 225, 332, 425
Sir John Kaye 79
Sir Syed Ahmed Khan 87, 100, 101
Sita Ram Goel 31
Six Point Program 207
Smith, Adam 382, 392
Smith, Joseph 131
social evolution 23, 223
social justice 161, 167, 243, 368, 396, 397, 426
socialism 108, 109, 141, 161, 167, 244, 245, 248, 251, 277, 291, 396, 398
Soomro, Allah Baksh 172
Søren Kierkegaard 110
Soviet Red Army 209
Soviet Union 148, 151, 260, 294, 321, 325, 423, 437
Special Theory of Relativity 120
Spencer Lavan 116
Sri Baijnath 94
state-deity 31
Subhas Chandra Bose 134
Suez Crisis 298
Sufi/Sufis 32, 34, 70, 232, 338, 346, 357
Sufi saint 32
suhoor 362
Suhrawardy, H. 190, 201, 202, 269
Sukarno 300, 301, 398
sulh-i-kul 37
Sultan Said bin Taimur 224
Sulzberger, C.L. 186, 258
Sunnah 70, 181, 296, 304
Sunni 4, 6, 36, 37, 39, 69, 81, 90, 92, 116, 131, 132, 139, 164–166, 168, 200, 216, 239–241, 256, 281, 283, 284, 287, 295, 296, 299, 303, 305, 306, 315, 337, 359, 367, 369, 374, 377, 402, 404, 424, 434
superorganism 383
Supreme Court of Pakistan 216, 220, 339
surkh hai, surkh hai. Asia surkh hai" 397, 398
Swami Vivekananda 110
Swaraj 180
Syed, Anwar 140, 145
Syed, G.M. 145, 399
Syed Ahmad Barelvi 38, 69
Syed Ameer Ali 79, 191, 297
Syed Mahmud 82
Syed Qutb 38, 107, 135

tabarra 165
taghut 289
Tahir Kamran 135
Tahir-ul-Qadri, Dr. 286
Tahzeeb-ul-Akhlaq 85
tajdeed 178
Taliban 15, 33, 35, 38, 40, 70, 104, 106, 117, 215, 219, 232, 241, 276, 281, 292–296, 300, 301, 303, 306, 307, 309, 319, 333, 334, 337, 338, 340, 345, 352, 364, 369, 391, 405, 407, 408, 410, 411, 413, 414, 418, 422, 424, 425, 431
Talleyrand, C. 396
Tanzeem-ul-Madaris 433
taqleed 86
taqriz 83, 84
tarana-e-Hindi 123, 124
Tarikh-e-Firishta 49
Tariq Ki Dua 105
Tariq Rahman 21, 41, 59
Tarjuman-ul-Qur'an 175, 182, 193
tax-to-GDP 427
tazia 165
Technical and Vocational Education and Training 432
Tehreek-e-Labbaik Pakistan 4
Tehrik-e-Taliban Pakistan 410
thawb 363
theocracy 129, 131, 132, 139, 144, 155–157, 164, 279, 403
theodemocracy 102, 131, 132
theology 26, 34, 63, 77, 80, 86, 114, 135, 142, 281, 282, 289
Thomas Arnold 106, 107
Tipu Sultan 46, 49, 71, 134
Tiwana, Malik Khizar Hayat 172
Treaty of Westphalia 348, 424
Truman, Harry 327
Trump, Donald 327, 350
Tuhfat-ul-Muwahhidin 68
Tulu'-e-Islam 114
Two Nation Theory 11, 12, 14–16, 21, 22, 28, 43–45, 78, 96, 97, 143, 146, 156, 159, 200, 221, 239, 240, 246, 254, 264, 267, 270, 271, 346, 368, 394, 416, 420, 422, 437

Udham Singh 71
ulema 37, 38, 63, 82, 87, 94, 165, 171, 172, 175, 178, 181, 281, 406
Umayyads 295
ummah 129, 131, 132, 271, 285, 295–300, 307, 399
UN General Assembly 388

454 Index

UN Security Council 414
Unionist Party of Punjab 172
United Jihad Council 405
United Nations 250, 280, 386, 421
United Provinces 53, 58, 72
United States 13, 23, 107, 144, 147, 148,
    155, 164, 167, 174, 179, 234, 273, 279,
    292–294, 300, 306, 311, 316, 319–321,
    325, 332, 334, 337, 341, 350, 371, 375,
    388, 391, 398, 401, 403, 410, 413, 415,
    422, 437
Universal Declaration of Human Rights
    272, 367
universalism 12, 122, 136, 245
University Grants Commission 94, 262,
    274, 402
urban slums 426
Urdu 10, 15, 26, 31, 41, 42, 48, 50, 53,
    58, 59, 69, 71, 78–84, 89, 93, 96, 97,
    100, 102–105, 107, 108, 111–113, 116,
    123, 125, 130, 134–136, 138, 145, 152,
    158, 172, 174, 181, 182, 186, 187, 200,
    205–209, 218, 224, 249, 253, 255, 257,
    264, 268, 270, 316, 318, 354, 357, 358,
    360, 362, 363, 365, 372, 373, 386, 399,
    402, 423
Usmani, Ishrat Hussain 396
Usmani, Shabbir Ahmed 165, 367
USS Enterprise 211
USSR 273

Vatican 53, 280
Vedic 26, 27, 29, 41, 119, 192
velayat-e-faqih 282
Victory Day 209
Vikings 30
Vindhyas 353

wahdat-i-deen 182
Wahhabi 68, 69, 77, 82, 83, 87, 99, 181,
    299, 303, 408
wajib-ul-qatl 87
War of Independence 10, 50, 72, 269
watan 33
wataniyyat 175
water harvesting 384
Watson, J. 354
Weinberg, Steven 117

West Pakistan 14, 129, 199, 200, 203, 204,
    206, 208, 209, 211, 212, 214, 215, 273,
    395, 397
White Man's burden 43
White Paper 207, 217
Wignaraja, K. 252, 259, 421, 438
Wilfred Cantwell Smith 95, 106, 126,
    128, 138
William Dalrymple 53
William James 120
William Metcalfe 53
William Shakespeare 118
William Wilson Hunter 54
Wolpert, Stanley 154, 169
World Punjabi Congress 358
World Trade Center 279, 405
World Wildlife Fund 384

Yadhav, Kulbhushan 229
Yahweh 117
yajooj-majooj 86
Yathrib 270
Yaum-e-Shuhada 323
yavanas 24
Yazid 287, 369
Yusuf, Hajaj-bin-, 360

Zaheer, Hasan 202
Zahiruddin Babur 36
Zaidi, Hasan 350, 376
Zaidi, Mosharraf 320
Zaidi, Zawar Hussain 154
zakat 283, 402
Zaman, Fakhar 358
zamindar 61, 65
zamindari 202, 249
Zarb-e-Azb 411
zarb-e-tauleed 386
Zardari, Asif Ali 228, 232, 326, 335
Zehra, Nasim 404
Zeno's Paradox 120, 121
Ziarat Residency 219
Ziauddin, M. 423
Zindah Rood 116, 127
Zinn, Howard 437
Zionism 141
Ziya Gökalp 80
Ziyad, Tariq bin 105

Printed in the United States
by Baker & Taylor Publisher Services